Entrepreneurship Marketing

Small and medium-sized enterprises (SMEs) dominate the market in terms of sheer number of organisations; yet, scholarly resource materials to assist in honing skills and competencies have not kept pace. This well renowned textbook guides students through the complexities of entrepreneurship from the unique perspective of marketing in SME contexts, providing a clear grounding in the principles, practices, strategies, challenges, and opportunities faced by businesses today.

SMEs now need to step up to the terrain of mobile marketing and consumer-generated marketing and utilise social media marketing tools. Similarly, the activities of various stakeholders in SME businesses like start-up accelerators, business incubators, and crowdfunding have now gained more prominence in SME activities. This second edition advances grounds covered in the earlier edition and has been fully updated to reflect this new, dynamic business landscape. Updates include:

- A consideration of social media imperatives on SME marketing;
- Discussion of forms of capital formation and deployment for marketing effectiveness, including crowdfunding;
- Updated international case studies drawn from diverse backgrounds;
- Hands-on practical explorations based on real-life tasks to encourage deeper understanding.

This book is perfect for students studying SMEs, Marketing and Enterprise at both advanced undergraduate and postgraduate levels, as well as professionals looking to obtain the required knowledge to operate their businesses in this increasingly complex and turbulent marketing environment.

Sonny Nwankwo is Emeritus Professor at the University of East London, UK, and the Provost of the Nigerian Defence Academy (NDA), Nigeria. He is Visiting Professor at universities across Africa, Australia, Europe, and North America. Prior to joining academia, he was a customer services manager in the telecommunications industry.

Ayantunji Gbadamosi is Research Coordinator and Chair of the Research and Knowledge Exchange Committee at Royal Docks School of Business and Law, University of East London, UK. His research interests are in Consumer Behaviour, SME Marketing, Marketing to Children, and Marketing Communications.

Entrepreneurship Marketing

Principles and Practice of SME Marketing

Second Edition

Edited by Sonny Nwankwo and Ayantunji Gbadamosi

LONDON AND NEW YORK

Second edition published 2020
by Routledge
2 Park Square, Milton Park, Abingdon, Oxon, OX14 4RN

and by Routledge
52 Vanderbilt Avenue, New York, NY 10017

Routledge is an imprint of the Taylor & Francis Group, an informa business

© 2020 selection and editorial matter, Sonny Nwankwo and Ayantunji Gbadamosi;
individual chapters, the contributors

The right of the Sonny Nwankwo and Ayantunji Gbadamosi to be identified as the
authors of the editorial material, and of the authors for their individual chapters, has
been asserted in accordance with sections 77 and 78 of the Copyright, Designs and
Patents Act 1988.

All rights reserved. No part of this book may be reprinted or reproduced or utilised in
any form or by any electronic, mechanical, or other means, now known or hereafter
invented, including photocopying and recording, or in any information storage or
retrieval system, without permission in writing from the publishers.

Trademark notice: Product or corporate names may be trademarks or registered trademarks, and are used only for identification and explanation without intent to infringe.

First edition published by Routledge 2010

British Library Cataloguing-in-Publication Data
A catalogue record for this book is available from the British Library

Library of Congress Cataloging-in-Publication Data
Names: Nwankwo, Sonny, editor. | Gbadamosi, Ayantunji, editor.
Title: Entrepreneurship marketing : principles and practice of SME marketing / edited
    by Sonny Nwankwo and Ayantunji Gbadamosi.
Description: Second edition. | Abingdon, Oxon ; New York, NY : Routledge,
    2020. | Includes bibliographical references and index.
Identifiers: LCCN 2019050174 (print) | LCCN 2019050175 (ebook) | ISBN
    9781138585225 (hardback) | ISBN 9781138585232 (paperback) | ISBN
    9780429505461 (ebook)
Subjects: LCSH: Marketing—Management. | Entrepreneurship. | Small
    business—Management. | New business enterprises—Management.
Classification: LCC HF5415.13 .E58 2020 (print) | LCC HF5415.13 (ebook) |
    DDC 658.8—dc23
LC record available at https://lccn.loc.gov/2019050174
LC ebook record available at https://lccn.loc.gov/2019050175

ISBN: 978-1-138-58522-5 (hbk)
ISBN: 978-1-138-58523-2 (pbk)
ISBN: 978-0-429-50546-1 (ebk)

Typeset in Goudy
by Apex CoVantage, LLC

Contents

Preface	vii

1 Marketing in small and medium-sized enterprises: an introduction 1
MIKE SIMPSON, NICK TAYLOR, AND JO PADMORE

2 Small and medium enterprises marketing: innovation and sustainable economic growth perspective 13
ABDULLAH PROMISE OPUTE

3 The role and relevance model of marketing in small and medium-sized enterprises 31
MIKE SIMPSON, NICK TAYLOR, AND JO PADMORE

4 The entrepreneurship marketing environment 46
AYANTUNJI GBADAMOSI

5 Buyer behaviour in the 21st century: implications for SME marketing 72
AYANTUNJI GBADAMOSI

6 Revisiting entrepreneurship marketing research: towards a framework for SMEs in developing countries 97
RICHARD SHAMBARE, JANE SHAMBARE, AND WELLINGTON CHAKUZIRA

7 Managing products and customer value: implications for SME marketing 112
AYANTUNJI GBADAMOSI

8 Choosing the right pricing strategy 131
P. SERGIUS KOKU

9 The reality of distribution faced by SMEs: a perspective from the UK 147
DAVID BAMBER

10 Marketing communications for the SME 162
TECK-YONG ENG AND GRAHAM SPICKETT-JONES

11 Internet marketing 174
PAUL DOBSON AND VISH MAHESHWARI

CONTENTS

12 Retailing and SME marketing   189
MEE LEING OOI AND HSIAO-PEI (SOPHIE) YANG

13 Small and medium-sized enterprise retailing in the UK   202
OGENYI OMAR AND PETER FRASER

14 Relationship marketing and networks in entrepreneurship   222
SUE HALLIDAY

15 Internal marketing and service excellence in SMEs   244
HINA KHAN

16 Crowdfunding of SMEs   262
SANYA OJO AND ENTISSAR ELGADI

17 International entrepreneurship and small and medium-sized enterprises   275
KEVIN IBEH AND MATHEW ANALOGBEI

18 Born global SME in contemporary markets   287
OFER DEKEL-DACHS, AMON SIMBA, AND HELENA KLIPAN

19 Cross cultural marketing strategies: for small and medium-sized firms   300
ROBIN LOWE, ISOBEL DOOLE, AND FELICITY MENDOZA

20 Marketing planning in small businesses   324
FRANCES EKWULUGO

21 Contemporary issues in entrepreneurship marketing:
sustainability, ethics, and social responsibility   337
SONNY NWANKWO AND DARLINGTON RICHARDS

22 The future of SME marketing and operations: critical change drivers   359
EMMANUEL ADUGU

23 Religion and the SME   375
ANDREW LINDRIDGE

24 SMEs and market growth: contemporary reflections on why
and how they grow   387
RULA M. AL ABDULRAZAK AND SHADI A. RAZAK

25 Developing entrepreneurial marketing competencies   400
BARRY ARDLEY, NICK TAYLOR, AND JIALIN (PENNY) HARDWICK

26 Marketing in the informal economy: an entrepreneurial
perspective and research agenda   412
NNAMDI O. MADICHIE, ANAYO D. NKAMNEBE, AND IGNATIUS U. EKANEM

List of contributors   429
Index   439

Preface

Undoubtedly, remarkable advances have been made to enrich understanding Entrepreneurship Marketing either by extending its theoretical and discursive properties or developing situated appreciations of its temporal and spatial dimensions. Paradoxically, narrative evidence from those who research and teach the subject continues to reveal growing complexities and tensions as they seek to overcome the problematics of comprehensive teaching resource support. It is common knowledge that much of the established marketing knowledge and associated programmes of study largely reflect axioms of large businesses. It is partly for this reason that high business failure rates among SMEs are consistently attributed to a failure on the part of scholars to appreciably interrogate the temporal and spatial dimensions of marketing in the context of SMEs or deal with the differences in marketing operations. The sheer scale of socioeconomic challenges confronting societies and the need to scale-up actions to achieve economic stability and growth gives rise to a central role for entrepreneurship. Making progress on these fronts would require carefully studying, analysing, documenting, and understanding strategic marketing actions involved in value-defining, value-developing, and value-delivery processes for achieving and maintaining the desired level of performance among SMEs.

In many ways, this second edition of *Entrepreneurship Marketing* stretches theoretical and discursive aspects of the field. In doing so, new directions and agendas are introduced; some potently emergent themes and perspectives are focussed. All of these, despite the underpinning eclecticism of the subject area, give impetus to the growing dynamism and the need to continue to re-scope the landscape of SME Marketing.

Today's entrepreneurs are confronted with more complex opportunity structures and new challenges. Accordingly, they need to become more dynamic, more innovative, and even more skilful in order to successfully navigate the profoundly evolving challenges and complex opportunity structures. For this reason, those who are involved in producing and disseminating knowledge on this very important topic of **entrepreneurship marketing** need to refine their taken-for-granted assumptions about entrepreneurs, markets, and strategies. This has not been the case so far with respect to a variety of textbooks designed for teaching and for personal development purposes. More fundamentally, those who teach the subject are frustrated with many of the existing sector-specific textbooks due to the apparent lack of depth and sufficient insights in exploring the dynamic interface between marketing and entrepreneurship. Many texts focus primarily on the broad spectrum of large company oriented treatments and make only cursory references to SMEs. This can be all too confusing to students, many of whom are left wondering whether the difference between SME marketing and marketing for large-scale enterprises is only superficial.

PREFACE

The need and motivation for SME-focussed analyses remain unquestionably obvious, hence this revised edition. It is presented to explore the roles of marketing in shaping SMEs' entrepreneurial identities; it assembles, probably for the first time in a pedagogical manner, original and insightful contributions aimed at illuminating the field and, very importantly, charting new directions for teaching the subject of entrepreneurship marketing. Accordingly, we present this second edition as a compendium of teaching and learning resources, put together with a clear target user-group in mind, and each chapter is contributed by those who themselves are involved in teaching and researching the subject. It is hoped that the book should be able to:

- Help students to develop a coherent understanding of marketing processes in SMEs;
- Provide students with an understanding of marketing strategies adopted by successful SMEs and how lessons learned might be transferred to new situations.

The uniqueness of this book is better appreciated when considered alongside what it delivers. Essentially, we aim to help students to achieve the following:

- Explore the fundamentals of marketing within the context of SMEs in such a way that clearly distinguishes the treatment of SME marketing from the knowledge of marketing associated with managing the large organisations; explicate the similarities/overlap in principles but using appropriate illustrations to contextually delineate the boundaries;
- Develop an understanding of the nature of the marketing environment within which SMEs operate; consider the causal textures and factors that influence SMEs; examine the techniques and tools of marketing analyses (and planning) and the various means that are available for formulating appropriate marketing;
- Identify, understand, and critique the role and function of marketing in SMEs in order to present a detailed and comprehensive discussion of available alternatives by which SMEs can obtain marketing intelligence and other various inputs, and how to make effective use of them;
- Examine the marketing mix elements of SMEs and discuss the peculiarities associated with managing each of these effectively within the constraints of SMEs, whilst being sensitive to the variability in terms of scope and size of SMEs;
- Present a well-grounded treatment of export market orientation and internationalisation of SMEs in the face of pervasive forces of globalisation, franchising capabilities, and information technology across both product and service offerings;
- Explore the role of the internet in marketing and shaping the frontiers of entrepreneurship, critical competencies for entrepreneurship marketing (specifically dealing with risk management, service quality, managing competition, innovation, growth, failure crises, and strategic turnarounds), social networks, and relationships in SME marketing, issues around the SME marketing challenge of multiculturalism, the impact of dominant sociocultural values (e.g., religion, sustainable consumption, ethics, and social responsibility) on entrepreneurship marketing.

An important feature of this book is that it deals directly with 'people issues' (i.e., everydayness of entrepreneurship marketing interactions) and has the underlying objective of preparing students for the realities and complexities of entrepreneurialism. To challenge limited perspectives of the real world of entrepreneurship marketing, we have included treatments that focus on the pervasive impact of technology on SME marketing operations, as well as

PREFACE

country and less-discussed informal economy cases/analyses. The significance of this book is substantial and stands to focus our attention and direct our energies while shedding new light on ways in which SME marketing can and does operate – beyond the conventional large organisation treatments. Many of the new roles of marketing in SME contexts and 'real issues' that matter in unpacking how SMEs engage their markets and valuable implications for growing and sustaining entrepreneurship are captured in this book.

As editors, we are not oblivious of the demands (presumably overbearing sometimes) we placed on our contributing authors in the face of the highly pressured environment in which we all work. We are sincerely very grateful for the contribution. This book would not have been possible without the commitment to scholarship demonstrated by distinguished academics and researchers whose highly significant contributions resulted in this unique ensemble. We would also like to acknowledge the support of our handling staff at Routledge, particularly Sophia Levine and Emmie Shand, who have proved to be great people to work with. We hope that students will find this book as exciting to use as we have had putting it together.

Sonny Nwankwo
Ayantunji Gbadamosi
University of East London

Chapter 1

Marketing in small and medium-sized enterprises
An introduction

Mike Simpson, Nick Taylor, and Jo Padmore

LEARNING OBJECTIVES

After reading this chapter, you will be able to:
- Define what we mean by small and medium-sized enterprises (SMEs) and why there is a need for theoretical developments in the area of SME marketing;
- Critically review the extant literature on marketing in SMEs;
- Consider the relationship between marketing, strategic thinking, and small firm survival;
- Discuss the reasons why big business marketing does not appear to be transferable to small and medium-sized enterprises;
- Discuss how small and medium sized businesses have adapted marketing to their particular context.

INTRODUCTION

The application of marketing principles is widely accepted as the way in which larger companies generate profits and grow. The supporting marketing literature has been developed over many years and has generally focussed on established large organisations. In contrast, the literature surrounding small and medium-sized enterprises (SMEs) and their marketing efforts is still in the development stage. This chapter explores how the established principles of marketing apply to small and medium sized enterprises. The relationship between marketing and strategic thinking is explored and in particular the extent to which some SMEs feel that marketing is not relevant to their business needs. There is evidence to suggest that the formal approaches to marketing that have been established for larger organisations do not appear to be easily transferrable to SMEs. However, if these companies are not utilising these principles to generate success then what are they using, and how does this inform our strategic view of marketing practice in SMEs? Marketing exists to facilitate exchanges. Exchanges of value as perceived from both the supplier and the receiver. Core to the understanding of value exchange is the notion that the supplier offers something of less value than they receive in return. Of course the opposite is also true for the receiver, in that the value of goods and services received is of greater value than the cost of obtaining them. The resultant satisfaction is shared among both parties.

The following chapter now examines the nature of SME organisations and how they differ from larger organisations. In addition the relationship to marketing is explored to reveal how SMEs organisations manage to create value that promotes profitable exchanges leading to customer satisfaction.

DEFINING SMALL AND MEDIUM-SIZED ENTERPRISES IN CONTEXT

Definitions of small and medium-sized enterprises (SMEs) vary widely from country to country. Most research defines SMEs by the number of employees. In the UK, SMEs are defined as businesses with fewer than 250 employees, and in the European Union they are defined as independent businesses with less than 25% owned or controlled by another enterprise(s) and with fewer than 250 employees (EU, 2005). The European Union also places stipulations on the turnover and balance sheet figures such that micro businesses (one to nine employees) should not exceed 2m Euro turnover, small businesses (ten to 49 employees) should not exceed 10m Euro turnover and medium sized businesses (50–249 employees) should not exceed 50m Euro turnover (EU, 2005). In some countries the definition of an SME varies by industry sector as well as number of employees and turnover figures.

Small and medium-sized enterprises are an important part of all economies, accounting for 99% of businesses in the UK. Worldwide SMEs account for in excess of 99% of all businesses and are by far the largest contributor to employment and the gross domestic product of nations. Therefore, SMEs are a source of job creation and contribute both innovation and competition to the market. Some, but not all, SMEs grow to be big businesses. Government policies are often aimed at growing SMEs to create employment or to ride out periods of economic crisis and yet many SMEs either cannot grow or choose not to expand beyond what can be managed and controlled by the owner-manager. Some owner-managers choose a life-style rather than to grow their business and this view affects the way SMEs behave. Owner-managers also define success in different ways (e.g., being happy rather than wealthy; having a manageable business rather than creating a large business they could not control themselves; simply having enough money and enough freedom to do as they wish). These issues only serve to complicate any theoretical developments in the area of marketing in SMEs.

Research has found that SMEs faced the following problems:

- Sales and Marketing (in 40.2% of SMEs)
- Human Resource Management (15.3%)
- General Management (14.3%)
- Production/Operations Management (8.6%).

(Huang and Brown, 1999)

Sales and marketing is often the most dominant problem encountered by SME operators and yet has been acknowledged to be the most important of all business activities and essential for the survival and growth of small businesses (McKenna, 1991; O'Brien, 1998). The areas of marketing with the most frequent problems in SMEs were promotion and market research (Huang and Brown, 1999). The reasons for this were that SMEs lacked the financial resources to employ specialists, that the resource constraints limited the ability of the company to search for information and that a lack of a management information system limited the use of data already held within the organisation.

Thus, the typical SME has limited resources, limited cash flows, few customers, is often engaged in management 'fire-fighting', concentrates on current performance rather than taking a strategic focus, often has a flat organisational structure, has problems with sales and marketing, and possibly has high staff turnover (Hudson et al., 2001). The dynamic forces (both internally and externally) affecting SMEs create a very different environment in which marketing activities take place by comparision with larger and often long established stable businesses that are capable of manipulating the business environment to a degree.

PREVIOUS RESEARCH ON MARKETING IN SMALL AND MEDIUM-SIZED ENTERPRISES

It is generally accepted that the basic principles of marketing are universally applicable to large and small businesses (Siu and Kirby, 1998; Reynolds, 2002). The study of marketing in SMEs has been recognised as a problematic area for researchers for over 20 years (Chaston and Mangles, 2002; Siu and Kirby, 1998). SME marketing in practice is thought to be largely done though networking (Gilmore et al., 2001) or a combination of transaction, relationship, interaction, and network marketing (Brodie et al., 1997). More recently, the use of internet marketing (Chaffey et al., 2000; Sparkes and Thomas, 2001) or e-commerce (Rayport and Jaworski, 2001) has become popular in all types of businesses including SMEs. However, academic research appears unable to resolve a number of questions about small businesses and their relationship with and the use of marketing. Siu and Kirby (1998) point out that empirical evidence has been generated in an ad hoc manner because of a general absence of a systematic approach to the subject. Insufficient knowledge about marketing in small business remains and a small business marketing theory specifically related to the understanding and knowledge of strategic marketing is needed (Siu and Kirby, 1998).

MARKETING MODELS FOR SMEs

Research on small businesses and their marketing activities has been largely limited to explanations of certain types of behaviour observed in small businesses (e.g., Hannon and Atherton, 1998; Smith and Whittaker, 1998; Huang and Brown, 1999), or on the search for factors that are missing or present barriers in smaller businesses, accounting for their apparent inability to apply or use marketing ideas and concepts that were often developed for larger businesses (e.g., Barber et al., 1989; O'Brien, 1998; Freel, 2000). Theory development in SMEs research seems to be somewhat limited in general. The work that has been done is more applied in nature, taking the form of prescriptive or descriptive frameworks and 'models', on how to apply certain business and management theories to the smaller business (e.g., Carson, 1990; Brooksbank, 1996; Valos and Baker, 1996; Brooksbank, 1999). Some authors are investigating the applicability of alternative paradigms based on creativity, semiotics and art, and employing alternative methodologies such as biography (Fillis, 2002).

Work specifically on marketing models in SMEs has resulted in six interlocking exploratory and qualitative models (Carson, 1990), while Hannon and Atherton (1998) suggested a matrix relating strategic awareness to planning effectiveness. Moller and Anttila (1987) devised a marketing capability framework, which was used to collect data with 36 Finnish and Swedish companies but they described their model as 'a qualitative tool for examining the 'state-of-the-art' of marketing in small manufacturing companies' (Moller and Anttila, 1987, p. 185). This model consists of two major components: the external and internal field of marketing capability (see also Simpson and Taylor, 2002 and Simpson et al., 2006).

THEORETICAL APPROACHES TO MARKETING IN SMALLER BUSINESSES

According to Romano and Ratnatunga (1995), marketing in small businesses can be categorised as:

- Marketing as a culture: defined as analysis of consumer needs and wants and assessment of competitiveness of small enterprises;
- Marketing as a strategy: defined as strategy development to enhance actual and potential market position of small enterprises;
- Marketing as tactics: defined as analysis of the 4 Ps (Product, Price, Place, and Promotion) to influence the performance or growth of small enterprises.

Romano and Ratnatunga (1995) also identified seven methodologies and three study objectives. However, Romano and Ratnatunga (1995) admit that the categorisation of marketing in SMEs is somewhat arbitrary and invited the reader to devise their own categories.

Siu and Kirby (1998) identified four theoretical approaches to marketing in small firms:

- Stages/Growth model
  The stages/growth model suggests that any model of small firm marketing must take into account the stage of development of the business but does not explain how the changes occur or account for the effects in variability of marketing skills between different owner-managers. The stages/growth model does not allow for leap-frogging due to technological advances such as the use of the internet.
- Management Style approach
  The management style approach acknowledges the limitations and constraints of the small firm (resources and capabilities) and provides a useful explanation for the poor development of marketing in small firms but does not explain the marketing practices actually used by small firms.
- Management Function model
  The management function approach acknowledges that marketing is both an important business function and an essential concept in small firm growth and survival, but many owner-managers simplify and misunderstand marketing as the 4Ps or interpret marketing as advertising. The management function approach has been vigorously criticised and few small business researchers have adopted this approach (Siu and Kirby, 1998).
- Contingency approach
  The contingency approach acknowledges that various factors affect the small firm's marketing performance and that there is no universal set of strategic choices that is optimal for all businesses regardless of their resources or business environment in which they operate. The contingency approach is positioned between two extreme views, which state that universal marketing principles exist and are applicable to all firms, or that each small firm is unique and each situation needs to be analysed separately (Siu and Kirby, 1998).

There is no grand unifying theory, the marketing concepts may be the same, but the process of implementation is different in each firm. Excellent reviews of the literature in this complex area can be found in Hill (2001a, 2001b) and Siu and Kirby (1998).

MARKETING, STRATEGIC THINKING, AND SMALL FIRM SURVIVAL

It is questionable whether small businesses need to practice marketing at all to survive and grow (Hogarth-Scott et al., 1996) although McLarty (1998) has found some evidence of strategic marketing in a growing SME. The study by Hogarth-Scott et al. (1996) concluded that small business owner-managers were often generalists, not marketing specialists, and complex marketing theories may not be appropriate for small businesses and probably would not aid in the understanding of their markets. Nevertheless, marketing was practiced to some degree by small businesses. In most cases competitive advantage was based on quality and service, while those competing on price were in the highly competitive markets with little or no product differentiation and low entry barriers (see Campbell-Hunt, 2000, for a discussion on how cost leadership and differentiation strategies can be combined). Product differentiation was a source of competitive advantage in some businesses while others were looking for niche markets (Hogarth-Scott et al., 1996). It would appear that marketing did contribute positively to small business success and the ability to think strategically. This view is supported to some extent by the much earlier work of Rice (1983) where it was clear that there was a difference between big business strategic rational planning and that carried out in small businesses. This difference was due to the amount of data collected about the external business environment by small companies compared to large companies and how this data was analysed. Small businesses collected considerably less data and in a more ad hoc fashion. Yet owner-managers were aware of the strategic nature of their decisions and Rice (1983) suggested that perhaps businesspersons gather enough information to allow them to make decisions at a 'permissible' level of probable success. It could be argued that today SMEs have access to much larger amounts of information and greater computing power than was available 27 years ago (see Rice, 1983), but this is still considerably less than that available to large organisations. SMEs owner-managers still have very little time to devote to the analysis of information for strategic decision making and therefore the comments of Rice (1983) still appear valid.

Hannon and Atherton (1998) noted that the level of strategic awareness of owner-managers appears to be strongly influenced by the personal competence of the owner-managers and the type, uncertainty and complexity of the business. In businesses where customer relationships were well defined and relatively stable, strategic awareness was often low. This was due to their perception of the external business environment being narrowly defined and stable. In companies that experienced fast growth and turbulent market conditions the level of strategic awareness was uniformly high and the motivation for a continually better understanding of the external business environment was strong (Hannon and Atherton, 1998).

PLANNING AND PERFORMANCE

The relationship between planning sophistication and financial performance was studied by Rue and Ibrahim (1998). Their results clearly showed that those SMEs with greater planning sophistication also showed greater growth in sales as reported by executives. Yet on objective measures such as return on investment (ROI) performance Rue and Ibrahim (1998) reported these were not affected. We note here that ROI (or Return on Capital Employed, ROCE) is a poor performance measure (Frecknall Hughes et al., 2007). Rue and Ibrahim (1998) suggest that small businesses with a sophisticated planning process may reap the benefits of these efforts in the long term. However, Perry (2001) suggested that SMEs using sophisticated planning activities (including written business plans) may enhance their chances of survival and success.

MARKETING ORIENTATION AND PERFORMANCE

There is some debate among academics as to the value of a marketing orientation and how it relates to the success of the firm (Narver and Slater, 1990, Henderson, 1998). Pelham (2000) quoting Levitt (1960) suggests that firms who adopt a marketing philosophy/marketing orientation and convert it into actions should have superior performance. However, Pelham (2000) also points out that there are firms that manage to be successful without embracing this concept but by emphasising technical or production capabilities. Henderson (1998) claims that there is no such thing as marketing orientation and that adopting those ideas inherent in a marketing orientation can be shown to account for only 10% of business performance. Harris (1998) contends that since market orientation can be viewed as a form of culture, the impediments to market orientation are categorised via a contemporary organisational culture framework. Thus, Harris (1996) found that obstacles to market orientation could be classified as assumptions, values, artefacts or symbols. However, the view from the retail shop floor (Harris, 1998) suggests a similar set of obstacles to those found by Harris and Watkins' (1998) study, namely: apathy, instrumentality, limited power, short-termism, compartmentalisation, ignorance, and weak management support. The solutions proposed involved, *inter alia*, education and empowerment of retail shop floor workers (see also Carson, 1993; Carson et al., 1995).

Denison and McDonald (1995) point out that studies have consistently shown that firms which were marketing orientated, or competent practitioners of marketing, performed better in terms of return-on-investment (ROI) and market share. However, ROI can be affected by operational changes and is not a good measure of performance. Rafiq and Pallett (1996) found some limited evidence that marketing orientated UK engineering firms were more likely to have higher profits. Again, profit is not such a good indicator of performance in SMEs as companies' choices regarding pay policy on remuneration and the way they run their operations can reduce their profit and therefore their tax obligations.

The main inhibitor of marketing effectiveness in UK businesses in the late 1980s and 1990s was poor implementation of basic marketing (Denison and McDonald, 1995). This finding is supported by research carried out by Brooksbank et al. (1999). There are many other orientations or approaches that might be adopted by a firm and so a marketing orientation may only be relevant under certain business conditions. The business environment in which SMEs operate is dynamic and may well lend itself to a variety of successful approaches and strategies.

SME MARKETING IN PRACTICE

Marketing in practice in small firms seems to rely on personal contact networks (Hill and Wright, 2001; Gilmore et al., 2001; Brodie et al., 1997; O'Donnell and Cummins, 1999) and is often driven by the particular way in which an owner-manager does business. According to Gilmore et al. (2001), marketing in SMEs is likely to be haphazard, informal, loose, unstructured, spontaneous, and reactive, conforming to industry norms. Gilmore et al. (2001) showed that because of networking there was much more communication between the SME owner-manager and his/her competitors than is usually reported in the literature and that competing firms might be quite supportive of each other. Similarly, networking with customers usually involved building a relationship with one or two important individuals in those

MARKETING IN SMEs

companies. Should those individuals leave then the relationship with the company would dissolve (Gilmore et al., 2001; see also Hill et al., 1999; Johnsen and Johnsen, 1999). Hence, SMEs owner-managers recognised that building relationships was vital to a company's success and they invested considerable time and effort in maintaining good relations with regular clients (Gilmore et al., 2001). The creation and existence of effective networking was concerned with maximising marketing opportunities and ensuring the enterprise's survival and development (Gilmore et al., 2001).

CONCLUSIONS

There is no clear definition of marketing in SMEs, and those definitions of marketing that do exist either relate to larger businesses or are linked to entrepreneurial behaviour in smaller businesses. There are many theoretical and practical approaches to investigating marketing in SMEs and none of these approaches seems to be generally accepted. There is no grand unifying theory of marketing in SMEs. In addition, marketing in SMEs does not appear to evolve or mature even when the market conditions and business activities change considerably (Brooksbank et al., 1999).

The measurement of the performance of SMEs appears to be problematic. There is very little objective data relating marketing activity to business performance in SMEs, yet there are claims by academics and managers that marketing activities do improve business performance. The performance of SMEs is difficult to assess because of normal fluctuations in activities arising from year to year. This is further exacerbated by the potential to manipulate the measures such as ROCE and ROI, which are typically used to measure performance. One of the general problems with accounting ratios is that there is no absolute definition as to what constitutes a 'correct' ratio and many of the ratios used suffer from wide variation year on year because of operational changes within the SME.

Although marketing is an important business function, its role within the organisation and its relevance with regard to the business environment in which the company operates has a complex relationship (Moller and Anttila, 1987). In fact, it is so complex that many other strategies and orientations seem to be equally successful in SMEs (Huang and Brown, 1999; Carter et al., 1994). This makes investigating marketing in SMEs and relating these marketing activities to business performance extremely problematic.

CHAPTER REVIEW QUESTIONS

1. After reading this chapter, what conclusions can be drawn about marketing in small and medium sized enterprises? In your response try to list both positive and negative aspects.

2. An SME owner-manager believes he has developed a new in car audio system that allows drivers to play an iPod through a voice activated command. He believes it is unique and will be a fantastic success. He has built a number of samples and the initial tests prove the device is working but he is yet to show it to any potential customers. The manager wants to market the product but has no formal marketing knowledge and comes to you as a marketing student to ask for advice. What do you say?

3. Try to construct a formal theoretical model of marketing in small and medium sized enterprises that relates company performance to the various concepts,

theories, methods, activities, and approaches of marketing. Explain how such a model might be tested.

4. Carry out your own review of the literature on the use of marketing in small and medium-sized enterprises. Do we know which concepts, theories, methods, activities, and approaches to marketing improve the performance of the company? What recommendations would you give to a small and medium-sized enterprise based on this critical review of the literature?

5. What are the main problems facing researchers investigating the use of marketing in small and medium-sized enterprises? How might these problems be overcome?

CASE STUDY: ELECTRICAL EQUIPMENT LTD.

Introduction

Max Carter stared out across his desk for what was to be the last time. Retirement and a new life in the South of France beckoned. Max had worked for Electrical Equipment Ltd (EEL) for most of the company's existence, rising through the ranks to become Marketing Director. EEL is a small UK based company manufacturing and selling alarm, signal, control and communications equipment for use in potentially explosive atmospheres such as the oil, gas, and chemical industries. The company has expertise in hazardous area applications and has full in-house manufacturing capability and excellent design and development capabilities. The sales team consider themselves to be sales engineers and have considerable technical expertise when dealing with customers in this market. The barriers to entry into this market are high due to the requirements of formal certification bodies in the UK, Europe and the USA. The company had a turnover of £8.6m and a gross margin of 50% in 2008.

Corporate Plan

In 2005, Max had devised a corporate plan with the Managing Director, Tim Whitlow, to grow the company turnover to £10m within five years. Central to Max's strategy was the development of a complementary range of standard (non-explosive atmosphere capability) audio equipment. This new range would broaden the portfolio and allow for cross selling of equipment. Max thought that in every hazardous environment, there would be an equally non-hazardous situation that still needed audio communications. This was additional business and would allow the sales turnover to increase whilst making sales visits and sales account management more efficient. Tim Whitlow agreed to Max's proposal after some considerable discussion. However, the sales engineers were not completely convinced by this approach.

Operations and Logistics

The standard (non-ex) audio products contain unsophisticated technology and Max decided it would be more efficient and cheaper to have these built in Taiwan. However, this introduced a delivery lead time from the Taiwan company to the UK of up to three months. This type of standard (non-ex) loudspeakers are readily available from other competing companies and so to stay competitive EEL felt next day delivery was essential. In order to do this EEL keep a full range of these (non-ex) loudspeakers at the factory and has £0.5m of stock.

New markets

In addition, EEL are actively pursuing higher value market segments for overseas markets by improving their products and gaining higher levels of certification. The company had also designed a range of explosive atmosphere (Ex) compatible process control devices. These process control devices are very popular and have an increasing rate of demand such that they are likely to become the industry standard for these type of explosive atmosphere (Ex) compatible process control devices.

Competitors

EEL's main competitor is Norloud (a Norwegian Company) they have a similar product range and have 20 years of experience in the market. Norloud is very difficult to dislodge from this market and part of the decision to move into the commercial (non-ex) compatible loudspeakers, was to try to take some of the market share from Norloud. Other competitors crowd the market offering selected niche products to highly defined markets. However, EEL are able to offer a one-stop shop for industrial audio, and thus save customers time and expense in searching for alternatives. Unfortunately, this strategy came at a cost for EEL. Procurement came under increasing pressure and found some difficulties in dealing with a Taiwanese supplier for the first time. The production team were trying to come to terms with new products and operating systems resulting in delays in meeting deliveries. The sales engineers reported mixed feelings about having to sell what they considered standard high street shop audio equipment, leaving their real competence underutilised. In short, the company was under pressure on a number of fronts. Max consulted the company information detailed in tables 1, 2, and 3 and decided to write to his fellow directors.

December 2009

Max Carter's last memo as Marketing Director reads as follows:

> "The commercial (non-Ex) compatible loudspeakers are a major burden on the sales department and the company as a whole. In order to generate revenue these products are time and resource intensive, hard to differentiate on product characteristics, require sharper pricing and produce lower margins than our other products. I would like to discuss this problem and see what we can do at our next Board meeting."

Tables of data were appended to the memo and are shown below.

CASE QUESTIONS

1. You have just taken over as the new Marketing Director and your job is to produce an outline strategic marketing plan for Electrical Equipment Ltd.
2. As a separate report/memorandum to your own department, you should identify any potential problems with the implementation of your strategic marketing plan. Indicate any potential solutions to these problems in your report/memorandum.

OTHER QUESTIONS

1. If you had been Tim Whitlow, the Managing Director, in 2005 what would have been your response to Max Carter's proposal to grow the company? What alternative course(s) of action were available to the company in 2005? Critically evaluate the options available.
2. Use Porter's Five Forces to analyse the current position of the company and comment on the potential strategies available to Electrical Equipment Ltd.
3. Carry out a Strengths, Weaknesses, Opportunities and Threats (SWOT) analysis on the current position of the company and comment on your answer.

Use the Boston Consulting Growth-Share Matrix to analyse the data in Tables 1.1–1.3. Comment on the results of your analysis and suggest a way forward for the company.

Table 1.1 Financial Information on Electrical Equipment Ltd (EEL) and the contribution from the standard non-explosive atmosphere products from 2005

Item \ Year end	2005	2006	2007	2008
Total Turnover for EEL (£m)	4.7	6.4	8.0	8.6
Gross Margin for EEL (%)	57	50	50	50
Contribution from non-Ex Products (£m)	–	0.8	0.97	1.0
Gross Margin on non-Ex Products (%)	–	35	31	35

Table 1.2 Details of the products for Electrical Equipment Ltd (EEL) (2009)

Product Description	Average Price (£)	Gross Margin on the item (%)	Number of Competitors on each item
Call Points (Ex) (EE Ltd)	100	50	1 main comp.
Status Lamps (Ex) (EE Ltd)	500–1000	40–50	2
Beacon/strobes (Ex) (EEL)	175	60	3
Sounders/Horns (Ex) (EEL)	200	60	3
Loudspeakers (Ex) (EEL)	130	40	2
Commercial Loudspeakers (non-Ex)	30	30	UK: 10 and 50 internationally

Table 1.3 Market information on Electrical Equipment Ltd (EEL) Ex and non-Ex products in 2009

Product	Market Growth Rate (%)	Market Share (£m)	Largest Competitor (£m)
Ex Products	5.8	7.6	4
Non–Ex Products	0.0	1.0	3.0

Note: (Ex) denotes the product is suitable for use in potentially explosive atmospheres and (non-Ex) denotes the product is not suitable for use in potentially explosive atmospheres.

REFERENCES

Barber, J., Metcalfe, J. and Porteous, M. (1989) Barriers to Growth: The ACARD Study. In Barber, J. and Metcalfe, J. (Eds.), *Barriers to Growth in Small Firms*. Routledge Publishers, London.

Brodie, R. J., Coviello, N. E., Brookes, R. W. and Little, V. (1997) Towards a paradigm shift in marketing? An examination of current marketing practices. *Journal of Marketing Management*, 13, 383–406.

Brooksbank, R. (1996) The BASIC marketing planning process: A practical framework for the smaller business. *Marketing Intelligence and Planning*, 14(4), 16–23.

Brooksbank, R. (1999) The theory and practice of marketing planning in the smaller business. *Marketing Intelligence and Planning*, 17(2), 78–90.

Brooksbank, R., Kirby, D. A., Taylor, D. and Jones-Evans, D. (1999) Marketing in medium-sized manufacturing firms: The state-of-the-art in Britain, 1987–1992. *European Journal of Marketing*, 33(1/2), 103–120.

Campbell-Hunt, C. (2000) What have we learned about generic competitive strategy? A meta-analysis. *Strategic Management Journal*, 21, 127–154.

Carson, D. (1990) Some exploratory models for assessing small firms' marketing performance: A qualitative approach. *European Journal of Marketing*, 24(11), 5–49.

Carson, D. (1993) A philosophy for marketing education in small firms. *Journal of Marketing Management*, 9, 189–204.

Carson, D., Cromie, S., McGowan, P. and Hill, J. (1995) *Marketing and Entrepreneurship in SMEs: An Innovative Approach*. Pearson Education Limited, Harlow, UK. ISBN 0-13-150970-5.

Carter, N. M., Stearns, T. M., Reynolds, P. D. and Miller, B. A. (1994) New venture strategies: Theory development with an empirical base. *Strategic Management Journal*, 15, 21–41.

Chaffey, D., Mayer, R., Johnston, K. and Ellis-Chadwick, F. (2000) *Internet Marketing*. Prentice Hall, Harlow, England. ISBN 0-273-64309-6.

Chaston, I. and Mangles, T. (2002) *Small Business Marketing Management*. Palgrave Publishers, Basingstoke, UK. ISBN0-333-98075-1.

Denison, T. and McDonald, M. (1995) The role of marketing: Past, present and future. *Journal of Marketing Practice: Applied Marketing Science*, 1(1), 54–76.

European Commission (2005) *The new SME definition: User guide and model declaration*. Enterprise and Industry Publications, Brussels.

Fillis, I. (2002) Small firm marketing theory and practice: Insights from the outside. *Journal of Research in Marketing & Entrepreneurship*, 4(2), 134–157.

Frecknall Hughes, J., Simpson, M. and Padmore, J. (2007) Inherent limitations in using financial ratio analysis to assess small and medium sized company performance. Working paper 2007.01. The Management School, University of Sheffield. www.sheffield.ac.uk/management/research/papers/2007.html.

Freel, M. S. (2000) Barriers to product innovation in small manufacturing firms. *International Small Business Journal*, January–March 2000, 18(2), Issue (70), 60–80.

Gilmore, A., Carson, D. and Grant, K. (2001) SME marketing in practice. *Marketing Intelligence and Planning*, 19(1), 6–11.

Hannon, P. D. and Atherton, A. (1998) Small firm success and the art of orienteering: The value of plans, planning and strategic awareness in the competitive small firm. *Journal of Small Business and Enterprise Development*, Summer 1998, 5(2), 102–119.

Harris, L. C. (1996) Cultural obstacles to market orientation. *Journal of Marketing Practice: Applied Marketing Science*, 4(2), 36–52.

Harris, L. C. (1998) Barriers to market orientation: The view from the shop floor. *Marketing Intelligence and Planning*, 16(3), 221–228.

Harris, L. C. and Watkins, P. (1998) The impediments to developing a market orientation: An exploratory study of small UK hotels. *International Journal of Contemporary Hospitality Management*, 10(6), 221–226.

Henderson, S. (1998) No such thing as marketing orientation – a call for no more papers. *Management Decision*, 36(9), 598–609.

Hill, J. (2001a) A multidimensional study of the key determinants of effective SME marketing activity: Part 1. *International Journal of Entrepreneurial Behaviour and Research*, 7(5), 171–204.

Hill, J. (2001b) A multidimensional study of the key determinants of effective SME marketing activity: Part 2. *International Journal of Entrepreneurial Behaviour and Research*, 7(6), 211–235.

Hill, J., McGowan, P. and Drummond, P. (1999) The development and application of a qualitative approach to researching the marketing networks of small firm entrepreneurs. *Qualitative Market Research: An International Journal*, 2(2), 71–81.

Hill, J. and Wright, L. T. (2001) A qualitative research agenda for small to medium-sized enterprises. *Marketing Intelligence and Planning*, 19(6), 432–443.

Hogarth-Scott, S., Watson, K. and Wilson, N. (1996) Do small businesses have to practice marketing to survive and grow? *Marketing Planning and Intelligence*, 14(1), 6–18.

Huang, X. and Brown, A. (1999) An analysis and classification of problems in small business. *International Small Business Journal*, 18(1), 73–85.

Hudson, M., Lean, J. and Smart, P. A. (2001) Improving control through effective performance measurement in SMEs. *Production Planning & Control*, 12(8), 804–813.

Johnsen, R. E. and Johnsen, T. E. (1999) International market development through networks: The case of Ayrshire Knitwear sector. *International Journal of Entrepreneurial Behaviour and Research*, 5(6), 297–312.

Levitt, T. (1960) Marketing myopia. *Harvard Business Review*, July–August, 24–27.

McKenna, P. (1991) Marketing is everything. *Harvard Business Review*, January–February, 65–79.

McLarty, R. (1998) Case study: Evidence of a strategic marketing paradigm in a growing SME. *Journal of Marketing Practice: Applied Marketing Science*, 4(4), 105–117.

Moller, K. and Anttila, M. (1987) Marketing capability – A key success factor in small business? *Journal of Marketing Management*, 3(2), 185–203.

Narver, J. C. and Slater, S. F. (1990) The effect of market orientation on business profitability. *Journal of Marketing*, October, 54, 20–35.

O'Brien, E. (1998) The DTI marketing initiative: The experience of 35 young Scottish companies. *Journal of Small Business and Enterprise Development*, Autumn 1998, 5(3), 219–227.

O'Donnell, A and Cummins, D. (1999) The use of qualitative methods to research networking in SMEs. *Qualitative Market Research: An International Journal*, 2(2), 82–91.

Pelham, A. M. (2000) Market orientation and other potential influences on performance in small and medium-sized manufacturing firms. *Journal of Small Business Management*, January 2000, 38(1), 48–67.

Perry, S. C. (2001) The relationship between written business plans and the failure of small businesses in the U.S. *Journal of Small Business Management*, 39(3), 201–208.

Rafiq, M. and Pallett, R. A. (1996) Marketing implementation in the UK engineering industry. *Journal of Marketing Practice: Applied Marketing Science*, 2(4), 13–35.

Rayport, J. F. and Jaworski, B. J. (2001) *e-Commerce*. McGraw-Hill, Boston, USA. ISBN 0-07-112052-1.

Reynolds, P. L. (2002) The need for a new paradigm for small business marketing? – What was wrong with the old one? *Journal of Research in Marketing & Entrepreneurship*, 4(3), 191–205.

Rice, G. R. (1983) Strategic decision making in small businesses. *Journal of General Management*, 9, part 1, 58–65.

Romano, C. and Ratnatunga, J. (1995) The role of marketing: Its impact on small enterprise research. *European Journal of Marketing*, 29(7), 9–30.

Rue, L. W. and Ibrahim, N. A. (1998) The relationship between planning sophistication and performance in small business. *Journal of Small Business Management*, October 1998, 36(4), 24–32.

Simpson, M., Padmore, J., Taylor, N. and Frecknall-Hughes, J. (2006) Marketing in small and medium sized enterprises. *International Journal of Entrepreneurial Behaviour and Research*, 12(6), 361–387 (ISSN 1355-2554).

Simpson, M. and Taylor, N. (2002) The role and relevance of marketing in SMEs: Towards a new model. *Journal of Small Business and Enterprise Development*, 9(4), 370–382 (ISSN 1462-6004).

Siu, W. and Kirby, D. A. (1998) Approaches to small firm marketing: A critique. *European Journal of Marketing*, 32(1/2), 40–60.

Smith, A. and Whittaker, J. (1998) Management development in SMEs: What needs to be done? *Journal of Small Business and Enterprise Development*, Summer 1998, 5(2), 176–185.

Sparkes, A. and Thomas, B. (2001) The use of the internet as a critical success factor for the marketing of Welsh agri-food SMEs in the twenty-first century. *British Food Journal*, 103(5), 331–347.

Valos, M. and Baker, M. (1996) Developing an Australian model of export marketing performance determinants. *Marketing Intelligence and Planning*, 14(3), 11–20.

Chapter 2

Small and medium enterprises marketing
Innovation and sustainable economic growth perspective

Abdullah Promise Opute

LEARNING OBJECTIVES

Grounded on the sustainability thinking, this chapter provides a collection of core issues around small and medium entrepreneurship marketing discourse. The learning outputs from the chapter include:
- Understanding the term and attributes of an entrepreneur;
- Understanding the sustainability logic of entrepreneurial activity;
- Understanding small and medium entrepreneurship marketing;
- Recognising the important role of customer orientation and strategic marketing in SME marketing;
- Understanding innovation approach to SME marketing;
- Understanding how to optimise the economic growth impact of SMEs.

INTRODUCTION TO THE CHAPTER

Economies are facing intense challenges globally to figure out strategies for ensuring sustainable economic growth. One central priority in the sustainable economic growth focus is the need to curb the progressive rise in unemployment and underutilisation of skills. The importance of this economic focus has been recognised by United Nations Economic Programmes (UNEP). Indeed, the United Nations Sustainable Development Goals, which provides a blueprint for achieving a sustainable future for all by 2030, emphasise core sustainable economic growth indicators, for example no poverty (goal 1), zero hunger (goal 2), and decent work and economic growth (goal 8), among others. For developed and developing countries alike, small and medium-sized enterprises are instrumental to economic growth and sustainability.

Grounded in the strategic marketing foundation as a critical approach for customer orientation and boosting organisational performance, this chapter lauds the importance for innovation oriented SMEs. Given the aforementioned unemployment and skills underutilisation challenge, the pertinence for boosting and sustaining the economic growth and sustainability development impact of SMEs has become a prominent matter of interest to both academics and policymakers. On that background, the importance of the theoretical framing of this chapter cannot be underestimated. Next, 'entrepreneurial marketing' and fundamental significance to this chapter's theoretical framing is explained.

ENTREPRENEURIAL MARKETING

'Entrepreneurial marketing' (EM) – which 'describes the marketing activities of small and new ventures' (Kraus et al., 2010, p. 20) – has been lauded as an important issue given its significant role in the economic activities of such firms. Broadly viewed, EM does not necessarily relate to only small ventures, hence it is also conceptualised as 'the proactive identification and exploitation of opportunities for acquiring and retaining profitable customers through innovative approaches to risk management, resource leveraging and value creation' (Morris et al., 2002, p. 5). Thus, there are two perspectives of EM:

- The quantitative perspective of entrepreneurial marketing which emphasises the quantitative aspect of the company as marketing for small and new ventures; and
- The qualitative perspective of entrepreneurial marketing which stresses the qualitative aspect and portrays marketing with an entrepreneurial spirit (marketing by entrepreneurs).

Both perspectives are two sides of the same coin as marketing activities that are driven by entrepreneurial features (such as innovative, risk-oriented, and proactive spirit) are also relevant to quantitative characteristics (smallness and newness) (Kraus et al., 2010). While entrepreneurship is often connotated with innovativeness and risk-taking, it has been documented that small and new ventures are rarely innovative but rather imitative (e.g., Kraus et al., 2010), rarely technology oriented (e.g., ZEW, 2007), and not risk oriented (e.g., Bhidé, 1999). Recognising these strategic shortcomings and negative economic growth impact, the focus in this chapter is on small and medium enterprises (SMEs). Invoking Kraus et al.'s (2010) theoretical framing which combined the definition of marketing of the American Marketing Association (AMA) and two conceptualisations of entrepreneurship (entrepreneurial orientation and entrepreneurial management), entrepreneurial marketing conceptualisation in this chapter reflects marketing activities that take into account innovativeness, risk taking, proactiveness, and strategic pursuit of opportunities towards profitably satisfying customers.

Next, small and medium-sized enterprises are explained, as well as their link to economic growth. Following that, customer orientation and strategic marketing are discussed. Thereafter, SMEs are explained from the point of innovation and sustainable economic growth. Then chapter conclusions are presented.

SMALL AND MEDIUM-SIZED ENTERPRISES (SMES) AND ECONOMIC GROWTH

For developed, as well as developing, countries, small and medium-sized enterprises, as entrepreneurial ventures, are tremendous economic growth contributors. At this point, it is important to understand who the entrepreneur is. An entrepreneur has been defined diversely. In defining the term 'entrepreneur', contributors have used several attributes to capture the meaning of the term. Box 2.1 captures some definitions of an entrepreneur.

BOX 2.1: SOME DEFINITIONS OF AN ENTREPRENEUR

The entrepreneur is one who takes the risk of *being self-employed* (Cantillon, 1756), while Knight (1921) described the entrepreneur as one who takes *non-quantifiable risks*, and profits from such risk bearing. In another view, Weber (1930) described entrepreneurship as the expression of *cultural values*. In defining entrepreneur, Schumpeter (1931) emphasised the *innovative attribute* and posits that an entrepreneur is an individual experimenting with new combinations. Barth (1967) simply described the entrepreneur as a *social agent for change*.

Describing an entrepreneur, Kraus et al. (2010) portrays a perspective that incorporates strategic orientation and marketing logic and commented thus: '"entrepreneurship" is an adjective that describes an approach to marketing that embraces the opportunities of the marketplace in terms of an effective implementation of price, place, promotion, and product tactics (four Ps) by being risk-taking, innovative, and proactive' (p. 21).

Taken together therefore, and from the business point, an entrepreneur is an individual who strategically organises or operates a business (or businesses) and ensures that the core marketing elements of products (or services), price, place, and promotion are effectively implemented towards profitably satisfying the customer. Armed with foresight, drive, and ambition, an entrepreneur takes risk and seeks to solve business or consumer problems. Some typical qualities of an entrepreneur include:

- Being open-minded;
- Being proactive;
- Willingness to take risks;
- Readiness to leverage an opportunity; and
- Being innovative.

Being Open-Minded: Open-mindedness has been identified as a central attribute of an entrepreneur who desires to be successful. Even the smartest and most highly successful people stay open to new and diverse ideas, and this allows them to see opportunities ahead of them and better ways of solving problems. Staying open minded allows entrepreneurs to strategise effectively, taking into consideration the cues from varying viewpoints.

Being Proactive: According to Merriam-Webster, being proactive implies 'acting in anticipation of future problems, needs, or changes'. Proactivity is a core operational feature of successful organisations. To optimise the business potentials, take opportunities, and compete effectively, an entrepreneur must be active and initiate carefully planned actions towards achieving desired goals.

Willingness to Take Risks: Risk taking is a core attribute of an entrepreneur. The willingness to take risk is the motivational component that prompts entrepreneurs to invest time and effort into seeking successful transformation of identified potential opportunities. Not taking risks can stifle a new business and hinder it from progressing beyond the infant stage. Entrepreneurs are however not blind risk takers; rather the risks are carefully thought out and the potential benefits weighed up.

Readiness to Leverage an Opportunity: An entrepreneur aims strategically to organise operational activities towards profitably satisfying the customer. Entrepreneurial decisions are therefore processed towards achieving positive outcome. Among others, decisions made include identifying and leveraging opportunities.

Being Innovative: Innovativeness is a core attribute of an entrepreneur. Success-driven entrepreneurs constantly search for innovations and new ways of reinventing their ideas. Whether innovations are internally or externally driven, entrepreneurs always push for new and better ways to process and implement their business plans and improve their value added creation by ways of marketing and or products based innovation strategies. To effectively grow their business through innovation, successful entrepreneurs reflect and adopt changes when necessary.

Given its instrumental importance to developed and developing economies, SMEs are increasingly being leveraged as economic activity medium (see Table 2.1). The plausibility of SMEs as economic growth contributors is also documented in Table 2.1.

Table 2.1 *Small and medium-sized enterprises and economic impact*

1.	Small and medium businesses are growing in developed as well as emerging economies	Welsh et al. (2014)
2.	As at 2007, there were 1,063,000 women entrepreneurs and 4,847,000 male entrepreneurs	Welsh et al. (2014)
3.	The *Global Entrepreneurship Monitor Women's Report* (GEM) documents over 100 million women in 59 countries launched and grew a new business venture in 2010. These countries represent more than 52% of the world's population and 84% of the world's gross domestic product (GDP)	Kelly et al. (2011)
4.	The number of small and medium enterprises (women) is increasing and contributing to jobs and wealth in many societies	Brush et al. (2010)
5.	Small and medium (family) business is very much widespread around the world. Spain, Austria, Italy, Germany, Switzerland, Norway, and the United Kingdom are typical countries of the European Union with a high level of family business	Petlina and Koráb (2015)
8.	Majority of companies belong to the sub-sector of family businesses and generate the most of new jobs in various countries	Ramadani and Hoy (2015)
9.	Small and medium-sized enterprises aid economic growth in developed and developing countries	Mitchell and Reid (2000)
10.	Small and medium-sized enterprises represent 99% of the global business population	Azudin and Mansor (2017)
11.	In Malaysia, small and medium-sized enterprises represent 97.3% of registered businesses as well as contribute 36% of gross domestic product of the nation	Azudin and Mansor (2017)
12.	Small and medium business (family businesses) contributed a 4.8% increase in total employment growth in the period 2006–2007 in Italy	Colombo et al. (2014)

Table 2.1 (continued)

13.	Small and medium (family) businesses account for more than two-thirds of all businesses and contribute significantly to wealth, competitiveness, and job creation in their countries;	Donckels and Frohlich (1991)
	estimates show that in the USA, 40 to 60% of the gross domestic product (GDP) is created by small and medium (family) businesses	Ward and Aronoff (1991)
14.	Small and medium (family) businesses contribute to economic growth through technological development and expansion into foreign markets	Morck and Yeung (2003)
15.	In India, small and medium (family) businesses generate about 79% jobs and account for two-third of GDP	Bernard (2013)

CUSTOMER ORIENTATION AND STRATEGIC MARKETING

The customer is visualised as being a king (Kennedy and Laczniak, 2016), hence the central focus of marketing is on the customer. In the modern day market landscape, customer orientation is a *sine qua non* for competing effectively in the market. Especially in this age of digital revolution where market boundaries are vastly disappearing through the enabling influence of multi-media devices in connecting to customers and across markets (Opute, 2017). Competing effectively in such digital norm requires an operational strategy that recognises the importance of drawing closer to the customer (Opute, 2020). For SMEs to effectively fulfil their role as sustainability and economic growth agents, they must be customer oriented.

Customer orientation implies the extent to which a firm channels its efforts towards responding effectively to the needs of the customer. An important marketing variable, customer orientation implies a customer driven business culture that culminates in best value creation for the customer. As Luo et al. (2008) note, the positive performance impact of customer orientation derives from the resulting trust. Building and consolidating this trust is of significant importance to SMEs that aspire to achieve sustainability and economic growth impact. Therefore, customer orientation may not only imply drawing closer to the customer but also cultivating long-term relationship with them. By doing both, organisations would position themselves to effectively build and consolidate trust.

Within the philosophy of employing a customer focus, a critical operational initiative relates to strategic orientation – a core enabler of entrepreneurial innovativeness (Kim, Kim and Yang, 2012). This importance of strategic orientation is recognised in this chapter, and in line with the entrepreneurial marketing emphasis in this chapter, strategic marketing is explained next.

Strategic marketing

The marketing landscape is increasing immensely in dynamism and challenges. Staying competitive in these circumstances requires organisations that are committed to embracing a suitable strategy to effectively respond to customers' stimuli as well as environmental and competitor pressure. SMEs must embrace proactive strategic marketing initiatives that enable them to shape their goals and survival.

The concept of strategic marketing has evolved over the last few decades and has been enhanced by inputs from the domains of marketing, strategic management, and industrial organisation (IO) economics. According to Meyer (1991, p. 828), strategy is crystallised around one central question: 'What causes certain firms to outperform their competitors on a sustained basis?'. Reinforcing and extending that substance, Varadarajan (2010, p. 133) proposed the following as issues fundamental to strategic marketing: (1) What explains differences in the marketing behaviour of competing businesses in the marketplace? and (2) What explains differences in the marketplace and financial performance of competing brands/product lines/businesses?

The underlying thesis of this chapter is that SMEs can be major actors in the wheel of sustainability and economic growth. To fulfil economic growth role, they must embrace customer orientation and critically ensure a suitable strategic marketing approach. Given the increasing dynamism in the modern day marketplace, characterised by tremendous technology revolution, a robust strategic marketing strategy approach that outplays competitors in adequately creating value for customers is essential. Such a strategic marketing approach would yield desired financial performance that drives and sustains economic growth impact of SME. Recognising aforementioned issues fundamental to strategic marketing, this chapter invokes Varadarajan's (2010, p. 126) viewpoint – strategic marketing encompasses organisational, inter-organisational and environmental phenomena concerning:

- The behaviour of organisations in the marketplace in how they interact with and respond to consumers, customers, and competitors stimuli as well as other external constituencies, in the operational efforts of creating, communicating, and delivering products and services that offer value to customers at a profit; and
- The general management responsibilities from the point of the boundary spanning relationship of the marketing function with other interfacing functional areas in the organisations.

The centrality of customer value creation in driving organisational strategy is undisputed. Consequently, the strategic marketing designs of an organisation must align to that value creation focus. In other words, strategic marketing is one major tool for implementing the customer value creation plan of an organisation. Fundamentally, a core task of strategic marketing is to address the question of how the marketing strategy of a business is shaped by both demand side and supply side factors. Effectively negotiating this task requires a strategic marketing orientation that is proactively tailored to offer suitable responses to the multiple stimuli (customers, competitors, and external environment). SMEs must ensure a strategic marketing approach that pursues and leverages closeness to customers in effectively delivering best value to customers through product/service offers and use of suitable marketing strategy. To optimise strategic marketing effectiveness, organisations must also ensure appropriate marketing strategy, i.e., integrated range of decisions that reflect the organisation's priorities concerning products (or services), markets, marketing activities, and marketing resources for creating, communicating, and delivery of products (or services) that meet the expectation of customers, and in so doing, meeting the objectives of the organisation. Essential in that strategic marketing orientation is an information seeking focus that enables SMEs to understand and respond effectively to competitors and other stimuli in the market.

For SMEs that have the operational capacity that involves functional boundaries, the strategic marketing activity will include also the optimal alignment of the functional areas towards symbiotic interdependence, effective marketing strategy implementation, and profitably satisfying the customer.

SMEs: INNOVATION AND SUSTAINABLE ECONOMIC GROWTH

A central underpinning foundation to the theoretical framing of this chapter relates to the entrepreneur-centred view, which contends that outcomes are contingent on the features and action models of key decision makers in SMEs. In that view, human agency is a critical factor that explains the strategic choices made for organisations. Thus, the entrepreneur-centred view challenges the assumption that SMEs strategic choices can be adequately explained by considering only a firm's external contingencies and its structural characteristics (Geppert and Clark, 2003; Hsieh et al., 2019). Invoking the entrepreneur-centred view, the theorising of this chapter considers the individual entrepreneur or group of decision makers in SMEs as the focal point as discovering or enacting of opportunities are strategic actions within their functional tents. Being innovation oriented is a strategic approach that decision maker(s) in SMEs must embrace towards boosting their performance and economic growth contribution.

Innovative firms gain a competitive advantage over their competitors. SMEs have the potential to be a significant contributor to sustainable economic growth. When strategically maximised, that potential can lead to highly customer oriented SMEs that play a major role in the national economic wheel. Importantly, SMEs that achieve such a pivotal economic role do not only create employment and utilisation of skills in their immediate operational environment but also drive the economic wheel, nationally and even globally, by keeping the economic chain active, an outcome that creates employment opportunities and further lubricates the economic chain. Consequently, SMEs that attain this pivotal capacity undergo a cycle transformation.

To achieve that sustainable economic growth impact, SMEs must embrace innovative strategy in their operations. SMEs must be proactive, willing to take risks and embrace initiatives that enable them to become or remain innovative in ensuring effective customer orientation in a marketplace that is progressively gaining in intensity and dynamism. Innovation can take different forms (see Figure 2.1):

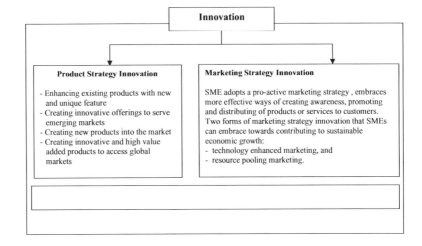

Figure 2.1 Types of Innovation for SMEs

Source: Author

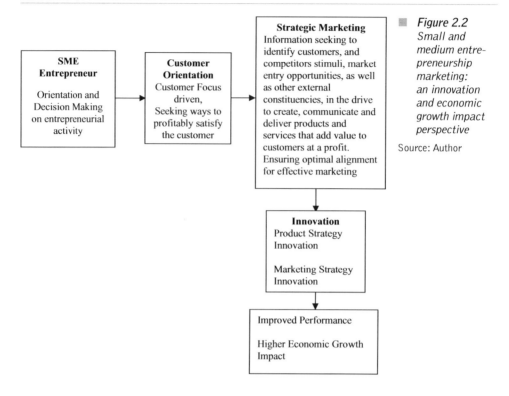

Figure 2.2 Small and medium entrepreneurship marketing: an innovation and economic growth impact perspective

Source: Author

Product Strategy Innovation: Innovation is a critical component of product differentiation strategy and product innovation is a fundamental competitive strategy component (e.g., Hsieh et al., 2019). Product strategy innovation includes: (1) innovative product offering – creating products that are already existing in the market but with new and unique features that appeal to the interest of customers; (2) innovative product offerings that serve emerging markets; (3) innovative product offerings – creating new products that did not exist previously in the market; and (4) innovative and high value-added products that serve a worldwide clientele.

Marketing Strategy Innovation: Innovation can take the form of marketing strategy, whereby the SME adopts a proactive approach that embraces new and effective ways of creating awareness, promoting and distributing of products or services to customers beyond the geographical domain where the SME is located. There are two forms of marketing strategy innovation that SMEs can embrace towards contributing to sustainable economic growth: technology enhanced marketing and resource pooling marketing.

- *Technology Enhanced Marketing*: This is a marketing strategy innovation approach where the entrepreneur leverages technology to boost the marketing of services or tangible products. The world is changing tremendously, and there is enormous power in the way technology and social media is used to drive marketing and in accessing market segments. Social media and technological devices offer entrepreneurs, including SMEs a medium for accessing markets beyond the geographical boundaries where the enterprise is situated. Using such technological and social media devices, entrepreneurships (including SMEs) can access a pool of customers in diverse social groups, and also aid their internationalisation.

- *Resource Pooling Marketing*: This is a marketing strategy innovation approach which involves a collaborative strategy where SMEs join forces with other firms in other locations who serve other product and market segments and leverage their network to help in marketing each other's products or services in their individual market domains for their mutual benefit. SMEs can also gain international orientation through this approach as they, overtime, gain foreign market knowledge and perceptions of opportunities through their resource pooling marketing.

CONCLUSION

Figure two summarises the conceptual framework of this chapter. Organisation formation and innovation are not only core to the entrepreneurship construct (Schumpeter, 1942) but also a differentiator of what is and what is not entrepreneurial (Covin and Miles, 1999; Covin and Miller, 2013). Grounded in that foundation, this chapter points to the importance of innovation-based SMEs as a strategic way of responding effectively to the increasing pressure to achieving sustainable economic growth. While innovativeness is the ability to produce innovation, the strength of this ability is reflected by the emergent innovation process outcome, for example new product/service introductions (and new market penetrations), market acceptance, and sustainable economic growth generation input.

Achieving such sustainable economic growth input requires SMEs that are not only innovation oriented but also cultivate risk taking ability and proactiveness. SMEs must exhibit a persevering orientation that utilises knowledge seeking attitude to penetrate new market territories, an operational approach that has been proven to facilitate early and accelerated internationalisation of SMEs (Li et al., 2015; Hsieh et al., 2019). SMEs must be bold in their operational approach, show willingness to take opportunities, take a step into the unknown – exploiting networks and opportunities to access markets (including international markets), embracing new strategies of production and service and more effective ways of marketing products and services.

Within the proposed proactive drive, SMEs should embrace strategic marketing orientation that shifts from the traditional customer engagement to online and technology-based options towards improving the innovation of products and services. Additional to the customer engagement benefits, such online and technology-based strategic marketing options can be exploited to take advantage of opportunities, for example accessing customer and market segments beyond the geographical location of the SMEs – internationalisation.

Entrepreneurial activities drive economic growth, and SMEs contribute immensely in that connection. Achieving the economic growth impact of SMEs hinges however on the extent to which the entrepreneurial activities are effectively implemented towards profitably satisfying the customers. To fulfil their role as lubricants of the economic wheel of societies, SMEs must be strategically oriented, proactive, innovative, and risk taking, and exploit opportunities, not only in their product (or service) offerings but also in their marketing dynamics. SMEs must embrace an entrepreneurial strategy that recognises and leverages the nuances of exploratory and exploitative innovation to optimise their ability to profitably satisfy customers and impact economic growth.

REVIEW QUESTIONS

1. Who is an entrepreneur? What are the characteristics of an entrepreneur?

2. What role do SMEs play in the economic growth of a country?

3. Explain the term 'entrepreneurial marketing'.

4. What role do you think customer orientation plays in SME marketing, and what steps can SMEs take in the way of recognising and leveraging the importance of customer orientation?

5. With digital revolution becoming a norm in the 21st century, market boundaries are vastly disappearing. What are the threats and opportunities of such development for SMEs?

6. Taking into consideration the dynamism in the 21st-century marketplace, what is the importance of strategic marketing to SMEs; identify critical strategic marketing steps that SMEs can take towards enhancing their competitive advantage.

7. Define and explain the importance of innovation to entrepreneurship. What innovative steps can SMEs take to enhance their value creation to customers and economic growth impact of SMEs?

8. Sustainability and economic growth will continue to be matters of importance to global economies: discuss what steps SMEs can take to effectively fulfil their role in the economic growth chain.

CASE STUDY: TOYOTA PRIUS: A CASE IN NEW PRODUCT DEVELOPMENT

"The Prius is solid evidence that the ponderous development process that produces new automobiles is finally on the brink of a genuine technological breakthrough."[1]

– Popular Science Magazine, July 1997

"We believe that clearing environmental hurdles and offering an attractive driving experience are critical for cars to thrive in the 21st century."[2]

– Hiroyuki Watanabe, Senior Managing Director, Toyota in 2003

Introduction

In December 1997, Toyota Motor Corporation (Toyota) of Japan launched its hybrid vehicle Prius in the Japanese market. This was one of the first mass-produced hybrid vehicles in the world. The Toyota Hybrid System (THS) combined an internal combustion engine fuelled by gasoline with an electric motor.

Prius achieved a balance between high mileage and low emissions and was the upshot of the company's initiative to produce environment-friendly automobiles

SMALL AND MEDIUM ENTERPRISES MARKETING

and its goal of manufacturing the 'Ultimate Eco Car'. The Prius generated much enthusiasm in the industry as it was both efficient and stylish.

The car was known to be safe and conformed to Japanese environmental pollution standards. Having sold more than 100,000 units worldwide by 2002, it was the bestselling hybrid car model in the world.

Further refined models were introduced in 2000 and 2003. Prius was introduced in the US market in 2000, after Toyota conducted a study of the US market and consumer preferences. Leveraging the research findings, various strategies were developed for this market. The new improved Prius sold for same price as the original Prius. These strategies helped Prius to successfully penetrate the tough US market even though it was based on a new concept of a hybrid car. In 2001, the Automotive Engineering International recognised Prius as the 'world's best engineered passenger car'.

By 2002, it was being sold in North America, Japan, Europe, Hong Kong, Australia, and Singapore. Analysts opined that the demand for hybrid cars would rise because of the unstable oil prices and the growing need for environment friendly products.

Commenting on the future of green technologies and on Prius in particular, Chris Giller of Grist.org said, 'In the marketplace, green technologies and industries are among the fastest growing and most innovative developments. The Toyota Prius has defied every prediction to become the must-have car. The organic food business doubles every time you blink. Renewable energy, emissions trading, environmentally conscious investing: many of the most exciting advances in environmental thinking are happening in the private sector'.

Background Note: Toyota

Toyota's history goes back to 1897, when Sakichi Toyoda (Sakichi) diversified into the textile machinery business from his traditional family business of carpentry. He invented a power loom in 1902 and founded the parent organisation of Toyota, the Toyoda Group, in the same year. In 1926, Sakichi invented an automatic loom that stopped operating when a thread broke.

This prevented the manufacture of imperfect cloth. (Calling attention to problems and rectifying them at the earliest later became an important part of the Toyota Production System (TPS)). The same year, Sakichi formed the Toyoda Automatic Loom Works (TALW) to manufacture automatic looms.

Sakichi's son Kiichiro, an engineer from Tokyo University, was more interested in automobiles and engines than the family's textile business. In 1929, he traveled to the US and Europe to study the manufacturing processes in car factories there. After returning to Japan, he spent his time studying car engines and experimenting with better ways to manufacture them.

In the early 1930s, Kiichiro convinced his father to launch an automobile business and in 1933, Sakichi established an automobile department within

TALW. The first passenger car prototype was developed in 1935. In 1936, Sakichi sold the patent rights of his automatic loom to a company in England to raise money to set up a new automobile business.

Hybrid Cars

Ferdinand Porsche manufactured the first hybrid-electric car in 1898. In the 1960s, a few attempts were made to manufacture hybrid cars by applying turbine engines to the production of the vehicles. A turbine-powered race car was introduced in 1967, with the turbine engines powering the wheels through a mechanical transmission.

The need for cleaner and more efficient vehicles led to the development of hybrid vehicles in the 1970s. In 1970, a program called the Federal Clean Car Incentive (FCCI) was started by the US government. This program led to the development of a hybrid prototype in 1972.

The program was scrapped in 1976 by the Environmental Protection Agency (EPA) of the US. In 1993, another program called the Partnership for a New Generation of Vehicles (PNGV) was launched in the US. The partners in the program – Chrysler, Ford, GM, and a few governmental agencies – developed hybrid prototypes but never commercialised them.

Knowledge Management at Toyota

According to analysts, Toyota's success in both the local and global markets was based on its gaining a competitive advantage through implementation of innovative and path-breaking ideas on its production floors. Toyota had focussed on learning from the very beginning.

At Toyota, knowledge sharing was intertwined with its people-based enterprise culture, referred to as the Toyota Way. The five key principles that summed up the Toyota Way were: Challenge, Kaizen (improvement), Genchi Genbutsu (go and see), Respect, and Teamwork.

The Toyota Way recognised employees as the company's strength and attached great importance to developing human abilities through training, coaching and mentoring. The principles of 'Respect for People' and 'Continuous Improvement' were at the core of the Toyota Way. Most experts agree that the TPS system at Toyota worked by combining its explicit, implicit, and tacit knowledge.

The Original Prius

The original Prius was powered by the THS. The THS was an advanced version of the EMS. THS is a power train that combined an internal combustion engine and an electric motor. It was based on the series/parallel hybrid system. It contained a power split mechanism that divided and sent power through two passages.

The First Generation Prius

In 2000, Toyota introduced its first generation model of the Prius in the US, Europe, and other markets. This model was also called Prius NHW11 or Prius

SMALL AND MEDIUM ENTERPRISES MARKETING

Classic. A few modifications were made to the vehicle to meet vehicle standards for California, USA. Modifications were made to the engine by increasing the horsepower from 58 to 72.

Marketing the First Generation Prius in the US

For Toyota, marketing the first generation Prius in the US was a challenge. Commenting on the launch of Prius in the US market, Senior Vice President and General Manager of Toyota Motor Sales, Don Edmond (Edmond) said, 'Frankly, it was one of the biggest crapshoots I've ever been involved in. Not because we lacked confidence in the quality of the product, or the logic of the concept, or the significance of this breakthrough technology. The challenge was to convince U.S. consumers that hybrid technology was more than a science project'.

The Second Generation Prius

Toyota began evaluating the popularity of its first generation Prius in the market soon after it was launched. The evaluation was based on the price, performance, and social aspects of the product as seen by buyers and potential customers.

The Testing

The most important feature of the new Prius was its enhanced safety. The company had worked towards child safety, reducing the impact of collisions to a remarkable degree.

Outlook

Toyota expected higher demand for the new Prius than the earlier versions. Edmond said, 'We are targeting a sales volume of 36,000 for the first full year. That's three times our sales target for Prius (original) when it launched in the U.S.'.

Sources: (1) Annual Report, 1998, www.toyota.co.jp (2) Yuri Kageyama, "Toyota Unveils Beefed-Up Hybrid," www.cbsnews.com, April 17, 2003. (3) Automotive Engineering International is a magazine published by the Society of Automotive Engineers. The magazine contains latest information about the technology, and the products manufactured. (4) Grist.org (Grist Magazine) was an online magazine providing environmental news. Grist was a nonprofit organisation established in 1999 and headquartered in Seattle, Washington. (5) Chip Giller, "The Environment's New Bling," www.boston. com, April 21, 2005. www.icmrindia.org/casestudies/catalogue/Marketing/Toyota%20Prius.htm

QUESTIONS

1. As shown in the case study, Toyota Motor Corporation (Toyota) of Japan launched its hybrid vehicle Prius in the Japanese market in December 1997. One of the first mass-produced hybrid vehicles in the world, this product was a huge global success and contributed to Toyota's recognition on the global stage. Based on the facts in Box 1:
   a. Identify and discuss the strategic marketing initiatives in the operational modus of Toyota Motor Corporation (Toyota) of Japan.
   b. Identify and discuss the innovation based features of the operational modus described in Box 1.

c. Identify and discuss the market penetration (internationalisation) approach and its effectiveness to the competitiveness of Toyota Motor Corporation (TMC).
d. Discuss how the combination of the steps in questions (a, b, and c) enables the economic growth impact of TMC (Toyota) of Japan.

2. As shown in the case study, TMC (Toyota) of Japan began as a family carpentry business and passed through several forms of diversification and transformation. Based on the facts in Box 2:
   a. Discuss the term entrepreneurial drive and explain the entrepreneurial drive influence on the diversification and transformation reflected in Box 2.
   b. Discuss the process to internationalisation that SMEs may pass through.
   c. Identify and discuss the strategic processes used by TMC (Toyota) of Japan.
   d. Identify and discuss the innovation features reflected in Box 2.
   e. Pinpoint the learning and knowledge management steps taken and discuss how learning and knowledge management culture aid the growth of SMEs and economic growth contribution.

3. As shown in the case study, TMC (Toyota) of Japan faced a challenge in marketing the First Generation Prius in the US: Based on the facts in Box 3:
   a. Pinpoint the core features of this challenge.
   b. Identify and discuss the strategic marketing and innovation steps taken to effectively address this challenge.
   c. Discuss how the steps taken in b would enable Toyota' economic growth contribution.

LET'S REASON TOGETHER

Daniel Platt Limited: a case study in engineering entrepreneurship

Introduction

William Wilkes, Roof Tile Technical Manager at Daniel Platt Limited and an experienced brick layer and roofer, recognised the problem precisely. 'Builders using clay roof tiles often find that they cannot get the roof tiles they need when they need them, especially when working on the valley area of a roof where two pitches meet.' During 170 years of manufacturing natural clay floor tiles, Daniel Platt had to adapt to market needs in an entrepreneurial way on many occasions, and this problem for builders presented an opportunity to create new customers.

Delving into the niche market for clay roof tiles was one such entrepreneurial response when the wider market for ceramic products became increasingly competitive. Having made the move, maintaining a strong, distinct position in the selected niche was vital in order to maximise the value of the opportunity. The introduction of a flexible product design would enable the right products to be available ex-stock.

Routinely, builders might have to wait for up to eight weeks because a particular specification to fit the pitch of the roof they were working on was not available. The

SMALL AND MEDIUM ENTERPRISES MARKETING

implications in terms of time lost and negative cash flow are significant, as jobs cannot be completed within contractual terms. Producing only one type of fitting instead of three would reduce stock levels and improve product availability resulting in more satisfied customers and increases in sale revenue.

Additional Information

The Engineering Issue

Roofs are constructed with different levels of pitch (slope), most commonly 40, 45, and 50 degree pitches, each one requiring a different 'fitting' which is in fact the term used to describe the angle between the two wings of a valley tile. The task was to design a single tile that would fit all three angles. 'It was relatively easy to get it right for two angles but all three required more consideration to ensure the aesthetics and the functionality of the tile were right', William Wilkes explained.

The process began with a cardboard template, progressed to a metal angled support plate, and then to a piece of extruded clay placed on the support plate and cut to required shape. Different angles were tried and tested on a metal frame roof construction fitted with boards and tile laths and located within Daniel Platt's manufacturing facility. The selected best fits were then fired and placed on to the test roof. It was a long and meticulous design engineering process. As the valley tiles do not feature the 'nibs' that hold regular roof tiles on the laths, precision engineering was essential as the valley tiles at every angle must be supported by the regular tiles.

Innovative Actions Support

Daniel Platt's capacity to exploit the opportunity was considerably enhanced by the support of the Innovative Actions Programme, West Midlands. This regional development agent provided a mechanism for encouraging companies to think differently and for making innovation 'real' and effective. Daniel Platt's entrepreneurial skills and engineering capability were boosted and a product that may have otherwise never reached the market was successfully created. The team provided David Platt with funding to support the research and product development processes, including a coaching and mentoring service.

The universal valley tiles are currently on test with the building trade, and positive feedback is already being received. Sales of roof tiles are now providing customers for one third of the company's total output.

4. mini-case-studies – case studies entrepreneurship

Accessed on 30 May, 2019, from: www.coursehero.com/file/13024027/4-mini-case-studies/

Question:
Using an innovative approach, this company has been able to effectively respond to the challenge faced by the company. Identify the nature of innovation in this case and explain the proactive steps taken towards staying competitive.

TECHNOLOGY, SMES, AND THE 21ST CENTURY

Entrepreneurship, and indeed SMEs, are gaining increasing importance as a vehicle for job creation and economic growth. For economies to adapt effectively and achieve the aforementioned dual outcomes, SMEs are increasingly embracing innovative strategies. 'Innovation and entrepreneurship power economic growth' (Florida et al., 2017, p. 87). Entrepreneurial innovation enables SMEs to creatively respond to market challenges. In the 21st century where technologies are evolving tremendously and massively impacting how we live and organise our activities, SMEs must respond to, and leverage, this evolvement. On the one hand, due to information and communication technology, customers are not only able to stay connected with other consumers globally but also access the global market, a development that increases the competition challenge that business faces. On the other hand, SMEs can leverage the technology advancement to enable them respond effectively to market stimuli. In other words, SMEs must embrace suitable strategic marketing approach to compete effectively. Doing that requires that SMEs enforce innovative approaches in their entrepreneurial activity. SMEs can leverage technology to implement product strategy innovation through (1) innovative product offering with unique features that appeal to the interest of existing customers, (2) innovative product offerings that serves emerging markets, (3) innovative product offerings leading to new products in the existing market, and (4) innovative and high value added products that serve the global market. Also, SMEs can leverage technology to implement marketing strategy innovation that embraces new and effective ways of creating awareness, promoting and distributing of products or services to customers beyond the geographical domain where the SME is located. SMEs can adopt two options in that regard: (1) technology enhanced marketing and (2) resource pooling marketing.

Questions:
1. What entrepreneurial steps can SMEs take towards effectively fulfilling their role as economic growth drivers?
2. How does technology impact entrepreneurial activity of SMEs?

REFERENCES

Azudin, A. and Mansor, N. (2017) Management accounting practices of SMEs: The impact of organizational DNA, business potential and operational technology. *Asia Pacific Management Review*, 23(3), 222–226.

Barth, F. (1967) On the study of social change. *American Anthropologist*, 69, 661–669.

Bernard, H. R. (2013) Family-owned businesses–the backbone of Indian economy. Available at: http://www.kpmgfamilybusiness.com/family-owned-businesses-backbone-indias-economy/

Bhidé, A. V. (1999) *The Origin and Evolution of New Businesses.* Oxford University Press, New York.

Brush, C. G., Carter, N. M., Gatewood, E. J., Greene, P. G. and Hart, M. M. (2010) *Women Entrepreneurs and the Global Environment for Growth.* Edward Elgar Publishing, Inc, Boston, MA.

Cantillon, R. (1756) *Essai sur la nature du commerce en général,* Gyles, R., London and Paris.

Cavusgil, S. T. and Knight, G. (2015) The born global firm: An entrepreneurial and capabilities perspective on early and rapid internationalization. *Journal of International Business Studies*, 46, 3–16.

Colombo, M. G., De Massis, A., Piva, E., Rossi-Lamastra, C. and Wright, M. (2014) Sales and employment changes in entrepreneurial ventures with family ownership: Empirical evidence from high-tech industries. *Journal of Small Business Management*, 52(2), 226–245.

Covin, J. G. and Miles, M. P. (1999) Corporate entrepreneurship and the pursuit of competitive advantage. *Entrepreneurship Theory and Practice*, 23(3), 47–63.

Covin, J. G. and Miller, D. (2013) International entrepreneurial orientation: Conceptual considerations, research themes, measurement issues, and future research directions. *Entrepreneurship Theory and Practice*, 38, 11–44.

Dana, L. P. and Dana, T. E. (2005) Expanding the scope of methodologies used in entrepreneurship research. *International Journal of Entrepreneurship and Small Business*, 2(1), 79–88.

Day, G. S. (1984) *Strategic Market Planning: The Pursuit of Competitive Advantage*. West Publishing Company, St Paul.

Day, G. S. and Montgomery, D. B. (1997) Call for papers. *Journal of Marketing*, 61(April), 100–101.

Day, G. S. and Montgomery, D. B. (1999) Charting new directions for marketing. *Journal of Marketing*, 63(Special Issue), 3–13.

Deshpande, R., Farley, J. and Webster, F. (1993) Corporate culture, customer orientation, and innovativeness in Japanese firms: A quadrad analysis. *Journal of Marketing*, 57, 23–37.

Donckels, R. and Fröhlich, E. (1991) Are family businesses really different? European experiences from STRATOS. *Family Business Review*, 4(2), 149–160.

Florida, R., Adler, P. and Mellander, C. (2017) The city as innovation machine. *Regional Studies*, 51(1), 86–96.

Geppert, M. and Clark, E. (2003) Knowledge and learning in transnational ventures: An actor-centred approach. *Management Decision*, 41, 433–442.

Hsieh, L., Child, J., Narooz, R., Elbanna, S., Karmowska, J., Marinova, S., Puthusserry, P., Tsai, T. and Zhang, Y. (2019) A multidimensional perspective of SME internationalization speed: The influence of entrepreneurial characteristics. *International Business Review*, 28, 268–283.

Hunt, S. D. (2015) The theoretical foundations of strategic marketing and marketing strategy: Foundational premises, R-A theory, three fundamental strategies, and societal welfare. *AMS Review*, 5(3–4). doi:10.1007/s13162-015-0069-5.

Hunt, S. D. and Morgan, R. M. (1995) The comparative advantage theory of competition. *Journal of Marketing*, 59(April), 1–15.

Iwu, C. G., Opute, A. P., Nchu, R., Eresia-Eke, C., Tengeh, R. K., Jaiyeoba, O. and Aliyu, A. (in press) *The International Journal of Management Education*.

Kelly, D. J., Bosma, N. and Amoros, J. E. (2011). Global Entrepreneurship Monitor 2010 Global Report. Available at: https://entreprenorskapsforum.se/wp-content/uploads/2011/02/GEM-2010-Global-Report.pdf (accessed October 21, 2019).

Kennedy, A.-M. and Laczniak, G. R. (2016) Conceptualisations of the consumer in marketing thought. *European Journal of Marketing*, 50(1/2), 166–188,

Kennedy, K. N., Goolsby, J. R. and Arnould, E. J. (2003) Implementing a customer orientation: Extension of theory and application. *Journal of Marketing*, 67(October), 67–81.

Kim, Y., Kim, W. and Yang, T. (2012). The effect of the triple Helix system and habitat on regional entrepreneurship: Empirical evidence from the US. *Research Policy*, 41(1), 154–166.

Klewitz, J. and Hansen, E. G. (2014) Sustainability-oriented innovation of SMEs: A systematic review. *Journal of Cleaner Production*, 65, 57–75.

Knight, F. (1921) *Risk, Uncertainty and Profit*. Houghton Mifflin, Boston.

Kraus, S., Harms, R. and Fink, M. (2010) Entrepreneurial marketing: Moving beyond marketing in new ventures. *International Journal of Entrepreneurship and Innovation Management*, 11(1), 19–34.

Li, L., Qian, G. and Qian, Z. (2015) Speed of internationalization: Mutual effects of individual-and company-level antecedents. *Global Strategy Journal*, 5, 303–320.

Luo, K., Hsu, M. K. and Liu, S. S. (2008) The moderating role of institutional networking in the customer orientation – trust/commitment – performance causal chain in China. *Journal of Academy of Marketing Science*, 36(2), 202–214.

Meyer, A. D. (1991) What is strategy's distinctive competence? *Journal of Management*, 17(1), 821–833.

Mitchell, F. and Reid, G. C. (2000) Problems, challenges, and opportunities: The small business as a setting for management accounting research. Editorial. *Management Accounting Research*, 11(4), 385–390.

Morck, R. and Yeung, B. (2003) Agency problems in large family business groups, *Entrepreneurship Theory and Practice*, 27(4), 367–382.

Morris, M. H., Schindehutte, M. and LaForge, R. W. (2002) Entrepreneurial marketing: A construct for integrating emerging entrepreneurship and marketing perspectives. *Journal of Marketing Theory & Practice*, 10(4), 1–19.

Narver, J. C. and Slater, S. F. (1990) The effect of a market orientation on business profitability, *Journal of Marketing*, 54(October), 20–35.

Norton, R. (1997) Some things economists actually agree on. *Fortune*, October 13. http://archive.fortune.com/magazines/fortune/fortune_archive/1997/10/13/232523/index.htm.

Opute, A. P. (2014) Cross-functional bridge in dyadic relationship: Conflict management and performance implications. *Team Performance Management*, 20(3/4), 121–147.

Opute, A. P. (2017) Exploring personality, identity and self-concept among young consumers (Chapter Five). In *Young Consumer Behaviour: A Research Companion*. Routledge (Taylor and Francis), London. ISBN: 978-0-415-79008-6 (hbk).

Opute, A. P. (2020) Teamwork and customer service (Chapter 14). In *Customer Service Management: A Strategic and Operational Perspective*. Taylor and Francis, London.

Opute, A. P., Madichie, N. O., Hagos, S. B. and Ojra, J. (in press) Entrepreneurship behaviour of African minorities in the UK: Demystifying cultural influence. *International Journal of Entrepreneurship and Small Business*. Available at: https://www.inderscience.com/info/ingeneral/forthcoming.php?jcode=ijesb

Petlina, A. and Koráb, V. (2015) The Structure of family relationships within the family wine trading business in the Czech Republic. *Enometrics XXII, Peer–Reviewed Conference Proceedings*. 1. Brno. s. 52–58.

Porter, M. E. (1996) What is strategy? *Harvard Business Review*, 74(November–December), 61–78.

Ramadani, V. and Hoy, F. (2015) Context and uniqueness of family businesses. *Family Businesses in Transition Economies*, DOI 10.1007/978-3-319-14209-8_2.

Schendel, D. E. (1991) Editor's comments on winter special issue. *Strategic Management Journal*, 12(Winter Special Issue), 1–3.

Schumpeter, J. (1931) *Theorie der wirtschaftlichen Entwichlung*, Dunker und Humblat, Munich and Leipzig.

Schumpeter, J. A. (1942) *Capitalism, socialism, and democracy*. Harper and Brothers, New York.

Slater, S. F., Hult, G. T. M. and Olson, E. M. (2010) Factors influencing the relative importance of marketing strategy creativity and marketing strategy implementation effectiveness. *Industrial Marketing Management*, 39, 551–559.

United Nations Sustainable Development Goals Vision 2030. www.un.org/sustainabledevelopment/sustainable-development-goals/ (Accessed on 28 January 2019).

Varadarajan, R. (2010) Strategic marketing and marketing strategy: Domain, definition, fundamental issues and foundational premises. *Journal of the Academy of Marketing Science*, 38(2), 119–140.

Varadarajan, R. (2015) Strategic marketing, marketing strategy and market strategy. *Academy of Marketing Science Review*, 5, 78–90. DOI 10.1007/s13162-015-0073-9.

Ward, J. L. and Aronoff, C. E. (1991) Trust gives you the advantage'. *Nation's Business*, 79(8).

Weber, M. (1930) *The Protestant Ethic and the Spirit of Capitalism*. Scribner, New York (translated by Talcott Parsons from 'Die protestantische Ethik und der Geist des Kapitalismus', Archiv fur Sozialwissenschaft und Sozialpolitik, 1905, revised 1920) pp. 20–21.

Welsh, D. H. B., Memilie, E., Kaciak, E. and Ochi, M. (2014) Japanese women entrepreneurs: Implications for family business. *Journal of Small Business Management*, 52(2), 286–305.

ZEW (2007) Start-ups zwischen Forschung und Finanzierung: Hightech-Gründungen in Deutschland. Springer-Verlag, Mannheim.

Chapter 3

The role and relevance model of marketing in small and medium-sized enterprises

Mike Simpson, Nick Taylor, and Jo Padmore

LEARNING OBJECTIVES

After reading this chapter, you will be able to:
- Discuss the origin of the role and relevance model;
- Present the role and relevance model of marketing in SMEs;
- Discuss the strategies within the model;
- Explain how the model can be used to aid practitioner SMEs;
- Critically evaluate the likely value of the model for analysing and predicting the behaviour of SMEs;
- Present the model in application using case study organisations

INTRODUCTION

This chapter introduces the role and relevance model of marketing in SMEs. The model aims to explain how and why SMEs approach the action of marketing the way they do. The role of marketing examines the level of marketing activity in an organisation. At a basic level, this could be a job description title such as marketing officer or as part of a list of duties undertaken by an individual or team such as sales force or account manager. On a recent site visit to a Lincoln based agricultural SME, I was taken to the sales office. On route, we passed a door with a notice, 'Marketing Department'. Does this tell us anything about the nature of the marketing activity in the company? Probably not very much, but it is a start and we can assume that there is some level of marketing activity going on. The role of marketing in SMEs can be hidden; it is quite likely that an SME will not be so formally structured and marketing activities may be employed in a rather more organic fashion. In a second company visit, the finance director of a construction company explained that everyone in the company could handle most of the jobs. It would not be unusual for the production manager to make sales calls to clients. A third example is a transport company, who often say that their best marketing people are their drivers. It is the drivers who sit in the cafés and talk to other drivers and they often discuss which haulage load is going where and who is the end customer. This information is fed back to the office in an unstructured ad-hoc way but is in fact a form of market research and does lead to new business being found. Nobody at the company has a job title of 'Marketing Manager', but it is clear that marketing is a key activity in the company.

This is then compared with the relevance of marketing to the organisation. The relevance level indicates the competitiveness of the organisation's markets. Markets which are seen to be highly relevant are characterised by their competitive nature. Competitors sharing similar selling propositions striving to compete and establish advantages will often be characterised by the need for market information and the ability to compile and execute marketing actions. Highly relevant markets are seen as demanding for marketing resources, hence the relationship between the role that marketing plays in an organisation can be directly compared with the relevance that marketing has to an organisation's markets.

Therefore, this chapter explores how the established principles of marketing apply to small and medium-sized enterprises (SMEs). The underpinning work for this chapter was initiated through case studies of organisations allowing the authors to explore the use of marketing principles and practices in SMEs. This study suggested that the achievement of competitiveness for SMEs was reliant on the relationship between the role that marketing plays in an organisation and its relevance to market conditions. These findings were then used to conduct a survey involving a large number of SMEs. The findings enabled the authors to understand the way in which SMEs struggle with the use and value of marketing within their daily business activities. Key to this understanding is the relationship between the role and relevance of marketing in SMEs. The chapter presents a model that goes a long way to explaining the behaviour of SMEs with regard to marketing. The model appears to be viable and could be used to analyse and diagnose the situation regarding marketing within SMEs.

THE ROLE AND RELEVANCE MODEL OF MARKETING IN SMEs

The role and relevance model of marketing in SMEs has been thoroughly investigated and tested. The research methods adopted included literature search, the development and administration of a pilot questionnaire to selected SMEs, a large-scale survey of SMEs within a 60km radius of Sheffield, UK. In total 853 questionnaires were distributed, and 143 usable completed questionnaires were returned, giving a response rate of 17%. In addition, interviews with managers of SMEs and local interest groups and associations (Chamber of Commerce and Industry, Engineering Employers Federation, SME owner-managers, Institute of Management, etc.) were employed to further test the findings. The final results have been published in the *International Journal of Entrepreneurial Behaviour & Research* and the *Journal of Small Business & Enterprise Development* (Simpson et al., 2006; Simpson and Taylor, 2002).

The model offers a straightforward way of diagnosing the situation within an SME. The simplicity of the model allows for a clearer understanding of what is often a complex and messy situation within these companies and their business environment. Some findings suggest a positive link between a company's financial performance and its approach to marketing within the model.

THE ORIGINS OF THE MODEL

The origins of the work were formed when investigating government funded organisations that offer employment to disabled people. Very often these companies were suppliers to the local authority with virtually guaranteed business at set prices. In such a company would marketing have any part to play in the organisation's activities? Would there be a role for a marketing function, a marketing officer, a need for market analysis, for planning and for marketing implementations, in fact would marketing be totally irrelevant in such circumstances? This initial work was then extended to other SMEs with varying levels of business guarantees. These guarantees are viewed in the context of each company's competitive environment. Does the level of dynamic market conditions in itself affect the resources and activities the company directs towards marketing? The aim of this work was to evaluate how the need for marketing in these organisations varies with different market conditions. Would a company operating in a highly competitive market have a far higher developed marketing activity and would it be recognisable in comparison to theoretical principles? Would we see a comparative weakening of the role of marketing in companies that exhibited less challenging market conditions? The model put forward in this chapter not only attempts to explain the nature of marketing in SMEs but goes further to offer potential strategies that companies can adopt to change their competitive position and become more market dominant.

SOME BACKGROUND AND HISTORY

Early work on the role and relevance model began with research on Supported Employment Enterprises (SEEs). Supported Employment Enterprises are commercial enterprises that provide meaningful, gainful employment, training, and development opportunities for people with a disability. They are often owned and operated by local authorities or charitable trusts. Hence, Supported Employment Enterprises are run specifically to provide employment. SEEs, with the exception of Remploy, which is a very large government funded diverse business employing disabled people, represent a unique sector of small and medium sized enterprises. It was discovered that the conventional use of marketing activities, tactics and strategies were either not used, not understood, were not known or the organisations were simply prevented from using public money (via the local authority) for marketing purposes. Yet under these conditions these businesses were expected to compete with other businesses (not all of which were SMEs) in an open market in order to continue to employ and (re-)train disabled workers (see Box 3.1.) (Simpson et al., 2001a, 2001b).

Following a large number of individual case studies and a national survey of these SEEs (Simpson et al., 2001a, 2001b) it became clear that there were significant differences between the various companies being studied. There were very big differences in the way these businesses were managed, and the degree of autonomy and entrepreneurial activity varied immensely between organisations. Despite SEEs being a relatively specialised selection of SMEs there was a very wide range of activities being undertaken by these companies and a very large number of industrial sectors were represented. The use of marketing techniques varied from sophisticated marketing planning activities that were translated into detailed implementation plans to almost openly hostile approaches to marketing often precipitated by local authority interventions. Existing models and frameworks proved to be unsatisfactory in explaining this behaviour or they were focussed on entrepreneurial marketing approaches (Carson et al., 1995). This led to some early speculative frameworks and models being developed that could explain the behaviour of these companies. One of the speculative models that seemed to have some general applicability to both SEEs and SMEs was the role and relevance model of marketing.

BOX 3.1: THE CASE OF BARROW INDUSTRIES

Introduction

Barrow Industries is a Supported Employment Enterprise. They employ people with disabilities who may lack the skills and confidence to gain normal employment. The aim is that the employees gain work based skills, grow in confidence and are able to enter open employment. This in turn creates a vacancy at Barrow for a new recruit and the cycle continues. Whilst doing this, Barrow Industries are also expected to be profit generating. Support from the public sector is provided in the form of grants and funding to help them achieve these aims. In reality, Barrow makes losses and employees feel too comfortable to want to move into the private sector. The current product range now consists of kitchen furniture (sink units) and uPVC windows. The company's turnover is around £1.1m with roughly 60% of income coming from uPVC windows and 40% from kitchen furniture. Some 95% of the work is for the local authority who use the products for council owned properties. The company pays competitive wage rates for the industry and this would appear to stifle progression of disabled workers into open employment.

Marketing at Barrow Industries

Marketing is not represented at all well in the organisation although the assistant manager has been on an organised marketing course in the past. The company does not see much reason or need for marketing at present because of the ties with the local authority. If the constraints placed on the company by the local authority were to be removed, then the managers felt that the company could expand into other markets and possibly find enough work to double in size. Barrow Industries is not an integrated marketing organisation. It has no marketing department and therefore there is little marketing impact on other departments within the company. The consequences of this are that no marketing research is initiated, no one visits customers and no effort is taken to measure the effectiveness of the company activities. The company business plan contains a single side of A4 regarding marketing strategy. The sales and promotion plan involves sending brochures/price lists to large organisations and offering custom-built windows and kitchen units as required. The strategy relies on the fact that the company is the nominated supplier to a major local authority.

Head Office: A centralised approach

The local authority has considerable control over the marketing (and demarketing) activities of the company in that taking advantage of marketing opportunities is actively discouraged. The committee cycle for decision making means that quick responses to new developments are almost impossible. The manager of the company has to seek approval for expenditures as small as £150 despite having the responsibilities of running a £1.1m turnover business!

The company has a great opportunity to sell to the public and businesses and possibly double in size, employ more disabled workers and become profitable. However, this would require greater resources for marketing and sales and an increase in the workforce to meet demand. The huge constraints placed on the business by the local authority means that there is no autonomy for the managers to run the business.

Case questions

1. Would a company with a guaranteed customer have any need for marketing?
2. How would you advise the Managing Director of Barrow Industries to address the issue of
   a. the internal market;
   b. the external market, ensure you discuss the implications of any actions undertaken.
3. Where would you place Barrow Industries on the role and relevance model of marketing used in this chapter? Justify your choice.
4. What action could Barrow Industries reasonably take to improve their marketing efforts? Could they aspire to be a marketing-led organisation?

THE ROLE AND RELEVANCE OF MARKETING

The model presented in Figure 3.1 was developed to explain and describe the relationship between the concepts of role and relevance of marketing within SEEs and later expanded into other SMEs. The terminology used tries to describe the type of organisation that would be placed in each quadrant within the matrix.

Figure 3.1
The role and relevance of marketing: the new model

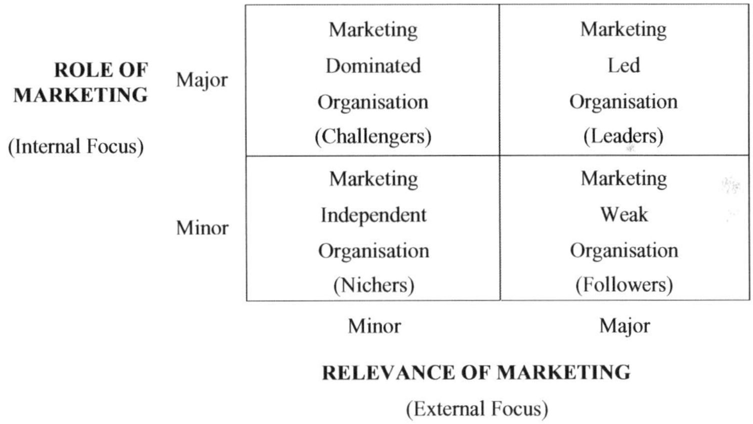

Figure 3.2
Routes or strategies to becoming a marketing led organisation

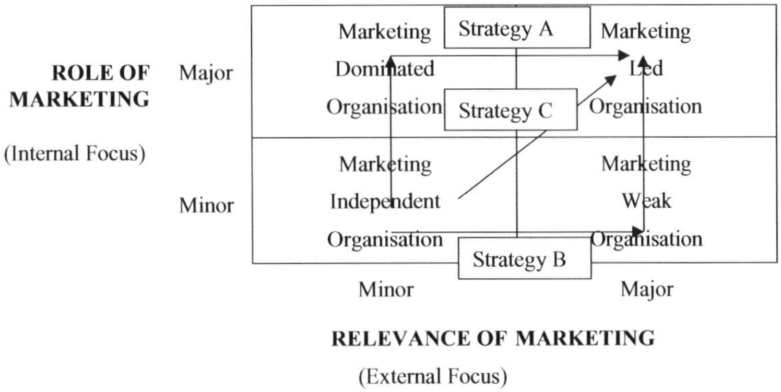

THE ROLE DIMENSION

The role of marketing within an organisation can be viewed as an internal focus on the use of marketing by the organisation. So that, if marketing plays a big role in the organisation then marketing would be expected to be included in all business plans and be used as a way of generating strategies and planning the future of the organisation. Marketing would be expected to take up a significant amount of the time spent by senior managers both in planning and in implementing marketing activities. It would also be expected that the organisation would have a marketing orientation with the trappings of a marketing department with sufficient staff, resources, and a reasonable budget. Marketing strategies and plans would be developed, monitored, and evaluated in a systematic way by organisations where marketing plays a major role within the organisation.

THE RELEVANCE DIMENSION

The relevance of marketing examines the need for marketing by the organisation when operating within the company's particular business environment. The focus of attention here is on the external need for marketing so that the company can remain competitive within its business environment. For example, in a highly competitive industry or a very dynamic industry a company would need a major marketing effort in order to compete and maintain market share. A company not doing this would soon lose market share or be overtaken by changes in the market, which were not anticipated. However, in a less competitive and stable industry marketing would be less relevant to the future of the organisation. This is especially true if the organisation has little or no ambition or ability to grow. It may be that these limitations are artificially imposed but so long as the market remains stable then the relevance of marketing maybe regarded as minor. Much of this discussion is already well known to marketers (Porter, 1980).

Dimensions of Role of Marketing	Dimensions of Relevance of Marketing
Time and effort spent on: • Producing business plans for the future. • Creating marketing strategies and plans. • Developing new products or services. • Designing advertising campaigns. • Maintaining the marketing information database. • Producing publicity and press releases. • Analysing competitor's offerings. • Evaluating the performance of marketing strategies and plans. • Tracking the performance of the various promotional and advertising activities. **Marketing Organisation/Structure:** • Marketing department. • Number of personnel in marketing. • Director level representation. • Marketing database.	**Business environment assessment:** • Guaranteed business. • Survival against competition. • Important for expansion of the company. • Highly competitive market. • Could not survive without marketing. • Doing fine without marketing. • More help is needed with marketing. • Intense rivalry between competitors. • Threats from substitute products/services. • Threats from potential new entrants. • Power of Suppliers/buyers. **Ambitions of the Business:** • Need for growth of the company. • Need for market penetration. • Need for market share. • Need for new products within the market. • Need to diversify to grow and develop.

Figure 3.3 Some of the dimensions of role and relevance

The categories in the role and relevance model

Given the two dimensions listed previously this leads to four logically distinct categories or quadrants in the model (see Figure 3.1).

Marketing led organisation (major relevance and major role of marketing)

In a marketing led organisation, marketing is very important to the company's success and plays a major role in the strategic direction of the organisation. Marketing is regarded as highly relevant in this type of organisation because competition is very fierce in the markets the organisation serves. Hence, marketing consumes a lot of organisational effort, but the rewards are seen in maintaining and improving the market share of the organisation against tough competition. Noting that SMEs, even the larger ones, usually have small market shares or serve niche markets. The organisation would be expected to have a strong marketing orientation and whole-heartedly adopt and adhere to the principles and practices of marketing. Such an organisation would be expected to have a marketing department with a reasonable budget, representation of the marketing function at director level on the Board of Directors and the marketing function should have a significant effect on the strategy adopted by the organisation. Such an organisation might be viewed as having adopted best practice business sense in dealing with its external business environment. Such a company might be viewed as a SME leader in the industry.

Marketing dominated organisation (minor relevance and major role of marketing)

In a marketing dominated organisation, marketing would be seen as dominating the strategy making process, using a lot of resources and producing a lot of plans, which may not be very useful because of the markets the organisation serves. This is an unbalanced or mismatched approach. Markets served by this type of organisation would be guaranteed business with, say, a local authority or much larger company that is the major or sole customer of the organisation. Hence, marketing may be seen as an unnecessary burden or that the organisation has aspirations to be a supplier outside the present circumstances but has not yet achieved this. In the first case, the marketing department may be powerful and be able to resist reductions in resources. In the latter case, the marketing department may have been deliberately boosted to achieve greater market share or penetrate new markets and eventually become a marketing led Organisation in the model (see Figure 3.1). Such an organisation might be viewed as an SME challenger in the industry. Any particular case would need to be investigated to decide between these two scenarios. Ideally, there should be a fit between the company's aspirations, corporate strategy and the business environment in which they find themselves. Where there is no clear reason for such a large concentration of resources and effort on marketing, then the company could be described as a marketing dominated organisation, and the strategic necessity of such an approach would need urgent attention at senior management level.

Marketing weak organisation (major relevance but minor role of marketing)

A marketing weak organisation could be seen as requiring marketing expertise and effort to maintain its market share and grow in the market it serves. Hence, marketing would be highly relevant for the organisation to survive in the longer term against existing competitors but the organisation spends little time and effort on marketing activities. Such an organisation would be termed a marketing weak organisation in the model (see Figure 3.1) and as such mismatched with the needs of its business environment. The idea that these companies might be called SME followers might be considered. For example, such an organisation would have a very poor marketing effort and may, perhaps, have a sales orientation with a fixation on price rather than any other attribute of the product or service offered. The organisation would have no marketing department and have few or no staff able to formulate marketing strategy or carry out basic marketing tasks. Again, there are two simple scenarios to deal with. The first scenario is of a truly ignorant and dysfunctional organisation which is unaware of the benefits that marketing can offer and is struggling to maintain its position against its competitors – a marketing weak organisation. The second scenario is of an organisation that has no intention of growing and is content to remain small within its chosen market or, alternatively, has tried some marketing but has seen little or no reward for these efforts and has abandoned such marketing efforts, again, being content to remain small within its chosen market – an SME follower. The first scenario can be rectified with some training and effort so long as the business environment indicates that the rewards for marketing effort are there to be had, usually verified via market research. The second scenario could also be rectified but it is likely that complacency has set in and the situation is irretrievable in the minds of the senior managers within the organisation. Sometimes being small and less proactive can be used as a survival strategy when the managers feel they have no need to grow and that they are comfortable as they are. This would be an SME Follower strategy.

Marketing independent organisation (minor relevance and minor role)

A marketing independent organisation is similar to a marketing dominated organisation except that it has not been burdened with a big commitment to marketing (see Box 3.1). Using the same example of guaranteed business with, say, a local authority or much larger company that is the major or sole customer of the organisation, then here we see there is a balance between the organisation's effort in marketing and the needs of the business environment. There is a balance because the organisation may have few aspirations beyond the present tied circumstances with the large customer and does not need to engage in marketing efforts to ensure survival. Hence, the role played by marketing is minor and the relevance of marketing is minor because competition is effectively absent altogether. Such an approach could be called an SME nicher.

The weakness of this approach is that the future of the organisation is directly linked to the future of its major customer and the organisation has no other strategy or resources to rely upon. Such an organisation could be termed as a marketing independent organisation as it does not rely upon marketing strategies or marketing initiatives to generate sales. This situation may have been safe in the past but the problems facing local authorities and other large organisations are growing and this may well lead to difficulties in the future for an organisation adopting this approach.

Strategies which may be adopted with the new model

In developing this new model we have attempted to follow the basic idea of strategic portfolio management:

Regardless of the particular layout chosen for the matrix, the basic idea behind the portfolio concept remains the same: the position (or box) that a business unit occupies within the matrix should determine the strategic mission and the general characteristics of the strategy for the business.

(Bettis and Hall, 1981)

Strategy 1. develop the business in one or both dimensions

This is where a company has determined that it needs to develop either its commitment to marketing by increasing the time and effort spent in that area, or it needs to pay greater attention to the changes in the business environment to capitalise on its investment in marketing. That is, the firm is moving up the matrix to increase the role of marketing (e.g., from a marketing weak to marketing led organisation). Alternatively, the firm is moving across the matrix from left to right as it becomes more aware of external influences and wishes to capitalise upon the existing role that marketing is playing (e.g., from marketing dominated to marketing led organisation). An alternative view, which would be less attractive, is in moving from marketing independent to a marketing weak organisation. Although, this might prove to be a more natural strategy for a growing SME.

Strategy 2. stay in the same position

This is where a company has determined that it is in the right position in the matrix for the business environment in which it operates and the role that marketing plays within the company. Such a position might be in the marketing led organisation category or the marketing independent organisation category depending upon circumstances. It is unlikely that companies in the marketing weak category or marketing dominated category would adopt this view, as there are clear imbalances in these categories.

Strategy 3. reduce the commitment of the firm in one or both dimensions

This is where a company has determined that it has invested too heavily in marketing and the business environment suggests that much of this effort is unnecessary. The company may well choose to move from marketing dominated towards marketing independent (or even marketing led towards marketing independent) where it has obtained a secure future with a large contract guaranteed for a long time with, say, a local authority or other large organisation. However, such an approach would also depend upon the ambitions of the company regarding growth and diversification. If ambitions were limited or restricted in some way by limited resources or by the desire of the owner-manager for a simple business strategy then this approach may be valid.

Strategy 4. eliminate the commitment of the firm in one or both dimensions

This is where a company has determined that it does not require marketing and is very similar to the previous strategy but here the owners/managers have no desire to grow the business. This strategy may also be adopted in the short term where the firm has cash flow problems and a relatively stable and reliable customer base. However, this strategy will, in the longer term, have a negative effect on the performance of the organisation.

Assumptions

Given the strategic options included it was assumed that SMEs might want to become marketing led organisations. The rationale for this thinking was that it was suspected from our research that these types of organisations would perform better and therefore have stronger financial results over time that could be used to reinforce the company's position in the longer term. It was also noted that SMEs often start from humble beginnings and that for some owner-managers growth of the business is the only way to ensure that the business survives and returns a profit, or at least pays the owner-manager's salary and expenses. While we appreciated that many SMEs were unable to grow and develop and that many owner-managers did not wish to grow their business, the model must provide some guidance according to the principles outlined by Bettis and Hall (1981) on how a company could grow and develop by moving through the matrix in Figure 3.1. Therefore, we suggested that an SME may choose to become a marketing led organisation via three basic routes or strategies through this framework. These three approaches are illustrated in Figure 3.2.

Strategy A (marketing independent to marketing dominated to marketing led): a proactive approach that would consume a lot of resources initially but would allow the organisation to actively search for opportunities within the desired marketplace.

Strategy B (marketing independent to marketing weak to marketing led): a reactive approach in which the demands of the marketplace in which the company operates/intends to operate demand a stronger role for marketing.

Strategy C (marketing independent to marketing led): is the normative response where any business environment changes are matched closely with a response from the company by increased marketing effort. "Strategy C" appears to be rare in SMEs in our experience.

BOX 3.2: THE CASE OF GRIPPLE LIMITED

Gripple Limited, based in Sheffield, UK, (www.Gripple.com) was started in 1988 and has grown to a position in 2010 where the company currently employs 230 people and has a turnover of approximately £23m. The company manufactures a patented device for joining, securing and tensioning wire known as a 'Gripple'. The company has seen excellent growth in turnover with 40% increase in several years during the 1990s and intends to increase turnover to £40m by 2012. The product has been systematically improved, developed and new patents obtained over the last ten years so that the company now targets four distinct markets. These are the fencing and vineyard trellising market, the construction market, wire rope connectors and pallet strapping. The Gripple devices were designed to hold a variety of sizes of wires and steel ropes but with the advantage of being fully adjustable for tensioning and positioning.

The company operates in two divisions an Industrial Division and an Agricultural Division. The company has a marketing department with a marketing director and a marketing assistant however, everyone in the organisation is marketing orientated. Marketing of the products is sophisticated, and the promotional material is of high quality. Target markets are systematically identified and attacked. New product development is seen as vital for the company to grow with 30% of income expected to come from products developed in the last three years. The strategy is to identify new geographic markets with each new product and systematically attack each market. Margins are kept up by doing much of the work themselves and selling directly to the customer via its own offices abroad rather than via agents and distributors. The company prefers to be close to both its customers and suppliers and has developed good working relationships. The company uses videos of the products and their applications for both the Gripple and Hang-Fast system. These are useful as product outlines and as training videos. The promotional literature consists of well-designed glossy brochures, quarterly newsletters and press releases on latest developments within the company. The company takes every opportunity to use the media with any new developments. Everything the company does appears to be driven by a marketing orientation. The premises are the very attractively converted Old West Gun Works in Sheffield. The layout of the factory and the offices is very pleasant, open plan and welcoming to visitors. Products are on display in the reception area. The company uses appropriate high technology to design, manufacture, and control the production of Gripples and has highly trained staff on single status contracts who are also shareholders in the business. The company invites both local university students and industrialists into the company to discuss latest developments. The company sees itself as a leader in the field and an example to other manufacturing companies locally, regionally, and nationally and has won a number of awards for innovation, best new product, and best factory. The company uses every opportunity for PR and media coverage of its activities.

The marketplace in which the company operates is extremely competitive with numerous different types of wire joining devices. Competitors appear to be ruthless in infringing patents and trademarks. The company has recently successfully defended its rights in the US courts when a company produced a product almost identical to the Gripple called the 'Grabber'. The Gripple Hang-fast system is seen as a replacement for traditional screw threaded steel rod and struts. Breaking into this market has been hard but is now being seen as a good method of expansion for the business. Marketing is highly relevant to the future prospects of the company and marketing plays a very strong strategic role within the company. Marketing has significant impact on the strategic thinking and strategy making process within the company. The overall score using Kotler's (1977) approach to marketing effectiveness is 27 out of 30, which is superior/excellent.

Questions
1. In your opinion, where does Gripple Limited fit into the Role and Relevance Model of Marketing discussed in this chapter? Justify your answer.
2. Given that the company has ambitions to increase turnover to £40m in 2012, what advice would you give to the managing director of this company? Do you foresee any problems with the company's approach?

CONCLUSIONS

The role and relevance model of marketing remains fairly robust but with a few shortcomings due to the concentration on classical marketing strategy and practices and the omission of postmodern marketing such as networking, internet marketing, e-commerce, and e-business. However, there is considerable evidence in the literature that SMEs are also weak in the use of internet methods of marketing (see Sparkes and Thomas, 2001). The omission on network marketing is perhaps a more serious matter (see O'Donnell and Cummins, 1999) that may affect the position of some SMEs in our model and again should be investigated further.

It is worth noting that:

> Theories are construed as speculative and tentative conjectures or guesses freely created by the human intellect in an attempt to overcome problems encountered by previous theories and to give an adequate account of the behaviour of some aspects of the world or universe.
>
> (Chalmers, 1982, p. 38)

This is exactly the view we have taken with the model discussed in this chapter. It is not definitive but merely a theoretical development that has been thoroughly tested. It is a step forward that may prove to be a useful development and allow or prompt further discussion of the issues of marketing in small and medium-sized enterprises.

Criticism has been received regarding the delineation of the relevance of marketing. The main criticism is that this concept is less well defined and operationalised since it is the result of attempting to define the external business environment and the aspirations of the company with a limited number of questions. These questions may not capture the full impact of the external business environment in which these companies operate. The questions also relied heavily on classical approaches to marketing and business environment issues (e.g., Porter, Ansoff). The position on this axis is also the result of the owner-managers' interpretation of the external business environment and the aspirations for the future of the company. This is dependent upon the owner-managers' own perceptions and strategic awareness, which would be expected to vary considerably across this sample of SMEs (see Hannon and Atherton, 1998). A more carefully selected set of questions may improve the delineation of the concepts plotted on this axis and result in a more robust model.

The model and original data collected also leads to the conclusion that 'Marketing Led' organisations perform better and invest more in marketing and this result was expected (Denison and McDonald, 1995). The scatter of data points in the original work could be indicative of SMEs adopting 'Strategy B', the reactive strategy (see Figure 3.2), through the matrix. Follow-up interviews established that 'Strategy B' is often the most convenient way for SMEs to adopt marketing practices and that often enlightened employees are frustrated by their company's lack of enthusiasm for marketing and the company's confusion of marketing with advertising and selling. Some notable exceptions using the proactive approach of 'Strategy A' were also found but these were often strategically orientated and highly motivated SMEs with a dynamic, well trained, and committed management team. Differentiating between 'Strategy A', the proactive approach, and 'Strategy C', the incremental approach, through the matrix was hard to do using the interviews and the telephone interviews in the original research. However, it appeared that few companies were adopting these strategies and that 'Strategy B' was the preferred approach. This result tends to suggest that the stages/growth approach (Siu and Kirby, 1998) may have an effect as many SMEs only felt ready for marketing after reaching a certain size or level of turnover. These SMEs also felt that marketing was only appropriate when the competitive environment required a more carefully considered strategic approach (see McLarty, 1998) and when the company had the resources to implement a marketing programme. Some owner-managers were more hostile towards marketing and thought it expensive and not very effective. Owner-managers with poor experiences of marketing consultants generally took this view.

There is evidence that the role and relevance model of marketing offers some new insights into the behaviour of SMEs regarding marketing. However, there are differences in approach to researching marketing in SMEs and there are different approaches adopted by SMEs towards marketing (Brodie et al., 1997). We recognise that our paradigm may well have left many questions unanswered, particularly where very young companies are involved. However, the Role and Relevance model does show that SMEs can be categorised to some extent and that these categories do make intrinsic sense of the situation. The categories in the model are good descriptors of the companies studied in our opinion. The original quantitative results are not enough to understand fully what is going on in these companies. Some results appear to partially support other models and ideas such as the stages/growth model (Siu and Kirby, 1998) or the idea that marketing does not evolve in these companies (Brooksbank et al., 1999) and may even regress. This suggests to us that the situation in SMEs regarding their approach to marketing is complex, dynamic and probably influenced by many more factors than we have been able to capture and examine in this work. We conclude that our model is firmly positioned as a contingent model (Siu and Kirby, 1998) but that other factors, which manifest themselves as data in support of other approaches, are probably superimposed on companies in this sample. The sample of SMEs used in our original research may be biased due to the use of mailing lists from local interest groups, whose members may well be more responsive to this type of research. While the Role and Relevance model may be imperfect, it is self-consistent, adaptable, and extendable, and additional questions could be included and scored in a modified questionnaire to cover internet marketing, e-commerce, customer relationship marketing, and networking, for example.

We also conclude that some companies have a clear idea of what they are doing about marketing and strategy, but many do not know what they are doing and are 'Marketing Weak'. The model does offer some new insights into marketing in SMEs and from our results there appear to be certain basic requirements for 'Marketing Led' SMEs, that is: a marketing database, an active business plan, marketing representation at board level, and a marketing department. This result is not new and is not simply an artefact of the data collection method in our opinion but does suggest some agreement with the ideas of marketing orientation. The original study did find some limited evidence that 'Marketing Led' SMEs had a better financial performance than SMEs in other categories in the model.

Finally, the role and relevance model of marketing in SMEs appears to be a practical and useful theory and has been qualitatively applied over the last few years by undergraduates, postgraduates, and a few practitioners when analysing case studies and real companies.

MANAGERIAL AND POLICY IMPLICATIONS

Given the descriptions of the type of SME and the kind of business environment in which they operate it is possible to qualitatively and also quantitatively determine the quadrant in which a particular SME is positioned. It is then possible to give advice on the strategies, tactics, and general marketing approaches that might be used to improve the situation of the SME and develop the SME into a marketing led company. As a diagnostic tool the role and relevance model is quite useful in this respect. However, we would caution that overly prescriptive approaches to marketing for SMEs would not be beneficial and that careful analysis

MIKE SIMPSON, NICK TAYLOR, AND JO PADMORE

and interpretation of the particular business situation in which an SME operates should be investigated more thoroughly using many more tools and techniques. That is, the model is a guide that explains only some of the behaviour of SMEs. However, as a starting point for managers and consultants it is a useful approach.

CHAPTER REVIEW QUESTIONS

1. Given the features and dimensions of role and relevance shown in the table in Figure 3.3, what other features, activities, concepts, ideas and dimensions of marketing might be used to expand the lists in Figure 3.3. How might the (expanded) lists shown in Figure 3.3 be operationalised so that reliable data might be collected to populate the model? Justify your answer.

2. Critically review the recent literature concerning marketing in small and medium sized enterprises. Try to examine alternative theoretical approaches and compare and contrast these approaches with the role and relevance model of marketing in SMEs outlined in this chapter.

3. Discuss the way(s) that the performance of SMEs might be determined. Try to establish a methodology that would prove or disprove that marketing led organisations in the role and relevance model were performing better than those SMEs in other categories in the model.

REFERENCES

Bettis, R. A. and Hall, W. K. (1981) Strategic portfolio management in the multi-business firm. *California Management Review*, 24(1), 23–38.

Brodie, R. J., Coviello, N. E., Brookes, R. W. and Little, V. (1997) Towards a paradigm shift in marketing? An examination of current marketing practices. *Journal of Marketing Management*, 13, 383–406.

Brooksbank, R., Kirby, D. A., Taylor, D. and Jones-Evans, D. (1999) Marketing in medium-sized manufacturing firms: The state-of-the-art in Britain, 1987–1992. *European Journal of Marketing*, 33(1/2), 103–120.

Carson, D., Cromie, S., McGowan, P. and Hill, J. (1995) *Marketing and Entrepreneurship in SMEs: An Innovative Approach*. Pearson Education Limited, Harlow, UK. ISBN 0-13-150970-5.

Chalmers, A. F. (1982) *What Is the Thing Called Science? An Assessment of the Nature and Status of Science and Its Methods*, 2nd ed. Open University Press, Milton Keynes.

Denison, T. and McDonald, M. (1995) The role of marketing past, present and future. *Journal of Marketing Practice: Applied Marketing Science*, 1(1), 54–76.

Hannon, P. D. and Atherton, A. (1998) Small firm success and the art of orienteering: The value of plans, planning and strategic awareness in the competitive small firm. *Journal of Small Business and Enterprise Development*, Summer 1998, 5(2), 102–119.

Kotler, P. (1977) From sales obsession to marketing effectiveness. *Harvard Business Review*, November–December 1977, 67–75.

McLarty, R. (1998) Case study: Evidence of a strategic marketing paradigm in a growing SME. *Journal of Marketing Practice: Applied Marketing Science*, 4(4), 105–117.

O'Donnell, A. and Cummins, D. (1999) The use of qualitative methods to research networking in SMEs. *Qualitative Market Research: An International Journal*, 2(2), 82–91.

Porter, M. E. (1980) *Competitive Strategy: Techniques for Analysing Industries and Competitors*. Free Press, New York.

Simpson, M., Padmore, J. and Taylor, N. (2001) Marketing in supported employment enterprises. Part 2. The national survey results. *Journal of Small Business and Enterprise Development*, 8(4), 301–309.

Simpson, M., Padmore, J., Taylor, N. and Frecknall-Hughes, J. (2006) Marketing in small and medium sized enterprises. *International Journal of Entrepreneurial Behaviour and Research*, 12(6), 361–387 (ISSN 1355-2554).

Simpson, M. and Taylor, N. (2002) The role and relevance of marketing in SMEs: Towards a new model. *Journal of Small Business and Enterprise Development*, 9(4), 370–382. (ISSN 1462-6004).

Simpson, M., Taylor, N. and Padmore, J. (2001) Marketing in supported employment enterprises. Part 1. Case studies. *Journal of Small Business and Enterprise Development*, 8(3), 233–244.

Siu, W. and Kirby, D. A. (1998) Approaches to small firm marketing: A critique. *European Journal of Marketing*, 32(1/2), 40–60.

Sparkes, A. and Thomas, B. (2001) The use of the internet as a critical success factor for the marketing of Welsh agri-food SMEs in the twenty-first century. *British Food Journal*, 103(5), 331–347.

Chapter 4

The entrepreneurship marketing environment

Ayantunji Gbadamosi

LEARNING OBJECTIVES

After reading this chapter, you will be able to:
- Understand the meaning of marketing environment;
- Discuss the nature of the SMEs Marketing environment;
- Differentiate between the external and internal marketing environment of SMEs;
- Understand the impact of Macro- and Microenvironmental factors on the marketing activities of SMEs;
- Explain environmental scanning and why it is important in SME marketing;
- Discuss the relevance of SWOT analysis to SME marketing;
- Understand how SMEs cope with the turbulence in the marketing environment.

INTRODUCTION

No business exists in a vacuum. Irrespective of the size and scale of their operations, business organisations operate within environments which either directly or indirectly influence how they plan, organise, and execute their marketing activities. Similarly, regardless of whether they are small and medium scale enterprises (SMEs) or large corporations, these environments contain certain factors and forces that combine to impinge on how they relate to their customers. Therefore, it is logical to state that having an in-depth understanding of the marketing environment is very fundamental to the study of SME marketing. Now, let us first consider a working definition of marketing environment that will guide our discussion in this chapter. We may simply define marketing environment as the totality of factors and actors that both presently influence or in the future might influence how marketers go about satisfying the needs and wants of their target market.

From this definition, we can deduce that organisations interact with the various elements of the environment and the extent to which they are able to do this effectively is significantly determined by the characteristic of the organisation involved. This is where the distinction between the context of SMEs and large corporations can be appreciated. Although, there is a clear lack of consensus on what constitutes the definition of SMEs as they vary with sectors, and most importantly across different countries of the world, there is agreement that they are smaller in many ramifications when compared to their large corporation

THE ENTREPRENEURSHIP MARKETING ENVIRONMENT

Figure 4.1
SME marketing environment

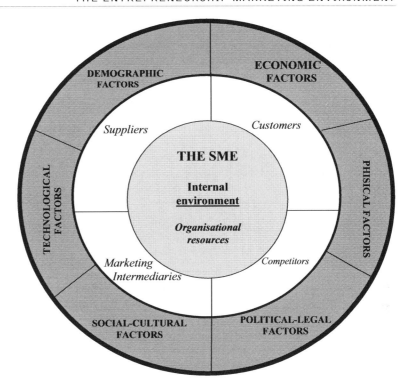

counterparts. This suggests that the impact of the environmental factors on these organisations, and the way they also respond to them might be dissimilar, hence our need to look into marketing environment in the context of SMEs.

THE NATURE OF THE SME MARKETING ENVIRONMENT

Although SMEs have limitations that sometimes distinguish them from large corporations, the marketing environment where they operate is *multifaceted* and *dynamic* as it is the case for other organisations. This explains why an SME cannot assume that consumers' taste and needs two years ago will still remain the same now or assume that the laws governing the importation of their productive inputs will remain the same perpetually. The constant interaction of these many dynamic factors comes with some degree of uncertainty; hence the marketing environment is *complex*. Let us now consider the categories and each of these factors for a better appreciation of how they impact the marketing activities of SMEs.

In its broad sense, marketing environment can be categorised into internal and external environments, and the external also be categorised further into macro and micro factors. These different categorisations explain the marketing environment from the perspective of the closeness of each of the factors to the SMEs, and also indicate the extent of control that they have in fine-tuning the factors towards satisfying their target markets.

Internal marketing environment

The internal marketing environment of SMEs consists of those factors within the organisation including financial resources, human resources, production facilities, and other factors that can be categorised as part of the organisation's resources. By their nature, SMEs have considerable level of control on these factors and could manipulate or combine them in various forms towards responding to threats or opportunities in the external marketing environment and consequently providing the goods and services needed by their target market.

External marketing environment

Some factors are external to business organisations and exert considerable influence on how they function to achieve their objectives. These factors are shown in Figure 5.2. Owing to the nature of the external environment factors, they are uncontrollable for SMEs. These factors can be classified further on the basis of whether their effects relate to all organisations or a particular organisation. Those external factors that are quite broad in scope and by nature influence the marketing activities of all business organisations are called *macroenvironmental factors*. Basically, they are economic factors, political-legal factors, sociocultural factors, technological factors, demographical factors, and physical environmental factors. The other group of factors that are though external, are regarded as particularly related and very close to the firm are *microenvironmental factors* which consist of customers, competitors, suppliers, and channel members. Each of these factors is now discussed in turn.

MACROENVIRONMENT OF MARKETING

Economic environment

Considerable factors under economic environment are interest rate, inflation rate, unemployment rate, income distribution, savings, credit availability, and a host of others. Hence, it is logical to state that this part of the marketing environment embraces the overall health of the economic system in which SME operates. More specifically, it deals with the management of demand in the economy. Thus, it is very crucial for SME marketers to understand the effects of these economic variables because they influence costs, prices, and demand for their goods and services. Government often directs the affairs of the economy through the use of interests rate controls, taxation policy, and its expenditure. Hardly is there any better example to cite here than the prevailing global economic crisis. The effect of this on consumer spending has led to several undesirable changes in business organisations. These include downsizing, rationalising resources more than ever before, and in some cases folding up.

The economy that is characterised with high level of inflation, unemployment will pose great challenges to SMEs operating in that environment. From the international marketing perspective, marketing activities like exporting, franchising, and direct foreign investment depend greatly on how healthy the economy of the host country is. SMEs operating at this level need to know the level of economic development in prospective countries to be targeted. Similarly, at that level, knowing the exchange rates between countries is imperative for the success of SMEs. They also need to gauge relevant indicators such as the Gross Domestic Products (GDP) and the Gross National Product (GNP) of the economy for assessing how healthy it is at any point in time. Summarily, SMEs must be aware of the standard and cost of living of the society where they operate as doing this will go a long way to indicate areas of opportunities that could be explored to them.

48

Political-legal environment

This dimension of the marketing environment has to do with government regulations of businesses in all ramifications and the existing relationships between businesses and government. Imagine a society where there are no regulations; things will go in different directions and anybody would like to invest in any type of business in such a society. In this situation unscrupulous business operators might produce any product without due care of what happen to who is going to consume them. At best, the situation will be chaotic. This brings in the relevance of the political/legal sector of the marketing environment. Basically, this part of the environment consists of laws, public officials, legislative bodies, courts, and political structures and actors that work interactively to regulate business transactions in a particular society. It is a fundamental part of the macroenvironment that SMEs cannot afford to ignore as it determines what they can do or cannot do in their marketing activities. There are a variety of these legal frameworks. Examples include regulations on business formation, laws on pricing, competition, mode of distribution, method of marketing communications, and employment to mention but few. One of the key challenges of this environment is that SMEs have to be familiar with the existing laws that guide commercial activities not only at the federal level but also at the state and local levels. In most cases, they will also have to consider international laws guiding business practices, either because they buy some of their inputs from oversea companies or because they have business commitments abroad. The following are examples of rules and regulations in the UK and EU that are relevant to SMEs and could have impact on their marketing activities.

The information in Table 4.1 is the Small Business Act for Europe which was adopted in June 2008. It indicates the commitment of the European Union to promoting the growth of SMEs in the region and that the body recognises the significant roles of the SMEs in the economy and works towards improving the sector through the partnership approach. The effort is aimed at improving the overall approach to entrepreneurship in the EU and provides SME-friendlier business environment in the form of various packages that could encourage SMEs to grow. The onus is on the SMEs to explore the opportunities in the package and similar provisions for the benefits of their entrepreneurial endeavours.

Table 4.1 Small Business Act for Europe

10 principles to guide the conception and implementation of policies both at EU and Member State level concerning SMEs

- I. Create an environment in which entrepreneurs and family businesses can thrive and entrepreneurship is rewarded
- II. Ensure that honest entrepreneurs who have faced bankruptcy quickly get a second chance
- III. Design rules according to the "Think Small First" principle
- IV. Make public administrations responsive to SMEs' needs
- V. Adapt public policy tools to SME needs: facilitate SMEs' participation in public procurement and better use State Aid possibilities for SMEs
- VI. Facilitate SMEs' access to finance and develop a legal and business environment supportive to timely payments in commercial transactions
- VII. Help SMEs to benefit more from the opportunities offered by the Single Market
- VIII. Promote the upgrading of skills in SMEs and all forms of innovation
- IX. Enable SMEs to turn environmental challenges into opportunities
- X. Encourage and support SMEs to benefit from the growth of markets

Source: http://eurlex.europa.eu/LexUriServ/LexUriServ.do?uri=COM:2008:0394:FIN:en:PDF a set of new legislative proposals which are guided by the "Think Small First" principle: (Accessed on 10/04/10)

Table 4.2 is an extract of the legislation that relate to sales of goods in the UK. These like many others are in place to ensure a harmonious market system where parties to commercial transactions will have something to use as a frame of reference for their dealings. Table 4.3 highlights the rights of the consumers in relation to their marketing interactions. It covers their shopping rights, rights to have the products that will be fit for the intended purposes, the right to get a refund when this is not the case, and directions on how to get help and what to do if things go wrong in their transactions.

Table 4.2 Sale of Good Acts 1979 (c.54) – Part II: Formation of the contract

Contract of sale

1) A contract of sale of goods is a contract by which the seller transfers or agrees to transfer the property in goods to the buyer for a money consideration, called the price.
2) There may be a contract of sale between one part owner and another.
3) A contract of sale may be absolute or conditional.
4) Where under a contract of sale the property in the goods is transferred from the seller to the buyer the contract is called a sale.
5) Where under a contract of sale the transfer of the property in the goods is to take place at a future time or subject to some condition later to be fulfilled the contract is called an agreement to sell.
6) An agreement to sell becomes a sale when the time elapses or the conditions are fulfilled subject to which the property in the goods is to be transferred.

Source: Office of Public sector information: Part of the National Archives (www.opsi.gov.uk/RevisedStatutes/Acts/ukpga/1979/cukpga_19790054_en_3) (Accessed on 13 March 2010)

Table 4.3 Consumer rights and where to get help

Shopping rights
When you go shopping anything you buy is covered by a law called the Sale of Goods Act 1979. This means that when you buy a product it should be:
- as described
- fit for purpose
- of satisfactory quality

As described
This means that the item you buy should be the same as any description of it. A description could be what the seller has said to you about the item or something written in a brochure.

Fit for purpose
What you buy should be able to do the job that it was made for. Also, goods should be fit for any specific purpose you agreed with the seller at the time of sale. For example, if you were looking to buy a printer and asked the seller if it would work with your computer then that advice has to be correct.

Refunds
You can get your money back if an item is:
- faulty (it doesn't work properly)
- incorrectly described
- not fit for purpose

If you find that the item doesn't meet these requirements you can ask for your money back, as long as you do so quickly. Alternatively, you can request a repair or replacement or claim compensation.
You do not have a right to a refund if you:
- change your mind about a product
- decide you do not like it

THE ENTREPRENEURSHIP MARKETING ENVIRONMENT

▓ *Table 4.3* (continued)

Receipts and proof of purchase
You don't have to have a receipt to get a refund. However a seller can ask you to provide some proof of purchase. This could be a credit card bill or bank statement.

Items bought in a sale
If you buy anything in a sale you are still covered by the Sale of Goods Act. You wouldn't get a refund if:
- you were made aware of a fault before the sale
- the fault should have been obvious when you bought the item

Where to get help if things go wrong
First, ask the company to put things right – put your complaint in writing. If you are still not happy you may have to take the matter to court. Contact your local Citizens Advice Bureau for advice.
You can also get in touch with the local council's Trading Standards office.

Your rights when you buy a service
If you are using a service such as hiring a builder or using a mechanic then you are covered by the Supply of Goods and Services Act 1982. This means that any goods supplied must be of satisfactory quality and any service you buy must be:
- carried out with reasonable care and skill
- carried out within a reasonable time and at a reasonable charge (if no charge is agreed in advance)

What 'reasonable' means will be different in each case. If you have a problem, you may need to ask the Citizens Advice Bureau what 'reasonable' is for your situation.

What to do if you have a problem
If you have a problem, contact the service supplier straight away to sort out the problem.
If you are still not happy, check if they belong to a trade association. An example would be a carpenter belonging to the Federation of Master Builders. You will find trade association details on a company's adverts and bills. The association may be able to help you settle a dispute.
If you can't sort out the problem, you may have to go to court. Contact your local Citizens Advice Bureau for advice.
Product safety and recalls
If you are worried about the safety of anything you have bought, for example a child's toy, contact your council's trading standards office.
You can also contact Consumer Direct.

Source: www.direct.gov.uk/en/Governmentcitizensandrights/Consumerrights/DG_182935 (Accessed on 13 March 2010)

All of this legislation guiding business practices have been put in place for a number of reasons which can be summarised as: (1) to protect companies from each other such as preventing unfair competition; (2) to protect consumers from unfair business practices such as deceptive advertising; and (3) to protect the interest of society against unrestrained business behaviour (Kotler et al., 2008). Therefore, SMEs do not only need to have a good knowledge of these existing regulations and guidelines but also need to adhere to them.

In the UK, there are many regulatory bodies some of which are government-instituted while some are not and their impact on how SMEs conduct their marketing activities cannot be underestimated. Examples include the Office of Communications (Ofcom) which is the communication regulator that regulates TV and radio sectors, fixed line telecom and mobiles, plus the airwaves over which wireless devices operate in the UK. It works independently of the government towards concentrating solely on protecting the interest of

51 ▓

citizens and consumers (www.ofcome.org.uk/what-is-ofcom). Another example is the Office of Fair Trading (OFT), which has the mission of making markets work efficiently and effectively for consumers in the UK by promoting and protecting their interest. It ensures that businesses are fair and competitive (www.oft.org.uk). Of course there a good number of more organisations that have no direct linkage to government but equally influence marketing indirectly. Trade Associations and pressure groups are non-governmental, yet often drive home their points on acceptable standards of conduct from marketers. In some countries, especially the developed ones, like United States, and UK, activities of consumer movements are more pronounced. The consumerists in their philosophy strive to bring marketers to conform to standard that enhances consumers' welfare. The basic rights of consumers often advocated in consumerism are highlighted in Table 5.4:

The first four of the consumer rights listed in Table 4.4 have their origins as the declarations of former US president John F. Kennedy, while the last four are new additions by consumer movement through Consumer International. SMEs need to be aware of these rights and the implications they have for their transactions as they work towards satisfying their target markets.

Sociocultural environment

The sociocultural environment encompasses marketers' relationship with the society and the culture of that society. It reflects how people live in relation to their day-to-day activities which could have very close link to what they buy, why they buy them, where they buy them, how they buy them, and how often they buy them. This is why it is stated that culture influences our perception of things (Gbadamosi, 2004). In this sense, this segment of marketing environment is undoubtedly important to SMEs and worth being diagnosed thoroughly. Essentially, factors that make up the sociocultural environment include the religious beliefs, the languages, the type of food consumed, the mode of dressing, and family patterns. Since SMEs directly or indirectly produce goods and services for people in the society, such products must be positioned in such a way that conforms to the mores and values of that society as most consumers are strongly influenced by their sociocultural settings. In many instances the sale of a product that is forbidden in one society might be culturally accepted in several other societies. For instance, selling flowers could be a very successful venture in

Table 4.4 Basic rights of consumers

	Consumers' Rights
1.	The right to safety
2.	The right to be informed
3.	The right to choose
4.	The right to be heard
5.	The right to satisfaction of basic needs
6.	The right to redress
7.	The right to education
8.	The right to a healthy environment

Source: www.consumersinternational.org/Templates/Internal.asp?NodeID=95043 (Accessed on 16/03/2010)

the UK as consumers use them to express their emotions such as for love and bereavements. The use of flowers on Valentines' day, the Christmas period, and Mothers' Day is on the increase and indicates how successful this business has been in this cultural setting. However, this is unlikely to be the case in most developing countries where people crave for other things to express their feelings in similar contexts.

Another major change in sociocultural environment is the changing role of women in the society (Lamb et al., 2010). The surge in the number of women in employment also has considerable implications on societal consumption patterns. In the past, women used to have far less employment opportunities as the belief in the society was that women's role was in the home. Obviously this trend and belief has changed in recent times. The publication of the Office for National statistics indicates that figures of women's employment are 56% and 70% respectively for 1971 and 2005 (ONS, 2006), while the figure for January to March 2019 is 71.8% (ONS, 2019), and this marked increase also reflects in the number of jobs that women do now compared to figures during decades earlier. *The Focus on Gender* publication of the Office of National statistics shows that both men and women filled similar jobs estimated at about 13.6 million each compared to the case in 1985, when men filled more jobs than women with the difference of 2 million jobs (ONS, 2008). Meanwhile, the ONS data shows that gender pay gap fell to 8.6% for year 2018 in respect of full-time employees, while the figure is close to zero for full-time employees aged 18–39 (ONS, 2019). Family consumption pattern has equally changed in line with all these societal changes. Indeed, as SME often target relatively small customer groups, tracking these changes will give them directions on how to achieve competitive advantage. The knowledge of this environment will equip them such that the product or service they offer to the targeted niche could be distributed through the right outlet, priced effectively, and promoted in such a way that will reach the target audience effectively. For instance their marketing communication messages, which used to be designed to appeal to only husbands, might change to that which appeal to the couple in light of the changes in family buying roles.

TECHNOLOGICAL ENVIRONMENT

Technological environment which embraces the technical skills and equipment that enhance the conversion of inputs into outputs is pivotal to the success of businesses and the society. The simple process of how this takes place is demonstrated in Figure 4 2:

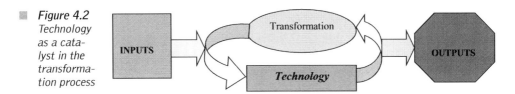

Figure 4.2 Technology as a catalyst in the transformation process

It supports wealth creation and has a very strong influence on marketing activities. It is therefore not surprising that the trend all over the world shows that technology is constantly changing. We now have several inventions that make marketing transactions more efficient and effective compared to what used to be in place several years back. The changes to computing, telephoning, and printing in recent times are just some examples of how technological environment changes, and influences marketing of goods and services. Although due to financial constraints some of these businesses may not be able to afford some of the newly developed highly sophisticated equipment meant for production of goods that could give them economies of scale, they could engage in inter-organisational relationships (IOR) to achieve this. In such an arrangement, two or more establishments can pull their resources together towards buying the new inventions that will give them the opportunity to satisfy their target markets. The stiff competition in the market cannot allow small businesses to remain complacent with old equipment and processes. They have to be up to date with inventions and also explore the opportunities towards gaining competitive advantage in the marketplace. Linking this discussion to Figure 2.3, it is apparent that having the right inputs into the transformation process is important and significantly determines the type of outputs that will come out of the system. The BBC programme titled *Dragons' Den* features several inventions and how entrepreneurs have used them to improve their production processes especially in terms of alternative raw materials or equipment that will improve their production processes. Such inventions further emphasise the dynamic nature of this environment.

Reflecting on how we have described technology so far and the prevailing changes in this environment, it is clear that the role of research cannot be trivialised. It aids inventions in various forms – introduction of a variety of new products and services; and increasing productivity in organisations where such new processes are adopted. For instance, the advent of smartphones, tablets, social media, and several computer software packages to the information communication technology (ICT) sector has transformed the world of business in recent times and touches our lives every day. Many of these developments offer marketers the opportunity to be more efficient and effective at creating value for their customers. Today, improved technology has widened the scope of online marketing transactions. It allows marketers to communicate more effectively with their target audience, while the customers could also relax and place order for products and services from home. SMEs that are sensitive to development and inventions in the world of technology will be better able to achieve competitive advantage in their market domain. Overall, this part of marketing environment contributes towards improving the standard of living of the people in the society.

Nevertheless, despite all the highlighted opportunities in this environment, it is noteworthy to state that changes in it could constitute challenges for marketing activities, especially at the small and medium scale level. Since the changes in this environment happen independently of the pace that a particular organisation embraces them, businesses that are not willing to move with the trend will be left behind, and might lose its competitive edge, market share, and profits to the businesses that are making the most of the developments. Interestingly, consumers are not oblivious of these changes hence are becoming more demanding and sophisticated accordingly. So, keeping up to date with the trend in the technological development is not an option but a necessary course of action for businesses that want to survive in this age.

PHYSICAL ENVIRONMENT

Tracking the changes in the physical or natural environment is crucial to businesses. No doubt, these changes are beyond the control of SMEs, albeit they could present opportunities for marketing activities, or poses threats to their successful marketing practices. If we consider it from the marketing perspective, the relevance could be discussed from numerous perspectives. As noted by Armstrong and Kotler (2009), marketers need pay particular attention to several trends in the natural environment which include shortages of raw materials, increased pollution, and increased government intervention. Considering these points critically, they offer directions to SMEs on how to explore opportunities. Monitoring these developments in the physical environment will inform marketers of the existing gaps that they could fill with their innovations that could provide alternative raw materials or reduce pollution. There have been unprecedented concerns about managing the environment from government and other well-meaning groups in the society in recent times. The clamour by researchers and environmentalists that countries have to reduce their carbon emission has been on for a while. Their core message is that, if these issues are not addressed early enough, the consequences will be undesirable and grave for the society in the future. For instance, shortage of raw materials could have enduring effects on many businesses including SMEs. One of the implications of the shortage of raw materials is that it may lead to substantial increase in the costs and prices of goods that require such scarce resources. This will also have a multiplier effect on the competitive advantage of such establishments unless they are able to research into and develop cost-effective alternatives. They will most likely lose their share of the market to others who have cost-effective inputs as the increase in the associated costs may not be easy to pass to the consumers who have free access to competitors' offerings. Viewing this from the opportunity perspective, some businesses including SMEs have also realised the trend in the waste and pollution being generated by other businesses and now explore it as a business opportunity by managing such wastes on their behalf.

Demographic environment

Demographic environment covers issues about the market populations, based on factors like age, household structure, gender, race and ethnicity, income, and location. Like other macro-environmental factors discussed earlier, this segment of the marketing environment is beyond the control of the SMEs, yet they have far-reaching implications on their marketing activities. The demographic mix of people varies from one society to another. This is one of the reasons why it is difficult to have 'one-size-fits-all' marketing strategies when operating in various societies especially for international marketing. As an example, Table 4.5 relates to the United Kingdom. It presents the population estimates and projections of the country for periods from 1971 to 2026. Looking at this table closely, one would notice that the population is ageing, stated differently, the older generation groups are increasing in number; and the trend is expected to continue for the next few decades. Among the reasons cited for this trend in the population statistics are fall in death and birth rates (ONS, 2009).

From a global perspective, it has been projected that about 60% of the population of the less-developed countries will be urban in 2025 (Boyd et al., 2002). These projections and speculations are of special relevance for marketing of goods and services in the society. Trend in a population's age distribution provides useful indicators of demands for products and services. It could also provide better insight into needs and wants of the target markets, and offers opportunities to design specific marketing programmes to serve the markets. The most populous of the various age categories in the society will likely provide good opportunities for marketers. On the other hand, in light of their limitations, small businesses could also note the trend of specific small groups that could constitute viable niches so as to be able to design appropriate marketing mix to satisfy their specific needs thereby avoid direct competition with large corporations.

Apart from age and geographical settlement, categorisation of people on the basis of family structure, social class, income, race and ethnicity, and lifestyle could be very rewarding to small businesses in their marketing planning. The shopping patterns of bachelors and newlyweds are likely to be different from that of large families with children. To a considerable extent, income could also be a reflection of people's purchases. For example, a study

AYANTUNJI GBADAMOSI

Table 4.5 Population[1]: by sex and age (thousands)

	Under 16	16–24	25–34	35–44	45–54	55–64	65–74	75 and over	All ages
Males									
1971	7,318	3,730	3,530	3,271	3,354	3,123	1,999	842	27,165
1981	6,439	4,114	4,036	3,409	3,121	2,967	2,264	1,063	27,412
1991	5,976	3,800	4,432	3,950	3,287	2,835	2,272	1,358	27,909
2001	6,077	3,284	4,215	4,382	3,856	3,090	2,308	1,621	28,832
2007	5,895	3,788	3,936	4,578	3,941	3,546	2,398	1,835	29,916
2011	5,961	3,846	4,235	4,314	4,292	3,592	2,636	2,018	30,893
2016	6,187	3,647	4,707	4,043	4,487	3,642	3,052	2,324	32,088
2021	6,485	3,490	4,784	4,318	4,217	4,045	3,153	2,761	33,253
2026	6,557	3,670	4,553	4,787	3,957	4,238	3,230	3,322	34,313
Females									
1971	6,938	3,626	3,441	3,241	3,482	3,465	2,765	1,802	28,761
1981	6,104	3,966	3,975	3,365	3,148	3,240	2,931	2,218	28,946
1991	5,709	3,691	4,466	3,968	3,296	2,971	2,795	2,634	29,530
2001	5,786	3,220	4,260	4,465	3,920	3,186	2,640	2,805	30,281
2007	5,615	3,580	3,924	4,670	4,039	3,686	2,660	2,887	31,059
2011	5,682	3,613	4,200	4,375	4,413	3,744	2,883	2,958	31,868
2016	5,909	3,420	4,572	4,092	4,620	3,796	3,323	3,156	32,887
2021	6,202	3,272	4,591	4,321	4,323	4,242	3,438	3,549	33,938
2026	6,271	3,453	4,368	4,691	4,048	4,448	3,512	4,155	34,946

[1] Mid-year estimates for 1971 to 2007; 2006-based projections for 2011 to 2026.

Source: ONS, Correction Notice: Social Trends No. 39 (2009), as obtained from Office of National statistics; Government Actuary's Department; General Register Office for Scotland; Northern Ireland Statistics and Research Agency

of low-income consumers' purchases of grocery products indicates that, in some cases their preferences are at variance from people at the other end of the spectrum of income distribution (Gbadamosi, 2009). Some ethnic groups are noted as constituting good market for certain products, while sometimes people in a geographical location might have peculiar needs that may be different from those outside the location. In the UK, leading supermarkets such as Tesco, Morrison's, and ASDA now have product lines with items that appeal to ethnic minority groups in the society. The change in the trend of immigration has introduced opportunities to small businesses that could identify and explore them. The establishment of *Obalende Suya*, a London-based Nigerian restaurant launched in 1987 which has been an instant hit among the African immigrants (Madichie, 2005) is an example of how small businesses are exploring the trend in demographic environment for marketing purposes. All these are examples of diversities in demographic environment with potent implications for marketing activities in the SME context.

ACTIVITY 1: IN-CLASS ACTIVITY

Think of a business that you will like to do in the future and discuss with two or three other members of your class which marketing opportunities you could get from the changes in each of these Macro-environmental factors in relation to this business.

THE ENTREPRENEURSHIP MARKETING ENVIRONMENT

MICROENVIRONMENT OF MARKETING

Figure 4.3 shows the interactions among the microenvironmental factors. It indicates that the SMEs source its inputs such as raw materials, machineries, human resources, and money from the suppliers and use them in the transformation process to yield the needed output as explained earlier in Figure 4.3. The output that they obtain from this process could either be sold directly to the customers or through intermediaries.

As shown in Figure 4.3, there is a possibility that the competitors will have relationships with each of the parties in the microenvironmental system of the business. While it is possible that they source their inputs from the same supplier, they could also be using the same intermediaries for the distribution of their offerings to the target customers who also have the liberty to buy from any organisation that best satisfies their needs including the competitors. Let us now explore each of these elements in turn to see how they influence marketing activities of SMEs.

Customers

Customers constitute a major element of the microenvironmental factors. Essentially, marketing is about satisfying customers whether in the context of small and medium scale enterprises or large corporations. Thus, having the right information about them and delighting them is crucial for successful marketing practice. Marketers need to be familiar with trends associated with the purchases of their customers and maintain very good relationship with them. Logically, customers are the boss in the marketing system as they dictate which organisation will stay in business and which should leave the scene. Fundamentally, one of the constraints of SMEs in comparison to large corporation is finance. However, this cannot be regarded as a tenable excuse for not being able to satisfy their target markets. Hence, most SMEs often target niches with clearly identifiable set of needs that they would be able to satisfy within their constraints. Otherwise the customers will shift their loyalty to organisations that will give them optimum benefits in their transactions. Hence, SMEs are expected to design their marketing strategies to revolve around satisfying their customers as shown in Figure 4.4.

As marketing activities are applicable to transactions involving the sale of physical goods and services, the figure shows the marketing mix elements consisting of the 4 Ps (product, price, place, and promotion) and the extended marketing mix elements for services (process, physical evidence, and people) being managed holistically towards satisfying the customers. This is considered useful as there are many examples of SMEs in the service sector just as there are a good number of them that offer physical products to their customers. Lawyers, Accountants, Teachers, Musicians, Information Technology Operators, and Fitness coaches are examples of service-oriented SMEs commonly noticed in the British

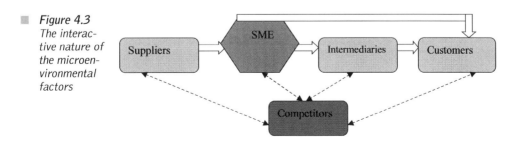

Figure 4.3
The interactive nature of the microenvironmental factors

Figure 4.4 Customer as the centerpiece in marketing transactions

marketing environment. In fact, in most cases when organisations offer physical products to their customers, the total package of transaction still includes some elements of services. Nevertheless, the point being made here is that in all of these marketing transactions, customers will always occupy a pivotal position for the organisation to succeed in the marketing environment. The logic in this argument is that satisfied customers are not only likely to make a repeat purchase but are also likely to inform others of their positive experience in the form of *positive word-of-mouth* communications. On the other hand, dissatisfied customers may not only stop buying from the organisation but are also likely to spread the *negative word-of-mouth* to friends and neighbours of their dissatisfaction with the transactions. So far, it is evident that organisations exist because there are customers. Accordingly, the whole of this book in one form or another is about how small and medium size enterprises (SMEs) could satisfy their customers efficiently and effectively better than competitors.

Competitors

One of the dramatic changes that have taken place in the marketing system in recent times is the increasing scale of competition in the marketplace. As consumers have more access to information and are more equipped to select among competing offerings, marketers including SMEs are no longer guaranteed patronage except they are willing to outperform their rivals in the business setting. In order to be able to survive and succeed, business organisations compete for virtually all resources needed – men, money, materials, and machines. In fact, as shown in Figure 4.3, competitors are not only vying to get the pounds that the customers have to spend, their activities could also permeate the entire marketing system including the link to the suppliers of resources needed, intermediaries, but are also after information on how the SME operates. SMEs may face competition from various sources. This may be from organisations of comparable scale or large corporations, such competition may also be within or outside the industry, and it could even come from previous employees. In fact, customers of an organisation may also be potential competitors (Montgomery and Weinberg, 1979). This is why it is very important for them to identify all current and

THE ENTREPRENEURSHIP MARKETING ENVIRONMENT

potential sources of competition for their business. Such effort will give them information on the gaps in the markets and their competitive advantage. Hence, when entering into battle with their direct competitors SMEs should first consider whether it is necessary, as there may be some customers in the market who can be profitably served without venturing into head-on competition (Hill and O'Sullivan, 2004). Nonetheless, this does not necessarily suggest that marketers should always avoid competition. It has been noticed that even when faced with highly competitive environment, innovative smaller firms can survive and even prosper (Lamb et al., 1999). Small businesses could concentrate on niches that have specific needs that could be met within their limited resources. Above all, SMEs should be sensitive to competition – their number, their mode of operations, their market share, their marketing mix elements, and their strengths and weaknesses. If this is done effectively, they stand a better chance of succeeding even in the volatile marketing environment.

Suppliers

As businesses engage in exchange to satisfy their customers, they also obtain their inputs from various other organisations known as the *suppliers* (see Figure 4.4). The role of suppliers in the marketing system as a microenvironmental factor is vital and could take several forms. Some supply the raw materials needed by SMEs to produce their final output. Banks and lending agencies provide the needed capital. NATWEST, HSBC, Barclays, and many other banks in the British Marketing environment have various funding schemes for SMEs in the form of loans and overdrafts. Employment agencies that provide the needed human resources as at when needed, consultancy firms that provide business advice, advertising agencies, and marketing research firms are all examples of suppliers that influence how SMEs relate to their customers. Losing a key supplier of raw materials, component parts, or critical services can sometimes create inconceivable disruption to production flow which would affect how SMEs satisfy their customers. Thus, as these organisations monitor their markets, and other environmental factors, they also need to be aware of trends and changes in the activities of their suppliers. Besides, they need to create and maintain very good relationship with them. Similarly, it is important for them to pay particular attention to issues like suppliers' innovations, deals with rivals, supply shortages, delays or quality concerns, strikes or requirement difficulties, legal actions or warranty disputes, supply costs and price trends, and new entrants into the supply chain (Dibb et al., 2001). Indeed, the qualities of relationship businesses have with their suppliers will influence how well they are able to serve their target markets and how successful they can be in their marketing environment.

Intermediaries

Intermediaries of SMEs are individuals or other organisations that mediate between them and their customers by engaging in the distribution of their goods and service. Stated differently, they act as the link between production and consumption and bridge the gap between the two ends in the marketing system. Examples include the wholesaler, retailers, and agents. In a production setting, while the producing SMEs provide customers the form utility, intermediaries provide time, place and possession utility. Fundamentally, the ultimate consumers of the products could not be deemed to have been totally satisfied until they have the product needed at the right time and be able to buy it at the right place. As indicated so far intermediaries occupy pivotal position in the marketing system for most organisations, but they are considered especially relevant for small businesses that need their services to make their products available in areas where they could not ordinarily be able to reach due to their financial limitations. This explains why most small business owner/managers would be very keen to have the support of major intermediaries for a wider distribution of their products. Before Levi Roots, a British producer of *Reggae Reggae Sauce*, pitched his Jamaican sauce on the BBC programme, *Dragons' Den* in 2007, the product was yet to be known. However, the opportunity he had through this television appearance and the networks that developed afterwards sparked distribution opportunity for this product in major British supermarkets which has now made the product widely known and successful in the British marketing environment. In most cases, SMEs do not adopt conventional distribution methods, and sometimes combine several methods whenever applicable to respond to environmental threats. Essentially, it is important to note that intermediaries constitute one, and an important element of the microenvironment and any strategic change to them and their activities could also have strategic implications for the SMEs in their bid to satisfy their customer.

ACTIVITY 2: IN-CLASS ACTIVITY

Reflect on your recent purchases of three products or services from an SME in your locality and discuss with two other members of the class how the customer-oriented approach of the SME has contributed to your satisfaction or how its disregard for this has left you dissatisfied.

Environmental scanning and analysis

Having discussed various environmental factors that influence the marketing activities of SMEs, we will now examine environmental scanning and analysis and their relevance to the success of SMEs. *Environmental scanning* simply involves collecting information about the forces that make up the environment. It is about acquiring relevant information to guide the organisation's future course of action (Aguilar, 1967). Thus, conducting SMEs' environmental scanning would involve collecting information related to the economy, taxation, exchange rates, interest rate, legislations, competitors' characteristics, political and legal factors, demographics, sociocultural factors, customers, suppliers, physical environment, and a host of others as highlighted earlier in the discussion of marketing environmental factors. As noted by Saxby et al. (2002), it allows managers to become instantly aware of factors in the environment that could significantly influence their activities in the organisation, especially in relation to their strategic direction.

While environmental scanning basically deals with obtaining information about the environmental factors, *environmental analysis* has to do with assessing and interpreting the information gathered in the course of scanning the environment. Scanning and analysis of the environmental factors are interconnected and work interactively. As changes in marketing environment can lead to opportunities and threats, SMEs would be better positioned in the marketplace if they engage in environmental analysis after the scanning. Although most of these forces are beyond their control, scanning and analysis combined together often yield far-reaching benefits.

In order to be able to obtain relevant information, SMEs would need to explore various sources including websites, trade publications, and newspapers. The rigorousness in conducting environmental scanning actually varies from firm to firm. This is an area that has been widely explored in the business literature (Miles and Snow, 1978; McDaniel and Kolari, 1987; Slater and Narver, 1993; Saxby et al., 2002). One of these contributions which have been widely explored and applied differently is that of Miles and Snow (1978) in which the authors developed a typology of strategic behaviour of firms in relation to their environmental scanning. This perspective indicates that firms could be classified as Prospectors, Analysers, Defenders, or Reactors. The prospectors are firms that scan the environment proactively and actively seek to identify and explore opportunities, and tend to be creator of change in their industry, whereas the Defenders have narrow product-market domain and tend not to search for opportunities outside their domain of operation (McDaniel and Kolari, 1987). The Analysers exhibit both the behaviour of the Prospectors and the Defender, hence they explore new products from a relatively stable base of customer (Slater and Narver, 1993). The Reactors rank below the other three in their qualities and attitudes towards growth and environmental monitoring (Slater and Narver, 1993). They do not demonstrate consistent strategy rather they simply respond to pressures from the environment as they come (McDaniel and Kolari, 1987). For a long time, this postulation has been widely used, adapted and explored in various forms. But our key interest in this view lies in its emphasis that firms vary in how they approach their strategic choice and environmental scanning activities.

Saxby et al. (2002) present a model which incorporates the environmental scanning approach of firms and generic strategy into various organisational culture types. Their work is an improvement on an earlier work of Deshpande et al. (1993). In the original model of Deshpande et al. (1993), a two by two matrix which produces four quadrants labelled separately – Clan, Advocacy, Market, and Hierarchy – was developed. In this work, the Clan describes firms that are internally focussed and flexible in how they manage things. In this postulation, firms in the Market culture tend to be market oriented and their major goal is about getting profits through competitive advantage (Saxby et al., 2002). They are the opposite of the Clan. This model shows the Advocacy to be flexible and market-oriented, whereas the Hierarchy which is the converse of the Advocacy describes firms that are basically concerned with a stable organisational settings and emphasises orderliness (Saxby et al., 2002).

The core message of Saxby and others which they emphasise in their model (see Figure 5.5) is that there is a compelling need to incorporate environmental scanning approaches and generic strategy into these various organisational culture highlighted. Thus, they suggest four environmental scanning approaches to be the *Informal* for the Clan, *Exploratory* for the Advocacy, *Analytical* for the Market, and the *Disciplined and Structured* for the Hierarchy. Saxby et al. (2002) made an interesting and noteworthy conclusion from the study. They contend that if a manager operates in on quadrant but adopts an inappropriate environmental method, the firm will either be missing valuable information or wasting their resources. Indeed, this postulation also indicates and supports the view that firms are not the same and do not approach the scanning of environment in the same way. The implications of these extant perspectives on environmental scanning are remarkably relevant to our understanding of SMEs' environmental scanning.

An argument in the same direction but perhaps in a simplified form is presented in this chapter, as shown in Figure 2.6, that some SMEs often ignore environmental scanning on the excuse that it amounts to a waste of their time and do not really add anything significant to their marketing transactions. They are shown as category A and depicted as *The Vulnerable*. Another category of SMEs do it passively merely to conform to certain exigencies such as obtaining loan from banks, but often abandon it afterwards and probably revisit it when

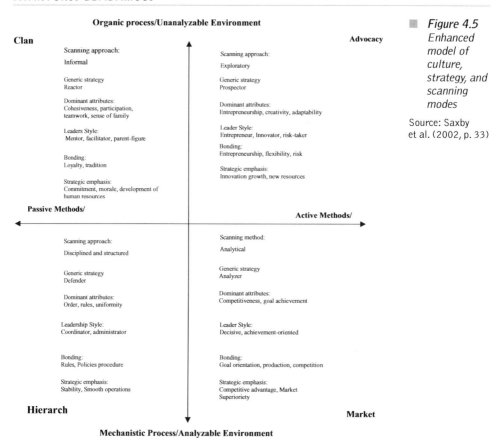

Figure 4.5 Enhanced model of culture, strategy, and scanning modes

Source: Saxby et al. (2002, p. 33)

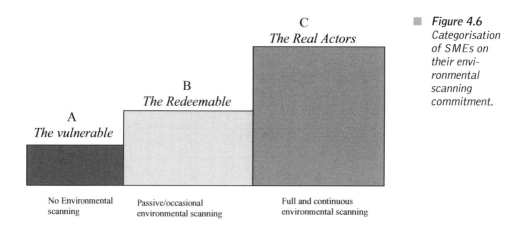

Figure 4.6 Categorisation of SMEs on their environmental scanning commitment.

similar needs arise in the future. SMEs in this category are described here as *The Redeemable* (category B) which might survive the environmental turbulence as the consciousness of the owner-managers to opportunities might be triggered in the course of the occasional scanning of their marketing environment albeit not proactively commissioned. Nonetheless, there are some SMEs which might actively and continuously scan their marketing environment to identify opportunities and threats in it. This latter category of SMEs shown as category C stands to benefit in many ramifications from such active commitment to environment scanning. They are described as the *Real Actors* as they explore the market and engage in innovative marketing within the constraints militating against their survival in the turbulent marketplace.

Since environmental factors are dynamic, multifaceted and complex, overall, a thorough diagnosis of these factors will provide useful information to the SMEs on that will serve as input to their marketing decisions such that will enable them to be able to satisfy their competitors and have a competitive advantage.

SWOT analysis: analytical tool in entrepreneurial marketing

The popularity of the SWOT analysis as an analytical tool which could be used by organisations in their planning activities is not in doubt. The term SWOT is an acronym for Strength, Weaknesses, Opportunities, and Threats.

Essentially, conducting a SWOT analysis involves identifying opportunities and threats associated with the firm in the marketing environment, and acknowledging its strength and weaknesses. In other words, SMEs are expected to complete the boxes in Figure 4.8 and use the output in their planning process. Doing this is expected to be closely linked to the environmental scanning and analysis of the organisation. This is because firms scan their marketing environment for opportunities that they could explore and to be aware of the threats associated with these environmental factors as shown in Figure 4.7.

As shown in Figure 4.8, opportunities and threats exist in the external marketing environment of SMEs. Changes in this layer of the marketing environment could present excellent opportunities for the firms and if spotted and explored, such opportunities could make such businesses become winners in the marketplace. For example Ngamkroeckjoti et al. (2005) found that SMEs that scan their environment will be better able to develop appropriate new products. This is because such firms would have noticed the changes in the environmental factors and be able to match their innovations with the needs of their market.

Unlike opportunities which connote positive developments in the marketing environment, the threats are the converse (see Figure 4.8). As we experience changes in the marketing environment, SMEs are confronted with equivalent challenges in relations to these

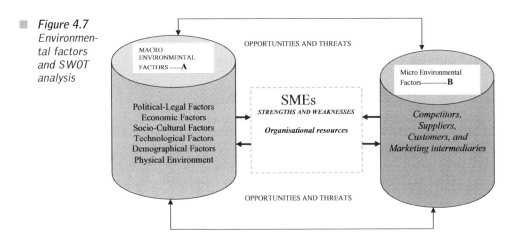

Figure 4.7 Environmental factors and SWOT analysis

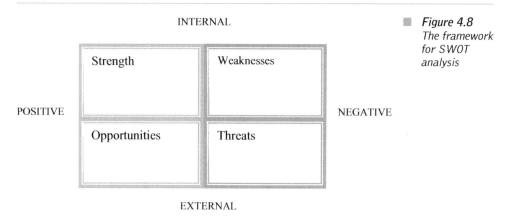

Figure 4.8
The framework for SWOT analysis

factors. So, this reiterates the turbulent nature of the marketing environment. Besides the high level of uncertainty confronting SMEs, it is also noteworthy that the turbulence varies in degree in relation to various industries in the marketing environment. But, it is expected that industries with high levels of turbulence will experience unpredictable changes and an unstable competitive landscape (Gango and Agarwal, 2009). In addition, a change in one factor in the marketing environment can trigger changes in several other ones. For example, a change in government might affect policy on taxation and small businesses, which could also have effects on the economy and the sociocultural factors. However, environmental scanning could help SMEs in this turbulence by enhancing their marketing decision-making activities, as doing it implies that they are most unlikely to be met unaware by these changes.

The strengths and weaknesses of the organisation are internal and are essentially organisational resources, processes, culture, and other similar factors which could be fine-tuned to exploit the opportunities and cope and with the threats in the marketing environment. As popular as SWOT analysis is, some who use it apply it shoddily and realise very little benefit from it. In order to be able to obtain optimal benefits from using SWOT analysis as an analytical tool for achieving success in the marketing environment, Piercy and Giles (1989) provide very useful guidelines which are making it focussed: it should be applied with shared vision, it should be targeted at enhancing the value of the customer (customer orientation), it should incorporate environmental analysis, and it should be applied to allow for structured strategy generation.

SMEs' response to the marketing environment

So far, we have established that SMEs are confronted with environmental turbulence and other associated threats in the external environment. Although the turbulence of the marketing environment often affects all business organisations, the characteristics of SMEs suggest they are more vulnerable than larger enterprises.

The existing literature indicates that SMEs have some noteworthy distinguishing characteristics in comparison to larger enterprises. Wong and Aspinwall (2005) provide a long list of the characteristics of small businesses classified into clusters of factors: ownership and management, structure, culture and behaviour, system, processes and procedures, human resources, and customers and market. Examples of these characteristics in their list are that such firms are mostly started, owned, and dominated by the entrepreneurs, simple and less

THE ENTREPRENEURSHIP MARKETING ENVIRONMENT

complex structure, flexible structure and information flow, multi-tasked owner-manager, low degree of specialisation, and unified culture. Others are simple planning and control system, informal evaluation, flexible and adaptable process, closer and information relationship, normally dependent on a small customer base which are mostly local and regional market with few international, more frequent and closer contact with customers, and many know their customers closely – personally and socially (Wong and Aspinwall, 2005). Based on a body of literature, Chen et al. (2006) also state that some or all of these features could be used to distinguish SMEs from large firms:

- Flexibility and volatility;
- Skill (or expertise) shortage;
- Very limited market power;
- Market behaviour mainly affected by partners, or competitors.

Another view emphasises that they are small in size, constrained by a general lack of financial resources which also suppresses their growth potential, and externally they do not have any control over their environment (Carson et al., 1995).

Essentially, despite the variations in the number of these characteristics highlighted, one could still see the point of convergence between these views that they are small in many ramifications compared to large enterprises that are financially sturdy and more systematic in their marketing approaches. Hence, these tend to inhibit the extent to which they are able to explore opportunities in their marketing environment.

Nonetheless, if these characteristics are critically examined, one will note that SMEs also have several tools at their disposal that they could use to succeed in the volatile marketing environment. These include their use of personal contact network (PCN), flexibility, informality, less complex structures and procedures, and their closeness to their customers.

To respond to the environment, SME could obtain and clarify information about the environment from friends, business associates, customers, suppliers, and several others that they have contacts with. This could provide them with needed information about environment that would serve as very useful input to their marketing decisions. Exploring their links to all these individuals or organisations in their network can lead to many opportunities which they ordinarily may not be able to get without being in the link. This social networks offers small firms invaluable opportunity of exploring their marketing environment. Laere and Heene 's (2003) also note that networks have now become critical and are forms by which SMEs in fast-changing and highly competitive market could gain competitive success.

Moreover, although SMEs are relatively small compared to large enterprise, they have the advantages of being flexible, and closeness to their customers as they often target niches, they could explore these as ways of responding to the environment. They can use this to know the needs and wants of their customers closely and then design appropriate marketing mix elements that will make them achieve their marketing objectives. Their flexibility also implies that they are more likely to be able to change their internal factors quickly to adapt to the changes in the marketing environment to meet the needs of their customers. However, not all SMEs are aware of this, as is evident in the high rate of small business failure. As the turbulence in the marketing environment intensifies, SMEs that will survive are those who are ready scan the environment, be innovative, explore their characteristics as strengths for gaining a competitive advantage, and be customer-focussed.

65

SUMMARY

All organisations operate within their marketing environment, which influences how they are able to serve their customers. However, the extent of which they respond to the environmental forces varies with the type of organisations. SMEs are known to be smaller in many ramifications compared to large enterprises hence are unlikely to respond to the environment in the same way. These environmental factors could be classified into internal and external. While the former are within the organisation and could be fine-tuned by the SMEs to be able to satisfy their customers effectively, the same cannot be said of the latter. Thus, SMEs are expected to fine-tune their internal factors in such a way that would make them get the best out of the external environment. Essentially, this environment consists of organisational resources like its personnel and others that are often used to operate within the environment.

The external environment can also be categorised further into macro and microenvironmental factors. Macroenvironmental factors are broad in scope and affect all organisations. Examples are economic factors, political/legal factors, socio cultural factors, and technological factors. However, micro factors are very close to the particular SME and influence how the business operates to satisfy its target market. The basic micro factors are customers, competitors, intermediaries, and the suppliers. Given the uncertainties and complexities associated with these environmental factors due to their continuous changes, businesses are expected to collect information about the factors and analyse it to give them direction for their marketing decisions. This process is known as environmental scanning and analysis.

SMEs respond to marketing environmental factors through their marketing advantages which include flexibility and closeness to their customers. These also give them opportunity to respond quickly to the needs of their customers who are in most cases niches with specific identifiable characteristics within the larger markets. These also give them the opportunity to enjoy customers' loyalty.

KEY TERMS
- Marketing Environment SME
- Macroenvironment Microenvironment
- Environmental Scanning Uncertainty
- Opportunities Threats
- Strengths Weaknesses
- Loyalty Flexibility
- Resource Constraints Entrepreneurship

REVIEW QUESTIONS

1. Identify two areas that technological advancement could be of benefit with respect to an SME that intends to establish its retail business in one of the European countries and discuss two ways that you think it could suffer setback for not matching up with trends in the technological environment.

2. Enumerate and discuss two of the macroenvironmental factors that you think a small scale web designer should be sensitive to. Rationalise your response.

66

THE ENTREPRENEURSHIP MARKETING ENVIRONMENT

3. Assume that Joe Mosi, the owner of a local business which sells body lotion in your neighbourhood, has just appointed you as the new marketing manager in his establishment. Your new challenge is to highlight the relevance and impact of socio-cultural environment, demographic environment, intermediaries, and suppliers to marketing in that type of business to your subordinates in a forum organised by the chief executive. What are the main highlights that will feature in your presentation?

4. Mrs. Joy Margaret Samson is proposing to go into the business of manufacturing and marketing of baby foods. However, Favour Honey, her confidant, has advised her that she needs to consider very important factors in the environment while pursuing this investment. Being the chosen consultant, explain these factors in detail and use appropriate diagram to support your explanation.

5. Examine the roles of regulatory agencies in the marketing of edible products in your country. Give SME-related examples to justify your standpoint.

6. What in your own opinion distinguishes macroenvironmental factors from micro environmental factors? Use one for each of the two types of environment to robustly exemplify your viewpoint.

7. What is environment scanning? How is it different from environmental analysis? Use SMEs examples to support your viewpoint.

8. Conceptually explain the relevance of sociocultural environment to an SME Fitness club business owner in your locality.

9. Examine the specific impacts of the economic environment on a small-scale furniture firm based in an urban centre of your country. Illustrate your points with current and relevant examples.

CASE STUDY: BREXIT, BUSINESS UNCERTAINTY AND SMEs IN THE UK MARKETING ENVIRONMENT

The UK referendum conducted on Thursday, 23 June 2016, to leave the European Union (EU) was a significant and historic event in the world political system. This has been noted by many commentators as a sign of great turbulence in the business environment. It is hard to argue that this is not the case as many political office holders including Prime Ministers have had to quit their jobs over the uncertainty surrounding this development. It is convenient for one to simply dismiss this development as merely political, but the impact permeates every part of the business environment. Economically, the fall in the value of the British pounds was one of the early signs that accompanied the announcement of the referendum result. Similarly, some business establishments, both SMEs and large corporations, have had to change their strategies and structures in order to still be relevant in the marketplace. There are rumours that the Bank of England may further increase the interest rate to cushion the effect of instability in the system. This has been met with counter rumour that such an increase cannot even be considered immediately due to how fragile the economy has been. This makes the uncertainty in business to be significantly heightened. Uncertainty constitutes one of the biggest complaints of businesses around Brexit, as indicated in a recent article published in *Trust Shops*, entitled "Business After Brexit: What Changes for UK Businesses?" As the final arrangement between the European Union (EU) and the United Kingdom on how to organise the exit is yet to be finalised, most consumers are delaying some spending decisions to avoid being caught up in any unfavourable financial consequence of the conundrum. A clear and commonly stated example is that of transactions involving properties. Investors in properties have heard the lingering rumour that house prices may be significantly affected. Hence, they are delaying making commitment to such investments which in turn affect many other important issues. Estate agents, stockbrokers, and other stakeholders in property business experience a similar trend of slowdown in market.

The challenge for the UK SME is surviving in the midst of economic uncertainty, as all of the environmental factors are closely interlinked. The change in economy is inextricably linked to sociocultural system that explains peoples' consumption of goods and services. In a similar vein, these are all linked to the changes that take place in the political scene of the country which also has multiplier effects on the technological dimension of the business environment. Statistically, it has been noted that about one third of SMEs delay activities around growth and investment as a result of the uncertainty that surrounds Brexit. Information available from small business website shows that 19% of SMEs indicate that they are on the brink of folding up as a result of a lack of guidance associated with Brexit, while 8% of these businesses are already engaging in redundancies for cost savings. This number far outweighs 4%, which is the proportion that is working on hiring staff to work in their establishments. Going by the recent tracker information from Bibby SMEs, on the average, SMEs plan to invest around £64,600 in their business as at the first quarter of 2019, which is a far cry from the £103,648 for a similar purpose cited in 2018. The challenges associated with this Brexit uncertainty does not only apply to local business activities but also influences transactions across national borders. Small business publications indicate an unprecedented low level of export plans among these small businesses, which is at only 27%, whereas the figure for the previous year indicates a 42% proportion. To many business owners, this is a real threat to the sustainability of the establishment if no serious action is taken to address the trend. Mike Cherry, who is the Chairman of the Federation of Small Businesses (FSB), clamoured that government can help businesses in a number of ways. He noted that small firms in the Netherlands and Ireland have benefited from vouchers that aid their access to advice, useful equipment, as well as upskilling that could help future-proof their businesses in relation to changes in trade arrangements. According to him, the UK government could provide soft loans to small businesses for this purpose.

Meanwhile, available information still shows that about 8% of these small businesses predict that their businesses will benefit from Brexit. While this position raises some degree of optimism about opportunities in the marketing environment concerning this development, the proportion of the business that indicates this position is relatively small. So, whether the change will be a force for good or bad is unclear. As many small businesses are involved in transactions with other SMEs and large corporations in various other countries, it is now more imperative than before to ensure that they make the most of the limited resources at their disposal. It has

THE ENTREPRENEURSHIP MARKETING ENVIRONMENT

been suggested that part of the ways for small business to survive after Brexit is to embrace technology and innovation. So, the prevalent digital tools could be explored as a form of competitive advantage.

Questions

Questions

1. Apart from the specific examples cited in this case, using information from the internet, newspapers, other media, or your experience; select two SMEs operating in different sectors of the UK economy and explain how the complexity of the environment could influence their operations.
2. What advice would you give to new small business planning to begin operation next summer in the UK marketing environment to succeed in the highlighted uncertainty?
3. To what extent do you agree with the claim made in the case study that technology and innovation could be significant to how SMEs deal with uncertainty around Brexit?
4. Explain how the information provided in this case about Brexit relates to micro-environmental factors of SMEs in the food industry.

Sources

Small Business (2019), One third of SMEs delay growth and investment, citing Brexit uncertainty, 16th April, 2019

https://smallbusiness.co.uk/one-third-of-smes-delay-growth-and-investment-citing-brexit-uncertainty-2547311/ (Accessed, 21th, May, 2019)

Small Business (2019), 'Small business growth plans stall ahead of original Brexit date', 29th May, 2019, https://smallbusiness.co.uk/brexit-growth-plans-2547218/ (Accessed, 1st June, 2019)

Eisenberg, A. (2019), 'Business After Brexit: What Changes for UK Businesses?, Trusted Shops, 16th April, 2019

https://business.trustedshops.co.uk/blog/brexit-damage-european-market/(Accessed, 29th May, 2019)

Percy, S. (2019), A force for good or bad? What Brexit could mean for small businesses, The telegraph, 8th February, 2019

www.telegraph.co.uk/business/challenges/brexit-for-small-businesses/(Accessed, 21st May, 2019)

TECHNOLOGY, SME, AND THE 21ST CENTURY:

Big data and the contemporary SME

Conventionally, the data obtained by organisations in the form of market intelligence are analysed to aid such companies in their decision-making endeavours towards creating and delivering value to the customer. Meanwhile, in recent times, data sources opportunities available to businesses are far more than what we used to have several decades before now. Some of these come from social media activities of

69

the organisations, the Internet of Things (IoT) and many other sources. Accordingly, despite the multiplicity of sources, firms are expected to manage these data effectively to achieve notable results that could aid the business survival. This brings in the notion of Big Data. In their definition, Sivarajah et al. (2017: 263) explained the term as 'the artefact of human individual as well as collective intelligence generated and shared mainly through the technological environment, where virtually anything and everything can be documented, measured, and captured digitally, and in so doing transformed into data'. This is a significant development in the technological dimension of the contemporary marketing environment. Interestingly, this relevance of Big Data (BD) is as to large organisations as to SMEs, in that the latter category of business also has a significant amount of data at its disposal as a result of developments in the world of technology.

Reference

Sivarajah, U., Kamal, M. M., Irani, Z., & Weerakkody, V. (2017). Critical analysis of Big Data challenges and analytical methods. *Journal of Business Research, 70,* 263–286.

Question:

Select any two SMEs operating in different sectors of the economy in your country; make a list of sources of their market intelligence. Compare and contrast these sources and explain how Big Data has transformed the landscape of SME marketing.

GROUP TASK: LET'S REASON TOGETHER

Do you think that not-for-profit small organisations need to perform environmental scanning and analysis? Share your response with two members of your class and compare your viewpoints.

REFERENCES

Aguilar, F. J. (1967) *Scanning the Business Environment.* Macmillan, New York, 1–18.

Armstrong, G. and Kotler, P. (2009) *Marketing: An Introduction,* 9th ed. Pearson Education Inc., New Jersey.

Boyd, Jr. H. W. B., Walker, Jr. O. C., Mullins, J. W. and Larréché, J. (2002) *Marketing Management: A Strategic Decision-making Approach,* 4th ed. McGraw-Hill Companies, Inc., New York, 76–77.

Carson, D., Cromie, S., McGowan, P. and Hill, J. (1995) *Marketing and Entrepreneurship in SMEs: An Innovative Approach.* Pearson Education Ltd, Essex.

Chen, S., Duan, Y., Edwards, J. S. and Lehaney, B. (2006) Toward understanding inter-organizational knowledge transfer needs in SMEs: Insight from a UK investigation. *Journal of Knowledge Management,* 10(3), 6–23.

Deshpande, R., Farley, J. U. and Webster, F. E. Jr (1993) Corporate culture, customer orientation, and innovation in Japanese firms: A quadrad analysis. *Journal of Marketing,* January, 23–37.

Dibb, S., Simkin, L., William, M., Pride, W. M. and Ferrell, O. C. (2001) *Marketing: Concepts and Strategies.* Houghton Mifflin, Boston.

Ganco, M. and Agarwal, R. (2009) Performance differentials between diversifying entrants and entrepreneurial start-ups: A complexity approach. *Academy of Management Review,* 34(2), 228–252.

THE ENTREPRENEURSHIP MARKETING ENVIRONMENT

Gbadamosi, A. (2004) Cultural Dimension of Comparative Management and Administration. In Ogundele, O. J. K. (Ed.), *Comparative Management and Administration – A Book of Readings*. Concept Publication, Lagos, 111–137.

Gbadamosi, A. (2009) Cognitive dissonance: The implicit explication in low-income consumers' shopping behaviour for 'low-involvement' grocery products. *International Journal of Retail and Distribution Management*, 37(12), 1077–1095.

Hill, L. and O'Sullivan, T. (2004) *Foundation Marketing*. Pearson Education Limited, Essex, 72–73.

Kotler, P., Armstrong, G., Veronica, W. and Saunders, J. (2008) *Principles of Marketing*, 5th ed. Pearson Education Limited, Harlow.

Laere, K. V. and Heene, A. (2003) Social networks as a source of competitive advantage for the firm. *Journal of Workplace Learning*, 15(6), 248–258.

Lamb, Jr., C. W., Hair, Jr., J. F. and McDaniel, C. (1999) *Essentials of Marketing*. South-Western College Publishing, Ohio.

Lamb, C. W., Hair, J. F. and McDaniel, C. (2010) *MKTG*, 3rd ed. South-Western Cengage Learning, Mason.

Madichie, N. (2005) Marketing assessment of Nigerian foods in the United Kingdom. Paper Presented at the Academy of Marketing Conference, 4–7 July, Deblin Institute of Technology, Dublin.

McDaniel, S. W. and Kolari, J. W. (1987) Marketing strategy implications of the Miles and Snow typology. *Journal of Marketing*, October, 19–30.

Miles, R. E. and Snow, C. C. (1978) *Organizational Strategy, Strcuture, and Process*. McGraw-Hill, New York.

Montgomery, D. B. and Weinberg, C. B. (1979) Toward strategic intelligence systems. *Journal of Marketing*, 43, Fall, 41–52.

NgamKroeckjoti, C., Speece, M. and Dimmitt, N. J. (2005) Environmental scanning in Thai food SMEs. *British Food Journal*, 107(5), 285–305.

ONS (2006) News release: New report points rise in women in work, 23rd March. www.statistics.gov.uk/pdfdir/wim0306.pdf (Accessed on 22 March 2010).

ONS (2008) Focus on gender, 26 September.

ONS (2009) Correction notice: Social trends: No 39 – 2009 Edition, National Statistics, Harlow, http://www,statistics.gov.uk/downloads/theme_social/Social_Trends39/Social_Trends_39.pdf (Accessed 26 October 2010).

ONS (2019a) Gender pay gap in the UK: 2018. www.ons.gov.uk/employmentandlabourmarket/peopleinwork/earningsandworkinghours/bulletins/genderpaygapintheuk/2018 (Accessed 1 June 2019).

ONS (2019b) Labour market overview, UK: May, 2019. www.ons.gov.uk/employmentandlabourmarket/peopleinwork/employmentandemployeetypes/bulletins/uklabourmarket/may2019 (Accessed 1 June 2019).

Piercy, N. and Giles, W. (1989) Making SWOT work. *Marketing Intelligence and Planning*, 7(5/6), 5–7.

Saxby, C. L., Parker, K. R., Nitse, P. S. and Dishman, P. L. (2002) Environmental scanning and organizational culture. *Marketing Intelligence and Planning*, 20(1), 28–34.

Sivarajah, U., Kamal, M. M., Irani, Z. and Weerakkody, V. (2017) Critical analysis of Big Data challenges and analytical methods. *Journal of Business Research*, 70, 263–286.

Slater, S. F. and Narver, J. C. (1993) Product-market strategy and performance: An analysis of the miles and snow strategy types. *European Journal of Marketing*, 27(10), 33–51.

www.statistics.gov.uk/cci/nugget.asp?id=1654 (Accessed on 22 March 2010).

Wong, K. Y. and Aspinwall, E. (2005) An empirical study of the important factors for knowledge-management adoption in the SME sector. *Journal of Knowledge Management*, 9(3), 64–82.

Chapter 5

Buyer behaviour in the 21st century
Implications for SME marketing

Ayantunji Gbadamosi

LEARNING OBJECTIVES

After reading this chapter, you will be able to:
- Explore the consumer decision making process and how the understanding of this could aid SMEs' marketing practices;
- Discuss the nature of factors that influence consumer behaviour and their implications for SME Marketing;
- Discuss the organisational buying decision process and the corresponding SMEs' actions for value creation in that context;
- Analyse factors influencing decisions of organisational buyers and how these influence SMEs' marketing approaches for targeting this market.

INTRODUCTION

It is now a well-acknowledged point that SMEs are established regularly in most societies. Entrepreneurs are driven by passion for creativity and the need to make a difference to the society where they operate. They help in job creation, playing significant roles in the global marketing environment and constitute over 90% of establishment in most societies. As an example, it has been noted that SMEs represent 99% of millions of businesses that are existing in the European Union (EU) (Gilmore, 2011). A thorough look at virtually every sector of the economy in the marketing environment will reveal something new somewhere intended for creating value for the customers. This sounds good for the economy in many ramifications. Summing these perspectives up from their review of the literature, Grimmer et al. (2018) indicates the importance of SMEs in relation to innovation, serving niche markets, social mobility, economic variety and integration, and activation of competition. Unfortunately, most of these businesses die prematurely. In some cases, this happens almost immediately after the introduction of the business while in other cases, it happens a few months after the establishment of the business. A number of reasons could be given for the failure of these businesses. In some cases, the product design is rather shoddy, or the prices are not right in several other cases. There are also reasons around the fact that the distribution strategy adopted may be inappropriate for the product or inappropriate marketing communication strategies. It is also common that these business ideas lack the appropriate fund required to survive in the competitive environment. Meanwhile, one of the usually taken-for-granted points is the lack of appreciation of the fit of the products to the needs of the consumers. So, the question of what consumers buy, why they buy them, where they buy them from, and how often they engage in these transactions are among the salient questions that should drive SMEs' activities in the marketplace. Accordingly, in this chapter, we will be examining the factors that propel people's consumption decisions, the stages in the buying decision-making process, issues around organisational buying decision process, and how they relate to the SME in the contemporary marketing environment. We will now first turn attention to the stages in the consumer decision-making process.

CONSUMER DECISION-MAKING PROCESS

Before the consumer pick a brand of fragrance, a type of shoe, the service of an event planner, or any other market offering over other alternatives, they usually go through a number of stages in the purchase process. It is important for the SMEs to be aware of this in order to be able to know what are usually involved in each of these stages and how they could design their marketing strategies to be of fit for these stages. Before we examine these stages, it is important to indicate that, at this stage, in this section of the chapter, attention is being focussed on consumption that take place for self-gratification. This refers to cases such as purchase for personal or household consumption, as a gift for people, or for other related purposes and not for resale or for use in business organisations.

The consumer decision-making process consists of the stages depicted in Figure 5.1. In this, it is shown that consumers begin the 'journey' leading to the purchase of a particular market offering from the stage of need recognition.

NEED RECOGNITION

At this stage, the consumer recognises the gap between her current (actual) state and the desired state. Therefore, the displeasure of a consumer with the current hairstyle compared to the desired stage of her looking beautiful with a new freshly made hairdo will trigger the need to approach a hairstylist. A common misconception about this stage among some SMEs is that even if a product is not needed, consumers could be persuaded to buy the product if the firm that developed it is seen to be innovative. However, such assumption is misplaced as meeting needs are very crucial to consumers transaction especially as they are keen to achieve value for any transaction they engage in. This desire for value and the prevalence of a good number of options available to consumers on how to meet the needs this day and age indicates that SMEs have to be customer driven to survive the marketplace. As expected, the scope of the competition is wider than merely competing with other small businesses in the locality, consumers are exposed to market offerings from various organisations of various sizes and hold no allegiance to any except those meeting their needs. A firm may have passionately spent considerable amount of effort and other resources on developing a product that is not needed by the people.

Figure 5.1 Consumer decision-making process

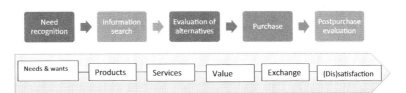

This could be tantamount to casting those resources down the drain. One of the ways by which this challenge could be addressed is to engage in research that will reveal these gaps in the market that should drive the firm's innovation. If done effectively, this is expected to reveal the market niches that could be filled in the market. A full discussion of entrepreneurial marketing research has been covered in Chapter 6 of this book. A closely related view on this is the notion of value co-creation which has been noted as core to success for contemporary marketing practice. The main issue in value co-creation is that consumers are not passive receivers of market offerings supplied by the business but are active participants in the creation of brand equity and their own value-in-use (Lusch and Vargo, 2006; Millspaugh and Kent, 2016).

INFORMATION SEARCH

When the consumer recognises the need to buy a product or service, more often than not, they engage in search for information that could lead to getting the needed item. A number of factors make this an important step that could not be ignored by SMEs in how they operate in the marketplace. These factors are associated with the changes in the market environment such as technological and sociocultural factors. For example, to get information relating to products or services, the significant improvement in the digital world has made it easier for the consumers to obtain the required details through the internet with the use of several devices like phones, and tablets for 'on the go' customers. Most of these customers are now on various social media platforms engaging with one another and businesses in relation to marketplace information. So, it is now very compelling for SMEs to follow the trend, embrace technology, and be discoverable when consumers are in need of information relating to their market offerings.

Conventionally, the sources of information that could be explored by the consumer vary and could be categorised differently. Hence, we will look at a commonly used categorisation which are: internal and external. The internal sources of information relates to the consumers' past experiences with respect to the purchase of that product. A consumer's experience after a transaction involving a plumbing business will go a long way to determine whether or not the firm's services could be used subsequently when the need arises. Every other source outside of the individual's personal experience and sources of information could be regarded as external. Examples here include friends and family sources, trade organisations' publications, print media, electronic media, and several others. If SMEs have positioned their market offerings to be consistent with the need of the target market, it is also essential to ensure that the business and the brand are well positioned within the systems where it could be discovered when the consumer is searching for information. This relates more to the notion of integrated marketing communications. This involves coordinating marketing communication tools such that a clear, consistent, reliable, and competitive message is delivered in relation to the organisation and its market offerings (Fahy and Jobber, 2019). Hence, within the relative financial constraints of the SMEs, they are expected to have a coherent marketing communications package that will position their offerings effectively in the marketplace to be among what the consumer will consider in the decision-making process.

EVALUATION OF ALTERNATIVES

At the stage of information search, consumers are usually inundated with options. This is one of the key advantages accruing to consumers because of competition that take place among business organisations. Consumers could have options from large organisations that are usually at advantage in some ramifications compared to SMEs, several small businesses are also competing for success with various products and services. At this stage, consumers evaluate the alternatives on the basis of certain criteria developed for this choice. Some of the key criteria that could be used are:

- Price;
- Quality;
- Convenience/Availability;
- Reliability;
- Comfort;
- Eco-Friendliness;
- Durability.

It is important to note that the list is not exhaustive but more importantly, the criteria that will be used by the consumer will be a function of many factors, such as the nature of the product and the characteristics of the consumer. For instance, the criteria to use for the selection of which accountant to choose will be different from the one that will be used to select a web developer, which will also be different to what will be used when considering which restaurant to visit for a meal. While there is a challenge for small businesses in relation to large corporate organisations that are significantly endowed with resources, small businesses also have advantages in relation to niche targeting, closeness to their customers, and flexibility to make changes to explore marketing opportunities in the environment. Ultimately, the consumer develops a list of criteria that will offer her value in the transaction. The implication of this stage is quite significant for the SMEs. It is important to ensure that the business' unique selling propositions (USP) is clearly highlighted to the consumers for them to be able to make it a choice among many when considering what to buy.

PURCHASE

Having evaluated the alternatives, the consumer decides to buy the one that offers the most value. Contemporary marketing is driven by value, which could be defined, from several aspects related to the transactions. The product itself is expected to be a source of value to the consumer in terms of how it fits the intended use. Price is another point of value. For example, it has been reported that consumers at the lower end of income spectrum are driven by price, buy no frills items, and do not consider higher prices to be indication of good quality (Gbadamosi, 2009). Similarly, the mode of distribution could be a source of value to the consumer. The development in technology has made it easier for consumers to order products or services and modernise the delivery system. Consumers all over the world are now more connected to businesses than ever before. The internet usage rate as a percentage of the population for 2019 was put at 35.9% for Africa, 51.7% for Asia, 86.6% for Europe, and 89.1% for North America (Internet Word Stat, 2019). The onus is on businesses to have a holistic way of delivering value to the consumer. Essentially, it is important for SMEs to have well defined target markets and design its strategies towards meeting their needs. It is also useful to know those making the actual purchase and/or purchase decisions in order to be able to reach them with appropriate marketing programmes. In a family setting, the following buying roles are usually identified:

- Initiator – initiates the idea to buy the needed products/services;
- Influencer – his/her views support the idea to buy the needed products/services;
- Decider – makes the decision around the purchase of the needed items;
- Buyer – makes the actual purchase of the products/service;
- Gatekeeper – controls the flow of information between the business organisation, and the family;
- User – uses the product.

Irrespective of their sizes, whether large corporation or SMEs, it is important to know the dynamics associated with these roles and how they change over the years so that appropriate marketing strategies could be put in place for the best results that deliver value to all of the parties involved.

POST-PURCHASE EVALUATION

The stage of post-purchase evaluation is characterised with checking the experience after the purchase or use of the product with the need identified at the early stage of the process. It is about checking whether the product or service that constitutes the focus of the transaction delivers in relation to the need identified. On this, there are a number of possibilities. The need identified may have been met and it is possible that the product or service in question exceeds expectations. There is also the possibility that the products or services are found to have performed less than expectation. The first two cases often result in satisfaction while product's performance below expectation results in dissatisfaction. Customer satisfaction has been notably regarded as a core part of business success as it tends to result in repeat purchase and loyalty. Meanwhile, customer loyalty has a reverberating significance in business. It is often stated that effort required to generate sales from existing customers tends to be less than the one expended in attracting new customers. A myopic view of marketing is to simply focus on transactional approach rather than embracing relationship marketing which ensures that long-term relationship between the parties are given utmost attention. It has been noted that the multitasking activities of SMEs could mean that they may not give priority to Customer Relationship Management (CRM) (Gilmore et al., 2001; Hutchinson et al., 2015).

A good number of measures could be put in place to ensure customer satisfaction. Apart from ensuring that the market offerings are designed to conform to the consumers' needs, engaging in periodic evaluation in the form of customer satisfaction surveys would go a long way to indicate whether the customers are actually getting value from their transactions. Besides, this can also lead to customer devotion. As emphasised in the study of Hassan and Casaló Ariño (2016), consumers are defending the brand within Facebook brand communities. Consumers who are satisfied can defend brand through informing, clarifying, and explaining the position of the organisation in the form of sharing their own personal experiences in relation to the brand towards protecting it. So, this will encourage positive word-of-mouth (WOM) communications that could counter any negative impressions that may have been created by others about the brand or the business. This is closely linked to the notion of customer retention which has been widely acknowledged as resulting in reduced costs associated with sales and marketing when compared to what it will take to acquire new customers (Gronroos, 1989, 2000).

UNDERSTANDING FACTORS INFLUENCING CONSUMER BEHAVIOUR: THE KEY SUCCESS FACTORS FOR THE SME

When making their consumption decisions, consumers are influenced by a myriad of factors. Some of these could be categorised as personal factors, while others involve the consumers' interactions in their sociocultural settings (social cultural factors) and marketing stimuli. It is imperative for SMEs to have a good knowledge of this as that will help them in the design of their marketplace strategies.

Figure 5.2 brings all of these factors together. We will now turn attention to each of these and most importantly consider their implications for SMEs.

CONSUMERS AS INDIVIDUALS – PERSONAL FACTORS

The decisions around people's value-oriented transactions could be driven by factors that are personal to them which are: Income, Age and Lifecycle, Occupation, Lifestyle, Personality, and Self-concept. Some of these personal factors which are psychological in nature are motivation, perception, learning, and attitude.

The people's income is a fundamental part of their consumption decision making system, as marketing revolve around engaging in exchange of something of value between

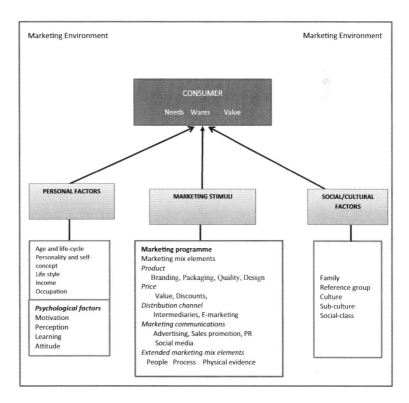

Figure 5.2 Major influences on the consumer decision making

Source: Adapted from Gbadamosi (2019a)

the transacting parties. This suggests that high-income earners are likely to exhibit certain consumption pattern different from those outside of this group. We can see some evidence of this around us in various ways. Restaurant patronage, clothing usage, and grocery consumption are among the many indications that highlight people's income in relation to their consumption. Similarly, some products and services are age-related. Clearly, some inventions around us are typically directed at children, while others will appeal to middle-aged, and several others to consumers of older generation. For a very long time, the common contentions around family consumption often depict children as passive members with very little relevance to decision making. The changes in the marketing environment now render this arguments weak in that the children of today are notably actively involved in the consumption decisions of their household. Parents are considering the requests of their children as crucial for several purchases such as the choice of holiday destination, the specific restaurant to visit, and clothing types to use among many others. A related phenomenon is the family life cycle, which is about how individuals and family members experience changes over time in relation to their households. Some of the key factors that are commonly used to determine the family life cycle are marital status, age, the number and age of children, and the couple's retirements and death. One of the key benefits of knowing this dynamics for entrepreneurial decisions in relation to segmentation, targeting, and positioning approach is similar to reasons for having in-depth knowledge of how a person's occupation informs their consumption decisions. Personality could be defined as the unique distinguishing psychological characteristics we could use to identity a person or group of people (Kotler and Armstrong, 2018). So, it is about what uniquely explains an individual's feelings, thoughts, and behaviour (Kassarjian, 1971; Szmingin and Piacentini, 2018).

When considering how to target consumers, businesses sometimes use people's activities, interests, and opinions, which have been commonly noted with the acronyms of AIO. These items describe peoples' lifestyles, which tends to indicates peoples' consumption patterns. We can get a much deeper sense of this from how Solomon et al. (2016) explain it – our consumption patterns indicate how we choose to spend our time and money. One of the things that we can notice from this issue is that it is reasonably broad and also somehow closely linked to several other factors that influence our consumption decisions like self and reference groups. Given the broad significance of this factor, SMEs have a lot to gain from having an in-depth analysis of consumers' lifestyles. It is common to note that lifestyle could give us a different consumption pattern than what could be obtained from other factors like age and gender. For example, our interests in recycling and politics are examples of what explains our lifestyle and may not be age related. Personality is what makes an individual unique. In the way Schiffman et al. (2010: 136) put it, the following three points are key to the discussion of the term:

- It reflects individual differences;
- It is consistent and enduring;
- It can change.

A closely related factor to personality is an individual's self-concept, which is about how we perceive ourselves, our beliefs about ourselves, and how we evaluate them. Fundamentally, consumers operate in many contexts. Accordingly, they tend to have multiple selves reflecting different aspects of these representations. A simple way for us to explain this lies

Table 5.1 Consumer self: illustrations and examples

	Type of self	Indication	Illustration/Examples
1.	Actual self	A more realistic view of how one sees himself or herself.	This sows the qualities an individual currently has and those s/he lacks
2.	Ideal self	How one would like to see himself or herself	This focusses on achieving the missing qualities
3.	Social self	How the consumers feel other people see them	This emphasises one's consciousness of others and their impression of his or her current state
4.	Ideal social self	How consumers would like to be seen by others	This closely explains consumers'' drive towards the fulfilment of social needs
5.	Digital self	How one sees himself or herself or seen by others in the digital social media platforms such as Facebook and Instagram	Updating online presence with desirable photos
6.	Extended Self	The external objects that consumers use as part of their identities	Possessions like clothing, cars, furniture, and homes that form part of the people's identities

in acknowledging that consumers have the actual self and the ideal self, which are in most cases different. Consumers engage in consumption activities, buying several products or paying for some services to bridge the gap between these two types of selves. The following table was developed based on the perspectives that have been expressed in academic literature (Solomon et al., 2016; Schiffman et al., 2012) on the topic.

PSYCHOLOGICAL FACTORS

Motivation is one of the key psychological factors that drives peoples' consumption behaviour. It addresses the issue of why consumers behave the way they do. Essentially, motivation takes place when someone's unmet needs become aroused. The need refers to the state of felt deprivation as indicated by the gap between someone's actual state and the desired state. Meanwhile, there are a number of theories that have been developed over the years to explain this phenomenon. However, the detailed discussion of these theories is beyond the scope of this chapter. Hence, we will simply be looking at one of these which is very commonly discussed on this subject – Abraham Maslow's Hierarchy of Needs. As shown in Figure 5.3, Maslow (1943) in his seminal paper 'A Theory of Human Motivation', argues that human needs could be arranged in hierarchy order. In this theory, humans move through the hierarchy beginning from a physiological need through to a self-actualisation need that tops the hierarchy.

Perception as a psychological influence on human consumption is about how people select, organise, and interpret the stimuli they are exposed to. Consumers are exposed to many marketing stimuli, but how they select, organise, and interpret them could vary and will also be very crucial to their decision of how to react to competing market offerings such as those offered by SMEs compared to large organisations, or among the specific categories of organisation. There are many areas of marketing implication of consumer perception that

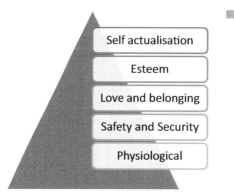

Figure 5.3 Hierarchy of needs

could be of great use to SMEs. For example, it is important for these businesses to address these and other related questions:

- What is the customers' perceived risk associated with buying our product or buying from us?
- What is the perception of our customer about the packaging or labelling associated with our market offerings?
- How do customers perceive the quality of our product/service in relation to competitors' offerings?
- How do the customers perceive the price of our products?
- Do the customer groups being targeted perceive that higher price being charged implies that the product involved is of high quality?
- What is the perception of the market about the image of our business?

In relation to these and other relevant questions, the firm's examination of the consumers' perception is usually valuable to strategic development on how a firm would position its offerings or reposition an existing product or service for better performance in the marketplace. The use of a perceptual map which shows how a product or service appears in the mind of the consumer compared to competing brands is increasingly popular. An example of this is illustrated using hypothetical illustrations of firms/brands around two dimensions of price and range of services offered by logistics companies.

X could be seen to have been positioned as a firm that offers a narrow range of services but charges a lower price compared to other firms in the business. We also can say that B charges relatively higher than E and offers a wider range of services. Other positions on the map could be explained in a similar manner (Figure 5.4).

Meanwhile, attitude can be defined as a learned **predisposition** to respond to stimuli in a consistently favourable or unfavourable way (Fishbein and Ajzen, 1975). Accordingly, consumers' attitude towards the market offerings of a business or its offerings could be positive or negative. By nature, attitudes are enduring and difficult to change. Hence, a key part of the relevance of this subject is for SMEs to position their offerings to be in tune with consumers' needs to generate positive attitude. Nevertheless, in some cases, firms may attempt to change consumers' unfavourable attitude towards its products or services. For example, as indicated in the literature (Lutz, 1975; Kerin and Hartley, 2019), some of the strategies for changing attitudes are:

- Changing beliefs about the extent to which a brand has certain attributes;
- Changing the perceived importance of attributes;
- Adding new attributes to the product.

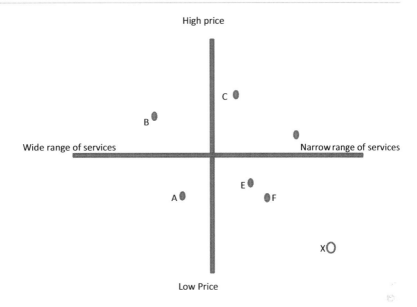

Figure 5.4 Perceptual map

Most consumers' decisions around what they buy, where they buy, and how they buy are related to learning. One of the simple and useful ways to explain learning is to conceptualise it as changes that occur in behaviour as a result of experience (Kotler and Armstrong, 2018). This perspective links recent action to past activities. However, Kerin and Hartley (2019) extend this further to show that learning indicates human behaviour that results from repeated experience and reasoning. As shown by these authors, we can claim that people learn by developing automatic responses to a situation built up through repeated exposure (behavioural learning) and through thinking, reasoning, and mental solving that does not involve experience (cognitive learning). There are a number of key points that we can tease out from these learning theories as related to marketing practice in the context of SMEs. Essentially, it is important for businesses and brands to have a good lasting impression in the mind of the consumers by ensuring that they have pleasant experiences from their transactions to encourage repeat purchase. This can result in sustainable loyalty. Many businesses are exploring this principle to their advantage in various ways such as product line extensions, family branding, and licencing. This is because, consumers are most likely to believe that a brand that has performed in one product category will most likely deliver value in subsequent extension of the brand in relation to other market offerings from the organisation.

Sociocultural factors

Consumers do not operate in a vacuum but interact with people in various contexts. As shown in Figure 5.2, people's consumption decisions could be linked to culture, subculture, family reference groups, and social class.

Culture is very fundamental to consumption. In their recent publication, Szmingin and Piacentini (2018) define it as the sum total of learned ideas, beliefs, values, knowledge, and customers that regulate the behaviour of members of a particular society. Some of the relevant issues we can infer from the definition is that culture is prescriptive, shared, and learnt. It patterns the behaviour of people of particular settings such as what food to eat, which clothes to put on, how to wear them, gift giving behaviour, meanings associated with specific seasons of the year, and a host of others. The societal values are shared. The notion of enculturation and acculturation are central to culture as they explain how it is learnt. Enculturation is about learning one's own culture while acculturation is about learning other people's culture. Each identifiable culture also has several subcultures. These consist of groups of people that have more close value system within a particular culture. Examples of subcultural systems are religions, geographical regions, racial groups, and nationalities (Kotler and Armstrong, 2018). The crucial role of family in consumption is an age-long issue, as it is a fundamental establishment that influences peoples' decisions in several ways. Schiffman et al. (2012) highlight three basic role of family that are particularly key to consumers as the following:

- Economic well-being (financial provision for consumption);
- Emotional support (love, affection, intimacy);
- Suitable family lifestyle (upbringing, experience, and goals in the family).

Another useful discussion associated with the relevance of family to consumer behaviour is the family buying roles, which is about the participation of the members of the family in the consumption system. Usually, the roles are:

- Initiators
- Influencers
- Gatekeepers
- Deciders
- Buyers
- Users

These roles are complementary, but it is also useful to note that the dynamics of these roles continue to change in contemporary societies compared to what we used to have several years before now.

Consumers tend to use other people as a form of reference when making decisions around consumption. They hold relevance for the consumers' decisions. This could be co-workers, roommates, fellow club members, people of religious organisations, and many others. These people help consumers when seeking or clarifying information. This is quite related to the word-of-mouth communications (WOM), which is about the spreading of the information relating to marketplace activities. The spread of the word through digital technologies in recent times (e-WOM) has widened the scope of this phenomenon over the years. We now have various functioning brand communities offline and online that influence activities of their members in respect of specific brands. The role of opinion leaders is very crucial in reference group arrangement. These are individuals who influence the action of others by offering opinions on issues of interest to the opinion seekers. The strong credibility of reference group members compared to commercial sources of information makes it very reliable and widely used among consumers.

Societies are usually characterised with some degree of differences among members in relation to factors such as income, wealth, and education. This is known as social class. As indicated by Armstrong and Kotler (2015), it is a society's relatively permanent ordered division such that members share interests, values, and behaviour. The categorisations vary from one society to another, and the proportion of those in each category also tends to vary with the overall economic structure or system of the country. An example of this is the seven social classes of 21st-century Britain that was developed by Professor Mike Savage from the London School of Economics, as reported by Horton (2015):

- Elite;
- Established middle class;
- Technical middle class;
- New affluent workers;
- Traditional working class;
- Emergent service workers;
- Precariat.

In Kotler and Armstrong (2018), the following American classifications are shown:

- Upper uppers;
- Lower uppers;
- Upper middles;
- Middle class;
- Working class;
- Upper lowers;
- Lower lowers.

In each of these classifications, the ordering indicates that those at the top classes are rated higher in relation to the endowment of some combination of these factors compared to those at the lower classes through to the bottom in the order indicated.

Overall SMEs are expected to be interested in all of these social cultural factors as they influence peoples' consumption. it is expected that the segmentation, targeting, and positions strategies of these businesses will take all of these into consideration. For instance, the study of Muhamad et al. (2016) on the degree of Islamic culture adoption in Malaysian SME hospitality industries found evidence that travellers' religiosity and hotel selection behaviour are strongly positively related.

MARKETING STIMULI

As shown in Figure 1, the marketing stimuli offered by a business constitutes a major category of factors that could explain consumers' marketplace decisions. To create and deliver value for the consumers, SMEs are expected to pay specific attention to how their products and services offered meet the consumer's needs. Similarly, the associated factors such as brand labelling and packaging could be determining factors of success for business in many cases.

As indicated at the introduction of this chapter, a number of reasons could be listed for the failure of small business. One of this revolves around price and pricing strategies. Setting the price too high or too low could have significant negative consequences for the firm, especially those at the early stage of their business span.

How would the product be distributed to ensure that they are available at the right time and the right place is a key question of relevance that cannot be disregarded by SMEs in their marketing strategy. The dynamics of roles and activities of the channel members are part of the marketing stimuli that could prompt consumers to act in favour of a particular brand over another. Accordingly, this should be approached with utmost effectiveness necessary. Meanwhile, the role of marketing communications at influencing consumption has been a long established issue. More often than not, we are drawn to buy certain items because of how such items have been favourably mentioned by marketers. The tools that are often commonly used to achieve integrated marketing communication could be presented as follows:

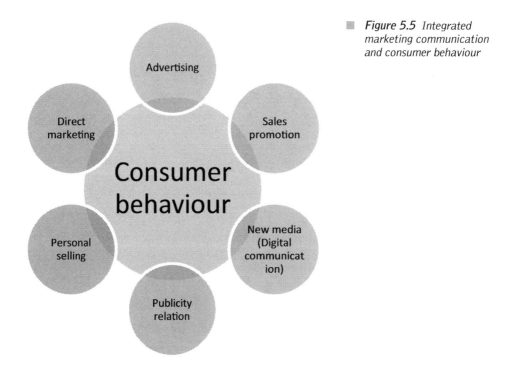

Figure 5.5 Integrated marketing communication and consumer behaviour

The extended marketing mix elements, namely people, processes, and physical evidence, could go a long way to prompt specific consumer action such as brand loyalty. As an illustration, we can imagine a firm with friendly employees that are committed to their roles towards satisfying the consumers with an efficient/stress-free service delivery process. If compared to its counterparts with characteristics opposite to these, all things being equal, the result is expected to be in favour of the customer-oriented business. Similarly, the physical evidence around things like furniture, building, logo, and many others tend to kindle positive responses from the consumer. Hence, paying attention to these would help SMEs towards succeeding in the marketplace.

CONSUMER INVOLVEMENT

Our decisions as consumers for different products and scenarios differ. For instance, the way we will act in the purchase of candy, bottled water, and duct tape would most likely be different from cases of purchases around a house and car. This difference is often linked to the notion of *consumer involvement*. So, with reference to Zaichkowsky (1985) in her paper 'Measuring the involvement construct', we can bring out a definition of the term 'involvement' as a person's perceived relevance of the object based on the inherent needs, values, and interests (Zaichkowsky, 1985; Solomon et al., 2016, p. 208). This is consistent with another more recent claim which indicates that it is the perceived relevance of a product to the consumer (Szmingin and Piacentini, 2018, p. 88). Given this definition, we can hold the view that consumers can be involved with various goal objects including product categories, brands, advertisements, media, decisions, or activities (Arnould et al., 2004; Peter and Olson, 2005). Within the context of these definitions and explanations, it is clear why the consumer decisions are often explained in the two-fold dichotomy of low and high involvement. So, in the low involvement scenario, the perceived risk associated with the purchase is relatively low, the available options or brands are only subjected to limited evaluation or no evaluation prior to purchase. On the other hand, in high involvement scenarios, the perceived relevance of the product; and the perceived risk are high hence, the consumers engage in extensive and significant pre-purchase evaluation. From a broad perspective, consumers' involvement with diverse objects results in different reactions. Some examples are stated by Sadarangani and Gaur (2002). In this, it is noted that consumers' involvement with products leads to a greater perception of differences in their attributes, perceptions of greater product importance, and a stronger commitment to brand choice. Similarly, when a consumer is highly involved in purchases, he or she tends to engage in a search for more information, spending more money, and spending more time searching for the right selection (Clarke and Belk, 1978; Sadarangani and Gaur, 2002). Also, as indicated by Zaichkowsky (1985) who also quotes Wright (1974), when a consumer is involved in advertisement, she or he tends to engage in more counterargument to the advertising.

Apart from the high-low dichotomy categorisation of involvement, there are several other conceptualisations of the term which have been noted by authors in the academic literature. It is noteworthy to consider one of these perspectives in the relevant literature (Rothschild and Houston, 1980; Parkinson and Schenk, 1980; Sheth et al., 1999; Assael, 1998) which could provide interesting explication of the term further. Hence, we can have the following involvement types as shown in the next figure:

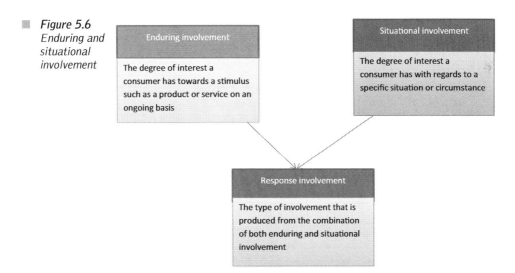

Figure 5.6
Enduring and situational involvement

Since response involvement combines both enduring and situational involvement, it could be said that it captures the complexity of extensiveness of behavioural processes that depict an individual's relationship to any given issue (Rothschild and Houston, 1980). Overall, there are significant implications for SME marketing in the discourse of consumer involvement. Essentially, since there is a link between consumer involvement, brand differences, and loyalty as demonstrated in the literature such as Jensen and Hansen (2006), it makes sense for SMEs to consider increasing consumer involvement in their market offerings. Some of the strategies for doing this has been identified as follows by Schiffman et al. (2012, p. 231):

- The use of sensory appeal;
- Unusual stimuli;
- Celebrity endorsement;
- Provide distinctive benefit to consumers;
- Forge relationship with customers.

These are closely consistent with those listed by Solomon et al. (2016, p. 212) based on an eclectic synthesis of various perspectives, which are more specifically related to increasing message involvement:

- The use of novel appeal;
- The use of prominent stimuli;
- Celebrity endorsement;
- Provide value that customer appreciate;
- Invent new media platform to grab attention;
- Encourage the viewers to think about actually using the product;
- Create spectacle where the message is itself a form of entertainment;
- Use consumer-generated content – letting the consumer make the messages.

THE BUYING BEHAVIOUR IN BUSINESS-TO-BUSINESS MARKETING: THE PLACE OF SMES

So far we have been discussing the importance of understanding the consumption behaviour of those buying for personal gratification and how SMEs could be well positioned to serve this. However, there are very many SMEs that also serve organisational buyers like those buying for resale, those buying as inputs to produce other products, and others like government and nonprofit organisations. Figure 5.7 shows these various markets.

This section is also very important in that while there are similarities between the two markets (B2C and B2B), there are also noteworthy differences between them which indicates that the approaches to be adopted by SMEs for targeting consumers buying for personal use will be different from those buying for business purposes. Some of these differences are highlighted as follows:

- Nature of demand;
  - Derived demand;
  - Relatively fewer than consumer market;
- Nature of the product or services involved;
  - Relatively technical;
  - Complex products;
- Buying process and participants;
  - Professional buyers;
  - Multiple influences in the buying centre;
- Reciprocal transactions;
- Buying criteria;
  - Economic and technical criteria.

BUYER BEHAVIOUR IN THE 21ST CENTURY

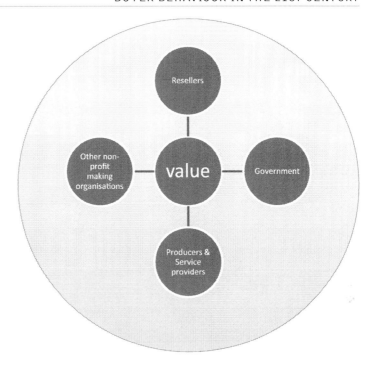

Figure 5.7
Organisational buyers

Having the knowledge of these differences is useful to know the inherent challenges in serving the two markets (consumer market and organisational market). Meanwhile, Azad and Hemmati (2013) indicate that the key differences in the internal marketing status between consumer and industrial goods SMEs revolve around the customer type. They specifically indicate that industrial goods SMEs tend to have direct and individual relationships with their customers compared to consumer goods SMEs.

ORGANISATIONAL BUYING DECISION PROCESS

Just as we have discussed in relation to consumers buying for ultimate consumption, there are stages involved in organisational buying processes. This is depicted in Figure 5.8 as adapted from some of existing literature such as Kotler and Armstrong (2018) and Hutt and Speh (2004):

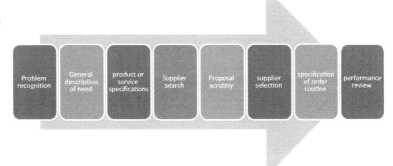

Figure 5.8
Organisation buying decision process

While some of the basic principles that underpin the decision for behaviour for ultimate consumer such as need or problem recognition, evaluation of alternatives, and post-purchase evaluation apply to business-to-business (B2B) scenarios, we can see that there are some differences in the two processes. Essentially, these include the formality of the process, the relative complexity of the process, and the collective involvement of some relevant members of the organisation. Those involved in the process by playing one role or another constitutes the **buying centre**. Just as we have for family buying roles discussed earlier, the members of the buying centre also known as decision-making units (DMU) play some complementary roles as shown in Figure 5.9, using the framework from Webster Jr and Wind (1972) as cited by Kotler and Armstrong (2018):

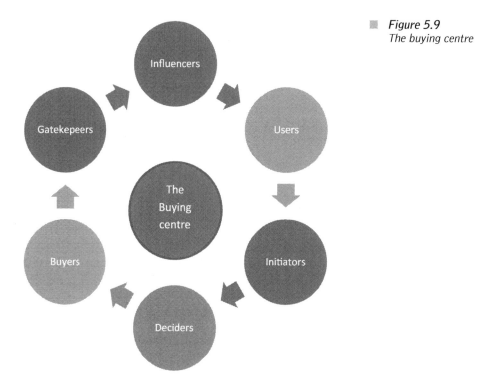

Figure 5.9
The buying centre

Their titles of the roles pretty much reveal what each of the roles stands for in relation to the relevance of each member of the organisation. For example, while the gatekeepers control how information flows in and out of the organisation, especially in relation to the buying centre, the buyers are members that engage in the actual purchase of the products or services needed. Meanwhile, the extent to which an organisation will adhere to the stages of the buying process is a function of the nature of the purchase it is confronted with. As the literature (Robinson et al., 1967; Hutt and Speh, 2004; Kotler and Armstrong, 2018) indicates, organisations could be confronted with any or a combination of these buying situations:

- Straight rebuy;
- Modified rebuy;
- New task.

An organisation engaging in a ***straight rebuy*** of what has been bought previously is familiar with the choice criteria and will simply approach the purchase in the form of a routine decision-making exercise whereas the one engaging in ***modified rebuy*** is interested in changing some of the factors associated with previous purchases in the new one. This could be in the form of changing the prices, suppliers, product specification, or other issues associated with the purchase. The third buying situation is the ***new task*** in which the organisation is approaching a purchase for the first time that is different from those that the company has experienced before. By the nature of this purchase the organisation is expected to engage fully with the buying process scrutinizing all the details and protocols to ensure that it has the best from the buying experience.

Apart from the buying situations, a number of key factors influence the organisations' choices of the needed products. These are highlighted in Figure 5.10:

Figure 5.10 Influences on organisational buying behaviour

Source: Adapted from Hutt and Speh (2004); Kotler and Armstrong (2018)

When dealing with organisational buyers, it is important for SMEs to be aware of these factors that influence how the firm and relevant members involved in the purchase behave. This will give them a competitive edge to be successful even in the volatile marketing environment when serving this market segment (B2B). As shown in the earlier figure, while organisation buying is corporate in nature, it is important to note that those making decisions are also influenced to an extent by factors that are individually related and interpersonal. For example, the age and experience of an organisation member might play a role in how s/he negotiates or interacts with the selling organisation, and there is a high possibility that a better interpersonal relationship between members in the buying centre will result in effectiveness on how they handle the purchasing role. By and large, it will be greatly beneficial if SMEs could analyse these factors in relation to the organisations being targeted towards meeting their needs effectively. This in turn will go a long way to determine whether such selling SMEs will get a repeat patronage when the buying organisation will be engaging in straight rebuy in future transactions. When targeting organisational buyers, the role of networking is key to success. It has been indicated that networking will be of great advantage, especially in their international marketing activities (Jones, 1999; Mikhailitchenko and Varshney, 2016).

TECHNOLOGY, SME, AND THE 21ST CENTURY

The change in the world of technology has strengthened the consumers' position as 'The King' in the marketplace. Over 4.3 billion representing 56.3% of the world's population have been noted as internet users (Internet World Stat, 2019). The consumer dictates the tune of the business and has a wide variety of options on how to obtain what is needed. The 21st-century consumers now crave convenience in virtually all of their transactions. The ease to compare the product prices, the fast delivery of the products ordered, and the clarity of information around the products or services in question offered are some of the key issues on top of the demand list of the contemporary consumer. Meanwhile, it is very common to often hear that SMEs' constraints around resources put them at a disadvantaged position in relation to their large enterprise counterpart in terms of how they could satisfy consumers in the marketplace. However, the development in the digital world now makes it easier for some of these firms to compete at a relatively manageable cost. Most of these small businesses are now on social media platforms such as Facebook, Instagram, YouTube, and Twitter, engaging with their various target customers. The increasing level of customer engagements with SMEs on these platforms in recent years is an indication that customer supremacy is fostering creativity in the use of digital technology. Meanwhile, the more we experience further growth in this technology system, the more cost efficient ways of satisfying customers emerge. Future possibilities on this are innumerable.

Questions

1. Considering the key factors that characterise SMEs in the European Union context, identify five businesses that fall into this category. Explore their websites thoroughly, identify their target market, and highlight specific evidence to show that they are using the opportunity of technological growth to satisfy their target customers.
2. In a group of three, agree on a type of business that you could start with a focus on targeting organisation buyers as the niche. Come up with appropriate brand name for this market offering, and your distribution methods. Discuss how you could use technology to make this business a success in relation to the target market.

GROUP TASK: LET'S REASON TOGETHER

Select any two business types from the list provided and discuss the following issues in relation to them.

a. What specific market niche could be targeted with these businesses? Give reasons for your chosen target consumer groups.
b. Present the unique core business propositions of these businesses.
c. What specific problems and threats do you anticipate could affect these businesses vis-à-vis the selected niches?
d. What actions do you think could be put in place to solve these problem?

e. Compare the points noted on these issues with other student groups in order to identify business specific differences as related to your choices.
     I. Estate agency;
     II. Insurance broker;
     III. Grocery stores;
     IV. Event planning;
     V. Gardening;
     VI. Transportation business;
     VII. Law firms;
     VIII. Accounting firms;
     IX. Cleaning and business support;
     X. Education.

CASE STUDY: OPPORTUNITY RECOGNITION IN THE UK ETHNIC MINORITY MARKET

One of the noticeable trends in the 21st-century marketing system is the increase in the number of ethnic minority groups in many developed nations, including the UK. People are driven to these societies for so many reasons such as search for greener pastures, moving closer to loved ones who are residents in the country, moving away from unpleasant experiences in the home country, and a host of several other reasons. The number of ethnic non-whites that are based in the UK by the 2011 census is 7.9 million representing approximately 14% of the population (ONS, 2019). The full details of specific ethic groups are presented in Table 5.2. Until recently, the impression in these societies among many people has been that all immigrants embrace the cultural values of the host countries in relation to food, clothing, and other consumption issues. However, the reality on the ground now shows that these consumers' quests for having a taste of home away from home is increasing.

Meanwhile, as there are many personal factors such as age, gender, personality, and attitude that drive these ethnic consumers in their choices on a daily basis, the significant role of ethnicity has come to the fore more prominently in recent times. One of the signs that pinpoint this is that most big supermarkets such as Tesco, ASDA, and Morrison's now have specific aisles devoted to 'World foods', indicating that the number of people demanding for these items is increasing. This ranges from specific food types to drinks that link peoples' memories to their countries of origin. So, consumers from the Caribbean, China, Nigeria, Ghana, or other places will see familiar brands on the shelves when shopping at these big supermarkets in the UK. Apart from these giant organisations making incursions into this developing market, the growing number of SMEs targeting these ethnic markets in the country is becoming more noticeable. Grocery items, clothing and fashion accessories, event planning, legal and immigration consultancy, and many others are some of the examples of businesses that are featuring many SMEs targeting niches of ethnic consumers in the country. This is becoming more noticeable in the cosmopolitan cities in the country like London, Manchester, and Liverpool, where the number of ethnic consumers is proportionally high.

One of the points that plays a key part in this development is the religious activities of the members and entrepreneurs (Gbadamosi, 2019b). The case of solidarity and networking activities among members of religious organisation are strengthening the operations of these businesses within the ethnic circle. For example, the Pentecostal church system is noted to be facilitating interactions among members by organising business directories through which ethnic businesses could be listed. Accordingly, members of the church could consult this directory when in need to get the services of a caterer, plumber, accountant, hairdresser, and a host of others. The idea here is that these ethnic consumers could be helped at the stage of the search for information after the recognition of the need for the product or service. While these ethnic consumers could consult friends, neighbours, and co-workers for information on how to meet their needs for ethnic products, the role played by these religious organisations is becoming more significant. At another level, these small businesses maintain close connections with members of these faith-based organisations such that when they have periodic worship gatherings involving many members from different parts of the country congregating at a particular location, these small businesses are always on the ground supplying essentials needed by the congregants including specific ethnic cooked foods. Similarly, they use such opportunity to share leaflets to create awareness of their services and share contact details of how they could be reached.

The strong bonds that exist among these ethnic consumers tend to serve as cues for brand management among SMEs in such a way that makes them competitive even when they are in competition with large organisations. The ubiquity of social media is another crucial way by which these businesses connect with their target niches. They update their customers on new items available, current market deals, business opening times, and a host of other useful details about the business. Some of these businesses use these digital platforms to capture post-purchase evaluations of their services, but in most cases the owner-manager rely on their informal personal interactions with customers to generate this information. Despite these efforts, the key question for these small businesses targeting ethnic markets is whether they are well positioned to cope with the threat from large organisations in this contemporary marketing environment.

Table 5.2

Ethnicity	Number	%
All	50, 075,912	100
Asian	4,213,531	7.5
Bangladesh	447,201	0.8
Chinese	93,141	0.7
Indian	1,412,958	2.5
Pakistani	1,124,511	2.0
Asian others	835,720	1.5
Black	1,864,890	3.3

BUYER BEHAVIOUR IN THE 21ST CENTURY

Table 5.2 (continued)

Ethnicity	Number	%
Black African	989,628	1.8
Black Caribbean	594,825	1.1
Black others	280,437	0.5
Mixed	**1,224,400**	**2.2**
Mixed White/Asian	341,727	0.6
Mixed White/Black African	165,974	0.3
Mixed White/Black Caribbean	426,715	0.8
Mixed other	289,984	0.5
White	**48,209,395**	**86.0**
White British	45,134,686	80.5
White Irish	531,087	0.9
White Gypsy/Traveller	57.680	0.1
White other	2,485,942	4.4
Other	**563,696**	**1.0**
Arab	230,600	0.4
Any other	333,096	0.6

Source: (ONS, 2019)

www.ethnicity-facts-figures.service.gov.uk/uk-population-by-ethnicity/national-and-regional-populations/population-of-england-and-wales/latest (Accessed, 22nd April, 2019)

QUESTIONS

1. Discuss the trend in sociocultural influence on UK ethnic consumers' buying behaviour as highlighted in the case study. To what extent do you think serving this segment is a sustainable business opportunity for SME in this marketing environment?

2. Select any three personal factors that influence ethnic consumer in the UK and explain how SMEs could explore the knowledge of these factors for their business advantage

3. Discuss the consumer decision making process using ethic consumers as an example and explain how SMEs could be proactive at each of these stages for successful marketing practice in the competitive marketing environment.

CHAPTER DISCUSSION QUESTIONS

1. Having a grasp on the knowledge of consumer behaviour has been severally noted as useful in marketing. Discuss how this knowledge could be of use to SMEs in this 21st century.

2. Enumerate the stages in the organisational buying processes; compare this to the process involved for consumers. What are the implications of the stages in these processes for successful marketing practice for SMEs targeting these two segments?

3. Assume you own a small fashion business in your country and would like to ensure that it survives in the volatile business environment. Given that having an understanding of key influences on consumption is crucial to success, select a target market to serve and discuss the main personal factors that could be relevant to this consumer segment while deciding whether to choose your brand or alternatives. In addition to this, indicate what action you will take to ensure that challenges associated with each of these factors are addressed in favour of your business.

4. Explain the difference between situational and enduring involvement? How relevant are these to SME marketing practice. Use specific examples to support your claims.

5. What key factors should SMEs targeting hospitals, retail giants, and government agencies be focussing on in relation to how these establishments select their needed products, services providers, and suppliers?

REFERENCES

Armstrong, G. and Kotler, P. (2015) *Marketing: An Introduction*, 12th ed. Pearson Education Ltd, Harlow.

Arnould, E. J., Price, L. L. and Zinkhan, G. M. (2004) *Consumers*, 2nd ed. McGraw-Hill/Irwin, Boston, 229–286.

Assael, H. (1998) *Consumer Behavior and Marketing Action*, 6th ed. South-Western College Publishing, Cincinatti, OH, 146–160.

Azad, S. and Hemmati, H. (2013). Marketing status in SMEs, industrial versus consumer companies. *Acta Universitatis Danubius. Œconomica*, 9(3), 37–48.

Clarke, K. and Belk, R. W. (1978) The Effects of Product Involvement and Task Definition on Anticipated Consumer Effort. In Keith, H. H. (Ed.), *Advances in Consumer Research*, vol. 5, Association for consumer Research, Ann Arbor, MI, 313–318.

Fahy, J. and Jobber, D. (2019) *Foundations of Marketing*, 6th ed. McGraw-Hill, London.

Fishbein, M. and Ajzen, I. (1975) *Belief, Attitude, Intention, and Behavior: An Introduction to Theory and Research*. Addison-Wesley, Reading, MA.

Gbadamosi, A. (2009) Cognitive dissonance: The implicit explication in low-income consumers' shopping behaviour for 'low-involvement' grocery products. *International Journal of Retail and Distribution Management*, 37(12), 1077–1095.

Gbadamosi, A. (2019a) A conceptual overview of consumer behavior in the contemporary developing nations. In *Exploring the Dynamics of Consumerism in Developing Nations*. Hershey, PA: IGI Global, 1–30.

Gbadamosi, A. (2019b) Women-entrepreneurship, religiosity, and value-co-creation with ethnic consumers: Revisiting the paradox. *Journal of Strategic Marketing*, 27(4), 303–316.

Gilmore, A. (2011) Entrepreneurial and SME marketing. *Journal of Research in Marketing and Entrepreneurship*, 13(2), 137–145.

Gilmore, A., Carson, D. and Grant, K. (2001) SME marketing in practice. *Marketing Intelligence & Planning*, 19(1), 6–11.

Grimmer, L., Grimmer, M. and Mortimer, G. (2018) The more things change the more they stay the same: A replicated study of small retail firm resources. *Journal of Retailing and Consumer Services*, 44, 54–63.

Gronroos, C. (1989) Defining marketing: A market-oriented approach. *European Journal of Marketing*, 23(1), 52–60.

Grönroos, C. (2000) *Service Management and Marketing: A Customer Relationship Management Approach*. John Wiley & Sons, Chichester.

Hassan, M. and Casaló Ariño, L. V. (2016) Consumer devotion to a different height: How consumers are defending the brand within Facebook brand communities. *Internet Research*, 26(4), 963–981.

Horton, H. (2015) The seven social classes of 21st century Britain – where do you fit in? The Telegraph, 7th December, Available at: https://www.telegraph.co.uk/news/uknews/12037247/the-seven-social-classes-of-21st-century-britain-where-do-you-fit-in.html (Accessed on 17th December 2019).

Hutchinson, K., Donnell, L. V., Gilmore, A. and Reid, A. (2015) Loyalty card adoption in SME retailers: The impact upon marketing management. *European Journal of Marketing*, 49(3–4), 467–490.

Hutt, M. D. and Speh, T. W. (2004) *Business Marketing Management: A Strategic View of Industrial and Organisational Markets*. South Western, Cincinnati, OH.

Internet Usage Statistics. (2019) Internet users and 2019 population stat. www.internetworldstats.com/stats.htm (Accessed on 25 May 2019).

Jensen, J. M. and Hansen, T. (2006) An empirical examination of brand loyalty. *Journal of Product & Brand Management*, 15(7), 442–449.

Jones, M. V. (1999) The internationalization of small high-technology firms. *Journal of International Marketing*, 7(4), 15–41.

Kassarjian, H. H. (1971). Personality and consumer behavior: A review. *Journal of Marketing Research*, 8(4), 409–418.

Kerin, R. and Hartley, S. (2019) *Marketing*, 14th ed. McGraw-Hill, Colombus, OH.

Kotler, P. and Armstrong, G. (2018) *Principles of Marketing*, global ed. Pearson Education Limited, Harlow.

Lusch, R. F. and Vargo, S. L. (2006) Service-dominant logic: Reactions, reflections and refinements. *Marketing Theory*, 6(3), 281–288.

Lutz, R. J. (1975) Changing brand attitudes through modification of cognitive structure. *Journal of Consumer Research*, 1(4), 49–59.

Maslow, A. (1943) A theory of human motivation: The basic needs. *Psychological Review*, 50, 370–396.

Mikhailitchenko, A. and Varshney, S. (2016) SME internationalization in emerging markets: Symbiotic vs. commensal pathways. *Journal of Marketing and Consumer Behaviour in Emerging Markets*, 1(3), 4–19.

Millspaugh, J. and Kent, A. (2016). Co-creation and the development of SME designer fashion enterprises. *Journal of Fashion Marketing and Management*, 20(3), 322–338.

Muhamad, R., Wong, E. S. K. and Abuduhaiti, M. (2016) Degree of Islamic culture adoption in Malaysian SME hospitality industries. *Current Issues in Tourism*, 19(3), 243–252.

ONS (2019), Population of England and Wales, www.ethnicity-facts-figures.service.gov.uk/uk-population-by-ethnicity/national-and-regional-populations/population-of-england-and-wales/latest (Accessed, 22nd April, 2019).

Parkinson, T. L. and Schenk, C. T. (1980) An empirical investigation of the S-O-R paradigm of consumer involvement. *Advances in Consumer Research*, 7(1), 696–699.

Peter, J. P. and Olson, J. C. (2005) *Consumer Behaviour and Marketing Strategy*, 7th ed. McGraw-Hill Companies Inc., New York.

Robinson, P. J., Faris, C. W. and Wind, Y. (1967) *Industrial Buying and Creative Marketing*. Allyn & Bacon, Boston.

Rothschild, M. L. and Houston, M. J. (1980) Individual differences in voting behavior: Further investigations of involvement. *Advances in Consumer Research*, 7(1), 655–658.

Sadarangani, P. H. and Gaur, S. S. (2002) Role of emotions and the moderating influence of product involvement in web site effectiveness. *Conference Proceedings at ITS 14th Biennial Conference, Challenges and Opportunities in the Digital Century. The Role of Information and Telecommunications*, Seoul, Korea, August.

Schiffman, L. G., Kanuk, L. L. and Wisenblit, J. (2010) *Consumer Behaviour*, 10th ed. Pearson Education Inc., New Jersey.

Schiffman, L. G., Kanuk, L. L. and Hansen, H. (2012) *Consumer Behaviour: A European Outlook*, 2nd ed. Pearson Education Limited, Harlow.

Sheth, J. N., Mittal, B. and Newman, B. I. (1999) *Consumer Behaviour and Beyond*. The Dryden Press, Orlando.

Solomon, M., Bamossy, G., Askegaard, S. and Hogg, M. (2016) *Consumer Behaviour: A European Perspective*, 6th ed. Prentice Hall, Harlow.

Szmingin, I. and Piacentini, M. (2018) *Consumer Behaviour*, 2nd ed. Oxford University Press, Oxford.

The Telegraph (2019) The seven social classes of 21st century Britain – where do you fit in? www.telegraph.co.uk/news/uknews/12037247/the-seven-social-classes-of-21st-century-britain-where-do-you-fit-in.html (Accessed on 28 April 2019).

Webster Jr, F. E. and Wind, Y. (1972). A general model for understanding organizational buying behavior. *Journal of Marketing*, 36(2), 12–19.

Wright, P. L. (1974) Analyzing media effects on advertising responses. *Public Opinion Quarterly*, 38, 192–205.

Zaichkowsky, J. L. (1985) Measuring the involvement construct. *Journal of Consumer Research*, 12(December), 341–352.

Chapter 6

Revisiting entrepreneurship marketing research
Towards a framework for SMEs in developing countries

Richard Shambare, Jane Shambare, and Wellington Chakuzira

LEARNING OBJECTIVES

By the end of this chapter, you should be able to:
- Define EMR;
- Distinguish EMR from conventional marketing research;
- Describe the elements of the EMR process;
- Identify key factors affecting EMR.

INTRODUCTION

Marketing is an inescapable necessity for any business (Kotler and Armstrong, 2016). This is particularly true in the contemporary business world that is characterised by precarity, chaos, and competition. Factors that once guaranteed business success yesterday are no longer relevant in today's globalised marketplace characterised by the internet and technology. To maintain competitive advantage and long-term survival, businesses conduct marketing research, which, in turn, determine present and future courses of action (Jones and Rowley, 2009). Marketing research, consequently, has developed into an important business function. However, the marketing research lessons in the literature are skewed towards large-scale enterprises (LSEs); and there is very little mention of entrepreneurship marketing research (EMR).

Recent findings point towards a misfit between conventional marketing approaches and small-scale enterprises (Hollensen, 2014). Several authors cite this misalignment as having a negative effect on the performance of small-scale businesses, as the principles of conventional marketing are hardly applicable to small and medium enterprises (SMEs) (Morris et al., 2002; Stokes, 2000). Consequently, there seems to be a consensus that EMR is more in tune with the marketing needs of SMEs (c.f., Coviello, Brodie, and Munro, 2000; Collinson and Shaw, 2001; Gaddefors and Anderson, 2008; Jones and Rowley, 2009; Malholtra, 2010; Morris et al., 2002). While the literature increasingly recommends SMEs to adopt EMR, there is very little guidance on how the former can implement the latter. This lack of guidance is viewed as a gap within the body of knowledge that this chapter seeks to address.

This chapter, therefore, examines the marketing programmes engaged by SMEs with a view to studying how these differ from conventional marketing. Finally, we consolidate these lessons into constructing an EMR framework. To this end, the chapter seeks to answer two research questions:

RQ1: Which structural features of SMEs necessitate them to engage in different marketing programmes from large corporations?

RQ2: What is entrepreneurship marketing research and how does it differ from conventional marketing research?

THE CENTRALITY OF MARKETING IN BUSINESS – BIG AND SMALL

Marketing is critical for the survival of any business, regardless of industry, sector, or size (Gaddefors and Anderson, 2008). All businesses, in one way or another, are involved in marketing. Marketing provides managers with tools to answer five key questions related to businesses:

- Which markets present opportunities for selling products?
- Which products to sell?
- To whom do we sell to?
- How much do we sell our products or service?
- How do we communicate to our market and through which channels?

Traditional marketing research framework

The traditional marketing research framework represents the systematic process through which managers utilise to conduct marketing research (Blumberg et al., 2011; Malholtra, 2010). It consists of five sequential phases designed to provide managers with marketing intelligence about the selected markets (Kotler and Armstrong, 2016). These phases, as shown in Figure 6.1 are problem definition, research design, research methods, analysis,

■ *Figure 6.1* The marketing research process
Source: Own construct

REVISITING ENTREPRENEURSHIP MARKETING RESEARCH

presentation, and implications of findings. As with scientific research, marketing research begins with the formulation of a problem statement. Thereafter, all the remaining activities in the marketing research cycle attempt to resolve the research problem.

In other words, the researchers' perceptions of the problem with respect to their ontological orientation (i.e., how they view the world) influences the research design, what kind of data to collect and from whom, as well as the methods of analysis. Given its routine nature and predictability, positivism became and still is favoured by marketers, especially those within LSEs. For that reason, traditional marketing research tends to be This inclination towards quantitative approaches largely grew out from having the marketing function to be more compatible other management functional areas such as financial management, budgeting, and operations management, which are predominantly quantitative.

WHAT ARE SMES AND HOW DIFFERENT ARE THEY FROM LSES?

To appreciate small-scale enterprises we, first, need to understand LSEs. LSEs are the traditional big businesses commonly referred to as corporations. For some time now, big corporations such as Coca-Cola, HSBC, IBM, Unilever, Toyota, and SAB Miller have been viewed as being the only form of (serious) business. These corporations have multiple branches and subsidiaries spanning across multiple industries or countries, which supposedly bring in big profits. In a world primed for economies of scale, bigger is always better – big companies raking in big profits. From this perspective, it is understandable that the last 100 years of literature projects an image that the only model for commercial enterprise exists in the form of big corporations.

The latter views began facing some resistance in the 1980s when entrepreneurship and SMEs emerged as themes in the mainstream literature (Jones and Wadhwani, 2006). From that point onwards, the potential of entrepreneurial ventures in sustaining profitable business ventures was realised. The World Bank (2019) estimates that there are at least 445 million micro-enterprises operating all over the world, today. By all accounts, these statistics indicate that SMEs are 'big business.' Commenting on the impact of SMEs on the global economy, the World Bank (2019) continues as follows:

> SMEs play a major role in most economies, particularly in developing countries. Formal SMEs contribute up to 60% of total employment and up to 40% of national income (GDP) in emerging economies. These numbers are significantly higher when informal SMEs are included. . . . In emerging markets, most formal jobs are generated by SMEs, which also create 4 out of 5 new positions.
>
> (World Bank, 2019)

The data, in part, explains the big hype about SMEs as critical elements of the world economy, particularly in developing countries.

What is an SME?

There is a multitude of SME definitions proliferated within the literature. Table 6.1 highlights some of these definitions.

In this chapter, we consider SMEs to be small businesses that behave entrepreneurially, i.e., enterprises in which the owners have a significant influence on the day-to-day

Table 6.1 Definitions of entrepreneurship

Author	Definition
Timmons and Spinelli (2004)	Entrepreneurship is a way of thinking, reasoning, and acting that is opportunity obsessed, holistic in approach and leadership balanced for the purpose of value creation and capture.
Frederick, Kuratko, and Hodgetts (2006)	Entrepreneurship is a process of innovation and new venture creation through four major dimensions – individual, organisational, environmental, process – that is aided by collaborative networks in government, education, and institutions.
Kearney, Hisrich, and Roche (2010)	Entrepreneurship is the process of creating something new with value by devoting the necessary time and effort, assuming the accompanying financial, psychic, and social risk and uncertainties and receiving the resultant rewards of monetary and personal satisfaction.
Nieman and Nieuwenhuizen (2015)	Entrepreneurship is the emergence and growth of new businesses. Entrepreneurship is also the process that causes changes in the economic system through innovations of individuals who respond to opportunities in the market.

Source: Moos (2014) and Nieman and Nieuwenhuizen (2015)

management and operations. Because of the close link between small businesses and their founders, the former often inherit the personalities of the latter. This is a stark contrast to LSEs, which rely on policies and systems for governance. Following this line of thought, therefore, owner-managed enterprises, one-person businesses, and even family businesses, naturally, fall within the SME category.

Structural features of SMEs that necessitate a different marketing approach

In this section, we examine the structural features of SMEs.

SMEs are small in size and scope
SMEs, as the name suggests, operate small operations in terms of size, production, and capital requirements. Being small is not necessarily a bad thing; it has its own advantages. Because they are small, SMEs are in a better position to specialise in the service of niche markets. For that reason, SMEs tend to offer goods and services to smaller geographic areas as compared to LSEs. This limited focus allows SMEs to create more personalised relationships with their customers, suppliers, and other stakeholders.

Owned by individuals or families
A vast majority of SMEs are either one-(wo)man or family businesses. As such, financing for these businesses is often restricted to owners' personal savings or loans from family and friends. Family owned SMEs often operate according to family traditions and values, even across generations. Over time, these businesses integrate into the community and become permanent features of their respective communities. Therefore, SMEs are more committed to serving their communities through highly personalised service and stronger customer relationships. A classic example of such commitment is seen in the case of Hoshi Ryokan – the

oldest family business in the world. Founded in 718, Hoshi Ryokan is a Japanese inn-keeping business operated by 46 generations of one family since its founding (Kamei and Dana, 2012). Clearly, with 46 generations of business and marketing intelligence being handed down from generation to generation, family businesses are able to assert their market dominance. This level of commitment often leads to effectuation – the process by which the business fully exploits its unfair advantage and its extraordinary marketing knowledge to its advantage (Dhliwayo et al., 2017).

Owners involved in day-to-day operations

SME owners play a dual role of owner-manager or owner-employee. Unlike in LSEs, there is always a direct line of communication between the owners of the business and its customers. SME management style tends to be very flexible; owners can make required changes quickly, which would ordinarily require pre-approval from the board of directors in the case of LSEs. Hence, this facilitates flexible decision making in all matters of the business, including marketing. Overall, owners' direct involvement has various marketing benefits. These include:

- SME owners' presence in the business promotes confidence on the part of customers;
- The owners' presence in the daily operations of the business reduces instances of agency problems. Moreover, business owners have the opportunity not only to interact directly with customers but also to learn about their businesses and the market, and also to draw lessons from past mistakes to improve marketing strategies;
- Unrestricted interchange of marketing information between owner-managers and customers;
- Faster implementation of marketing decisions;
- Long-term outlook on business. Independent SMEs owners and family firms think of years, and sometimes decades, ahead. This 'patience' and long-term perspective allows for a good marketing strategy and decision making.

Lean resource base

SMEs mostly rely on capital from their owners, whom we have identified are mostly individuals or families. As such, capital outlay is restricted to a bare minimum. A third of all SMEs' capital investment is in the form of entrepreneurs' savings, time, and energy (Chakuzira, 2019). Because their resource base is lean, entrepreneurs develop creativity to manage their businesses. This, therefore, triggers the existence of yet another interesting attribute of SMEs – creativity and innovation.

Creativity and innovation

By definition, SMEs emerge out of creativity and innovation. As such, creativity and innovation are embedded in virtually all aspects of SMEs including product development. Entrepreneurs often fuse innovation with business management to start new ventures. A case in point is Bank Zero in South Africa. Bank Zero was founded by Michael Jordaan, the former CEO of First National Bank (FNB), one of South Africa's leading banks. Bank Zero charges zero fees and offers a lot more transparency to customers by providing app-driven banking services. Commenting on the need for innovativeness in the South African banking industry, Michael Jordaan retorts:

> Facebook, WhatsApp, Twitter, and Instagram are the new normal for societies. Why shouldn't banks also innovate in this era of wider connectedness whilst still ensuring a

robust banking value proposition? Bank Zero is addressing these realities while employing cutting-edge technologies and delivering state-of-the-art security.

(Business Tech, 2018)

Clearly, Bank Zero is a combination of innovation and experience. Examples such as these are abounding in the literature such as social media marketing and Facebook marketing.

Tendencies towards informality

SMEs tend to be informal. Although the majority of medium-scale enterprises are formally registered businesses, a significant proportion of these started out as small informal entities. Formal or not, SME management style leans more towards informality than formality. Because owners are readily available, they can be consulted more frequently, which means less reliance on written down rules and procedures.

Characteristics of SMEs and their appropriate marketing responses

In the foregoing section, a number of features that both define and distinguish SMEs from LSEs were deliberated on. Having noted these, Table 6.2 seeks to identify some practical marketing responses, commonly applied by entrepreneurs.

Table 6.2 demonstrates that because of their nature, SMEs subscribe to different marketing ethos. The umbrella term for this marketing strategy is referred to as entrepreneurial marketing.

Table 6.2 SME marketing response

SME Characteristics	Marketing Response
Lean Resource Base	• Due to limited resources, SMEs rely on low-cost marketing approaches (e.g., word-of-mouth and social media marketing).
Creativity and Innovation	• Marketing research, therefore, amounts to personal interactions with customers.
Small Target Markets	• SME target markets are smaller as compared to LSEs. • Entrepreneurs act on first-hand market information. • Because entrepreneurs interact with customers all the time (e.g., a hairdresser gets immediate feedback from clients on the latest trends and market demands), there is no need for market surveys. • Since they are available all the time, SME owners can engage one-on-one with customers.
SMEs are owner-operated	•
SMEs provide customised service	• SMEs, particularly the micro and small enterprises, provide customised and bespoke services and products to customers. Continual customer input in the production process facilitates the co-creation of products and services. • In this regard, marketing research is irregular and highly customised to individual customers' unique needs.

Table 6.2 (continued)

SME Characteristics	Marketing Response
Community Businesses Flexible Management Style Small Distance between owners and customers	• SMEs are community businesses. They are initiated by community members for servicing the needs of the community. The business owner, being part of the community already has an idea of what the needs of the market are. Furthermore, as part of the community, the business (which is hardly separable from the owner – a community member) is involved is virtually all activities within the community (e.g., celebrations, attending fellowship and worship together, birthday parties, political and civic meetings). As such, the business, which is the proxy of the community member has a specific role to play in the community. For instance, a seamstress would be expected to make outfits for the annual community fair. Equally, a baker, within the community, would likewise be expected to bake cakes for the community.
Informal management style SMEs commodify Informality	• SMEs are largely informal. • Customers, in turn, have developed expectations that all SMEs could or should be informal. This behaviour is noticeable when customers often try to engage in price negotiation and haggling with the owner. • Customers are, therefore, empowered to want to negotiate with the owner because they know they are dealing directly with the owner and not an employee. • Some retailers often re-package items to reduce quantities to ensure that customers can afford smaller quantities of goods.

Source: Moos (2014)

WHAT IS ENTREPRENEURIAL MARKETING?

Morris et al. (2002:5) define EM as being 'the proactive identification and exploitation of opportunities for acquiring and retaining profitable customers through innovative approaches to risk management, resource leveraging and value creation'. EM essentially is an alternative philosophy to creating and capturing value from customers practiced mostly by start-ups, emerging and small firms. It is important to highlight that EM does not conform to the strict sequential form of positivism. In simple terms, EM is how SMEs create value from the coalescence of both marketing activities and entrepreneurial actions. Table 6.3 highlights some of the differences between EM and conventional marketing.

Table 6.3 demonstrates that the most distinguishing feature of EM is the role of the marketer within the firm. The traditional marketing perspective views marketing in absolute terms, in line with positivism. In traditional marketing scenarios, the marketer's role, in the traditional sense, involves the execution of two major functions: (1) to study the environment by means of environmental scanning; and (2) to coordinate the marketing mix for the purposes of exploiting the opportunities within the environment.

In contrast, in EM, marketers are change agents, both to the internal and external environment. Mark Zuckerberg is an archetypical example of such a change agent. Facebook has practically changed how people communicate. Within the organisation, marketers do more than just coordinating the marketing mix. The entrepreneurial marketer actively searches for innovative ways of creating new relationships for the firm with its customers, partners,

Table 6.3 Traditional marketing vs. entrepreneurial marketing

	Traditional Marketing	EM
Basic Premise	Facilitation of transactions and market control	Sustainable competitive advantage through value-creating innovation
Orientation	Marketing as objective, dispassionate science	Central role of passion, zeal, persistence, and creativity in marketing
Context	Established, relatively stable markets	Envisioned, emerging, and fragmented markets with high levels of turbulence
Marketer's role	Coordinator of the marketing mix, builder of brands	Internal and external change agent
Market approach	Reactive and adaptive	Proactive, leading the customer with dynamic innovation
Customer needs	Articulated, assumed, expressed by customers through survey research	Unarticulated, discovered, identified through lead users
Risk perspective	Risk minimisation in marketing actions	Marketing as a vehicle for calculated risk-taking; emphasis on finding ways to mitigate, stage, or share risks
Resource management	Efficient use of resources, scarcity mentality	Leveraging creative use of the resources of others; doing more with less; actions are not considered by resources currently controlled
New product/service development	Marketing supports new product/service development	Marketing is the home of innovation; the customer is a co-active producer
Customer's role	External source of intelligence	Active participant in firm's marketing decision process, defining product, price, distribution, and communication channels

Source: Morris et al. (2002)

external environment, and other stakeholders. In addition to existing relationships, the marketer tries to develop new markets. Unlike the structural approaches in traditional marketing tactics, the entrepreneurial marketer relies on soft skills – communication, empathy, innovation, and relationship management – to execute her function. Central to EM is the function of building relationships. Simply, the entrepreneurial marketer performs multiple roles ranging from being a change agent to an innovation specialist to a relationship manager.

ENTREPRENEURIAL MARKETING RESEARCH

Although it is noted that EMR is not a rigid process, we argue all EMR activities unfold in a pattern albeit it being different from market to market. The purpose of this section is, thus, to present the EMR framework. In earlier sections, we learned that LSEs depend

REVISITING ENTREPRENEURSHIP MARKETING RESEARCH

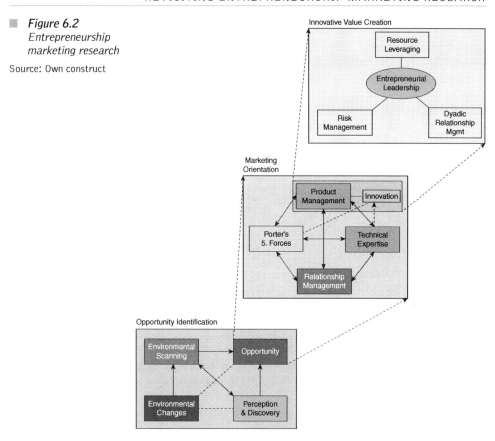

Figure 6.2
Entrepreneurship marketing research

Source: Own construct

on positivism to conduct research, which fundamentally is a top-down approach to marketing research. This involves, first, the assessment of existing environmental conditions, also known as environmental scanning (Jones and Rowley, 2009). Thereafter, marketers determine which marketing mix elements to address so as to capitalise on the external environment. Naturally, top-down approaches dictate the application of the five-step approach illustrated in Figure 6.1.

EMR, in contrast, unfolds from bottom-up (Stokes, 2000). It begins with the marketer identifying a business opportunity and then investigating approaches on how to build a business around the opportunity. Figure 6.2 illustrates the EMR framework.

Figure 6.5 quite literally demonstrates that EMR is a bottom-up exercise (Stokes, 2000; Stokes et al., 1997; Gaddefors and Anderson, 2008; Morris et al., 2002). The EMR process takes place in three distinct phases: opportunity identification, marketing orientation, and last, innovative value creation. These are briefly discussed next.

Opportunity identification

Opportunity identification is the first step in EMR. In this stage, entrepreneurs use their perceptive and discovery 'sixth senses' to analyse consumer needs vis-à-vis existing offerings on the market. The primary focus of this investigation is to identify possible improvements in the product or service offerings, for example, Google developed an improved web search engine.

Some examples of EMR approaches used in the opportunity identification phase

Entrepreneurship is a lived experience. Entrepreneurs, therefore, are engaged in a perpetual state of opportunity identification. These opportunities and business ideas are derived from people's experiences in their everyday lives. Marketing approaches used by entrepreneurs and SMEs in opportunity identification tend to be socially embedded mainly because of two underlying reasons. First, because SMEs are resource constrained, embarking on costly systematic top-down marketing approaches is not an efficient utilisation of resources. Beyond the monetary considerations of top-down approaches, the marketing philosophy of SMEs is skewed against large-scale marketing research. Rather, SMEs are primed for relationship oriented marketing approaches. Second, the spheres of influence or target markets for SMEs are comparatively smaller than those of LSEs. Because of this, the need for SMEs to engage in large-scale research for the purposes of generalising results to a bigger market automatically falls away. Therefore, entrepreneurs rely on various combinations of social mechanisms to gather information about market trends and consumer needs so as to observe environmental changes. The following are examples of social tools used by SMEs in identifying consumer needs and business opportunities:

1. ***One-on-one socialisation:*** this approach represents the simplest and the cheapest means of marketing for SMEs. One-on-one interaction with customers involves the entrepreneur initiating and maintaining relationships with individual customers. Through one-on-one socialisation, an entrepreneur creates opportunities for developing an in-depth understanding of customers' needs.

Let's reason together: Mogau's Seshoene's 'The Lazy Makoti'

Mogau Seshoene is a 31-year old South African entrepreneur based in Johannesburg. Before going into business, Mogau was an internal auditor. Today, she runs a vibrant cooking and dining experience business under the brand name 'The Lazy Makoti'. 'The Lazy Makoti' offers various services related to South African cuisine including cooking classes, selling traditional cutlery, developing recipes, publishing and selling recipe books. Mogau recounts her business as follows (Kemp, 2018):

> My journey began while I was working in a corporate setting, a friend of mine was getting married and knew that one of the expectations of her new family would be that she knew how to cook – and specifically traditional South African food. After trying with no luck to find a cooking school of some sort to take lessons on South African cuisine, she asked if I could teach her. I always had a great love for cooking. I gave her a few lessons after which she started to recommend my services to friends and family. And it literally snowballed from there. I left the corporate world and went to culinary school. I trained at the Saxon Hotel and started doing classes regularly. Fast forward to this year and I have just released my first cookbook, *The Lazy Makoti's Guide to the Kitchen.*
>
> When I started giving the cooking lessons, my friend would lament about how she's nervous that her in-laws would call her "the lazy Makoti" because she couldn't cook. I thought it was funny and relatable. This balanced between modern and traditional.

Source: https://city-press.news24.com/Trending/the-lazy-makotis-got-her-own-cookbook-20181118

LET'S REASON TOGETHER ACTIVITY QUESTIONS

- Using the four elements of opportunity identification in the EMR Framework, discuss how Mogau went about identifying the opportunity for her culinary and dining business.
- Search for the Lazy Makoti on social media (Facebook, Instagram) and describe how she is using social media in marketing her business.

2. **Social networks:** building social networks is instrumental for entrepreneurs. As the saying goes 'who you know is more important than what you know'. Entrepreneurs, therefore, invest a considerable amount of time in building social networks. Anis and Mohamed (2012) explain that social networks are the basis for social capital, which in turn leverages an entrepreneur's marketing efforts. From this social capital, entrepreneurs are able to initiate various marketing programmes.

3. **Social media:** technology is fast becoming an important arena for business development. Technology today serves the dual purpose of acting as a platform for trade and e-commerce as well as an advertising medium. Social media sites such as Facebook, Instagram, Twitter, LinkedIn, and Gumtree are increasingly being used platforms for advertising businesses and services. The two biggest advantages of using social media for SME marketing are:
   - Social media marketing is cost efficient;
   - A marketer is able to reach a large pool of potential customers.

Within the context of opportunity recognition, social media, in particular, Instagram, Twitter, and Facebook provide marketers with insights into the issues that are trending. That way, entrepreneurs are able to establish trends and topical issues that are likely to point the entrepreneur to ideas and beliefs held by the market. Social media, thus, acts as a repository for information.

Marketing orientation

Market orientation, according to Kohli et al. (1993), refers to the 'organization wide generation of market intelligence pertaining to current and future needs of customers, dissemination of intelligence horizontally and vertically within the organization, and organization-wide action or responsiveness to market intelligence'. Marketing orientation, in other words, is an attempt at creating a vehicle through which opportunities can be packaged into usable and sellable products. In this phase, the entrepreneur fuses his or her technical expertise as well as that of other stakeholders including accountants and bankers to create a product offering. In this phase, entrepreneurs define their business' value proposition in terms of the 4Ps. Marketing orientation, therefore, amounts to answering the following questions:

1. What resources are needed to ensure that my identified opportunity can sustain a business?
2. How can these resources be efficiently configured to guarantee profitability?
3. What partnerships do I need to realise my opportunity?
4. What are my 4Ps?
5. How will my value proposition be unique from competitors?

To answer these questions, the entrepreneurs utilises an elaborate network of partners and stakeholders. This network would enable him to utilise competitive tools such as Porter's Five Forces to evaluate the competitive positioning of his or her business.

Technology, SMEs, and the 21st century: Re-visiting Porter's five forces framework

Porter's five forces framework assists marketers to analyse competition within an industry. The framework posits that there are five forces that shape competition within an industry, namely:

1. The rivalry of existing competitors;
2. Bargaining power of buyers;
3. Bargaining power of suppliers;
4. The threat of substitute products and services;
5. Threat of entrants.

Traditionally, SMEs experience challenges in maximising the utility of Porter's Five Forces framework due to limited access to information. These limitations arise mostly from time and cost limitations. However, social media sites (e.g., Facebook, YouTube, Twitter, Instagram, and Reddit among others) have drastically changed things for SMEs. Information that once was exclusive to competitors can now be readily available on social media sites. For instance, by studying social media metrics such as the number of followers and analytics can be quite useful in providing some insights into the dynamics of a market. For SMEs, social media affords them with unique insights to not only understand the industry but also to gauge market responsiveness to competitors' marketing efforts. For instance, if a competing firm launches a new product, a marketer can track the popularity and growth of the market by studying comments and threads on social media such as Facebook posts, likes, and comments. The utility of social media is that it can be used to conduct competitive analysis.

TECHNOLOGY, SMES, AND THE 21ST CENTURY QUESTIONS

1. How has social media changed the way business analyse competition?
2. Select an SME in your area. Use at least two social media platforms to conduct a competitive analysis of the industry in which your selected firm belongs.

Innovative value creation

The final stage of the EMR framework is value creation. This is the entrepreneurial leadership phase. Entrepreneurial leadership is characteristically different from the other two phases. The value creation phase eventuates when the business is operational, whereas the preceding phases are merely hypothetical. To this end, the entrepreneur is concerned with three primary activities:

1. *Leveraging resources:* refers to creating partnerships that would allow entrepreneurs to leverage on other businesses' resources and networks. This is often achieved through the formation of networks and strategic partnerships.
2. *Risk management:* relates to the monitoring of the environment to protect the business from any harm.
3. *Dyadic relationship management:* this is perhaps is the most important aspect of EM. It relates to the formation of sustainable relationships with customers. These relationships help consumers identify a product. Consequently, dyadic relationship management an attempt on the part of entrepreneurs to constantly provide upgrades and improvements on innovations so that they continue to provide value for customers.

Effectively, these three phases the opportunity identification, marketing orientation, and innovative value creation constitute the EMR framework that we propose for SMEs. From Figure 6.5, as well as the foregoing discussions, it is clear that EMR is both fluid and non-formulaic (Morris et al., 2002). For that reason, positivism appears not to be an efficient paradigmatic position for EMR. Naturally, research specialists such as Malholtra (2010) argue that qualitative methodologies framed within constructivist research paradigms are more appropriate for entrepreneurs and SMEs (Doole and Lowe, 2003). Stokes et al. (1997) further elucidate that constructivism, unlike positivism, allows entrepreneurs greater freedom and creativity in the EMR process, as reflected in Figure 6.5. This line of thought suggests that because entrepreneurship is a sociocultural endeavour, entrepreneurs, therefore, ought to rely on their social senses to view the world.

With that said, it should be noted that the fluidity of the EMR process in Figure 6.5 be emphasised. This flexibility that Stokes (2000) defines as a bottom-up approach is that which makes qualitative research strategies more appropriate for entrepreneurial marketing. As such, EMR is considered most appropriate for SMEs.

CONCLUDING REMARKS

This chapter set out to present EM as an alternative philosophy, as practiced by SMEs. The inadequacies of conventional marketing approaches were highlighted, which necessitates alternative perspectives such as EMR. First, we presented the generic marketing research framework as applied by LSEs. Subsequent to this, we articulated the rationale behind the structured approach to traditional marketing research. We then outlined some characteristics of SMEs that render traditional marketing research approaches inappropriate and generally inapplicable within the SME context. Finally, the chapter proposed an EMR framework.

CASE STUDY: DELL COMPUTERS

In 1984, a college student named Michael Dell decided to found a computer company. Today it is one of the largest and best-known computer companies in the world. Here are some of the steps that Dell took in its earliest stages to get noticed in the computer market.

- **Define your customers** – Dell realised early that there was a hole in the market for customised business computers. Their first products were marketed to large and midsized companies looking to purchase many computers at once. It was only in the late 90s that they began to focus on personal computers for students and families.
- **Offer something new** – In the early 80s, computers were bought and sold primarily through retail stores. Dell took the then-radical step of selling directly to consumers, cutting out the retail middle man. This made it easy for business customers to place large orders and to customise each computer they purchased.
- **Go to where the customers are** – Dell marketed at electronics trade shows, in trade magazines, and in other avenues that corporate technology officers would follow. Advertising messages highlighted the ways that Dell computers were optimised for business customers.

- **Offer exceptional services** – Dell offered 24-hour technical support to all of its customers. This was a valuable service to customers who were only beginning to integrate computers into their businesses.

Source: www.marketing-schools.org/types-of-marketing/entrepreneurial-marketing.html

CASE STUDY REVIEW QUESTIONS:

1. Based on your knowledge of the EMR research process, did Michael Dell use the top down marketing approach or the EMR approach? Substantiate your answer in question one and briefly describe the phases of the marketing approach which Michael Dell used.
2. From the case study and the steps conducted by Michael Dell, can Dell be classified as an LSE or SME? (Give reasons for the choice of your answer.)

CHAPTER REVIEW QUESTIONS

1. Define the following terms:
   a. Entrepreneurship;
   b. Marketing research;
   c. Entrepreneurial marketing;
   d. Methodological fallacy;
   e. Ecological fallacy.

2. 'Marketing provides managers with tools to answer five basic questions'.
   a. List these five questions.
   b. Briefly discuss why it is important for business managers to answer these questions.

3. Discuss the process of the traditional marketing research process.

4. What is the difference between SMEs and LSEs?

5. Discuss the specific characteristics of LSEs and SMEs.

6. Distinguish between EMR and the top-down approach to marketing.

7. Explain how the structural features of small businesses necessitate different marketing approach among small businesses.

8. Suggest ways of obtaining relevant market and consumer information in an EMR context. Provide examples.

9. Using examples, distinguish between traditional marketing research and EMR.

REFERENCES

Anis, O. and Mohamed, F. (2012) How entrepreneurs identify opportunities and access to external financing in Tunisian's micro-enterprises? *African Journal of Business Management*, 6(12): 4635–4647.

Business Tech. (2018) Bank Zero has taken a big step closer to launching – here's how it's different from other SA banks [Online]. Available at: https://businesstech.co.za/news/banking/270041/bank-zero-has-taken-a-big-step-closer-to-launching-heres-how-its-different-from-other-sa-banks/ (Accessed 18 December 2019).

Blumberg, B., Cooper, D. R. and Schindler, P. S. (2011) *Business Research Methods*, 3rd European Edition. McGraw Hill, London.

Chakuzira, W. (2019) *Using a Grounded Theory Approach in Developing a Taxonomy of Entrepreneurial Ventures IN South Africa: A Case Study of the Limpopo Province*. University of Venda.

Collinson, E. and Shaw, E. (2001) Entrepreneurial marketing – A historical perspective on development and practice. *Management Decision*, 39(9): 761–766.

Coviello, N. E., Brodie, R. J. and Munro, H. J. (2000) An investigation of marketing by firm size. *Journal of Business Venturing*, 15(5–6): 523–545.

Dhliwayo, S., Mmako, N., Radipere, S. and Shambare, S. (2017) *Entrepreneurial Skills*. Van Schaik, Pretoria.

Doole, I. and Lowe, R. (2003) Cross Cultural Marketing for SMEs. In Rugimbana, R. and Nwankwo, S. (Eds.), *Cross Cultural Marketing*. Thomson, Melbourne.

Frederick, H., Kuratko, D. F. and Hodgetts, R. (2006). *Entrepreneurship: Theory, process and practice (Asia-Pacific Edition)*. Cengage Learning Pty. Ltd, Victoria, Australia.

Gaddefors, J. and Anderson, A. R. (2008) Market creation: The epitome of entrepreneurial marketing practices. *Journal of Research in Marketing and Entrepreneurship*, 10(1): 19–39.

Hollensen, S. (2014) *Global Marketing*, 6th ed. Pearson, Cape Town.

Jones, G. and Wadhwani, R. D. (2006) *Entrepreneurship and Business History: Renewing the Research Agenda*. Division of Research, Harvard Business School.

Jones, R. and Rowley, J. (2009) Presentation of a generic "EMICO" framework for research exploration of entrepreneurial marketing in SMEs. *Journal of Research in Marketing and Entrepreneurship*, 11(1): 5–21.

Kamei, K. and Dana, L.-P. (2012) Examining the impact of new policy facilitating SME succession in Japan: From a viewpoint of risk management in family business. *International Journal of Entrepreneurship and Small Business*, 16, 60–70.

Kearney, C., Hisrich, R. D. and Roche, F. W. (2010). Change management through entrepreneurship in public sector enterprises. *Journal of Developmental Entrepreneurship*, 15(04), 415–437.

Kemp, G. (2018) The lazy Makoti's got her own cookbook. *City Press*. Available at: https://city-press.news24.com/Trending/the-lazy-makotis-got-her-own-cookbook-20181118 (Accessed 28 April 2019).

Kohli, A. K., Jaworski, B. J. and Kumar, A. (1993) A measure of market orientation. *Journal of Marketing Research*, 30(4): 467–477.

Kotler, P. and Armstrong, G. (2016) *Principles of Marketing – A Global and Southern African Perspective*, 2nd ed. Pearson, Cape Town.

Malhotra, N. (2010) *Marketing Research: An Applied Orientation*, 6th ed. Pearson, Upper Saddle River, NJ.

Moos, M. N. (2014) *Evaluating the South African Small Business Policy to Determine the Need for and Nature of Entrepreneurship Policy*. DCom in Business Management, University of Pretoria.

Morris, M. H., Schindehutte, M. and LaForge, R. W. (2002) Entrepreneurial marketing: A construct for integrating emerging entrepreneurship and marketing perspectives. *Journal of Marketing Theory and Practice*, 10(4): 1–19.

Nieman, G. and Nieuwenhuizen, C. (2015) *Entrepreneurship: A South African Perspective*. Van Schaik.

Stokes, D. (2000) Putting entrepreneurship into marketing. *Journal of Research in Marketing and Entrepreneurship*, 2(1):1–16.

Stokes, D., Fitchew, S, and Blackburn, R. (1997) *Marketing in Small Firms: A Conceptual Approach*. Kingston University, Kingston.

Timmons, J. and Spinelli, S. (2004). *New Venture Creation: Entrepreneurship for the 21st Century*. McGraw Hill/Irwin, N. Y.

World Bank. (2019) *Small and Medium Enterprises (SME) Finance*. Available at: https://data.worldbank.org/. (Accessed on 26 March 2019).

Chapter 7

Managing products and customer value
Implications for SME marketing

Ayantunji Gbadamosi

LEARNING OBJECTIVES
After reading this chapter, you will be able to:
- Define a product;
- Discuss various classifications of products and the relevance to SMEs;
- Explain how SMEs could use branding & packaging in their businesses to create value and deliver value;
- Explain the stages in the product development and the relevance why this may not be strictly applicable in the SME context;
- Discuss the product life cycle in relation to SMEs;
- Explain how SME could use Diffusion process to achieve competitive advantage.

INTRODUCTION

Creating and delivering value to the target market is a core aspect of 21st-century marketing. In fact contemporary marketing has also taken this further to accentuate the notion of value co-creation between the customer and marketers (Vargo and Lusch, 2004) in such a way that indicates a paradigm shift in marketing (Gbadamosi, 2019). Meanwhile, at any level of marketing transaction – be it at the small and medium-size enterprise (SMEs) level or large corporation context – market offerings, or to put it simply, products, are at the heart of marketing activities. This is because they constitute one of the key elements of the marketing system (see Figure 7.1) and are at the centre of exchange process upon which other elements aimed at satisfying the needs of their target markets revolve. It could be described as the bone, the tendon, and the ligament of the system without which no marketing process can take place (Gbadamosi, 2000).

It is important for us to discuss product as an element of the marketing-mix in the context of SMEs for two reasons (our attention will be more concentrated on the first, as the other has been explored in another chapter of this book):

1. SMEs provide goods and services to their target markets and will need to understand issues and strategies associated with managing them effectively.

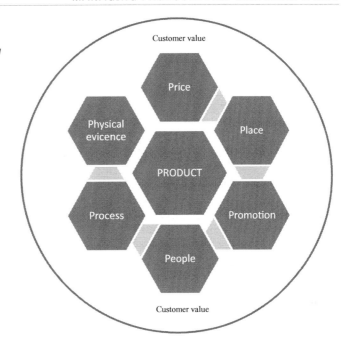

Figure 7.1
Product as a core element of the marketing system

2. They also buy goods from other organisations either for resale or use in producing the offerings that they offer to satisfy the needs and wants of their customers.

Therefore, this chapter examines product as a key factor in SME marketing transactions. But as we set to achieve this objective we will constantly reflect on common knowledge on product as the thread to weave and shape our discussion of managing products in small and medium-size enterprises. This is important because marketing activities in large corporations are largely at variance with what we have in SMEs in some ramifications (Carson and Cromie, 1990; Gilmore et al., 2001). As a platform for other key issues in the chapter, we now start with the definition of a product.

WHAT IS A PRODUCT?

At the mention of product, what often comes to mind are the tangible products like fast moving consumer goods such as bread, milk, detergent, salt, and this book you are reading. Yes! They are products indeed. However, it will be misleading to limit the definition or explanation of products in marketing context to these tangible items. This is because people do not buy these products as an end in themselves, rather they buy them because they are means to an end. Hence, a product is hereby defined as anything that can be offered to the target market for meeting their various needs. From this definition, product can be tangible materials like books and pen and can also be in the form of services such as those offered by teachers, lawyers, accountants, and management consultants; it can also be ideas. Hence, the local barbers and hairdressers that give their customers better looks, cleaning firms that keep the environment tidy, and the security firms that safeguard the neighbourhood, are indeed offering products though intangible in nature. To buttress this point further, we will now examine various classifications of products that SMEs could be offering to their customers or buying from their suppliers.

PRODUCT CLASSIFICATION AND OPPORTUNITY RECOGNITION IN SMEs

From a broader perspective, products could be classified on two bases:

1. on the basis of their attributes or;
2. on the basis of the type of consumers that use them.

If products are classified on the basis of the attributes they possess, then we can categorise them as durable products, non-durable products, and services.

Durable products are products that provide benefits to the user over a long time, as they can survive several uses after their purchase. Examples are cars and refrigerator. Conversely, *non-durable* products are those products that could only be used once or a few times after which there will be a need to replace them. Examples of this category are vegetables and fruits. *Services* are intangible products offered to the buyer to satisfy their needs and wants. They comprise activities and benefits upon which the values and satisfactions of the buyers are measured. Transportation services and public relations services are typical examples for this product category. There are several small businesses that offer these and many other services. In-depth discussion of service marketing in the context of SMEs is provided in a separate chapter which provides information on managing services in SMEs.

Considering product classification from the perspective of the type of consumers that use it reveals the dichotomy of consumer products and organisational products. Consumer products can be sub-classified further into *convenience products, shopping products, specialty products,* and *unsought products.* Organisational products on the other hand can also be classified further into *capital products, components and parts, accessory products, raw materials,* and *services.* These classifications are shown in Figure 7.2

While these classifications are closely related to what we will find in most common textbooks on principles of marketing, our key interest here is to understand how SMEs manage these array

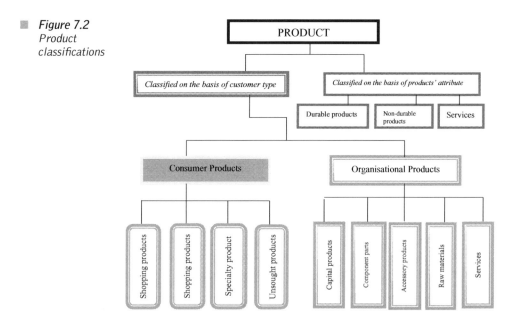

Figure 7.2 Product classifications

CONSUMER PRODUCTS: B2C MARKETING OFFERINGS IN SMEs

In many instances, SMEs offer products or services to buyers whose purpose of purchasing these items is for personal gratification. This could be in the form of using them personally or buying for friends, family members, or others who will ultimately use such items. In this context, products are usually categorised as *convenience products*, *shopping products*, *speciality products*, and *unsought products*.

Convenience products are the products which customers buy on a routine basis with little or no comparison of alternatives. They are usually low in price and are often bought without planning. The convenience of obtaining the product is emphasised more than loyalty to any particular brand. Examples are table salt, sugar, and detergents. If we reflect critically on our previous purchases, it will not take a long time to realise that small grocery stores located near our residence, motor parks, and train stations are exploring our need for convenience by providing these items at convenient locations and times. These indicate that while SMEs have limitations in relation to their influence in the marketplace, their size and flexibility could stimulate innovation and give them competitive advantage in the marketplace (Hill, 2001; O'Dwyer et al., 2009).

Shopping products can be described as products that consumers buy less frequently, and make considerable efforts to compare on the basis of quality, price, style, and suitability when making the purchase decision. As Brassington and Pettit (2007) explain this category, they represent more of a risk and an adventure to consumers. While the purchase of convenience products often involves no planning and little or no comparison of competing brands, the purchase of shopping products is typically a limited problem-solving decision. For purchases in this context, the buyer is willing to shop around to make comparisons of alternatives before the final decision is made. Examples of these products are clothing and computer laptop.

Specialty products are consumer products that are bought very infrequently, have unique features sought after by the buyers, and are very expensive such that they tend to approach the purchase with great care and engage in extensive problem solving. For these products, buyers are willing to pay a premium to get exactly the item needed and consumers tend to be loyal to specific brands in the purchase of this range of products. Cars, houses, services of civil engineers, and services of medical doctors are relevant examples of this category. In this age, the competition faced by SMEs from large businesses intensifies especially for those offering shopping and specialty products. This underscores the degree of challenges they face to survive in the marketing environment. One of the key strategies for small businesses to survive and succeed when operating in the sectors that provide these products is targeting niches with clear-cut identifiable needs and offering them unique products that are distinctively beneficial to them in relation to specific features covering issues of importance such as style, quality, and suitability. This will not only give them a space in the crowded marketplace but could also make them achieve a competitive advantage.

Unsought Products are products that the buyers are not aware are existing. In some cases, when they know that they exist they usually do not have enough zeal to buy them except such products or services are vigorously promoted to them. Examples are life insurance, and some home decoration materials. Since consumers do not usually engage in a purposeful search for these products, a lot of marketing communication efforts are required from the marketers to create product awareness. Although SMEs are constrained in terms of how much they could spend on marketing communications, there are some low-cost promotion methods that could be used for this purpose. In-store promotion, personal selling and social media could be very useful in this context. The key issue here is to keep it simple and effective, but not doing it at all puts the business at serious risk.

ORGANISATIONAL PRODUCTS: B2B MARKETING OFFERINGS IN SMEs

Organisational products are bought by other organisations for resale or for the purpose of using them to produce other goods. They vary in terms of the financial requirements and the degree of risk associated with the purchase. Basically, they are shown in Figure 7.2 and are now discussed in turn.

Capital products are products bought to aid the production of goods and or services in the buying organisation. They are bought infrequently, involve very substantial financial commitment. Due to the high risk associated with buying the wrong type, and the significance of the purchase, the weight of the inputs of several professionals who are experts in the relevant field to the decision is quite considerable. Therefore organisations often commit significant time and effort to the purchase as the purchase decision is considered strategic. Examples of products in this category are machineries and buildings. Offering these products would require considerable personal selling efforts on the part of the sellers as the sale requires close contact relationship between the parties. Besides, buyers will most likely require information and technical supports from the seller. With the huge investment in the purchase of these products, acquiring or offering them is arguably one of the major challenges confronting small businesses. Some firms often have to rely on borrowing or funding through various government initiated programmes to be able to scale the hurdle. In other instances, many SMEs will have to collaborate with one another to be able supply these items. Whichever form the transaction takes, conforming to buyers' specification remain a major rule in the relationship.

Component parts are products that are though finished products; are bought to form part of the products which the organisation offers to its target market. One example is in the car manufacturing firms where parts of cars such as tyres and other electrical materials are bought by car manufacturers to constitute their finished products. Similarly, to complete a house for a client, construction companies will need items like cement, bricks, woods, and many others which will all be skilfully combined together to become the useable befitting edifices after the construction. SMEs supplying these items need to be very conscious of the quality standard of the buyer and adhere to them. Attempt to fiddle with the quality of the component parts will most likely affect the final output of the buying organisation. One of the ways to thrive in the recent marketing environment would be for the firms to gain and maintain the trust of their clients. Breaching the quality standard and the trust of key customers could lead to severe breakdown of the relationship and severe consequence to enterprising targeting one or very few niches.

Accessory products are organisational products that the buyers use to meet their auxiliary needs. They are also used to facilitate the production of goods and services in the establishment but not as directly as in the case of components parts and usually the purchase does not involve the scale of risk and financial investment associated with the purchase of capital products. PCs, printers, telephones, bulbs, filling cabinets, and shredders are examples of this category of products. Many small and family businesses with very limited fund available may start from this level of marketing. Yet they need to be customer oriented and be conscious of competition. Issues like prompt-delivery, ease of ordering will more likely woo the buyers for product category.

Raw materials: these are usually in their natural form as inputs that need to go through the transformation process before the buyer could get the ultimate offerings intended to satisfy the target market. Examples include cocoa, timber, fish, and vegetables.

Services are intangible offerings bought by organisations to enhance the production of their goods and services to their customers. Maintenance and repair of machinery, cleaning of the premises, security services for organisations' properties, consultancy services are just a few examples of services as organisational products. There are many SMEs providing services to various target niches in the UK. This is closely related to the ease of starting some of these service businesses which require relatively little capital. For instance, Nwankwo and Gbadamosi (2009), in a study on Pentecostalism and entrepreneurial orientations among black ethnic minorities in London, report how these individuals are using the platform of their faith-based organisational affiliations to support their entrepreneurial ambitions. Some of these are lawyers, accountants, IT technicians, and barbers. These entrepreneurs acknowledge the ease of market entry in these service businesses and how their personal contact networks (PCN) within these circles have contributed to their success.

Reflecting on these categorisations, and due to resource constraints associated with the running of their enterprises, SMEs have relative limitations on the extent of the range of products that they could offer in their marketing activities. Accordingly, it is difficult for them to compete directly with large-scale enterprises. However, customers remain ever demanding and make comparisons among alternative offerings for certain categories of product. SMEs offering distinctive products are expected to explore their unique selling propositions (USP) in relation to quality and style to match the requirements of the targeted niches. For example, some SMEs target certain ethnic minority groups in the various multicultural societies such as in the UK, the US, and Canada; and they are fully committed to providing them with required products or services. This approach often encourages repeat purchase and loyalty and engenders a continuous good relationship between the two parties.

IN-CLASS ACTIVITY: THINK AND DISCUSS EXERCISE

In a group of three, reflect on what you have heard or read in the news recently and discuss how these have presented opportunities for you as a group of entrepreneurs and which product type you could use to explore these opportunities.

LEVELS OF PRODUCTS: IMPLICATIONS FOR SME MARKETING

In product planning and management, three interrelated levels of product are commonly discussed. These are the *core product*, the *actual product*, and the *augmented product*.

The core product (see Figure 8.3) describes the benefit that a customer buys when he or she buys a product. It is what allows customers to solve problems and satisfy basic needs which prompted the purchase of the product. The core product of a laptop computer bought by a customer is the ease of processing information and other things that the laptop facilitate. This area is one of the key challenges confronting most small businesses. While most small firms are innovative leading to the development of several products, some do not really

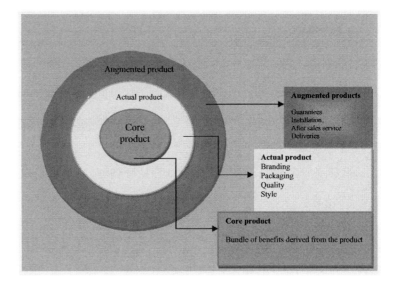

Figure 7.3 Levels of a product

consider how their innovations satisfy the needs of the target market and the gap they are filling in the market. Consequently this leads to sudden failure of such products.

The second layer in the levels is the actual product which encompasses elements like brand name, packaging, quality, and design that function together to offer the buyer the core benefits desired for purchasing the product. For very creative and right thinking entrepreneurs, this level of product is loaded with opportunities to transform their businesses. If well explored, it could actually be a way of gaining competitive advantage in the competing and volatile marketing environment. One of such ways is to ensure that the desired level of quality expected by the customers is not compromised. For small firms that are less endowed in major resources than larger corporations (Raymond and Croteau, 2006), ignoring the importance of quality is a gamble that can have very serious consequences. In fact, it has been shown that quality is an essential foundation for progressing to large-scale innovation for SMEs (McAdam and Armstrong, 2001). Similarly, despite the dominant role of large organisations in the competitive environment, the merits of branding to SMEs are far-reaching. Supporting this view, Wong and Merrilees (2005) argue that brand orientation might play a critical role in the growth of small firms. If the quality meets the customers' expectations, such buyers would be willing to associate with the brand.

The third layer, the augmented product offers additional benefits or services that often distinguish the marketers' offering from competitors'. Examples include after sales services, customer service, guarantee, and delivery. The size of SMEs, their flexibility, and closeness to their customers indicate that augmented product could be a veritable tool for them to achieve competitive advantage. They can fortify their relationship with their customers by building good customer services into their offerings. In this age, marketing is more about managing relationships than about the product in the transaction. An IT technician who calls his customers days after the service to gauge their satisfaction level is likely to get a repeat purchase and enjoy word-of-mouth communication from the customer than those who do not. The flexibility and closeness of these small firms to their customer also means that they could easily identify problems related to their offerings and adopt service recovery as necessary.

PRODUCT LINE/PRODUCT MIX

A product line is the group of closely related product items offered for sale by the marketer while a product mix is the collection of all products or services that an organisation offers to its market. Hence, a product mix will consist of all the product lines of an organisation. The number of product lines within the product mix is described by the *product width*, while the number of products within a product line is known as the *product line length*. Clearly, due to resource constraints, it is logical to acknowledge that, in comparisons to large enterprise, SMEs could only manage less *product width* and product *line length*. But in reality, many small businesses rush their innovations into the market, some hurriedly engage in *me-too* innovations, and over-diversify. This approach can considerably strain the performance of the existing products in the market. This is because such new investments might severely drain the available resources – financial and time – that could be better used on the existing products that are already performing well in the marketplace.

BRANDING

The American Marketing Association defines a brand as 'a name, term, sign, symbol or design, or a combination of them intended to identify the goods and services of one seller or group of sellers and to differentiate them from those of competitors' (AMA, 2010). This is a very useful definition as it clearly emphasises the major role of branding – distinguishing offerings. Another relatively close viewpoint states that it distinguishes a product or service from its unbranded counterpart through the sum total of consumers' perceptions and feelings about the attributes and the performances of the products (Jevons, 2005). This latter definition clearly brings in the relevance of consumers' perception. These two views strongly support the explanation of Wilson and Gilligan (1997) that branding provides the basis for a consumer franchise and, if managed effectively it could allow for greater marketing flexibility and a higher degree of consumer loyalty. It is therefore not surprising that large corporations including Coca-Cola, Pepsi, Nokia, and Tesco ardently devote resources to managing their brands. Clearly, the discussion of managing product in SME context will be incomplete without due reference to branding. As small businesses relate with their customers in the course of their marketing transactions, branding can be a way of maintaining a strong bond between the two parties if effectively used. Wong and Merrilees (2005) suggest that SMEs need to take a longer-term, investment approach to branding, and develop a strongly distinctive brand. They add that it is important for these businesses to develop an internal culture where all staff 'live the brand' on a daily basis and have a clear and consistent communication of their brand through marketing activities. All available official statistics indicate that SMEs constitute over 99% of the enterprises in the UK business environment. With this number of SMEs, the possibility of consumers being inundated with numerous competing offerings cannot be underrated. This brings in the relevance of brands which does not only distinguish the offering but could also lead to loyalty if the branded products satisfy the target customers, and above all offers the owner *brand equity* which is the positive return of the impact of the brand provided to the business. As a brand provides the owner with brand equity, the possibility of brand extension could be carefully explored for future inventions.

PACKAGING

One of the marketing stimuli closely related to managing product in SMEs is packaging. We must have received one product or another from our local stores in different boxes, delivered

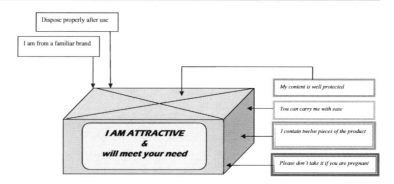

Figure 7.4 How packaging communicates with the buyer

to us in bags, or supplied to people on our behalf wrapped in papers of different sizes and colours. These experiences often live us as consumers with different feelings and sometimes prompt our future behaviour in relation to these offerings. This shows that packaging plays different roles and could be perceived differently by the buyers. Accordingly, effective packaging might contribute to factors that provide SMEs the key to satisfying their customers effectively better than competitors do.

Packaging plays several important roles in marketing transactions but can be broadly categorised as *functional* roles and *commercial* roles. When packaging attracts customers, projects the image of the product or that of the seller and communicates things about the seller, then it is deemed to be performing the commercial roles. When wondering why you have selected a brand of orange drinks, chocolate, gum, or detergent over another, the answer may as well be effective packaging. It communicates quality to the buyers and as many of consumers' purchases now take place in self-service commercial environments, the commercial role of packaging will continue to maintain its relevance in marketing systems.

On the other hand, the functional roles of packaging cover product containment, user convenience, and product preservation. Above all, an effective packaging strategy should make life easy for all the stakeholders – buyers, sellers, intermediaries, and the public. This last point directs our attention to something significant. Today's consumers in the UK and EU now crave for packaging that favours environmental friendliness. For instance, in 1994, the European Union (EU) accepted a proposal for packaging directive which is aimed at minimizing packaging waste in some ways such as reusing or recycling (Rundh, 2005). These additional considerations make it very challenging for SMEs to think of how best to improve the packaging; as ineffective and non-considerate packaging can be very frustrating not only to the consumers but to the stakeholders. Besides, consumers' attitudinal reactions to packaging also vary which indicate how compelling it is for firms to be customer driven in their choice of packaging designs for their products. For example, there is evidence which suggests that low-income consumers are not motivated to buy low-involvement grocery products by the attractiveness of the packaging but are greatly keen about its functional roles (Gbadamosi, 2009a). In fact, it is also shown that this consumer segment also thinks that manufacturers might be ripping them off to fund their promotion in the form of attractive packaging (Gbadamosi, 2009b). Now, the key issue for SMEs here is the increasing need for them to use their ability of innovation to design effective packaging that will be of good fit for the purpose – satisfy their customers, is cost effective, and portray the firm as a socially responsible establishment. This could give them competitive advantage where many other strategies are falling.

MANAGING PRODUCTS AND CUSTOMER VALUE

> **T&D2: THINK AND DISCUSS EXERCISE**
> Assume you are the owner/manager in a SME that has just introduced a new body lotion, discuss how you will go about designing your branding and packaging strategy in order to achieve competitive advantage in the marketing environment.

NEW PRODUCT DEVELOPMENT IN SMEs: INNOVATION, CREATIVITY, AND PECULIARITIES

The marketing environment of SMEs is turbulent and dynamic. Consequently, the needs and wants of the consumers being served also change rapidly as the factors in the environment. Hence firms are investing an increasing amount of resources and managerial attention to product innovation (Hyland et al., 2001). Indeed, small businesses will need innovation to be able to stay on in the game and survive the competition in their marketplace. So, what is innovation?

In a bid to answer the same question, Deakins and Freel (2003) revisited the Schumpeter's (1934) explanation of innovation. Five sources of innovation identified are (1) introduction of new product or significant improvement of the existing ones, (2) introduction of new method of production, (3) opening of a new market, (4) discovering a new source of supply of raw materials or half-manufactured good, and (5) creation of a new type of industrial organisation. After several decades of its publication, this referenced view is still very useful and offers us a broad scope of innovation. Adding to this all-encompassing view, Deakins and Freel (2003) state that innovation is different from invention as the former is holistic and involves the commercial application of the latter. Hence, this view is in tune with the claim that innovation derives from the ability to see connections, to spot opportunities, and to take advantage of them (Bessant and Tidd, 2007). Although resource constraints may impact SME's ability to explore innovation, evidence in the literature indicates that small businesses could be at an advantage in innovation especially due to their flexibility to explore opportunities as they come (Deakins and Freel, 2003). Now let us turn our attention to how SMEs develop new products.

From the beginning of this chapter we have established from the literature (Carson and Cromie, 1990; Gilmore et al., 2001) that there are differences in how SMEs and large corporations practice marketing. It is logical to state that this argument could be extended to how they develop new products.

Conventional marketing understanding indicates the process of new product development as depicted in Figure 8.5. This process starts with the generation of ideas, acknowledges that not all of the ideas generated would be useful, or feasible, so they have to be screened. The product ideas that have survived the screening stage would need to be transformed into the form that is understandable to the consumers who will use them – product concept. At the business analysis stage, costs, anticipated sales, and profitability prospects of the products are examined to gauge their overall economic viability. If the business analysis stage provides very promising outcome, then the actual product could be developed. As shown in this process, before launching the product fully, the firm is expected to offer the product to samples of the target market in selected geographical locations. This will give the firm the opportunity to access the fitness of its marketing strategies.

The first major issue of consideration here is that this process is systematic and assumes the significant relevance of group decision making. With this in mind, we are still prompted

121

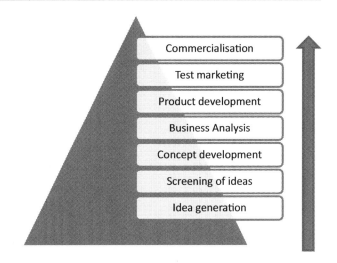

Figure 7.5
Stages in the new product development

to ask whether this process will be a good fit for SMEs. One of the ways to address this is to revisit the characteristics of SMEs as a platform for gauging the appropriateness of this conventional New Product Development (NDP) process in this context. The basic characteristics of SMEs identified by Carson et al. (1995) can be summarised as follows: they operate predominantly at a local or regional market rather than national or international market; they tend to have limited market share; and they are often owned by one person or a few individuals. These authors also add that small firms are independent in which case the owner/managers have ultimate authority to decide and manage the affairs of the enterprise; and the firms are generally managed in a personalised fashion. A shrewd look at the process and these characteristics will indicate that it is will be difficult to conclude that the two are perfectly compatible. However, this does not suggest that SMEs do not develop new product neither does it indicate that they are not innovative, rather it directs our attention to and justifies the need for a paradigm shift towards SME marketing within which NPD in SMEs can be robustly captured.

Indeed, new product development takes place in SMEs and entrepreneurs are not short of ideas. Nevertheless, many of such products fail prematurely. One of the common reasons for this is lack of finance to implement the concept. The significance of finance to the development of new products varies from one industry to another. As noted by Barringer and Ireland (2010), firms need to raise money to pay up-front costs associated with the lengthy product cycles in some industries. This can delay the implementation of new inventions or product ideas. In fact, in some instances, while the inventor is waiting for funds to develop the new product, the product idea may have been overtaken by newer inventions, thereby being rendered useless. From a different perspective, many owner-managers often venture into product development but skip many essential phases in the process. Some are too passionate about the product idea to the extent that they forget that such ideas must meet the needs of the target customers. There have been some cases of inventors introducing products into the market without having a thorough business analysis through which they will know whether they will be successful from a commercial standpoint or not. In some other cases, one will be wondering what is really new about the product that has just been developed by some SMEs, as such inventions do not really fill any gap in the marketplace or indicate the competitive advantage of the firm. The empirical study of Salavou and Avlonitis (2008) indicates that

SMEs vary in categories in relation to their product innovativeness. They identify three groups of SMEs on the basis of their product innovativeness as the straight imitator (low level), the product innovator (high level), and the concept innovator (moderate level). In this classification, the product innovators are explained as those that developed more radical variations of their existing offerings have a feel of what customer like or dislike about their existing product. Consequently, consumers would more readily adopt their invention compared to the other two. This typology is really helpful as it shows that while SMEs are noted to be adventurous about inventions, not all of these would readily satisfy the customers and be a commercial success.

Since, the need to develop new product is intensifying due to changes in taste of customers, the onus is on the SMEs to embrace effectiveness in their product development activities. SMEs need to operate between two walls. One is their characteristics and limitations and the other is the integrity of new product development process. This is consistent with the view of Carson et al. (1995) that SME marketers could practice *marketing adaptation* in which case they need not be ardently concerned about the rigour of marketing techniques but still maintain the integrity of the process. This means they are still following the process albeit loosely as it involves according due consideration to the peculiarities of these businesses.

PRODUCT LIFE CYCLE: IMPLICATIONS FOR MARKETING IN SMALL BUSINESSES

The term product life cycle (PLC) is very popular in the mainstream marketing literature. This popularity cannot be dismissed as mere academic exercise. Rather, the unwavering interest in the topic is because it is an invaluable tool for tracking the performance of products during their lifetime in terms of their sales trends. Essentially, the product life cycle indicates that we can explain the life of a product by likening it to that of human being. It holds that products too are introduced; they grow, mature, and reach the end of their life. It consists of four stages: introduction, growth, maturity, and decline; the stages differ with respect to the degree of market knowledge of the product, market acceptance of the product, and the prevailing competitive situation for the product. Hence, different marketing strategies are applicable in each of the stages. The stages are shown in Figure 7.6.

Figure 7.6
The product life cycle

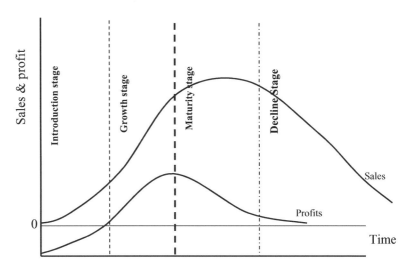

As the figure indicates, at the introduction stage, the product is still fresh in the market and requires all the entrepreneurial initiatives possible to be able to still maintain its presence at the scene. This stage is crucial, especially for products developed by SMEs, for a number of reasons. First, it requires heavy promotion investments to create awareness. There is a need for the firm to create the new product awareness through advertising. They need to encourage trial with sales promotion and encourage intermediaries to help push the product through the channel. Second, in spite of all these efforts, the new product is unlikely to generate profit at this stage, which can be very discouraging for an owner/manager who may have invested his or her life savings and secured loans to see the investment through. For SMEs with limited funds, this could be the most challenging of all the stages. Most new products fail at this stage. It has been estimated that the failure rate of new products range from 60% to 90% depending on the industry and the peculiar definition of product failure (Dibb et al., 2016). However, if new product development stages are handled carefully, especially in a customer-oriented manner, the effort can be very rewarding as the product enters its second stage – growth.

At the stage of growth, sales and profits grow but would also attract competitors. So, SMEs need to be very conscious of competition and emphasise and encourage repeat purchases. An empirical study on determinants of new product performance in small firms, O'Dwyer and Ledwith (2009), shows that competition orientation and product launch proficiency have strong links to new product performance. The closeness of the firm to the customers, and flexibility in their marketing, could be very useful tools to thrive at this stage as they may be able to gain the loyalty of their customers.

At the stage of maturity, sales growth levels off, and profits starts to fall. With many brands in the market at this stage, competition is still a major threat to small businesses. Hence effort should be directed at encouraging repeat purchase but this should also be a period that signals opportunity for the owner-manager to think of other innovations such as modifying the product in some forms.

The last of the stages of the PLC is the decline stage. Due to many reasons, which include change in consumer preferences, technological advancements, and very stiff competitive attacks from domestic or rival products, the sales of the product fall speedily. At this stage, SMEs might need to be more cost-conscious. They could reduce their spending on marketing communications and reduce the price of the product in order to be able to sell the existing stock. Firms at this stage would be considering the options of whether to bring the product back to live with investments or to just *let go*. This latter option could be a bitter pill for many SMEs to swallow, but if the product does not look promising, especially from a commercial standpoint, it appears logical to allow it to 'die' naturally and replace it with new inventions.

MANAGING DIFFUSION OF NEW PRODUCTS IN SMEs

There is growing evidence that there is no dearth of new product ideas and innovations among SMEs, but the palpable problem is that some of the new products they introduce fail. One of the major ways of addressing this concern is to understand the process by which their new inventions spread among members of a social system. This is known as the diffusion process (Rogers, 2003; Bessant and Tidd, 2007). Having this knowledge will help these firms on how they position their products in a customer-oriented manner.

Perhaps a good way to begin the discussion of product diffusion is to acknowledge frankly that the responses of people to new products vary. While some can be very enthusiastic and quickly receptive to new innovation, others tend to be very sceptical of these unfamiliar offerings. So, some individuals adopt new products early, while some will not until the very last days of the life of the new product. A widely referenced, seminal work on categorisation of people in terms of their adoption of new product is that of Rogers (1962) as reported by Kotler et al. (2008). This shows that there are five categories of adopters based on the speed at which they adopt the new product. These are the innovators, the early adopters, the early majority, the late majority, and the laggards.

The innovators are the first set of people who are interested in buying the product when it was newly launched into the market. They tend to be venturesome, young, well educated, have high income and take pride in owning something new. They constitute a relatively small – 2.5% of total of those who adopt the product. The early adopters who constitute the next 13.5% buy the new product after the innovators. They tend to be more community-oriented than the innovators, very influential in various groups they interact with, regarded as experts, and are likely to be opinion leaders (Lamb et al., 2010). Hence, they are often consulted by other groups who adopt the new product after them. The early majority follows the early adopters and are noted for adopting the new product before the average person. They are 34% of the total adopters of the product. The next 34% of those who adopt the new innovation are called the late majority. They rarely assume leadership role and do not adopt the new product until after a majority of people have tried it as they are sceptical. So, they are mainly prompted by word-of-mouth commutation to buy the product. The laggards are the last 16% of those who adopt the product. They are typically very suspicious and cautious of new inventions such that they don't buy the new product until when it is about to be or has been replaced by a newer model.

Apart from the knowing the categories of adopters of new products another useful information needed by SMEs are the factors that influence the how consumers adopt new product. These have been identified to be *relative advantage, complexity, compatibility, observability,* and *trialability* (Rogers, 2003; Bessant and Tidd, 2007). If we consider each of these factors critically, it is noteworthy that they have inherent lessons and implications for how SMEs manage their new products in their highly competitive environment. Essentially, consumers will be interested to know whether the new product offers benefits that they could not get from the existing ones (relative advantage). If so, such products have very high tendency of getting the attention of the target market. This is why it is important for SMEs to ensure that their inventions are filling gaps in the market. Moreover, if the new product is too difficult to understand or use (complexity), it might affect the rate at which it will be adopted. During the process of the new product development, if the integrity of the process involved is maintained, the problem associated with complexity could have been detected and dealt with earlier before it becomes available in the market. The extent to which the new product conforms to the existing cultural values and knowledge (compatibility) plays a key role in how quickly the product will diffuse. On this point, being customer-oriented could help SME to ensure that the product is consistent with extant values and knowledge. Also, if the benefits of using the product are easily observable, there is high tendency that the adoption rate of the product will be fast. Trialability is about the ease with which the new product could be tried in limited form or quantity.

These issues have a good number of useful implications for SME marketing. Since, SMEs typically target niches, and rely on personal contact network (PCN) for their marketing, it makes sense for them to identify and target the opinion leaders specially to get them involved in their offerings. As SMEs are resource constrained and might not be able to afford investing in large-scale marketing communication investment, they could engage the contact of opinion leaders to generate very useful word-of-mouth communications, which is notably credible in the parlance of marketing. Besides, SMEs could also use this knowledge for their marketing plan such that their segmentation, targeting, and positioning is done effectively in respect to these various characteristics of adopters.

Moreover, given that consumers' response to new products vary, knowing the various categories of adopters and the factors that influence how the new products diffuse will be tremendously useful. This will give them the opportunity to be able to position their products effectively in a customer-oriented approach.

SUMMARY

Product is a core element in marketing transactions for both the large scale and SMEs. As entrepreneurship is about opportunity recognition, having an understanding of how products are classified will be very useful to indicate which offerings could be best provided by SMEs to satisfy their needs.

Although products could be broadly classified on the basis of their attributes and the type of buyers that buy them, they are usually conceptualised as having three levels, namely the core product, the actual product, and the augmented product. This knowledge could help SMEs to understand the elements that provide value to the customers and be able to use their advantages of flexibility, and closeness to their customers to satisfy them better than competitors. Owing to their resource constraints, the length of products in a line that SMEs could manage would be relatively limited compared to large enterprise. However, they could concentrate on niches with special identifiable needs that they could meet effectively and efficiently better than competitors. As they operate in the turbulent marketing environment, their adequate understanding and effective use of marketing stimuli like branding, packaging, and quality could also be the veritable tools for them to obtain competitive advantage.

The process in the development of new products is systematic and impliedly involves group decision making. However, the characteristic of SMEs suggest there is a need for paradigm shift on how SMEs develop their new products and this would involve a balance of maintaining the integrity of the NPD and given due consideration to the characteristics of this type of business – marketing adaptation. Having developed new products, it is important for small businesses to realise that such products often pass through certain stages, with each having implications for success or failure of the product. However, the stage of introduction is noted to be very critical for small firms because of the initial investments and commitments which may not yield the expected profit immediately.

KEY TERMS
- Product SME
- Organisational products Consumer products
- Resource constraints Opportunity recognition
- Product Life cycle New product development
- Innovation Packaging
- Branding Product line
- Product mix Marketing mix

MANAGING PRODUCTS AND CUSTOMER VALUE

REVIEW QUESTIONS

1. What is a product? Discuss the relevance of product to the marketing system. Justify your viewpoint with examples in the SME marketing context.

2. Discuss various types of products, classified on the basis of their attributes and explain the usefulness of such knowledge to small business owners

3. Enumerate and discuss the major levels of products that must be considered by product planners. How can this knowledge help SMEs to gain competitive advantage?

4. To what extent might a SME which is involved in the marketing of cosmetic products and intends to operate in a European country use branding and packaging to their advantage?

5. Briefly discuss the stages in the new product development and explain why this many not be strictly amenable to the context of SMEs.

CASE STUDY: FRUGAL BUSINESS SERVICES LTD

It is clear that businesses are under unprecedented level of pressure this day and age to be customer-focussed in order to survive the turbulent marketing environment. While this challenge applies to all organisations irrespective of sector and size, its impact on SMEs is more pronounced. This relates to how they manage their market offerings, the way these are priced, as well as the strategies involved in distributing them to the target audience. It is also challenging figuring out how to manage the marketing communications in such a way that all of the target markets are reached effectively at the most cost efficient form. On a positive note, this challenge is prompting innovation and opportunity recognition among small businesses. This is the case with Peter Osezua whose passion for entrepreneurship and customer-orientation triggered his interest to establish Frugal Business Services Ltd on 24 November 2014. This passion permeates the entire business, including the activities of the five employees working in this establishment. Peter and his team at Frugal Business Services know that service business is quite different from those involving the sales of physical products that could be touched, felt, or tasted. The team at Frugal are not oblivious to the fact that services are essentially intangible, perishable, inseparable, and variable in relation to those rendering it and the circumstances involved. Hence, the approach at Frugal is to constantly evaluate customers' experience of their services so that action could be taken about any dissatisfaction reported. This has been the driving force and a key success factor of Frugal business strategy over the past couple of years.

The business of Frugal covers cargo shipment, courier services, logistics, and financial services. The organisation is very popular among customers in the UK who frequently send money and packages to their loved ones in various other countries outside the UK. The current customer-based of this organisation are mainly Africans, Afro-Caribbean, Asians, and East Europeans. The Innovation to start the Bureau de change business could be linked to the positive development in the

127

legal environment. Specifically, this is about the introduction of Small Payment Institution (SPI) by the Financial Conduct Authority (FCA) that gives authority to individual financial business owners to create a platform that allows customers to send or receive money from others abroad. Since Frugal is SPI licenced, the popularity of its financial transactions has soared recently among customers who think the mainstream banks offering similar services are becoming too bureaucratic for their liking. Frugal as a brand now resonates clearly with its customers across the country which gives the organisation competitive strength in relation to companies such as Western Union, RIA Money Transfer, Moneylink, and several others. Although it is still a small company, the watchwords for the operations have been trust, commitment, and integrity. The maxim at Frugal is that if the customers trust you for a great service, they will be loyal. So, they do not compromise on offering services that communicate integrity to their various consumer segments. Hence, it is not surprising that the customers are thrilled to engage in word-of-mouth communications of the services of the business to their friends, family members, and business associates.

While Frugal services are currently provided mainly in the United Kingdom, the plan of Peter, the owner-manager is to make the business global like competing organisations such as Western Union. He understands that there are customers with needs that revolve around these services in other countries. Hence, the plan for the next coming years is to reach countries like the United States (US) and other European countries that have yet to be reached. This passion for expansion is enthusiastically shared by staff members at Frugal Business Services Ltd, and they are confident of success with the specific aim to make their services accessible to customers irrespective of their ethnicity, race, sexual orientation, language, and religious background. Relying on the quality of service provided to its target customers over the years, the organisation has engaged in brand extension to other services. The business now has other establishments with related name. These are Frugal Communication Ltd and Empowerment Foundation. There are many other great plans for the future. This could be around retailing or creating value for other businesses in the form of Business-to-Business (B2B) transactions. Frugal believes that if the current product line succeeds and customer satisfaction is maintained, the effort it will take to convince buyers will be far less compared to if there is no record of accomplishment to build on.

Questions

1. Peter plans to expand his current business to other areas in the future. When planning the product for this future establishment, what product levels should he put into consideration towards satisfying the target market?
2. Explain the stages in the new product development process. Why do you think this conventional process may not be amenable to Peter's plan in his future business aspiration?
3. What advice would you give to Frugal Business Services to strengthen the brand equity of the organisation?

Source: Used with the kind permission of the Management of Frugal Business Services Limited for Educational purposes

MANAGING PRODUCTS AND CUSTOMER VALUE

Technology, SME, and the 21st century:

Electronic word of mouth communication (eWOM) and new product development among SMEs

One of the challenges of small businesses has been identified as limited resources, especially when compared to big multinationals. So, this could be a challenge in their resource allocation to marketing communications especially for new products. However, the development in the world of technology now makes digital communications such as the one done through social media easily accessible to SMEs, implying that they can now make favourable mention of their products to target audiences at relatively low costs. While it could be very challenging for new products at the stage of introduction in the Product Life Cycle (PLC), consumers who have tried and enjoyed the product or service often helps spread the message among friends, family members, and associates electronically. This electronic word of mouth (eWOM) usually strengthens brands, and aids quick diffusion of innovation among various consumer groups as any recommendation through this is considered credible by the receiver. This is because the sender of the message is independent of the brand. By and large, eWOM has opened great opportunities for SMEs to promote their product or services whether they are organisational products or those targeted at the ultimate consumers who buy for personal gratification.

1. Discuss the use and effectiveness of eWOM for SMEs whose business is the sale of organisational products as compared to those that deal in consumer products
2. Assume you are the owner-manager of a company that specialises in event management services. You have now spotted an opportunity to extend this business into baking and supplying cakes for special occasions. Which of the stages of the new product development (NPD) process would eWOM be useful for in relation to this product idea? Justify your answer with relevant explanation.

LET'S REASON TOGETHER

Group task: in-class activity

In a group of three, each member should think of any two products that could be sold to specific groups of students in your university and identify those groups. In a group discussion with your colleagues, explain how you could make this to be a commercial success and discuss the difficulties you may encounter in developing this product compared to if such products will be developed and offered by a large-scale multinational firm.

REFERENCES

American Marketing Association (2010) Marketing power: Dictionary. www.marketingpower.com/_layouts/Dictionary.aspx?dLetter=B (Accessed on 25 February 2010).

Barringer, B. R. and Ireland, R. D. (2010) *Entrepreneurship: Successfully Launching New Ventures*, 3rd ed. Pearson Education Inc., New Jersey.

Bessant, J. and Tidd, J. (2007) *Innovation and Entrepreneurship*. John Wiley & Sons Ltd., West Sussex.

Brassington, F. and Pettitt, S. (2007) *Essentials of Marketing*, 2nd ed. Pearson Education Ltd., Essex.

Carson, D. and Cromie, S. (1990) Marketing planning in small enterprises: A model and some empirical evidence. *Journal of Consumer Marketing*, 7(3), 5–18.

Carson, D., Cromie, S., McGowan, P. and Hill, J. (1995) *Marketing and Entrepreneurship in SMEs: An Innovative Approach*. Pearsons Education Ltd., Essex.

Deakins, D. and Freel, M. (2003) *Entrepreneurship and Small Firms*. McGraw-Hill Education, Berkshire.

Dibb, S., Simkin, L., William, M., Pride, W. M. and Ferrell, O. C. (2016) *Marketing: Concepts and Strategies*. Cengage, Hampshire.

Gbadamosi, A. (2009a) Low income consumers' reactions to low-involvement products. *Marketing Intelligence and Planning*, 27(7), 882–899.

Gbadamosi, A. (2009b) Cognitive dissonance: The implicit explication in low-income consumers' shopping behaviour for 'low-involvement' grocery products. *International Journal of Retail and Distribution Management*, 37(12), 1077–1095.

Gbadamosi, A. (2019) Marketing: A Paradigm Shift. In Gbadamosi, A. (Ed.), *Contemporary Issues in Marketing*. SAGE, London.

Gbadamosi, Tunji. (2000) Consumers' redemption: Whose responsibility? *International Journal of Management Sciences and Information Technology*, 1(1 April), 46–54.

Gilmore, A., Carson, D. and Grant, K. (2001) SME marketing in practice. *Marketing Intelligence and Planning*, 19(1), 6–11.

Hill, J. (2001) A multidimensional study of the key determinants of effective SME marketing activity: Part 2. *International Journal of Entrepreneurial Behaviour & Research*, 7(6), 211–235.

Hyland, P. W., Gieskes, J. F. B. and Sloan, T. R. (2001) Occupation clusters as determinants of organisational learning in the product innovation process. *Journal of Workplace Learning*, 13(5), 198–208.

Jevons, C. (2005) Names, brands, branding: Beyond the signs, symbols, products and services. *Journal of Product & Brand Management*, 14(2), 117–211.

Kotler, P., Armstrong, G., Veronica, W. and Saunders, J. (2008) *Principles of Marketing*, 5th ed. Pearsons Education Limited, Harlow.

Lamb, C. W., Hair, J. F. and McDaniel, C. (2010) *MKTG*, 3rd ed. South-Western Cengage Learning, Mason.

McAdam, R. and Armstrong, G. (2001) A symbiosis of quality and innovation SMEs: A multiple case study analysis. *Managerial Auditing Journal*, 16(7), 394–399.

Nwankwo, S. and Gbadamosi, A. (2009) Mediating the effects of black pentecostalism in entrepreneurial orientations. *Institute for Small Business and Entrepreneurship Annual Conference*, The Novas Centre, Liverpool, UK, 3–6 November.

O'Dwyer, M., Gilmore, A. and Carson, D. (2009) Innovative marketing in SMEs: A theoretical approach. *European Business Review*, 21(6), 504–515.

O'Dwyer, M. and Ledwith, A. (2009) Determinants of new product performance in small firms. *International Journal of Entrepreneurial Behaviour and Research*, 15(2), 124–136.

Raymond, L. and Croteau, A. (2006) Enabling the strategic development of SMEs through advanced manufacturing systems: A configurational perspective. *Industrial Management & Data Systems*, 106(7), 1012–1032.

Rogers, E. M. (1962) *Diffusion of Innovations*. Free Press, New York.

Rogers, E. M. (2003) *Diffusion of Innovation*. Simon & Schuster, New York.

Rundh, B. (2005) The multi-faceted dimension of packaging: Marketing logistic or marketing tool? *British Food Journal*, 107(9), 670–684.

Salavou, H. and Avlonitis, G. (2008) Product innovativeness and performance: A focus on SMEs. *Management Decision*, 46(7), 969–989.

Schumpeter, J. (1934) *The Theory of Economic Development*. Harvard University Press, Cambridge, MA.

Vargo, S. L. and Lusch, R. F. (2004) Evolving to a new dominant logic for marketing. *Journal of Marketing*, 68(January), 1–17.

Wilson, R. M. S. and Gilligan, C. (1997) *Strategic Marketing Management: Planning, Implementation and Control*, 2nd ed. Butterworth-Heinemann, Oxford.

Wong, H. Y. and Merrilees. B. (2005) A brand orientation typology for SMEs: A case research approach. *Journal of Product and Brand Management*, 14(3), 155–162.

Chapter 8

Choosing the right pricing strategy

P. Sergius Koku

LEARNING OBJECTIVES

After reading this chapter, you will be able to:
- Develop an appreciation for complexities in pricing;
- Develop pricing objectives;
- Develop appreciation for the interface between pricing decisions and law;
- Develop appreciation for the internal and external factors that affect pricing decisions;
- Be able to discuss pricing variables and the various pricing objectives;
- Understand the differences in the pricing process in SMEs and large organisations;
- Choose an appropriate pricing strategy;
- Be able to do simple calculations involving markup and break-even volume.

INTRODUCTION

Regardless of firm size, pricing is one of the most critical activities that take place within the firm. The importance of the pricing process to a firm lies in the fact that pricing is the only means through which a firm can generate revenue. A mistake in the process could be costly to the firm. Pricing mistakes may not only make the firm less profitable but also they can result in a firm's bankruptcy and its eventual closure.

Because of its importance, pricing has attracted a significant research effort in many academic disciplines such as marketing, economics, and law. Because it can be easily mimicked by competition, firms do not rely solely on price for their competitive strategy. However, price's uniqueness as a strategic tool is reflected in the fact that it is about the only corporate activity that goes by several different names, depending on the context. For example, it is referred to as a 'fare' in the transportation industry, a 'fee' in education and its related business, 'cover' in the entertainment industry, and 'price' in many other situations.

Regardless of what it is called, the primary objective of price is to cover all the costs incurred in making a product/service and to produce profit while it still appeals to the intended target market. The issue of whether products or services must be priced to maximise profit is a seemingly simple but in fact rather vexing one and will not be discussed in detail here. However, suffice it to say that, while some economists believe that pricing must be used as a tool to maximise profit, behavioural economists take the view that profit maximisation is not the object of the firm. Cyert and March (1963), for example, have argued that because of the interactions that take place within firms, the wide range of personal objectives that are held by the employees, as well as the constraints that exist, firms aim to achieve profits that would be satisfactory to their disparate stakeholders, instead of trying to maximise profits.

The concerns about pricing are not limited to large organisations alone. Small to medium-sized enterprises (SMEs) as well as nonprofit organisations such as universities, municipalities, and public hospitals are also equally concerned about pricing strategy. Governments in many countries are interested in the pricing practices of firms because of either their political or economic philosophies. Governments that are interested in the free- market economic system also tend to be interested in the pricing policy of firms in pursuit of their economic policies. Other governments might be interested in price controls in the pursuit of their social policies. Governments' interest in the pricing policies of firms is expressed in the laws that are passed and enforced. For example, to ensure free markets, governments pass and enforce anti-collusion laws and other laws that prohibit pricing practices that seek to stifle competition (Stigler, 1987).

To attain certain social objectives, governments pass and enforce price controls or price ceilings. The existence of laws concerning pricing also suggests that firms must not be concerned by profit-maximising objectives alone when they price; they must also be concerned about complying with existing laws on pricing. Firms that operate in several countries or different jurisdictions must be aware of the laws on pricing in the different countries/jurisdictions in which they operate, as there is no one universal law on pricing that is applied by every country (Koku, 2009).

The objective of pricing remains the same in both small and large organisations; however, those who set prices or play a key role in pricing differ. Prices of products and services are set in large organisations by product line managers in conjunction with marketing and sales departments or by a department that is solely responsible for pricing. On the other hand, prices are generally set by top management in SMEs. As such it is imperative for top management in SMEs to be thoroughly familiar with the issues associated with pricing of the products or services that they offer.

LAWS ON PRICING

It is consistent with economic theory of revenue maximisation for a firm to charge different buyers different prices. This is true for both large and small firms as well as for-profit and nonprofit organisations (Nagle, 1987). Let us take the case of universities and colleges, for example. These institutions charge consumers (students) different prices (tuition) based on where the students come from – such as in-state or out-of-state tuition, or national or international student tuition. They also do so by such other means as offering different scholarships and financial aid packages. Similarly, hospitals charge the insured and the uninsured different rates for the same treatment. Indeed, price discrimination is an ever-present phenomenon in business. However, because several states and countries have price discrimination laws that make certain types of price discrimination illegal, it is important that organisations know which types of price discrimination are permissible and where they are permissible.

Firms use different pricing strategies such as quantity discounts for retailers based on size and package and non-linear price schedules (where different segments exist), organisations

CHOOSING THE RIGHT PRICING STRATEGY

have to be careful about the issue of price discrimination, which is defined variously by different authors. According to Kent Monroe, price discrimination

> [w]henever there are price differences for the same product or service sold by a single seller that are not justified by cost or changes in the level of demand. Price discrimination also occurs when two or more buyers of the same product or service are charged the same price despite differences in the cost of serving these buyers.
>
> (Monroe, 2003, p. 250)

It is true that an organisation may be willing to charge different consumers different prices for the same product/service based on the consumers' willingness to pay the different prices. This could be done in an effort to generate more revenue for the organisation while selling the same number of units. Economists explain this phenomenon as an attempt by the organisation to extract all the potential gains from trade and argue that this practice is possible because the different consumers or consumer groups have different elasticity of demand. Alternatively, it has been argued that different consumers may, based on their perceived benefits, assign different values to the same product, hence their willingness to pay different prices.

Even though price discrimination as defined connotes charging different prices for the same product or service without cost justifications, the ambit of price discrimination could involve other business practices such as special promotions, rebates, and discounts (cash and quantity) that lead to price differences.

Price discrimination immediately evokes connotations of an illegal act, as discussed earlier. However, there are legally permissible or defensible price-discriminatory practices. How else could one explain the practice of students as a group being able to subscribe, through their universities, to a newspaper such as the *Wall Street Journal* or magazines at prices below newsstand prices, or senior citizens being able to buy bus tickets at a discount?

The permissible price-discriminatory practices are generally regarded as exceptions to laws, such as the antitrust laws. The most well-known exception is cost-based pricing, i.e., a firm can charge different consumers different prices for the same product if the cost for serving these consumers is different. The practical application of this exemption is seen in instances where a firm charges a consumer who buys in larger quantities a lower price than a consumer who buys the same product in a smaller quantity. This prepares the ground for what economists call block pricing.

By using block pricing, a seller could extract additional profits from similar consumers who face a similar downward-sloping demand curve. Take, for instance, a situation where a seller is selling a roll of 36-millimeter film for $4.00 per roll, and a buyer values the first roll of the 36 millimeter film at $4.00, but the second at $2.00. Because the two rolls of film will cost the buyer $8.00 ($4.00 each) the buyer will buy only one roll of film. However, the seller can get the buyer to buy the two rolls if s/he puts them together and offers them for $6.00. Here, the consumer who buys a pack of two rolls of film pays less per roll of film than the consumer who buys only one roll of film.

One of the major motivations behind the antitrust laws is the prevention of a monopoly that could result from predatory pricing. Thus, the law makes an exemption for different prices to be charged for the same product if it is certain that the firm will not emerge as a monopoly, or the practice is not designed to injure competitors. Such a case could be said to exist when a company is going out of business. It also allows price changes for obsolescence of goods that are seasonal and perishable or closing-out-a-line sales, and court sanctioned distress sales are also exempted.

THE ECONOMICS OF PRICING

Firms use their pricing strategy to serve several objectives. While generating revenue and profit are the obvious primary objectives, several secondary objectives exist. For example, the pricing strategy must not only complement the firm's distribution as well as its communication strategies but also the pricing policies should also be consistent with the nature of the product. A pricing strategy will not be complementary with the distribution strategy if a firm sells rare and expensive items, such as jewelry, using mass merchandisers. Similarly, the pricing strategy will not be complementary with the communication strategy if a seller advertises expensive jewelry using handbills (flyers) or tabloids. A pricing policy will be inconsistent with the product if a firm sells a high-quality product at a price at which consumers do not expect the product to sell.

These discussions suggest a number of issues. First, consumers often use price as an indicator of quality; thus, all things being equal, a high price is indicative of high quality. For this reason SMEs should be careful when they set price. A drastic reduction in price of a product that has been positioned as a high-quality product may only confuse buyers. They will think that the product's quality has also been drastically reduced. Price, in addition to serving as a signal, also serves as an indicator of value (Zeithaml, 1988). However, value is defined differently by different authors. Some authors defined value as

$$\text{Value} = \frac{\text{Perceived Benefits}}{\text{Price}}$$

However, others argue that consumers tend to define the value of a product in terms of its substitutes, hence

$$\text{Value} = \frac{\text{Perceived Benefits}}{\text{Price}}$$

In either case, the role of price as an indicator of value is clear.

In spite of numerous studies on the subject, how consumers exactly use price in their purchasing decisions largely remains not well understood. It is, however, clear that, regardless of the definition of value, consumers use other non-price variables such as the *perceived value* of the product or service in their buying decisions. Perceived value-pricing strategy is therefore an appropriate strategy for not only large firms but also for SMEs. The firm that uses this strategy will rely on non-cost variables. It will try to determine the buyer's perception of the product or service's value and price accordingly. As discussed earlier, this type of pricing strategy is more appropriate when the pricing decision is made to be consistent with all the other marketing variables. Regardless of how consumers use price information, it is clear that for some products consumers react to price changes by either purchasing more of the product or less of the product. This concept is known in economics as price elasticity of demand. It serves as one of the decision factors in changing price in many large organisations and should be used by SMEs also.

PRICE ELASTICITY OF DEMAND

The price elasticity of demand is defined as the degree of responsiveness in quantity demanded given a unit change in price. Algebraically, it is expressed as

$$E = \frac{\text{\% Change in Quantity Demanded}}{\text{\% Change in Price}}$$

There are a few points to note about E. Because it would be nonsensical to have dimensions, i.e., tons/price, the coefficient of elasticity does not have any dimensions. Furthermore, the absolute value of the coefficient is what is considered. Hence, in terms of the elasticity of demand, the effect of -2 is the same as the effect of 2 since $|-2|$ is the same as 2. The demand is said to be elastic when the absolute value of E is greater than 1 (for example, $3, -4$, 10, etc.), and is said to be inelastic when E is less than 1 (for example, 0.7, 0.65, 0.35, etc.).

The demand is generally elastic for goods and services that have substitutes. For example, one would expect the demand for products with close substitutes, such as for running shoes or laptop computers, to be price elastic. The same is true for services such as university education or retail stores that have several substitutes. For these goods, a unit change in price will result in more than a unit change in the quantity demanded. A percentage price change in tuition may result in a disproportionate change in the "demand" for education. The opposite is true for goods and services that do not have close substitutes. The demand for such products is price inelastic. The demand for quantity of common salt, for example, will not change significantly because of percentage price change – hence, such a demand is price inelastic.

Other factors that have been shown to affect the elasticity of demand include other uses of the product or service, and the ratio of the price of the product or service to the income of the consumer. Generally, the more uses for the product or service, the more elastic its demand. And the smaller the ratio of the price to the consumers' income, the less elastic its demand. On the other hand, the higher the ratio of the price to income, the more elastic its demand.

Some firms sell the same product or services at very different prices in different countries or geographic locations, not because of the additional costs incurred in making the products or services available, but because they price using the concept of the elasticity of demand.

Prices are lower at locations where there are many substitutes and higher at locations where there are no close substitutes. However, a firm risks being accused of dumping if it sells below 'fair market value' in foreign markets where there are close substitutes. Dumping could be a violation of the World Trade Organization's agreement between the signatory countries if it threatens material injury to an industry in the importing nation.

THE ISSUE OF CROSS-ELASTICITY

Cross-elasticity arises when the change in price of one product, let us say product A, affects the quantity of another product, let us say product B. Cross-elasticity plays an important role in a firm's pricing decisions, particularly if the firm sells several products that are used jointly, i.e., if some of the products are complementary. For example, razor blades and shaving sticks are complementary goods; therefore, an increase in the price of razor blades will more than likely affect the quantity of shaving sticks demanded. A firm that manufactures razor blades and shaving sticks will, therefore, have to take into consideration the effects of price change of one of the products on the other.

Similarly, the manufacturer of razor blades and shaving sticks will have to take into consideration the fact these products are used together into their initial pricing. A good strategy may be to sell the shaving stick at a much lower price, or even give it away free, and sell the razor blade at a premium, if the shaving sticks are designed in a way that the consumer has to buy the same manufacturer's razor blades. While complementary pricing strategy may be a common practice in large and multinational organisations, it is nonetheless germane to SMEs.

The availability and the price of close substitutes should also affect a firm's pricing decisions. As in the case of supplementary goods, a change in price of a product, let us say product C, affects the quantity demanded of its substitute, let us say product D, particularly if product D is a close substitute to product C. The concept of cross-elasticity is at work here again. The implication of cross-elasticity – not for SMEs only but for every firm – is that effective pricing decisions cannot be made by focussing only on margins; they also have to take into consideration the configuration of the entire market. This will include not only the other products that are made by SMEs and how they are used or demanded by the consumer but also the availability of close substitutes.

PRICING STRATEGIES

Two basic pricing strategies, full-cost pricing and variable-cost pricing, form the principal foundation for other strategies. Because it is intuitive and rather simple to understand, most managers tend to apply what is commonly referred to as a full-cost pricing strategy. The objective of this strategy is to recoup the costs that go into making a product plus a markup. Full costs can be divided into three parts as follows:

- The direct costs incurred in making the product or service. These direct costs are generally direct labor and direct material;
- The product's or service's share of the production fixed costs (overheads);
- The producer's markup.

The markup can be lowered or increased, depending on the competitive environment.

The variable-cost pricing comprises only the direct costs, which are the direct costs of materials and direct labor costs. It is evident from the components of variable costs that a firm cannot survive using only variable-cost strategy. In practice, firms use variable-cost pricing for limited objectives and only for a short duration. They can, for example, be used to build traffic to the store, but manufacturers have to be ever so careful in using this strategy because they can be accused of predatory pricing, which is illegal in many jurisdictions. Firms use variable-cost pricing also for products that are being discontinued.

Products can, in some extreme cases, be priced below cost. This strategy is sometimes referred to as distress pricing and used when a product has become obsolete. Under distress, pricing the product is simply priced at the cost of carrying it (that is, the cost of insuring the product and the space it occupies).

PRICING STRATEGIES FOR NEW PRODUCT INTRODUCTION

There are two primary new product introduction pricing strategies, which are known as skimming and penetration strategies. Skimming refers to new product introduction pricing strategy in which the initial price is high. This initial high price is lowered subsequently. There are several explanations for the use of skimming strategy. First, the innovating firm wants to recoup its investment in the new product as quickly as possible before competition sets in. Second, the innovating firm gets to enjoy economics of scale as the users of the new product grow in number. The firm then passes on to consumers, in the form of lower prices, the benefits (cost savings) of the economics of scale.

136

It is also reasonable to expect the innovating firm to develop cost-saving methods as it gets more experienced in making the new product. In order not to be underpriced by competition, the innovating firm also passes along these cost savings to the consumer. The skimming strategy is common in industries where new inventions require a substantial investment, such as the high technology industry and the pharmaceutical industry. Recent examples of new products in the high technology industry where skimming strategy has been used include digital watches, calculators, cellular phones, and iPods. Examples of skimming in the pharmaceutical industry include penicillin, the entire class of cholesterol-lowering drugs, and patches for smoking cessation.

The penetration pricing strategy with new products is said to be used when the new product is introduced with an initially low price and increased over time. Most new products fall into this category when they are introduced with coupons which are later on eliminated. Introducing new products or services with coupons amounts to the use of price penetration strategy as the coupons serve as a price subsidy, and their elimination will result in the consumers having to pay the full price.

Even though we have emphasized the introductory phase of the product or service in skimming and penetration strategies, the entire *product life cycle* presents distinct opportunities for the firm to implement a different pricing strategy. Thus, a firm could use one type of strategy (for example, penetration strategy) in the product or service's introductory phase. It may use the full-cost pricing approach in the growth phase, promotional pricing strategy in the maturity phase, and a loss-leader approach in the declining phase.

PRICING OBJECTIVES

Irrespective of whether the firm uses full-cost pricing or variable-cost pricing strategy, the pricing objectives have to be first clearly delineated. There are three basic objectives – the firm must decide whether it wants to maximise revenue, maximise its pre-tax profits or maximise its market share. Even though maximizing revenue or maximizing pre-tax profits objectives could result in the same approach, they are not always the same. Many large firms could set their price to maximise their revenue by estimating their demand function. However, such practices are not widely used by SMEs because their pricing decisions are generally made by one or a few individuals as opposed to an elaborate pricing department in large organisations.

A firm may have to sell at prices lower than its competition in pursing maximisation of market share as its objective.

PRICING WITH OTHER MARKETING VARIABLES

Even though pricing decisions are directed towards generating revenue, they cannot be made in isolation of other marketing variables such as the *product*, *place*, and *promotion*. Indeed, it is imperative that the pricing strategy be consistent with the firm's entire marketing strategy. The relationship between price and the *product* or *service* is the most obvious of the relationships between price and the product or service is the most obvious of the relationships between price and other marketing variables. The firm will lose credibility if the price is not consistent with the quality of product or service that the firm is offering. Similarly, a firm cannot sell expensive and high-quality offerings using a mass-distribution strategy. The distribution strategy will undermine the product quality as consumers will assume that because mass-distribution strategy is being used, the offering (product or service) might not 'truly' be a high-quality offering after all.

137

What about *promotion* and *place*? Just as an inappropriate distribution strategy will under- mine the firm's credibility and the effectiveness of its overall marketing strategy, so too will inappropriate use of promotion and place. Media that are reflective of the quality or caliber of product or service being offered must be used. For example, one would expect advertisements of a high quality watch that targets successful business-people to be carried in such business-oriented newspapers as *The Times*, the *Wall Street Journal*, *Time*, *Newsweek*, etc., but not in newspapers or magazines that are considered tabloids.

In much the same way as advertising, one would expect the place where such high-quality watches are being sold to be reflective of their class. Certainly, one would not expect such watches to be sold by street vendors on the sidewalk because watches that are sold on sidewalk by street vendors are usually thought to be of low quality or shady origin.

THE ROLE OF THE THREE Cs

The three Cs are Cost, Customers, and Competition. These three factors individually and collectively play a significant role in a firm's pricing decision. The role of cost in a firm's pricing decision is obvious as the firm must, at the very minimum, cover its production cost. The cost of production is directly traceable to the cost of the inputs – direct material and direct labor. If these costs are high the price of the product or service will also be high and vice versa. It is, however, important to note that the target customers will influence the quality of the input.

Given the importance of market segmentation in designing effective marketing strategies, it should be no surprise that an effective pricing strategy also calls for different prices for different consumer segments. For example, a newspaper publisher could sell to students at a price lower than the rack price. Similarly, senior citizens pay lower prices for certain services and products such as prescription drugs and public transportation. The elasticity of demand is the underlying economic argument behind charging different customer segments different prices. However, firms using this strategy have to be careful not to run afoul the strict price discrimination laws that are enforced in many jurisdictions. Price segmentation using such variables as race or religion is not permissible, at least not in the United States.

The price of competitors' products, particularly close competitors, also matters. Because price-sensitive consumers do take the price of close substitutes into consideration, a firm will do well to pay attention to those prices. Some firms may not be satisfied knowing just the price of competitors; they may also want to know how competitors arrived at such prices. Since they cannot ask their competitors directly, they engage in what is called reversed engineering. In reversed engineering a firm takes apart the competitor's product and prices each of the component parts. By so doing a firm may learn the actual cost of competitors' products and may also be able to estimate the markup on the product.

A firm that is armed with fairly accurate information on competitors' costs and markup will be in a better position to match competitors' prices. Hence, a common pricing strategy where products or services are similar is to match the price of the competition. Pricing to match competitors is, however, fraught with dangers. First, a firm can easily price below its cost or below its own required returns in an attempt to match competitors' prices. Second, matching competitors' prices can unintentionally lead to a price war in which every seller tries to underprice the competition.

CHOOSING THE RIGHT PRICING STRATEGY

RETURN ON INVESTMENT AND MARKUP PRICING

While pricing to match competitors is easy to implement, it does not take into consideration a firm's own cost of production or the required rates of return on its investments; it is, therefore, not a very useful strategy, at least in terms of realizing a firm's financial objectives. Markup pricing and return on investment pricing techniques incorporate the firm's financial objective in its pricing strategy.

Many firms in the services industry, such as law practices or accounting firms, practice markup pricing in which they add a standard markup on cost. How does the markup pricing work? Let us look at the following:

Direct labor cost/unit	= $10.00
Direct material/unit	= $5.00
Total fixed cost	= $100,000.00
Number of units produced	= 50,000.00

(For simplicity we can assume that all the units produced are sold.)

The direct cost per unit from the information included = $15.00 (i.e., $10 for direct labor per unit + $5.00 for direct material per unit). However, the total cost per unit will have to reflect each unit's share of the total fixed cost as well (this is one of the issues dealt with in cost allocation, which will not be discussed in this chapter). Since a total of 50,000 units have been produced, each unit's share of the total fixed cost is given as follows:

$$\text{Each unit's share of the total fixed cost} = \frac{\$100,000.00}{50,000.00}$$
$$= \$2.00$$

Therefore, the unit cost in producing the item = $17.00 (i.e., $15 + $2).

Now, let us assume that the firm applies a 20% markup on each unit produced. In that case the selling price will be as follows:

$$\text{Selling price of the product} = \frac{\text{Unit Cost}}{(1 - \text{Desired Markup})}$$
$$= \frac{17.00}{(1 - 20\%)}$$
$$= \frac{17.00}{.80}$$
$$= \$21.25$$

The consumer may, however, pay more than $21.25 for the item if the firm does not sell directly to the final consumer, but instead sells through intermediaries. Because the intermediaries also have to add on their desired markup, the product might end up costing significantly more than $21.25. The final price will depend on the number of intermediaries through whom the product passes to get to the final consumer.

Pricing strategies that discuss the role of the intermediaries are discussed in detail in distribution channels issues which we do not cover in this chapter. However, it is

139

important to know that a retailer, which many SMEs are, can apply markup as a percentage of its cost or its selling price. Take, for example, a retailer who buys an item for $20.00 and desires a 30% markup on cost – they will sell the item for $26.00 (i.e., $20 × 1.30). However, the same retailer who desires 30% markup on the basis of the selling price will sell the product for $28.57 (that is, $20/.7). It should be clear from this example that the price that the final consumers pay depends on whether the intermediaries apply their markup requirements using the cost price or the selling price as the basis.

In practice, particularly in small business settings, the owner or entrepreneur sets a profit goal and prices the product or service to achieve this goal. This type of pricing is referred to as target-return pricing. The attainment of the profit goal, however, involves the concept of break-even. In order for a firm to realise profit, the firm must first achieve a break-even volume, i.e., it must first sell enough to cover all the costs incurred in making the product. Therefore, the target-return price assumes having first attained a break-even volume. Let us assume here that the firm has invested $1 million in the project and desires 30% return on this investment. The break-even volume with the example given is derived as follows:

$$\text{Break-even volume} = \frac{\text{Fixed Cost}}{\text{Contribution}}$$

where contribution = Selling Price – Variable Cost which $= \$21.25 - \$15.00$

$$= \$6.25$$

Using the figures here:

$$\text{The break-even volume} = \frac{\$100,000.00}{\$6.25}$$
$$= 16,000 \text{ units}$$

The target-return price = unit cost + (desired return × investment)/unit sales. Here again, for the sake of simplicity, we dispense with the concept of the discounted streams of future income.

Using the figures in our example prior:

$$\text{Target return price} = 17.00 + \frac{(30\% + \$1,000,000.00)}{50,000}$$
$$= \$17.00 + 46.00$$
$$= \$23.00$$

VALUE PRICING

Even though value pricing may sound similar to perceived-value pricing, the two are not the same. The customer under the perceived-value pricing concept discussed earlier thinks the product or service is worth the price. However, under value pricing, the firm tries to set prices in a way that the price represents 'an extraordinary bargain for the consumer'. Thus, under value pricing, the firm not only charges price lower that its competitors, but it also gives better services and guarantees than its competitors.

OTHER PRICING STRATEGIES

Other pricing strategies that firms use include product line pricing, psychological pricing, and transfer pricing. Product line pricing strategy is used by firms that produce more than one product or more than one product line. Under this pricing strategy, different product lines may carry distinctly different prices. The cross-elasticity between products in a line is relevant to product line pricing, and so are the product positioning and the interrelations between the offerings within the line. The lowest-priced product in a line might be positioned as the traffic builder, while the highest-priced product might be positioned as the premium item.

Taking the psychological pricing approach can lead sellers to price a product or service such that the price ends in a 9. For example, it is believed that a pair of shoes selling for $49.99 conveys a cheaper price than the pair selling for $50.00. Whether this is effective or not is debatable, but the fact is that we are constantly bombarded or surrounded by evidence of such practices. The psychological effects of pricing also lead sellers to set high prices, regardless of the cost, for conspicuous consumption items such as jewelry and fur coats, or items that involve consumers' ego, such as perfume.

Closely associated with psychological pricing is the concept of reference price. Sellers don't really use reference price because a reference price is simply the consumer's benchmark price that the consumer uses to make certain purchases. When using reference price in their pricing strategy, sellers generally display their products with the products that they wish to be associated with in the mind of the consumer.

Transfer pricing is practiced in situations where the firm makes one or several components of a final product that it assembles at the same or a different location. In this case the firm could set the price of the component parts that are made within the firm in different departments in order to arrive at a predetermined price of the final product.

The internet has revolutionised the way business is done and has opened global markets that may have been cost prohibitive to SMEs. Suddenly, an SME in the UK or the US could, through a creative use of its website, receive orders from far away markets such as Singapore or Hong Kong, where it may not have actively participated previously. While these possibilities are exciting, they have also made pricing decisions for SMEs more complex. Because international markets involve other geographic locations that could be far away, SMEs now have to consider whether shipping charges, warehousing, insurance, and such associated costs should be reflected in their pricing decisions or dealt with separately.

Simply put, pricing decisions can be very involved and there is often a lot at stake whether the firm is a large multinational organisation or an SME. Because an easy international presence can be achieved through the internet, pricing decision makers should be both knowledgeable on the economics of pricing and also familiar with the legal issues relating to pricing in the different jurisdictions in which they market their products and services.

REVIEW QUESTIONS

1. Which three Cs are relevant to pricing?

2. Why should an organisation be familiar with the laws of the different states or countries in which it conducts business?

3. List the external factors that could affect an organisation's pricing.

4. What is price elasticity of demand and how does it work?

5. Is price discrimination always illegal?

6. Jane sells Wow Chocolate Cookies, which she makes using a secret recipe, through retailers. She sells the cookies to the retailers at $20.00 per box. Calculate (1) the price the retailers should sell the cookies to final consumers for if the retailers' policy requires a 20% markup on cost and (2) what the price would be if the retailers required a 20% markup on the basis of the selling price?

7. Labor costs at Apple, Microsoft, and IBM have increased from $35.00 per hour at each of these firms to $50.00 per hour. At Toshiba's Japanese plants, however, labor costs have remained at approximately $30.00 per hour. The difference in these costs gives Toshiba an advantage in which of the following types of cost?
   a. Fixed cost
   b. Variable cost
   c. Semi-variable cost
   d. Marginal cost
   e. Total fixed cost

CASE STUDY: SANDY'S SMARTPARKAPP

As she tells it, Ms. Sandy Otis said she always knew that working for someone else or for that matter a large corporation was 'not for her', and yet that was what she did for ten years after earning her bachelor's degree. At college she was studious and graduated within the top 1% of her graduating class. She majored in computer science and was recruited to work in the information systems' department with a major fortune 100 company after completing her bachelor's degree. She had interned with the same company, IGK, Inc., during her last two summers in college, so she said working there on full-time basis was like 'going home'.

Sandy's work was challenging, but she excelled. After five years she was promoted to join the international trouble shooting division. While most of the work done within this department was at the company's head office in New York, it also entailed some overseas travels which Sandy always looked forward to. However, after serving in this department for four years, Sandy thought the time had come for her to realise her dream – working for herself.

Even though she had dreamed of owning her own business, Ms. Otis did not take any business courses while in college. Instead she opted for honors courses in computer science which she enjoyed, so planning to start her own business was a time and energy consuming undertaking for her. She went to the local library regularly and read voraciously anything she came across on starting one's own business. She confided in a friend that she felt that she would more than likely make it to the level of senior middle management level within the next two to three years if she remained with the company, but she also felt that the time had come for her to make it on her own.

Ms. Otis has, over the years, been frustrated by parking problems whenever she went to work. So, she had been telling herself to design an "App" that could help solve parking problems. She took the "App" project more seriously now that she is seriously contemplating leaving IGK and works on the design every weekend during her spare

CHOOSING THE RIGHT PRICING STRATEGY

time. The App consists of sensors that are embedded at certain locations in the parking lot. These sensors communicate with a large (four feet by four feet) LCD board that is installed at the entrance of a parking lot and displays the numbers of the stalls in a parking lot that are not occupied. The sensors also communicate with cell phones.

Akain, the small town of a population of about 100,000 where Sandy comes from is located by a small meandering river that also has a small waterfall, an old military barrack, and a museum full of civil war era artifacts. It is said that the town's outskirts served as one of the battel fields for the civil war. Thus, the town is frequented by tourists who encounter parking problems during the summers. Accordingly, Sandy thought Akain's museum would be a good testing ground for her SmartParkApp. Sandy therefore enlisted the assistance of the museum manager in Akain, Ms. Davis, to test her device. With $20,000.00 (twenty thousand dollars) from her savings and $50,000.00 (fifty thousand dollars) from her two siblings ($25,000 or twenty-five thousand dollars each), she was able to buy and installed all that was necessary to test the App in the museum's parking lot. The device worked beautifully and was even covered in the local newspaper.

Now the challenge is twofold. First is to develop a viable business model, and the second is launch the product. Most of the expenses that Sandy incurs will come from assembling the LCD display board, the installation cables, and the sensors. She plans to initially import all the component parts of these devices, and have her workmen assemble them in the SmartParkApps factory, an old warehouse that she has purchased in Akain for $30,000 (thirty thousand dollars). Her value proposition is that SmartParkApp will make car park owners more efficient. The SmartParkApp will also help drivers (car park customers) to save time, especially in the mornings when they are rushing to get to work on time. They can easily know beforehand where vacant stalls are in the car park instead of 'circling' (driving around) the block to find a parking spot. Similarly, customers can ahead of time tell where the vacant stalls are when they are going for big events such as concerts or games. A SmartParkApp on a cell phone allows the cell phone to connect with all the car parks in the city or the area that have installed SmartParkApp sensors. A connection means the cell phone will display exactly what is displayed on a particular car park's LCD display. Hence all a driver needs is to purchase one SmartParlApp from a car park. These SmartParkApps will be renewed every 12 months and from any car park.

Even though Sandy does not exactly know how much to sell the 'app', her experience tells her that it cannot sell more than $15.00. She thought an ideal suggested retail price is $12.00 per year which averages to the cost of $1.00 per month, but this money does not go SmartParkApp, Inc., instead it goes to car park owners. SmartParkApp, Inc., only makes money from selling the LCD displays which it bundles with the sensors and the 'app'. The LCD display sells for $2,500.00 with a five-year, maintenance free warranty.

With additional $10,000 (ten thousand dollars) spent on buying materials and with labor from her two siblings and friends, Sandy was able to bring the old warehouse to the standards for her operations. The building now houses three offices, a showroom and the factory. Sandy wrote the codes for 'apps' herself and plans to update them periodically. However, she also plans to hire an assistant programmer,

143

three salespersons and five assemblers. Her potential customers are universities, large parking garage owners, and municipalities that own fee-paying car parking facilities (that is parking lots for which customers are charged to park).

Even though Sandy plans to use the personal selling approach to sell the SmartParkApp to car park owners, universities, municipalities, and major hotels, she has also created a nice website for the company and plans to use the digital media with such vehicles as Facebook, Instagram, and the like to create a buzz about her company and product. She is also leveraging her connections with free programming groups to enlist bloggers about the product. With a well-written business plan, additional $50,000.00 (making a total personal out of pocket contribution of $70,000.00), a loan of four hundred and thirty thousand dollars from her parents ($430,000.00), Sandy was able to convince a local banker to give her a line of credit for $1,000,000 (one million dollars). She values her own in kind investment in the business to be $1,000,000.00 (one million dollars) plus out of pocket cost at $70,000.00 (seventy thousand dollars).

The grand opening for SmartParkApp, Inc. (known for short as SmartPark) was held one Saturday morning in April, 2018. A local DJ was at hand and so were the mayor and the local pastor and many of Sandy's friends and former bosses from IGK. The food, drinks, music and all the giveaways at the Grand Opening cost Sandy $10,000 which she thought was high but rationalised the cost a good a good investment in advertising. Cognisant of the fact that she did not know any accounting or finance that could assist her to determine an appropriate pricing strategy that would enable her to succeed in business, she retained you as a consultant and provides you with the data that follows:

1. Selling price of the bundled LCD SmartParkApp system $2,500.00;
2. Investment in the business $1,500,000.00;
3. Direct labor per LCD display panel (this includes installation of the device for client companies) $300.00;
4. Direct material per LCD display panel (this includes cables and sensors needed for installation plus the app) $200.00;
5. Advertising and promotion $200,000;
6. Factory overhead $500,000.00.

Based on the data provided, calculate the following:

1. Contribution per unit:
   a. $3,500
   b. $2,000
   c. $2,500
   d. $1,500
   e. $1,000

2. Break-even volume in units:
   a. 300
   b. 250
   c. 350
   d. 220
   e. 150

CHOOSING THE RIGHT PRICING STRATEGY

3. Break-even in dollars
   a. 900,000
   b. 950,000
   c. 100,000
   d. 875,000
   e. 800,000
4. Unit volume needed to achieve $20,000 profit:
   a. 300
   b. 360
   c. 400
   d. 460
   e. 410
5. Suppose Sandy wants to realise 15% return on her investment at the end of the first year of operation. How much would that be?
   a. $125,000
   b. $225,000
   c. $200,000
   d. $175,000
   e. $100,000
6. How many LCD display panels will she sell during the first year to realise this objective?
   a. 100
   b. 110
   c. 80
   d. 90
   e. 120

Correct answers
1. $2,000
2. 350
3. 875,000
4. 360
5. $225,000
6. 90

LET'S REASON TOGETHER

Different sums of money were mentioned in the case, however, not all of them were used in the calculations. Why and why not?

TECHNOLOGY, SME, AND THE 21ST CENTURY

Advancement in technology, particularly in the field of electronic communication and its associated areas has dramatically transformed the way business is conducted in the 21st century, across the entire spectrum of organisations – multinationals, internationals, large corporations, medium-sized corporations, and small startups. While some small startups are using the internet as a means to get off the ground, some are using it to help them arrive at a market clearing price for their offerings. Examples include the use of E-bay, reverse auctions, and the use of cell phones by farmers in rural areas in Africa and else to get market prices for their produce. Can you think of other areas in which technology is being used in the 21st century to help SMEs determine prices?

REFERENCES

Brickley, James A., Smith, C. W. and Zimmerman, J. L. (1997) *Managerial Economics and Organizational Architecture*. McGraw-Hill, Boston, MA.

Cyert, R. N. and March, J. G. (1963) *A Behavioral Theory of the Firm*. Prentice Hall, Englewood Cliffs, NJ.

Koku, P. S. (2009) Which laws do your marketers know? Some legal issues on price discrimination. In *Conference Proceedings*, Academy of Marketing Science World Congress, 409–419.

Kotler, P. (1994) *Marketing Management, Analysis, Planning, Implementation and Control*, 8th ed. Prentice Hall, Englewood Cliffs, NJ.

Monroe, K. B. (2003) *Pricing: Making Profitable Decisions*. McGraw-Hill, New York, NY.

Montgomery, A. L. (1997) Creating micro-marketing price strategies using supermarket scanner data. *Marketing Science*, 16, 315–337.

Nagle, T. T. (1987) *The Strategy and Tactics of Pricing*. Prentice Hall, Englewood Cliffs, NJ.

Stigler, G. (1987) *The Theory of Price*. Macmillan, New York, NY.

Swan, A. C. and Murphy, J. F. (1999) *Cases and Materials on the Regulation of International Business and Economic Relations*, 2nd ed. Mathew Bender, New York, NY.

Zeithaml, V. A. (1988) Consumer perceptions of price, quality, and value. *Journal of Marketing*, 52, 2–22.

Chapter 9

The reality of distribution faced by SMEs
A perspective from the UK

David Bamber

> **LEARNING OBJECTIVES**
>
> *After reading the chapter, you should be able to*
> - Understand the **place** component of the marketing mix;
> - Gain insights into strategic and logistic distribution functions
> - Review the main tasks of distribution
> - Understand some of the complexities of distribution
> - Analyse the interconnections distribution functions using the UK real ale market
> - Analyse the case of an intermediary acting as a wholesaler to SME retails outlets

INTRODUCTION

In this chapter we will look at the distribution channels, looking at the situation faced by SMEs, but focussing on the UK SME brewery trade and public houses (pubs) operated by sole traders. Attention will be paid to the close links between; the supply chain, the distribution channels, the production of the product, the raw materials and the requirements of the consumers. There are independent partners that make either products or services available for the consumer or, indeed, other businesses. There may also be intermediaries: people in between the producer and the consumer, so that there are different structures for distribution channels. The purpose of those channels is to add some value to the transaction processes and, indeed, not just the transaction process but the relationship processes between producer and, ultimately, the consumer. The gaps between suppliers, manufacturers and consumers are breached by the distribution channels. Using the distribution channels, the goods are made available to the consumer where and when they are needed. Those distribution channels add value to the marketing chain as they create space and time utility for businesses further down the chain. Clearly, the task of distribution is to add value in some way or other to the product, or service, so that there will be benefits for the producer, the consumer and intermediaries.

There are several tasks of distribution: promoting products: informing the market about new products; contacting, building up personal relationships; sorting goods for use in connection with each other and adapting these to the consumer's needs. However, another function of distribution is to store the products so that they become available 'just in time', as needed by the consumer. Additionally, there will be breaking down of the bulk so that the large quantities produced become manageable for the consumer and retailer. Then clearly, as already mentioned, there is a transportation task. Hence, there are several functions connected with distribution and the flow of product between the two partners. Some flows are *forward flows* and others are *backward flows* and importantly some other flows concern exchange of information and knowledge. Physical distribution concerns shipment of products to the customer. This is the place component of the marketing mix. There are many decisions to be made concerning distribution and these are likely to include decisions about the market coverage, channel distribution, warehousing, order processing, transportation and inventory management.

DISTRIBUTION OVERVIEW

The distribution function supports the marketing processes that focus on the fulfilment of customer demand. So that successful distribution strategies allow the customer to access the product conveniently and provide pre- and post- purchase support for the business. There are two facets to distribution: the *logistical* and the *strategic*. The logistical distribution is called 'supply chain management' and this function sustains the strategic function. The logistics provide the regular transfer of goods, information and capital between different levels in the supply chain. It is the operation function that is informed by marketing intelligence. Whereas, the strategic distribution function provides a competitive advantage to the business within the distribution network. So, decisions about the strategic distribution function concern who, what, where, when, and which business partners are to be involved in the fulfilment of customer demands. Generally, that will concern the selection of intermediaries between manufacturer and retailer and may also involve certain service functions.

There can be different types of intermediaries, between the producer and the consumer, including wholesalers, agents, retailers, franchisees, the internet, overseas distributors, or alternatively there may be direct marketing from the producer straight to the consumer.

The wholesalers may split up the product into manageable sized packs for resale by a retailer. The wholesalers generally purchase products, taking ownership and 'title' of those goods, from the manufacturers and resell to retailers. Wholesalers often store the products before selling onto the retailer. As a range of products may be available from one wholesaler, the wholesaler may assume some other marketing activities producing brochures and promoting certain products. The agent, however, would generally be used in an international setting where it would be difficult or expensive for the producer to contact consumers directly.

The agent 'on the ground' secures an order for the producer or service provider and takes a percentage commission, or a flat fee, and would not usually take 'title' of any goods. Often agents are used by training institutes in the UK to recruit international students. A problem arises when agents are difficult to control, as they could serve several providers, playing one against another and potentially having a stronger allegiance to a rival. Where the agents operate in state-of-the-art markets, they would be expensive to train but could provide local knowledge and insights.

Retailers stand face to face with the consumer and are placed to have a strong relationship with the consumer. The consumer entering the typical retail outlet will be offered several brands and a series of goods, many of which will have been previously promoted by the retailer. The product's final selling price will most likely be determined by the retailer. Some retailers may offer services to the consumer as well as goods, for example large retailers of electronic products offer credit facilities and repair service insurance. Incidentally, in 1856 Edward Clark, the business partner of Issac Singer (inventor of the Singer® Sewing machine) developed a system for instalment selling and time payment purchasing that become the model for hire-purchase agreements. This provided people with low incomes an opportunity to own an expensive product that had the potential to help them earn money, through sewing, for themselves (Singer, 2007). Many large famous retail brands started life as SMEs, one such example is Marks and Spencer (M&S) which was founded by Michael Marks in 1884, when he opened a penny bazaar stall on Leeds' Kirkgate market (M&S, 2019).

Internet technology may be used at any point in the distribution channel and provides a facility with low set up costs. This e-commerce uses systems such as shopping basket software and PAYPAL© to transfer money from purchaser to seller, even when they are separated geographically. The internet thus has the potential to reach a dispersed international market, providing a wide market with niche products. Isaac Singer (Singer, 2010) operated one of the first businesses that used a form of franchising, offering licenses to entrepreneurs to sell sewing machines across the United States of America and to train customers in their use. A franchise is a right granted, through a legal agreement, to an individual, or group, to offer another company's goods or services, usually at a certain location or in a geographical territory. This allows the franchisor to distribute products or services to a large marketplace. This benefits the individual franchisees who gain trust from the customers who are loyal to the established corporate image and brand. The franchisor is also likely to provide and support an up and running business model. The downside for the franchisee is that they are usually tied to buy certain products from the franchisor, and they have not only to pay a one off start-up fee but also pay regular ongoing royalties.

The distribution channel stretches from the producer of raw materials and the providers of utilities through to the consumer. A short supply channel may involve just the manufacturer selling directly to the consumer, whereas a long distribution channel may involve indirect selling from the manufacturer, the wholesaler, intermediary agents, the retailer as well as the consumer. The shortest indirect channel is from the manufacturer to retailer to consumer channel and this may be the manufacture's preferred consumer marketing channel as it benefits from the close relationship of the consumer to the retailer. The main distribution tasks, all of which contribute to building a good relationship with the consumer and from which competitive advantage can arise, are summarised in Table 9.1. Those distribution tasks are represented by the acronym RAINCAPP.

Table 9.1 Tasks of distribution

Task	Description
Risk avoidance	The wholesaler assumes the risk of holding the stock
Adjusting	The distributor adjusts the offering to match the customer needs. This may cover aspects such as sorting, assembling and packaging
Information gathering	Intelligent information is selected, accumulated and distributed throughout the distribution channel
Negotiation	Agreements on price and other offers are brokered
Communication	The communication networks between manufacturer, distributors and consumer are facilitated.
Acquisition	Capital is acquired to distribution channel costs
Promotion	Offerings are placed, promoted and distributed
Physical distribution	Goods are transported and stored

From the manufacturer's perspective, the main aim of the distribution strategy is to expose the product to the widest possible market. Hence, from the manufacturing SMEs viewpoint, with relatively limited resources, the distribution decisions will extend from intense distribution through as many retail outlets as possible through to locally focussed distribution through a limited number of niche outlets. The SME faces the daunting prospect of being just a small voice calling '*me-too!*' in the already overcrowded marketplace, where the big international companies dominate. So how can SMEs compete against such power? The SME must develop strong relationships with the customers at all levels of the supply chain, develop itself into a reliable brand and establish a credible reputation. Additionally, the distribution channel it selects will need to be supported by an efficient and effective infrastructure that can deliver products reliably.

A NICHE MARKET

Let us now think about modern times and the distribution of beer, in particular **real ale** – so the beer can be taken to the outlets, the public houses and the supermarkets and the off licences. How is the beer moved around? It is moved around in containers and there are different kinds of containers, such as the barrel, which may be made from metal or, traditionally, of wood. There are tin cans and there are bottles. So, the brewer needs these things to transport the beer and they need a mode of transport. Traditionally the beer barrels were transported from the brewery to the pubs using horse-drawn carts called 'drays', which have found much favour in local communities in the North of England and elsewhere, where the shire horses, or dray horses, have come back into favour and are displayed ceremonially pulling perhaps six or eight large barrels of beer. These have been used as a status symbol for the re-emerging economy that is dedicated to quality, traditional and authentic values.

In the UK right up to the 1970s, the industry became dominated by a few key players producing low quality products. There was a backlash to the poor quality and consumers demanded better quality and a greater variety of products. In the 1970s, beer was typically bland. The mass producers had become complacent in the marketplace and were content on abandoning traditional brewing methods that had been passed down through generations; those brewing businesses having been originally small, medium-sized, and often one-man businesses. Now they had abandoned the quality that had been so insisted on by the original founders. The backlash came from a small organisation called the Campaign for Real Ale (CAMRA). CAMRA (2019) is a UK based consumer campaigning group that now has over 100,000 members. Unfortunately, the mass market is still served by multi-national companies producing low priced offerings for beer typically labelled as 'Smooth Bitter'. It is nitro-keg beer that has been chilled to ease the filtering off of any lingering yeast, making the beer sterile, before being pasteurised to enable chemical stability before being pumped up with nitrogen and offered to the customer.

BREWERY LOCATION

A major concern about location has to do with the transportation problem. Typically the objective is to minimise transportation costs. Here, the problem is where to locate a brewery and its various depots. Koksalan et al. (1995) considered the problem of selecting the best location for a new fourth brewery from alternative locations, for a large beer company in Turkey. Koksalan et al. (1995) noted that the main transportation costs arise when shipping malt from the two malt factories to the breweries and when shipping beer from the breweries to

300 different customer zones. Clearly, SMEs cannot afford the costs of employing high powered mathematicians to solve their day to day problems, as the larger Turkish brewer had, but they have similar location problems. One such problem was faced by Richard Baker (Doggart, 2009). Richard had worked in the Falklands on tourism and transport problems, but then decided to set up a brewery and first considered setting up on East Falkland. The problem was that the water quality was not right for the brewing process and the heavy cost of importation of raw materials would burden the potential brewery too much. On return to the UK, he set up in a partnership and formed the 'Bowland Brewery'. The location decision was resolved, and the brewery would be located in the Forest of Bowland, which is designated as an 'Area of Outstanding Natural Beauty' in rural Lancashire (Bowland, 2019). The location was chosen not only for the excellent availability of high quality water but also because of the large number of pubs in the area that are *free houses* and able to sell any type of beer they want, plus the landlords of those pubs have the skills required to keep the beer in the tip top condition that the consumer and producer demands. Hence, 90% of the Bowland Brewery production is retailed within a 30-mile radius of the brewery, which keeps transportation costs to a minimum.

THE RETAIL SECTOR

The retailer in this sector may be in competition with the wholesaler. The wholesaler may collect together different varieties of beer from different brewers – the manufacturers – and offer these to the retailers: a one-stop shop. Indeed, the retailers in this case may well be offered a great variety of beers. However, the wholesaler perhaps has not got the enthusiasm to seek out the small micro-brewers that may be scattered around the country. Therefore, the retailer may feel disenfranchised when using the wholesaler in not getting the bespoke new beer variety that the retailer and, indeed, his consumers are demanding. So if the retailer were to go to the wholesaler, although a variety of ales would be on offer, these are unlikely to be the new varieties. In this case, the retailer would necessarily need to approach the manufacturers in the micro-breweries themselves. A classic text on wholesaling fruit and vegetables is presented by Beckman and Engle (1951).

Alternatively, the retailer might decide from the very start that they will use their network of intelligence and, indeed, consumers because in this sector the boundary between consumer, retailer and manufacturer is often blurred. Kent and Omar (2003) provide a strategic and operational overview of retailing across different sectors. The retailer is likely to be a consumer and the manufacturer is also likely to be a consumer and maybe, as is seen in the Brewpubs, the manufacturer could be also a retailer. They have, in the micro-brewery, done away with the vertical competition and combined the processes of manufacture and distribution and retail into the one outlet. The retailer may go straight to the brewer and purchase those bespoke products that their consumers are demanding. In this case, they may become the consumer and travel around, stay overnight and collect three or four different barrels of beer from different producers, perhaps in one geographic area at a time. Supermarkets, such as E. H. Booth in the North of England, in recent years have been offering a wide variety of real ales in bottles. They offer over 200 bottled types, with 55 brewed locally in Lancashire, Yorkshire, Cheshire, and Cumbria (Booths, 2019) Perhaps; this is because they saw the lucrative business of the small SME off licence that was offering bespoke beers in bottles to the real ale drinker. The supermarket realised its potential and, with the initiative of offering the variety of real ales, gained an increase in its market share. Other supermarkets have followed suit, such as Morrison's and Sainsbury's. Now they too, offer real ale, often from local producers, from micro-breweries as well as macro and regional breweries.

THE WHOLESALER

One of the largest wholesalers of beer related products in the UK is 'H.B. Clark & Co. (Successors) Ltd.' Clark (2019). Clark & Co., not an SME, has a series of ten depots in the north of England, stretching from Stockport to Newcastle. They provide products and services for the beer trade, including beer festivals, tithed pubs, and free houses. Their promotional material states that they are a one stop shop: one call, one order, one invoice and one delivery. They have their own brewery but also take supplies of real ale from over 40 other breweries, many of which are SMEs. Typically, Clarks offer promotional discounts to 'bulk buyers': if several cases of one product are purchased then one case of another product could be free. Other supplies are on special offer. One group of the company, 'Fam draught minerals', offers a broad range of flavours of draught minerals through the provision of electric pumps and nozzle equipment to the bar top, saving the retailer time and effort in stocking and re-stocking fridges with bottles of Coke® and Lemonade. They also provide year-round technical service for the equipment. As far as wine products are concerned, they also offer specialist advice from wine experts, provide wine menus and glasses. They offer bar top distribution points, such as the 'Jagermeister Machine' (see Jagermeister, 2019) that dispenses the cooled herbal liqueur and the Guinness® Surger® that allows the lower volume vendor to stock and provide the customer with cans of Irish stout manufactured by Guinness, rather than maintain large volume of cask stout which would run the risk of spoiling if sales were not brisk enough. The Surger® provides the consumer with the stout with its traditional creamy head and has low maintenance costs. Hence, the wholesaler not only imports and sources bespoke branded products, distributes them to its depots, it also provides back-up services, promotional materials and specialist bar top point of sales equipment for SMEs and franchised retail outlets.

HORIZONTAL COMPETITION

Let us consider some kinds of horizontal competition within this sector of the beer trade. There are several outlets at the retail level. There is the supermarket. There are the off licences, specifically dedicated to selling mainly alcoholic products – beers, wines, and spirits – as their main products. There are the pubs; as we have seen there are the tied pubs, the tenanted, and the managed pubs. There are various sports, social and politically affiliated clubs. Then there are the breweries themselves and the micro-breweries. Additionally, it is interesting to note that there are innovative solutions in the retail sector concerning beer retailing. In Southport, the Inn Beershop is run by Peter Bardsley, who has been granted a special licence to retail not just beer but also use the retail shop as a cafe. Perhaps in this sector the laws of competition are broken and superseded by laws of cooperation and collaboration because Peter Bardsley's brother, Paul, runs the Southport Brewery (2019) and his other brother, John, runs Lancashire Heroes, an off licence in the same town, each is operating in a different way. Lancashire Heroes is a drink-in or take-out specialist ale shop that has over 300 different bottled beers, so the consumers' demands for variety and quality are satisfied (Siddle, 2019).

The micro-breweries themselves also, to some extent, work in cooperation. One micro-brewery might swap barrels with another micro-brewery so that when the retailer comes to collect beer, they may also offer their guest beer from the other micro-brewery that they have either a formal or informal agreement with, thereby giving the retailer increased choice. There is another type of retail outlet in this sector and it is the world-renowned beer festival. Typically, in the UK now each town will have at least one beer festival, if not two or three. They may be run by charities or the local branch of CAMRA. They may be run by individuals for profit or not for profit. A famous beer festival is held in the vaults of Liverpool Anglican Cathedral. Again this is a marketplace and a showcase for the brewers. The consumers benefit by having a wide range of beers available in one location.

SME RELATIONSHIPS WITH LARGER BREWERIES

It is interesting to note that even the largest breweries and the regional breweries probably started as SME family businesses, the Guinness business in the 1700s, for example was so heavily dependent on the building of new canals in Ireland to transport the barrels of beer. Many family businesses that took off were often then passed through the generations as they expanded. So like many micro-breweries that survived the first few years of business, they may expand from being a one person business to become family businesses before becoming even larger. Such was the history of Charles Hall, who was born in 1751 and was a farmer's son. In those days many of the farmers brewed beer for the farm workers and Charles Hall founded his own brewery in 1777. Maybe it was from the use of his entrepreneurial skills, learnt in the farm business from his father, which he was able to quickly to build up his own brewery business. Then, early in the business, he seized upon an opportunity to produce beer for the army and gained a contract to supply ale to the army camped near the coast of Weymouth during the Napoleonic Wars. Soon, George Woodhouse became his business partner, and, indeed, duly married Charles's granddaughter. The business took off from there and produced one of the traditional beers of England, based in the South West of England: Badger Ale. Badger Ale is now brewed by Hall and Woodhouse Limited, who have been producing real ale since the foundation by Charles Hall in 1777. Although they are now a fairly large regional brewer the brewing knowledge has been passed down through the generations of the Woodhouse family, with the top-quality ingredients always including Dorset spring water. Now Hall and Woodhouse have an estate of over 260 tenanted and managed pubs, mainly scattered along the south coast of England, in Devon and Kent. They have 180 tenanted pubs and 60 managed pubs with 1,181 employees, the size of which puts it outside the scope of the SME category, but they are intimately connected with those lone traders, small businesses who are tied to them through the agreements of the tenancy (Hall and Woodhouse, 2019).

CONTRACTUAL COMPLICATIONS

The situation, however, in the pub trade is not as simple as that presented in many textbooks, which often present the classical picture for large businesses. As with most SMEs who find themselves in a position of intense rivalry, there is the additional problem that may arise in the pub trade in the UK. That is that the pub might be actually owned by the brewery and the publican may just rent the pub from the brewery. Indeed, the publican is often a sole trader who is quite frequently in a business partnership with a personal partner. In this case, the publican, as a sole trader, has a tenancy agreement with the brewery. The situation may be a little less clear if the brewery employs a manager to run the pub for the brewery, and this means that the pub is sometimes called a 'managed house'. In that case, it may be that the brewery itself is an SME and the manager is an employee of that SME. Sometimes, when the contract tied between the self-employed publican and the brewery, the publican finances the pub with loans from the brewers themselves. However, in these cases where the publican rents the pub from the brewery, where the manager is paid by the brewery and where a financial agreement is made between the brewer and the publican, all of these lead to the situation where the brewer demands, as part of the contractual agreement, that the landlord actually purchases beer directly from them. The landlord is legally tied to purchase only from them and not from competitors. Such a contractual agreement gives the advantage to the brewer, so that the brewer receives a consistent demand for its products (Diallo, 2019). However, there may be problems for the consumer and, indeed, for the landlords themselves. In one particular region there may be a brewery which owns a majority of pubs in that area, so that it is very difficult within that small geographical area for the consumer to find any other products. This is, in CAMRA's view, a form of monopoly, or cartel, which is illegal in the UK. There is no competition as such from different breweries because each tied pub is tied in to buying product from that one particular brewer or from the holding company's beer list. Clearly, across the country there will be different breweries, but for the local person there will be no competition, or a risk of poor competition. Indeed, in some contractual agreements between landlord and brewery, the brewery may tie in the supply other things, such as soft drinks and spirits, and quite often these may be offered at inflated prices (Williams, 2009).

THREATS TO THE FREE ECONOMY

In contrast to the tied situation, the alternative situation does exist, but it is a rarer case in the UK, where the pub is a free house: free to purchase products from wherever it chooses. That means that it is not tied to any one brewery and it is free to purchase its product wherever it wants. So, this kind of pub, the free house, can then purchase different kinds of beer from different breweries. From 1989 to 2003, there was partial freedom for tied pubs when tied pubs were legally permitted to stock at least one extra beer from another brewery. This gave the consumers greater choice. The extra beer was often called the guest beer. However, that law was repealed in 2003. This led to certain representations being made by the consumer group CAMRA and others for the Office of Fair Trading to investigate the potential monopoly, at least at the regional level if not at the national level, caused by tying pubs into supply contracts with regional or national breweries.

DIFFICULTIES CAUSED BY WAREHOUSING HOPS AND RISING OIL PRICES

Warehousing itself has problems. One problem could be because a concentration of flammable product is stored in one location. Sure, the advantage to the purchaser would be a variety of products available at one location and a constant stream of products. However, when disaster hits, it hits the SME hard. Shortages in supply cause the price rises which must be passed on to the customer by the SME; that is, if supply can be guaranteed. It will be the larger firms that take up the remaining supply because they have the flexibility and the excess capital to absorb the price rises, so the SME is constantly under pressure from all sides; not only supply but also from economic demands.

An indication of the volatility of the sector is given by the number of openings and closures: from 1990 to 2009, 1108 breweries opened in the UK and 542 breweries closed. That means that over that period 566 new breweries were opened and remained open. It is particularly interesting to note that in one-year 1999 over 90 breweries had closed. Most of all those breweries are, or were, micro-breweries, employing a very small number of people, perhaps less than five. There were a small number of closures due to takeovers by larger breweries. The number of openings indicates the dynamic nature of business activity in the

THE REALITY OF DISTRIBUTION FACED BY SMEs

SME sector. It is a volatile business environment, but for 566 UK micro-brewery businesses in 2009, success had been continuing (see Quaffle, 2019 for upto date figures).

TECHNOLOGY, SMES, AND THE 21ST CENTURY

Figure 9.1 presents an overview of real ale distribution in SMEs and non-SMEs in the UK. There are a plethora of SMEs operating in different ways and at different levels of the distribution supply chain. Since 2005, micro-pubs and micro-breweries have seized the opportunity to work with smaller capacities but with much lower overheads than medium sized businesses. Most SME retail outlets have either a formally or informally appointed social media manager who posts daily updates on Facebook© and other social media platforms. Some remain reluctant to adopt mobile phone payment systems and even contactless card systems due to their associated perceived costs; often failing to factor in the speed of payment, increased speed of service and associated increase in customer traffic flow. Table booking systems are used in many SME bar and food outlets: open source software is available at OpenTable (2019). Such software allows Prevent diners from making multiple reservations for the same time, allocates times and tables to customers, remind diners about upcoming reservations, minimise and mitigate against no shows, and manage customer expectations by making diners aware of what a no-show means. Technology can empower the SME customer by presenting them with up to date customer specific information. For example, Preston Real Ale Tickers (PRAT) use a Facebook© group platform to send each other up to the minute information of offers available at specific venues. Britain's best pubs can be 'Tapped Into' using CAMRAs GBAPP (2019) UK's *Best-Selling Beer & Pub Guide* that is available as an app via Google-Play and The APP Store. Information is compiled and updated by users all over the UK. Similarly, the "Real Ale Finder" (2019) has two apps with one purpose, to connect the people who love real ale, craft ale, and real cider to their favourite pint wherever they are and an inventory management, tools and reports app for pubs that pushes up to date information notifications to real ale drinkers. There have been advances in 'hardware' as well as 'software' for example SIBA (2019) has reported that 'some of the major challenges for brewers are to make safe quality beer that maintains consumer confidence, while meeting retailer expectations and minimising both costs and wastage. This has been achieved in many microbreweries by using a simple rapid test, to determine the hygienic quality of their production equipment and working surface areas'. SIBA (2019) cites Langham Brewery as being a successful small independent steam-powered microbrewery near Midhurst and Petworth in the South Downs National Park. Stating that the brewery's success producing quality and consistent beer is due to maintaining high sanitation processes and keeping the operations spic and span. The brewery uses the SystemSURE Plus products from Hygiena International (2019) for the quick and accurate hygiene testing of surface areas.

QUESTION

1. Find out how JDWetherspoon (2019), a company with 900 pubs, uses its app for order placement and table service. Note the extra costs and benefits for the customer and for the business in using the a Indicate how such an app (or even a low-tech solution like a 'bell push system') may be used by an SME.

155

CONCLUSION

The variety of raw materials, brewers (manufacturers), distributors, retailers, and consumers are indicated in Figure 9.1. The intricate flow of transactions and product between each could only be worked out through detailed business case analysis, as there are not one or

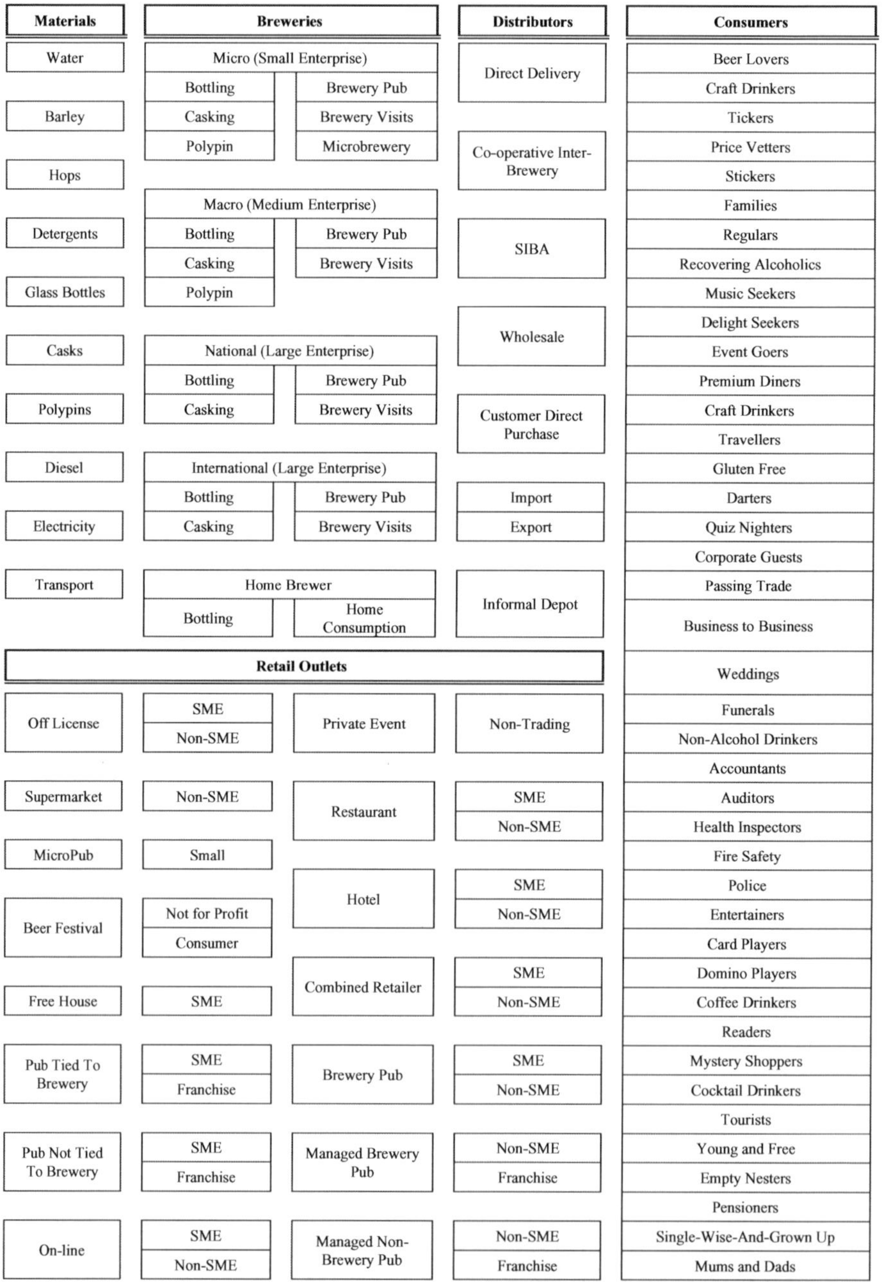

Materials	Breweries		Distributors	Consumers
Water	Micro (Small Enterprise)		Direct Delivery	Beer Lovers
	Bottling	Brewery Pub		Craft Drinkers
Barley	Casking	Brewery Visits		Tickers
	Polypin	Microbrewery	Co-operative Inter-Brewery	Price Vetters
Hops				Stickers
	Macro (Medium Enterprise)			Families
Detergents	Bottling	Brewery Pub	SIBA	Regulars
	Casking	Brewery Visits		Recovering Alcoholics
Glass Bottles	Polypin			Music Seekers
			Wholesale	Delight Seekers
Casks	National (Large Enterprise)			Event Goers
	Bottling	Brewery Pub		Premium Diners
Polypins	Casking	Brewery Visits	Customer Direct Purchase	Craft Drinkers
				Travellers
Diesel	International (Large Enterprise)			Gluten Free
	Bottling	Brewery Pub	Import	Darters
Electricity	Casking	Brewery Visits	Export	Quiz Nighters
				Corporate Guests
Transport	Home Brewer		Informal Depot	Passing Trade
	Bottling	Home Consumption		Business to Business
	Retail Outlets			Weddings
Off License	SME	Private Event	Non-Trading	Funerals
	Non-SME			Non-Alcohol Drinkers
				Accountants
Supermarket	Non-SME	Restaurant	SME	Auditors
			Non-SME	Health Inspectors
MicroPub	Small			Fire Safety
		Hotel	SME	Police
Beer Festival	Not for Profit		Non-SME	Entertainers
	Consumer			Card Players
		Combined Retailer	SME	Domino Players
Free House	SME		Non-SME	Coffee Drinkers
				Readers
Pub Tied To Brewery	SME	Brewery Pub	SME	Mystery Shoppers
	Franchise		Non-SME	Cocktail Drinkers
				Tourists
Pub Not Tied To Brewery	SME	Managed Brewery Pub	Non-SME	Young and Free
	Franchise		Franchise	Empty Nesters
				Pensioners
On-line	SME	Managed Non-Brewery Pub	Non-SME	Single-Wise-And-Grown Up
	Non-SME		Franchise	Mums and Dads

Figure 9.1 An overview of real ale distribution in SMEs and non-SMEs in the UK

even a few standard business models in this marketplace. Here, the exchange interactions between producers and retailers are assisted by distribution channels. The channels create time and space for the partners. The channels may also provide additional services that add value to the interactions. The cost for the SMEs of assuming distribution themselves would be prohibitive if it were not for the collaboration from potential rivals. The real ale trade relies on collaboration between brewers, and that to craft competition, rather than pure economic competition, so that high product quality standards are maintained, as is the product variety that is demanded by the consumer, who are quality vetters and new product seekers in this sector. The distribution is intimately connected with the supply of raw materials and is particularly susceptible to supply and price fluctuations. Systems such as the DDS can help ensure a constant demand for products from many small brewers and can provide large franchise chains with an endless supply of variety of products. Much trade, particularly between the micro-brewery and the free houses run by sole traders relies on strong interpersonal relationships and a knowledgeable support community. The franchise system that ties sole traders, as publicans, to large holding companies or breweries, can be beneficial to both stakeholders, but the holding company may extract a high price for its expertise and tied products and that could effectively lead to brewery owned monopolies at the local level. The consumer is far from being a silent partner in these transactions and not only demands quality products but also demands business sustainability based on traditional values and authentic production processes.

SUMMARY OF KEY POINTS

- Distribution is "Place" in the Marketing Mix;
- Distribution concerns placing the offer with the consumer through intermediaries;
- There are two entwined aspects to distribution: logistics and strategy;
- There are complexities connected with distribution;
- The real ale marketplace in the UK is driven by SMEs and the consumers demands for authentic quality products and variety;
- The niche SME sector is volatile;
- SMEs may be inexplicably tied in business to larger companies.

Innovations in distribution are being driven by SMEs

CHAPTER REVIEW QUESTIONS

1. Look up the lease agreements for Punch, Admiral, and Enterprise (now trading as 'Ei Group plc') on each company's website. Compare and contrast the leases and evaluate which might offer the best deal for (1) the leaser and (2) microbreweries.

2. Investigate how family brewery businesses, originally a small business, have grown into a larger business and what key events, particularly in terms of distribution, there were in the histories of those businesses. Resource websites: www.robinsons brewery.com/, www.Guinness.com and www.moorhouses.co.uk.

3. Review standard texts on distribution and, considering the perspectives of different stakeholders, compare and contrast the real ale business with another sector of your choice.

CASE STUDY: SOCIETY OF INDEPENDENT BREWERS ASSOCIATION (SIBA, 2019)

The Direct Delivery System (DDS) was launched in December 2003 by the Society of Independent Brewers Association (SIBA) of with the explicit aim of improving market access for the participating breweries via the estates of major pub companies. Almost 600 micro-breweries active in the British marketplaces, and these small brewers have limited resources with tight economic considerations that demands a short supply line that is as simple to operate. Generally, cask beer is unique to pubs and usually is consumed at the pub. Hence, the cask ale enthusiasts, who are not all members of CAMRA, place themselves as market leaders that continually drive quality improvement, consumer and producer responsibility along with authentic cultural heritage. More recently according to Honestbrew (2019) 'Craft Beer is very much carrying the torch of CAMRA, taking the fight to big beer, out to remove blindfolds for the world to see that a whole lot of cheap guff is being brewed. It differs from Real Ale as there are fewer restrictions when it comes to brewing, allowing for a far greater amount of experimentation and innovation in terms of styles and flavours. Craft Beer emphasises creativity and unique tastes over how much yeast lies in the bottom of the bottle or cask'. Craft beer drinkers maybe considered as a niche segment that caters for the younger beer drinkers that favour experimentation and creativity within a niche market that caters for traditionally made beers. Besides working with free houses, the DDS has a portfolio of four substantial non-brewery owned pub chains: Punch Taverns (Punch, 2019), Admiral Inns (Admiral Inns, 2019), Enterprise Inns Plc. (Enterprise Inns, 2019), and The Orchid Group. Three of the four companies operated tied partnerships with self-employed leases. The Orchid Group is a large company that employs managers to run its business outlets is one of 18 pub and restaurant chains, with over 1700 retail outlets, owned by Mitchells and Butlers (2019). Punch (2019) have a leased estate of 6,841 pubs. In those pubs the company has an agreement with the landlord who operates their own self-employed retail business, as an SME, but leases the pub from the company and agrees to operate the pub in certain ways. Punch Partnerships offers lease agreements with the business partners. The company does not directly manage these pubs but provides detailed support as part of the lease agreement, which is usually ten years long, see the Punch (2019) website for the latest business updates. The SME partner usually pays an index linked rent, which is periodically reviewed and based on a share of the pub profits. Clearly, this is a tied agreement as the SME partner is required to buy products; including all beers, cider and lagers, from the company but in some agreements with the exception of one guest ale. There is also a section in the agreement that covers the management of gambling machines and quiz machines in the pubs. Punch Taverns (2019) state that 'the agreements provide a low-cost entry into running a pub business with professional support'. So that assistance is provided by the company for the business processes such as finance, purchasing, human resource management, order taking and credit management, with a business relationship manager and customer administration support. Additional resources are provided to asset and personnel development. Admiral Taverns was formed in 2003, and in 2010 boasted an estate of over 2,000 public houses, the majority of which are located

THE REALITY OF DISTRIBUTION FACED BY SMEs

across the UK in city centres and in rural locations. Each pub we let is individual, just like our pub landlords, and we aim to make them focal points of their community. The company encourages the licensees to 'run the business their way', whilst still providing the much-needed operational support. Although the group was formed in 2006, it has grown to become the sixth largest managed pub company and restaurant company in the UK. In 2010, they had 6500 pub employees in the UK, which clearly places the business outside the SME designation. They have 8,590 outlets, restaurants and pubs outlets and the company is reportedly the 'best unbranded franchise in the world'. Eighteen percent of the stock comprises restaurants, 38% are pubs that serve bar meals, 25% are pubs that serve light snacks, and 19% are pubs without catering facilities. However, with the activation in 2005 of the Licensing Act (2003), setting up a small independent public house was relatively straightforward and micropubs have burgeoned in recent years in the UK, and the Micropub Association (2019) had 349 micropub members listed. A micropub, according to the Micropub Association (2019) is 'a small freehouse which listens to its customers, mainly serves cask ales, promotes conversation, shuns all forms of electronic entertainment and dabbles in traditional pub snacks', noting, 'there may be differences between the pubs; they may or may not have a bar, they might serve beer straight from the cask or through hand pumps. They share a philosophy: a simple pub with the focus on cask beer and conversation for entertainment, with the basic premise of KIS, KIS – Keep It Small, Keep It Simple'.

Questions

1. Find out how the DDS operates and identify the services that it provides for (1) free houses and (2) large pub chains.
2. What advantages do small independent breweries and micro-pubs gain by subscribing to the DDS?
3. Identify and undertake a review of one UK microbrewery using SIBA in its distribution strategy. Complete a 'Strengths Weaknesses Opportunities Threats' (SWOT) analysis for product distribution from the microbrewery.
4. There are other models of distribution, such as those organised by breweries themselves in collaboration with numerous other breweries. What advantages would such distribution systems have for (1) micro-pubs, (2) larger pubs, and (3) breweries compared with the SIBA model.

LET'S REASON TOGETHER

Imagine your team is going back in time to visit a pub (different teams should choose a different time: five years ago, ten years ago, 50 years ago, or 100 years ago). Use the resource websites: www.robinsonsbrewery.com/, www.Guinness.com and www.moorhouses.co.uk and resources from The Pub History Society (2019).

1. Explain what technology was used in your team's time and compare that to today's technology.
2. Explain what games were played in the pub in your team's time and compare that to today's games.

3. Explain what the drinking glasses looked like in the pub in your team's time and compare them to today's drinking glass, making special reference to any branding.

   Now, imagine your team is going forward in time to visit a new pub in that time zone (different teams should choose a different time: five years from now, 10 years from now, 50 years from now, or 100 years from now).

4. Imagine what technology may be used in the distribution process in your team's time and compare that to today's technology. *Hint:* look at 'future technology forecasts'. *Caution:* Do not take things for granted as one pub chain recently banned the use of mobile phones (Samuel Smiths, 2019).

REFERENCES

Admiral Taverns (2019) Admiral Taverns. www.admiraltaverns.co.uk (Accessed on 1 March 2019).

Associated Press (2006) Fire destroys Yakima hop warehouse, 3rd October 2006. www.spokesmanreview.com (Accessed on 1 March 2019).

Avis, A. (1995) *The Brewer's Tale: History of Ale in Yorkshire*. Radcliffe Press, London.

Beckman, T. N. and Engle, N. H. (1951) *Wholesaling: Principles and Practice*. Roland Press, New York.

Booths (2019) Booths super market. www.booths.co.uk/food-and-drink/ (Accessed on 1 March 2019).

Bowland (2019) Bowland Brewery. www.bowlandbrewery.com/ (Accessed on 1 March 2019).

CAMRA (2019) Campaign for real ale. www.camra.org.uk (Accessed on 1 March 2019).

CAMRAs GBAPP (2019) CAMRA real ale finder. Available at: https://gbgacamra.org.uk/ (Accessed on 1 March 2019).

Clark (2019) H.B. clark group of companies. www.hbclark.co.uk (Accessed on 1 March 2019).

Cyclops (2019) Cyclops©Beer. Available at: https://cyclopsbeer.co.uk (Accessed 1 March 2019).

Diallo, U. (2019) Pub companies 'Pubcos' and tied tenants. *FSB Policy Paper*, Federation of Small Businesses, London. www.fsb.org.uk (Accessed on 1 March 2019).

Doggart, A. (2009) The beauty of Bowland. *Fylde Ale*, Winter 2009, Issue 71, 6–7.

Enterprise Inns (2019) Enterprise inns. www.eipublicanpartnerships.com/ (Accessed on 1st March 2019).

Evans, J. (2004) *The Book of Beer Knowledge*. CAMARA, St Albans.

Hall and Woodhouse (2019) The hall and woodhouse business. www.hall-woodhouse.co.uk (Accessed on 1 March 2019).

Honestbrew (2019) Craft beer. Available at: https://honestbrew.co.uk/beer-bible/craft-beer-vs-real-ale/ (Accessed on 1 March 2019).

Hornsey, I. S. (1999) *Brewing*. Royal Society of Chemistry, Cambridge.

Hornsey, I. S. (2003) *A History of Beer and Brewing*. Royal Society of Chemistry, Cambridge.

Hygiena International (2019) SystemSURE Plus. www.hygiena.com/ (Accessed on 1 March 2019).

Jagermeister (2019) The herbal liqueur. www.Jagermeister.com (Accessed on 1 March 2019).

James, M. (2010) Beer ticking, personal communication from Michael James, real ale drinker.

JDWetherspoon (2019) www.jdwetherspoon.com/ (Accessed on 1st March 2019).

Jennings, P. (2007) *The Local: A History of the English Pub*. The History Press Ltd, Stroud.

Kent, T. and Omar, O. (2003) *Retailing by Tony Kent and Ogenyi Omar*. Palgrave Macmillan, New York.

Kirkstile (2019) The Kirkstile Inn. www.kirkstile.com (Accessed on 1 March 2019).

Koksalan, M., Haldun, S. and Kirca, O. (1995) A location-distribution application for a beer company. *European Journal of Operational Research*, 80(1), 16–24.

Koroneos, C., Roumbas, G., Gabari, Z., Papagiannidou, E. and Moussiopoulos, N. (2005) Life cycle assessment of beer production in Greece. *Journal of Cleaner Production*, 13(4), 433–439.

M&S (2019) Marks and Spencer Ltd. corporate.marksandspencer.com/ (Accessed on 1 March 2019).

McVicar, J. (2004) *New Book of Herbs*. Dorling Kindersley, London.

Micropub Association (2019) The MicroPub and MircoBrewery Association. www.micropubassociation.co.uk/ (Accessed on 1 March 2019).

Mitchells and Butlers (2019) Mitchells and Butlers. www.mbplc.com/ (Accessed on 1 March 2019).

160

THE REALITY OF DISTRIBUTION FACED BY SMEs

Oil Prices (2019) World oil prices. www.oilnergy.com (Accessed on 1 March 2019).

Okells (2019) Okells Brewery. www.okells.co.uk (Accessed on 1 March 2019).

OpenTable (2019) Booking System. Available at: https://restaurant.opentable.co.uk/ (Accessed on 1st March 2019).

OPSI (2002) The enterprise act, 2002. www.opsi.gov.uk (Accessed on 1 March 2019).

Parker, P. M. (2006) *The World Market for Iron or Steel Tanks, Casks, Drums, Cans, and Similar Containers with Capacity of Less Than 300 Litres: A 2007 Global Trade Perspective.* ICON Group International Inc., San Diego.

Parking, P. (2010) Beerticking the video. www.beertickersfilm.com (Accessed on 1 March 2019).

The Pub History Society (2019) www.pubhistorysociety.co.uk/index.html (Accessed on 1 March 2019).

Punch (2019) Punch Taverns. www.punchtaverns.com/ (Accessed on 1 March 2019).

Quaffle (2019) Breweries opening and closing. www.quaffale.org.uk (Accessed on 1 March 2019).

Real Ale Finder (2019) www.realalefinder.com/ (Accessed on 1 March 2019).

Samuel Smiths (2019) No more mobile phones. www.dailymail.co.uk/news/article-6867347/Pub-chain-Samuel-Smiths-BANS-drinkers-using-mobile-phones.html (Accessed on 1 March 2019).

SIBA (2019) Society of independent brewers. www.siba.co.uk (Accessed on 1 March 2019).

Siddle, J. (2019) Inn beer shop. *Southport Visiter.* www.southportvisiter.co.uk (Accessed on 1 March 2019).

Singer (2007) The history of the Singer® Sewing Machine. www.singer.com (Accessed on 1 March 2019).

Singer (2010) The history of the Singer® Sewing Machine. Available at: https://protect-eu.mimecast.com/s/5e7sCQ1ppFKNRDSxzUXn?domain=singer.com (Accessed on 17 December 2019).

Southport Brewery (2019) Southport Brewery. www.southportbrewery.co.uk (Accessed on 1 March 2019).

Sumner, J. (2005) Powering the porter brewery. *Endeavour*, 29(2), 72–77.

Warkentin, M., Bapna, R. and Sugumaran, V. (2001) E-knowledge networks for inter-organizational collaborative e-business. *Logistics Information Management*, 14(1–2), 149–163.

William, S. (2009) Is the pub 'tie' killing our locals? *Norwich Evening News*, 24. www.eveningnews24.co.uk (Accessed on 1 March 2019).

Zerodegrees (2019) A microbrewery. www.zerodegrees.co.uk (Accessed on 1 March 2019).

Chapter 10

Marketing communications for the SME

Teck-Yong Eng and Graham Spickett-Jones

LEARNING OBJECTIVES

After reading the chapter, you should be able to
- Understand differences in approach to marketing communications between large organisations and SME;
- Recognise the stages in a promotional campaigns for SMEs in the wider context of marketing communication planning;
- Identify the main marketing communications tools used by typical SMEs;
- Be able to consider the wider context of human communication in relation to networks of relationships.

INTRODUCTION

Why do we need to study marketing communication for SME?

The task of marketing communication is to plan and apply marketing communications tools like advertising, sales promotion, personal selling, and public relations. Marketing communication can cover practice across a wide range of marketing contexts, from large companies and political movements to small companies and individual traders. In the context of Small and Medium-Sized Enterprises (SMEs), marketing communication deserves to be examined separately. Unlike large organisations, few SMEs have a dedicated in-house marketing communication specialist or the resources to outsource role to specialist support agencies that deal with marketing communications like advertising, public relations and media buying. SMEs use marketing communication in ways more specific to their sector than to large organisations. This chapter examines the role of marketing communication for typical SMEs including the communication tools, the communications mix and the strategic perspective of a network approach to developing marketing communication strategy.

Definitions and terms of marketing communication concepts

Marketing communications (plural) deals with the methods and range of communications by which marketers may communicate, like television advertising or public relations. *Marketing communication* (singular) is a more encompassing and broader functional role

MARKETING COMMUNICATIONS FOR THE SME

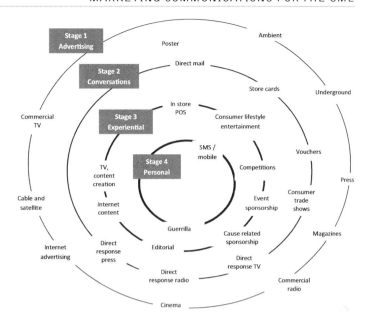

Figure 10.1
Typical campaign map for an integrated marketing communications launch campaign

Adapted from the launch of 118118, a presentation by agencies Naked, WCRS and Huge to D&AD's Xchange, 2004 (London School of Fashion, 1 September 2004)

that relates to the maintenance of social structure and associated relationships (van Riel, 1995). Both large and small companies use communications tools but larger organisations are more likely to focus on building the relationship customers have with a brand while SMEs are more likely to focus on driving sales leads and providing access to product information.

Large companies are also more likely to coordinate a range of communications tools to manage their brands and try to build customer relationships over time. This can be illustrated by the typical launch campaign for a major new brand, see Figure 10.1, when a campaign may move customers through campaign stages towards a deeper relationship:

- Stage 1: Advertising, to build awareness with media messages;
- Stage 2: Conversations, using direct channels of communication to capture data and build interest through involvement;
- Stage 3: Experiential, using opportunities for target customers to encounter brand information as part of their normal life;
- Stage 4: Personal, encourage customers to take ownership of a brand and personalising the relationship.

This is quite different from the typical way marketing communication is employed by SMEs. While there will be exceptions across a sector as broad as SMEs, taken as a whole marketing communications tools used by SMEs tend to have a coherent character relatively distinct from the communications mix favoured by large firms. SMEs tend to use the principle marketing communications tools (Fill, 2005) in specific ways (Spickett-Jones and Eng, 2006):

- **personal selling** has a priority;
- **PR** is mainly synonymous with publicity;
- **sales promotion** has limited explicit use reflecting that negotiated and incentive based pricing is regarded less as a promotional tool than as a way of establishing trading terms;

- **advertising:** there is a low emphasis on display advertising which reflects a perception of its limited usefulness;
- **direct marketing** is largely syndicated catalogues, mail-shots and blanket email.

Looking for patterns in the uses of marketing communications tools by SMEs, research (Spickett-Jones and Eng, 2006) suggests many SMEs focus on providing sales leads, establishing sales, or maintaining existing relationships. When sponsorship is used by SMEs often it may have no clear relationships with the equity or public standing of an SME, or any clear association with its products. Testimonials and writing articles for trade magazines are used by some SMEs to help build profile and credence in the marketplace, but these are rare examples of any attempt to enhance the market perceptions and public standing of an SME by using more widely seen marketing communications activity.

Marketing communication agencies specialise in developing creative ideas and marketing communication campaigns. Large companies frequently outsource much of their marketing communications activity to professional communication service agencies which are often SMEs. While SMEs specialising in marketing communications may provide large clients with advice over marketing communication strategy, they also tend to employ visible communication services for their own business in limited ways, classified advertising, and PR (Dyer and Ross, 2003).

Characteristics of SME marketing communication

Staff in an SME may see the role of marketing communication from a different vantage point compared to a management team working for a large organisation. For example, a large organisation may be concerned with brand equity while an SME may be concerned with the personal relationships of their most valuable customers. A multinational organisation may seek to manage the equity of its brands across international markets by deploying forms of mass communication, including media advertising. This sort of activity may

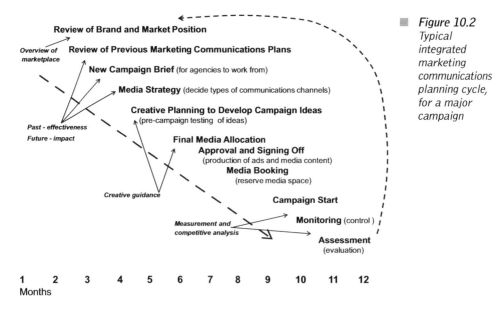

Figure 10.2 Typical integrated marketing communications planning cycle, for a major campaign

MARKETING COMMUNICATIONS FOR THE SME

involve considerable resources and additional specialist skills found outside the company and acquired through delegating tasks to outsourced communication agencies. However, SMEs lack the capacity to support remote markets, and they may not have the resources for mass media driven communications activity.

Although SMEs are confronted by limitations compared to large organisations, many SMEs operate successfully in carrying out marketing communication. A typical SME will tend to 'see' marketing communication as something they need to do occasionally to boost sales, i.e., marketing communications. However, though largely invisible as part of an explicit marketing strategy, the role of marketing communication in typical SMEs can be outlined as follows:

- SMEs tend to use marketing communication in an ad hoc way to support the network position of the organisation, to maintain the infrastructure and relationships the SME needs to survive in its environment;
- Few SMEs will identify with a strategic and functional role for marketing communication which is similar to that found practiced in larger organisation.

To understand SME marketing communication, it is necessary to consider how they seek to support a successful position in the marketplace and what they do in communications terms to support market relationships that sustain their position.

Strategically, SMEs tend to manage key relationships within their supporting infrastructure by regular marketplace interventions using close personal relationships. This means they can sense marketplace trends and make regular adaptations rather than need to use longer-term planning frameworks. As a result SMEs tend to have less need to devise conventional marketing strategies or to work with promotional campaigns where marketing communications activity has to show how it supports these strategies. Instead, the small size of SMEs encourages the sharing of roles and the fostering of relationships that develop into support networks because of key SME features:

- low bureaucracy;
- highly motivated staff;
- perceived shared-interest between staff and the enterprise;
- staff willing to use their natural relationship skills to strengthen the business.

The use made of marketing communications tools by SMEs suggests these organisations tend to deploy communications tools for short-term tasks rather than to support any defined strategic marketing objectives, or to build distinctive and sustainable competitive positions in their markets. Nevertheless many SMEs can be highly successful without this type of strategic planning behind their marketing communication. Since SME marketing communications activity is mostly sales driven and tactical (Spickett-Jones and Eng, 2006), it is appropriate to ask if marketing communication needs a strategic framework in an SME context. However, this partly assumes SMEs should behave like larger businesses and that they should be measured by similar approaches to strategic marketing and communication strategy. If perspectives on successful SMEs derived from conventional strategic marketing analysis fail to identify what sustains their success, it is appropriate to frame and examine SMEs marketing communication differently. Thus, the following sections discuss how SMEs marketing communication is practiced through communication technology and a network perspective.

165

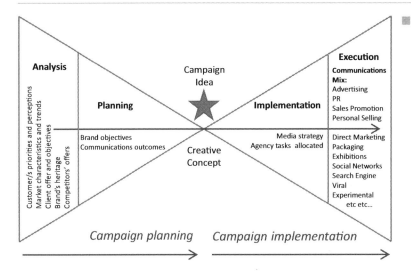

Figure 10.3 Typical cyclical marketing communication process for a large company campaign

Communication technology and marketing communication

In the midst of rapid development in communication technology it is easy to be swept along by hype attached to possible implications for marketing communication. It is valuable, therefore, to see marketing communication in its context as part of human activity, to see how different types of communication impacts on the way people operate in their social and physical environment. Neuroscientists suggest that an important part of human evolution can be attributed to the human brain's communication capacity. Unless there is a dramatic alteration to the way the human brain works, the usefulness of any development in communication technology is likely to be determined by the way the technology works with our existing brain capacity. Some neuroscientists (Kandel et al., 2000) believe this capacity evolved because of two related adaptations in our human ancestors: the need to develop *technology* to help exploit the environment, and the need to manage *cooperation* to create a cohesive social group. The same two forces are at work in the modern world when organisations seek to harness the power of marketing communication, via whatever technology, to build successful collaborations within the marketplace.

Technology as an enabler in communication contexts

According to Alan Stevens, founder of Media Coach and a social media consultant, 'The key thing about social media is not just broadcasting but measuring the impact of what you do'. He recommends companies to filter what other people are saying about their products and services, and provide immediate feedback (FT 16/17 Jan 2010). SMEs can take advantage of internet-based communication tools and software applications at a relatively low cost. For example, they can use the internet to recruit staff, respond to customer complaints, develop new business opportunities and monitor changes in the marketplace.

A communication technology's success will depend on the role it performs for human beings. How will a mode of communication help people achieve what they want to? The same will be true for an organisation. When people have a high level of commitment to an enterprise and when they come into close contact with other people in their marketing environment, marketing communication and human communication can become inextricably linked. For marketing communication, the key marketing environment is represented by **people.** So identifying the roles of key of different people is a vital aspect of marketing communications in the SME context:

- **Who.** Which people are most important and how to manage an appropriate relationship with different people will depend on the perceived importance of specific groups and individuals, and the scale of the market as well as the resources available;
- **What.** The type of relationship is feasible may depend on the available resources, **why** and **when** these relationships should be strengthened, and the access to suitable communications technologies to manage these relationships;
- **Where.** Key people in the marketing environment may be aligned to other organisations, perhaps in the supply chain, or they may work for suppliers of specialist services, like an advertising agency;
- **How.** In a networked economy every organisation must have a supporting 'infrastructure' and in essence that is what marketing communication is about. It enables an organisation to relate to the most critical parts of the marketing environment and do this in meaningful and appropriate ways in order to win support.

Marketing communication opportunities for SME

As technology helps the communication landscape evolve, conveying the value in a marketing proposition offers an increasingly wide range of options. This can create new layers of complexity in the practice of marketing communication in terms of the following challenges:

- New channels of communication contend with older modes of communication but rarely displace completely the more traditional and established media;
- People's capacity for focal attention is likely to have remained largely unchanged but it is now spread across a wider range of communication channels;
- The greater availability of interactive technologies has created an evolving communication landscape that contains growing opportunities to exchange information, often driven by the proactive efforts of people in the marketplace who seek information. This has created new opportunities for SMEs to become more visibility and accessible to a wider marketplace.

The changes in the communication landscape help to make this an exciting time to discuss marketing communication for SMEs. Once the communication roles and marketing objectives that support SMEs are better understood, there are now possibilities for many SMEs to gain access to wider markets via new channels of communication. With expanding technology and communication infrastructure offering new opportunities for promotion and trade, SMEs can access new ways to support a wider marker presence and grow their business compared to expensive traditional media channels, like television.

However, new methods do not necessarily mean a low-cost strategy. For example, maintaining a social network site or entertaining customers with a 'Twitter' feed may give a company's followers rewarding information but maintaining a credible presence on such sites takes resources and dedicated effort. When those who work in an SME are dedicated enthusiasts for what they do they may be keen to talk about their products and services, particularly to gain custom and support. However, to dedicate time and resources to do this online could distract from their main business, making the products and services that win the support of customers and perhaps give the staff a sense of achievement.

> ### *Exploring network opportunities*
> Social networking sites offer new opportunities through real-time interactive communication in networks. Divining Femininity is a case in point, when the co-founder, Vena Ramphal set up her company through a social media networking site, Twitter, with a co-founder. They launched their company with a tweet and were surprised to have more than 300 people view their posting in the first few hours (FT 16/17 January 2010).

As technologies mature, SMEs opportunities are likely to expand and become easier to access. Online channels are already starting to provide new entry points into different markets and new ways of communicating market value, even for very small SMEs. For example, independent artisan food producers (e.g., regional cheese makers, farmers raising rare breeds of livestock, brewers of traditional ales and specialty bakers) may carry the status of 'food heroes' in their local market. However good their products and however infections their enthusiasm may be for these products, if a producer can reach only the markets their personal contacts can access these markets will be strictly limited. Even though these producers may have limited personal skill and may lack the necessary resources to build a website or manage a presence on a social network site they may still access the services to do this by working in an alliance with those who do have such skills, and this can offer a model to make wider markets available to an SME at mutual benefit to all those in an alliance (see 'The Virtual Farmers Market' case).

A network perspective to marketing communication

More recently, marketing has embraced a network theory model, where organisations are not seen as insular and distinct from their marketing environment. SMEs are part of a network in an interconnected model where what can be achieved depends on other organisations as well as the demand the network is capable of serving. In a network model, resources that create a distinctive and sustainable market capacity may not be owned by a particular organisation but may belong to the network in the sense that it is the capacity to do things in an alliance of network capabilities that makes a particular strategy possible. This means that strategic resources may lie not in organisations, but between organisations in the network.

In this network model, some relationships between organisations will not be about competing with each other or negotiating to win the best trading terms. Instead, success may depend on mutual interests that deal with resolving tensions and risks between organisations over levels of competition and points of cooperation. The concept of business networks implies a blurred of organisational boundaries. This is a theoretical challenge to conventional strategic analysis models that tended to treat each organisation as a distinct entity.

168

So, instead of industrial economic theory's sharply defined boundaries, some authors argue business relationships are characterised by competition and cooperation, or coopetition (Bengtsson and Kock, 2000).

A network theory approach stresses the importance of both relationships and structural determinants on strategy. The notion of SMEs existing within a network of relationships shows how they are interdependent on the actions of other organisations within a value chain concept. Thus, an SME plays critical roles in developing and managing networks of relationships through how communication with the marketplace takes place. For SMEs marketing communication depends on:

- Considering the resources an SME can access, some within the network in and through the relationships it is possible to develop;
- Leveraging the role of marketing communication to build a suitable network that gives access to key resources via interactive technologies and networking tools;
- Identifying where there may be scarce resources and unbalanced dependencies on key network partners, to reduce over-dependency or map strategic opportunities, e.g., access new markets.

Going global through cross-relational networking

According to Mike Southon, many successful UK small businesses collapsed under the pressure of geographical expansion. This is due to the difficulty of setting up networks of relationships and knowledge across national borders to deal with the complex legal, taxation, compliance, and human resources issues ((FT 27/28 February 2010). In the context of cross-relational networks, SMEs competitiveness can be affected by access and knowledge of certain critical resources, which may not be directly connected to the business but have implications for strategic decisions such as the legal system and supply chains.

In a network perspective, SMEs that view the potential for relationships to affect each other in cross-relational actions will develop a deeper understanding of their competitive position (Eng, 2005). A cross-relational view accounts for not only impacts between relationships but also across relations, which play some part in supporting the overall network. For example, a test of the levels of dependency between organisations as a measure of the relationships *within* networks and *between* participants would demonstrate variation of control and dependence on critical resources for an exchange relationship in networks. For SMEs, there are strategic implications for choice and development of relationships as regards different levels of relationship stability or rates of change in the marketing environment. For example, when there is rapid change in the environment an SME is likely to require strong relationships with network partners who can give access to the character of this change, or partners in the network who operate where the market is most dynamic. Thus, it is advantageous for SMEs to adopt a cross-relational view of networks in order to:

- Identify critical relationships that support channels of marketing communication, which could include partners in networks of relationships not directly connected to an SME;

- Manage relationships that are critical but not directly connected by understanding the implications of their strategic actions at different levels of relationship;
- Develop sources of core competence through development and investment of selective key relationships in networks with cross-relational impacts on control and dependency.

CHAPTER SUMMARY

For decades there has been a bias in marketing communication which, to a large extent, has overlooked SMEs. One reason for this neglect is because of a perceived bias in what marketing communication is thought to be about. This bias comes from the role and success of specialist marketing communications services, like advertising agencies.

Agencies try to manage arms-lengths relationships with large markets for major clients, usually by trying to manage a sense of relationship people feel towards a brand. In a competitive world, clients want their promotional budgets to work as hard as possible, so agencies seek every greater synergy by combining different promotional tool, often in complex and integrated marketing communications campaigns. Because agencies tend to work with large companies to produce some of the most publically visible elements of marketing communications, like TV ads, these are often thought of as the pinnacle of good promotional practice. Being so public, many large-scale marketing communications campaigns give access to campaign materials for those who want to study marketing communication. This supports the idea that marketing communications 'is' what agencies do. This chapter highlights that the relatively large scale of marketing communications activity that agencies develop for large clients has tended to overshadow the deeper characteristics of SME marketing communication

This chapter deals with the basic communication tools employed by SMEs. In contrast to conventional marketing communication analysis, it can be seen that SMEs focus on communication strategies to enhance short-term survival rather than develop a grand marketing communication plan. SMEs utilise new technologies to combine their knowledge and skills with other partners and take advantage of new technologies. Apart from the cost-benefit advantage of technology and alliance relationships with complementary resources, this chapter presents a network perspective to identifying and examining marketing communication opportunities and channels. In a network view, SMEs have the potential to overcome resource limitations, exploit network capabilities, and identify and manage critical resources in the network. In particular, networks of relationships create inter-dependency, SMEs that manage and develop not only direct relationships but also indirect and cross-relations are more likely to develop and sustain their competitive position.

DISCUSSION AND REVIEW QUESTIONS

1. Identify three major differences of marketing communication between large and SMEs.

2. What are the main stages of a typical marketing communications campaign?

3. What are the marketing communications tools applicable to SMEs?

4. Which aspects of the new and digital communication environment most significant for SMEs and why?

MARKETING COMMUNICATIONS FOR THE SME

5. Interpersonal communications are often the most expensive and difficult to control but many SMEs rely heavily on forms of marketing communications that use such personal contacts; why?

6. Why an integrated marketing communication model does not reflect SMEs marketing communications practice?

7. Suggest three practical examples of how information communication technology and media have been used in marketing communication for SMEs.

8. How does a network perspective of marketing communications help SMEs identify new opportunities?

9. Give examples of interdependencies between SMEs marketing communication activities in networks of relationships.

10. Why is it important to examine cross-relational impacts of network relationships for developing competitive marketing communications strategy?

CASE STUDY – THE VIRTUAL FARMERS MARKET

In the UK the resurgence of interests in small scale artisan food production has been accompanied by the growth in farmers' markets that are now common across the UK. Often, these markets take place on specific days of the month and in basic and improvised venues that provide a place where local producers can showcase their wares, i.e., a focal point where the opportunity to pool significant levels of product inventory bring local producers and local customers together.

Using gaming technology, this model has now been extended to the 'Virtual Famers Market' (www.vfmuk.com/), a website that showcases inventory from a much wider geographical area and broader product range than a local farmers' market can offer. The challenge is to reproduce online enough of the distinctive 'essence' that customers respond to when they are drawn to a local farmers' market. One barrier is the lack of opportunity online to taste, touch, and smell the food.

Using up to date technology from the gaming industry the site is able to offer a supporting information architecture that blends product availability with marketing communication content. Doing this, the site resonates with customers' interest in food by providing topical information and newsworthy content about producers and their food passion. It does this alongside access to goods with accompanying video stories, offering customers access to a form of personable 'market patter', the sort of encountered that might be had at a farmers market, and largely made by the 'food heroes' themselves, the people who are responsible for the artisan products on sale. Typically these videos are made with the sort of disarming and naïve production values that have become widely familiar and accepted in a 'YouTube world'. In that way, the video content provides access to and insight into the character of the producer, and it does this with a sort of rustic and charmingly authentic mode of communication that suits the style of the goods these producers also bring to the market. It brings something of the experience to the customer, the essence of the local farmer's market on their computer screen.

By clicking the 'meet the producer' button next to different goods customers have access to the provenance of a product, in the form of the artisan producer. Via the extend reach this technology offers, the sometimes quirky and enthusiast personalities behind the goods can reach out to capture a wider market. This can be likened to the differentiation a major grocery brand might try to achieve with a TV adverting campaign, but in the Virtual Markers Market customer who buy a small producer's chocolate sauce also 'buy' the people who make that chocolate sauce. Policed by the mutual interest of other producers for stories to be authentic and supported by customers' perception of the 'authority' of the site's wider reputation, the goods on the site carry greater credence. In effect, this is not just a shopping site, by combing an opportunity to trade with a combination of promotional messages, marketing communication content, the site conveys information that can build the sense of trust to enhance the value of goods.

'Virtual Farmers Market' is, effectively, creating interest and potently loyalty among an already interested audience. This is using communication with the market to create interest, provoke trial and build reputation in the sort of engagement stages that management of brand equity via TV adverting has done for decades, but it offers this to small retailers, SMEs who might never win a listing with a major grocery retail chain. A sense of access to the 'real' people behind the products may give customers in the market a heightened level of authenticity which lends the goods distinctive appeal.

A site like 'Virtual Farmers Market' can combine a range of marketing functions in a converging platform, including commerce and marketing communication. Not only is it a potential media space for those who want to know more about artisan food, it is also a retail space making an inventory of attractive products more easily available and a promotional space where different producers can communicate the passion and points of difference they offer in the hope the market will react favourably towards these. In an age of increasing convergence, the communication of marketing relevant information, content delivered with up to date technology information, is likely to become increasingly available to SMEs even if the SEMs themselves do not host or manage the content directly. If the products and services are attractive enough this presents a market for those who are willing to make such services more visible and accessible.

Questions:

1. Logan Dairy makes handmade and award winning goat cheese in Yorkshire. The cheeses are sold from the farm but mainly to local delicatessens and restaurants throughout East and West Yorkshire. One of their most successful cheeses is rolled in freshly milled black pepper to give a light spicy crust to the cheese before it is packaged. What are the advantages and disadvantages for Logan Dairy of promoting their products using the Virtual Farmers Markets?
2. Why would customers want to buy Logan cheese from a local delicatessen and in what way does Virtual Farmers Market communicate values that would mimic those that promote the product's benefits, as expressed through channels.
3. What would you include in a communications mix to promote Logan Dairy's cheeses and why?

4. Boursin is a cream cheese made in France by the multinational group, Unilever. One of the varieties comes prepared with cracked black peppercorns, like one of the Logan Dairy's most popular cheeses. How would a company like Unilever differ in their approach to marketing communication from Logan Dairy, and why would this be different?

REFERENCES

Bengtsson, M. and Kock, S. (2000) Coopetition in business networks – to cooperate and compete simultaneously. *Industrial Marketing Management*, 29, 411–426.

Dyer, L. M. and Ross, C. A. (2003) Consumer communication and the small ethnic firm. *Journal of Developmental Entrepreneurship*, 8(1), 19–31.

Eng, T.-Y. (2005) An empirical analysis of the influence of cross-relational impact of strategy analysis on relationship performance in a business network context. *Journal of Strategic Marketing*, 13, 219–237.

Fill, C. (2005) *Marketing Communications*. Prentice Hall, Harlow, UK.

Kandel, E. R., Schwarz, J. H. and Jessell, T. M. (2000) *Principles of Neural Science*, 4th ed. MaGraw-Hill, New York.

Spickett-Jones, J. G. and Eng, T-Y. (2006) SMEs and the strategic context for communication. *Journal of Marketing Communications*, 12(3), September, 225–243.

van Riel, C. B. M. (1995) *Principles of Corporate Communication*. Prentice Hall, London.

Chapter 11

Internet marketing

Paul Dobson and Vish Maheshwari

LEARNING OBJECTIVES

After reading this chapter, you will be able to:
- To provide an overview about how SMEs can identify, target, gain and increase sales using the internet;
- To demonstrate an applied understanding of how to develop an organisations internet marketing to, identify, market, and engage customers;
- To evaluate applications of internet marketing by examining its relative impact on SMEs in developing customer friendly websites to gain sales by providing value-added customer experience.

INTRODUCTION

Internet marketing has changed the outlook for businesses in the way they promote their products and services and the how they engage with their existing and prospective customers. The use of internet in marketing activities is now a *norm* as all businesses (SMEs and MNEs) gain better customer interaction over range of social media platforms and websites. Internet marketing is commonly used terminology that includes variety of online communication channels such as digital marketing, social media marketing, search engine marketing, email marketing, and online. Internet marketing is carried out using multiple channels as it supports better and quick identification of customer journeys (Chaffey and Ellis-Chadwick, 2019) and could be very effective for small and medium-sized businesses (SMEs) to provide cost effectiveness and optimise growth.

The role of internet marketing and growth of social media channels goes hand in hand and has become active part of contemporary marketing activities among businesses including SMEs, both for interacting with diverse customer segments and understanding behavioural motives of existing and potential customers. Internet marketing and digital channels, including social media platforms, allow constant customer engagement by enabling sharing and building of content, this helps developing better customer relationship.

This chapter provides overview about how SMEs can identify, target, gain, and increase sales using the internet. Using examples and case studies we will demonstrate how to develop an organisations internet marketing to, identify, market and engage customers. We

INTERNET MARKETING

will discuss various applications of internet marketing and show how it will enable SMEs to develop customer friendly website, gain sales and increase the value of the sales generating a better customer loyalty potentially.

Furthermore, the chapter will also discuss how to target the social media marketing using the right platform at the right time, and how to improve the engagement of potential customer and sharing by current customers to help gain sales for SMEs.

DEFINING YOUR CUSTOMERS TO ENABLE EFFECTIVE AND EFFICIENT MARKETING

Customer personas have been used in traditional marketing and digital marketing for around 10 years (Chaffey and Bosomworth, 2019) and relative fictional characters are designed to represent key purchasing and purchase decision made by customers. If done effectively and better than the competition it can give a competitive advantage, as the SMEs targeting of digital marketing can be more effective and efficient than the competition. In addition, the increase in marketing ROI can enable a higher marketing to spend per customer acquisition and therefore a much great impact if the organisation requires.

Besides improving the targeting of digital marketing, the benefits of using personas also include (Dobson, 2017):

- Giving an organisation-wide understanding of the customer. This is important as this enables an SME to integrate it's marketing across the whole of the organisation plus as customer buying behaviour changes over time, front end staff can quickly identity and give an early warning to investigate the change in customer behaviour and quickly adapt the marketing;
- Enables website design and development to be improved so that the customer experience and satisfaction meets the customer needs better. This can lead to increase in conversion, sales, and capturing customer details, such as name and email, by focussing on the customer flow through the website;
- Help develop an integrated communication plan across all platforms and customer journeys;
- Improve data driven digital marketing as you know the characteristics and reasons behind the customer flow information.

It should be noted that for start-ups and SMEs starting to develop their customer persona, initially they may need to use secondary research such as trade magazines, plus information from internal qualitative feedback. Further development of the persona's using the analytics from the website and social media can be undertaken when customer traffic is entering and flowing through the organisation's website. This should include data driven evidence such as demographics, platforms, day/time of day the platform is used, and keywords used.

Typically, when working with SME's we talk to all front end employees and discuss the characters types of customers, both business to consumer and business to business. This will include the key areas that influence, trigger and act as a barrier or fear from purchasing and group together character types that are the same. We usually end up with between three and five personas.

An example of one of the personas that Valentine Clays initially developed for one of their evening events is in Figure 11.1 (see www.valentineclays.co.uk/). This included the key areas they wanted to initially develop to help understand the customers for this event.

175

Customer Persona A

Claire White – Young Professional

Background and Demographics	Channels	Goals
History: Business Student Sex: Female Age: 29 Current role: Finance manager Size of company: Medium Income: £ 32,000	Valentine Clay's Website Facebook Twitter Pinterest Instagram Email Linkedin	Short Term: To be able to network with other professionals in a similar position. Long Term: To progress in current rore or new role/position.

Daily Challenges
Limited time to socialise with friends and family due to work commitments.

Work stress.

Lack of opportunity to network due to the organisational structure at her workplace.

Common Objectives
Will I feel comfortable within this environment?

Are there any competing events nearby or other ways of socialising more suitable for myself?

Will I enjoy the activities held at this event?

Biggest Fears
Lack of other attendees, limiting the chance to network and socialise.

Feeling anxious in a new environment.

Availability of services such as secure car parking.

Change Expectations
Chance to relieve stress caused by work whilst still being able to network by socialising and having fun at a new event.

Relieves the pressure of hosting social events which may cause more stress dues to lack of time outside of work.

Content Criteria
Organisation takes feedback into consideration.

Email and social media updates/notifications about the running of the event.

Special offers due to customer loyalty at this event.

Awareness
- Internet research to find activities which encourage networking with people in a similar position
- Online research to find evening events which can be attended with friends
- Word of mouth
- PR - Articles and comments in newspapers etc.

Research
- Looking on the website
- Reading customer review's
- Check if the organisation is reputable
- Check price range

Decision
- Good reviews from people who have previously attended the ladies evening
- A good level of organisaiton and planning shown from the organisation
- Fits around her busy work schedule

■ *Figure 11.1* Customer personas

Source – The Author Paul Dobson from case study Valentine Clays (see www.valentineclays.co.uk/).

INTERNET MARKETING

Beside the persona characteristics a key area to map is what platform's they are using and when, is can be developed to target digital marketing on a more personalised basis to help ensure better marketing than competitors and improve marketing ROI.

THE CUSTOMER JOURNEY TO SALES AND LOYALTY

The customer journey creates a clear map, that demonstrates what marketing platforms and tools can be used and where in the customer journey these could be most effective. Starting with potential customers and their search pattern, then following the path to enable them to make a purchase. It is crucial that upfront engagement and consultation with customers is proactive to support informed decision making, resulting in positive conviction. As you can track customers, unless they restrict this, you can remarket to them if they've shown an interest. This enables you to target your paid marketing to potentially interested customers rather than those who may have no interest at all.

Understanding and improving the customer journey to enable lead nurturing can lead to a 50% increase in sales (Patel, 2019). The customer journey can be demonstrated as a conversation funnel that demonstrates the path and experiences potential customers make to get to your website and through your website. In addition it shows what digital marketing to use where to encourage each step of the way, from becoming aware of your products and services to becoming qualified leads and to purchasing. This is supported by analytics used in your social media and website to monitor and control the customer experience (CX).

A simpler version has been developed by Stec (2019) (Figure 11.2). In this customer journey to decide and purchase there are three key strategies (adapted from Stec, 2019)

- Awareness Stage: The potential customer has become aware of a need or requirement and has started to look for information and potential solutions;
- Consideration Stage: The potential customer has researched and has defined and to a large extent understands their problem or requirement;
- Decision Stage: The customer is preparing to buy and looking for the best solution/ purchase.

The customer journey does not stop here. SMEs can develop their internet marketing to increase sales for example; once the website has their initial purchase and card details before

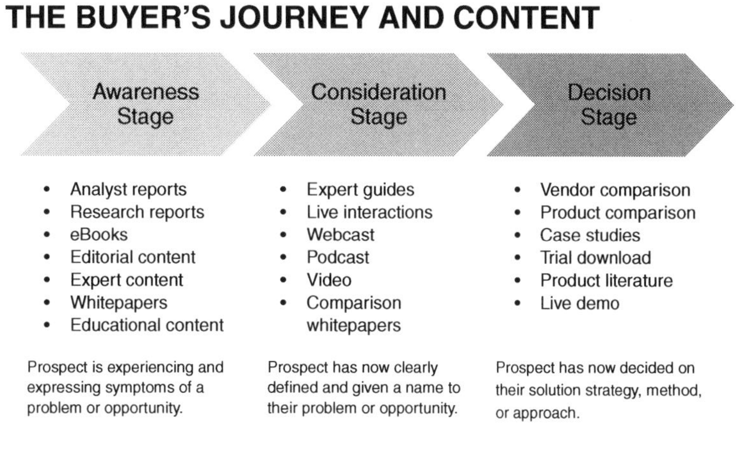

Figure 11.2 Customer experience

Source: (Stec, C. https://blog.hubspot. com/service/customer-experience)

THE BUYER'S JOURNEY AND CONTENT

Awareness Stage	Consideration Stage	Decision Stage
• Analyst reports • Research reports • eBooks • Editorial content • Expert content • Whitepapers • Educational content	• Expert guides • Live interactions • Webcast • Podcast • Video • Comparison whitepapers	• Vendor comparison • Product comparison • Case studies • Trial download • Product literature • Live demo
Prospect is experiencing and expressing symptoms of a problem or opportunity.	Prospect has now clearly defined and given a name to their problem or opportunity.	Prospect has now decided on their solution strategy, method, or approach.

confirming purchase, the website can aim to sell complimentary options via up/cross/down selling further products or help the customer become an advocate to help referral marketing.

Once this customer journey is mapped you can start to optimise it using analytics such as Google Analytics to improve conversation and sales. An integral part of this is optimising social media conversations.

It should also be noted that using Social Media you can bypass a lot of these stages to encourage potential customers to buy something they didn't know they wanted, e.g., via Facebook advertising.

SOCIAL MEDIA MARKETING

Social media activity is increasing in active viewers and impact. SME social media marketing is creating content to promote your business and products on various social media platforms such as Facebook, Instagram, LinkedIn, and Snapchat. This unique content should be tailored to the specific platform it's being shared on to help you boost conversions and increase brand awareness. For example, on Facebook short videos with no hashtags is more effective that straight text with hash tags for a variety of reasons. There are a variety of reasons why social media marketing works. This includes (adapted from Baker, 2019):

Develop brand awareness

A lot of potential customers are using social media on a regular basis at the top of the customer journey funnel (Top of Funnel) and these potential customers research not just on search engines such as Google but also social media platforms. An example is YouTube that has the second biggest social media platform, after Facebook, (Kallas, 2018), for the number of users that search for information. Regular quality use of social media helps reinforce and keep customers aware of brands as well. Using social media SMEs can also enhance customer engagement through comments and shares, and include links to your business website to increase sales. An example is the Auberge De Chabanettes Hotel and Spa (see http://aubergedechabanettes.com) with the support of a series of timed Facebook posts, became known as the hotel to go to for a high quality relaxing stay in the area.

Generating lead and conversation

Understanding the platforms and triggers that lead to sales can have a substantial benefit to organisations. As an example is using YouTube and Facebook led to an increase from a few subscribers to over 9600 on YouTube for the head chef of an Indian restaurant Latifs (as an example see www.youtube.com/watch?v=_weLAzB1nFk). This led directly to an increase in customer visits.

Developing lead and sales

If done correctly, sharing and discussing your products and services is a simple way of developing sales as your marketing to people who have an interest in your business or product in general. For example to increase sales during quiet periods Latifs effectively undertook the following:

INTERNET MARKETING

- Created content of meals when they knew from analytics that customers would start to think about their evening meal;
- Included offers and vouchers during quiet period of service on Facebook to their followers;
- Regularly produced YouTube videos that are promoted across other platforms, mainly Facebook, to increase brand awareness and engagement;
- Developed an integrated digital marketing campaign that took into account the future direction of the business, seasonality, staff holidays, etc.;
- Changed the profile from personal to business, for example with Instagram, to improve the analytics information.

Improve long term relationships with customers

Besides improving engagement and long-term sales from customers, advocate marketing is a very powerful form of marketing as people are more likely to read posts and shares from friends than from an organisation. If a business can encourage customers to share, e.g., via a competition, selfie or photographing the product, then the customers are marketing for the business. In addition businesses can interact with customers answering questions and asking about products. This can be an effective way of developing customers to help with new product development and understand changes in customer buying behaviour.

Business, community, and competitor analysis

Keeping an eye on discussions, concerns, what's working or not working with social media can help businesses plan and keep ahead of the customer buying behaviour curve. In addition, keeping an eye on the competition can also help ensure that the business social media branding is more distinctive and engaging than the competition.

SME business owners may see statistical reports about which social media platform is best for what type of users at what time. However, these reports are frequently the average millions or tens of thousands of users and sometimes many countries. The most reliable information SMEs can gain their customer statistics is from their own social media and associated google analytics which will be more targeted to their customer base.

PAID FOR ADVERTISING AND SEARCH ENGINE MARKETING

There are various forms of paid for advertising available online from social media advertising, for example advertising a Facebook post or search engine marketing. Typical search engine advertising can be seen at the top when a viewer has run a search results. These are usually noted to show that they're an advert by an AD or the note sponsored against it. An advantage of paid for advertising, especially compared to SEO/inbound marketing is that businesses can get fast results. In addition, as noted earlier, it can also be used for retargeting potential customers who have visited the business website or interacted with their social media and therefore are potentially more likely to be interested in buying. The targeting of this advertising has to be considered carefully and business need to consider the correct platform, demographics. SMEs considering Business to Business (B2B) advertising could consider LinkedIn, Facebook, and Twitter advertising, and with recent updates this advertising has the ability to become increasingly targeted. Google AdWords has an extensive analytics system plus the ability to build customised dashboards to help both the advertising and customer journey. This can highlight the keywords to use to attract customers and just

179

as importantly the analytics can show what words to avoid as gaining the wrong customers to the website can be both costly and affect the advertising quality ranking therefore making future advertising more expensive.

Although paid for advertising can demonstrate a clear return on investment and can have a fast response when started, a disadvantage is that when an organisation stops paying for these the adverts stop.

AFFILIATE MARKETING

The concept of affiliate marketing is very simple – affiliates make money by referring products from their website. Affiliate marketing provides an excellent platform for brands to test new products and services because payment is by results only (Maheshwari et al., 2019). High click through rates (CTR) can be achieved and sales increased at a fraction of the cost of other forms of digital marketing, Furthermore, affiliate marketing provides detailed metrics giving information such as the type of buyer coming from each affiliate source, which can feed into digital strategy development. So, for many, affiliate marketing is a key component of a digital strategy. That said, digital marketers must be wary of damage to their brand when considering affiliate marketing. The choice of affiliate and the tactics agreed with them is of paramount importance, as the partnerships represent your brand in one way or other. Heavy discounts, unsolicited emails, or pop-up advertisements are all to be avoided if you wish to protect the investment in your brand.

SMEs can benefit by using affiliate marketing in order to scope market; gauge customer needs and key influencers and reference groups to attain market share. This could result into optimised returns and resource efficiencies.

REFERRAL AND ADVOCATE MARKETING

Referral marketing is about enabling and incentivising your customers to advocate and encourage their friends to try a business product by put in place the tools to encourage, reward and track customer recommendations. A Nielsen report (Casey, 2017) noted that 83% of people trust recommendations from friends and family. Because the demographics of friends are usually similar and referral marketing is fairly easy to develop plus has many potential benefits, this type of marketing strategy can be customised by a variety of SMEs to reach different target demographics. An example is running refer-a-friend marketing campaign for local SMEs where we have seen how valuable referred customers can be. These referred customers spend more than customers from other channels and have a higher lifetime value. The key is to enable easy tracking and optimising of the scheme to maximise customer acquisition.

There are key areas to enable referral marketing:

1. Make an experience or post that people want to share such as a viral post;
2. Make the product or experience sharable, e.g., easy to photograph and share or make the post sharable on Facebook;
3. Ensure great customer service so that customer want to share a great experience;
4. Implement a referral programme with incentives;
5. Promote the programme.

To help develop and implement for your business, have a look at successful examples such as Dollar Shave Club and Dropbox.

EMAIL MARKETING

Email marketing is the use of email to develop a relationship with potential and current customers. Although there is increased legislation, such as GDPR, for email marketing, this is usually covered by the email marketing system, which also offers opt-in features, support for cart-abandonment, segmentation of marketing emails, etc., as part of its free package such as Mailchimp.

Done correctly, emails can be personalised and targeted such as birthday or special discounts on products to help increase sales. Ideally, SMEs should be capturing customers names and email address on their website as these are already targeted audiences and the SME can confirm that these customers have signed up to receive them. The three main advantages of email marketing is that they are easy and cheap to setup and run, and you can get and use analytics such as open-rates, click-through rates, and conversations, to see which type of emails are working for particular customer segments. Email marketing is also easy for SMEs to test the emails for example by A/B split testing and enhance to get a better return.

Newsletters can be sent by these email marketing systems to help provide customers of news releases, produce development and sales, supporting and technical information available on the business website, and special offers. All of these can help develop the SMEs brand and sales.

MOBILE MARKETING

Mobile marketing is a deliberate strategy to market to mobile phone users. With such a large number of people using the mobile to access information on the internet, it has become an increasingly substantial market. Mobile marketing for many organisations has become a necessity or they start to lose customers to better competitors. Mobile marketing has many strengths:

1. Reach – Most customers have and use their mobile phone, in a lot of cases from when they wake up and on-and-off throughout the day. As friends and family probably contact them through the mobile phone they're receptive to regularly looking at their mobile;
2. Personalisation – with advanced targeting and geolocation available SMES can target their mobile advertising when they know potential customers are in the area or even in the area of competitors and target specific demographic customer types including by customers hobbies/interests;
3. Trust – Mobile users are become more trusting of ecommerce, especially when it's backup by a trust-worthy payment system such as PayPal;
4. Cost Effective – With correct target marketing SMES can gain a high ROI on their marketing;
5. Improved customer engagement, loyalty, and branding.

There are key steps involved in developing the SME mobile marketing strategy. To start with, clear goals and objectives are required; this could be gaining leads, sales, or brand recognition. After this define the target audience personas and their characteristics so that the next stage of ensuring the website is mobile compatible and probably setup as with accelerated mobile pages, plus apps, if required, are developed with the target audience in mind. Finally this mobile strategy has to be integrated across the SME business operations and marketing so that customer enquiries and orders are sorted.

CONTENT CURATION

Content curation is the discovering, production, and promoting of quality, informative content. According to Curata (2014), the best in-class marketers create 65% of their own content, syndicate 10%, and research and curate the final 25% (Figure 11.3).

A lot of SMEs do not have the time to create original content or the finances to hire professional PR agencies to develop content new content. Therefore, for SMEs researching and developing quality content for their target audience could take up to 75% (Dobson, 2017). In addition there are fairly cheap platforms such as www.fiverr.com and www.freelancer.co.uk where freelancers can develop targeted content.

There are key benefits of content curation (adapted from Hootsuite, 2019). These are:

1. Be recognised as an expert. To help build the brand of the SME in the organisation can become been as an expert in their area. In today's fast paced business environment, SME business owners do not have a lot of time for research; therefore if customers find a key source of timely, informative, quality material, they can stick to one source instead of having to research, read, or listen to lots of areas, which might be a waste of time.
2. It's easier than creating your own. Although crating original content is important, it takes a lot of time and it's far easier to take and adapt other material that you can take, quote/adapt, and contextualise for your customers. Remember to reference the original work, e.g., via a hyperlink, and only quote small section do not copy and paste large sections as this is plagiarism.
3. Show you're in the game . . . or even ahead of the game. By noting new and up-and-coming information SMEs are demonstrating that they're not just in the game but fully informed. The very fact that the SME is researching to create content can help the SME informed but also helps highlight potential new opportunities or risks.
4. Grow your network to grow your business. Curating and sharing content can help the SME connect with leaders, influencers, and customers in the industry. As the SME develops conversations it can develop influence and more views.

The Content Marketing Institute (2019) suggests the key steps involved in developing and marketing content (Figure 11.4) is: Start with the contents purpose and goals, develop a clear understanding of why you are creating content, and what value it will provide.

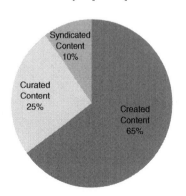

Figure 11.3 Curata's 2014 Content marketing tactics planner

Source: Curata (2014), Content Marketing Tactics. Available at www.curata.com/resources/ebooks/content-marketing-tactics-2014. Accessed 6th May 2019.

INTERNET MARKETING

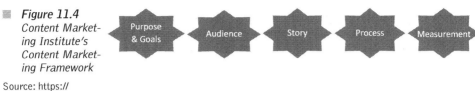

Figure 11.4 Content Marketing Institute's Content Marketing Framework

Source: https://contentmarketinginstitute.com/2019/09/refresh-content-marketing/

Next, understand the audience using the personas noted earlier. SMEs know who they're creating content for, and how they will benefit and want to read plus share it. The story is what specific, unique, and valuable ideas SMEs will build their content assets around. Can this be developed to help raise the SME profile/brand, gain leads, and get more views on the website. The process is how the SME will structure and manage your operations in order to activate their plans. For example, is this content going to be published via a timed post for by Hootsuite to Twitter? Finally, the measurement: how will you gauge performance and continually optimise your efforts such as analytics setup so that the SME can monitor results? Is this a call to action to achieve the objective, e.g., lead name and email addresses?

As is the case for all areas of internet marketing for SMEs, the measurement, understanding, and control is important for ensuring that the marketing is correctly targeted and getting results.

SEARCH ENGINE OPTIMISATION (SEO)

Search Engine Optimisation (SEO), or organic search as it used to be called (Fill and Turnbull, 2016), is to enhance the websites ranking and visibility of a search engine SERPs (Search Engine Result Pages). The key search engines such as Google, and in China Baidu, uses an algorithm to compare the content and other key data to the keywords and phrases used to search (Jerath et al., 2014). This should drive more customers to the website and increase engagement and sales. For example, HubSpot Research found that 77% of viewer research a brand before engaging with it (HubSpot, nd).

Nowadays most business understand the basics of SEO and why it is important (Fortin, 2019). However, developing and implementing an SEO strategy that enables improved ranking for key words to improve website visits and sales for SMEs is difficult. There are three types of SEO that SMEs should focus on. These are:

- On-page SEO: This is that the content on the web-pages are optimised for the keywords that the SMEs customers and potential customers will use when search for their products and services (Newman, 2013). As an example, the Auberge de Chabanettes, Small Boutique Hotel with Spa (see http://aubergedechabanettes.com/) had to include geographic local details in their website to be properly ranked for their customer keywords used in Google. The content and content curation of quality reading on a website is a key area, as this assists SEO but also improves the perception that viewers have of the organisation. Other areas of on-page SEO includes how the keywords are used in the webpage for example, in the headings and in the first few paragraphs, the length of informative text, image file names and alt tags, and how relevant the page is to the keywords.

- Off-page SEO: This SEO is affected by the number and quality of the links that are pointing to pages on the SMEs website. These 'backlinks' have become less influential with recent search engine updates but backlinks from influential and trusted websites such as the BBC plus relevant popular websites can have a strong impact on the SEO.
- Technical SEO: This refers to the website's architecture and server optimisation so that the search engines spiders/robots can effectively index the SME's website. It is important to note that the spider just sees text, so the website needs to be setup to ensure that this is carefully targeted. In addition, the website needs to have easy to find navigation and links for the spiders find, plus no dead links, i.e., to pages or websites that no longer exists. The website address (URL) should not be long, and it should not include unusual text characters. In addition, the website should not have duplicate content. The spiders searching of the SME's website can also be assisted by using sitemap and robots.txt files. The sitemap file lists all website addresses URLs on your site for the spider to search, and the robots.txt file informs search engines what website pages not to search.

MONITORING AND IMPROVEMENT OF AN SME INTERNET MARKETING

As noted earlier, monitoring and improvement is an important area in Internet Marketing. The internet is an ideal way to monitor and develop marketing for SMEs as SMEs can have access to live data using free-platforms such as Google Analytics. These can include dashboards to give easy to read up to date information on marketing performance, how this has led to sales and where the blockages are. According to Forbes there are ten online metrics that should be followed (Demers, 2014), These are:

1. Total website visit. This gives SMEs the overall picture how the website is doing and gives the initial picture before drilling down into the data to see further information such as demographics, what percentage of visit is via mobiles, etc. It is also important to filter out the spiders/robots of search engines as they can increase the number of website visits but are not potential clients.
2. New/returning sessions. Measuring the number of new can be used to see the effectiveness of marketing campaigns and the returning customers who come back. The new customers can be linked to social media campaigns using code supplied by Google analytics so that SMES can directly measure the effectiveness of the social media marketing.
3. Channel-Specific Traffic. The website visitors from search engines searches, from email typing the website address in, hyperlink in emails, social media or links from other websites can be tracked. This can be good for seeing which websites are linking to the SMEs website and how effective they are.
4. Bounce rate. The bounce rate is the number of website visitors who visit the site and leave without doing anything. This should be as low as possible as it can indicate the visitors who accidently visited due to incorrect keywords, tags or understanding of the SME's marketing. A high bounce rate can affect the cost of paid for advertising as it might indicate that they quality of the information website is not strong for what the viewers were looking for.

INTERNET MARKETING

5. Total Conversions. This measures the number who have undertaken an action on the website such requested further information or purchased something and is therefore an important measure. If this figure is low it can indicate a bad design in the website, marketing or the service or product being offered is poor or viewers were not interested. This is reinforced by behaviour flow where the SME can see how visitors are flowing through the website to the point of sales.

6. Lead to Close Ratio. This is the ration of sales to leads and is a measure of sales success. How well is the SME developing and following up leads to get sales. This can be developed by improving the customer flow and look at re-marketing to customers who have shown an interest.

7. Customer Retention Rate. SMEs can consider this ratio after they've been trading for around 12 months or more and is a measure of returning customers. Usually returning and loyal customers are have a lower cost to keep than marketing to gain new customers so this can have a direct impact on the profit levels of organisations.

8. Average Customer Value and Cost Per Lead. This can be useful to try and estimate the value of a customer per year to help give estimated annual sales, plus cost per lead is to understand how effective is the marketing ROI to gain new customers. Some SMES also calculate life-time value of customers to help realise the overall income potential from customers.

9. In addition there's a basket of social media ration such as: shares, reposts, mentions, reach, followers, and visits. However, these need to lead to sales, so this flow needs to be included as well.

A good way to learn and develop SME internet marketing is to look for best in class examples that can be understood and developed for the SME.

TECHNOLOGY, SME, AND THE 21ST CENTURY

The improving technology and it's customer interface has made it easier for SMEs to take control of their own online marketing. SMEs can easily develop and maintain their own websites using online systems such as Wix and Wordpress or get a subcontractor to develop the website fairly cheaply, for example using Freelancer or Fiverr. The basics of SEO can be done using plugins such as Yoast, removing the need to pay agencies for this, and social media marketing is becoming more targeted at the right audience, if done correctly. However, with the increasing number of platforms, such as Snapchat, WeChat, and TikTok, comes an increasing number of areas SMEs need to consider when online marketing to their customers. Although LinkedIn is known for its B2B marketing, increasingly Facebook is also an effective platform. Therefore, there is an increasing need for SMEs to monitor where their customers and potential customers are looking and how they're buying, or their competitors could gain market share by superior targeting of their online marketing. Fortunately, there are also online tools available to do this such as Google analytics, which includes free online training on how to do the basics with the system. In addition, SMEs need to stay up to date with changes in legislation, e.g., GDPR, and security risks by keeping their email system secure from phishing and website plugins up to date, etc.

Question 1: How will the expanding us of intelligent personal assistants (IPA) such as Amazon Alexa, iPhone Siri, and Google Assistant change the way clients interact with SME online marketing?

Question 2: How could SMEs monitor how their competitors are marketing online?

CASE STUDY

Valentine Clays is an expanding, family run manufacturer supplying clay bodies and raw materials to studio potters, education providers, and industry (see www.valentineclays.co.uk/). They have a close working relationship with the studio potter and the ceramic community for their new product development enabling them to develop ceramic clay bodies to suit the specific requirements of a long list of renowned British and international potters, education sector, and industry customers.

To help enable its close relationship with customers and the local community it runs regular events including charity events, pottery workshops, ceramics exhibitions by potters and corporate events under the banner love clay (see www.loveclay.co.uk/), and these are actively marketed online using Twitter, Facebook, and Instagram. They're using contemporary online marketing tools such as profiling, SEO, and targeted free social media marketing starting with their Loveclay ladies' evening that includes, gin tasting, pottery making, and chocolate tasting.

The first step, profiling, is to understand their Loveclay ladies' evening customers, including what platforms they use, when do they use these platforms, and what are they looking for. This is then combined with the results of the Google analytics, keywords, website audience information such as demographics, and customer behaviour to confirm or modify the results. This then creates a comprehensive customer profile that can then be used to support the targeted social media marketing.

The result is that their ladies' evening is a very successful event and usually fully booked. Attendees are fully aware of what to expect, with clear communication, including a pre-brief and photos of previous events. The percentage of returning customers is very high and helped enable attendees to become hobby potters. In addition, the attendees are helping with new product development by suggesting new ideas and events.

QUESTIONS:

Question 1: Should Valentine Clays consider paid for advertising for its Loveclay ladies evening and other events?

Question 2: How should Valentine Clays consider further develop their online marketing for all of their events and what do they need to be aware of?

Question 3: How can Valentine Clays use the online marketing processes outlined in the case-study to monitor for changes in customer behaviour?

Question 4: What online marketing could Valentine Clays consider with attendees after attending the event?

INTERNET MARKETING

END OF THE CHAPTER DISCUSSION QUESTIONS

1. Discuss the benefits of using personas in internet marketing in relation to an SME of your choice?
2. What are the key strategies of decision making for purchase in a customer journey?
3. Explain and discuss how SMEs can gain their customer statistics using social media and associated google analytics?
4. What are the key strengths of content curation for SMEs and how relevant content could be developed?
5. What role does continuous monitoring and improvement of internet marketing play for SMEs? Discuss with examples.

'LET'S REASON TOGETHER' BOX

As outlined by Smart Insights (2019), small businesses must always focus on their marketing budget. Making sensible choices about which campaigns are the most affordable and deliver the highest ROI should be top of their priority list. Doing so maximises available resources and offers the greatest potential to boost growth.

Question – Working together in groups or pairs, outline a strategy for your chosen SME that is working on a tight budget for growth using internet marketing tools. This should include how to target the social media marketing using the right platform at the right time and how to improve the engagement of potential customer and sharing by current customers to help gain sales.

REFERENCES

Baker, K. (2019) Social media marketing: The ultimate guide. Available at: https://blog.hubspot.com/marketing/social-media-marketing (Accessed on 6 May 2019).

Casey, S. (2016) Nielsen social media report. www.nielsen.com/us/en/insights/reports/2017/2016-nielsen-social-media-report.html. (Accessed on 6 May 2019).

Chaffey, D. and Bosomworth, D. (2019) Customer persona guide and template. www.smartinsights.com/guides/customer-persona-guide-and-template (Accessed on 6 May 2019).

Chaffey, D. and Ellis-Chadwick, F. (2019) *Digital marketing,* 7th ed., Pearson, UK.

Content Marketing Institute (2019) Content marketing framework. Available at: https://contentmarketinginstitute.com/2019/09/refresh-content-marketing/ (Accessed on 13 September 2019).

Curata (2014) Content marketing tactics. www.curata.com/resources/ebooks/content-marketing-tactics-2014 (Accessed on 6 May 2019).

Demers, J. (2014) www.forbes.com/sites/jaysondemers/2014/08/15/10-online-marketing-metrics-you-need-to-be-measuring/#640a027e76c1 (Accessed on 6 May 2019).

Dobson, P. (2017) SME and location digital marketing. Academy of Marketing – Place Marketing & Branding Special Interest Group – Inaugural SIG Meeting.

Fill, C. and Turnbull, S. (2016) *Marketing Communications: Discovery, Creation and Conversations,* 7th ed. Pearson, Harlow.

Fortin, D. How to create an SEO strategy for 2019. Available at: https://blog.hubspot.com/marketing/seo-strategy (Accessed on 14 May 2019).

Jerath, K., Ma, L. and Park, Y. H. (2014) Consumer click behavior at a search engine: The role of keyword popularity. *Journal of Marketing Research,* 51(4), 480–486.

Kallas, P. (2018) Top 10 social networking sites by market share statistics. www.dreamgrow.com/top-10-social-networking-sites-market-share-of-visits/ (Accessed on 6 May 2019).

Maheshwari, V., Lawrence, A. and Dobson, P. (2019) *Social Media Marketing* in Gbadamosi, A. *Contemporary Issues in Marketing: Principles and Practice.* SAGE Publications Limited, Thousand Oaks, CA.

187

Newman, T. (2013) *Social Media in Sport Marketing*. Holcomb Hathaway Publishers, Scottsdale, AZ.

Patel, N. (2019) How to build a conversion funnel that will triple your profits. Available at: https://neilpatel.com/blog/how-to-build-a-conversion-funnel-that-will-triple-your-profits/ (Accessed on 6 May 2019)

Stec, C. Customer experience: The beginner's guide. Available at: https://blog.hubspot.com/service/customer-experience (Accessed on 6 May 2019).

Chapter 12
Retailing and SME marketing

Mee Leing Ooi and Hsiao-Pei (Sophie) Yang

> **LEARNING OBJECTIVES**
>
> *After reading this chapter, you will be able to:*
> - To introduce the concept of Retailing, SME, SME Marketing;
> - To examine the marketing challenges of online SME retailers in the UK;
> - To evaluate the marketing challenges of offline SME retailers in the UK;
> - To identify the use of omni-channel approach by the UK SME retailers;
> - To analyse brand management in the context of the UK SME retailers.

INTRODUCTION

Retailing, the largest private employers in the UK, is employing 16.3 million people with a combined turnover of over £2 trillion, Small and Medium Enterprises (SMEs) is making a significant impact on economic growth as SMEs accounts for 99% of all UK private enterprises, 59.1% of private sector employment and 48.7% of private turnover (Resnick et al., 2016). Hence, Omar and Fraser (2010) suggested that the well-being of the UK economy depends partly in the role and performance of SMEs.

The aim of this book chapter is to introduce the concept of SME retailing by focussing on the particularities of firm size (only SMEs, not larger retailers), industry context (retailing), while the geographical context is the UK. In this chapter, you are going to consider Retailing and SME Marketing in the UK, including the concept of SME and SME Marketing, the marketing challenges of online versus offline SME retailers, the use of omni-channel approach, and brand management.

We will start the chapter first by introducing retailing, SMEs and SME Marketing, followed by the marketing challenges of online versus offline SME retailers. Third, we will discuss the use of omni-channel approach and conclude with the concept of brand management in the context of SME retailers.

RETAILING, SMES AND SME MARKETING

Definition of retailing

Retailing as 'business activities involved in selling goods and services to consumers for their personal, family, or household use' (Berman and Evans, 2010, p. 28), could either have a single shop or chains with more than one outlet (Omar and Fraser, 2010). The functions of retailing are, (a) the physical movement and storage of goods; (b) the transfer of title to goods; (c) the provision of information concerning the nature and use of goods; (d) the standardization, grading and final processing of goods; (e) the provision of ready availability; (f) the assumption of risk concerning the precise nature and extent of demand; and (g) the financing of inventory and the extension of credit to consumers (Baker, 1998, p. 238).

Definition of SMEs

There is no universal definition of small and medium-sized enterprises (SMEs). Definitions and criteria of SMEs varies widely by country and industry sector (Simpson, Taylor and Padmore, 2011). For example, first published in 1996, the SME definition of the European Commission specifies size gradation for micro, small and medium-sized firms based on three factors: headcount, annual turnover, and annual balance sheet total. That definition was revised in 2003 to reflect on economic changes (Commission of the European Communities, 2003) as follows:

1. Micro: less than ten employees, with a turnover of £2 million, and a balance sheet of £2 million;
2. Small: less than 50 employees, with a turnover of £10 million, and a balance sheet of £10 million;
3. Medium: less than 250 employees, with a turnover of £50 million, and a balance sheet of £43 million.

Marketing of SMEs

Despite of the disagreements on the definitions of SMEs, literature tends to agree that SMEs have fewer resources and finances than larger firms. As a result, Simpson et al. (2011) suggest that marketing activities in SMEs often emerge in specific forms, in line with its dynamic internal and external environments, significantly different to marketing practices in larger firms.

Due to limited resources, SMEs frequently face significant challenges with the strategic implementation of marketing practices. Marketing of SMEs is often informal, unstructured, driven by the particular preferences of the entrepreneur (Simpson et al., 2011), as well as reliant on the personal contact networks of the entrepreneur.

Features of SMEs

The size, resources, and structures of SMEs present a number of opportunities and challenges. The informal and less complex organisational structure of SMEs allows them to react more flexibly and quickly to opportunities in the market, in comparison to the lengthy bureaucratic and managerial set-up of larger companies (Wuest and Thoben, 2011). This is one of the ways in which SMEs can gain competitive advantage over larger firms.

190

RETAILING AND SME MARKETING

However, there are a number of marketing disadvantages associated with SMEs. In particular, SMEs need to deal with human and financial resource constraints. Often, employees in SMEs work across departments and attempt to adopt multiple roles simultaneously. Financial and human resource constraints are likely to mean that the quality and extent of SMEs' marketing operations are limited and insufficient in nature (Wuest and Thoben, 2011). However, despite these numerous constraints, SMEs can develop more innovative and 'nice' marketing strategies given their flexibility and specialist knowledge. This represents a two-sided coin for SMEs' marketing practices.

The marketing challenges of SME retailers in the UK

Unlike larger retail chains that have sophisticated public relations departments with undisputed lobbying power, SME retailers have little opportunity to influence government policy and have no clear strategic direction, which makes them even more vulnerable in a fast-changing competitive retailing environment.

Strategic marketing planning is a vital process in order for firms to achieve their marketing objectives, while this is often lacking in SMEs. Researchers have proposed that SMEs face constraints in carrying out structured, formalised, and strategic planning (Chaston and Mangles, 2002). In contrast to larger firms, strategic planning in SMEs tends to be informal, flexible and undocumented (Majama and Magang, 2017).

It is recommended for SMEs to develop marketing plans based on an understanding of a firm's internal and external factors. While SMEs cannot influence the external environment, they can attempt to enhance their internal structures, which could generate an in-depth, formalised, and strategic marketing planning that fits in with the surrounding contexts. Ekwulugo (2011) suggested SMEs to understand and adapt to the fluctuating external environment. Arguably, as SMEs are more flexible than larger firms, they are better equipped to adjust to changes in the external environment.

There are many theoretical and practical approaches to investigating marketing in SMEs, while there is no unifying theory of marketing in SMEs. It is found that marketing in SMEs are often linked to their entrepreneurial behaviour (Simpson et al., 2011). In the next section, you are going to learn the marketing challenges face by online SME retailers in the UK.

The marketing challenges of online SME retailers in the UK

Online retailing sector in the UK has reach £59.7 billion in 2017, and there is still much room for online retailers to grow, as the sector is forecasted to have double-digit growth through to 2023 (Mintel, 2018). Di Fatta et al. (2018) asserts that e-commerce has become an increasingly important conduit for all firms, but more significant for SMEs that have a limited geographical reach in comparison to chain retailers. However, according to Royal Mail Press (2018), just above two thirds (68%) of UK online SME retailers currently sell overseas, while 80% of online SME retailers sell to Europe, followed by the US (35%), Canada (31%), and Asia (17%).

Due to limited resources, many SMEs lack basic digital skills or do not have the capacity to take advantage of new digital technologies, leading to less productive or innovative in the online retailing provision. In particular, Nripendra et al. (2019) highlighted key barriers for the adoption of digital technologies by SMEs that are, (1) perceived cost, (2) perceived risk, (3) lack of technology knowledge, (4) changes in business strategy and process, and (5) customer trust and confidence. 'Perceived cost' is the top barrier that stop SMEs to adopt

191

technologies, while 'perceived risk', demonstrated by how personal opinions affect the willingness to adopt to technology in SMEs, also has a great significance on the outcome of technology adoption of SMEs (Rana et al., 2019).

Digitalisation is rapidly changing the retailing landscape (Seethamraju and Diatha, 2019), especially in the area of digital payments. Some SMEs are not exploiting the use of digital technologies in areas such as identifying customers and what they want, automating production, enhancing human resource and finance processes, as they are not making use of cloud computing and remote server access. Digital technology and digital skills allow online SME retailers to benefit from digital platforms, such as social media and online selling and payments as well as emerging technologies, such as artificial intelligence, robotics, and 3D printing. In addition, digital technology allows online SME retailers to improve market intelligence, increase local competitiveness and access global markets and knowledge networks at relatively low cost (House of Commons Report, 2019).

Failure to adopt digital technologies could potentially threaten the business model of SME retailers, given changing consumer habits and preferences and increasing competition from retailer chains as well as larger online retailers (Seethamraju and Diatha, 2019). In the light of new technology trends, retailers are advised to focus on consumers rather than on devices. For example, different age groups use the internet in distinct ways, with the younger groups focussing more on leisure and entertainment, while consumers over 50 years old are becoming an important demographic for online retailing, relying more on tablet and smartphone use (Wrigley et al., 2015).

THE MARKETING CHALLENGES OF OFFLINE SME RETAILERS IN THE UK

External forces, such as internet retailing, the rise of 'convenience cultures' and car ownership, have altered consumers' use of brick and mortar retailing, such as shopping at UK High Streets, town centres, or retail shops located in local communities (Ntounis and Parker, 2017). 'Convenience culture', which draw consumers to smaller store format of retailers nearby, alongside the increasing levels of online shopping, have created complex structural changes in the way UK consumers shop. Moreover, the multi-channel reality has implied that some offline SME retailers find it hard to react.

However, the rise of online shopping does not suggest the 'death of physical space' in retailing. Rather, for offline SME retailers, it points towards the need for different formats and changes in business models as well as the use of floorspace. Evidence suggests that growing numbers of consumers are less convinced by the costs-versus-benefits balance of the out-of-centre superstore/retail park proposition and have therefore sought convenience at the local level and in the community (Wrigley et al., 2015). It could therefore bring business opportunities to offline SME retailers.

Research showed that offline SMEs retailers concern about bureaucracy and record keeping, as the regulatory impact can result in reduced competitiveness and impeded growth for SMEs (Schmidt et al., 2007). It is important for offline SME retailers that are located in High Streets or local communities, to consider the needs of their various stakeholders, including town teams, other retailers, service providers, and local government. One of the major challenges faced by SME retailers is identifying and communicating their market position, in particular, the maintenance of up-to-date information on catchments (Millington and Ntounis, 2017).

Though consumers enjoy the convenience of shopping online, an enjoyable offline town centre shopping experience are still needed by consumers. There is a need for different stakeholders in local communities, such as town teams, SMEs retailers, service providers, and local government, to operate together as a 'network' rather than individually, in order to enhance the vitality of town centres (Wrigley et al., 2015). For example, some new 'pop-up' store formats are bringing community-oriented forms of consumption back to the High Streets (Hubbard, 2017), while the complex nature of the High Street still requires all stakeholders to work together effectively, in order to develop the basic knowledge and resources that could help local communities to co-create sustainable town centres (Ntounis and Parker, 2017).

One of the new 'pop-up' store formats is the concept of running a micropub, in which a small-scale venue selling real ale to take over a vacant shop premise, usually in smaller or struggling town centres. The rapid take-up of the micropub concept has attracted considerable attention, suggesting a model for retail regeneration based on community mindedness and a close relationship between business owners and customers (Hubbard, 2017).

Researchers (Millington and Ntounis, 2017) also suggested that knowledge exchange in place management between various stakeholders of High Streets can help inform offline SME retailers the identification of new marketing strategic objectives, project planning, and delivery. Collaborative forms of engaged scholarship, such as conducting suitable market research in local communities, can generate knowledge for offline SME retailers and test alternative ideas and different views of a common problem. In addition, Parker et al. (2017) proposed a place management framework to regenerate High Streets, which consisted of repositioning, reinventing, rebranding and restructuring strategies (4R's of regeneration). Offline SME retailers can apply the 4R's framework and answer key questions such as:

1. Do we need more information (repositioning)?
2. Do we want to change something (reinventing)?
3. Do we need to communicate more effectively (rebranding)?
4. Do we need to work out who is responsible for what (restructuring)?

However, following the given consideration, offline SME retailers still need to understand the impact of technology on consumption and how consumers of different age groups embrace on-the-go technologies during their town centre visit, and whether this plays a significant role in enhancing town centre vitality (Wrigley et al., 2015). Similarly, more evidence is needed by offline SME retailers on the effectiveness of community-led online platforms in town centre revitalisation.

As disused earlier, for consumers who seek convenience at a local/community level, economic cost-saving is not the only issue. Rather, those consumers might be seeking authenticity, traceability, responsible sourcing, and community-sustaining consumption (Wrigley et al., 2015). Apart from assessing local knowledge and real-time data, offline SME retailers should possess a clear and shared understanding of the identity and function of their towns. Moreover, in order to attract consumers to continue shopping in local communities or at High Streets, offline SME retailers need to reflect on the complexity of understanding and analysing market repositioning as well as developing coherent marketing strategies (Millington and Ntounis, 2017).

THE USE OF OMNI-CHANNEL APPROACH BY THE UK SME RETAILERS

While larger retailers are increasingly moving ahead with their omni-channel strategies, evidence suggested that the UK SME retailers still lack skills in channel management, as only four in ten SME retailers (38%) have a physical store as well as a presence online, while additional popular channels for SMEs are still catalogues (14%), telephone (21%), and exhibitions (12%). Nevertheless, over half of SME retailers (52%) are planning to sell through new channels (Royal Mail Press, 2018).

Multi-channel management is the design, deployment, coordination, and evaluation of channels to enhance customer value through effective customer acquisition, retention, and development (Neslin et al., 2006; Verhoef et al., 2015). Retailing literature has so far debated the differences between concepts including multi-channels, cross-channels and omni-channels retailing, suggesting the following definitions (Beck and Rygl, 2015; Yrjola et al., 2018),

1. Multi-channel retailing is the set of activities involved in selling merchandise or services through more than one channel, whereby the customer cannot trigger channel interaction and/or the retailer does not control channel integration.
2. Cross-channel retailing focuses more on the customer's or the retailer's point of view. From the customer's point of view, cross-channel retailing enables the customer to trigger either partial channel interaction through all channels or full interaction through more than one channel (but not all widespread channels).
3. Omni-channel retailing is the set of activities involved in selling merchandise or services through all widespread channels, whereby the customer can trigger full channel interaction and/or the retailer controls full channel integration.

With most consumers today using a combination of online and mobile search in their path to purchase, utilising appropriate channels is key to gain success in retailing. For example, SME retailers can offer in-store picks-ups as well as in-store returns from online orders (Telegraph, 2016). Omni-channel retailing influences the success, development and growth of SMEs as well as online and offline operations in various ways. There are three different areas in which the omni-channel retail could affect the operations of SME retailers (Pertiwi et al., 2016). First, technological factors, as the success of omni-channel is dependent on the availability and use of technology in SMEs. Therefore, a positive outlook is needed by SME retailers to the adoption of technology among the management team, in order to set aside financial, managerial, and technical resources to aid in adoption of omni-channel retailing. Second, SME retailers need to consider the environmental factors, including competitors, customers, suppliers, and external support systems, that influence the implementation of omni-channel retailing. Finally, individual factors are affected by SME managers. A majority of SMEs are run by a single manager who oversees and allows for the activities taking place within the firm. Therefore, the success of attaining profitable omni-channel retail entirely depends on the manager's perception, attitude, culture, and behaviour.

Due to the advent of the online channel and ongoing digitalisation, retailing has changed dramatically in the last two decades (Beck and Rygl, 2015; Yrjola et al., 2018). SME retailers need to make decision concerning to what extent they should implement omni-channel integration (Cao and Li, 2018). SME retailers looking to embrace omnichannel user experiences should reconsider what their store is for. The opportunity for the SME retailers is to create an engaging and entertaining experience in the store, which complements the digital one (Telegraph, 2016).

In the UK, the online channel has become very dominant and can be considered a disruptive development (Christensen and Raynor, 2003). Therefore, some scholars have promoted the move from a multi-channel to an omni-channel retailing model (Rigby, 2011;

Verhoef et al., 2015). It is challenging in a short term, while SME retailers' long-term goal should be on delivering an effective and emotionally engaging brand experience across their own e-commerce and mobile sites, social media, physical stores, and delivery partners (Telegraph, 2016).

Omni-channel retailing offers SME retailers new routes for interaction with their customers, such as via social media, providing SMEs valuable customer opinions on products as well as improving additional support and customer service. Omni-channel management should be seen as the synergetic management of the numerous available channels and customer touchpoints, in such a way that the customer experience across channels and the performance over channels is optimised (Verhoef et al., 2015).

As the retailing industry evolves towards a seamless omni-channel retailing experience, 'the distinctions between physical and online will vanish, turning the world into a showroom without walls' (Brynjolsson et al., 2013, p. 23). The opposite of showrooming also occurs, which is referred to as web rooming, where shoppers seek information online and buy offline. SME retailers are therefore suggested to do cross-channel promotions (Telegraph, 2016).

Omni-channel retailing is not an easy project for SME retailers to take up, especially for micro to small firms because it requires expertise that most times increases expenditure and increases the firm size. Therefore, SMEs are advised to ensure they use adequate strategies instead of trial and error methods that may cost the enterprise unnecessary expenses and losses (Pertiwi et al., 2016).

BRAND MANAGEMENT IN THE CONTEXT OF UK SME RETAILERS

SMEs, as the pillar of the UK economy, contribute to the country growth in terms of employment, wealth creation, and poverty reduction. However, SME retailers face fierce pressure from competition and rapidly changing external environments. Consequently, branding has become a crucial corporate activity to assure a sustainable growth for SMEs (Raki and Shakur, 2018). However, due to smaller marketing budgets, SME retailers often lack a coherent branding strategy, but trying to break through in a crowded marketplace by using all tools at their disposal to create a more personalised, targeted, and buzzworthy marketing (Nielsen, 2018).

Explored the meaning of 'retail brand' on SMEs, Mitchell et al. (2012) confirmed that the owner-manager (OM) is central to the brand management function in SME retailoring. Despite of the important role of OM in SMEs, it was found that when facing marketing challenges and barriers, OMs are often unsure whether marketing will be worth their precious time and expenditure out of SMEs' limited resources (Resnick et al., 2016).

Heding et al. (2008) identified two additional brand management perspectives, that are the emotional and the cultural approach. Within the emotional approach, the brand construct is extended as a central tenant within brand communities, as a conveyor of an emotional brand story as well as a basis for an intimate brand customer relationship. The cultural approach of branding, on the other hand, takes into account the sociocultural perspective of the brand construct, which is perceived as a cultural artefact, given the elevated role of consumption within a postmodern society (Heding et al., 2008).

Literature suggested that SME retailers use branding to avoid price competition, provide added value to customers and achieve differentiation from larger retailers. Two key features of brand management are discussed by scholars (Mitchell et al., 2015), including brand centrality and customer centrality. Brand centrality means moving from product features or consumer-based associations to a more strategic outlook, whereby brand identity (i.e., the corporate brand) takes on a greater significance to the firm, focussing more on the relational and emotional paradigms (Heding et al., 2008). On the other hand, customer centrality is the extent to which consumers are involved in the brand creation process, seeing consumers as the receiver and ultimately the co-creators of brand meaning.

In brand management, SME retailers need to first formulate the brand strategy, then to construct brand identify, and finally evaluate brand equity (Mitchell et al., 2015). First, SME should focus on branding strategy, viewing branding as an important strategic activity, which reinforces the reputation of the SME and allows the business to grow, compete, and survive. SME retailers tend to have a much narrower portfolio, which means it could be risky for the business if their product is not right. Therefore, successful SME retailers are winning by focussing on research (Nielsen, 2018) to inform how the branding strategy should be conducted and on what products.

Second, SME retailers should construct brand identity. SMEs tend to derive their brand identity from the OM, who acts as a brand manager, a brand strategist and a champion for the brand. The vision of OMs is fundamental in embedding key attributes of brand identity in SMEs. Finally, SME retailers should evaluate its brand equity. OMs should recognise the benefits and value of the brand to the SMEs. Normally, SME retailers do not formally measure brand equity, while viewing brand performance more as an informal and subjective approach. However, the study of Mitchell et al. (2015) suggested that the daily interaction between OMs and customers of SMEs is vital to how the brand equality was appraised.

In addition, Resnick et al. (2016) presented a four-attributes frame as the SME self-branding model. It suggests that the personal brand of the OM becomes the identity for the SME through a unique set of skills, often honed to suit his/her particular market context and customer set. The SME self-branding model focussing on the role of the OM, whose individual personality creates and shapes the SME and affect the ability of SMEs to work closely with customers. OMs of SME retailers are therefore advised to (1) focus on being both fast and smart, (2) prioritise their strongest innovations, (3) understand how every decision make could impact the size of company revenue, (4) create a compelling retail story for visibility on shelf and online, and (5) experiment on small number of variables in small universe before implementing ideas in a large scale (Nielsen, 2018).

SUMMARY OF KEY IDEAS

- The size, resources, and structures of SMEs present a number of opportunities and challenges. The informal and less complex organisational structure of SMEs allows them to react more flexibly and quickly to opportunities in the market, in comparison to the lengthy bureaucratic and managerial set-up of larger companies. However, the challenges of SMEs often come from human and financial resource constraints.
- SMEs face constraints in carrying out structured, formalised, and strategic planning. While SMEs are aware of the importance of strategic planning, they often lack the capabilities, resources, and skilled personnel to conduct it effectively. Thus, in contrast to larger firms, strategic planning in SMEs tends to be informal, flexible, and undocumented.
- Taking advantage of the potential benefits, such as customer intelligence gathering, transaction efficiencies, transparency, and extended customer reach, SME retailers can modernise their business model in the digitised environment and remain competitive. Failure to adopt digital technologies could potentially threaten the business model of

RETAILING AND SME MARKETING

SME retailers, given changing consumer habits and preferences and increasing competition from retailer chains as well as larger online retailers.

- The rise of online shopping does not suggest the 'death of physical space' in retailing. Rather, for offline SME retailers, it points towards the need for different formats and changes in business models as well as the use of floorspace. Evidence suggests that growing numbers of consumers are less convinced by the costs-versus-benefits balance of the out-of-centre superstore/retail park proposition and have therefore sought convenience at the local level and in the community. It could therefore bring business opportunities to offline SME retailers.

- Omni-channel management should be seen as the synergetic management of the numerous available channels and customer touchpoints, in such a way that the customer experience across channels and the performance over channels is optimised.

- In brand management, SME retailers need to first formulate the brand strategy, then construct brand identify, and finally evaluate brand equity. SME should first focus on branding strategy, viewing branding as an important strategic activity, which reinforces the reputation of the SME and allows the business to grow, compete, and survive. Second, SME retailers should construct brand identity. SMEs tend to derive their brand identity from the OM, who acts as a brand manager, a brand strategist, and a champion for the brand. Finally, SME retailers should evaluate its brand equity. OMs should recognise the benefits and value of the brand to the SMEs.

CASE STUDY – GOUSTO

The online grocery market was still in its infancy in 2012 but is worth £18bn in 2018 (Elite Business Magazine, 2018). Busy lifestyles were taking a toll on people's ability to cook healthy and nutritious food from scratch, yet the percentage of food going to waste in people's homes was still high.

Gousto, a British meal kit retailer, was founded by Timo Boldt and James Carter in June 2012. The founding mission of Gousto was to transform the online grocery market by dramatically embracing the mega-trends of grocery land, which were sustainability, health, convenience and online. Gousto aims to eliminate food waste. Gousto turns the logic around by first asking customers what they want, and only then buying the ingredients they have asked for.

First, Gousto offers convenience. The brand makes customers' lives easier by saving them time, money and reducing stress with pre-portioned ingredients, easy to follow recipes and delivery straight to their door. Second, Gousto delivers quality, as the brand uses British meat, responsibly sourced fish, and free-range eggs. Gousto also uses local, seasonal produce from British farms wherever possible.

Gousto changes the way consumers order fresh food. Ultimately, Gousto wants consumers to stop shopping at mainstream UK supermarkets (physical and online) and use the service of Gousto. The brand recently launched a customer-facing Artificial Intelligence (AI) recipe recommendation tool, through which half of customer orders are now placed. Gousto also prioritizes the majority of its investment in technology to accelerate business growth.

Gousto applies AI and machine learning to three areas of Intellectual Property (IP). The first area is consumer-facing, which offers personalisation. Second, Gousto

197

aims to improve its automation factory supply chain. Third, AI connects personalisation and supply chain to improve productivity and efficiency (Growth Business, 2018).

By investing in AI and machine learning, Gousto has the potential to run much more efficiently than mainstream UK grocery stores' offline or online offering, especially in reducing food waste. AI is now identifying market gaps in the menu of Gousto and helps the brand answering key questions such as, 'what are the trends', 'what are the gaps', 'what do consumers really want', and 'why do consumers want it'? The brand claims to do research and development as well as innovation through AI. Gousto offers more choice to customers than competitors by driving factory and logistics efficiencies through the use of automation and data.

Gousto's meal kit service offers over 30 weekly recipes and delivers seven days per a week. In comparison to competitors, it has the shortest lead time of 3 days, and the lowest price point, starting at £2.98 per meal (Techcrunch, 2019).

Due to its success, Gousto has been voted best recipe kit service by media, such as the Independent, the Guardian, the Metro and Time Out London. In December 2015, Gousto raised £9m in funding from BGF Ventures, MMC (Gousto, 2019). In October 2016, Gousto's co-founder Timo Boldt was awarded IGD's 'Young Entrepreneur of the Year' award (Gousto, 2019). Gousto has so far raised £28.5m from venture capital investors, aiming to be responsible for 400 million meals in UK homes by 2025 (Telegraph, 2018).

Gousto is a purpose driven business, with a passion for getting more UK consumers cooking and in turn improving the health of the nation. Gousto wants to create value for customers where it really matters, rather than just "building tech for the sake of tech" (Growth Business, 2018).

Discussion questions on Gousto, the case study
1. What are the competitive advantages of Gousto?
2. How does Gousto compete against larger UK retailers, utilising digital technologies?

DISCUSSION QUESTIONS ON THE CHAPTER

- Discuss the marketing challenges of online SME retailers in the UK;
- Evaluate the marketing challenges of offline SME retailers in the UK;
- Identify the use of omni-channel approach by the UK SME retailers;
- Analyse the brand management approaches by the UK SME retailers.

LET'S REASON TOGETHER

Identify a well-known SME retailer in the UK and answer the following questions based on the company's marketing practices:

- How does your chosen SME retailer compete against larger retailers using online and/or offline marketing strategies?

TECHNOLOGY, SME, AND THE 21ST CENTURY

SME retailers often do not know what technologies are available, how technologies are used by competitors, and whether they are optimising the technologies that they do have.

SME retailers are therefore suggested to take advantage of digital payment systems as well as other digital technologies, including mobile, social media, and analytics. Ultimately, the use of technology can help SMEs to deliver efficiencies, especially on managing staff time, allow better access to store data, enhance data creation, modification, and analysis.

DISCUSSION QUESTION FOR TECHNOLOGY, SME, AND THE 21ST CENTURY

- How can technology be used better by SMEs in the 21st century, to gain competitive advantages against rivals who are larger retailers?

REFERENCES

Baker, M. J. (Ed.). (1998) *Macmillan Dictionary of Marketing and Advertising*. Palgrave Macmillan International Higher Education, London.

Beck, N. and Rygl, D. (2015) Categorization of multiple channel retailing in Multi-, Cross-, and Omni-channel retailing for retailers and retailing. *Journal of Retailing and Consumer Services*, 27, 170–178. Available at: https://doi.org/10.1016/j.jretconser.2015.08.001.

Berman, B. R. and Evans, J. R. (2010) *Retail Management: A Strategic Approach*, 11th ed. Prentice Hall, Boston, MA.

Brynjolsson, E., Jeffrey Hu, Yu and Rahman, Mohmmad S. (2013) Competing in the age of omnichannel retailing. *MIT Sloan Management Review*, 54(4), 23–29.

Cao, L. and Li, L. (2018) Determinants of retailers' cross-channel integration: An innovation diffusion perspective on omni-channel retailing. *Journal of Interactive Marketing*, 44. 10.1016/j.intmar.2018.04.003.

Chaston, I. and Mangles, T. (2002) *Small Business Marketing Management*. Palgrave, Hampshire.

Christensen, Clayton M. and Raynor, Michael E. (2003) *The Innovator's Solution*. Harvard Business Press, Boston.

Commission of European Communities (2003) *DG Enterprise: Final Report of the Expert Group on Enterprise Clusters and Networks*. Commission of European Communities, Brussels.

Di Fatta, D., Patton, D. and Viglia, G. (2018) The determinants of conversion rates in SME e-commerce websites. *Journal of Retailing and Consumer Services*, 41, 161–168.

Ekwulugo, F. (2011) Marketing Planning in Small Business. In Nwankwo, S. and Gbadamosi, A. (Eds.), *Entrepreneurship Marketing: Principles and Practice of SME Marketing*. Routledge, London, 356–366.

Elite Business Magazine (2018) Timo Boldt tells the £56.5m investment story of Gousto. http://elitebusinessmagazine.co.uk/finance/item/timo-boldt-tells-the-565m-investment-story-of-gousto (Accessed on 27 March 2019).

Gousto (2019) Gousto's founder: 'I'm fed up with food waste.' www.gousto.co.uk/blog/stopping-food-waste (Accessed on 27 March 2019).

Growth Business (2018) Why recipe box firm Gousto is coming to eat supermarkets' lunch. www.growthbusiness.co.uk/why-recipe-box-firm-gousto-is-coming-to-eat-supermarkets-lunch-2555382/ (Accessed on 27 March 2019).

Heding, T., Knudtzen, C. F. and Bjerre, M. (2008) *Brand Management: Theory, Research Practice*. Routledge, London.

House of Commons Report (2019) Business, energy and industrial strategy committee small businesses and productivity, Fifteenth Report of Session 2017–2019. Available at: https://publications.parliament.uk/pa/cm201719/cmselect/cmbeis/807/80702.htm.

Hubbard, P. (2017) Enthusiasm, craft and authenticity on the high street: Micropubs as 'community fixers'. *Social & Cultural Geography*, DOI: 10.1080/14649365.2017.1380221.

Majama, N. S. and Israel 'Teddy' Magang, T. (2017) Strategic planning in small and medium enterprises (SMEs): A case study of Botswana SMEs. *Journal of Management and Strategy*, 8(1), 74–103.

Millington, S. and Ntounis, N. (2017) Repositioning the high street: Evidence and reflection from the UK. *Journal of Place Management and Development*, 10(4), 364–379.

Mintel (2018) UK online retailing market report. Available at: https://store.mintel.com/uk-online-retailing-market-report (24 July 2019).

Mitchell, R., Hutchinson, K. and Bishop, S. (2012) Interpretation of the retail brand: An SME perspective. *International Journal of Retail & Distribution Management*, 40(2), 157–175. Available at: https://doi.org/10.1108/ 09590551211201883.

Mitchell, R., Hutchinson, K., Quinn, B. and Gilmore, A. (2015) A framework for SME retail branding. *Journal of Marketing Management*, DOI:10.1080/0267257X.2015.1063531.

Neslin, Scott A., Grewal, D., Leghorn, R., Shankar, V., Teerling, M. L., Thomas, J. S. and Verhoef, P. C. (2006) Challenges and opportunities in multichannel customer management. *Journal of Service Research*, 9(2), 95–112.

Nielsen (2018) Why small brands are stealing the spotlight. www.nielsen.com/ca/en/insights/news/2018/perspectives-why-small-brands-are-stealing-the-spotlight.html (Accessed on 27 March 2019).

Ntounis, N. and Parker, C. (2017) Engaged scholarship on the high street: The case of HSUK2020. *Journal of Place Management and Development*, 10(4), 349–363.

Omar, O. and Fraser, P. (2010) The role of small and medium enterprises retailing in Britain. University of Hertfordshire Business School, Working Paper.

Parker, C., Ntounis, N., Millington, S., Quin, S. and Castillo-Villar, F. R. (2017) Improving the vitality and viability of the UK High Street by 2020: Identifying priorities and a framework for action. *Journal of Place Management and Development*, 10(4), 310–348.

Pertiwi, E., Guihua, N. and Pingfeng, L. (2016) The influence of omni-channel retailing on Indonesian SMEs online and offline business operations. *Innovation and Management*, 746–752.

Raki, S. and Shakur, M. M. A. (2018) Brand management in Small and Medium Enterprises (SMEs) from stakeholder theory perspective. *International Journal of Academic Research in Business and Social Sciences*, 8(7), 392–409.

Rana, Nripendra P., Barnard, D. J. J., Baabdullah, Abdullah M. A., Rees, D. and Roderick, S. (2019) Exploring barriers of m-commerce adoption in SMEs in the UK: Developing a framework using ISM. *International Journal of Information Management*, 44, 141–153, ISSN 0268-4012, Available at: https://doi.org/10.1016/j.ijinfomgt.2018.10.009.

Ravi Seethamraju, R. and Diatha, K. S. (2019) Digitalization of small retail stores, challenges in digital payments. In Proceedings of the 52nd Hawaii International Conference on System Sciences.

Resnick, S. M., Cheng, R., Simpson, M. and Lourenço, F. (2016) Marketing in SMEs: A "4Ps" self-branding model. *International Journal of Entrepreneurial Behavior & Research*, 22(1), 155–174.

Rigby, D. (2011) The future of shopping. *Harvard Business Review*, 89(12), 65–76.

Royal Mail Press (2018) Majority of UK SME online retailers are confident sales will increase in 2018. www.royalmailgroup.com/en/press-centre/press-releases/royal-mail/majority-of-uk-sme-online-retailers-are-confident-sales-will-increase-in-2018/ (Accessed on 28 March 2019).

Schmidt, R. Ä., Bennison, D., Bainbridge, S. and Hallsworth, A. (2007) Legislation and SME retailers – compliance costs and consequences. *International Journal of Retail & Distribution Management*, 35(4), 256–270. Available at: https://doi.org/10.1108/09590550710736193.

Simpson, M., Taylor, N. and Padmore, J. (2011) Marketing in SMEs. In Nwankwo, S. and Gbadamosi, T. (Eds.), *Entrepreneurship Marketing: Principles and Practice of SME Marketing*. Routledge, New York.

Techcrunch (2019) A further £18M funding lands on Gousto's plate. Available at: https://techcrunch.com/2019/01/06/a-further-18m-funding-lands-on-goustos-plate/?guccounter=1 (Accessed on 27 March 2019).

Telegraph (2016) Omnichannel retail tips for small businesses. www.telegraph.co.uk/connect/small-business/business-solutions/omni-channel-retail-tips-for-smes/ (Accessed on 29 March 2019).

Telegraph (2018) Meal kit maker Gousto delivers £28.5m investment. www.telegraph.co.uk/business/2018/03/12/meal-kit-maker-gousto-delivers-285m-investment/ (Accessed on 27 March 2019).

Verhoef, P. C., Kannan, P. K. and Inman, J. J. (2015) From multi-channel retailing to omni-channel retailing: Introduction to the special issue on multi-channel retailing. *Journal of Retailing*, 91(2), 174–181.

Wrigley, N., Lambiri, D., Astbury, G., Dolega, L., Hart, C., Reeves, C. and Wood, S. (2015) British high streets: From crisis to recovery? A comprehensive review of the evidence. Available at: https://core.ac.uk/download/pdf/30341672.pdf (Accessed on 28 March 2019).

Wuest, T. and Thoben, K. (2011) Information management for manufacturing SMEs. In IFIP International Conference on Advances in Production Management Systems 2011, Springer, 488–495.

Yrjola, M., Saarijarvi, H. and Nummela, H. (2018) The value propositions of multi-, cross-, and omni-channel retailing. *International Journal of Retail & Distribution Management*, 46(11/12), 1133–1152. Available at: https://doi.org/10.1108/IJRDM-08-2017-0167.

Chapter 13

Small and medium-sized enterprise retailing in the UK

Ogenyi Omar and Peter Fraser

LEARNING OBJECTIVES

After reading this chapter, you should be able to:
- Understand the current issues and trends in SME retailing in the UK;
- Appreciate the key features and competitive position of SME retailing;
- Gain basic knowledge of the benefits and drawbacks of SME retailing;
- Recognise the challenges and opportunities facing the owner-managers in competing with larger retailers.

INTRODUCTION

Small and medium retail companies in cities and town across the UK tend to face many operational problems including: increased market competition from larger chains across the country; changing consumer shopping habits, insufficient levels of financial investment; low business and management skills, poor knowledge of current legislation, lack of sector-specific support systems, and poor staff training in retail marketing. In spite of these numerous problems, small and medium-sized enterprise (SME) retailers play an important role in providing to the cities and towns in terms of product, services, and retail formats. Meanwhile, the contribution made by these SME retailers to the landscape in the UK is often not recognised or given due regard by performance indicators, which fail to address their input into the socio-economic activities of the UK high streets. Being small tends to be a handicap in a business environment because the problems faced by SME retailers in the UK are directly applicable to SME retailers in many other countries in Europe and North America.

In the UK, SME retailers have been largely ignored in the past for so long and their contribution to the local community in which they are based is only just beginning to be appreciated. Unfortunately, unlike the larger retail chains that have sophisticated public relations department with undisputed lobbying power, SMEs have little opportunity to influence government policy because they do not always have a common voice. Also, unlike the larger chains that have a clearly defined business and marketing strategy many SME retailers have no strategic direction which makes them even more vulnerable in such a fast changing competitive environment.

The purpose of this chapter is to review the operational dimensions of small and medium enterprise retailers in the UK and highlight the difficult retailing issues faced by these retailers in the fast changing and competitive UK retail environment. The chapter documents the contribution made by the SME retail sector and identifies the critical success factors taking their disadvantage due to size into consideration.

The chapter is structured as: following the introduction, the overview of the general retail environment is briefly explored. This is followed by a theoretical review; SME retail sector examination; impact of competition on growth strategy; contributions and critical success factors; and finally, a forecast and future outlook.

DEFINITION OF SMES IN RETAILING

It is important to note that, in general, there is no single official universal definition for a small firm (Mukhtar, 1998). However, the US Small Business Administration (SBA) has traditionally defined 'small businesses as fewer than 500 employees' (SBA, 2001). While its size standards were recently revised to vary by industry as defined by the North American Industrial Classification System (NAICS), with the exception of the wholesale trade, the size maximum for most sectors remains at 500 employees. Meanwhile, other studies that have followed this definition of small businesses may have failed to detect and discriminate the differences and nuances between the 'larger' small firms for example, a firm with 450 employees and £15m in revenues and truly small firms for example, a firm with seven employees and £30,000 and £450,000 in sales (Haksever, 1996; Ibrahim et al., 2001; Sawyer et al., 2003). Since there is no unanimous agreement as to the definition of SME, it is important to always search the current literature for other definitions of small businesses.

According to Mukhtar (1996), a wide range of definitions are used in practice. The Wiltshire Committee's definition of SMEs is often used by researchers and states that:

> it is a business in which one or two persons are required to make all the important management decisions such as finance, accounting, personnel, purchasing, processing or servicing, marketing, selling, etc., without the aid of internal specialists and with specific knowledge in only one or two functional areas.
>
> (see Berryman, 1983)

The European Commission offers a more exacting definition; and its definition for SMEs, first adopted in 1996, specifies size gradations for micro, small, and medium-sized firms based on three factors: headcount, annual turnover, and annual balance sheet total (see Mukhtar, 1998). Recently, that definition was revised to reflect economic changes since 1996 (Commission of the European Communities, 2003) as follows:

1. Micro: ten or fewer employees, with a turnover of €2 million, and a balance sheet of €2 million;
2. Small: up to 50 employees with a turnover of €10 million, and a balance sheet of €10 million;
3. Medium: up to 250 employees, with a turnover of €50 million, and a balance sheet of €43 million.

OGENYI OMAR AND PETER FRASER

In specific retailing terms, there are three approaches to defining and classifying retail firm size in the UK. The first definition concerns less than 100 employees (officially medium-sized and small enterprises, with small defined as less than ten employees and medium defined as between ten and 100 employees). The second definition typical for the retail sector takes the number of outlets as a measure, with single shops and chains (consisting of more than one outlet). The third definition takes sales volume as a measure for classification.

EXHIBIT 1 HARPO'S: A SINGLE RETAIL OUTLET

Harpo's, a single outlet retailer of secondhand records, CDs, DVDs, and music books, has just won the award for 'Coketown's best independent retailer' for the second year in succession. At the start of the business there is only a basic website. It seemed workable enough but was not very exciting or informative. John, in his mid-fifties, married with three grown daughters from his first marriage, made it clear that he has no business background or training. In his earlier years he started a civil engineering degree but dropped out as he couldn't cope with mathematics on the course. In order to earn a living, John said he began working on a market stall in another city selling secondhand records. His father, a wealthy civil servant, had never really been reconciled to the way in which his son bought and sold secondhand records for a living. But ever since John could remember he'd loved records and he relished trading, moving on from the stall to run a record shop. Then he wanted to live in the country with his then girlfriend, and they were offered a small cottage outside Coketown. John used all his savings as a deposit on the cottage and took out a mortgage.

Needing to earn a living in Coketown, in 1976, he set up Harpo's with a partner. Simon. Simon had previously run a similar business and so John felt confident going into business with him. To assist with startup costs they obtained a bank loan of £500. Six years later in 1983, he bought out his business partner for £10,000 – he had found that his partner liked to spend money whereas John was more cautious and wanted to have more control over events. The current premises represents the third location for Harpo's. Harpo's is still operating as a sole trader though John has occasionally considered whether or not to convert it to a company in order to take advantage of the protection afforded by limited liability. One of his friends, an experienced businessman told him that this would be a wise move, especially for the future value of the business. The business has two main product areas, one being the sale of tickets to events (mainly local pub gigs amounting to 50% of sales) and the other being the sale of secondhand records, CDs, DVDs, and music books.

The business has developed a lot since being founded in the late seventies. John said that although it had changed, the business has evolved over the years rather than made any sudden jumps. What changes had he seen? Technology apart, his audience tends to be made up of either those in their forties or fifties or students. He gets a buzz when he sees students come in. After all these years he still enjoys pricing records. His staff have been with him long term and they all have different skills. For example, if you ask his manager, he can give the 'A side' to any quoted 'B side'. One of his people keeps his knowledge up to date, being a DJ. One of his daughters,

SMALL AND MEDIUM-SIZED ENTERPRISE RETAILING

the youngest (Bridget) also works in the shop, although John explained that this is because she does not know what to do with her life rather than the fact that she wants to be part of the business. Of course, staffs occasionally leave. Apparently one of his employees left amicably and went to work in a similar shop in the capital. When they talked by phone his ex-employee explained his new boss just looked up the catalogue price and applied that to each item, although in all likelihood it would remain on the shelf. John explained that he never did this, this was not London and he needed to shift stock.

In the end there were certain heuristics or rules of thumb that John had developed over his years in business. He summarised these as follows: look after your staff; pay your bills on time; save for retirement immediately you start (he hadn't and said he would retire tomorrow if he could); work long hours; anything you can do yourself, do yourself; always be nice to people – you never know when you might need a favour, don't ask any of your staff to do anything you wouldn't do yourself. Always do your own bookkeeping. This not only saves money but more important helps you keep your finger on the pulse of the business. In particular, said John, pay your tax and pay it on time, then the VAT man wouldn't come near. The best thing he learned at school, he said, was perhaps surprising. After he obtained an 'O' level in wood-work, he was able to do his own shop-fitting activities. Even better, in the early days he did shop-fitting jobs for cash – once for a bank manager. This meant that he was able to keep his 'cash flow' positive. He'd only ever had to fire one person and that was for poor timekeeping. As to the future, he wondered about downloading music and how long it would take before it affected his business.

CHARACTERISTICS OF SMALL AND MEDIUM-SIZED ENTERPRISE RETAILERS

The operation of an SME retailing business may seem an attractive proposition to the person who 'wants to be his own boss'. In general, there are few people who do not feel that they could run a small business successfully. But in the public interest several European countries demand some form of qualification and/or experience before setting up a small retail business. However, there is no law preventing people without qualifications or experience from owning a small business. Some characteristics can be ascribed to many small and medium enterprise retailing including long hours of operation, legal restrictions, an enormous volume of bookkeeping and accounting involving the complications of value added tax (VAT), National Insurance contributions, and income tax. In practice, the experience of many small and medium enterprise retailers is likely to deter many prospective retailers, especially the intending self-employed people as the situation in Exhibit 2 highlighted.

EXHIBIT 2 THE BARBER SHOP

Bill, after years of experience working for others as a barber, is determined to open a business of his own. He strikes a deal with a prominent Chicago hotel. He will

205

open his business in their flagship property, a gigantic 2000 bed hotel where he will have exclusive barber rights. Even better, if he is successful in the larger premises he has there, he will be offered the opportunity to develop smaller shops throughout the nation-wide chain. Bill commits everything he has to his enterprise but quickly discovers that his business is not performing to expectations.

- hotel visitors rarely stay for more than two to three days and often have their hair cut before coming to town;
- being inside a hotel, and unable to advertise his presence on the street, he attracts virtually no passing trade;
- alongside his hairdressing business he offers a shoe shining service, which seems to be attractive. These chairs are nearly always full, but the contribution made to profit scarcely dents his heavy overheads.

Bill is worried about the future prospects for his business if things continue as they are, and he has asked you as his friends what you think he should now do. Draw up an outline action plan and advise him.

The lack of 'know-how' at the start and expertise in merchandising or stock control in the succeeding years can cause a small retailer to feel isolated and uncompetitive. Although there are several sources of help both official and non-government agencies (NGOs) but only few small enterprise retailers are aware of them. For this reason, the government, through the Department of Industry, has set up a series of Small Firms Information Centres and issued a series of free guides for small firms.

As per the discussion so far in this chapter, things are not all that bad for small enterprise retailers; and there are some good advantages of self-employment. For example, Blankson and Omar (2003) found that 'an inherent advantage SME retailers usually possess is a rapport with their customers and the locality', which is difficult for large stores to achieve. Similarly, the flexibility of service to suit parochial needs, and informality of retail service procedures can build up goodwill and especially attract the timid customer who is overawed by large sophisticated stores.

The SME retailer's convenience aspect of being close to the local community should not be overlooked. Many SMEs open until late and serve the local community in such a way that they cannot be dismissed lightly as uneconomical or old fashioned. They form a very necessary and useful part of social life in the communities they operate. The traditional wholesaler is one of the props of the average private shopkeeper. His representative will call regularly on the shop, take orders and show samples, give advice and credit and supply in small quantities from the ranges of many manufacturers. For example, some wholesale pharmacists make daily deliveries of prescriptions to their client retailers.

A fair proportion of SME retailers is affiliated to voluntary groups and chains with whom they agree to buy the bulk of their supplies while retaining their independence. Through this loyalty to the group, SME retailers benefit from low prices, advertising, a supply of promotional aids, advice, and often financial help in re-equipping the business. The grocery voluntary groups are known as 'Symbol' groups, incorporating a number of wholesalers under their brand and lately developing their own-branded merchandise. Another source of supply to the SME retailer is the cash-and-carry warehouse. These are usually situated

SMALL AND MEDIUM-SIZED ENTERPRISE RETAILING

where occupancy costs are low, and the costs of sales representatives, delivery, and credit are completely eliminated. By passing on these savings a cash-and-carry warehouse can sell at near to wholesale cost, gaining net margins from bulk-buying discounts. The most important feature of the cash-and-carry warehouse is that it should not sell to the public.

STRUCTURAL OUTLINE

The Office for National Statistics (ONS) counts more than 81,000 enterprises in the UK retail sector, with only 200 of them not belonging to the medium-sized and small group. About 95% of the enterprises are typified as small and less than 5% as medium. According to figures from ONS, more than 75% of the outlets in the UK retailing belong to single operating firms, and less than 25% are regarded as multiple chains (see Table 13.1). The market share (in terms of sales) of small business is less than 10% and the market share of medium-sized business is about 15%. The multiples and the cooperatives have the largest share of the market. This share of the UK retail market tends to vary significantly among

Table 13.1 Classification of British retailing

Type	Features
1. Multiple chain retailing e.g., Next, ASDA, M&S.	Defined as having more than ten outlets and having: • Standardised products • Competitive prices • Creating customer familiarity with the store's corporate image • Own brand ranges of products
2. Co-operative retailing e.g., CWS, CRS	• 19th-century origins; stronger in the North than in the South • Original philosophy of fairness and consumer control • Lack of coordination between the different co-ops • Process of distributing dividends has reduced amount available for investment in new stores and locations • Conflict of interest between those that see them in original terms and those who see them as more commercial entities • Poor market focus and market image
3. Department stores e.g., Selfridges, House of Fraser	• Emerged in the 19th century as a development of the drapery trade • Purpose to sell a wide variety of products under one roof as much as possible to middle classes • Currently groups attempt to standardise facilities as far as possible
4. Independent retailers	• Fewer than ten outlets • Major decline in total shop numbers due to fall in-independents • Financially incapable of changing or too conservative • Personal service counts for much of the surviving trade
5. Voluntary chains e.g., SPAR, Londis	• Small business create buying and marketing strengths through contractual relationship
6. Franchises e.g., Benetton, Body Shop, McDonald's	• Agreements between retailers and franchisees offering local expertise and money in exchange for marketing system of the franchise

(continued)

207

Table 13.1 *(continued)*

7. Mail Order e.g., Littlewoods, Next Directory, Lands End	• Traditionally a means of enabling poorer households to buy on credit • Market for traditional catalogues declining • Updating through telephone ordering targeted product ranges
8. Door-to-door selling e.g., Kleene Eeze, Betterware	• A declining form of selling, created by urbanisation and easy access to high densities of population. Household goods are successfully distributed in this way
9. Mobile Shops e.g., Groceries, fruit and vegetables, fish and chips	• Reach consumers distant from local shops, e.g., housing estates and rural areas, as independent stores on wheels
10. Informal selling e.g., Dorling Kindersley, Anne Summers	• Party plan shopping based on a local agent organising friends and neighbours to look at products in an informal home environment
11. Periodic markets e.g., Camden Lock market, Petticoat Lane, London	• The oldest form of exchange • Many street markets confute to find success in fresh products, low price clothing and household goods. Some markets become established and trade daily in a specialised area

different retail sectors as for example the market share of small business in the food sector is only 11%whereas small business in books claims more than 50% of the market.

The UK retail sector is one of the largest employers and more than a quarter of these persons are active owners and their family members, a typical characteristic of small firms. In that regard, the UK retail sector is definitely dominated by small and medium enterprise retailers.

In addition to the existing categorisation of different ways of distributing goods and services it is possible to note the emergence of new retail concepts, originating in the US or Europe including discount warehouses, 'Category Killers', which enjoy continued growth in less competitive sectors with wider ranges and lower prices, for example Toys R Us, Pet City, and IKEA, and discount food retailers such as Netto and ALDI.

RETAIL INDUSTRY RESTRUCTURING

In recent years, and more fundamentally, UK retailing is being restructured by the growth in larger store sizes and decline of independent retailing seem to accompany each other. The UK has higher than average retail concentration in almost all sub-sectors: the ten largest retailers combined have 37–38% of all retail sales. In food retailing concentration is increasingly apparent as regional multiples such as Wm. Low, and now weaker national chains, such as Summerfield, have been acquired by stronger competitors.

During the 1980s, relaxation of planning policy enabled property developers and retailers to create new shopping centres, retail parks, and, largest of all, regional shopping centres. Lakeside and The Metro Centre in Gateshead are typical of these extensive facilities. Larger stores sizes were made possible by development and resulted in wider product assortment, the development of new products and spacious, customer oriented shopping environments. As result the traditional town centre shopping areas and suburban parades have declined. This may be due partly to local and central government policies on retailing.

SMALL AND MEDIUM-SIZED ENTERPRISE RETAILING

Table 13.2 *Percentage share of retail sales by top five multiples in sub-sectors*

Product Sector	% Share of Sales
Grocers	66
DIY	63
Mixed good	61
Chemists (excluding Boots co)	58
Electrical goods	36
Clothing	33

Source: Compiled from Key Notes, 2008

ORGANISATION OF SMALL RETAILER

Small retailers generally use simple arrangements because they contain only two or three levels of personnel for example, the owner-manager and employees. In most cases, the owner-manager personally runs the business and oversees workers (Berman and Evans, 2001:368). The owner-managers of a single store may be the entire organisation and as such when they go to lunch or go home, the store closes. But as Levy and Weitz (2004: 282) observed, 'as sales grow, the owner-managers employ others to work for them'. In a small business organisation such as the type in Figure 13.1, coordinating and controlling employee activities is easier than in a large chain stores. The owner-manager simply assigns tasks to each employee and watches to see that these tasks are performed properly. Since the number of employees is small, small enterprise retailers have little specialisation (Blankson and Omar, 2003). At the same time, Blankson and Omar (2003) also documented that each employee performs a wide range of activities, while the owner-manager is responsible for all management tasks of the firm.

As sales increase, specialisation in management may occur when the owner-manager employs additional or an external consulting team. Figure 1 illustrates the common division of management responsibilities into merchandise and store management. The owner-manager continues to perform strategic management tasks. The store manager may be responsible for administrative tasks associated with receiving and shipping merchandising

Figure 13.1
Organisation of a small retailer

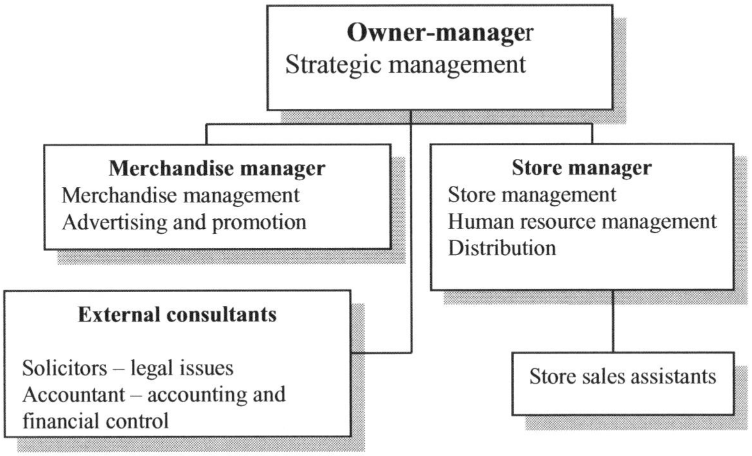

209

and managing the employees (Levy and Weitz, 2004). The merchandise manager who is sometimes referred to as the buyer may handle the advertising and promotion tasks as well as the merchandising tasks. Often the owner-manager contracts with an accountant to perform accounting and financial tasks while the solicitors handle the legal store issue. As the small enterprising retailer continues to grow, it may expand to become a medium enterprise retailer subsequently, provided it operates within the government regulations.

Some SME retailers may only own one retail unit but others may own several units in several locations. In the UK, there are almost 2.2 million small to medium enterprise retailers accounting for nearly 35% of total retail store sales. One-half of small enterprises are run entirely by the owners and/or their families. These small enterprise retailers generate just 3% of total UK retail sales and many of them have no paid employees.

The high number of SME retailers in the UK is associated with the ease of entry into the retail marketplace (McGoldrick, 2002). As a result of low capital requirements and relatively simple licensing provisions, entry for many kinds of small retail enterprises is easy. The investment per employee in retailing is usually much lower than for manufacturing firms. Retailer licensing, although somewhat more stringent in recent years, is still a matter of routine. Each year, tens of thousands of new retail businesses, most of them small independent retailers, open new businesses in the UK. The ease of entry into retailing is accompanied by and reflects the low market shares of many SME retailing firms in many goods/service categories. However, in the grocery retail category for example, where large chains are quite strong, the four largest grocery retailers account for more than 65% of sales.

Since a great deal of competition is due to the relative ease of entry into retailing it is undoubtedly a strong factor in the high rate of retail business failures among the newer SME retail entrants. The Office for National Statistics (ONS) estimates that one-third of new UK retailers do not survive their first year and two-thirds do not continue beyond their third year. Most of these failures involve small independent retailers. On an annual basis, a large number of these small enterprise retailers do go bankrupt in addition to the thousands of small retailers that just close down due to inability to compete in a rapidly changing sector of the UK economy. In spite of this high rate of failures SME retailing has a variety of advantages as well as some disadvantages. These advantages and drawbacks are listed in Table 13.3.

Table 13.3 Benefits and drawbacks of SME retailing

Advantages	Disadvantages
There is great deal of flexibility in choosing retail formats and locations, and in devising strategy. Because only one store location is involved, detailed specifications can be set for the best location and a thorough search undertaken. Uniform location standards are not needed, as they are for chain stores. In setting strategy, small retailers do not have to worry about being too close to other company stores and have great latitude in selecting target markets. Since many SMEs have modest goals, small customer segments may be selected rather than the mass market. Product assortments, prices, store hours, and other factors are then set consistent with the market.	In bargaining with suppliers, SMEs may not have much power because they often buy in small quantities. They may even be bypassed by suppliers or limited in the products made available to them. Reordering may also be tough if minimum order requirements are too high for them to quality. In order to overcome this problem, a number of SMEs, such as DIY stores, have formed buying groups to increase their power in dealing with suppliers.

SMALL AND MEDIUM-SIZED ENTERPRISE RETAILING

Table 13.3 *(continued)*

In so far as small enterprise retailers run only one store, investment cost for leases, fixtures, workers, and merchandise is very low. In addition, there is no duplication of stock or personnel functions. Responsibilities are clearly delineated within a store as identified earlier in this chapter.	Most small and medium enterprise retailers typically cannot gain economies of scale (low per-unit costs due to handling many units at one time) in buying and maintaining inventory. Due to financial constraints, small assortments are bought several times per year rather than large orders once or twice per year. Thus, transportation, ordering, and handling costs per unit are high.
SME retailers often act as specialists and acquire skills in a niche of a particular goods/service category. They are then more efficient and can lure shoppers interested in specialised retailing.	Operations are often very labour intensive, sometimes with little knowledge of computer technology. Ordering, taking inventory, marking items, ringing up sales, and bookkeeping may be done manually. This is less efficient than using computers (expensive for some small retailers in terms of the initial investment in hardware and software although costs have fallen significantly). In many cases, owner-managers are unwilling or unable to spend time learning how to set up and apply computerised procedures.
SMEs exert strong control over their strategies, and the owner-operator is typically on the premises. Decision making is usually centralised and layers of management personnel are minimised.	By virtue of the relatively high costs of television advertising and the large geographic coverage of magazines and some newspapers (too large for firms with one outlet), SMEs are limited in their access to advertising media and may pay higher fees per advertising compared to regular users. Yet, there are various promotion tools available for creative SME retailers.
There is a certain image attached to small and medium enterprise retailers, particularly small ones that chains find difficult to capture. This is the image of a personable retailer with a comfortable atmosphere in which to shop.	A crucial problem for family run retail business is an overdependence on the owner's resources. Often, all decisions are made by this person, and there is no continuity of management when the owner-manager is ill, on vacation, or retires. The leading worries at family run retail business involve identifying successors, the role of non-family employees, and management training for family members. Long-run success and employee morale can be affected by overdependence on the owner.
Small and medium-sized enterprise retailers are able to sustain consistency in their efforts since only one geographic market is usually served and just one strategy is carried out. For example, there cannot be problems due to two branch stores selling identical items at different prices.	There is a limited amount of time and resources allotted to long-run planning. Since the owner is intimately involved in daily operations of the firm, responsiveness to new legislation, new products, and new competitors frequently suffers.

(continued)

211

Table 13.3 *(continued)*

Almost all the SMEs have 'independence'. Owner-managers tend to be in full charge and do not have to fret about stockholders, board-of-director meetings, and labour unrest. They are often free from union work and seniority rules. This can enhance labour productivity.

Owner-managers usually have a strong entrepreneurial drive. They have personal investments in their businesses, success or failure has huge implications, and there is a lot of ego involved.

THE UK GOVERNMENT POLICY AND RETAILING

The UK economy is characterised by many unique relations between retailers and their suppliers. The 'balance of power' in this relationship has changed significantly in the past four decades in favour of the largest retailers, and this trend has been highlighted particularly in the grocery supermarket field. In a realistic sense, SME retailers have not benefited much from such a shift in power relationship. The largest supermarket operators have been able to take advantage of their structural market power, the use of information technology, and generally increasingly sophisticated management to achieve considerable cost savings not just in traditional merchandise purchases but also in newer areas such as fresh produce and petrol, as well as in the area of retailer-dominated physical distribution management. It is, however, debatable whether the development of such retailer-supplier relations is beneficial for consumers.

In one form or another, the government exerts considerable influence over a number of aspects of retailing in the UK. The broadest way in which to understand this is to put it in the context of consumer protection (see Omar, 1999). This can be interpreted as a vast range of government action designed to ensure that the final consumer is best served and protected in a whole range of final consumption activities (see also Swann, 1979; Smith and Swann, 1979; Howe, 2003). As a particular example only, shop opening hours are regulated in ways that have implications for both retailing competition and consumer service (Davidson and Ervine, 1992). In this respect the UK retailing environment is particularly liberal, and since 1994 there have been few restrictions on shop opening hours. As Kent and Omar (2003) acknowledged, 'across the United Kingdom there is now an increasing incidence of 24-hour grocery supermarket opening in addition to the widespread availability of smaller scale "convenience stores", and Sunday trading is also both widespread and popular with shoppers'. Beyond this, the two principal areas of government intervention in retailing in the United Kingdom are competition policy and land-use planning regulations. These are however few of the challenges that SME retailers may face in their daily operations.

CHALLENGES TO SME RETAIL SECTOR

Small and medium enterprise retailing has long been a feature of the British economy, providing valuable local economic and social resources. However, the sector is facing the challenge of a continually changing retail environment. Also the sector is highly dependent on family human and financial resources, which greatly increases the potential negative

SMALL AND MEDIUM-SIZED ENTERPRISE RETAILING

economic and social impacts of the failure of small retailers to respond to these challenges adequately. Challenges to the SME retail sector in the British economy could be classified into external and internal challenges.

External factors

The small and medium enterprise retail sector in general is a traditional feature of the British economy. This sector plays an important role in the maintenance of strong economic and social resources in many towns and cities throughout Britain. However, according to Welsh et al. (2003) commenting on the challenge to c-stores remarked that:

> these organisations are increasingly under threat from a number of external factors, including changing demographics, increased competition and changing consumer behaviour that combine to present an ongoing challenge to their survival and future development opportunities (see also Baron et al., 2001).

Economic and social change, competition from multiple retailers and location difficulties combine to create inadequacies in the SME retail environment. Economic development in the UK brings with it a higher standard of living for the British communities and a greater share of resources devoted to retailing. This is true for all the developed countries of Europe and North America. Retail stores of various types are more numerous and larger than elsewhere; and customer choice becomes more sophisticated. The major outcome of this development however, is that retailing has become more sensitive to changes in social, economic, fiscal, and demographic. Examples of such external factors that have most influence on retailing may include birth rate, lending rate, fashion, public opinion, employment levels, social behaviour, and government legislation among many others.

It is obvious that an increase in birth rate will normally result in population growth with a consequent increase in demand. Specifically, the effect will be felt by SME retailers catering for children. In the same way, the effects of an increase in the banks' lending rate will have several repercussions on the SME retail operation, including the higher rate for hire purchases, bank overdrafts, and less consumer spending power.

In terms of changes in public opinion, the effect can be drastic and drive away customers. Anti-smoking campaigns for example has a direct effect on Pubs and their businesses; and also has direct impact upon the retailing of tobacco. This is also related to changes in fashion which extends beyond the mere design of clothes. For example, the mini-skirt was responsible for the change to tights from stockings. Current changes in social behaviour

Table 13.4 Factors affecting SME retailing

External Factors	Internal Factors
• Changes in the UK economy	• Reasons for self-employment
• Changes in government policy	• Owner's business experience
• Changes in local authority policy	• Owner's educational backgrounds
• Private sector initiatives	• Owner's business training and skills
• Changes in the economies of scale	• Influence of role models in the family
• Changes in retail technology	• Influence of role models in the community
• Changes in demographic characteristics	• Influence of cultural or religious values
	• Family support and encouragement

Source: Welsh et al. (2003)

for example, trends towards more foreign travel, more leisure, and more DIY results in new kinds of merchandise for SME retailers. Finally, transport systems and environmental plans are all additional problems which face the SME retailers.

Generally the threats to the survival of SME retailers are related to operating costs, the availability of financial capital for reinvestment and bulk supply problems (Baron et al., 2001). Many small enterprise retailers are unable to price their goods and services at a competitive level because many of their customers are aware of the supermarket prices. In addition, Smith and Sparks (2000) highlighted the fact that changing the expectations of consumers and their needs may require the retailer to introduce new technology which may cost them more financial resources to install.

MINI CASE STUDY OF A MULTIPLE BUTCHER SHOP

George, 42 and a butcher by trade, had inherited with his brother a small multiple founded by his grandfather. He and his brother are about to open a fourth butcher's shop in the High Street to add to their long established three. It will open on 1 December in time for the Christmas and New Year peak, and despite all his experience this development feels like a quite a gamble. Thinking of the new year, George shrugged. He hadn't been thinking of expansion but had been approached to find out what rent he would be interested in paying, the premises having stood empty for a while. He suggested a figure and they came to some agreement. He has warned his staff that the new shop will mean less favourable conditions as they will have to stay open into the evening and work split shifts. He has 70 staff across the three shops; several have retired lately and another aged 70 is going to go in the New Year. None have been replaced. He may have to consider redundancy at some stage, but he was not the first owner-manager to give me the impression that he puts paying his own staff first.

- I raised this issue of local food, local shops. Would there be a move away from supermarket shopping as a result? He was skeptical, as he was about websites. His company has one but has never made much headway with it.
- I asked about the apparent decline in cooking due to a rise in the use of prepared meals. Did he find his staff had to give more advice now? Well he said certainly we do more preparation – chicken breasts with stuffing, a really good quick meal all pre-prepared. And we do a lot of barbecue portions – 'though this hasn't been a good year for barbecues'. George and his brother employ their own baker so prepare all their own pies and cooked foods. This part of the business was very profitable.
- If the consumer market is a struggle, what about B2B sales? George was clearly very frustrated. The City Council now has as its meat supplier a company based in another city 50 miles away. Public sector bodies talk quality, local businesses and food miles, said George, but when it comes to the crunch all they care about is price. He more or less got an admission to this effect from a woman when he phoned up afterwards (later I thought privately that any council might be in legal trouble if they didn't take the lowest price). The same, we eventually discussed, goes for NHS and University and other contract purchasers. He commented that he knows all his suppliers, and he couldn't say that of the successful bidder.

Internal factors

Specific to small business retailing is the concern with respect to the age of owner-managers. Many owner-managers have the average age of 58 years with almost 30 years in small retail businesses. This means that they are not likely to be very knowledgeable in the area of retail technology and current retail trends sufficient enough to compete. Welsh et al., have remarked that:

> the lack of knowledge of modern retail methods and small business management results in an inability to implement and interpret the controls necessary to facilitate sound management practice and prolonged business development.
>
> (Welsh et al., 2003)

Although age may be a concern but it is not the only determining factor to SME retail success. Many other internal factors such as the location of the business and its links with the local community, family participation and assistance, relevant skills of other store assistants, plus the amount of funds available for reinvestment will all contribute one way or the other to small business success. Welsh et al., quoted both Storey (1994) and Basu and Goswami (1999) as identifying that 'the willingness of the owner-manager to respond to the challenge of the changing retail environment may also be affected by age, reasons for business entry, and issues related to family and community influences, ethnic background and business succession' (see Welsh et al., 2003).

The size of every small business cannot be ignored as being small hinders effective competition. Being small in size is a disadvantage in that sufficient financial resources may be a problem and large or bulk merchandise purchases may be beyond a small enterprise and may not therefore reap any economies of scale. Suppliers and retail banks may only agree to a limited amount of merchandise and funds respectively. In that SME retail business is likely to face many operational restrictions including the employment of staff, and sources of supply. Although, small and medium-sized enterprise retailers face all these market challenges they are able to provide their customers with needed services and fill a niche or gap in the UK retail marketplace.

Impact of recession

The global economic downturn has affected small and medium size retailers severely in recent years more than the large chains in the UK. Besides the large retailers, the unorganised retail segment, comprising mainly the small and medium-sized companies, also suffered a major setback as their financial resources and revenue declined in real terms. With customers keeping away from bulk and expensive purchases, business volumes of retail stores have fallen drastically. This situation is therefore raising concern among the SME retailers that operate usually on small margins.

Meanwhile, as is usually the case when things are not working well, retailers are beginning to take the restructuring route to streamline their operations and drive down losses. An increasing number of SMEs are reviewing their strategies and evaluating various aspects of their administration including financial options, risks, marketing strategy, and resource management. In view of the current market dynamics, retailers are focussing on introducing value-retail and less capital intensive formats that would help them nullify the adverse effects of the global economic deceleration. Some SME retailers are also adopting more effective business models such as specialty retail stores to draw consumers and revive sales.

EXHIBIT 3 SHOP-IN-SHOP FORMAT

The most favoured format among the UK SME retailers is the shop-in-shop format. Most small and medium sized retailers are shifting and opting for this business structure because it facilitates and enhances revenue generation; and also allows optimum space utilisation. In order to adopt this format, SMEs undertake shop refurbishment and at the same time reduce their shelf space for those products which do not sell well. By using this format small retailers are able to offer in a displayed space 'freebies' and discounts to augment their sales. In addition to offering discounts and restructuring their business operations, SME retailers are taking adequate measures to improve their supply chain management; using computer technology to improve the efficiency of their distribution and logistics networks; and revamp their customer service provision to attract customers in order to come out of economic recession.

As a result of the difficult times that SMEs are going through, it has become important for small and medium enterprise retail companies to restructure their businesses (Hogg et al., 2003). In particular, those SME retailers with less money to invest are reformatting their outlets and explore alternative money generation options to draw more customers. Many SMEs are shifting their stores to formats which require less financial and labour investments and have high business potential in order to boost their flagging sales.

RETAIL MARKET COMPETITION

With the emergence of the discount retailing format in the 1970s and 1980s, and the proliferation of discount chains, 'category killers', and other mass-merchandisers such as John Lewis, M&S, Tesco, ASDA/Wal-mart, Sainsbury, and many others dominating the British retailing market with their national coverage and low priced offerings achieved through economies of scale. Resulting from the high market concentration, it is possible to assume that small and medium enterprise (SMEs) retailers may not be able to find any competitive space in the UK retail sector. Meanwhile, in spite of high rate of business failures among the SME retailers, many others are doing good businesses and competing well in the British retail market (Kent and Omar, 2003, p. 80).

Both Miles and Snow (1978) and Porter (1985) consistently argued that 'firms with clearly defined strategies tend to outperform those without such clarity'. Based on Porter's view of the firm, larger retailers such as Marks & Spencer, John Lewis, etc., are more able to leverage internal and external resources through economies of scale in price reduction across product lines; and the use of sophisticated technologies to manage inventories. These larger retailers are also able to use computer technology (the World Wide Web) to reach a wider customer segment by adopting cost leadership and/or product differentiation strategies. As for the SME retailers, one of the key efficient methods of competing against the larger retailers is to employ focus strategies to capture a segment of the target market not adequately served by the multiple retailers.

The adoption of such focus strategies may demand an SME retailer to go beyond the traditional positioning strategy in order to meet the needs of various customer segments, and target the merchandise and retail practices to them appropriately (Bennison and Hines, 2003). This suggested approach is a suitable strategy for an SME retailer with specialised retail marketing skills to compete in a niche retail market. It is possible for such an SME retailer to use its skill to establish strategic position and emphases on superior product quality and customer service as its critical success factor (Omar, 1995). In the UK, SME retailers who are successful within their communities are those that lay greater emphases on market and/or product segmentation involving a focus strategy (Kent et al., 2003). The competitiveness of SMEs in the UK retail sector is based therefore on a combination of a set of complementary resources and competencies, which converge in pursuit of a specific strategic position.

Continuous and successful existence in the UK retail sector is based on location advantages that enable ease of access to targeted customer segments. In that case, SME retailers who have no retail marketing skills but nevertheless have the following attributes are more likely to become better competitors. These attributes include the following:

- a keen understanding of the community marketplace;
- actively engaged in the day-to-day operations of the small retail business;
- offer quality products at a competitive price;
- provide superior customer service;
- employ knowledgeable and motivated assistants;
- receive adequate support from suppliers;
- adapt to relevant local retail culture;
- have good community linkages;
- have a positive business image.

All these attributes, when put together and deployed to pursue a focussed differentiation strategy targeting relatively narrow customer segments, makes an SME retailer highly competitive in the marketplace.

CONCLUSIONS

Retailing is a significant part of the total UK economic activity as it is to all the other European countries. Small and medium-sized enterprise retailers also represent a fair propotion of such national contribution as could be seen from the contents of this chapter. In general, retailing is of importance to the government as well as the consumers not only because of its economic contribution alone but also because of its size and market power of individual retailers; and the evidence that suggests that retail market do not necessarily work in a perfect competition (Howe, 2003).

This chapter briefly discussed the operation of small and medium enterprise retailers noting their economic and social contributions; their characteristics; and some impediments to their operation. The chapter has highlighted the lack of skills and know-how of many SME retailers at the start of their business that may bring an end to many of them within a year of business start-up. In all a good business practice calls for the development of a strategy to encompass all aspects of the business, from start up position, compete with other retailers to succession or close down. This will then place an enterprise in a position to respond proactively to changes in the external retail environment and maximise available opportunities.

As has been discussed in this chapter, the limited availability of alternative resources in small and medium enterprises involving only the owner-managers and members of their family places increased focus on the skills and attitudes of the propriator. However, one of the critical success factors in SME retailing is being aware of the changing external environment in order to develop suitable retail marketing strategies to meet the challenges.

Finally, and in summary, some of the specific issues relevant to all SME retailers therefore include: (1) the lack of resources, primarily management time and skills; (2) long hours of opening in order to compete with large retailers and meet the needs of shoppers who seem to take for granted increasing availability (for example, UK shops open noticeably longer hours than those say in France and Germany – these long opening hours usually result in owner-manager fatigue and lack energy to maintain and develop strategic outcomes); (3) failure to delegate – this is a function of lack of staff to take on tasks as well as an unwillingness to do this; (4) failure to monitor the competition and take ideas from them to maintain development; (5) lack of previous experience/training/education in the business sector; and (6) failure to pay attention to basic promotion in particular branding and the external appearance of the shop, from shop and brand name to promotional signage to paintwork and signposting of opening hours.

The owner-manager needs to constantly question how the shop would be seen by a customer. Thus, the key advantages of SME retailing lie in the ability to be flexible and having the motivation for personal selling and to develop a relationship with the customer. Related to this is the importance of focus, to differentiate the product range from that of a multiple retailer and develop an offering that would not emphasise price.

REVISION QUESTIONS

1. Small and medium-sized enterprise retailing has been defined in variety of ways. Using the knowledge gained after reading this chapter, define the term 'small and medium sized enterprise retailing' as you understand it.

2. What are the main differences between small and medium enterprise retailing and multiple retailing in terms of retail operation?

3. In your opinion, what do you consider to be the critical success factors in SME retailing in the UK?

4. Discuss how you think small enterprise operating from one store in a particular local community could attract customers to the store.

5. Describe the contributions made by SME retailing to the British economy.

6. Perhaps one of the major key success factors in SME retailing is to identify a value-based strategy for responding to challenges in retail environment. Explain briefly how SME retailers could respond to challenges in UK retail environment.

7. Using the knowledge gained from reading this chapter, evaluate the advantages and disadvantages of SME retailing.

8. SME retailers are increasingly under threat from a number of external and internal factors. Discuss the effects of these factors and explain how the threat could be minimised.

9. Evaluate how SME retailers could best cope with the impact of economic recession in the UK.

10. Explain how SME retailer could take advantage of their location proximity to their customers in the face of intense retail competition from the multiples.

CASE STUDY: BRITISH SHOPPERS HIT BY INFLATION SHOCK

Rapid rising prices and a weak pound have brought the shock return of inflation according to the government official sources. The government's official measure, the Consumer Prices Index (CPI), jumped from 3% to 3.2% in November 2009. It stunned the city economists, who had predicted a fall to 2.6% only. The increase was also attributed to rising supermarket prices and many small and medium-sized enterprise retailers' decision to reverse the 2.5% cut in VAT brought in by the government in an attempt to stimulate the economy. Gas prices went up by 33% year on year. Another major contribution to the rise in the CPI came from fresh vegetables, which have gone up 23.8% in a year and almost 5% in a month.

The Office for National Statistics (ONS) said carrots, cucumbers, and courgettes were among those rising fastest in price. Other foods that have gone up dramatically include pizza and mayonnaise. A spokesperson for the British Retail Consortium, said: 'the weak pound has increased the cost of imported food, such as fruits and vegetables, which aren't harvested in Britain at this time of year'. 'The weak exchange rate has also made UK produce more attractive for overseas buyers, restricting supplies of beef and lamb at home and pushing prices up. Non-food goods such as clothing, footwear and some electrical goods are cheaper than they were this time last year.'

A spokesperson for the ONS said 'the inflation figure was much higher than expected, with the exchange rate probably to blame for now' transport prices also rose, reflecting an increase in the price of petrol of 3.2% per litre between January and February 2009. ONS statistician added that the cut in VAT from 17.5% to 15%, which was introduced in December 2009, was being reversed on the high street. It can be seen that many prices returned to the previous selling price in November 2009 or even gone beyond that, and that is quite widespread'. The broader measure of inflation, the Retail Prices Index (RPI), did fall slightly, from 0.1% to 0.0%, but this was also less than expected. Most forecasts predicted that the RPI, which includes the cost of housing, would go negative for the first time since March 1960, ushering in a period of deflation.

The RPI is widely used by employers as a benchmark for wage increases and its fall to zero means that most workers will get a pay freeze or only a nominal rise this year. The Chief Economist at the Chartered Institute of Personnel and Development, said, 'for millions of workers, this will be a spring and summer of pay depression, as pay rises give way to widespread pay freezes or pay cuts'. 'For the vast majority of workers, accustomed as most of us are to an annual boost to our pay packets, a pay freeze or pay cut will feel like a hardship, especially while the CPI measure of inflation continues to rise'. RPI inflation at below zero could lead to lower incomes for pensioners and reduced returns for savers. The unexpectedly high level of inflation forced the Bank of England's Governor to write a letter to the Chancellor explaining why it is still above the 2% target.

Economists pointed to prices that are expected to fall over the coming months. Gas and electricity prices, though sharply higher than a year ago, are now starting to subside as the effect of cheaper oil starts to flow through. They also said that the latest rise in the CPI was unlikely to deter the Bank of England from continuing with quantitative easing or keeping interest rates at 0.5% for an extended period.

Questions

1. Explain the effects of inflation and how rising prices may negatively affect what consumers buy and consume.
2. The retail price index (RPI) is widely used by employers as a benchmark for wage increases. Discuss why the fall or decrease in RPI may be a great worry for SME retailers and their employees.
3. The weak exchange rate has made UK produce more attractive for overseas buyers, restricting supplies of beef and lamb at home and pushing up prices. Explain what you understand by this statement.

Sources: Compiled from various sources for the purpose of classroom teaching only

REFERENCES

Baron, S., Harris, K., Leaver, D. and Oldfield, B. (2001) Beyond convenience: The future for independent food and grocery retailers in the UK. *International Review of Retail, Distribution and Consumer Research*, 11(4), 395–414.

Basu, A. and Goswami, A. (1999) South Asian entrepreneurship in Great Britain: Factors influencing growth. *International Journal of Ebntrepreneural Behaviour & Research*, 5(5), 251–275.

Bennison, D. and Hines, T. (2003) Retailing for communities: Issues of inclusion and exclusion. *International Journal of Retail & Distribution Management*, 31(8), 385–388.

Berryman, J. (1983) Small business failure and survey of the literature. *European Small Business Journal*, 1(4), 47–59.

Berman, B. and Evans, J. R. (2001) *Retail Management: A Strategic Approach,* 8th ed. Prentice Hall, New Jersey.

Blankson, C. and Omar, O. E. (2003) Marketing practices of African and Caribbean small businesses in London, UK. *Qualitataive Marketing Research: An International Journal*, 5(2), 123–134.

Davidson, F. P. and Ervine, W. C. H. (1992) Legal Issues in Retailing. In Howe, W. S. (Ed.), *Retailing Management*. Macmillan, London.

European Commission (2003) 'What is an SME?', Internal Market, Industry, Entrepreneurship and SMEs, https://ec.europa.eu/growth/smes/business-friendly-environment/sme-definition_en (Accessed on 28 January 2020).

Haksever, C. (1996) Total quality management in the small business environment. *Business Horizons*, 39(2), 33–41.

Hogg, S., Medway, D. and Warnaby, G. (2003) Business improvement districts: An opportunity for SME retailing. *International Journal of Retailing & Distribution Management*, 31(9), 466–469.

Howe, S. (2003) *Retailing in the European Union: Structures, Competition and Performance*. Routledge, London.

Ibrahim, A. Bakr, Soufani, K. and Lam, J. (2001) A study of succession in a family firm. *Family Business Review*, 14(3), 245–258.

Kent, A. E. and Omar, O. E. (2003) *Retailing*. Palgrave Macmillan, Basingstoke.

Kent, T., Dennis, C. and Tanton, S. (2003) An evaluation of mentoring for SME retailers. *International Journal of Retail & Distribution Management*, 31(8), 440–448.

Levy, M. and Weitz, B. A. (2004) *Retail Management*, 5th ed. McGraw Hill/Irwin, New York.

McGoldrick, P. J. (2002) *Retail Marketing*, 2nd ed. London: McGraw-Hill.

Miles, R. E. and Snow C. C. (1978) *Organizational strategy, structure and processes*. New York: McGraw Hill.

Mukhtar, S. M. (1996) A case for gender-based entrepreneurialism, business competence development, and policy implications: A global perspective. Paper Presented at Forging Global Alliances.

Mukhtar, S. M. (1998) Business characteristics of male and female small and medium enterprises in the UK: Implications for gender-based entrepreneurialism and business competence development. *British Journal of Management*, 9(1), 41–51.

Omar, O. E. (1995) Retail influence on food technology and innovation. *International Journal of Retail & Distribution Management*, 23(3), 11–16.

Omar, O. E. (1999) *Retail Marketing*. Financial Times/Pitman, London.

Porter, M. E. (1985) *Competitive Advantage*. Free Press, New York.

Sawyer, O. O., McGee, J. and Peterson, M. (2003) Perceived uncertainty and firm performance in SMEs: The role of personal networking activities. *International Small Business Journal*, 21(3), 269–290.

SBA (2001) Frequently Asked Questions – Advocacy: The Voice of Small Business in Government, https://www.sba.gov/sites/default/files/FAQ_Sept_2012.pdf (Accessed on 28 January 2020).

Smith, A. and Sparks, L. (2000) The role and function of the independent small shop: The situation in Scotland. *International Review of Retail, Distribution and Consumer Research*, 10(2), 205–206.

Smith, P. and Swann, D. (1979) *Protecting the Consumer: An Economic and Legal Analysis*. Martin Robertson, Oxford.

Storey, D. (1994) *Understanding the Small Business Sector*. Routledge, London.

Swann, D. (1979) *Competition and Consumer Protection*. Penguin, Harmondsworth.

Welsh, R., Bent, R., Seamon, C. and Ingram, A. (2003) The challenge to C-stores: Edinburgh South Asian responses. *International Journal of Retail & Distribution Management*, 31(8), 408–417.

Chapter 14

Relationship marketing and networks in entrepreneurship

Sue Halliday

LEARNING OBJECTIVES

After reading this chapter, you will be able to:
- Explain how a relational, networking perspective to marketing enables collaboration which, in turn, creates innovation, knowledge and, therefore, competitive advantage in entrepreneurship;
- Discuss how relationships and networks combine as strategic resources in entrepreneurship to create the desired outcome of valued customer experience;
- Demonstrate ability to apply this understanding to gain knowledge of the business world and test own ideas for setting up in business;
- Demonstrate your skills in entrepreneurial marketing using the contents of this chapter to apply solutions to the case study.

INTRODUCTION

Relationships and networks are vital to entrepreneurship and marketing. New businesses need to be entrepreneurial in their marketing as well as in their business ideas. Research indicates that greater profits lie in the direction of developing on-going relationships with customers, despite the necessary costs of investing in both product and service quality, and in relation building competences (Chaston, 1997).

Indeed, relationships are at the heart of marketing. In the US a new definition of marketing was produced in 2004, the first for decades, and it included the word 'relationships'. That definition was hotly contested and has now been adapted to the current definition:

> Marketing is the activity, conducted by organizations and individuals, that operates through a set of institutions and processes for creating, communicating, delivering, and exchanging market offerings that have value for customers, clients, marketers, and society at large.
>
> (American Marketing Association, 2007)

This chapter will focus on the topics of Relationship Marketing and Networks at this interface of entrepreneurship and marketing. It covers:

RELATIONSHIP MARKETING AND NETWORKS

- Roots of Relationship Marketing (RM);
- The Six Markets Model of RM;
- What is a Relationship?;
- The Two Core Concepts of RM – Trust and Commitment;
- Current Context for Entrepreneurial RM;
- Two Fundamental Propositions for Entrepreneurial RM Today;
- Networks for Entrepreneurial RM;
- Future Direction of RM and Networks.

We conclude with a short case study on Dovetail – Workers in Wood Ltd, for you to apply all the content of this chapter to a real-life example of a small sustainable business. Questions are best answered as a team activity.

ROOTS OF RELATIONSHIP MARKETING

Relationship Marketing, historically, links three other concepts: services marketing, network/interactive industrial goods marketing and Total Quality Management (see Christopher et al., 1991; Gummesson, 1991). One effect that certainly impacts upon the SME is that even in large firms all are involved in marketing. The term part-time marketer (PTM) was coined to emphasise this broader marketing function, which now includes internal Part-Time Marketers (PTMs) such as top management, telephonists and external PTMs such as consultants, dealers, customers, media, investors. This change means that the smaller firm will find it easier to ensure that its employees are trained and expecting to act as marketers, whatever their specialism.

Figure 14.1
The Six Markets Model of RM

Source: Originally in Christopher et al. (1991)

These six markets are the stakeholders where relationships can be built to grow the entrepreneurial business. These six markets are where relationships and networks take place and so we see this model in action in the case study at the end of this chapter. Read this carefully and you will be able to apply this model in practice.

WHAT IS A RELATIONSHIP?

Once relationships rather than transactions are at the heart of marketing, understanding is needed into how customer relationships are formed, with models that focus on relationships, not transactions (Webster, 1992). Gummesson introduced the '30 Rs' for companies to work out their own specific relationship portfolio – as you can see this covers all of life:

Classic market relationships

1. Supplier and customer
2. The customer – supplier – competitor triangle
3. Network – distribution channels

Special market relationships

4. Full-time marketers and part-time marketers
5. Customer and service provider
6. Many-headed customer and many-headed supplier
7. Relationship to the customer's customer
8. Close versus distant relationship
9. Dissatisfied customer
10. Monopoly relationship: customer or supplier as prisoner
11. Customer as 'member'
12. Electronic relationship
13. Parasocial relationships, with symbols and objects
14. Noncommercial relationship
15. The green relationship
16. The law-based relationship
17. The criminal network

Mega relationships

18. Personal and social networks
19. Mega marketing – the real 'customer' is not always found in the marketplace
20. Alliances change the market mechanism
21. The knowledge relationship
22. Mega alliances change the basic conditions for marketing
23. Mass media relationship

Nano relationships

24. Market mechanisms are brought inside the company
25. Internal customer relationships

RELATIONSHIP MARKETING AND NETWORKS

26. Quality providing a relationship between operations management and marketing
27. Internal marketing – relationships with the employee market
28. Two-dimensional matrix relationship
29. Relationship to external providers of marketing services
30. Owner and financier relationship

So you can see that there is a greater richness in relationship marketing which:

> sees marketing activities as part of a larger context, inside as well as outside the company, which shall be beneficial to all parties in the long run, preferably also in the short run. Relationship marketing is a process, a chain of activities. It stresses flows and context. It represents a holistic attitude to marketing.
>
> (Gummesson, 1991, p. 14)

KEY LEARNING POINT:
There is a huge range of possible relationships for the SME to focus on in their marketing strategy. As a small business do not overlook the social context when thinking about marketing.

When is a relationship a relationship?

It has been suggested that a relationship could only be said to exist when customers choose to use the language of interpersonal relationships – e.g., *my* builder/consultant/jeweller. Therefore the richest approach is to focus on the customer's perspective in relationships and on any benefits they acquire from entering a relationship rather than undertaking a discrete set of transactions. It has been found that three primary types of benefits are appreciated (Gwinner et al., 1998). Interestingly, confidence benefits were most highly prized, across the firms looked at, followed by social benefits and finally special treatment benefits. Confidence is defined as covering the sense of reduced anxiety, faith in the trustworthiness of the provider, reduced perceptions of anxiety and risk, and knowing what to expect.

Confidence creation is a relatively straightforward tool for entrepreneurs to include in their relationship marketing plans. Relationships act to reduce risk, since what is not known or understood, (such as the expertise of the builder or the marketing consultant or kitchen designer) is mitigated by personal knowledge of the builder, consultant or designer. This is one way in which trust is such an important element of relationship marketing – we will give further thought to this topic shortly.

Relationships are important to the SME. Research early on in the development of relationship marketing (Crosby et al., 1990) found that effective relationship selling will be most critical when the:

- service is complex, customised and delivered over a continuous stream of transactions;
- environment is dynamic and uncertain in ways that affect future needs (demand) and offerings (supply).

This is where the entrepreneur is likely to be growing his/her business.

225

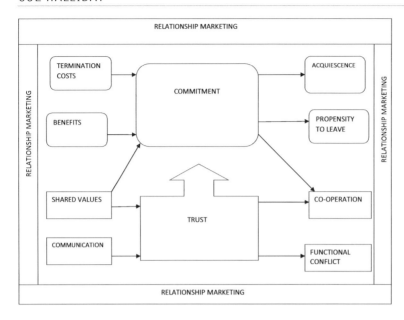

Figure 14.2 Model of Relationship Marketing (Trust and Commitment as core)

Source: Adapted from Morgan Hunt Trust Commitment Model of Relationship Marketing

THE TWO CORE CONCEPTS FOR RM – TRUST AND COMMITMENT

The Morgan Hunt Model of Relationship Marketing (Figure 14.2) gives us two core concepts for RM – Trust and Commitment.

TRUST

According to both buyers and sellers, trust is by far the most important factor characterizing a good relationship. It is relevant to SMEs to consider trust as part of societal norms, as part of the glue of social capital and contributing to the continuous web of business and social relations. Markets are part of society – they are what is called socially embedded, for far more than mere economic behaviours take place within the business arena. This is obvious when we reflect for a moment on how entrepreneurial behaviour varies across cultures. Singaporean Chinese are known for the persistence and work ethic that leads entrepreneurial businesses to thrive. Equally and connectedly, the family is supportive of this approach to business. In the UK corporate life is seen as far more 'natural' – and success is often understood as linked to the size of the company worked for. Again, from an era of greater social stability, many in their sixties and seventies in the UK are retiring on company pensions earned from long term employment in one company. Younger generations in the UK have learned from the 'me' decades and from the 1980s and the whole Thatcher period, that to thrive it is possible and profitable to set up in business for oneself. So marketing is situated in the context of social norms – and the likelihood to trust is part of that social context. In a recent review of entrepreneurship and its links to marketing social networking and relationships with customers and other stakeholders are seen as being at the foundation of entrepreneurial marketing (Hills et al., 2008). Social networking is of course primarily a social norm.

RELATIONSHIP MARKETING AND NETWORKS

> **KEY LEARNING POINT:**
> Relational competence and skills in creating contexts conducive to trust are essential for the SME.

Figure 14.3 Responses to uncertainty according to perceptions of risk.

opportunism_____ trust _____regulation

In the face of uncertainty, all writers on the topic of trust wrestle with where to place trust on a continuum with regulation at one end and opportunism at the other (see Figure 14.3). Opportunism calculates that it is not worth calculating further, and it may also involve an understanding that advantage can be taken of another's vulnerability or lack of knowledge. Regulation ensures that optimal calculations are made, according to criteria of risk aversion, that information is fully shared and that vulnerability cannot be exploited. An option to reduce uncertainty between these two extremes is to trust, either initially ('placed trust') or increasingly during a process of relationship building ('trust as response'); another option is to take a risk (Halliday, 2004). Attitudes to risk vary, from risk aversion, through risk neutrality to risk seeking, and the entrepreneur's attitude to risk is a hotly contested issue. Are they risk takers? Or do they seek to reduce risk and to gain control by skills and knowledge which act to mitigate what might be risks if taken by others?

> This is part of the broader realm of business life and is also part of social relationship building.

> Trust is the reliance by one person, group or firm upon a voluntarily accepted duty on the part of another person, group or firm to recognize and protect the rights and interests of all others engaged in a joint endeavour or economic exchange.
>
> (See Hosmer, 1995 p. 392)

This definition embraces obligations and interests. In this way, trust is deeper than reliance on either promise or competence. Trust implies the personal characteristic of trustworthiness on the part of the trusted. Blanket trust rarely exists – rather we trust someone in a constrained context and/or for a particular purpose (Blois, 1999).

How does trust work?

Placed trust

'Placed trust' is a trusting act, which enables initial understanding for the service delivery, or alliance, or whatever dependence is involved. For the antecedents to 'placed trust' are out there, in society, in social norms, in communally understood competences, in scripts and roles and characters (Pavis, 1998). Relevant to SMEs is that 'placed trust' is an outcome of prior expertise and reputation building. Reputations depend on the 'embeddedness' of interactions in structures or networks of social relations (Raub and Weesie, 1990). This highlights the importance of another of the areas for networking in the six markets model: influence markets. The social context for the entrepreneur is critical to her success.

227

In evaluating the successful functioning of 'placed trust', there is the interesting conundrum of how to evaluate the other's competence. Not to do so would open up the debate about trust to charges of irrationality once more and we have seen that not to have grounds for believing in this competence would be naiveté. If trustworthiness is to be assessed prior to entering a relationship, how then is the evaluation to be made? Would trusting an incompetent professional (or entrepreneur) be trusting or naïve? We can answer that it is trust, 'placed trust' because the context indicates that it is reasonable to assume competence. This gives a place for branding in entrepreneurial marketing, for within the act of trusting there is the expectation of a technically competent role performance, and branding can sum this up for the consumer in the form of an understood code in a symbol.

This is an important message for entrepreneurs: entrepreneurs benefit from a good social reputation.

So, 'placed trust' depends on the trustworthiness of the other, and these societally embedded expectations are largely, by their very nature, met. When they are not (as in the English scandal of the murderous family doctor in Yorkshire) there is outrage and horror. 'Placed trust' is robust, but is betrayed by such flouting of social norms. Researchers working on an MBA cohort found what they described as surprisingly high levels of initial trust. But let us consider this context. All students had successfully passed a selection process. All had very similar ambitions in joining the programme. For this context and purpose, as fellow-MBA students, they could trust one another (i.e., place trust in one another). This is 'placed trust' and not the trust in response to the other's actions.

Commitment

Trust as response

Trust in response to the other's actions is the kind of trust most written about and it is understood in the literature to contribute to loyal purchasing by creating commitment (see Morgan and Hunt model at Figure 14.2). It is the expectation of fairness that breeds commitment instead of the alternative over time, in conditions of dependency, of a desire to escape. Commitment in a mutually beneficial relationship is needed for profitability and for high levels of word-of-mouth recommendations; this is built upon 'trust as response' to behaviours on the service provider's part to create commitment to marketing relationships. Mutuality in relationships requires matching 'trust as response' with trustworthiness rather than reciprocal trustfulness. This trust can therefore be used in creating marketing relationships.

Entrepreneurs succeed when they build trust – this is often not articulated as a marketing strategy, but as a result of interpersonal connections. Here we can see how central an element trust-building is to the creation of a good entrepreneurial marketing strategy and plan. Trust as a response is most likely to create both repeat custom and new custom with friends of the customer – it creates commitment.

See the case study for a worked example of this informal relationship marketing strategy.

SPOTLIGHT ON SERVICE QUALITY

Customer perceptions of service quality are more important than any managerial or professional definition of quality internal to the organisation (see Parasuraman et al., 1985). Understanding the customer and the components of service quality in the mind of the customer can therefore give competitive edge to the service organisation. From a focus on services marketing the spotlight is on service quality: expressed simply, companies providing high service quality, as perceived by their customers, tend to be the most profitable companies. Small businesses have the ability to grow and to be sustained by relatively fewer customers and so customer recommendation, as we demonstrate in the case study at the end of this chapter, is a key relational marketing strategy for the entrepreneur.

A major conceptual contribution from services marketing scholars has been to see that perceived service quality is the difference between expected service and perceived service. This gap can be a major hurdle in attempting to deliver a service which consumers would perceive as being of high quality. Ten determinants of service quality were tabulated as: access; communication*; competence; courtesy*; credibility; reliability*; responsiveness*; security; tangibles; understanding/knowing the customer*. Those denoted with an asterisk are linked clearly and directly to the quality of the relationships, that, in our case, the entrepreneur or the SME itself has created. Those customers who seek a relationship in their business decisions will form profitable targets for the SME skilled in relationship development. In this way, segmentation of customers by relational and service quality expectations will often be useful in seeking competitive advantage.

KEY LEARNING POINT:
Creating customer perceptions of high-quality relationships enables competitive advantage to be developed by the firm in the marketplace.

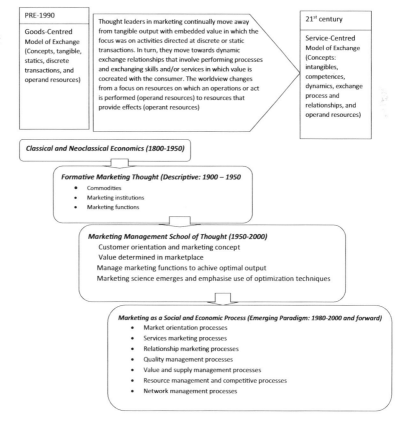

Figure 14.4 Evolving to a new dominant logic for marketing

Source: (Vargo and Lusch, 2004, p4)

CURRENT CONTEXT FOR ENTREPRENEURIAL RELATIONSHIP MARKETING

A study of entrepreneurial marketing as a newly establishing discipline within marketing (see Morris et al., 2002) emphasized that entrepreneurial marketing has a twin focus in interesting ways: a focus on innovation and creativity and a focus on relationship building to obtain a wider resource base. The former clearly takes from the entrepreneurship literature and practice, and the latter focus is developed from the Relationship Marketing approach discussed in this chapter.

Service-dominant logic to marketing

Relationship Marketing in SMEs now also needs to be understood as fitting in the latest theoretical context: the 10 Foundational Premises of Service-dominant Logic (see Vargo and Lusch in the list of articles at the end of the chapter). For the focus on relationships that has been described in this chapter has led to a re-evaluation of the marketing discipline. It has led to leaders of marketing thought in the United States proposing what they call a new logic to marketing – what they termed a new dominant logic – the service-dominant logic (see Vargo and Lusch, 2004).

They charted developments in marketing (see Figure 14.4) as a move from Marketing Management as very much a function within the firm to a services marketing emphasis on process to the latest manifestation of this process focus, termed 'Network management processes'.

> **KEY LEARNING POINT:**
> Consider how each of the ten foundational premises of the service-dominant logic to marketing fits relational, networking SMEs.

Table 14.1 Service-dominant logic foundational premise modifications and additions

FP's	Original Foundation Premise	Modified Foundation Premise	Comment/Explanation
FP1	The application of specialised skills and knowledge is the fundamental unit of exchange	**Service** is the fundamental **basis** of exchange	The application of operant resources (knowledge and skills), 'service,' as defined in S-D logic, is the basis for all exchange. Service is exchanged for service
FP2	Indirect Exchange Masks the Fundamental Unit of Exchange	Indirect Exchange Masks the Fundamental **Basis** of Exchange	Because service is provided through complex combinations of goods, money, and institutions, the service basis of exchange is not always apparent

RELATIONSHIP MARKETING AND NETWORKS

Table 14.1 *(continued)*

FP3	Goods are a distribution mechanisms for service provision	Goods are a distribution mechanism for service provision	Goods (both durable and non-durable) derive their value through use- the service they provide
FP4	Knowledge is the fundamental source of competitive advantage	**Operant resources are** the fundamental source of competitive advantage	The comparative ability to cause desired change drives competition
FP5	All economies are services economies	All Economies are **service** economies	Service (singular) is only becoming more apparent with increased specialisation and outsourcing
FP6	The customer is always a co-producer	The customer is always a **co-creator** of value	Implies value creation is interactional
FP7	The enterprise can only make value propositions	The enterprise **cannot deliver value, but** only offer value propositions	Enterprises can offer their applied resources for value creation and collaboratively (interactively) create following acceptance of value propositions, but cannot create and/or deliver value independently
FP8	A service-centred view is customer oriented and relational	A service-centred view is **inherently** customer oriented and relational	Because service is defined in terms of customer-determined benefit and co-created it is inherently customer oriented and relational
FP9	Organisations exist to integrate and transform microspecialised competences into complex services that are demanded in the marketplace	**All social and economic actors are resource integrators**	Implies the context of value creation is networks of networks (resource integrators)
FP10		**Value is always uniquely and phenomenologically determined by the beneficiary**	Value is idiosyncratic, experiential, contextual, and meaning laden

Source: (Vargo and Lusch, 2008)

These are still being formulated and tested out by academics but clearly these ten premises make interesting research questions for student dissertations at undergraduate or postgraduate levels. It is also interesting to note how closely these new foundational premises connect with the focus of this chapter: networks and relationships are seen as fundamental building blocks for marketing and co-creation of customer value. Here innovation is sourced from understanding how, variously, customers integrate resources to create a valued experience.

The core idea relevant to this chapter is encapsulated in

FP8 A service-centred view is inherently customer-oriented and relational.

The latest additional premise is key for entrepreneurs tempted to focus on their new business proposition:

FP10 Value is always uniquely and phenomenologically determined by the beneficiary.

The two foundational premises of clear relevance to relationship marketing and networking in SMEs are:

FP4 Knowledge is the fundamental source of competitive advantage; it is gained by co-creation of value with customers and networks.

FP7 The enterprise can only make value propositions.

TWO FOUNDATIONAL PREMISES FOR ENTREPRENEURIAL RM TODAY

Knowledge is the fundamental source of competitive advantage; it is gained by co-creation of value with customers and networks

We have seen that entrepreneurial marketing can gain from understanding marketers as actors playing evolving, dynamic roles in a process of adaptation. And how can parties adapt if they cannot learn? Learning is central: Day has noted that organisations continuously learn about their markets through the linked processes of market sensing and sense making (see Day, 2002). Our focus here is on the need to take this aspect of organisations when implementing a marketing programme. This is neatly modelled by Sinkula et al. (1997), who link together gathering market-based information for marketing programmes with organisational learning (see Figure 14.5).

The opportunity, the perception of a gap in the market, when accompanied by the important question 'Is there a market in the gap?' is the other key concept that unites these two disciplines. Information is the oxygen of marketing: marketers get market information in the form of feedback on customer service, on new ideas from customers, of research on

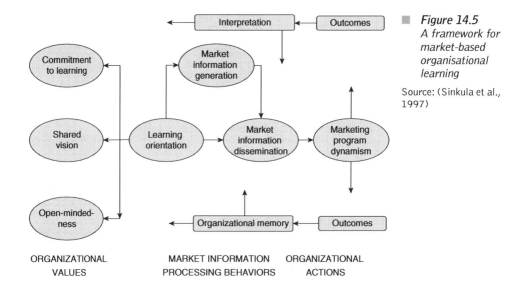

Figure 14.5
A framework for market-based organisational learning

Source: (Sinkula et al., 1997)

RELATIONSHIP MARKETING AND NETWORKS

why people are not or are no longer customers; for the entrepreneur this is often intuition, innovation and connectedness via the Personal Contact Network (we will mention this in more detail later). What thinking has linked a focus on competences, on the entrepreneur and the marketer as individuals capable of creating personal networks and of having knowledge and intuition to share? Relationship Marketing links these ideas.

The enterprise can only make value propositions

For the SME this means that to a large extent, innovation is co-created with customers.

Once we have identified as key issues relational management, learning and meaning creation, and management we have the heart of the innovative process under scrutiny.

Value is created by so-called 'toolkits for user innovation and design' (see Franke and Piller, 2004), a method of integrating customers into new product development and design. These 'Toolkits' allow customers to create their own product, which in turn is produced by the manufacturer. Over the past few years many more firms have turned to the internet as mechanism for communicating with their customers. Significantly the internet enables manufacturers to communicate directly with their customers without the need for intermediaries such as retailers and wholesalers. It also provides the opportunity for firms to interact with customers, in particular with a collection of customers, and for customers to interact with customers. By interacting with potential customers on technology capabilities possessed by the firm opportunities for deploying and utilising this technology may emerge. That is, genuine new product opportunities may be developed.

Somehow, the communications need to foster closeness – as Drucker writes: 'for communications to be effective, there has to be both information and meaning. And meaning requires communion' (2001, p. 341). This is all in fact easier for the entrepreneur and the small business, relying on interpersonal skills and networking.

To emphasise this important connection of the customer with value we can add in a model that overtly links cashflow to customer relevance. For relevance, read value. Hills and Singh's book (2000) *Research at the Marketing/Research Interface* provided a model of the small firm (see figure 14.6). It is an important insight to link cash flow to the core business idea and, by this means, to value:

> The functional entity produces goods and services. Its relevance to customer's needs essentially determines how the firm's cashflow from operations changes. As customer relevance increases, cashflow from operations increases. As customer relevance decreases, cashflow from operations is reduced.
>
> (p. 198)

Entrepreneurial marketing therefore continues to have as its focus: retaining customers. Therefore, a key marketing process becomes the development of business relationships (see Gummesson, 1997).

> **KEY LEARNING POINT:**
> The successful SME is inherently customer-oriented and relational.

233

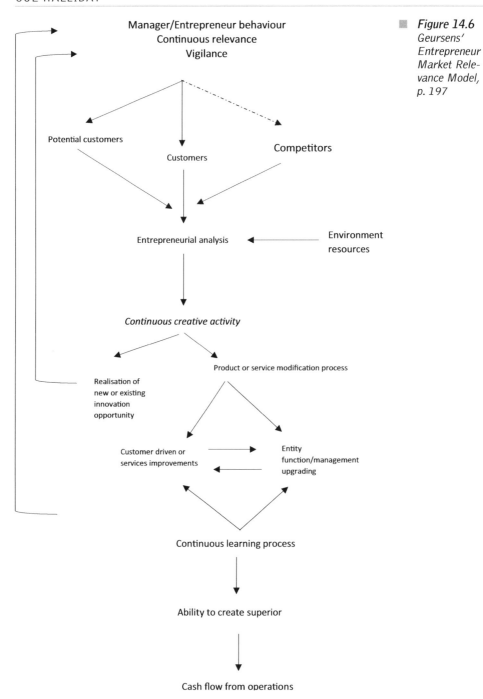

Figure 14.6 Geursens' Entrepreneur Market Relevance Model, p. 197

NETWORKS FOR ENTREPRENEURIAL RM

We have seen and discussed how Vargo and Lusch, in 2004, charted developments in marketing as a move from Marketing Management as the real focus of the discipline, in which it is very much a function within the firm and a study of that function, to the perspective

RELATIONSHIP MARKETING AND NETWORKS

from the 1980s of Marketing as a Social and Economic process. Services marketing emphasized processes and those that focussed on the customer led to the development of customer relationship marketing. Additional perspectives on value and quality, much as discussed in this chapter, followed and the latest manifestation of this process focus was termed 'Network Management Processes'.

Kay (1993) suggests that the *external linkages* that a company has developed over time and the investment in this network of relationships (generated from its past activities) form a distinctive competitive capability.

What is a network?

At some basic level, the first network into which human beings are, quite literally, born, is the family. In classes on a Master's programme on Entrepreneurship not only does the UK attract a great many students from overseas, but those students are most often drawn from cultures where the family business predominates as a structure of size and ownership. Recent research reviewed the whole area of family businesses and found that they tend to out-perform non-family firms (see Ibrahim et al., 2008). Reasons given are various. They are found to be nimbler, more active in the community and both more quality and more customer-oriented. Certainly the last three of these factors can be related directly to personal orientations in a family business. And so the actual network of the family is the basic network for the entrepreneurial firm. Non-family firms can emulate the focus on these areas without becoming a real blood-related family!

Personal Contact Networks (PCNs) have been focussed upon by previous textbook writers (see Carson et al., 1995; Bjerke and Hultman, 2002). These can be seen as assets to the firm. They are not for sale. They are only realizable by the persons creating them. The feel is essentially personal, and they will provide knowledge, market information, and opportunities for learning that match the flexible unstructured approach to business development favoured by entrepreneurs. Although the scale is personal, it may be that new members of the PCN are sought for their ability to contribute a missing resource for the entrepreneur – be that resource finance, technical know-how, or access to particular new markets. This is how networking fits into growing the entrepreneurial firm and finding the resources to feed this growth.

Another perspective on a network can be gained by looking at the network surrounding a patient who, once pictured as the centre of a complex network of service providers, can be re-imagined as, effectively, a network manager in a healthcare setting.

This addresses the complexity in a network. These can be small if they depend on real-time interpersonal knowledge – research on church size in the UK indicates that whilst if the membership stays at 120–150 people feel they know each other, once a church reaches 200 there are too many members for all of them to even know the names of every member nor to recognise them on sight. However, with the advent of the internet and Web 2.0 individuals can be part of much larger, complex, but virtual, networks. Social networking is still in its early days, but clearly there is potential for the SME in being part of this mostly social, but partly business, networking medium. Gummesson (2009) notes that network theory can tackle complex networks. He coins the phrase 'Many-to-Many' marketing and charts out a range of opportunities for the marketer who studies the 'Anna' network. In a 2006 article (see Gummesson, 2006), he defines this version of marketing practice as the description, analysis and utilisation of the network properties of marketing.

For the SME it is sufficient to note that they will be in a network and that a good marketing practice is to map that network and then plan how to develop the sets of relationships

235

that it includes. Where does this small business fit into the 'Many-to-Many' setting? How many networks is it part of? And the question for marketing action is around prioritizing some actors in the network with whom maximum value can be co-created.

Developing marketing through the use of formal business networks

The key point of looking at networks is to develop the business by using them as a method of growth. Networks will be made up of people from across those six markets introduced earlier (see Figure 14.1). Rocks et al. (2005) noted a diverse range of members of networks used by SMEs in the grocery sector in Northern Ireland: 'other owner/managers within the channel, sales teams, channel intermediary, retailing and manufacturing firms, people within the food industry, distributors, agents, consumers, buying teams, UK multiples, symbol wholesales, consultancy firms, PR agencies, and trade associations' (p. 87). These networks were found to be flexible, but very stable and this was key to the value created within them. These were found to be formal, rather than informal, social networks.

Collaborative competence in networks

A useful framework for thinking about where the entrepreneur needs to collaborate to successfully grow the business is the Six Markets Model (see Figure 14.1). The influence markets are those people who can make or break a small business' reputation. Many small firms can be strengthened by being recommended by mediators – perhaps professionals in their field such as accountants, lawyers and bankers. Small companies competing internationally might employ the local business club to recommend their work in global locations. Referral markets are even closer to the business in the sense that they can actually refer business to the small firm. Many industries have lists of approved suppliers – being part of the network is absolutely crucial. As is building a good relationship with customers, providing excellent after sales care and so creating business through word-of-mouth (WOM) recommendation. (See the case study for an example of a business built on WOM). Supplier markets, for the smaller business, will depend on interpersonal skills – the existence of finance at a competitive rate of interest or at the right time can come down to good relationships with bankers. The entrepreneurial business is in fact likely to be at the hub of a network of suppliers – see the case study for a fully worked example of this. Another textbook on Entrepreneurial Marketing (see Bjerke and Hultman, 2002) talks of the small firm becoming a virtual firm – or the hub of the network rather than one focussed on the organisation itself – a focal firm. This virtual firm is a series of linked members of a network, most probably connected electronically, where innovation is shared and learning fostered. In this way marketing for the SME is not just a smaller version of marketing in the large transnational firm.

We have seen, that collaboration is critical, and for the SME then the outcome will not only be business contacts but also, less tangibly and no less importantly, learning. For Hamel et al. (1989) lament that where

> the Japanese have generally learnt more than their UK or US partners, this is not due to oriental deviousness, but to occidental indolence. The key to competing through collaboration is to have the mindset to learn.
>
> (p. 147)

Ongoing challenge

Creating positive, profitable relationships across networks, both informally but also in structured ways, formally, in networks that are constellations of networks, is the constant challenge for the entrepreneurial business. Improving investor relations is hitting the headlines as an outstanding requirement for the SME seeking a listing (see Independent, 2010). This competence presents a key challenge for you in understanding and, in due course, practising entrepreneurship marketing.

FUTURE DIRECTION OF RM AND NETWORKS

Relationship Marketing is perhaps no longer new; however, it is still of great relevance to the entrepreneur as it can be seen as that which links a business, its customers and the other stakeholders in the firm. For entrepreneurs, who may find it easy to focus on their innovative service or product, the key message is that interpersonal relationships, sometimes mediated electronically, are part of building a sustainable (and therefore, for serial entrepreneurs, a saleable) business.

It has become established as an approach to marketing; a number of European professors set up a research project to assess relationship marketing's future as a way of doing business, to predict its likely strength in 2015 (see Bonnemaizon et al., 2007). They found four themes current and likely to determine the future in Relationship Marketing.

- Increasingly, RM will become a focus on a network of relationships connected to a business.

This perspective on the future is relevant to entrepreneurial companies because this is such a central feature of any successful entrepreneur's business. That this is to become more central essentially gives the SME competitive advantage. It also underlines that the wannabe entrepreneur needs to focus here when developing personal competences to set up in business.

- An element of this will be complex databases hold customer related data and using ICT to measure the value of relationships to the business.

This is of great relevance to the growth-minded entrepreneur/SME, as it a reminder of the investment needed to turn a Personal Contact Network (PCN) into a foundation for significant development.

- Firms will have to involve customers less by selling to them, more by genuinely creating a two-way flow of information in order to play a role more in creating value with them rather than in delivering value to them.

This perspective on the future is relevant to entrepreneurial companies because this, once again, is a central competence for the SME and so, once again, as this moves centre-stage, so the SME gains competitive advantage.

- Consumer experience will be increasingly important. Yet this is less susceptible to management by the business.

This perspective on the future is relevant to entrepreneurial companies because the greater personal contact and the greater social embeddedness of the firm, the easier it is to influence the customer experience. 'Experiential marketing' (see Schmitt, 1999) views consumers less as rational decision makers who care about functional features and benefits, and more as emotional human beings who are concerned with achieving pleasurable experiences. The personal, central role of the entrepreneur in the SME plays to this more emotional approach to marketing. This is increasingly important. For a key idea is to be found in the Prahalad and Ramaswamy book *The Future of Competition: Co-Creating Unique Value with Customers* (see list of readings at the end of the chapter) is that the power over the value chain will increasingly be in the consumer's head and hands and that winning firms will be able to co-create value with their customers. The good news is that the flexibility and customer-responsiveness that this implies on the part of the firm is well-suited to the entrepreneurial SME.

REVIEW QUESTIONS

1. List out the benefits to customers of being in a relationship with an SME.

2. Why should an SME focus on relationship building in its marketing strategy?

3. Write out in one sentence your idea for setting up an entrepreneurial business.

4. List out the benefits to the customer of using your goods and/or services.

5. Give examples of businesses you can think of that would benefit from relational selling.

6. Are you a person who trusts easily? Are you trustworthy? List out why customers for your business idea should place their trust in you.

7. Now, write out your business idea in one sentence, making sure you include what potential value to them you are offering. Reflect on how this differs from your answer to Q.3.

8. What new understanding does a focus on relationships and networks give to the core entrepreneurship concept of innovation?

9. How do learning, knowledge and innovation connect?

10. Where is value to be found in the entrepreneurial business?

CASE STUDY: DOVETAIL – WORKERS IN WOOD LTD.

John Kirby set up in business over 20 years ago just as the fitted kitchen was becoming an established requirement for the new homeowner. Large department stores all had fitted kitchen departments and John saw the opportunity to offer a more personal service to the top end of this market for those who could pay for this customisation. Each kitchen is made by their skilled team of workers at their workshop in Hampshire.

Background

Houses have always had kitchens – somewhere to prepare cooked food. For the elite in British society the kitchen was where servants produced food. After the First

World War households became smaller; and by the 1950s space was at a premium in most middle class houses. Efficiency led to the design of the fitted kitchen. In 2001 the UK fitted kitchens market was worth £3.2bn annually. Modest growth was predicted for the 2002–2006 period; however in 2006 sales of fitted kitchens grew by 16%. In 2004, one SME in this area had invested in machinery and manufacturing space that produced one typical kitchen every 2 minutes*! The market is dependent upon the economy; when the housing market is on the move it benefits from upgrades upon each sale cycle of the house.

The distribution chain is dominated by outlets such as MFI and IKEA and contains smaller DIY outlets and builders' merchants as well as very many smaller, more customised options.** At the most expensive end the chain stretches to the small team of craftsmen. Here we find, at this top end of the range, Dovetail – Workers in Wood Ltd. where the average price of the kitchen is £50 000. To match this, John and his team maintain exceptional standards of craftsmanship and service. These kitchens are built to last (the website includes a customer commenting that her 8 year-old kitchen remains great).

Dovetail design, project-manage, hand-craft, and install their kitchens. They make a virtue of their small size to relate to their customers personally. Their website addresses issues in working in a small team: ' We play to our strengths and make up for each other's weaknesses'.

Customers

Customers are the lifeblood of this business, as they are of any business. The order book has steadily grown over 20 years, and John has been able to move from having three or four months' work planned ahead to nearer a year of bookings. The firm has produced approximately one kitchen a month over the last decade. Last year the UK recession began to bite and the order pipeline began to shorten to three to four months. This led John to advertise. His experience of this has been grim. He found himself competing with companies with much bigger advertising budgets, such as Smallbone of Devizes***. He is finding that the potential customer was much more doubtful of his firm's capacity and therefore takes much more persuasion. The customer is also likely to be pursuing two or three companies at the same time, so that even if the kitchen is purchased, Dovetail's chance of success is reduced to one in three. Nevertheless this sales channel now produces three or four kitchens a year, which is proving useful in the current recession, which has had a strongly negative impact on the housing market as a whole.

This experience has led John to value even more highly his past customer base. For they act as a vital referral market for the company.

Ninety percent of Dovetail's customers come to the firm via recommendation from friends. These friends have, albeit at secondhand, experienced the new Dovetail kitchen and indeed, doubtless, heard the saga. Therefore they are immediately confident that Dovetail can produce a great kitchen for them. They understand the prices charged, and will have a feel for the way that John involves his customers in the design as much as they wish. So his new customers have already learned what it is like to do business with Dovetail before they themselves commit to purchase. This is the value of the referral market. What does this cost Dovetail? Well, very little, in the sense that although John has wondered about paying for these referrals, it really is a natural part of the process of producing delighted customers. So the real cost is to produce continuous excellent service.

Customer comments are quoted on the website: 'We simply love our new kitchen. John and his team were amazingly patient in working and re-working the design until we had something with which we were completely happy. They made many suggestions that we would never have thought of (such as built-in bins and crockery drawers instead of cupboards) and persuaded us to think boldly at times'.

'Dovetail was recommended to us by close friends and John Kirby and his team met the brief, they were alone in this. We enjoyed the relationship of working up the design, selecting materials and details with them'.

There is a strong technical element to their work: 'We were delighted with the kitchen that Dovetail built for us. It was a difficult space with some very strange angled walls but John Kirby came up with some creative solutions and managed to incorporate everything that we wanted'.

Spotlight on service quality

For the business to flourish by obtaining referrals, the service quality has to be high. They get the basics right: 'The kitchen was also built on time and within budget'. 'You produced and installed a product of the very highest quality. The process was enjoyable and the result provides endless pleasure'. 'From the very start to the final fitting the service and quality was faultless'. 'The installation went very smoothly and, if any problems did crop up, they were overcome without us hearing about them'. In this market repeat custom has been rare. John's rural customers do not move house very often. Once they have bought their kitchen, they do not need another. He can count on the fingers of one hand those who have moved and so asked him to supply a second kitchen – and that includes a couple of customers who asked him to renew the kitchen in their second-home! John does not admit to being influenced by fashion claiming that he offers timeless classics. However, there are undoubtedly echoes of current fashion trends in his kitchens and he and his customers are undoubtedly attuned to what is being reported in the fashionable magazines.

Therefore, a key influence market is the glossy magazine selling dreams of the desirable country home interior. However, John has found that winning PR on his kitchens generates only very poor sales leads. These potential customers may share dreams of the aspirational kitchen with his clients on the website – they may not share their ability to pay. For a small company like Dovetail, with no one detailed to answer the phone all day, the volume of enquiries generated is also a headache. John now considers that this route to market is not profitable for him, as a small entrepreneur.

Networks

Suppliers are absolutely critical to his business success. And it is from them Dovetail effectively wins repeat business. Plumbers, electricians, architects and interior designers all recommend him to their customers again and again. John views this network of collaborators in the successful design and fitting of a kitchen as part of the team. He comments 'You can never find the perfect supplier. I have learned to

RELATIONSHIP MARKETING AND NETWORKS

work with a good one and to bring them along during the process. I consider it my job to manage them: if they mess up, I mess up'.

Recruitment is an issue for Dovetail. It is a small team that depends on each member performing well for each customer. It is a series of complicated tasks that is a learning experience for each project – John does not want to lose the skills and knowledge built up in the business. However, over the years he has employed new staff and has learned to go to the schools to catch them young. He asks the Design teachers in local schools and colleges, with whom he carefully builds personal relationships, who of the youngsters has the essential, if elusive, spark. He uses their experience to drive his choice of new apprentices.

Once members of staff join the company John knows that he needs to create a climate that encourages them to perform to their potential and to stay. They celebrate the end of every project with an evening out – perhaps down at a local bowling alley. Over the years he has played host and even social worker, offering to arrange money management counseling for members of staff.

If there is one key to his success in terms of living his dream of setting up his own business he has found that it is all about relationships rather than all about his original profession: master carpenter. Relationships mean that customers and company can put up with a lot from each other. What is the key to his business success? 'If you are not perceived as trustworthy you have nothing to offer anybody'.

Questions

1. Do you see evidence of customer value being co-created with customers? List this out.
2. Map out the stakeholders that might feature in a marketing plan for Dovertail using the Six Markets Model to do so.
3. Do you think the Six Markets Model of relationship marketing is a good way to understand this small business?
4. What do you think are the three key success factors in this business? Why?
5. Why has John not grown his company larger over time? List out the issues in growing the entrepreneurial firm and how relationships and networks might act as both enablers and constraints.
6. Draw up a plan to double the size of the firm over the next three years.
7. Do you think this is a good idea? Justify your plans and/or your doubts.

www.dovtetail.tc
*
www.jtcfurnituregroup.com
**
www.joneskitchens.co.uk
***
www.smallbone.co.uk

REFERENCES

American Marketing Association. (2007) Definition of Marketing. Available at: http://www.marketing power.com/aboutama/pages/definitionofmarketing.aspx

Bjerke, Björn and Hultman, Claes M. (2002) *Entrepreneurial Marketing: The Growth of Small Firms in the New Economic Era*. Edward Elgar Publishing, Cheltenham.

Blois, Keith J. (1999) Trust in business to business relationships: An evaluation of its status. *Journal of Management Studies*, 36(2), 197–217.

Bonnemaizon, Audrey, Cova, Bernard and Louyot, Marie-Claude (2007) Relationship marketing in 2005: A delphi approach. *European Management Journal*, 25(1), 50–59.

Carson, David (2004) 'Towards a research agenda'– a report to the SIG meeting January 04 University of Stirling.

Carson, David, Cromie, Stanley, McGowan, Pauric and Hill, Jimmy (1995) *Marketing and Entrepreneurship in SMEs: An Innovative Approach*. Pearson Education, Harlow.

Chaston, Ian (1997) How interaction between relationship and entrepreneurial marketing may affect organizational competencies in small UK manufacturing firms. *Marketing Education Review*, 7(3), 55–65.

Christopher, M., Payne, A. and Ballantyne, D. (1991) *Relationship Marketing*, Butterworth Heinemann, Oxford.

Crosby, L. A., Evans, K. R. and Cowles, D. (1990) Relationship quality in services selling: An interpersonal influence perspective. *Journal of Marketing*, 54(3), 68–81.

Dawber, Alistair (2010) 'LSE looks to tackle problem of AIM investor relations'. *Independent*. 15 March, 42.

Day, George S. (2002) Managing the market learning process. *Journal of Business and Industrial Marketing*, 17(4), 240–252.

Drucker, Peter (2001) *The Essential Drucker*. Harper Business, New York.

Franke, N. and Piller, F. (2004) Value creation by toolkits for user innovation and design: The case of the watch market. *Journal of Product Innovation Management*, 21(1), 401–416.

Gummesson, Evert (1987) The new marketing – developing long-term interactive relationships. *Long Range Planning*, 20(4), 10–20.

Gummesson, Evert (1991) Marketing-orientation revisited: The crucial role of the part-time marketer. *European Journal of Marketing*, 25(2), 60–75.

Gummesson, Evert (1997) Relationship marketing as a paradigm shift: Some conclusions from the 30R approach. *Management Decision*, 35(4), 267–272.

Gummesson, Evert (1999) *Total Relationship Marketing*, 2nd ed. Butterworth-Heinemann, Oxford.

Gummesson, Evert (2002) Relationship marketing in the new economy. *Journal of Relationship Marketing*, 1(1), 37–57.

Gummesson, Evert (2006) Many-to-many Marketing as Grand Theory: A Nordic School Contribution. In Lusch, Robert F. and Vargo, Stephen L. (Eds.), *The Service-Dominant Logic of Marketing: Dialog, Debate and Directions*. M.E. Sharpe, London.

Gummesson, Evert (2008) *Total Relationship Marketing*, 3rd ed. Butterworth-Heinemann, Oxford.

Gummesson, Evert (2009) In Baker, Michael and Saren, Michael (Eds.) (2010) *Marketing Theory*. Sage Publications, London.

Gwinner, Kevin P., Gremler, Dwayne D. and Bitner, Mary Jo (1998) Relational benefits in services industries: The customer's perspective. *Journal of the Academy of Marketing Science*, 26(2), 101–114.

Halliday, Sue Vaux (2004) How 'placed trust' works in a service encounter. *Journal of Services Marketing*, 18(1), 45–59.

Hamel, Gary, Doz, Yves L. and Prahalad, C. K. (1989) Collaborate with Your Competitors – and Win. In Ghauri, Pervez N. and Prasad, S. Benjamin (1995) (Eds.), *International Management, A Reader*. Dryden, London,146–154.

Hills, Gerald E., Hultman, Claes M. and Miles, Morgan P. (2008) The evolution and development of entrepreneurial marketing. *Journal of Small Business Management*, 46(1), 99–112.

Hills, Gerald E. and Singh, Robert P. (2000) *Research at the Marketing/Entrepreneurship Interface*. Institute for Entrepreneurial Studies, Chicago.

Hosmer, Larue Tone (1995) Trust: The connecting link between organizational theory and philosophical ethics. *Academy of Management Review*, 20(2), 379–403.

RELATIONSHIP MARKETING AND NETWORKS

Ibrahim, Nabil A., Angelidis, John P. and Parsa, Faramarz (2008) Strategic management of family businesses: Current findings and directions for future research. *International Journal of Management*, 25(1), 95–110.

Kay, J. (1993) *Foundations of Corporate Success*. Oxford University Press, Oxford.

Kok, Robert A. W., Hillebrand, Bas and Biemans, Wim G. (2003) What makes product development market oriented? Towards a conceptual framework. *International Journal of Innovation Management*, 7(2), 137–162.

Langeard, E., Bateson, J. E. G., Lovelock, C. H. and Eiglier, P. (1981) *Services Marketing: New Insights from Consumers and Managers*. Marketing Science Institute Working Paper, Cambridge, MA

Morris, Michael H., Schindehutte, Minet and LaForge, Raymond W. (2002) Entrepreneurial marketing: A construct for integrating emerging entrepreneurship and marketing perspectives. *Journal of Marketing Theory and Practice*, 10(4), 1–19.

Palmer, Adrian (1994) Relationship marketing: Back to basics? *Journal of Marketing Management*, 10(7), 571–579.

Parasuraman, A., Zeithaml, V. and Berry, L. L. (1985) A conceptual model of service quality and its implications for future research. *Journal of Marketing*, 49(3), 41–50.

Pavis, Patrice (1998) *Dictionary of the Theatre – Terms, Concepts and Analysis*. University of Toronto Press, Toronto.

Prahalad, C. K. and Ramaswamy, Venkatram (2002) Co-opting customer competence. *Harvard Business Review*, 78(1), 34–39.

Prahalad, C. K. and Ramaswamy, Venkatram (2004) *The Future of Competition: Co-creating Unique Value with Customers*. Harvard Business School Press, Cambridge, MA.

Raub, W. and Weesie, J. (1990) Reputation and efficiency in social interactions: An example of network effects, *American Journal of Sociology*, 96(3), 626–654.

Rocks, Steve, Gilmore, Audrey and Carson, David (2005) Developing strategic marketing through the use of marketing networks. *Journal of Strategic Marketing*, 13(2), 81–92.

Schmitt, B. (1999) Experiential Marketing. *Journal of Marketing Management*, 15(1–3), 53–67.

Sinkula, James M., Baker, William E. and Noordewier, Thomas (1997) A framework for market-based organizational learning: Linking values, knowledge and behavior. *Journal of the Academy of Marketing Science*, 25(4), 305–318.

Vargo, S. L. and Lusch, R. F. (2004) Evolving to a new dominant logic for marketing. *Journal of Marketing*, 68(1), 1–17.

Vargo, S. L. and Lusch, R. F. (2008) Service-dominant logic: Continuing the evolution. *Journal of the Academy of Marketing Science*, 36(1), 1–10.

Webster, F. E. (1992) The changing role of marketing in the corporation. *Journal of Marketing*, 56(4), 1–17.

Chapter 15

Internal marketing and service excellence in SMEs

Hina Khan

LEARNING OBJECTIVES

After reading this chapter, you will be able to:
- Understand the influence and importance of internal customers on service excellence for SMEs;
- Understand the importance of internal marketing as an approach to achieve service excellence particularly for SMEs;
- Explain investigate specific issues relating to the implementation of a service excellence approach in relation to internal marketing in SMEs;
- Explore to what extent service excellence can be implemented in practice in SMEs.

INTRODUCTION

In today's highly competitive business environment, satisfying customer needs in a way that enables an organisation to achieve a sustainable advantage has become an extremely difficult task for any organisation particularly for SMEs (Small and Medium-sized Enterprises). Furthermore, this has become an even more difficult task for those SMEs that provide services that are intangible, inseparable, perishable and variable in nature.

Thus, service organisations constantly strive to achieve a competitive advantage through implementing different strategies which enables them to overcome the challenges associated with marketing a service. '**Service excellence**' has been seen as one such strategic approach that can be adopted by any type of the organisation, particularly by SMEs which have a flexible organisational structure, which enables them to obtain the required employee buy-in for such strategy compared to other types of large organisations with complex structures.

However, achieving service excellence does require lots of investment on a variety of resources such as personnel, money, materials, methods and time. Hence, for SMEs, the lack of sufficient capital required to invest in growing resources would act as a major barrier to maintain service excellence on an ongoing basis. Furthermore, to implement service excellence in SMEs, excellent analysis, planning, implementation and controlling skills, and inter-functional coordination within the organisation are also essential. Hence, effective

INTERNAL MARKETING AND SERVICE EXCELLENCE

utilisation of limited resources, expertise, and assistance from external parties has become crucial for Sees. However, the lack of expertise, the limited access to latest technology and lack of sufficient funds to invest in processes and to make improvements in the physical environment where the service is delivered have made it extremely difficult for SMEs to achieve a competitive advantage.

Nevertheless, 'the employees' who deliver the service to the external customers, or who receive different kinds of service as an internal customer of the organisation, seem to play a major role for SMEs. Hence, many SMEs strive to differentiate themselves on the basis of the *people factor* because it is the employees who represent the organisation: the only live resource which interacts with customers and makes or breaks deals for a company. Hence, managing employees or the people factor effectively has become crucial, making an effective internal marketing strategy to become a critical success factor in achieving service excellence for SMEs. Often, SMEs lack of resources, both financial and non-financial, and therefore implementing service excellence could be seen as a cost rather than a strategic resource. But, internal marketing could be a cost effective competitive strategy that SMEs could rely on to become successful. Thus, this chapter aims to provide an understanding on how a firm can achieve service excellence and the role that internal marketing plays in order to successfully implement service excellence within an organisation, with particular emphasis on SMEs.

SMES AND SERVICE MARKETING

Defining service

According to Kotler (2000) a service can be defined as 'any activity or benefit that one party can offer to another that is essentially intangible and does not result in ownership of anything'. Providing a similar view, Lovelock and Wirtz (2007, p. 10) describes service as a 'deed or performance', and that it is 'ephemeral-transitionary and perishable'.

What makes services different from physical goods?

Even though many similarities can be found between product and service marketing practices, there are specific characteristics of a service that makes it different from that of physical goods. These include

- Intangibility;
- Inseparability;
- Perishability;
- Heterogeneity;
- Lack of ownership.

A brief description of each of these characteristics is provided in table 15.1

SERVICES MARKETING AND ITS IMPORTANCE

The 7 Ps of services marketing

The marketing activities of any kind of organisation are normally concentrated around the traditional 4 Ps or the product, price, place, and promotion. However, the distinctive characteristics possessed by services such as intangibility, inseparability, perishability and heterogeneity have made it essential for marketers to successfully market services to its customers.

245

HINA KHAN

Table 15.1 Characteristics of a service

Service characteristics	Description
Intangibility	Unlike physical goods, services do not possess any tangible aspect or they cannot be felt or tasted. Moreover, they do not possess any physical presence, therefore the service receiver does not have an assurance of what they will receive or to what extent it will meet their needs.
Inseparability	Since the production and the consumption of the service occur simultaneously, it cannot be separated from the person providing it.
Heterogeneity	It is very difficult to provide a consistent service all the time due to the differences that occur when delivering the service mainly due to human variables.
Perishability	Services cannot be stored as physical goods.
Lack of ownership	Unlike the physical goods, services do not result in any transfer of property. Hence no ownership can be gained.

Thus, Gronroos (1978, p. 600) suggests that the 4 Ps (product, price, place. and promotion) that make up the marketing mix were extended to the 7 Ps to include three additional Ps; physical environment, processes, and people, in order to take account of the challenges posed by services marketing due to its unique differences from that of physical goods.

A brief description on each element that makes the 7 Ps is provided in Table 15.2.

Despite the aforementioned unique differences of services compared to tangible goods, the overriding need to identify and satisfy customer needs in a way that meet or exceed their expectations have made it essential for service organisations to integrate specific service marketing tools to achieve and develop a 'service excellence' oriented organisation.

Table 15.2 The 7 Ps of marketing

Marketing mix element	Description
Product	Product is the tangible good or intangible benefit offered to a customer in order to satisfy their needs.
Price	Price is the amount that a customer needs to pay in order to obtain the product or service.
Place	Place refers to the distribution method used to deliver the product to the customer.
Promotion	Promotion includes all forms of communication methods that a marketer may use to communicate with the target audience.
People	People refer to the service personnel who deliver the service. The appearance and the behaviour may have a greater impact on the quality of the service provided.
Process	This includes all sorts of procedures which are used to provide service.
Physical evidence	Physical evidence refers to the layout, appearance, the setting of the environment where the service is delivered. This also includes the brochures or any kind of equipment used to tangibilise the intangibility of the service provided.

INTERNAL MARKETING
What is internal marketing?
Internal Marketing was first proposed as a solution to the problem of delivering consistently high service quality during the 1980s. An early definition from Berry (1981), as quoted by Ahmed and Rafiq, (2003, p. 4), was 'viewing employees as internal customers, viewing jobs as internal products that satisfy the needs and wants of these internal customers while addressing the objectives of the organisation'.

Internal marketing is a management philosophy and accordingly requires management to 'create, encourage and enhance understanding of and appreciate the roles of employees in the organisation'. Gronroos (1978, p. 8); Parasuraman et al. (1991, 433p) defines internal marketing as 'attracting, developing, motivating and retaining qualified employees through job products that satisfy their needs'. Ahmed and Rafiq (2003, p. 10) agrees and defines internal marketing as 'a planned effort using a marketing-like approach, directed at motivating employees, for implementing and integrating organisational strategies towards customer orientation'. In order to create a service and customer orientated culture among employees, service organisations are increasingly trying to adopt the concept of internal marketing (Kang and Alexandris, 2002, p. 278).

KEY ELEMENTS OF INTERNAL MARKETING
According to Ahmed and Rafiq (2003), there are five key elements of internal marketing as follows.

1. **Employee motivation and satisfaction**
Internal marketing acts as a vehicle for staff acquisition, motivation and retention, which in turn leads to increased productivity and external service quality (see Figure 15.1).

2. **Customer orientation and customer satisfaction**
If internal marketing is to be successful, it should be customer oriented or focussed on anticipating and satisfying customer needs. Hence, internal marketing can be considered as a tool that promotes customer oriented behaviour among staff members.

3. **Inter-functional coordination and integration.**
Internal marketing has a strong impact on each and every employee working within an organisation, regardless of the division or function (for example, whether they belong to marketing, human resource management or finance is of little consequence). Therefore, internal marketing requires an effective co-ordination and integration of all of the functions within the organisation.

4. **Marketing like approach**
Internal marketing seeks to identify and satisfy the needs of the internal customers/employees. Internal marketing is integrated into marketing planning just like other marketing

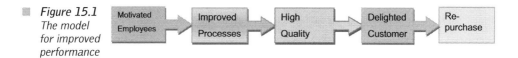

Figure 15.1 The model for improved performance

activities. Thus, internal marketing also adopts a marketing-like approach to satisfy internal customers by offering benefits and incentives to keep them loyal as well as to attract the best employees.

5. Implementation of specific corporate and functional strategies

In order to successfully implement internal marketing, it is essential for an organisation to integrate both corporate strategies related to internal growth and functional strategies for different functions within an organisation. However, despite the rapidly growing literature on internal marketing, not many organisations actually apply the concept in practice. They add that the number and range of activities and definitions available has led to difficulties in the implementation and adoption of the concept (Ahmed and Rafiq, 2003).

OBJECTIVES OF INTERNAL MARKETING

The objectives of internal marketing are to get the 'commitment of the employees to strategies and tactics of the firm and to create an environment where they feel motivated' (Blois and Gronroos, 2000, p. 506). It is the 'people factor in most cases that drives the customers away' and whilst firms believe in learning more about consumers' perceptions of their products and services, they 'invest very modestly in learning about what makes their employees act the way they do' (Wheeler, 2006, p. 97).

ADVANTAGES AND DISADVANTAGES OF INTERNAL MARKETING

There are numerous benefits that a firm can achieve through internal marketing (e.g., low employee turnover, greater service quality, and a rise in service satisfaction. Furthermore, it is suggested that an effective internal marketing strategy also helps an organisation to buy-in employees to implement change within an organisation. Thus, it can be suggested that through establishing effective internal marketing strategy any organisation, particularly SMEs can benefit effectively. Whilst the associated high cost with initiating an internal marketing programme would have a negative impact for the SME in the short term, it will deliver an added value in the long run (Iacobucci and Nordhielm, 2000).

IMPLEMENTING SERVICE EXCELLENCE

Service excellence defined

Service excellence is all about behaviour and attitudes of employees within an organisation. It's as much about the people within the organisation as the clients it is serving. Excellent, motivated people will have a 'can do' attitude and be prepared to go that extra mile for clients; however, it is how to motivate employees through internal service excellence that this chapter focuses on.

This subject is very interesting and highly relevant in today's competitive service industry. Services marketing and internal marketing are fascinating fields of academic study, which are firmly embedded in the real world. It is a very real topic for discussion because as consumers, we 'consume' services as part of our everyday life and can relate to the feeling gained from receiving excellent customer service and in the same respect know how it feels when the service does not live up to our expectations.

Significance of achieving service excellence for SMEs

In order to constantly deliver high quality products and services profitably, it requires 'an organisation to attain, sustain, and enhance the overall level of product and service excellence' (Swart and Duncan, 2005, p. 487). This is achieved by 'continually providing satisfaction of customer requirements and through utilising the efforts of everybody in the company' (Swart and Duncan (2005, p. 487). However, as customer expectations are increasing, 'service excellence is becoming a major competitive platform if only because current service is mostly so poor' (Quinn and Humble (1993, p. 60). However, the quality service movement is often accused of being 'merely slogans, fad and hot topics' (Farner et al., 2001, p. 350)

Furthermore, the processes are the means 'by which a company harnesses and releases the talent of its people to provide high performance. Moreover the improvement in performance can be achieved only by improving the processes by involving people' (Oakland, 2001, p. 99). Figure 15.1 shows an alternative model for improved performance by involving all employees within an organisation by seeking to continually improve their processes. Prabhu and Robson (2000, p. 312) also raise the issue of employee-related practices and suggest a significant association between those practices and operational performance.

Service excellence encourages people to care for one another and work with the same goal in mind. It makes them feel valued and as a result they enjoy their job which can only have a positive effect on external client service as shown in Figure 15.1.

Service excellence is associated with the motivation and the value of team working and being able to differentiate through high levels of external and internal service. Thus, service excellence means being part of an environment where you are motivated, developed, and valued and where you are happy to go that extra mile to deliver a better service to clients, both internally and externally (Khan and Hedley, 2009). Moreover, by 'consistently delivering high quality services in a profitable manner require an organisation to attain, sustain, and enhance the overall level of service excellence'. This is achieved by continually providing satisfaction of customer requirements and 'through utilising the efforts of everybody in the company' (Swart and Duncan, 2005, p. 487). This leads to delighted customers and as a result, repurchases as shown in Figure 15.1.

USE OF INTERNAL MARKETING AS A MEANS TO ACHIEVE SERVICE EXCELLENCE

The role of the PEOPLE factor in implementing service excellence in SMEs

For most companies today, the people are the company, it is therefore paramount that an organisation must 'use and manage the most important resource in order to achieve customer satisfaction' (Kanji, 2007, p. 5). An organisation needs to get their training and development right so that front line staff can infuse customers with their enthusiasm and commitment which then can have a positive effect on overall business.

SMEs need to get the internal dynamics right and recognise that internal customers' needs to be satisfied in order to meet the needs of external customers. Everyone in the organisation needs to 'deliver to others and more importantly to the clients'. Service excellence is about 'going beyond the client's expectations and leaving them with the feeling that they feel valued as a client. However, service excellence starts with employees in order to delight customers, organisations need to delight their employees too' (Chaston, 1994, p. 45; Atkinson, 1990)

The role of employees as brand ambassadors in implementing service excellence in SMEs

Thus, service excellence should not be referred to as an approach or programme but as a journey. The workforce should be aware that it's an ongoing journey. Hence, it should not be called a programme as that would infer that it (service excellence) would come to an end. Service excellence should be a way of life for the organisation. It should evolve but hopefully never end (Khan and Hedley, 2009).

The role of employees as brand ambassadors in implementing service excellence in SMEs

Companies must 'adapt their products and or services to remain competitive in the marketplace' (Krell, 2006, p. 50). Companies need to keep updating their products and offerings in order to keep up with the change in the marketplace, trends, customers' demands and their competitors' offerings. If the changes are vast, 'a company's brand may no longer accurately reflect what it offers. Thus, requiring a brand overhaul' (Krell, 2006, p. 50). Many companies opt for re-branding in order to enhance the company's overall image. However, re-branding can present a risk to the company, which increases if the company wrongly begins the re-branding campaign with its customers before getting buy-in from employees on the new brand (Krell, 2006). The employees are at the heart of implementing all these changes whether it is an introduction of a new product or service feature or rebranding of the current brand. It is the employees who actually make it happen, especially in the service sector, where employees are the brand.

In order to gain this buy-in from employees it is important that they feel 'their contribution is valued, their needs and personal priorities are recognised and that their participation makes a difference to them personally' as well as to the 'organisation as a whole' (Krell, 2006). Effective communication can 'strengthen both intellectual and emotional buy-in' (Krell, 2006). Particularly for SMEs this process is even more crucial because of lack of resources and specialist expertise. The following model, REBRAND, illustrates the process of implementing re-branding or a change for the SMEs. The model demonstrates the importance of employees' participation in the process as well as highlighting the external and internal barriers faced by the company when going through a change.

The REBRAND model provides a useful framework that SMEs can use to REBRAND themselves through employees. REBRAND stands for:

As shown in the model, the process of REBRAND starts from recognising internal and external brand barriers that would create a negative impact or hinder the effective rebranding process within an organisation particularly for SMEs. These barriers could be both internal and external to the organisation. Internal barriers could include barriers such as resistance to change, lack of motivation of the employees and the top management commitment, lack of strong leadership as well as the perception that money spent on developing the brand is a cost rather than an investment. This perception correlates with the reality of limited finance being available, especially for SMEs. The barriers external to the organisation would be low brand awareness within target markets and low levels of brand equity, which need to be overcome in order that to attract more customers.

All other elements such as enhancing brand awareness, brand equity, building a positive organisation culture, recruiting employees with specific skills and a positive attitude, seeking relevant aid from experts and external parties who can provide resources and expertise which are crucial for SMEs, developing strong relationships with employees and stakeholders could be regarded as the 'ways and means' through which an SME can achieve their ultimate goal of rebranding, which is providing an excellent internal and external service to both internal and external customers through empowering employees. The arrows represents the ongoing nature of the process and the knock-on effect on each act has on each element.

250

INTERNAL MARKETING AND SERVICE EXCELLENCE

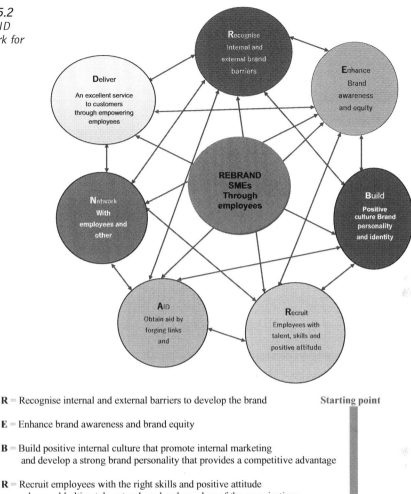

Figure 15.2 REBRAND framework for SMEs

R = Recognise internal and external barriers to develop the brand **Starting point**

E = Enhance brand awareness and brand equity

B = Build positive internal culture that promote internal marketing
and develop a strong brand personality that provides a competitive advantage

R = Recruit employees with the right skills and positive attitude
who would ultimately act as brand ambassadors of the organisations

A = Aid or seek help, emphasise the importance of seeking aid from other
parties such as experts, forging links, and working in partnership in order
to overcome brand barriers and to obtain skills and resources, which
SMEs often lacked due to the limited capital availability.

Ways and means

N = Networking includes developing strong relationship with employees and all
the other key stakeholders who influence and who are affected by the
actions of the organisation

D = Deliver; this could be considered as the final end result of rebranding which is
delivering an excellent service to both internal and external customers through
empowering employees in a way that delights them

End result

Furthermore, the model suggests that a strong internal culture and effective internal communication can help drive the brand and company as employees feel empowered. The employees will therefore communicate consistent positive messages and work together towards common goals. The barriers external to the organisation are low awareness and perception within target markets and low levels of brand equity, which need to be overcome in order that the organisations attract more customers. This is why the role of brand aiders is vital, in helping to overcome the external barriers (Khan and Ede, 2009).

BARRIERS THAT SMES NEED TO OVERCOME IN ORDER TO IMPLEMENT SERVICE EXCELLENCE

There are several factors and forces that may act as a barrier for an SME to successfully achieve service excellence within the organisation. Some of the major barriers are explained in the following.

Lack of initial buy-in from employees

The major limitation to service excellence is the initial lack of 'buy-in' from employees and the fact that many people tend to be cynical of the idea. People may take it seriously as a management technique as time goes on. When companies hire the right people and the right processes are in place, it leads to a change in the culture. Some critics say that service excellence is a term that is sometimes over used.

Lack of resources

Investing in both financial and non-financial resources are key to successfully implement service excellence within an organisation. For SMEs which are normally set up using the capital of individual owners, may lack essential financial and non-financial resources which are required to develop structures and processes and provide training to employees. Hence, a lack of resources is one of the major barriers to successfully implementing service excellence within SMEs.

Lack of top management commitment

Since most of the owners and managers are concerned about the short term return on investment, obtaining the commitment of top management to implement service excellence, which is costly and time consuming, to deliver return on investment can be difficult.

Lack of professional expertise

Many SMEs lack professional expertise required to implement service excellence and associated processes such as managing change. Furthermore, they also lack the financial resources required to employ 'experts' externally as consultants to the organisation. They may further lack the new managerial skills which may require managing such processes effectively. Hence, when implementing service excellence which requires a range of expertise, knowledge, and managerial skills, this lack of professional expertise may also act as a barrier to effective implementation of service excellence for SMEs.

Resistance to change

However, service excellence plays a crucial role when a company is introducing change. You can tag a lot of things on the service excellence process. It makes it easier to sell change. However, the danger is that it gets used for everything and goes too far. Things that are irrelevant can get the service excellence tag (Khan and Hedley, 2009). This concurs with Farner et al. (2001, p. 393) who suggest that this new idea is just new terminology and is a case of disregarding quality service movements as 'slogans' and a 'fad'. The concept of internal customers is criticised that detracts an organisation from the real customer. However, every organisation will have a number of people who are cynical and see something like service excellence as a new management fad that will pass with time.

Inability to retain high-calibre staff

The flat organisation structure of SMEs often makes it difficult for employees to realise their career goals and potential to grow within the organisation. This often contributes to a frustrating working environment which compels many experienced and skilled staff to move to another organisation. Hence, when implementing an initiative such as 'service excellence', which is an ongoing process, this inability to retain high-calibre staff can hinder the effectiveness and efficiency of SMEs to implement service excellence.

PRACTICAL IMPLICATIONS OF THE BARRIERS AND CHALLENGES FOR SMES

There are several practical implications for service sector organisations, particularly SMEs. First, the relationship between a motivated workforce and a successful organisation can be achieved by implementing service excellence as shown in Figure 15.3. Communication between teams throughout the organisation is crucial. Recruiting the right people in the first instance is also vital in providing service excellence for clients. The attitude of employees plays a large role in contributing to the overall culture of a firm and is therefore important to ensure that all employees buy into the culture of the organisation accepting and living the values of the organisation. Service excellence is also considered a continuous journey, ever evolving but never ending. Hence, it helps organisations to create synergy. Figure 15.3 shows the relationship found.

Figure 15.3 The relationship between internal customers, service excellence, and a winning organisation

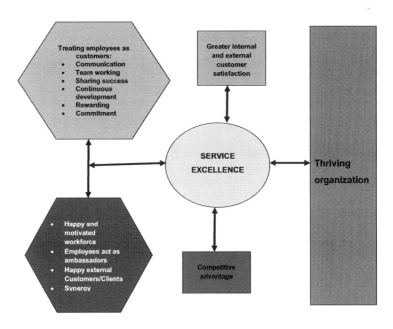

Figure 15.4 The IMPLEMENT steps to overcome barriers when implementing service excellence

ACTIONS THAT CAN BE TAKEN FOR SUCCESSFUL IMPLEMENTATION OF SERVICE EXCELLENCE IN SMES

The following section presents the steps that can be taken by an SME to overcome the barriers when implementing service excellence. The steps are defined as IMPLEMENT:

Identify areas to be improved

By identifying what prevent SMEs from achieving service excellence is crucial to successfully implementing service excellence. This could be achieved by identifying what kind of investments are required, what skills and knowledge need to be developed, and what processes and procedures need to be employed to achieve service excellence. Addressing these will enable SMEs to develop service excellence oriented culture which in turn ensure effective implementation of service excellence within the company.

Motivate employees

Employee motivation and job satisfaction leads to service excellence, which in turn has a positive effect on external customers. Basically, happy employees equal happy customers. This is apparent when an organisation looks after the well-being of their workforce and trains them to ensure they are happy and committed. People, in their ability to provide excellent service both inside and outside the organisation aids organisational success. This is supported by a number of authors including Gilthorpe (2006), Pfeffer (1998), and Oakland (2001), who are of the general consensus that people based strategies are highly effective in relation to organisational performance.

Plan the activities

Appropriate planning of how service excellence will be achieved in the organisation, how the limited resources available for an SMEs will be utilised effectively and efficiently will be vital for a successful implementation of Service excellence within an organisation. Analysing

INTERNAL MARKETING AND SERVICE EXCELLENCE

the organisation environment, identifying what kind of changes and resources required at the beginning of the planning stage will provide SMEs an opportunity to determine what strategies and tactics needs to be adapted if service excellence is to be achieved. Conducting a gap analysis of current level of service satisfaction and required level will also enable an SME to identify areas that need attention and plan appropriate strategies to close the gap in order to gain competitive advantage and achieve service excellence.

Lead

Leadership is crucial for the successful implementation of any kind of initiative within an organisation. For SMEs which are limited by expertise and financial resources, a task and people oriented leadership would be essential to buy-in employees to implement required changes which are essential to achieve service excellence. By providing task oriented and people oriented leadership, leaders would be able to ensure goals are achieved on time and the issues that arise related to employee satisfaction are managed and addressed simultaneously.

Employ the right people

Recruiting the right people also aids service excellence. By selecting the right people who fit the culture of the organisation, the organisation will undoubtedly be highly successful. This can be achieved by 'attracting, developing, motivating, rewarding and retaining qualified employees through job prospects that satisfy their needs' (Parasuraman et al., 1991; Varey and Lewis, 2000, p. 176). This also implies the similarity between service excellence and internal marketing and how the two are interlinked and can overlap. Whilst there is a degree of bias to be found from the authors, there is enough evidence to support the claim. The research has proven that service excellence can give a clear indication into the importance of treating employees as customers and also the relevance of a service excellence approach to differentiate a service organisation. This chapter explored how a service excellence approach can help to differentiate an organisation by focussing on motivating internal customers that leads to improved external service quality which brings, in turn, customer loyalty, retention, and long-term financial success (Gilbert, 2000). Clearly, the task of developing and maintaining a service excellence approach and application of internal marketing can be a long process and enthusiasm from management and employees alike can ensure that the approach is successful and in return differentiate a business.

Managing inter-functional coordination

Service excellence promotes interaction between all teams within the organisation. Team working is essential and is seen by customers both internally and externally as a key differentiator between firms. By having a workforce that genuinely cares about each other, work for each other towards the same goal, service excellence can be achieved. Openly encouraging employees to seek to improve their processes and giving them an outlet to share their ideas helps to make them feel they can contribute to the organisation (Khan and Hedley, 2009). It really makes a difference, giving them a sense of importance. People at all levels in the organisation need to have input into the direction of the organisation (Nixon, 1998). It is also recommended that sharing success and giving praise to employees who have done a great job, however insignificant, can give the workforce an incentive to work better and to go that extra mile to meet expectations, thus, making them committed to the organisation.

255

Educate

When implementing service excellence within a SME, educating internal customers about how the implementation would take place, what the organisation expect from each and every individual employee and as a team from them, likely changes that would affect employees, the short- and long-term benefits that employees would gain through service excellence and how it would contribute to the growth of the organisation would enable SMEs to reduce employee resistance and implement service excellence successfully.

Negotiate

Conducting effective negotiations between the management and employees would be crucial to avoid barriers such as employee resistance and lack of commitment, which are essential for successful implementation of service excellence. This would also help SMEs to develop and maintain effective inter-functional coordination and positive relationship between the management and employees.

Take actions

Once service excellence is implemented within a SME, it is essential to carefully monitor all the people processes and physical evidence by taking appropriate actions to avoid failures to ensure the success of strategy employed. Furthermore, as stated earlier, service excellence should be promoted as an ongoing journey and not just a programme as the programme comes to an end.

Does service excellence really matter for SMEs?

Having weighed up the various arguments for and against internal marketing and service excellence, it is concluded that there is sufficient evidence to show that there is a link between a motivated workforce, service excellence and a successful organisation. Although it is also noted that there is, as yet, no definitive measure of service excellence as such but repeat business from clients gives a good indication of this, together with the implementation of employee satisfaction surveys to understand the workforce as a whole and how their needs can be met (Khan and Hedley, 2009). Thus, having an understanding that looking after your people is key to providing excellent service and that meeting their needs is also as important as meeting those of the external clients. The objectives of internal marketing are to get the commitment from employees to create a motivated working environment. It is essential to note that internal customers are seen as just as important as the external customers (Blois and Gronroos, 2000).

CHAPTER SUMMARY

This chapter, first, defined the services and identified that services differ from tangible goods due to their unique characteristics such as intangibility, inseparability, heterogeneity, and perishability. These make it difficult particularly for SMEs to differentiate themselves from the competition. Hence, this chapter suggested that service excellence can be used as a strategic approach that can be used by SMEs to differentiate themselves from the competition. Furthermore, this chapter also identified that effective management of people can enable SMEs to implement service excellence successfully.

INTERNAL MARKETING AND SERVICE EXCELLENCE

Hence, in this chapter, the extent to which internal marketing can be used as a technique to implement service excellence within SMEs were identified. Furthermore, the linkage between service excellence and the importance of the role employees play and how it can indeed be the link between a happy and motivated workforce and a successful organisation are also explained in the chapter. By understanding this relationship, it should help SMEs to implement such a management method in order to achieve synergy and further raise the bar in already highly competitive marketplaces.

Thereafter, the objectives, relative advantages and disadvantages associated with implementing service excellence for SMEs were identified. It was also identified that lack of initial buy-in from employees, lack of resources, lack of professional expertise, and several other factors act as a barrier when implementing service excellence within SMEs effectively.

Finally, actions that can be adopted by SMEs to overcome these barriers are also identified. This can be achieved by integrating the IMPLEMENT framework presented in the chapter.

REVIEW QUESTIONS

1. With the help of examples, discuss the role employees play in implementing service excellence.

2. How can an SME achieve REBRAND through employees? Discuss by evaluating the model (Fig 16.2) REBRAD framework for SME's.

3. Critically evaluate challenges/barriers that SME's may face when implementing service excellence?

4. How can an organisation improve its core competences and achieve synergy by implementing service excellence?

5. Explain what role internal marketing plays in implementing service excellence in an SME?

CASE STUDY: AJD ELECTRONICS – SUNDAY TRADING IN THE 21ST CENTURY

AJD Electronics is small family business that sells electronic home appliances situated in the heart of a city centre. It has been operating for the last 15 years and has grown from sole proprietor to employing seven staff, four full-time and three part-time. The company used to open six days a week from Monday to Saturday. However, due to customer demands and increasing competition – particularly from online retailers – the company has decided to open seven days a week – Monday to Sunday. It has been noticed, since opening on Sunday, that the overall weekly sales have increased.

The owner of the company has pointed out that more and more people are shopping on Sundays and in terms of sales Sunday is the second busiest day of the week. In order to keep and increase the company's market share and to maintain their competitive position in the marketplace, the company is keen to adapt to these changes and stay in touch with future retail trends and changing consumer shopping behaviour. Moreover, one of the essential traits of the company's success has been to embrace change and be innovative with products and services it offers to satisfy customers and increase efficiency in order to compete effectively.

Nonetheless, in order to implement this change successfully the working hours of the current workforce need to be reviewed and new terms and conditions to be implemented. Concerns were raised by the employees, particularly full-time staff as they felt that it would increase the operating cost of the business, would affect their family lives and social commitments. They also felt refusal to work on Sundays may also affect their future prospects in the company. No premium pay was offered to work on Sundays; however, extra time off has been offered as an incentive to work on a Sunday. Full-time staff raised concerns that part-time staff don't have full knowledge about the products and are not fully trained as it was not considered viable to invest in their training and development due to high turnover. It was felt that they could be dismissed easily. Thus, part-time staff felt insecure in their jobs. Some part-time staff felt that Sunday opening hours would increase employment and provide them with an opportunity to earn extra income (Khan, 2018)

Both full-time and part-time workers felt that the company should offer more incentives to work on a Sunday. Moreover, they strongly felt that their future prospects within the company and rights should be protected. However, if more incentives were not offered, they would not work on a Sunday.

Despite all these concerns raised by the employees, the company insisted on opening on Sunday as it strongly believed that the increase in sales outweigh the operating costs of the business. It also pledged that staff with religious commitments will not be forced to work on a Sunday. Furthermore, it is paramount for the company to embrace changing consumer habits and their desire to shop on Sunday in order to remain competitive and successful.

Questions

1. How can service excellence help the company to implement this change?
2. Identify strategic and operational challenges that the company should consider prior to adopting the change to open on Sundays?
3. How can the company use 'internal marketing' to bring around the employees and bridge the divide?
4. How can service excellence help the company to satisfy both internal customers (employees) and external customer needs?

Reference: Khan, H. (2018) Sunday is the new Saturday: Sunday trading reforms and its effects on family-run SMEs, employees and consumers. *Journal of Small Business and Enterprise Development*, 25(6), 960–984, https://doi.org/10.1108/JSBED-02-2018-0055

INTERNAL MARKETING AND SERVICE EXCELLENCE

LET'S REASON TOGETHER: GROUP TASK

Sarah Jones' embarks on a new adventure – scenario

Sarah Jones is a fashion designer and works for one of the famous luxury designer labels. She has dedicated her life to fashion and has a vast in depth knowledge of the fashion industry. She wants to launch her own designer label online and hire three full-time employees to begin with. Sarah's aim is to adopt service excellence to implement her business strategies as she believes it will enable her to retain staff, promote loyalty and as a result happy customers. She believes happy and motivated employees means happy customers.

One of her customers has suggested that she should design jeans which 'make you feel attractive' regardless of your size. Sarah also likes this idea, as a few of her customers have expressed similar interest in a product of that nature. She is convinced that the market is 'crying out' for such a style. She is unsure about how to segment and communicate with the target market. She is also contemplating offering the new tailor made jeans to everyone regardless of their age or gender. She has developed a business plan to evaluate the potential and imminent competitors in the marketplace. She wants to offer tailor made jeans to suit individual require-ments. She aims to offer state of the art technology which scans customer's body images when ordering the tailormade jeans. This would allow her to create jeans which suit individual body shapes. She also wants to develop an online platform which offers customers to share ideas, provide instant feedback, and keep track of their order. She wants to keep in touch with her customers on a regular basis. So, in order to engage with today's tech-savvy consumers, she intends to launch online vid-eos appearing in them herself. This would allow her to interact with the customers directly and create a personal touch. She would also use the online videos/chats to promote her new designs and offers online as it is an easy way to reach consumers at an affordable cost. She wants to hire a marketing consultant who would help her investigate female and male buying habits, what is perceived as 'attractive' and what do they consider good value for money. She also wants to develop a strategy to spread positive e-word of mouth to promote her new small business.

Task

How can service excellence help Sarah to create brand awareness and e-word-of-mouth in today's technologically driven marketplace?

TECHNOLOGY, SME, AND THE 21ST CENTURY

Service excellence and keeping up with the future!

It is vital for a business to adapt to new technology to compete effectively. One of the challenges SMEs may face is to embrace change and implement new technol-ogy for a number of reasons, for instance, lack of finances, skills, or awareness.

However, some may argue that SMEs are all about people, their staff, managers, suppliers, and customers whom are all people. So, for all business, particularly SMEs, staff are their greatest assets and customers are key to their survival. Moreover, it is paramount to keep both staff and customers satisfied. Service excellence promotes fostering innovative technologies to implement business process to achieve high level of efficiency. These processes help staff to deliver the best service and positive customer experience which result in repeat purchase as a result help a company to gain and sustain competitive advantage. SMEs need to achieve profitability by differentiating their products and services, implementing service excellence and continuous innovation. Thus, business must incorporate new technology and service excellence to enhance company's functional strategies, processes, and values. Outdated processes and systems result in delay in service, frustrated staff, unsatisfied customers, and an out of touch business which cannot keep up with its marketplace, customer demand, and competitive offerings, hence, endangering its future.

Task

How can implementing service excellence facilitate a small family business help adopt new technologies to enhance its current process and practices? As a marketing consultant, develop a guide for a small family run business of your choice and outline clearly how it would improve the company's core competencies.

REFERENCES

Ahmed, P. K. and Rafiq, M. (2003) Internal marketing issues and challenges. *European Journal of Marketing*, 37(9), 1177–1186.

Atkinson, P. E. (1990) *Creating Culture Change, the Key to Successful Total Quality Management*. IFS, Bedford.

Berry, L. L. (1981) The employee as customer. *Journal of Retail Banking*, 3 March, 25–28.

Blois, K. and Gronroos C. (2000) *The Marketing of Services*. Oxford University Press, Oxford.

Chaston, I. (1994) Internal customer management and service gaps within the UK manufacturing sector. *International Journal of Operations and Production Management*, 14(9), 25–56.

Dubrovski, D. (2001) The role of customer satisfaction in achieving business excellence. *Journal of Total Quality Management*, 12(7 & 8), 920–925.

Evans, J. R. and Lindsay, W. M. (2005) *The Management and Control of Quality: International Student Edition Thomson*, South Western, Singapore.

Farner, S., Luthan, F. and Sommer, S. M. (2001) An empirical assessment of internal customer service: Managing service quality. *Journal of Marketing*, 11(5), 350–358.

Gilbert, G. R. (2000) Measuring internal customer satisfaction. *Journal of Managing Service Quality*, 10(3), 178–186.

Gill, J. and Johnson, P. (2002) *Research Methods for Managers*, 3rd ed. Sage Publishers, London.

Gilthorpe, G. (2006) Lessons in service excellence. *Legal Marketing* April/May, 31–33.

Gronroos, C. (1978) A service-orientated approach to marketing of services. *European Journal of Marketing*, 12(8), 588–602.

Harari, O. (1991) Should internal customers exist. *Management Review*, 82(6), 31–333.

Kang, D. J. and Alexandris, K. (2002) Measurement of internal service quality: Application of The SERVQUAL battery to internal service quality. *Journal of Managing Service Quality*, 12(5), 278–291.

Kanji, G. K. (2007) *Measuring Business Excellence*. Routledge, Taylor and Francis Group, London.

INTERNAL MARKETING AND SERVICE EXCELLENCE

Khan, H. and Ede, D. (2009) How do not-for-profit SMEs attempt to develop a strong brand in an increasingly saturated market. *Journal of Small Business and Enterprise Development*, 16(2), 335–354, 1462–6004.

Khan, H. and Hedley, K. (2009) Implementing service excellence to become a winning organisation. *Academy of Marketing Science Conference*, Oslo, Norway, 22–25 July 2009.

King, A. S. and Ehrhard, B. J. (1997) Empowering the workforce: A commitment to cohesion exercise. *Empowerment in Organisations*, 5(3), 139–150.

Kotler, P. (2000) *Marketing Management*. Millennium Edition. Prentice Hall, Englewood Cliffs, NJ.

Krell, E. (2006) Branding together. *HR Magazine*, 51(10), 48–54.

Longenecker, C. O. and Scazzero, J. A. (2000) Improving service quality: A tale of two Operations. *Journal of Services Marketing*, 10(4), 227–232.

Lovelock, C. and Wirtz, J. (2007) *Service Marketing, People, Technology, Strategy*. Pearson, Harlow.

Mitchell, A. (2005) Differentiate all you want, but its back to the basics every time. *Marketing Week*, 11 August 2005, 28–29.

Nixon, B. (1998) Creating the future we desire – getting the whole system into the room. *Journal of Industrial and Commercial Training*, 30(1), 4–11.

Oakland, J. S. (2001) *Total Organisation Excellence: Achieving World Class Performance*. Butterworth Heinmann, London.

Parasuraman, A., Berry, L. L. and Zeithaml, V. A. (1991) Refinement and reassessment of the SERVQUAL scale. *Journal of Retailing*, 67(4), 420–450.

Pfeffer, J. (1998) *The Human Equation: Building Profits by Putting People First*. Harvard Business School Press, Boston.

Prabhu, V. B. and Robson, A. (2000) Achieving service excellence – measuring the impact of leadership and senior management commitment. *Managing Service Quality*, 10(5), 307–317.

Quinn, M. and Humble, J. (1993) Using service to gain a competitive edge: The PROMPT approach. *Long Range Planning*, 26(2).

Reed, J. and Vakola, M. (2006) What role can a training needs analysis play in organisational change? *Journal of Organisational Change Management*, 19(3), 393–407.

Sharma, N. and Patterson, P.G. (1999) The impact of communication effectiveness and service quality on relationship commitment in consumer, professional services. *Journal of Services Marketing*, 13(2), 151–170.

Steward, T. (1997) Another fad worth killing. *Fortune*, 119–120.

Swart, W. and Duncan, S. (2005) A methodology for assuring the quality human performance. *International Journal of Computer Integrated Manufacturing*, 18(6), 487–497.

Turnois, L. (2004) Creating customer value: Bridging theory and practice. *Journal of Marketing Management*, 14(2), 12–23.

Wheeler, A. R. (2006) Retaining employees for service competency: The role of corporate brand identity. *Journal of Brand Management*, 14(1/2), 96–113.

Wisner, J. D. and Stanley, L. L. (1999) Internal relationships and activities associated with high levels of purchasing service quality. *Journal of Supply Chain Management*, 35(3), 25–35.

Chapter 16

Crowdfunding of SMEs

Sanya Ojo and Entissar Elgadi

LEARNING OBJECTIVES

After reading the chapter, you should be able to:
- Understand the constraints associated with start-up financing while reviewing funding options available to SMEs/entrepreneurs;
- Evaluate the crowdfunding mechanism as an alternate funding platform available to a new business start-up;
- Appraise the processes and procedures of crowdfunding as a finance option for a business venture;
- Recognise the effects of asymmetric information in the principal-agent relationship between the entrepreneur and the crowdfunders;
- Analyse the drawbacks of crowdfunding mechanism as a source of enterprise financing.

INTRODUCTION

Small and medium-sized enterprises (SMEs) play a very important role in any country's economy as vital generators of employment and income, and as drivers of development and innovation. SMEs represent a key role in the growth of the European Union (EU) economies. According to Golić (2014), 99% of European businesses today are concentrated in SMEs, which usually consist of up to 250 employees and 90% of those companies are micro-businesses employing ten or fewer workers. In the EU, there are 40 SMEs per 1000 residents indicating that SMEs represent the most key source of new employment; creating more than 4 million new jobs every year (e.g., Petković and Tešić, 2013). Even at the height of the 2008 financial crisis SMEs were able to create the greatest number of new jobs (European Commission, 2013). It is such that more than 66% of all employees work in SMEs in Europe, though in the developing countries this percentage is much higher (Golić, 2014).

Yet, SMEs/entrepreneurs have problems of access to finance provided by banks and other traditional sources of capital (De Buysere et al., 2012). Problems of access are exacerbated by insufficient collaterals, lack of cash flows, and the existence of huge information asymmetry between them and investors/financial establishments. Belleflamme et al. (2014) noted that many SMEs/entrepreneurs fail to persuade banks to grant them loans to finance their ventures and projects because of their inability to prove their businesses' viability. The global economic and financial crisis of 2008 was a watershed movement as SMEs have continued to experience restricted access to orthodox finance. While the strategy for economic rescue dealt mainly with banking systems and policy, the SMEs were left without the necessary attention and resources for their business.

SMEs AND ACCESS TO FUNDING

SMEs/entrepreneurs raise fund through several traditional sources such as bootstrapping; friends, families, and fools (3 Fs); business angels; bank loans; business grants; and venture capital. Bootstrapping is a situation in which an entrepreneur starts a business venture with little capital, relying on money (e.g., personal savings) other than outside (external) investments. An individual is said to be bootstrapping when she/he attempts to form and build a business from personal finances or the operating revenues of the new business. Bootstrapping as a form of financing may place unnecessary financial risk on the entrepreneur and may not provide enough investment for the business to become successful at a reasonable rate. Friend, Families, and Fools (3 Fs) source refers to money received as support from close friends, families, and well-wishers. This funding type is regarded as an emotional investment. The entrepreneur is able to convince her/his friends and families to invest in the business with the understanding of repayment as soon as possible. Fool investment really refers to investment by people who are neither friends and family nor professional investors. In short, they know nothing about the business but decided to invest in a venture through the persuasion (sweet talk) of the entrepreneur. However, if the business fails, friends, and family investment is likely to affect personal relationship and may turn into a lifelong debt, and a fool investment will most likely turn into a lifelong enmity. Business angels' investment refers to the informal market for access to start-up funding from wealthy individuals who ask for a proportion of the business equity. This type of investment is often difficult to access as investors are knowledgeable and ask tough questions from applicants (i.e., entrepreneurs).

Bank loans represents the formal route to business financing and can be obtained when the entrepreneur convinces the bank official of the credibility of, not only of the business but also of his/her integrity (e.g., creditworthiness). However, banks are not easily convinced and they often demand collateral which many SMEs/entrepreneurs may not be able to provide (De Buysere et al., 2012). Business grant represents free money to help a new start-up at the early stage of development. The money does not have to be repaid unlike in other traditional methods when individual investments have to be paid back either in cash or in kind. But grants funds are limited and not many SMEs/entrepreneurs are able to access them. Venture capital is a type of funding for a new or growing business, which usually comes from venture capital firms that specialise in building high-risk financial portfolios. With venture capital, a venture capital firm gives funding to a start-up in exchange for equity in the business. Access to this source could be difficult because it is regulated and investors have expert knowledge and may not be easily persuaded by entrepreneurs, particularly those who have little business experience.

Consequently, due to the different constraints attached to the traditional sources of funding, many SMEs/entrepreneurs are unable to access fund (e.g., Udell, 2015). Thus, they are constantly faced with funding challenges that affect their development and their expansion, particularly during economic recessions. Yet, access to finance has been emphasised as a key factor in the development, growth and success of SMEs (Ou and Haynes, 2006). The pressure to find alternative sources of funding is unending, hence, exploring alternative sources of funding has steadily increased and a funding avenue that is gaining momentum is crowdfunding.

Crowdfunding is facilitated by the extensive access to the internet and the widespread of social networking activities. Crowdfunding technique allows SMEs and entrepreneurs the chance to raise funds for their ventures and projects using the internet to contact many individuals. Each individual donates a contribution, which may be small, but all together makes a good amount of finance that helps to achieve the main goal of the SMEs/entrepreneurs. It is the case that across all areas of financing, SMEs/entrepreneurs are building crowdfunding platforms that enable private individuals ('the crowd') to use their savings to invest and lend directly to SMEs (Rees-Mogg, 2013). Accordingly, crowdfunding offers SMEs/entrepreneurs a recourse to alternate source of non-conventional funding arrangement.

CHAPTER OBJECTIVES AND STRUCTURE

This chapter intends to shed light on crowdfunding, including its antecedence, characteristics, and utility, particularly how it can help to serve SMEs/entrepreneurs funding requirements. It is the case that crowdfunding supports most businesses that are unable to access traditional funding methods, which is why it has become such a viable option for business start-ups (Hollas, 2013). Hence, this chapter analyses the mechanism of crowdfunding, its processes, merits and demerits, and implications in the context of raising funds for-profit and nonprofit projects and causes. The chapter is structured as follows: section 1 deals with the conceptual analysis of the crowdfunding model; section 2 has the discussion on the contextual analysis of the crowdfunding model; section 3 undertakes a critical appraisal of crowdfunding and section 4 summarises and discusses the implications of crowdfunding model as an alternative source of fundraising for SMEs/entrepreneurs projects and ventures.

CONCEPTUAL ANALYSIS OF THE CROWDFUNDING MECHANISM

Background

From the marketing perspective, crowdfunding demonstrates the evolving role of the consumer in marketing relationships. The consumers' role has evolved over time to expose a steady increase in the acknowledgement of their utility (Lusch et al., 2007). Ordanini et al. (2011) noted that, initially, the consumers had been treated as an ordinary recipient (Functional School), then considered as a vital source of information (Market Orientation), later regarded as co-producer (Service Marketing), afterward seen as innovative partner (Lead User Theory), and subsequently beheld as co-creator of value (Service-Dominant Logic). Presently, the consumers' role has been extended to include investment support in the trending crowdfunding event (Ordanini et al., 2011). Crowdfunding is a process in which people network and pool their money together, typically through the internet, in order to invest in and support efforts initiated by other people or organisations (Ordanini, 2009). Crowdfunding involves a mix of entrepreneurship and social network participation, and its principle is grounded in the decision of some individuals to pay for production and promotion of a product, rather than buying it, and bear the risk associated with that decision (Ordanini et al., 2011).

Explaining crowdfunding

Crowdfunding has recently emerged as a novel method of securing funds for entrepreneurial ventures, without having to provide venture capital or other traditional sources of finance (Mollick, 2014). Ordanini (2009) asserts that crowdfunding is a process of raising money

CROWDFUNDING OF SMEs

for a new project proposed by a person(s) through the collection of small to medium-size investments from several other individuals (i.e., the crowd). De Buyser et al. (2012) define crowdfunding as a combination of efforts of several individuals who all agreed to be a part of a network and pool their wealth (via the internet) to support certain projects/ventures which is started by other people or organisations. Likewise, Belleflamme et al. (2014, p. 8) claim that 'crowdfunding involves an open call, mostly through the internet, for the provision of financial resources either in form of donation or in exchange for the future product or some form of reward to support initiatives for specific purposes'. By emphasising the idea that crowdfunding is based on close cooperation between three parties; investors, intermediaries, and entrepreneurs, Valanciene and Jegeleviciute (2013) describe crowdfunding as a method of establishing a connection between entrepreneurs who raise funds for their business and new investors who represent the source of fund and are ready to invest their small contributions through internet intermediaries. Other views of crowdfunding present it as a financial mechanism and capital formation strategy, which act as a source of funding for start-ups, micro-enterprises, and SMEs (Pazowski and Czudec, 2014).

Various actors are involved in the crowdfunding events. The first group (initiators) are the people who put forward the proposals and/or the ventures to be financed. These individuals intend to use crowdfunding to access funding from genuinely interested backers and secure direct access to the market. The second group (investors) involves people who are prepared to fund the ventures, tolerate the risk, and anticipate a certain payoff. This group co-produced the output and selects (and sometimes develops) the offers they considered able to generate the maximum benefit. The third group (intermediary) consists of the crowdfunding organisations that connect the first group (initiators) with the second group (investors). Crowdfunding events have been enhanced by contemporary technological advances, which provide new opportunities and developments where consumers can utilise, generate, and adapt content and intermingle with other users through social networks (Ordanini et al., 2011).

Models of crowdfunding

Models of crowdfunding function as a donation-based fundraising device for SMEs/entrepreneurs' creative projects or social causes (e.g., medical/education/sports) to procure money from many individuals for a common goal usually organised through an online funding portal. Several crowdfunding projects give rewards to contributors, and these rewards could differ and could be proportionate to the amount of money contributed. Rewards may include items of a creative work or products produced with the funding, specific or customised incentives (e.g., signed works or promotional goods), or public recognition. A diverse set of relevant crowdfunding operations that vary in terms of risk/return for the consumer/investor and the type of consumer involvement are available.

Thus, crowdfunding activity can be separated into one of the following types: Equity-based crowdfunding, reward-based crowdfunding, debt-based crowdfunding, litigation crowdfunding, and donation-based crowdfunding.

Equity-based crowdfunding – this is a crowdfunding approach employed to obtain investment money, and contributors receive equity in the ensuing business. It represents a shared effort made between individuals to support the causes of other individuals (entrepreneurs) or SMEs in the form of equity. Donors/contributors may act as investors and obtain shares directly, or the crowdfunding service (intermediary) may act as a nominated agent (Ritobaan, 2013). Although this type of funding is prohibited in many countries (e.g., India), it is legal in the US following the enactment of the JOBS Act (Jump-start Our Business

265

Start-ups) in 2012, whose aim is to provide access to capital for the innovative firms that need investment capital from a pool of small investors (Hollas, 2013).

Reward-based Crowdfunding – this type, also known as 'non-equity' funding, has gradually become very popular, with a 230% increase in 2012 (Hollas, 2013). This form could be used to fund initiatives that support the free development of software, sponsorship of motion pictures, scientific research, development of inventions, and other related ventures/projects. Reward-based funders anticipate a return from the project.

Debt-based crowdfunding – describes processes such as 'Peer-to-Peer' (P2P) lending, 'marketplace lending' and 'crowdlending'. Borrowers generate campaigns to achieve their financial needs, and lenders contribute towards the objective for a stake (Hollas, 2013).

Litigation crowdfunding – in this type, the litigant appeals for a monetary donation to fund a court case, and the investors have the chance to get more than the initial investment if the case is won. Alex Salmond, the erstwhile First Minister of Scotland, raised money from this type of crowdfunding in 2018 (Moore, 2018).

Donation-based crowdfunding – this is a crowdfunding trend in which people are less dependent on charities to help them achieve their philanthropic aims: for example, individuals raising fund to sponsor personal or social causes (Third Sector, 2018).

Policy and regulatory frameworks

Many developed countries have or trying to enact policies and regulations aimed at easing the development of crowdfunding activities while addressing concerns about transparency and protection of investors. For example, the European Commission sets up (in 2014) the European Crowdfunding Stakeholders Forum (ECSF), an expert group that will assist the Commission in raising awareness, promoting transparency, developing training modules and exchanging best practices (OECD, 2014). In the US, the government instituted Jump-start Our Business Startups (JOBS) Act in 2012 to offer explicit legal support to crowdfunding investment. This Act defines the rules that apply to different types of investors and firms that canvas for funds, e.g., it states that entities cannot offer or sell securities to the public unless (1) the offering is registered with the SEC, or (2) there is an available exemption from registration (Mitra, 2012).

Regulatory difficulties constrained crowdfunding mechanism. By nature, it is not possible to regulate the offer as 'private placements to accredited investors' as it is regarded as a public offering of securities, which is greatly regulated in most countries (Cusmano, 2015, p. 58). The regulatory regime in such a situation is usually complicated, time-consuming, and expensive, and it can be prohibitive for the entrepreneurs or small businesses attempting crowdfunding (Helmer, 2011; Mitra, 2012). To prevail over such problems, some crowdfunding platforms establish 'investment clubs' that prospective funders can join, in which case, the regulatory provisions are less strict, as members of the club are considered qualified investors who need less protection compared to the 'general public' (Helmer, 2011; Cusmano, 2015, p. 58).

CRITICAL EVALUATION OF THE CROWDFUNDING MECHANISM

The advantages

Rees-Mogg (2013) argues that crowdfunding will likely continue to grow in years to come for a number of reasons. First, crowdfunders/investors get decent returns on their investment compared to other investment portfolios. Second, it is quicker to access money through

CROWDFUNDING OF SMEs

crowdfunding, for instance, a crowd equity fundraising will take 30–60 days compared to six to 12 months via traditional routes. Third, due to the internet, the market is massive, as billions of individual investors can connect with SMEs at the snap of a finger. Last, regulations around crowdfunding are currently light, so the crowd can just get on with it, and besides, the crowd itself is largely self-regulating (Rees-Mogg, 2013). Aside from the listed growth reasons, there are other advantages that the crowdfunding mechanism has over traditional financing routes. Some are discussed in the following.

To start with, SMEs/entrepreneurs may need external support to start their projects or to evaluate the social potential of their products. Crowdfunders (investors), as opposed to venture capital funds, do not require having a special understanding of the industry. It has been suggested that the crowdfunders as group/audience can sometimes be more efficient in predicting and solving problems in a company than individuals or teams. Consequently, there will be more chance for the project/venture to receive effective advice from crowdfunders in the long run (Schwienbacher and Larralde, 2012).

It is also the case that crowdfunders, as a crowd, would be more capable and efficient than a few numbers of equity investors. Besides, crowdfunding reduces investors' risk, not only because of the smaller amount of money of their contributions but also because they can become consumers to the product when launched in the market. In comparison, project/venture funded by equity (or orthodox financing) will require a large advertising campaign for product promotion (Schwienbacher and Larralde, 2012). In crowdfunding, management control is retained over the business as crowdfunders do not have the right to such control over the company. In other words, crowdfunding allows SMEs/entrepreneurs to raise their fund without losing their decision-making rights and privileges (Valanciene and Jegeleviciute, 2013).

Furthermore, compared to other forms of financing, crowdfunding removes the geographic obstacles between the entrepreneurs and the investors as it enhances sustainable communities' development, allowing people to invest in their communities. In this regard, it is worth mentioning that most companies will allocate their projects within their geographical area but will be able to raise funds globally (Valanciene and Jegeleviciute, 2013). In other words, crowdfunding enables local ventures/projects to attract global investors. Albeit, this is also possible with some other forms of traditional financing. It is also the case that SMEs/Entrepreneurs can use the response of crowdfunders as a useful indicator to gauge the market prospect of their proposed products/projects. For example, the demand for a product is expected to be high if investors signify a great interest in investing in the product's project, especially if it is expected that crowdfunders are the probable consumers of the project (Schwienbacher and Larralde, 2012).

In addition, crowdfunders contribute to the creation and improvement of a product/service which means they participate in creating value for the business. In other words, crowdfunding allows a SME/entrepreneur to reduce the cost needed to improve new products and the time required to create or improve new products.

The disadvantages

On the other hand, the disadvantages and challenges of crowdfunding reviewed by De Buysere et al. (2012) can be summarised in the following narrative. First, fraud is possibly the most critical disadvantage of crowdfunding. The possibility for funders to unknowingly provide funds for scams or fraudulent projects is ever present and constitute a potentially high risk on the crowdfunding platforms. The risk for fraud increases in this type of

267

finance because the pool of crowdfunders does not have the personal interaction or real knowledge of the actual project, beyond what is accessible on the crowdfunding website (a case of asymmetric information). In addition to this, the geographical area between the SMEs/entrepreneurs and crowdfunders can inhibit the funder from physically overseeing and observing the projects/ventures. In this regard, it is suggested that fraud can be prevented if the social network portals allow funders to carry out a search on the business and the SMEs/entrepreneurs before reaching or making an investment decision on a certain project or business.

Second, the practical experience of crowdfunding indicates that setting the value of the business/project by the SMEs/entrepreneurs initiating the crowdfunding process can be problematic. This is particularly difficult when evaluating the cost that cannot be estimated prior to the establishment of the business/project (such as intellectual property or estimations on market size and scale). This could lead to miscalculation, either through undervaluation or overvaluation by the SMEs/entrepreneurs, which could also be a significant problem for the funders. However, to avoid this problem, some crowdfunding platforms allow the SMEs/entrepreneurs to be flexible with the amount of fund/equity offered over the course of the campaign. Another solution to this problem is allowing the SMEs/entrepreneurs to first specify the amount of equity and the number of shares and then call on the potential crowdfunders to bid for the equity or shares. Funders who pay for the most equity or number of shares then win the equity/shares.

Third, currently, there is no agreed model to display data used for presenting investment projects across crowdfunding platforms. While open source accounting data standards do exist, they have not yet been widely adopted by crowdfunding platforms. In addition to this, founders are not obligated to provide any type of controlled data when pitching a project. However, this can be resolved by establishing a common body to operate standards, which can assist in foster a legal regime of transparency in the crowdfunding industry. Fourth, crowdfunders often are not expert investors and therefore may be unable to objectively measure the risks involved when investing in certain ventures/projects.

Other setbacks exist. Compared to orthodox financing, the crowdfunding industry is more vulnerable to the risks of cyber-attacks, identity and payment data theft, as well as money laundering (OECD, 2014). Furthermore, since investors usually lack experience and their individual investment is generally small, there is little incentive or capability to intervene in case of malpractice or misapplication (Belleflamme et al., 2014). Crowdfunding channel possibly will be less suitable for business models that are based on complex intangibles or innovations in very high- tech and advanced fields that require investors' specific expertise (Collins and Pierrakis, 2012). On such occasion, however, the crowdfunding apparatus may attract a group of investors that seek ventures that have some measure of innovation in specific fields, for example, engineers, scientists, IT experts, or individuals with visions of future applications (Helmer, 2011). In addition to funding, these individuals may also bring in knowledge, experiences, and networks to influence business strategies and skills (OECD, 2014).

Crowdfunding may also be unsuitable to finance firms whose business information and financial details are too sensitive to be shared with a large number of prospective investors simply because of the difficulties involved in arranging non-disclosure agreements with all the investors. Moreover, crowdfunding may be unsuitable for businesses that are intensely capital – intensive in early stages or those that require the types of post-investment support,

CROWDFUNDING OF SMEs

which only institutional investors can provide (Collins and Pierrakis, 2012; Helmer, 2011). Additionally, crowdfunding activities require good infrastructures such as reliable internet connection, stable power supply, and access to the banking sector for both entrepreneurs and investors' financial transactions.

SUMMARY AND IMPLICATION

Generally, crowdfunding can be regarded as a process of raising capital to help turn promising ideas into business realities by connecting entrepreneurs with potential supporters (investors). Currently, crowdfunding is an internet-based method of fundraising in which individuals solicit contributions for projects on specialised websites. Thus, crowdfunding provides an innovative source of alternate funding for SMEs and entrepreneurs alike. The reinforcement of this dynamic alternative funding process has the potential to improve the financial environment for SMEs, entrepreneurs, and ideas' initiators.

As a prospective method of financing projects or business ventures, crowdfunding has become a source of capital acquisition, an alternative to the existing traditional ways of funding (e.g., banks, stock exchanges, incubators, etc.). This generates the opportunity to acquire economic benefits for a variety of different operators in the marketplace. The establishment of such an electronic platform is valuable from an economic point of view since it fills certain niches, improves the speed of financial transfers, their volumes, values, and cutting down transaction costs. However, crowdfunding has some drawbacks including many barriers to development, particularly economic and legal. The awareness of crowdfunding mechanism, safety, and ease behind the transaction will be key for the market to achieve its potential. This calls for a measure of regulatory intervention to ensure transparency and to maintain the integrity of the crowdfunding event. Albeit, policy and regulatory interventions must be minimal to avoid jeopardising the novelty of the crowdfunding system. Over regulation may render the crowdfunding mechanism to become another conventional financing contrivance antagonistic to SMEs/entrepreneurs funding requirements.

TECHNOLOGY, SME, AND THE 21ST CENTURY

The web 2.0 technology and innovation of financial instruments combined with global trends on social platforms networking to directly facilitate the rapid growth of crowdfunding. Web 2.0 (social web) are websites that underscore user-generated content, participatory culture, ease of use, and compatibility with other systems, products, and appliances for end users.

Social networking websites (social media) are intensely altering consumers' behaviours in many ways in the 21st century such as in the way they are connected, the way they gather information, and the way they are inspired by trends from around the world. Equally, the social media provides a channel for firms/sellers to engage with consumers anywhere in the world. It is fashionable for firms (large and small) to initiate social media communities for members to exchange ideas to resolve a problem or pool their efforts to generate favourable exchange conditions for their own benefit.

As an internet-based activity, crowdfunding cannot be practise in the absence of good infrastructures such as reliable internet connection and regular electric supply. The exciting thing about crowdfunding is the nature of its community environment and how it is conducted through the practices of viral social networking and marketing.

Questions:
1. What infrastructural facilities are required for the crowdfunding mechanism?
2. Describe the technology architecture for the crowdfunding processes.

REVIEW QUESTIONS

1. What are the different categories of crowdfunding mechanism?

2. Which type of people can seek fund or invest on a crowdfunding platform?

3. What are the advantages and disadvantages of the crowdfunding methods?

4. Discuss the policy and regulatory environment around the crowdfunding mechanism.

CASE STUDY: AN ENTREPRENEUR'S CROWDFUNDING EXPERIENCE

Introduction
Elizabeth, a graduate of International Marketing from a London university, plans to float a business venture she has been nurturing for a while. The business idea, which is an internet-based jewellery shop, is grounded on creating novel jewellery sets from different inorganic materials such as ivory, carved stone, bone, seashells, animal teeth, animal hair, eggshells, wood, amber, and glass. She plans to source materials from all over the world, while selling her products to customers globally through the internet.

Essentially, Elizabeth anticipated a well-structured business plan will help her to secure £50,000 seed money to get her project off the ground. Much of the money is planned for use to source the organic materials and procurement of tools, pay for the web domain, advertising, and logistics (e.g., costs of looking for recycled materials).

Sourcing finance for business venture
In her efforts to secure funding, Elizabeth first considered bootstrapping: a means of resourcing a new business without engaging in the conventional methods of finance. She created a limited range of costume jewelleries from recycled material such as beads, buttons, and shells, which she sold at good margins to her friends and families. She then turned to friends, families and fools (3 Fs): sourcing start-up capital from 'friends, family and foolhardy investors'. Elizabeth secured a firm commitment of £10,000 from her friends and family to support her venture.

To gain the rest of her seed money, Elizabeth began to seek business angels: wealthy individuals who provide capital for a start-up in exchange for a proportion of the company's equity. Elizabeth pitched her internet shop to business angels but failed to secure funding. Initially, she pitched to an altruistic investor in the belief that her business's environment-friendly credentials will appeal to the investor. Failing to secure investment, Elizabeth approached others including a hedonistic angel investor who is supposedly attracted by the excitement of creating something new, and an economic investor who might be spurred by the profit potentials of the business. The feedbacks she received from these pitches suggest that the investors, aside from looking at the merit of the business proposal, are more interested in the entrepreneur's personality and set-up. For instance, Elizabeth was asked about her 'team' on more than one occasion during her pitches and one of the investors asked her to come back when her business is 'up and running'. Thus, Elizabeth realised that her failure may not be unconnected with the inability to personally convince the investors of the viability of her venture. It is the case that the entrepreneurs' personality, e.g., the entrepreneurs' experience, skills, and drive, and how they come across have been shown to be the most significant aspect for angel investors when deciding to make an investment.

Without angel investors, Elizabeth pursued a bank loan – the formal market for access to start-up capital for new ventures. Elizabeth's application for a business loan from her bank was unsuccessful as the bank's Small Business Adviser was sceptical of her business proposal. For instance, the bankers were unconvinced the business can generate the amount of revenue (£95,000.00) shown on Elizabeth's business plan in the first year of trading, also, the marketing and advertising budget (£12,500.00) is deemed unrealistic, especially, for a new start-up going into a contested marketplace. However, the bank adviser suggested Elizabeth look at the option of crowdfunding to raise money.

The crowdfunding campaign

Elizabeth, based on her failed bank loan experience, realised that planning is key to a successful crowdfunding exercise, thus she enlisted the support of an experienced mentor (Juliana) to guide her. First, her mentor asked her to agree on a timeline and begin a 'pre-crowdfunding' campaign on a website the mentor has used in the past. This made Elizabeth realise that crowdfunding process is indeed time consuming and is going to take much effort to execute.

Juliana impressed it on Elizabeth that the key to a good crowdfunding pitch entails the ability to clearly and succinctly explain what her business does and what needs it meets. This two information are crucial to kindle the potential investors' interest and the basis to articulate all other requisite information such as probable market size, pricing, route to profitability, exit, etc. Elizabeth was also warned to avoid any temptation to paint a picture that is unrealistic as potential investors are likely to be experienced business people who will not invest in a proposition they sense lacking integrity. According to Juliana, it is good to be honest and respond comprehensively to a potential investor's question or query, as others will also read

> it. Being honest and upfront helps to build trust, which is an essential ingredient in crowdfunding. Building credibility with investors must be a priority especially for a venture with no prior record.
>
> ### Student activity:
> 1. Appraise the specific problems Elizabeth met getting seed money for her venture.
> 2. What are the key issues to take into consideration to achieve a successful crowd-funding campaign?
> 3. Critically evaluate the crowdfunding model against other funding resources for a new start-up such as Elizabeth.

REFERENCES

Achrol, R. S. and Kotler, P. (1999) Marketing in the network economy. *Journal of Marketing*, 63(4), 146–163.

Belleflamme, P., Lambert, T. and Schwienbacher, A. (2014) Crowdfunding: Tapping the right crowd. *Journal of Business Venturing*, 29(5), 585–609.

Cermak, D. S. P., File, K. M. and Prince, R. A. (1994) A benefit segmentation of the major donor market. *Journal of Business Research*, 29(2), 121–130.

Collins, L. and Pierrakis, Y. (2012) *The Venture Crowd. Crowdfunding Equity Investment Into Business.* NESTA, UK.

Cusmano, L. (2015) New approaches to SME and entrepreneurial financing: Broadening the range of instruments. *OECD*, Annual Report, 1–109.

De Buysere, K., Gajda, O., Kleverlaan, R. and Marom, D. (2012) A framework for European crowd-funding. http://evpa.eu.com/wpcontent/uploads/2010/11/European_Crowdfunding_Framework_Oct_2012.pdf.

Dell, K. (2008) Crowdfunding. *Time*, 15 September, 51–52.

Edvardsson, B., Gustafsson, A. and Roos, I. (2005) Service portraits in service research: A critical review. *International Journal of Service Industry Management*, 16(1), 107–121.

Edvardsson, B. and Olsson, J. (1996) Key concepts for new service development. *Service Industries Journal*, 16(2), 140–164.

European Commission (2013) Report from the Commission to the European Parliament, the Council, the European Economic and Social Committee and the Committee of the Regions. http://ec.europa.eu/regional_policy/how/policy/doc/strategic_report/2013/strat_report_2013_en.pdf

Fleming, L., Mingo, S. and Chen, D. (2007) Collaborative brokerage, generative creativity, and creative success. *Administrative Science Quarterly*, 52(3), 443–475.

Freear, J., Sohl, J. E. and Wetzel Jr., W. E. (1994) Angels and non-angels: Are there difference? *Journal of Business Venturing*, 9(2), 109–123.

Fuller, J. (2006) Why consumers engage in virtual new product developments initiated by producers. *Advances in Consumer Research*, 33, 639–646.

Golić, Z. (2014) Advantages of crowdfunding as an alternative source of financing of small and medium-sized enterprises. *Zbornik radova Ekonomskog fakulteta u Istočnom Sarajevu*, (8), 39–48.

Guy, B. S. and Patton, W. F. (1989) The marketing of altruistic causes: Understanding why people help. *Journal of Consumer Marketing*, 6(1), 19–30.

Helmer, J. (2011) A snapshot on crowdfunding, Working papers firms and regions (R2/2011), Fraunhofer Institute for Systems and Innovation Research ISI, Karlsruhe.

Hollas, J. (2013) Is crowdfunding now a threat to traditional finance? *Corporate Finance Review*, 18(1), 27–31.

Howe, J. (2006) The rise of crowdsourcing. www.wired.com/wired/archive/14.06/crowds_pr.html.

Hoyer, W. D., Chandy, R., Dorotic, M., Krafft, M. and Singh, S. S. (2010) Consumer co-creation in new product development. *Journal of Service Research*, 13(3), 283–296.

Kleemann, F., Voss, G. G. and Rieder, K. (2008) Un(der)paid innovators: The commercial utilization of consumer work through crowdsourcing. *Science, Technology and Innovation Studies*, 4(1), 5–25.

Kotler, P. and Andreasen, A. (1991) *Strategic Marketing for Nonprofit Organizations*, 4th ed. Prentice Hall, Englewood Cliffs, NJ.

Lakhani, K. R. and von Hippel, E. (2003) How open source software works: "free" user-to user assistance. *Research Policy*, 32(6), 923–943.

Lusch, R. F., Vargo, S. L. and O'Brien, M. (2007) Competing through service: Insights from service-dominant logic. *Journal of Retailing*, 83(1), 5–18.

Mitra, D. (2012) The role of crowdfunding in entrepreneurial finance. *Delhi Business Review*, 13(2), 67–72.

Mollick, E. (2014) The dynamics of crowdfunding: An exploratory study. *Journal of Business Venturing*, 29(1), 1–16.

Moore, S. (2018) Alex Salmond is using crowdfunding to signal his power. That's wrong. www.theguardian.com/commentisfree/2018/aug/30/alex-salmond-crowdfunding-scottish-independence.

Muñiz Jr, A. M. and O'Guinn, T. C. (2001) Brand community. *Journal of Consumer Research*, 27(4), 412–432.

OECD (2014) *New approaches to SME and entrepreneurship finance: The case of crowdfunding*. OECD, Paris, CFE/SME(2013)/7/REV2/ANN1.

Ordanini, A. (2009) Crowd funding: Customers as investors. *The Wall Street Journal*, 23 March, r3.

Ordanini, A., Miceli, L., Pizzetti, M. and Parasuraman, A. (2011) Crowd-funding: Transforming customers into investors through innovative service platforms. *Journal of Service Management*, 22(4), 443–470.

Ou, C. and Haynes, G. W. (2006) Acquisition of additional equity capital by small firms – Findings from the national survey of small business finances. *Small Business Economics*, 27(2), 157–168.

Ouwersloot, H. and Oderkerken-Schroder, G. (2008) Who's who in brand communities and why? *European Journal of Marketing*, 42(5/6), 571–585.

Parkhe, A., Wasserman, S. and Ralston, D. A. (2006) New frontiers in network theory development. *Academy of Management Review*, 31(3), 560–568.

Pazowski, P. and Czudec, W. (2014) Economic prospects and conditions of crowdfunding. *Human Capital Without Borders: Knowledge and Learning for Quality of Life*. Proceedings of the Management, Knowledge and Learning International Conference 2014, ToKnowPress.

Petković, S. and Tešić, J. (2013) SMEs and Entrepreneurship Development and Institutional Support in Republic of Srpska (Bosnia and Herzegovina). In Ramadani, V. and Schneider, R. (Eds.), *Entrepreneurship in the Balkans*. Springer, Berlin, Heidelberg.

Prahalad, C. K. and Ramaswamy, V. (2004) Co-creation experiences: The next practice in value creation. *Journal of Interactive Marketing*, 18(3), 5–14.

Rees-Mogg, M. (2013) Why crowdfunding is increasingly popular for SME financing. www.theguardian.com/media-network/media-network-blog/2013/jan/31/crowdfunding-sme-finance-kickstarter-funding.

Ritobaan, R. (2013) Crowdfunding: Sideshow or headline act? Available at: https://web.archive.org/web/20130426053445/www.cfo-insight.com/financing-liquidity/alternative-finance/crowdfunding-sideshow-or-headline-act/.

Rutherford, S. (2000) *The Poor and Their Money*. Oxford University Press, Delhi.

Schau, H. J., Muñiz Jr, A. M. and Arnould, E. J. (2009) How brand community practices create value. *Journal of Marketing*, 73(5), 30–51.

Schwienbacher, A. and Larralde, B. (2012) Crowdfunding of Small Entrepreneurial Ventures. In Cumming, D. (Ed.), *The Oxford Handbook of Entrepreneurial Finance*, Chapter 13, Oxford University Press, Oxford.

Sullivan, M. K. and Miller, A. (1996) Segmenting the informal venture capital market: Economic, hedonistic, and altruistic investors. *Journal of Business Research*, 36(1), 25–35.

Third Sector (2018) The future of fundraising: Is crowdfunding the wave of the future? www.third sector.co.uk/future-online-giving-expert-report/article/1460657.

Udell, G. F. (2015) SME access to intermediated credit: What do we know, and what don't we know? Reserve Bank of Australia, Conference Volume.

Valanciene, L. and Jegeleviciute, S. (2013) Valuation of crowdfunding: Benefits and drawbacks, *Economics and Management*, 18(1), 39–47.

von Krogh, G. and Spaeth, S. (2007) The open source software phenomenon: Characteristics that promote research. *Journal of Strategic Information Systems*, 16, 236–253.

Wetzel Jr., W. E. (1983) Angels and informal risk capital. *Sloan Management Review*, 24(4), 23–34.

Chapter 17

International entrepreneurship and small and medium-sized enterprises

Kevin Ibeh and Mathew Analogbei

LEARNING OBJECTIVES

After reading this chapter, you will be able to:
- Explain the concepts of internationalisation and SMEs;
- Discuss international entrepreneurship and clarify the synonymous sense in which it is used with SME internationalisation in this chapter;
- Discuss the key facilitate factors for international entrepreneurship;
- Examine the major challenges and barriers to international entrepreneurship;
- Highlight appropriate managerial and policy approaches for promoting international entrepreneurship levels among SMEs.

INTRODUCTION

This chapter discusses international entrepreneurship (IE) among small and medium-sized enterprises (SMEs). It begins by outlining the relevant learning objectives and explaining key concepts, including internationalisation and SMEs. Next, the emerging area of 'international entrepreneurship' is explicated. This is followed by separate sections on the key facilitators and major barriers to international entrepreneurship. The final section summarises the chapter and outlines managerial and policy implications.

INTERNATIONALISATION AND SMEs

The term **'internationalisation'** is widely employed to describe the process of increasing involvement in international operations (Welch and Luostarinen, 1993; Bell et al., 2004). Not long ago, engagement in international activities was dominantly reserved for large, well-established organisations, typically multinational enterprises (MNEs). This, however, changed with the significant advances made over the past few decades in transportation, information and communication technologies, and in global regulatory, financial, and institutional environments. Smaller enterprises now increasingly operate outside their domestic markets under different arrangements, much like their larger counterparts (Ibeh, 2000; Fletcher, 2004). Some of these SMEs also appear to be creating new international ventures significantly earlier in their corporate history than their more traditional counterparts

(Rennie, 1993; Knight and Cavusgil, 1996; Autio et al., 2000; Oviatt and McDougall, 1994; Borchert and Ibeh, 2008). This phenomenon was a major impetus for the emergence of international entrepreneurship as a distinct research field (McDougall and Oviatt, 2000a; Coviello and Jones, 2005; Zahra, 2005).

Internationalisation or international entrepreneurship can be undertaken through a variety of international market entry and development modes, including exporting (direct and indirect); licensing; franchising; management contracts; contract manufacturing; turn-key contracts; contractual joint ventures; strategic alliances; equity joint ventures; mergers and acquisitions; and wholly owned subsidiaries (Ibeh, 2000). To these can be added inward internationalisation approaches such as importing and licensing-in. These modes are associated with varying levels of strategic control and rewards, resource needs, costs, and risks, and opportunities and threats (Westhead, 1993; Bell and Young, 1998; O'Farrell et al., 1998). Given SMEs' typically low resource base, they tend to serve international markets from their domestic bases, mainly via direct, indirect, or internet-based exporting. This explains why much of the SME internationalisation or international entrepreneurship literature pertains to exporting activity (Ibeh, 2006).

The repeated references to SMEs highlight the need for a proper definition of the concept. This is undertaken in the following paragraphs.

Small enterprises have been variously defined (Carter and Jones-Evans, 2006). The Bolton Report (1971), one of the earliest attempts in this regard, highlighted the following defining criteria:

- independent (not part of a large enterprise);
- managed in a personalised manner (simple management structure);
- relatively small share of the market.

This definition has, not surprisingly, been faulted on a number of grounds over the years. These include the relative nature of the concept of 'independence' (some firms may be legally independent but depend entirely on a larger enterprise for their economic activity) and the lack of clarity that often surrounds knowing when the locus of control shifts from the owner-manager to a functional or hierarchical management structure in a growing business (Storey and Johnson, 1987; Woods et al., 1993; Storey, 1994).

A more robust definition was introduced by the European Union in 1994, and updated in 2004. This distinguishes between three types of smaller enterprises, micro, small, and medium-sized enterprises, associated with the employee, turnover, and asset limits outlined in Table 17.1.

Table 17.1 SME Categories

Enterprise category	Head count	Turnover	Balance Sheet
Micro	< 10	€2m	€2m
Small	< 50	€10m	€10m
Medium-sized	< 250	€50m	€43m

Source: Carter and Jones-Evans (2006, p. 10)

These three size groups make up what is termed small and medium-sized enterprises (SMEs). It is important to note that some EU countries have adopted their own interpretation of SMEs. Beyond Europe also, there is a wide variety of definitions. Hong Kong sees SMEs as manufacturing enterprises with fewer than 100 employees or non-manufacturing with fewer than 50 employees. The US defines and SME as employing fewer than 500 employees. All of these make it difficult to compare SMEs across countries (Carter and Jones-Evans, 2006).

INTERNATIONAL ENTREPRENEURSHIP

International entrepreneurship refers to a new research field that has recently emerged at the entrepreneurship-international business interface. It has been defined as a combination of innovative, risk-seeking behaviour that crosses national borders and is intended to create value in organisation (McDougall and Oviatt, 2000b). Also described as the discovery, enactment, evaluation, and exploitation of opportunities across national borders to create future goods and services (Oviatt and McDougall, 2005), its essential contribution has been to illuminate a phenomenon, 'international new ventures' (INV), largely ignored by the entrepreneurship and international business theories; the former generally views new firm formation as a locally embedded process, while the latter does not really posit a role for smaller and inexperienced firms in the international markets (McNaughton, 2003).

The recent upsurge of interest in International entrepreneurship actually represents a return to Schumpeter's (1934) classic characterisation of entrepreneurship as the creation of new markets. At the heart of entrepreneurial activity is innovation (Hitt et al., 2001). Schumpeter (1934) distinguished between invention and innovation, with invention being the discovery of an opportunity and innovation being the exploitation of this opportunity (Alvarez and Busenitz, 2001). International entrepreneurial success requires not just the discovery of a valuable innovation but also that the innovation be introduced successfully to world markets (Acs et al., 2001) or, in Schumpeter's terms, the creation of new markets. This is the essence of international entrepreneurship.

What the IE research field has done, therefore, is to make INVs, born globals, and internationalising SMEs the main focus of concerted scholarly attention. This, as McDougall and Oviatt (2000a) noted, implies the search for more INVs and international entrepreneurs (see Quadrant II) and, more importantly, understanding the activities and key facilitating factors associated with this category of firms.

▨ *Figure 17.1*
Organisational Types and Contexts

Source: McDougall and Oviatt (2000a).

TYPE OF ORGANISATION

Entrepreneurial

Large, Established

GEOGRAPHICAL SCOPE

	Domestic	International
Entrepreneurial	I	II
Large, Established	III	IV

Factor facilitating international entrepreneurship

Oviatt and McDougall's (1994, 1995) early work on the international entrepreneurship research stream points to a number of key underpinning factors for successful international entrepreneurship. According to these authors, new ventures tend to possess certain valuable assets, use alliances and network structures to control a relatively large percentage of vital assets, as well as have a unique resource that provide a sustainable advantage that is transferable to a foreign location (Oviatt and McDougall, 1994, 1995). Scholars have developed the essential elements into a set of key international entrepreneurship facilitating factors. These are discussed under three broad categories, specifically decision maker factors, firm-specific advantages and firm's environmental factors – see Table 17.2.

Decision maker factors

Most SME internationalisation researchers are agreed on the central role of entrepreneurs, in their various manifestations as founders, decision makers or managers, in the internationalisation process (Miesenbock, 1988; Ibeh and Young, 2001). Entrepreneurs, or individuals carrying out entrepreneurial actions (Andersson, 2000; Oviatt and McDougall, 1995), are the most important agents of change. They are typically associated with the capacity and willingness to take risks in realizing their judgments, to be innovative and to exploit business opportunities in a market environment (OECD, 2000). Their individual-specific attributes (knowledge, relationships, experience, training, skills, judgement, and ability to coordinate resources) facilitate the recognition of new opportunities and assembling of socially

Table 17.2 Sample facilitating factors for international entrepreneurship

Source	Characteristic	Indicative Research
Decision maker	A global vision	Oviatt and McDougall (1995)
Decision maker	Prior international experience	Reuber and Fischer (1997)
Decision maker	Internationally proactive	Knight (1997)
Decision maker	Highly networked	Coviello and Munro (1995)
Firm	Possesses knowledge-intensive assets	McDougall et al. (1994)
Firm	Possesses high quality, differentiated products	Knight and Cavusgil (2004)
Firm	Provides a superior level of service	McDougall et al. (2003)
Firm	Pursues aggressive growth	Oviatt and McDougall (1994)
Firm	Pursues niche strategy	Andersson and Wictor (2003)
Firm's Environment	Offers helpful support programmes	Alvarez (2004); Carlos et al. (2008)
Firm's Environment	Offers quality supporting infrastructure	Lado et al. (2004)

Source: Adapted from Borchert and Ibeh (2008).

complex, value adding, and advantage creating resources (Schumpeter, 1950; Barney et al., 2001; Alvarez and Busenitz, 2001; Gabrielsson and Kirpalani, 2004).

Miesenbock's (1988) early remark that the key variable in small business internationalisation is the decision maker of the firm, who decides starting, ending, and increasing international activities, powerfully captures the dominant view on this issue. In small firms, the decision power is often concentrated in the hands of one or a few persons, and the CEO has a unique and influential role in the organisation (Chandler and Jansen, 1992). Bloodgood et al. (1996) found that more international work experience among top managers was strongly associated with greater internationalisation of new high-potential firms in the US. Also, Westhead et al. (2001) found that older founders with more resources, denser information and contact networks, and considerable management know-how were significantly more likely to become exporters, especially where industry-specific knowledge and experience were important. McDougall et al. (2003) suggested that managers of international new ventures had significantly greater international, industry, and technical experience than their counterparts with domestic new ventures. Zucchella et al. (2007) found that founder-specific drivers were the most significant factors in SMEs internationalisation. Coviello and Jones (2005) evidently agreed and called on researchers to incorporate entrepreneurial behaviour into models of internationalisation.

International new venture scholars have further highlighted the importance of decision maker's commitment in facilitating international entrepreneurship, with more recent work reinforcing the relevance of both affective commitment and continuance commitment (Gabrielsson et al., 2008). As these authors noted, affective commitment refers to the initial commitment stemming from the global orientation of the entrepreneur, while continuance commitment refers to the decision maker's continuing fidelity to the internationalisation venture beyond initial take-off (Gabrielsson et al., 2008). Relatedly, evidence also suggests that decision makers with more positive attitudes towards exporting and more favourable perceptions of exporting risks, costs, profits, and growth tend to exhibit greater international entrepreneurial behaviour (Ibeh, 2003).

Firm-specific advantages
Previous research has underlined the importance of a range of firm-specific factors in facilitating international entrepreneurship behaviour. One often investigated characteristic is firm size (variously measured by employee number, sales, ownership of capital equipment, financial capability or a combination of them), which is sometimes viewed as a proxy for the firm's resource base. Although findings on the impact of firm size on international entrepreneurship behaviour have been mixed, the balance of evidence suggests its importance, particularly in initiating international activity (Dean et al., 2000; Ibeh, 2006). Another characteristic that appears to influence international entrepreneurship is firm background, including previous experience of extra-regional expansion, inward internationalisation (Andersson et al., 2004; Ibeh, 2006), or international experience (Baldauf et al., 2000; Lado et al., 2004). The type of product/service marketed by a firm or the nature of its industry (e.g., extent of globalisation) can also be a crucial facilitating factor (Tyebjee, 1994; Ibeh, 2006).

There is an even stronger body of evidence that favourably links international entrepreneurship with firm capabilities and competencies (Francis and Collins-Dodd, 2004; Ibeh, 2005; Sapienza et al., 2006). Among the most critically regarded of these capability factors is the firm's stock of knowledge assets, including technological and R&D knowhow and market learning (Autio et al., 2000; Knight and Cavusgil, 2004; Rialp et al., 2005). This appears to have gained increased resonance in the recent international entrepreneurship literature and is widely appreciated across different internationalisation research traditions. Indeed, the Uppsala model (Johansson and Vahlne, 1977, 1990) actually suggests experiential market knowledge as the driving force of the firm's incremental evolution along the internationalisation path. Relational capabilities are also highly valued, as established networks are considered vital for the early internationalisation of new ventures (Coviello, 2006). The literature also suggests that relationships may provide a firm with access to key resources possessed by external parties, including knowledge, technology, social capital, market contacts, thus enabling it to bridge possible gaps to its internationalisation (Håkansson and Snehota, 1992; Eriksson et al., 1998; McLoughlin and Horan, 2000). Such network-based resource augmentation has been identified as an important trigger for rapid internationalisation (Oviatt and McDougall, 1997; Autio et al., 2000; Vissak et al., 2008).

Other important firm-specific capabilities highlighted in the international entrepreneurship literature include: research and product development; systematic market research; relational capabilities; distribution, delivery and service quality; and advertising and sales promotion. The possession of these capabilities and competencies enables a firm to identify the idiosyncrasies in the foreign markets, develop the necessary marketing strategies and implement them effectively, thus achieving higher export performance (Cavusgil and Zou, 1994; Wheeler et al., 2008).

Firm's environmental factors

Aspects of the SME's operating environments – industry, domestic market, and foreign market environments – may affect international entrepreneurship behaviour positively or adversely (Carlos et al., 2008; Wheeler et al., 2008). Previous integrative reviews, indeed, suggest that the so-called 'push' (e.g., adverse home market conditions, small domestic market) and 'pull' factors (e.g., and attractive market opportunities abroad) exert strong effects on initial IE behaviour (Leonidou, 1995). This is particularly given that SMEs tend to lack the necessary resources to control their operating environment (Ibeh, 2006). Taking domestic market factors for instance, research evidence suggests that firms generally perform better when faced with a benign domestic environment (Robertson and Chetty, 2000). This could be indicated, for example, by the availability of helpful public and private sector internationalisation support programmes (Alvarez, 2004), which typically act as an external resource bank from which firms can gain knowledge and experience, create or develop existing international networks, and undertake more sophisticated foreign market analysis (Carlos et al., 2008).

Foreign market factors also usually influence firm's international entrepreneurship behaviour. For example, government restrictions or pressures in the target market have been known to affect firms' internationalisation efforts by increasing or reducing their capacity and effectiveness (Beamish, 1993; Cavusgil and Zou, 1994; Baldauf et al., 2000; Dean et al., 2000; O'Cass and Julian 2003). The levels of infrastructural development, cultural similarity and market competitiveness have also been identified as important factors. The evidence largely associates that more international entrepreneurship activity is likely to occur if the foreign markets are culturally similar and have higher levels of infrastructural development (Lado et al., 2004).

BARRIERS TO INTERNATIONAL ENTREPRENEURSHIP

SMEs are known to face several challenges and impediments as they attempt to initiate, develop or sustain international entrepreneurship activities. These constraints – resource-related, attitudinal, psychological, structural, strategic, operational – have been the focus of considerable research among internationalisation and international entrepreneurship researchers (Leonidou, 1995; Hamill, 1997; Wright et al., 2007; OECD, 2009). The first named author offered a particularly useful four-category framework of internationalisation barriers, thus:

- Internal-domestic – Problems from within the firm such as lack of personnel with requisite knowledge and experience, negative perception of risk in selling abroad, etc.
- Internal-foreign – These are problems faced by the SMEs in the foreign market environment as a result of their limited ability in, for example, modifying products or communicating with foreign customers.
- External-domestic – These set of barriers typically originate from the SME's domestic environment and they include impediments such as complex documentations, inadequate infrastructure, and lack of necessary government support.
- External-foreign – The barriers in this category are experienced in the international markets and are not firm-specific. Examples include foreign government imposed restrictions, language and cultural differences, and difficulties associated with establishing reliable overseas contacts.

A recent OECD report on this topic seems to highlight internationalisation barriers of the mainly internal-domestic kind – see the following:

> Limited firm resources and international contacts as well as lack of requisite managerial knowledge about internationalisation have remained critical constraints to SME internationalisation. These resource limitations, especially of a financial kind, seem particularly prevalent among smaller, newly internationalising firms.
>
> (OECD, 2009)

The reference to the particular prevalence of financial constraints among smaller, newly internationalising firms reinforces previous evidence that firms at different stages of the internationalisation process typically encounter different sets of internationalisation problems (Bell, 1997). Born global firms investigated by Gabrielsson et al. (2008) deal with not only exporting risks but also limited finance and challenges associated with the global character of their operations. Another important finding to note is that decision maker and firm characteristics often influence how well SMEs respond to perceived internationalisation barriers (Ibeh, 2006).

CHAPTER SUMMARY AND IMPLICATIONS

This chapter has discussed international entrepreneurship among SMEs, identifying key facilitating factors and impediments to greater international entrepreneurship activities. Its focus on international entrepreneurship complements previous research on international business and entrepreneurship, which have respectively focussed on large multinational enterprises (MNEs) and SME venture creation and management within the domestic context (Gabrielsson et al., 2008). The chapter, thus, reinforces the reality that firm size and age are no longer prerequisites for international business (Autio et al., 2000; Rialp et al., 2005), as SMEs are now actively involved in international business like their larger counterparts.

In this new enterprise-keen world, born globals, international new ventures, global start-ups, and similar SME actors are known to internationalise at or near inception, facilitated by their key decision makers, firm-specific advantages, and aspects of their operating environment. Their positive international entrepreneurship behaviour is also typically enabled by a robust capacity to neutralise and overcome varying forms of internationalisation barriers/constraints.

The foregoing offers an outline of what needs to be done at managerial and policy levels to enhance the prospect of achieving the much needed boost in international entrepreneurship activities. For SME managers or decision makers, the emphasis, briefly stated, should be on capacity upgrading initiatives aimed at replicating the kind of attributes and capabilities identified as critical facilitators of international entrepreneurship. Policymakers seeking to promote greater international entrepreneurship among SMEs might benefit from pulling at both of the major levers highlighted in the preceding paragraph. That is, designing and delivering support programmes to better equip SMEs with the earlier noted facilitating factors, whilst also taking practical steps to eradicate or minimise the prevalence of internationalisation barriers and constraints.

REVIEW QUESTIONS

1. Comment on the view that successful international venturing is synonymous with excellent marketing.

2. Based on a brief desk research (preferably online), identify a born global firm from any industry of your choice and discuss the key factors that seem to have facilitated this firm's early entry into international markets.

CASE STUDY: CMK'S INTERNATIONAL NEW VENTURES

CMK, a small, rapidly growing Canadian developer and manufacturer of quality, easy-to-use diagnostic kits, generates some 90% of its revenues internationally, via exports to over 65 countries and JV operations in the Netherlands. It was founded in the late 1990s by a physician owner-manager whose previous work in developing countries alerted him of significant levels of unmet demand. CMK's first markets were, thus, international rather than domestic, particularly as it had limited opportunities in the latter.

Partly owing to its limited experience and resources, CMK mainly served its international markets through distributors. It developed lasting relationships with these distributors, which facilitated the speedy introduction of its innovative products in international markets. The first sets of markets entered, Turkey, Jordan and Iran, were those where the owner had worked and had contacts. CMK subsequently targeted other markets, namely Azerbaijan, Bulgaria, Cyprus, Greece, and subsequently Saudi Arabia and Kuwait. By the end of its second year in business, CMK had successfully entered nine international markets. Later international expansion involved less reliance on CMK owner's personal contacts. Rather, the company used a variety of channels in locating distributors and entering new markets in North and Latin America, Southeast Asia, Europe, and the Middle East. By the end of its fourth year, CMK had successfully established its products in some 30 markets around the world.

INTERNATIONAL ENTREPRENEURSHIP AND SMEs

In addition to a rapid internationalisation drive, CMK also prioritised the development of its manufacturing operations. The enhanced reputation thus gained enabled it to joint venture with its distributor in the Netherlands to enable local production of its diagnostic kits. This allowed it to better serve markets in Europe, the Middle East, and Africa (the firm entered a number of African markets in recent years), and to be more responsive to sudden changes in demand. For CMK, the ability to control manufacturing was of paramount importance since it wanted to ensure quality and also reduce cost. With the success of this Netherlands operation in, CMK is considering similar international ventures in Turkey and other markets. This suggests a new phase in its international development – that of a direct foreign investor.

QUESTIONS

1. Comment on the role of CMK's owner-manager in the establishment of this company's international ventures. Which particular decision maker attributes helped CMK in its international opportunity recognition and exploitation?
2. Would you describe CMK as a born global firm? Explain your answer making appropriate references to the literature. Which firm-specific factors would seem to have facilitated CMK's international entrepreneurship?
3. CMK essentially relied on foreign distributors to serve its international markets in its first few years of internationalisation. Why? Which challenges or constraints should this company be mindful of as it seeks to progress its new phase of international development? What advice would you offer CMK?

Source: Adapted from Borchert and Ibeh (2008)

REFERENCES

Acs, Z. J., Morck, R. K. and Yeung, B. (2001) Entrepreneurship, globalisation, and public policy. *Journal of International Management*, 7, 235–251.

Alvarez, R. (2004) Sources of export success in small and medium-sized enterprises: The impact of public programs. *International Business Review*, 13, 383–400.

Alvarez, S. A. and Barney, J. B. (2001) How entrepreneurial firms can benefit from alliances with large partners. *Academy of Management Executive*, 15, 139–148.

Alvarez, S. A. and Busenitz, L. W. (2001). The entrepreneurship of resource-based theory. *Journal of management*, 27(6), 755–775.

Andersson, S. (2000) Internationalisation of the firm from an entrepreneurial perspective. *International Studies of Management & Organisation*, 30(1), 63–92.

Andersson, S., Gabrielsson, J. and Wictor, I. (2004). International activities in small firms: Examining factors influencing the internationalization and export growth of small firms. *Canadian Journal of Administrative Sciences/Revue Canadienne des Sciences de l'Administration*, 21(1), 22–34.

Andersson, S. and Wictor, I. (2003). Innovative internationalisation in new firms: born globals–the Swedish case. *Journal of international Entrepreneurship*, 1(3), 249–275.

Autio, E., Sapienza, H. J. and Almeida, J. G. (2000) Effects of age at entry, knowledge intensity, and imitability on international growth. *Academy of Management Journal*, 43(5), 909–924.

Baldauf, A., Cravens, D. W. and Wagner, U. (2000) Examining determinants of export performance in small open economies. *Journal of World Business*, 35, 61–79.

Barney, J., Wright, M. and Ketchen, D. J. Jr (2001) The resource-based view of the firm: Ten years after 1991. *Journal of Management*, 27(6), 625–641.

Beamish, P. W. (1993) The characteristics of joint ventures in the People's Republic of China. *Journal of International Marketing*, 1, 29–48.

Bell, J., Crick, D. and Young, S. (2004) Small firm internationalisation and business strategy: An exploratory study of knowledge-intensive and traditional manufacturing firms in the UK. *International Small Business Journal*, 22, 23–56.

Bell, J. and Young, S. (1998) Towards an Integrative Framework of the Internationalisation of the Firm. In Hooley, G., Loveridge, R. and Wilson, D. (Eds.), *Internationalisation: Process, Context and Markets*. Palgrave Macmillan, London.

Bell, S. (1997) Globalisation, neoliberalism and the transformation of the Australian state. *Australian Journal of Political Science*, 32(3), 345–367.

Bloodgood, J., Sapienza, H. J. and Almeida, J. G. (1996) The internationalisation of new high-potential U.S. ventures: Antecedents and outcomes. *Entrepreneurship Theory and Practice*, 20, 61–76.

Bolton Committee (1971) *Report of the Committee of Enquiry on Small Firms*, Cmnd 4811. HMSO, London.

Borchert, O. and Ibeh, K. I. N. (2008) The Quintessential Born-Global: Case Evidence from a Rapidly Internationalising Canadian Small Firm. In Ndubisi N. (Ed.), *Internationalisation of Business*. Arah Pendidikan Books, Kuala Lumpur.

Carter, S. and Jones-Evans, D. (2006) *Enterprise and Small Business – Principles, Practice and Policy*. 2nd ed. Prentice Hall, Harlow.

Cavusgil, S. T. and Zou, S. (1994) Marketing strategy-performance relationship: An investigation of the empirical link in export market ventures. *Journal of Marketing*, 58 (1), 1–25.

Chandler, G. N. and Jansen, E. (1992) The founder's self-assessed competence and venture performance. *Journal of Business Venturing*, 7(3), 223–236.

Coviello, N. E. and Munro, H. J. (1995) Growing the entrepreneurial firm: Networking for international market development. *European Journal of Marketing*, 29(7), 49–61.

Coviello, N. V. (2006) The network dynamics of international new ventures. *Journal of International Business Studies*, 37(5), 713–731.

Coviello, N. V. and Jones, M. V. (2005) Internationalization: Conceptualizing an entrepreneurial process of behaviour in time. *Journal of International Business Studies*, 36(3), 284–303.

Dean, D. L., Menguc, B. and Myers, C. P. (2000) Revisiting firm characteristics, strategy, and export performance relationship: A survey of the literature and an investigation of New Zealand small manufacturing firms. *Industrial Marketing Management*, 29, 461–477.

Eriksson, K., Johanson, J., Maikgard, A. and Sharma, D. D. (1998) Experiential knowledge and cost in the internationalisation process. *Journal of International Business Studies*, 28(2), 337–360.

Fletcher, D. (2004) International entrepreneurship and the small business. *Entrepreneurship and Regional Development*, 16, 289–305.

Francis, J. and Collins-Dodd, C. (2004) Impact of export promotion programs on firm competencies, strategies, and performance: The case of Canadian high-technology SMEs. *International Marketing Review*, 21, 474–495.

Gabrielsson, M. and Kirpalani, V. H. M. (2004) Born globals: How to reach new business space rapidly. *International Business Review*, 13(5), 555–571.

Gabrielsson, M., Kirpalani, V. H. M., Dimitratos, P., Solberg, C. A. and Zucchella, A. (2008) Born globals: Propositions to help advance the theory. *International Business Review*, 17, 385–401.

Håkansson, H. and Snehota, I. (1992) *Developing Relationships in Business Networks*. Routledge, London.

Hamill, J. (1997) The internet and international Marketing. *International Marketing Review*, 14(5), 300–323.

Hitt, M. A., Ireland, R. D., Camp, S. M. and Sexton, L. D. (2001) Guest editors' introduction to the special issue strategic entrepreneurship: Entrepreneurial strategies for wealth creation. *Strategic Management Journal*, 22(6/7), 479–491.

Ibeh, K. I. N. (2000) Internationalisation and the Small Firm. In Carter, S. and Jones-Evans, D. (Eds.), *Enterprise and Small Business*. FT Prentice Hall, Harlow.

Ibeh, K. I. N. (2003) Toward a contingency framework of export entrepreneurship: Conceptualisations and empirical evidence. *Small Business Economics*, 15(1), 49–68.

Ibeh, K. I. N. (2005) Toward greater firm-level international entrepreneurship within the UK agribusiness sector: Resource levers and strategic options. *Management International Review*, 45(3) (Special Issue), 59–81.

Ibeh, K. I. N. (2006) Internationalisation and the Smaller Firm. In Carter, S. and Jones-Evans, D. (Eds.), *Enterprise and Small Business*, FT Prentice Hall, Harlow.

Ibeh, K. I. N. and Young, S. (2001) Exporting as an entrepreneurial act: An empirical study of nigerian firms. *European Journal of Marketing*, 35(5/6), 566–586.

Johansson, J. and Vahlne, J. (1977) The internationalisation process of the firm – a model of knowledge development and increasing foreign market commitments. *Journal of International Business Studies*, 8(1), 23–32.

Johansson, J. and Vahlne, J. (1990) The mechanism of internationalisation. *International Marketing Review*, 7(4), 11–23.

Juan Carlos, G., Levine, R. and Schmukler, S. L. (2008) Internationalisation and the evolution of corporate valuation. *Journal of Financial Economics*, 88, 607–632.

Knight, G. A. (1997) *Emerging Paradigm for International Marketing: The Born Global Firm*. PhD thesis, Michigan State University.

Knight, G. A. and Cavusgil, S. T. (1996) The born global firm: A challenge to traditional internationalization theory. *Advances in International Marketing*, 8, 11–26.

Knight, G. A. and Cavusgil, S. T. (2004) Innovation, organizational capabilities, and the born-global firm. *Journal of International Business Studies*, 35(2), 124–141.

Lado, N., Martinez-Ros, E. and Valenzuela, A. (2004) Identifying successful marketing strategies by export regional destination. *International Marketing Review*, 21, 573–597.

Leonidou, L. C. (1995) Empirical research on export barriers: Review, assessment and synthesis. *Journal of International Marketing*, 3(1), 29–43.

McDougall, P. P. and Oviatt, B. M. (2000a) International entrepreneurship: The intersection of two research paths. *Academy of Management Journal*, 43(5), 902–906.

McDougall, P. P. and Oviatt, B. M. (2000b) International Entrepreneurship Literature in the 1990s Directions for Future Research. In Sexton, D. L. and Smillor, R. W. (Eds.), *Entrepreneurship 2000*. Upstart Publishing, Chicago, IL, 291–320.

McDougall, P. P., Oviatt, B. M. and Shrader, R. C. (2003). A comparison of international and domestic new ventures. *Journal of international entrepreneurship*, 1(1), 59–82.

McDougall, P. P., Shane, S. and Oviatt, B. M. (1994) Explaining the formation of international new ventures. *Journal of Business Venturing*, 9, 469–487.

McLoughlin, D. and Horan, C (2000) The production and distribution of knowledge in the markets-as-networks tradition. *Journal of Strategic Marketing*, 8, 89–103.

McNaughton, R. (2003) The number of export markets that a firm serves: Process models versus born-global phenomenon. *Journal of International Entrepreneurship*, 1(3), 297–311.

Miesenbock, K. J. (1988) Small businesses and exporting: A literature review. *International Small Business Journal*, 6(2), 42–61.

O'Cass, A. and Julian, C. (2003) Examining firm and environmental influences on export marketing mix strategy and export performance of Australian exporters. *European Journal of Marketing*, 37, 366–384.

OECD (2000) *Is There a New Economy?* First Report on the OECD Growth Project, OECD, Paris.

OECD. (2009) *Top Barriers and Motivations for SME Internationalisation*. Report of the Working Party on Small and Medium sized Enterprises and Entrepreneurship. OECD, Paris, Available at: http://www.oecdorg/dataoecd/16/26/43357832.pdf (Accessed 23 August, 2010).

O'Farrell, P. N., Wood, P. A. and Zheng, J. (1998) Regional influences on foreign market development by business service companies: Elements of a strategic context explanation. *Regional Studies*, 32, 31–48.

Oviatt, B. M. and McDougall, P. P. (1994) Toward a theory of international new ventures. *Journal of International Business Studies*, 25(1), 45–64.

Oviatt, B. M. and McDougall, P. P. (1995) Global start-ups: Entrepreneurs on a worldwide stage. *Academy of Management Perspectives*, 9(2), 30–43.

Oviatt, B. M. and McDougall, P. P. (1997) Challenges for internationalization process theory: The case of international new ventures. *Management International Review*, 37(2), 85–99.

Oviatt, B. M. and McDougall, P. P. (2005) Defining international entrepreneurship and modeling the speed of internationalisation. *Entrepreneurship Theory and Practice*, 29 (September), 537–553.

Rennie, M. W. (1993) Born Global. *McKinsey Quarterly*, 4, 45–52.

Reuber, A. R. and Fischer, E. (1997) The influence of the management team's international experience on the internationalization behaviors of SMEs. *Journal of International Business Studies*, 28, 807–825.

Rialp, A., Rialp, J. and Knight, G. A. (2005) The phenomenon of early internationalizing firms: What do we know after a decade (1993–2003) of scientific inquiry? *International Business Review*, 14(2), 147–166.

Robertson, C. and Chetty, S. K. (2000) A contingency-based approach to understanding export performance. *International Business Review*, 9, 211–235.

Sapienza, H. J., Autio, E., George, G. and Zahra, S. A. (2006) A capabilities perspective on the effects of early internationalization on firm survival and growth. *Academy of Management Review*, 31, 914–933.

Schumpeter, J. A. (1934) *The Theory of Economic Development*. Harvard University Press, Cambridge, MA.

Schumpeter, J. A. (1950) *Capitalism, Socialism and Democracy*. Harper and Brothers, New York.

Storey, D. J. (1994) *Understanding the Small Business Sector*. International Thomson Business Press, London.

Storey, D. J. and Johnson, S. (1987) *Job Generation and Labour Market Change*. Palgrave Macmillan, London.

Tyebjee, T. T. (1994) Internationalisation of high tech firms: Initial vs. extended involvement. *Journal of Global Marketing* 7(4), 59–81.

Vissak, T., Ibeh, K. I. N. and Paliwoda, S. (2008) Internationalising from the European Periphery: Triggers, processes, and trajectories. *Journal of Euro Marketing*, 17(1), 35–48.

Welch, L. S. and Luostarinen, R. K. (1993) Inward-outward connections in internationalization. *Journal of International Marketing*, 1(1), 44–56.

Westhead, P. (1993) *A Matched Pairs Comparison of Exporting and Non-Exporting Small Firms in GB*, Working Paper (19. Small and Medium Enterprise Centre, Warwick Business School, Warwick.

Westhead, P., Wright, M. and Ucbasaran, D. (2001) "The internationalisation of new and small firms: A resource-based view. *Journal of Business Venturing*, 16, 333–358.

Wheeler, C. N., Ibeh, K. I. N. and Dimitratos, P. (2008) UK export performance research 1990–2003: Review and theoretical framework. *International Small Business Journal*, 26(2), 207–239.

Woods, A., Blackburn, R. and Curran, J. (1993) *A Longitudinal Study of Small Enterprises in the Service Sector*. Small Business Research Centre, Brunel University.

Wright, M., Westhead, P. and Ucbasaran, D. (2007) Internationalisation of small and medium-sized enterprises (SMEs) and international entrepreneurship: A critique and policy implication. *Regional Studies*, 41(7), 1013–1029.

Zahra, S. A. (2005) A theory of international new ventures: A decade of research. *Journal of International Business Studies*, 36(1), 20–28.

Zucchella, A., Palamara, G. and Denicolai, S. (2007) The drivers of the early internationalisation of the firm. *Journal of World Business*, 42, 268–280.

Chapter 18

Born global SME in contemporary markets

Ofer Dekel-Dachs, Amon Simba, and Helena Klipan

This chapter focuses on how small born global enterprises utilise new opportunities arising from technological advancement to overcome challenges affecting their internationalisation process.

LEARNING OUTCOMES

- To understand the nature of Born Global SMEs (BGSs);
- To develop an understanding of the differences between traditional processes of internationalisation and those adopted by BGS;
- To develop an awareness of how digitalisation affects the appearance and strategy of BGSs;
- To understand the concepts of cloud technology, crowdsourcing, co-creation and open innovation;
- To develop an awareness of business ecosystems and how they influence the internationalisation strategy of SMEs with a born global mindset;
- To appreciate why global start-ups are challenging to manage and yet increasing in prevalence.

INTRODUCTION

The 21st century epitomises an era in which international markets are increasingly converging into a common trading arena – a concept often described as globalisation (Pieterse, 1994; Ribau et al., 2018; Yayla et al., 2018). Consequently, new business models and strategies emerge to pursue the opportunities globalisation has to offer. One notable development in conjunction with evolutionary trends in globalisation and advanced information and communications technologies is the rise of *born global* firms (BGFs) (Rennie, 1993). These firms are increasingly becoming key contenders in international markets, which were once dominated by multinational enterprises (MNEs) (Hisrich et al., 1996). This chapter aims to develop the reader's understanding of this emerging phenomenon in the global business arena by providing nuanced theoretical and practical business insights.

BORN GLOBAL FIRMS

The concept of BGFs was first brought up by Rennie (1993) in his study on how small to medium sized enterprises (SMEs) in Australia were competing with established firms in the export markets. Oviatt and McDougall (1994) understood these types of firms as international new ventures (INVs). They conceptualised them as business organisations that from the beginning derive their competitive advantage from their trade in international markets. The interest in the success of BGFs led to several studies bringing light into different facets of their businesses.

Their strategic business approach is centred around flexibility, entrepreneurship, and trade in international markets (Oviatt and McDougall, 2005; Rialp et al., 2005). Competitive conditions arising from globalised markets are disproving traditional beliefs about firm internationalisation which often advocate a stepwise process of engaging in international trade (e.g., Johnson and Vahlne, 1977; Doole and Lowe, 2012; Keegan, 2014; Cavusgil and Knight, 2005; Gabrielsson and Kirpalani, 2012; Hisrich et al., 1996; Simba and Ndlovu, 2015). Li and Ferreira (2006) and Simba (2015) agree that BGFs constitute certain risk-taking behaviours, a proactiveness and a vision to anticipate economic events which are not considered in traditional approaches. BGFs can rapidly internationalise their operations regardless of their resources base (Freeman et al., 2013; Lin and Si, 2019; Zucchella et al., 2018). They take advantage of opportunities that exist in markets that span beyond their immediate proximity, termed *accelerated internationalisation* by Shrader et al. (2000).

However, being young, small, and operating under resource constraints makes the early internationalising firm vulnerable (Zucchella et al., 2018). A misstep may not only threaten their growth but their survival as well which makes the selection of the *right* target market(s) and the timing of entry imperative for them (Keegan, 2014). BGFs achieve extra revenue and profits on international markets while reducing their home-market dependence, limiting the threat of home market saturation and responding to unmet market needs (Leonidou et al., 2007; Bell, 1995; Madsen and Servais, 1997). They use integrated international marketing channels to access a diverse customer base (Keegan, 2014), adapting in line with the needs of individual markets and clients (Sharma and Blomstermo, 2003). Their market selection is defined by a broad scope and high number of target countries which they can enter at the same time and very early in their life (Johnson and Vahlne, 2009). The following sections will show how BGFs overcome their foreignness and liability of outsidership in their approach to international markets (Bembom and Schwens, 2018; Johnson and Vahlne, 2009).

DIGITALISATION

The digital landscape has changed remarkably in the past decades, and new advances in technology continuously transform the way businesses operate today (Ragatz, Handfield and Petersen 2002; Loane, 2005; Glavas et al., 2017), improving their efficiency and providing new ways of coordinating their activities (Gilmore and Pine, 2000; Verity and Hof, 1994). By removing constraints of both distance and time, the internet can facilitate the instant establishment of virtual branches throughout the world; allowing direct and immediate foreign market entry to the smallest of businesses Bennett (1997). Maloff (1995) found out that customers care very little about the physical size or remoteness of a supplier, provided they receive high quality products at fair prices. Information and communication technology (ICT) can reduce cost, improve transparency and provide new ways to reach under-served consumers (Ayoubi et al., 2014). One example is the introduction of the mobile phone technology in emerging countries which opened new business opportunities for its users, especially in areas lacking landline telephone systems (Aker and Mbiti, 2010), allowing them to reach customers wherever they are and to expand into e-commerce and m-commerce services (Koenaite, Chuchu, and de Villiers, 2019).

CLOUD TECHNOLOGY

BGFs often have limited IT resources, such as insufficient internal IT expertise, few technically skilled employees, tight access to financial capital, and few slack resources (Kuan and Chau, 2001; Salmeron and Bueno, 2006; Street and Meister, 2004). Yet, due to their various business uncertainties, BGFs may not be willing to immediately invest in permanent IT solutions. With the introduction of *the cloud* technology (Eckman, 2008), data has become more available anywhere at any time, thereby facilitating the way firms carry digital content to the international marketplace (Simba, 2015). The cloud enables ubiquitous, convenient, and on-demand network access to a shared pool of computing resources with minimal management effort, provider-user interactions, and time (Mell and Grance, 2009; Armbrust et al., 2010), thereby fostering the rise of entirely new business models (Greengard, 2010). Cloud technology has small upfront investments and flexible pay-for-use payment mechanisms which allow BGFs to proactively adopt advanced information systems while maintaining relatively low transaction and switching costs (Greengard, 2010).

CROWDSOURCING

The term crowdsourcing was introduced by Jeff Howe (Howe, 2006, 2008) who described crowdsourcing as a concept that depicts the way a firm takes a function once performed by its employees and outsources it to an undefined (and generally large) network of people in the form of an *open call*. Crowdsourcing shares its basic principles with web 2.0 based social networks, where a user gets feedback from other users on a topic of their choice. Particular to crowdsourcing is that it consists of an actual externalisation of product or service sourcing to the *crowd* or internet users that respond to the call. The strengths of this model are based on the non-discriminatory nature of participation (Pénin, 2008). It invites individuals, commercial firms, not-for-profit making organisations and/or communities, in other words the *crowd* to participate (Burger-Helmchen and Pénin, 2010). Participants can be either complementary, i.e., each individual performs a small fraction of the activity, or each individual tries to perform the activity as a whole. Entrepreneurial firms such as BGFs would not rely on a single supplier or on a small number of suppliers but rather launch *an open call* (Greengard, 2010).

For BGFs that are known for their ability to operate with limited resources (Simba, 2013), the *open call* approach offers the tools they may require for survival in the various markets they enter. It enables BGFs to take part in new projects and develop new competences in the long run. However, this model also presents a critical limitation: for a given problem, there are usually several solutions that correspond to different trade-offs or technical paths. Thus, BGFs need to assess the quality of the variety of options provided by the crowd. The selection of suitable solutions can be menaced by information overload (or, *infobesity*). If large companies can partially cope with this problem, it constitutes a crucial challenge for BGFs due to their limited capacity to dedicate time and specific resources to activities that are non-core business (Kittur et al., 2013).

CO-CREATION AND OPEN INNOVATION

Armed with new tools and dissatisfied with available choices as a result of globalisation, consumers increasingly want to interact with firms, influencing every part of the value chain and thereby co-create value (Prahalad and Ramaswamy, 2004). Co-creation refers to the joint creation of value during the interaction process between the firm and the customers (Grönroos, 2000; Vargo and Lusch, 2004; Ehrenthal, 2012). In contrast to traditional marketing practices, it considers customers as active players and parts of the firm during the interaction process to equally co-produce and co-create value for mutual benefits (Prahalad and Ramaswamy, 2000; Vargo and Lusch, 2004; Baldwin and Von Hippel, 2011; Gummesson et al., 2014; Ehrenthal, 2012; Grönroos, 2011; Vargo and Lusch, 2004). Baldwin and Von Hippel (2011) and others (e.g., Franke and Shah, 2003) focus on stakeholders' engagement in strong knowledge sharing and co-development in communities. Within these communities, users have been shown to share ideas, knowledge, and inventions freely towards firms and other users (Harhoff et al., 2003).

To seize global opportunities, firms will need to engage in propitious value co-creation activities that typically involve cross-border exchange of resources including human capital (Nair, 2015). Entrepreneurs need to identify those market gaps, methods and strategies that help in value co-creation and initiate cross-border ventures (Nair, 2015). In order to co-create value with customers, small firms like BGFs abandon traditional one-sided communication. Instead, their aim is to convert communication into a dialogue with the *crowd* (Vargo and Lusch, 2004). This dialogue is not necessarily controlled or even initiated by the firm. With the advent of social media, this dialogue can be initiated as a customer-to-customer conversation with the marketer observing but not necessarily directly participating (Vargo and Lusch, 2004). Prahalad (2004) regards dialogue, access to, transparency of information, and risk assessment as the building blocks of this co-creation.

The rise of co-creation paves the way for novel forms of innovation that seem extremely suited to BGFs (Mention et al., 2016). Innovation is highly critical for BGFs because of the nature of their market that spans multiple countries (Parent-Thirion et al., 2012). For these types of firms, enhancing their own competences, innovative products, and processes might prove to be the key to their development, or even survival (OECD, 2006). As a result, research and development processes in BGFs diverge from traditional knowledge generation to knowledge-brokering, from closed to open innovation, from research and development to connect and develop, and from competition to cooperation (Chesbrough, 2003; Mention et al., 2016). For BGFs, who have limited resources, user-centric development and validation of innovations by a network of stakeholders placed in target markets can play an important role in speeding up the innovation process (Mention et al., 2016).

NETWORKS AND STRATEGIC ALLIANCES

Digitalisation has led to a revolution in collaboration among firms. New types of business ecosystems are emerging in which customer needs are no longer satisfied my marketing efforts from within one company's value chain but from a network of partnerships worldwide (Alqahtani and Uslay, 2018). BGFs seem to use this development in their response to customer needs: By the creation of digital business ecosystems, they can gain access to resources and expertise with which they are equipped to face large companies as equals in the international marketplace.

290

Networks and strategic alliances are key aspects for young businesses such as BGFs in dealing with market and operational challenges arising from the international marketplace (e.g., Acosta et al., 2018; Fladmoe-Lindquist and Aharoni, 1993; Madsen and Servais, 1997; Simba, 2013; Wach and Wehrmann, 2014; Welch and Welch, 1996). Networks are defined as a linked set of nodes, consisting of people or organisations (Cooke, 2001; Breschi and Malebra, 2005). They are distinct from hierarchical or market relationships in their reliance on reciprocity, collaboration, complementary independence, and orientation towards mutual gain (Larson, 1992).

Empirical evidence illustrates the importance of networks in a firm's resource access (Vicente and Suire, 2007; Jack, 2010). According to Oviatt and McDougall (1994), a network of relationships is important for entrepreneurs and an asset in accelerating the internationalisation process of their firms. Ohmae (1989) considered network alliances mandatory, especially for firms that operate in the high technology industry. Consistent with Ohmae's views, Simba and Ndlovu (2015) investigated five BGFs that operate in biotechnology in the United Kingdom. They found that these entrepreneurial companies employed strategic alliances as a mechanism for their international marketing efforts. Ciravegna et al. (2018) described the role of activeness and networks as catalysts to the early internationalisation process of Chinese BGFs. Likewise, Bembom and Schwens (2018) underlined the importance of networks for the early internationalising firm and emphasised the need of adapting networks in response to changing resource requirements throughout the firm's internationalisation process.

Similarities between network partners, network partners' skills, and external factors, particularly strong market competition, can bind network partners together (Bembom and Schwens, 2018; Freeman et al., 2013 Simba, 2015) and constitute a driver for collaboration in their response to market transformations. Clearly, this network perspective underlines the importance of establishing strong relationships and that these partnerships continue to facilitate access to existing and new resources (Ahuja, 2000; Burt, 2017), enabling BGFs to create new market opportunities and to develop competitive advantage (Hakansson, 1982).

CONCLUSION

This chapter discussed changes in the contemporary international marketplace and the subsequent rise of born global firms (BGFs). It brought light into the understanding of what distinguishes BGFs from traditional firms and how those firms adapt their business approach in relation to their targeted markets. BGFs are *born* into a networked digitalised business world. They skip traditional paths of growth and meet customers in new ways derived from opportunities technological advancement offers. Profiting from the wide reach of the internet and thereby saving on various investment cost, BGFs are able to quickly and efficiently reach markets beyond their ultimate proximity. Their business approach builds on collaboration, co-creation, and flexibility while actively seizing the momentum of global technological advancement.

TECHNOLOGY, SMES, AND THE 21ST CENTURY

Technological advancement has made it possible for modern SMEs to access markets that are beyond their immediate boundaries. The increased availability of sophisticated communication technologies, integrated payment systems and IT-enabled logistics has played a major role towards making it possible for SMEs to trade their products and/or services in international markets. In advanced countries including the US, UK, Canada, and Australia and in established economic trade regions such the EU, ASEAN, NAFTA, etc., IT-related policies, for example, have been at the top of many economic development debates. But, regardless of this considerable focus on technology-based systems in many countries, SMEs that engage in international entrepreneurship continue to face a multitude of challenges. For example, in the multiple countries into which they often venture, development in the infrastructure is meant to facilitate the application of technology-enabled systems, yet still lags behind. In countries where the infrastructure which is needed to implement technology is in place, SMEs often pinpoint the prohibitive costs for acquiring new and advanced equipment to seamlessly integrate their own systems. Furthermore, the unauthorised access to web-enabled systems and cyber security issues have also been problematic for SMEs. The search for solutions to these problems remains a puzzle for the business community, in particular.

It is clear that while technology unlocks business opportunities for modern SMEs, it also brings significant challenges. Thus, a major issue with technology-for-business-development in the 21st century requires a holistic approach to its implementation without which its benefit may still be farfetched for ambitious SMEs.

DISCUSSION

1. What do you suggest for SMEs that intend to take advantage of the advancements in technology by expanding their operations into foreign markets but are restricted by limited financial resources for acquiring technology-enabled systems?

2. What should happen to turn the debate on implementing technology-based systems in different countries into action?

3. What advice would you give to modern SMEs that are sceptical about implementing technology-enabled systems such as web-based systems because of security issues?

CASE STUDY 1: TOMATO PRODUCTION IN THE MOUNTAINS OF NEPAL

The following case study is based on a real-life transportation problem affecting many farmers in the mountains of Nepal. It gives you the opportunity to apply the concept of crowdsourcing to a real-life situation.

Discussion: Discuss in the classroom the various ways in which food is generally transported from where it is produced to the local market or shop. (You can, for example, talk about rail, lorries, boats, planes, bicycles, etc.)

Many farmers in Nepal grow their crops (including tomatoes) on the mountainside. To sell them at the local market, they need to transport them to the bottom of the mountain, but it's a long and hazardous journey and they need to cross rivers and cliffs. Tomatoes are quite easily squashed, so they need to be transported with care.

Your task:

1. Search the internet for tomato farms in the Nepalese mountains. Find out how far these farms are from any transportation system. Now plan a crowdsourcing project that will help these farmers to find a solution for their logistical problem.

BORN GLOBAL SME IN CONTEMPORARY MARKETS

2. Now, work in small groups to design your campaign that will lead to a new model for the transportation of as many tomatoes as possible at the same time from the top of the mountains to the market without squashing them.
3. After you have developed your model and campaign, you can watch the following video produced by the charity 'Practical Action' and see the solution they have developed.

https://practicalaction.org/video-aerial-ropeways-nepal

CASE STUDY 2: AFFORDABLE AND CLEAN ENERGY

It's hard to imagine a life without energy – no energy to charge your mobile phone, to provide you with light in the evenings or to cook your food. If we want enough energy for everyone on the planet, we are going to need to find more renewable, sustainable and affordable solutions. The Sustainable Development Goals (SDGs) are 17 goals that were put together by global leaders from many countries around the world to end poverty, protect the planet and ensure prosperity for all by 2030. One of these, Global Goal 7, is about ensuring access to affordable, reliable and modern energy services and increasing substantially the share of renewable energy in the global energy mix. This shows us how important this topic is in lifting people out of poverty. Today, 1.6 billion people live their lives without any access to electrical energy – that's about one out of six people on our planet. To find out what life might be like without electrical energy and how having energy changes lives watch the following video: youtube.com/watch?v=usISdE-WSWU

Your task:
1. In your group, conduct a research with the help of the internet to get an idea of ways of energy production in different parts of the world.
2. Design in your group a global project based on open innovation. Consider how you can involve individuals from all over the world in developing an alternative energy solution. Here are some ideas to get you going:
   - Small-scale wind power: producing energy from wind power is one solution used in the developing world. You could investigate when this type of energy is used and contrast the differences between wind turbines in Europe and in the developing world. The challenge you create could be about building a working model of a wind turbine that could be used either in Europe or in a country in the developing world. To see examples from the developing world, go to practicalaction.org/smallscale-wind-power-1.
   - Solar power: solar energy can be produced rather cheaply. It can be used to produce electricity for lighting, heating, and cooking as well as for powering generators in machinery used by small businesses. You could design a project around making use of this source of energy. For an example of how solar power can be used to pump water, refer to practicalaction.org/solar-powered-water-pumps. To see how solar power can change lives go to practicalaction. org/videos-energy and watch the videos 'Dying for a drink' and 'How one lamp makes a difference'.

293

- Hydro power: producing energy from water is something that can be done on a medium/large scale in certain areas. You could design a project around building a model system suitable for your own location or for somewhere in Kenya. For general information on micro-hydro go to practicalaction.org/micro-hydro-power. For information on micro-hydro in Kenya watch bit.ly/2ccHqiE
- Biogas: biogas is a technology being piloted on a relatively small scale in Europe. Consider, if there are any projects near you. In the developing world, biogas is often a welcomed by-product of a household waste disposal system. You could design a project around creating a small and safe biogas system. Have a look at this video about biogas in Bangladesh: practicalaction.org/video-marvellous-microbes
- Biomass: many kinds of fuels can be used for cooking. People in the developing world change from using wood and dung fuel to kerosene and liquid-petroleum gas (LPG) when they can afford it. Your project could be about what kind of wood has the greatest energy content or which materials make the best biomass.
- Products powered by renewable energy: Many products we use such as phones are powered by electricity from the national grid which may include some electricity produced by renewable energy sources but is mostly electricity produced by burning fossil fuels. How about a project that designs a way of powering a common product such as a phone or a tablet using renewable energy source?

Useful links:

Global issues: Global issues that affect everyone and aims to show how most issues are interrelated

- globalissues.org

GNESD: publications and data related to energy and energy access

- gnesd.org

Greenbiz: Article on the fight over how to power the developing world

- greenbiz.com/article/fight-over-how-power-developing-world

Power for All: A collective of organisations dedicated to delivering universal energy access before 2030

- powerforall.org/#energy-access-imperative

Practical Action: General and technical information on energy solutions

- practicalaction.org/technical-briefs-schools-energy
- practicalaction.org/energy
- practicalaction.org/blog/category/programmes/energy

- practicalaction.org/energy-image-gallery

Renewable World: a charity tackling poverty through renewable energy

- renewable-world.org

The Independent: article on how the developing world spends more money on renewable energy than the developed world

- bit.ly/indengart

UN Global Goals: information about Global Goal number 7

- un.org/sustainabledevelopment/energy
- globalgoals.org/global-goals/modern-energy/
- youtube.com/watch?v=H2ULDepMiEk

Worldometers: basic 'real time' data including data on energy

- worldometers.info

TEACHING CASE STUDY: THE INTERNATIONALISATION OF XENOGESIS

XenoGesis is a drug discovery company geographically located in the East Midlands in the UK. The biopharmaceutical company is the brainchild of Dr. Richard Weaver – a drug discovery expert and a former employee of AstraZeneca. As part of Astra-Zeneca's restructuring exercise, the pharmaceutical giant closed its Charnwood R&D facilities in Loughborough, UK, between 2010 and 2011 (Stringer 2010) and Lund facilities in Sweden (Peters and Monck, 2012), making 1600 scientists, including Richard, redundant. Faced with the possibility of unemployment, he established a small drug discovery firm as a contract research organisation (CRO) in 2011 with only three employees including himself.

Richard understood very well his small firms' resource limitations including financial, human and knowledge capital, but that was not to deter him from growing his business. With that in mind he set up his services in a business incubator – BioCity. This initial move at the inception of his CRO was intended to reduce the impact of its resource limitations. Setting up his business in a place where his organisation was surrounded by other companies from a diverse range of industries, covering marketing, accounting, IT services, drug manufacturing, and commercialisation services, helped him to access the support he needed at the early stage of his organisation.

Central to his services were specialised laboratories and BioCity proved to be the right place for his business. BioCity as a regional science hub had connections with well-established networks that practiced open science, i.e., science hubs that facilitate work in collaborative projects. These included Boston Metropolitan Area,

Europe Enterprise Network, Medilink, and the Golden Triangle of Cambridge, London, and Oxford. Given that XenoGesis was resident at BioCity, the company was exposed to these connections. Gauging from Richards itinerary and the connections he established since the inception of his company, there is ample evidence of XenoGesis' international orientation.

The involvement of local and international institutions provided a steady flow of scientific knowledge he desperately needed. Plus, the firm's board of directors consist of scientists who had vast experience in drug discovery and had international reputation. In addition to the array of resources XenoGesis was privy to at BioCity, Richard continued to drive the company's international agenda. By 2012, he was taking part in annual conferences such as the Barcelona Bio Science Exhibition to showcase his discoveries and to source international partners. The connections he established included other companies, both, domestically and internationally, that were involved in drug discovery and, more importantly, XenoGesis' customers with whom they work from discovery through to full drug development. According to Richard, XenoGesis' clients are global, which perhaps implies that his company values international trade.

As of 2014, the drug discovery company had managed to develop strategic alliances with companies, including commercial partners, customers and research partners in the US, Canada, and Europe. In 2015, 69% of its sales were generated through its international contracts and its overall turnover per annum amounted to £3m and its workforce had grown from three people in 2011 to 25 people in 2018. Another sign that indicates that the company is growing is the recent opening of its new state-of-the art facilities at BioCity's new premises in Nottingham.

Questions

1. How can the rise of Cloud technology, the new generation of Born Global business models, and open innovation could help XenoGesis to achieve growth?
2. Discuss the main motivations for XenoGesis to adopt open innovation practices: benefits and challenges
3. Can a small company such as XenoGesis gain competitive advantage over large companies in implementing open innovation strategies?

REFERENCES

Acosta, A. S., Crespo, Á. H. and Agudo, J. C. (2018) Effect of market orientation, network capability and entrepreneurial orientation on international performance of small and medium enterprises (SMEs). *International Business Review*, 27(6), 1128–1140.

Ahuja, G. (2000) Collaboration networks, structural holes, and innovation: A longitudinal study. *Administrative Science Quarterly*, 45(3), 425–455.

Aker, J. C. and Mbiti, I. M. (2010) Mobile phones and economic development in Africa. *Journal of Economic Perspectives*, 24(3), 207–232.

Alqahtani, N. and Uslay, C. (2018) Entrepreneurial marketing and firm performance: Synthesis and conceptual development. *Journal of Business Research*. Available at: https://doi.org/10.1016/j.jbusres.2018.12.035 (Accessed on 29 March 2019).

Armbrust, M., Fox, A., Griffith, R., Joseph, A. D., Katz, R., Konwinski, A., Lee, G., Patterson, D., Rabkin, A., Stoica, I. and Zaharia, M. (2010) A view of cloud computing. *Communications of the ACM*, 53(4).

Ayoubi, R., Bayoumi, M. and Ayoubi, R. (2014) Real-time parallelized hybrid median filter for speckle removal in ultrasound images. In *2014 IEEE Global Conference on Signal and Information Processing (GlobalSIP)*. IEEE, 65–68.

Baldwin, C. and Von Hippel, E. (2011) Modeling a paradigm shift: From producer innovation to user and open collaborative innovation. *Organization Science*, 22(6), 1399–1417.

Bell, J. (1995) The internationalization of small computer software firms: A further challenge to stage theories. *European Journal of Marketing*, 29(8), 60–75.

Bembom, M. and Schwens, C. (2018) The role of networks in early internationalizing firms: A systematic review and future research agenda. *European Management Journal*, 36(2018), 679–694.

Bennett, R., 1997. Export marketing and the internet: Experiences of web site use and perceptions of export barriers among UK businesses. *International Marketing Review*, 14(5), 324–344.

Breschi, S. and Malebra, F. (2005) *Clusters, Networks and Innovation*. Oxford University Press Inc., New York.

Burger-Helmchen, T. and Pénin, J. (2010) The limits of crowdsourcing inventive activities: What do transaction cost theory and the evolutionary theories of the firm teach us? In *Working Papers of BETA (Bureau d'Economie Théorique et Appliquée)*. Strasbourg.

Burt, R. S., 2017. Structural holes versus network closure as social capital. In *Social capital*. Routledge, New York, 31–56.

Chesbrough, H. W. (2003) The era of open innovation. *MIT Sloan Management Review*, 44(3), 34–41.

Ciravegna, L., Kuivalainen, O., Kundu, S. K. and Lopez, L. E. (2018) The antecedents of early internationalization: A configurational perspective. *International Business Review*, 27(6), 1200–1212.

Cooke, P. (2001) Regional innovation systems, clusters and the knowledge economy. *Industrial and Corporate Change*, 10(4), 945–974.

Doole, I. and Lowe, R. (2012) International Marketing Strategy, Analysis, Development and Implementation. In Ainscow, A. and Darby, L. (Eds.), *Cengage Learning EMEA*, 6th ed. South Western, Cengage, 1À440.

Eckman, J. (2008) *We've Only Just Begun: Web 2.0 and Its Impact on the Modern Enterprise*. Presentation at the Web 2.0 Congress, Hamburg.

Ehrenthal, J. C. (2012) *A Service-Dominant Logic View of Retail on-Shelf Availability*, Doctoral dissertation, Rohner+ Spiller AG.

Fladmoe-Lindquist, K. and Aharoni, Y. (1993) *The Impact of Bargaining and Negotiating on the Globalization of Professional Service Firms*. Routledge, London.

Franke, N. and Shah, S. (2003) How communities support innovative activities: An exploration of assistance and sharing among end-users. *Research Policy*, 32(1), 157–178.

Freeman, S., Deligonul, S. and Cavusgil, T. (2013) Strategic re-structuring by born-globals using outward and inward-oriented activity. *International Marketing Review*, 30(2), 156–182.

Gabrielsson, M. and Kirpalani, V. H. M. (2012) *Handbook of Research on Born Globals*. Edward Elgar Publishing, Cheltenham.

Gilmore, J. H. and Pine, B. J. (2000) *Markets of One: Creating Customer Unique Value Through Mass Customisation*. Harvard Business School Press, Boston.

Glavas, C., Mathews, S. and Bianchi, C. (2017) International opportunity recognition as a critical component for leveraging internet capabilities and international market performance. *Journal of International Entrepreneurship*, 15(1), 1–35.

Greengard, S. (2010) Cloud computing and developing nations. *Communications of the ACM*, 53(5), 18–20.

Grönroos, C. (2000) Creating a relationship dialogue: communication, interaction and value. *The Marketing Review*, 1(1), 5–14.

Grönroos, C. (2011). Value co-creation in service logic: A critical analysis. *Marketing Theory*, 11(3), 279–301.

Galvagno, M. and Dalli, D. (2014) Theory of value co-creation: A systematic literature review. *Managing Service Quality*, 24(6), 643–683.

Hakansson, H. (1982) *International Marketing and Purchasing of Industrial Goods: An Interaction Approach*. John Wiley and Sons, Chichester.

Harhoff, D., Henkel, J. and Von Hippel, E., (2003) Profiting from voluntary information spillovers: How users benefit by freely revealing their innovations. *Research Policy*, 32(10), 1753–1769.

Hisrich, R. D., Honig-Haftel, S., McDougall, P. P. and Oviatt, B. M. (1996) International entrepreneurship: Past, present, and future, *Entrepreneurship Theory and Practice*, 20(4), 5–8.

OFER DEKEL-DACHS, ET AL.

Howe, J. (2006) The rise of crowdsourcing. *Wired Magazine*, 14(6), 1–4.

Howe, J. (2008) *Crowdsourcing: Why the Power of the Crowd Is Driving the Future of Business*. Crown Publishing Group, New York.

Jack, S. L. (2010) Approaches to studying networks: Implications and outcomes. *Journal of Business Venturing*, 25(1), 120–137.

Johnson, J. and Vahlne, J-E. (1977) The internationalisation process of the firm. *Journal of International Business Studies*, 8(1), 23–32.

Johnson, J. and Vahlne, J. -E. (2009) The Uppsala internationalization process model revisited: From liability of foreignness to liability of outsidership. *Journal of International Business Studies*, 40(9), 1411–1431.

Keegan, J. W. (2014) *Global Marketing Management*, 8th ed. International Edition. Pearson Education, Essex.

Knight, G. A. and Cavusgil, S. T. (2005). A taxonomy of born-global firms. *MIR: Management International Review*, 15–35.

Kittur, A., Nickerson, J. V., Bernstein, M., Gerber, E., Shaw, A., Zimmerman, J., Lease, M. and Horton, J. (2013) The future of crowd work. In *Proceedings of the 2013 Conference on Computer Supported Cooperative Work*. ACM, 1301–1318.

Koenaite, M., Chuchu, T. and Venter de Villiers, M. (2019) The impact of mobile banking on the adoption of banking products and services in South Africa, using the technology acceptance model. *Journal of Business and Retail Management Research* 13(3):93–103.

Kuan, K. K. and Chau, P. Y. (2001) A perception-based model for EDI adoption in small businesses using a technology – organization – environment framework. *Information and Management*, 38(8), 507–521.

Larson, A. (1992) Network dyads in entrepreneurial settings: A study of the governance of exchange relationships. *Administrative Science Quarterly*, 37(1).

Leonidou, L. C., Katsikeas, C. S., Palihawadana, D. and Spyropoulou, S. (2007) An analytical review of the factors stimulating smaller firms to export: Implications for policy-makers. *International Marketing Review*, 24(6), 735–770.

Li, D. and Ferreira, M. P. (2006) The evolutionary model of entrepreneurial firms' dependence on networks: going beyond the start-up stage. *Notas Económicas*, 24(6), 48–63.

Lin, S. and Si, S. (2019) The influence of exploration and exploitation on born globals' speed of internationalization. *Management Decision*, 57(1), 193–210. Available at: https://doi.org/10.1108/MD-08-2017-0735 (Accessed on 19 February 2019).

Loane, S. (2005) The role of the internet in the internationalisation of small and medium sized companies. *Journal of International Entrepreneurship*, 3 (December), 263–277.

Madsen, T. K. and Servais, P. (1997) The internationalization of born globals: An evolutionary process? *International Business Review*, 6(6), 561–583.

Maloff, J. (1995) The virtual corporation – the internet gives companies a myriad of new ways to support telecommuters and reinvent themselves. *Internet World*, 6(7), 46–51.

Mell, P. and Grance, T. (2009) Effectively and securely using the cloud computing paradigm. *NIST, Information Technology Laboratory*, 2(8), 304–311.

Mention, Anne-Laure and Torkkeli, M. (2016) *Open Innovation: A Multifaceted Perspective (Bridging Theory and Practice)*, *(Part 1 and 2)*. World Scientific, ISBN: 24248231.

Ohmae, K., 1989. The global logic of strategic alliances. *Harvard Business Review*, 67(2), 143–154.

Oviatt, B. M. and McDougall, P. P. (1994) Toward a theory of international new ventures. *Journal of International Business Studies*, 36(1), 45–64.

Parent-Thirion, A., Vermeylen, G., Van Houten, G., Lyly-Yrjänäinen, M., Biletta, I. and Cabrita, J. (2012) *Eurofound. Fifth European Working Conditions Survey*. Publications Office of the European Union, Luxembourg.

Pénin, J. (2008) More open than open innovation? Rethinking the concept of openness in innovation studies. In *Working Papers of BETA (Bureau d'Economie Théorique et Appliquée)*. Strasbourg.

Peters, K. and Monck, C. (2012) Delivery of a Science and Enterprise Park at Loughborough – Phase 1 Report. Available at: https://www.charnwood.gov.uk/files/documents/loughborough_science_and_enterprise_park_phase_1_report/Science%20%26%20Enterprise%20Park%20Phase%201%20Report.pdf

Pieterse, J. N. (1994) Globalisation as hybridisation. *International Sociology*, 9(2), 161–184.

Prahalad, C. K. (2004) The blinders of dominant logic. *Long Range Planning*, 37(2), 171–179.

298

Prahalad, C. K. and Ramaswamy, V. (2000) Co-opting customer competence. *Harvard Business Review*, 78(1), 79–90.

Prahalad, C. K. and Ramaswamy, V. (2004). Co-creation experiences: The next practice in value creation. *Journal of Interactive Marketing*, 18(3), 5–14.

Ragatz, G. L., Handfield, R. B. and Petersen, K. J. (2002). Benefits associated with supplier integration into new product development under conditions of technology uncertainty. *Journal of Business Research*, 55(5), 389–400.

Rennie, M. (1993) Born global. *McKinsey Quarterly*, 4, 45–52.

Rialp, A., Rialp, J. and Knight, G. A. (2005) The phenomenon of early internationalizing companies: What do we know after a decade (1993–2003) of scientific inquiry? *International Business Review*, (14), 147–166.

Ribau, C. P., Moreira, A. C. and Raposo, M. (2018) SME internationalization research: Mapping the state of the art. *Canadian Journal of Administrative Sciences/Revue Canadienne des Sciences de l'Administration*, 35(2), 280–303.

Salmeron, J. L. and Bueno, S. (2006) An information technologies and information systems industry-based classification in small and medium-sized enterprises: An institutional view. *European Journal of Operational Research*, 173(3), 1012–1025.

Sharma, D. D. and Blomstermo, A. (2003) The internationalization process of born globals: A network view. *International Business Review*, 12, 739–753.

Shrader, R. C., Oviatt, B. M. and McDougall, P. P. (2000) How new ventures exploit trade-offs among international risk factors: Lessons for the accelerated internationalization of the 21st century. *Academy of Management Journal*, 43(6), 1227–1247.

Simba, A. (2013) The role of global R&D networks in generating social capital for born-global bio-tech firms: A multi-case approach. *International Journal of Entrepreneurship and Small Business*, 20(3), 342–362.

Simba, A. (2015) A new model of knowledge and innovative capability development for small born-global bio-tech firms: Evidence from the East Midlands, UK. *International Journal Entrepreneurship and Innovation Management*, 19(1/2), 30–58.

Simba, A. and Ndlovu, T. (2015) The entrepreneurial marketing management and commercialization arrangements of born-global bio-enterprises: The case of UK companies. *Journal of Small Business and Entrepreneurship*, 27(2), 143–170. DOI: 10.1080/08276331.2014.994696.

Small, A. P. E. C. and Medium Enterprises Working Group. (2008) *Removing Barriers to SME Access to International Markets*. OECD publishing.

Street, C. T. and Meister, D. B. (2004) Small business growth and internal transparency: The role of information systems. *MIS Quarterly*, 473–506.

Stringer, H. D. (2010) Housing design and sustainable economic development in the East Midlands. East Midlands Development Agency, Nottingham.

Vargo, S. L. and Lusch, R. F. (2004) Evolving to a new dominant logic for marketing. *Journal of Marketing*, 68(1), 1–17.

Verity, John W. and Hof, Robert D. (1994) The Internet: How it will change the way you do business. *Business Week*, 14 November, 80–86, 88.

Vicente, J. and Suire, R. (2007) Informational cascades vs. network externalities in locational choice: Evidences of 'ICT Clusters' formation and stability. *Regional Studies*, 41(2), 173–184.

Wach, K. and Wehrmann, C. (2014) Entrepreneurship in International Business: International Entrepreneurship as the Intersection of Two Fields (chapter 1). In Gubik, A. S. and Wach, K. (Eds.), *International Entrepreneurship and Corporate Growth in Visegrad Countries*. University of Miskolc, Mickolc, 9–22.

Welch, D. E. and Welch, L. S. (1996) The internationalization process and networks: A strategic management perspective. *Journal of International Marketing*, 4(3), 11–28.

Yayla, S., Yeniyurt, S., Uslay, C. and Cavusgil, E. (2018) The role of market orientation, relational capital, and internationalization speed in foreign market exit and re-entry decisions under turbulent conditions. *International Business Review*, 27(6), 1105–1115.

Zucchella, A. Hagen, B. and Serapio, M. G. (2018) *International Entrepreneurship*. Edward Elgar Publishing Limited, Northampton, MA. ISBN:9781785365454.

Chapter 19

Cross cultural marketing strategies
For small and medium-sized firms

Robin Lowe, Isobel Doole, and Felicity Mendoza

LEARNING OBJECTIVES

After reading this chapter, you will be able to:
- Develop an appreciation of the challenges and opportunities facing small medium-sized enterprises (SMEs) in internationalising across cross cultural markets;
- identify and compare the different strategic approaches to cross cultural marketing adopted by SMEs;
- Understand the factors that drive SME internationalisation;
- Contrast the alternative segmentation strategies of SMEs developing cross cultural marketing strategies;
- Understand the role that relational strategies play in cross cultural SME marketing.

INTRODUCTION

There is an apparent dichotomy in the development of SMEs. For a few of the most successful SMEs, growth rates seem to be accelerating as they pursue opportunities across the world at an ever faster pace, driven and supported by the latest advances in information and communications technology. For many other SMEs, no matter where in the world they are situated, competition seems to increase. SMEs that have had a traditional and secure niche in the local business community are increasingly coming under attack from worldwide competition. It seems that no matter how small and specialised the local grocery or bookstore is, it has become part of the global market and has to compete with the global giants, such as Wal-Mart and Amazon.com.

Small and medium sized firms (SMEs) have always been of great importance to the local or national economy because they create wealth and employment and frequently initiate innovation. The majority of smaller firms, however, are a less powerful force outside their home territory. Indeed, many SME's, despite what may be competitive advantage in the product and service offering at home and significant marketing capability, never move into international markets at all. However, the changes in the international trading environment, particularly information and communications technological developments, are increasing the opportunities for SME's to become considerably more important in the future global economy, both in fast growing business sectors, and in specific market niches, where innovation in mature industry sectors can lead to new opportunities for the smaller firm.

For many firms exporting is the first significant step in cross cultural marketing. It is the stage in the internationalisation process where firms recognise that cross cultural markets provide the advantage of considerably expanded market potential with relatively little commitment and limited associated risk. Cross cultural marketing, when defined as the marketing of goods and/or services across national and political boundaries becomes the means by which SMEs can seek market expansion.

WHAT IS AN SME?

A number of definitions of the small and medium-sized firm sector exist but the most commonly used terms relate to the number of employees in the company. The European Union, for example, defines a small firm as employing between zero and 49 employees and a medium firm as employing between 50 and 249 employees.

The UK government estimates there were 4.8 million private sector enterprises in the UK at the start of 2008, of these 99.9% were classed as SME's. The number of people employed by SMEs was estimated at 13.7 million, and their combined turnover was £1,500 billion. However because the SME classification includes sole operators (estimated at 24.4% of total enterprises) as well as quite sophisticated businesses, it is not particularly useful for segmenting the smaller firms' sector.

In this chapter, therefore, the review of smaller firm strategies is not restricted to firms with a specific number of employees but instead, to those businesses in general which think and act like small and medium-sized enterprises. Typically their strategies are closely linked to their owners' knowledge, capability and ambition. Indeed they often become the very personification of their owner and are thus strongly influenced by the home country culture. This is something we will be discussing later in the chapter.

The reason for adopting this stance is that, for example, a garment-making firm with 250 employees has a very restricted capacity to internationalise, whereas a 250 employee financial services or computer software company could be a significant international player. Many quite large businesses have operated in the same way for decades, perhaps exporting to the same customers in the same countries for years. They are unwilling or unable to seek out new markets and stick to what and who they know. Such firms take business decisions within the 'inner' management group as they have done for years and in much the same way that family owners of small firms take decisions.

Whilst family businesses share many of the problems of any business the complexity of personal family relationships presents additional challenges. Often, members of the extended family have a financial or emotional interest in the firm and feel that their often conflicting views about strategy should be taken into account. The loyalty and commitment of families to each other does offer stability, however, and where members of the extended family are located in different countries they can help with setting up a new arm of the business in a new market by providing financial support there, help with the supply chain, and finding customers. Asian family firms have been particularly successful with this.

Many of the fastest growing international small firms very rapidly grow through the 250 employee ceiling without making significant changes to their international strategic approach. Typically the primary focus of small firms is on the short term and finding new customers and meeting their requirements. When the firm has a successful product or service, the managers are often reluctant to change it. However, without fully realising it,

301

the model and approach to their home and nearby markets is usually based around their detailed knowledge and an understanding of the needs of their customers. The danger is that, due to their lack of resources and expertise, these firms often do not take time to develop the same close relationships with customers in their new markets and instead may simply appoint an intermediary dealer or distributor to be the primary contact with customers. If they are unable to adapt their business mode and strategy quickly enough to take account of the different market conditions, social culture, and ways of doing business, the firm might underperform.

Our discussion in this chapter therefore relates to issues such as these that do not significantly affect strategy development in the largest multinational firms that have real global power but are central to strategy development in smaller firms. Small firms are not small versions of larger firms but are driven by very different demands and a significantly different mindset.

THE IMPORTANCE OF SME ACTIVITY IN CROSS CULTURAL MARKETING

Of the huge number of SMEs only a small percentage, perhaps less than 5%, has the ambition and capability to grow significantly. How many of them are likely to be involved in cross cultural marketing is difficult to estimate.

The British Chamber of Commerce suggest that 25% of small and medium-sized firms export occasionally and 38% frequently, but only 21% export over half of their turnover. Recent research suggested of the 100 fastest growing firms in the UK, 50% did not show evidence of any export activity and less than 15% of the firms achieved more that 50% of their turnover from exports

The SME sector has also become more important as a creator of wealth and employment due to the downsizing in global firms. Large global firms are reducing their workforces across the world, and concentrating on increasingly out-sourcing their non-core components, often to smaller firms. Employment in the public sector has been decreasing during this same period due to the extensive privatisation of public sector owned utilities and agencies, such as gas, electricity, water, and telephones. Further to this an increased volume of public sector services, such as cleaning and catering have been contracted out to private organisations. In many countries this has left the small and medium-sized firms sector as the only significant growing source of wealth and employment.

The role and contribution of small and medium sized firms in the exports of an economy has however received increasing attention. The interest reflects both a national government concern with generating greater exports and the increasing focus on competitiveness in cross cultural markets by SMEs themselves.

However despite this many SMEs ignore the potential of their products and services to be marketed across cultures and concentrate instead on their domestic markets. Even in the 21st century many SMEs regarded exporting as an *add on activity* and so withdraw from international markets when orders in the home market improve or conditions on international markets became unfavourable. By contrast, a small but significant minority succeed on international markets and show a strong commitment to further expansion in their international activities. Grimes et al. (2007) developed a profile of the internationalising firms and it is possible to use this to characterise firms at each stage of internationalisation.

302

CROSS CULTURAL MARKETING STRATEGIES

ILLUSTRATION 1 THE AFRICAN CONTEXT

African cultural dynamics are evident not only in the management of SMEs and family owned enterprises in Sub-Saharan Africa but in larger and state owned corporations (Darley and Blankson, 2008). Overseas companies seeking to do business with them would benefit therefore from an increased awareness of African cultural values and beliefs.

There are four main areas for consideration for overseas businesses wishing to make links with African companies: organisational behaviour, buyer-seller interaction, collaborative partnerships, and negotiation.

Organisational behaviour

The concept of *ubuntu* or reciprocity means that management policies respect elders, allow for fulfillment of social obligations, and recognise the role of symbolism and religion as well as the authority of position with hierarchy.

Buyer-seller interaction

Particular consideration should be given to nonverbal communications, context, and notions of authority. As respect for elders is important it follows that authority increases with age. This has an impact on the choice of style for a sales presentation as well as the choice of representative making the pitch.

Collaborative partnerships

In the African context networks and relationships are vital to the success of SMEs. African firms attitude to collaborative partnerships are characterised by extensive communication, consultation, and interaction.

Negotiations

The African negotiation strategy tends to take on a problem solving approach in order to identify options suitable to both parties. The negotiated outcomes should promote the development of a long-term relationship and aim for long term goals. Hierarchy is an ever present influence in the negotiation process.

With these factors in mind SMEs can be categorised as follows:

DOMESTIC SMES

The vast majority of SMEs provide lower income per hour than is possible from employment in another organisation. Examples of this are the small convenience store where the whole family might be involved in the enterprise. Community enterprises are typically supported by public funds because they are seen as not simply providers of employment but also as change agents in achieving greater social inclusion, better health, and improved education and housing. The challenge for them, as they achieve success in economic regeneration, is how to convert from their initial 'social funding dependency' to become businesses within the mainstream business community.

The impact of this segment on the economy is limited because over the long term the number of births of new companies is often cancelled out by the number of deaths. Over

303

shorter periods, however, the segment can be dramatically affected by changes in the national economy in general, and the local economy in particular (for example, if a major local employer closes down and has a knock-on effect on dependent businesses). New businesses in this sector can have a high displacement effect on the existing business base. For example there are a relatively fixed number of hairdressers, local shops, car mechanics and market traders that are needed in the local economy and, in order to succeed, the new local businesses have to take customers from the existing firms, so putting them at risk.

Cross cultural marketing, therefore, has little relevance to the majority of these businesses other than where it poses the threat of competition. In practice however, a few lifestyle firms find a business formula, sometimes by accident, that is viable in cross cultural markets, and so the firm becomes more ambitious as the opportunity for growth is realised.

ILLUSTRATION 2 KENNY'S BOOKSHOP

Family run bookshop Kenny's branched out from the high street by offering its products online over 20 years ago. Exports now account for 70% of their turnover and they have a warehouse of over 1 million titles in order to fulfill order from all over the world. In the last few years they have been granted the lucrative status as official supplier to the National Library of China.

Conor Kenny, the owner of the Galway based business, advises SMEs not to be put off exporting just because there are already large competitors in the global marketplace. He reminds SME's that there may always be a niche for them that the big players have overlooked.

Kenny's USP is specialist Irish-interest titles however another important tool in the fight to make a sale, according to their web sales manager, Karen Golden, is price. They use price comparison technology to continually compare and re-price their products in order to keep one step ahead of the competition. This doesn't prevent them working collaboratively with the competition however. Kenny's acts almost like a cooperative by carrying listings of booksellers on its website as a means of attracting buyers to the site.

NETWORKED SMEs

For many SMEs the resources required to familiarise themselves with foreign markets are limited so the opportunity to gain this information through their current networks and relationships is vital. According to Agndal and Chetty (2007) there are two key types of relationships: business relationships at the level of the organisation, for example with suppliers and distributors, and social relationships which are reliant on the involvement of an individual.

Crick and Chaudhry (2010) in a study of UK based Asian owned businesses conclude that Asian transnational entrepreneurs increase their competitiveness by maximising their relationships with contacts in their country of origin. By having a strong trusted network which includes family and friends they were able to develop collaborative ventures, access resources, and set up manufacturing operations in India to compete with cheaper imported goods from, for example, China.

Mangold and Faulds (2009) point out that consumer like to network with likeminded people. Social networking media is increasingly used by SMEs as a means of accessing consumer feedback as well as a cost effective marketing communications tool. Advances in technology have enabled businesses to develop a networking platforms and blog sites which encourage users to generate content and interact with other clients. Mulhern (2009) says that this usage of digital media promotes extended understanding of the consumer and encourages loyalty.

ILLUSTRATION 3 MASALA MASALA

Masala Masala was set up by London based lawyer Priya Lakhani when she saw a gap in the market for fresh, healthy, authentic Indian sauces. To see how her sauces would fair in the mass market, she tested them on her non-Indian friends with positive results.

This sense of community and sharing has been incorporated into the business model via a blog facility on their website which allows the general public to swap recipes. The company website and Facebook group also promotes The Masala Masala project, which offers a homeless person in India a hot meal for every pot of sauce sold. It pays charities, including Save the Children, to feed slum dwellers in Mumbai and Tamil Nadu in the south.

SUPPLY CHAIN SMEs

The downsizing that has occurred in many global firms as a response to the global slow down since 2009 has led firms to think about what is their core competence and answer the question what business are we really in? The response to this question has led a number of firms operating globally to identify those components and services which were parts of the overall product offer but which they regard as being peripheral to their business. As a result of this many of these large corporations have decided to outsource more of their supplies.

In a study of Indian SMEs within the manufacturing sector, it was observed that developing their position in the supply chain was given strategic importance when considering competitive advantage. This is because most Indian SMEs supply components or parts to larger organisations and original equipment manufacturers (Singh et al., 2010).

Loane (2006) found that internet usage had become essential to supply chain SMEs for them to upgrade their business processes and operations in order to collaborate effectively with their multinational clients.

SMEs WITH CONCENTRATED EXPANSION INTO FOREIGN MARKETS

Whether as the result of an unsought opportunity or necessity through saturation in the domestic market, many SMEs internationalise by targeting a limited number of overseas markets. Steve Smith, chairman of consultant Quest Worldwide, advises small businesses to identify emerging markets in fast growing cities such as Shanghai and focus on them one at a time (*Sunday Times* October 19, 2008).

In a 2007 study of small or medium-sized British retailers, it was found that organisations that traded in the luxury goods market chose to focus the internationalisation strategy on fashionable cities around the world such as Paris and New York as well as trading on their

English style to increase their appeal to overseas markets (Hutchinson, Alexander, Quinn, and Doherty).

SMEs WITH DISPERSED EXPANSION INTO FOREIGN MARKETS

Many SMEs internationalise by targeting customers rather than countries. This is typical in niche markets where the SME offers adapted products or services to meet the customer specification. The geographical location of these customers is less relevant and may result in the business trading all over the world.

Some SMEs view dispersed expansion as a way of minimising the risk of dependency on concentrated foreign markets, overcoming the constraints of a small domestic market and maximising on opportunities identified through marketing research activities. According to McNaughton (2003), these firms may set out to reach a number of markets at once or may add to their portfolio, learning from past experiences.

BORN GLOBAL SMEs

Within this segment are hyper growth firms that typically experience growth in turnover and employees in excess of 100% over a three-year period. Typically they identify and exploit a unique and defendable niche in the market and develop products and services that are 'leading edge'. These are the firms that tend to make the news. In the last few years many technologically based businesses have found it necessary to be extremely ambitious in order to survive and grow and are 'born global'. These companies market their products and services around the world, and thus face the challenges of cross cultural marketing from the first days of their existence. However, it is likely that the majority of new technology innovations will be relatively less culturally sensitive, and thus require a less locally adapted marketing approach, than products and services that are competing in more traditional business sectors.

According to Andersson (2004) the attitude of the owner or director of a firm in the early stages of development is very important in high growth industries. Firms led by entrepreneurs with a positive attitude to early internationalisation tend to integrate this approach into their company culture.

THE INTERNATIONALISATION PROCESS

Motivations and barriers

In many cases the SME will have overcome significant attitudinal barriers as they begin to look on cross cultural marketing as akin to looking for new customers in the next town, next state or on another coast. According to Andersson (2004) cultural differences can vary from industry to industry as well as from region to region therefore analysis of these differences must be carried out at industry level.

Traditionally areas which firms have identified as barriers to internationalisation centre on:

- Fear of bureaucracy;
- Trade barriers in foreign markets;
- Transportation difficulties;
- Lack of trained personnel;

306

CROSS CULTURAL MARKETING STRATEGIES

- Lack of incentive to move out of the domestic market;
- Lack of coordinated government assistance;
- Unfavourable conditions in international markets;
- Slow payment by buyers;
- Lack of competitive products;
- Payment defaults;
- Language barriers.

Thus, for many SMEs their expansion into international markets can be a result of them overcoming such fears due to necessity when the environment in which they are operating becomes unfavorable and so the expansion into international markets becomes a matter of survival. Adverse environmental stimuli can include such things as:

- adverse domestic market conditions;
- downturn in their local economy;
- increased competition from international suppliers;
- the demands of their customers to supply them internationally;
- the need to reduce unacceptable levels of inventories;
- a downturn in the home market meaning they have excess capacity;
- The need to spread the risk of business across several markets.

Equally, however, the stimuli to SMEs developing internationally can be a deliberate proactive strategy to develop the business further, in which case the stimulus to do so could be due to such things as:

- the company identifying specific attractive profit and growth opportunities;
- seeing competitive advantage in other markets through the repositioning of their product or service;
- public policy programmes for export promotion;
- the changing of foreign country regulations to provide opportunities;
- the realisation their company possesses a differential advantage in key export markets;
- the presence of an internationally minded manager;
- the opportunity to better utilise management talent and skills;
- management beliefs about the value of cross cultural marketing.

If a company sees only limited growth opportunities in the home market for a proven product it may well see market diversification as a means of expansion. This could mean new market segments within a domestic market but it may well mean geographic expansion in foreign markets. Thus companies try to spread risks and reduce their dependence on any one market. For example BF Rail, a firm in the north of the UK traditionally obtained 90% of its sales from one customer – the company controlling the coal mines in the region in which it was located. When many of the coal mines began to close, BF Rail soon realised if they were to survive they needed to pursue a strategy of market diversification through international expansion.

Alternatively the firm may identify market gaps. The proactive company with a well-managed marketing information system may identify foreign market opportunities through its research system. This could, of course, be by undertaking formal structured research or by identifying opportunities through a network of contacts scanning international markets for potential opportunities.

307

An economic recession can provide opportunities for internationalisation for entrepreneurs and SMEs. In particular, during an economic downturn SMEs can exploit the favorable exchange rates to trade overseas and offset the weakness in the domestic market. On the other hand, however, difficulty accessing finance from risk averse lenders can make SMEs vulnerable.

The capability that that the World Wide Web has to bring together disperse and fragmented markets has been a significant factor affecting SME internationalisation. It has had the effect of enabling specialist suppliers to reach a global audience, niche suppliers to create a global niche business, and supply chain members to more effectively contribute to the value chain of major internationals. Loane (2006) observes that small entrepreneurial organisations demonstrate significant internet usage to support their overseas activities. In particular she notes that the internet and associated technologies are used not only for communications via email or social networks and marketing via websites but also as a knowledge building tool, a distribution channel, and a means of enhancing business processes.

CATEGORIES OF INTERNATIONAL DEVELOPMENT

According to a report by the British Chamber of Commerce, firms competing on cross cultural markets can be categorised by examining their attitudes and behaviour towards competing internationally. They can be categorised into four segments:

- **Opportunists** make up 37% of SME exporters and tend to be the smallest type of business in terms of employee numbers and turnover. They are reactive when it comes to export sales, do not research markets or develop written export strategies or rely on export sales. They sell directly to the customer rather than an agent or a distributor and do not tailor their services or products.
- **Developers** make up 17% of SME exporters. They are also reactive and tend not to research markets although they may have some level of strategy in place. In contrast to opportunists, their export turnover is 50% of their total annual turnover and there will be limited adaptation of products and services.
- **Adaptors** make up 26% of SME exporters. Their export turnover is also around 50% and they have a dispersed global presence. Although they may carry out some limited research they tend to learn as they go along and adapt accordingly. They are well positioned for export growth and demonstrate an awareness of missed opportunities.
- **Enablers** make up 20% of SME exporters. They are proactive and make strategic choices about which markets to move into. They demonstrate an awareness of their customers' requirements and tailor their products and services to meet them.

MODES OF ENGAGEMENT

In the early stages of international development SMEs may treat cross cultural markets as purely short-term economic opportunities to be pursued in order to maximise short-term profit. As firms become more involved in international markets they treat the resulting business opportunities as strategic to company development. Successful firms invariably build a distinctive competitive position across a range of cross cultural markets. In examining cross cultural marketing in SMEs, the type of mode of engagement employed and how firms build a competitive advantage across a range of markets, is therefore an important area of consideration.

CROSS CULTURAL MARKETING STRATEGIES

In exploiting cross cultural market opportunities to generate revenue from international markets, SMEs have a number of modes of engagement to choose from. The main options we will consider in this section are as follows:

- direct exporting;
- indirect exporting;
- licensing.

In choosing an appropriate method of engagement there are a number of marketing and environmental factors, such as the nature and power of competition, the existing and anticipated tariff and non-tariff barriers and the nature of the product itself, company factors, such as its size and financial resources, skills, ambition, and attitudes to international trade to take into account. However, firms consider three key strategic criteria too. The different methods of engagement require considerably different levels of investment. The methods offer very different levels of involvement in the market. For example, handing over many of the marketing activities in another country to an intermediary means the company may have little direct control over the marketing mix in that country, for example, its image, market positioning, and reputation. Finally, the methods pose different levels of risk to both finances and reputation if the new market venture underperforms or fails.

Indirect exporting

For firms that have little inclination or few resources for international marketing, the best option is to allow others to sell their products overseas. Indirect exporting allows them to benefit from opportunities that arise, such as selling excess capacity with the least possible convenience and expense. This method means that low levels of investment are needed and their involvement in the market will be low. Whilst financial risk is normally low problems can occur because of the firm's disconnection from the market. If the customer demand changes suddenly the indirect exporter may not become aware until it is too late to respond.

Direct exporting

Direct exporting is perhaps the most common form of international development and typically involves more proactively in carefully selecting and managing an agent or distributor to handle the export sales. To be successful the exporter and intermediary must both be motivated and committed to the activity and be prepared to make the necessary investment in time and resources to understand the overseas market share, the marketing operations, and decision making in order to reduce the potential risk.

Licensing

For innovative small firms with creative new products and services, the challenge is to maximise the global sales potential before competitors find a way to exploit similar ideas and market opportunities. The investment required to do this alone is beyond the resources of most small firms and licensing provides an opportunity to achieve global sales and a significant income stream without the expense of production or hiring marketing, sales and operations staff. Licensing might include brands, products, characters, software, themes, and technology and process know-how.

309

STRATEGY DEVELOPMENT

The strategy development process

Having considered the various categories of SME modes of engagement in internationalisation, we now turn to the factors which influence the strategic marketing development of SMEs.

There are an infinite number of strategies that an SME can adopt, but as they become more sophisticated they increasingly focus on meeting the needs of their chosen markets and differentiating their offer from that of their competitors.

The principal approach to cross cultural strategy development follows three stages (normally referred to as segmentation, targeting, and positioning – STP markets):

1. Identification of the various consumer *segments* that exist within the business sector, using the various segmentation methods. It is important for SMEs to define cross-border segments with clearly identifiable requirements that it is able to serve.
2. The firm must then *target* the segments which appear to be most attractive in terms of their size, growth potential, the ease with which they can be reached, and their likely purchasing power.
3. In seeking to defend and develop its business the firm needs to *position* its products or services in a way that will distinguish them from those of its local and international competitors and build up barriers which will prevent those competitors from taking its business. Of course by specifically positioning to meet the requirements of its chosen segments (e.g., for a premium product), it may also be saying to other segments that it cannot met their needs (e.g., for an inexpensive product).

INTERNATIONAL MARKETING SEGMENTATION

Market segmentation is the strategy by which a firm partitions a market into submarkets or segments that are likely to manifest similar responses to marketing inputs. The aim is to identify the markets on which a company can concentrate its resources and efforts. That way it can achieve maximum penetration of that market, rather than going for perhaps a market-spreading strategy where the company aims to achieve a presence, however small, in as many markets as possible. The two main bases for segmenting international markets are by geographical criteria (i.e., countries) and transnational criteria (i.e., individual decision makers.)

Country based segmentation

The traditional practice is to use a country based classification system as a basis for selecting international markets to enter. The Business Portfolio matrix, shown in Figure 19.1 encourages companies to classify potential target countries in three categories:

Primary markets are the best opportunities for long-term strategic development. Companies may want to establish a permanent presence in these countries and so conduct a thorough research programme. Firms expect to earn at least 30% of export turnover in primary markets.

Secondary markets are where opportunities are identified but political or economic risk is perceived as being too high to make long-term irrevocable commitments. As a result these markets would be handled in a more pragmatic way due to the potential risks

310

CROSS CULTURAL MARKETING STRATEGIES

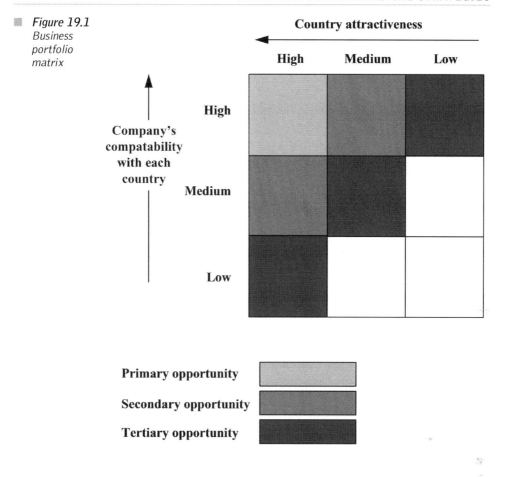

Figure 19.1 Business portfolio matrix

identified. A comprehensive marketing information system would be needed to continually monitor the situation. Usually secondary markets account for between 10–30% of export turnover

Tertiary markets are the catch-what-you-can markets. These markets will be perceived as high risk and so the allocation of resources will be minimal. Objectives in such countries would be short-term and opportunistic; companies would give no real commitment and would not carry out significant research.

Figure 19.1 illustrates the Business Portfolio matrix. The horizontal axis evaluates the attractiveness of each country on objective and measurable criteria (e.g., size, stability, and wealth). The vertical axis evaluates the firm's compatibility with each country on a more subjective and judgmental basis. Primary markets would score high on both axes.

It has long been recognised that SMEs, when operating on cross cultural markets, identify their primary markets as the ones where they feel most culturally at ease. Thus, the perception of the firm is that the psychological distance between the international market and their home market (known as the psychic distance) is relatively small. In cross cultural marketing the psychic distance effect is usually a function of the firm's perception of risk and their knowledge of foreign market conditions. Firms will reduce the degree of commitment and risk exposure in markets where the gap is perceived to be much wider and these they term as tertiary markets.

The approach is a particularly useful device for a company operating in a portfolio of markets to prioritise market opportunity. Once the prime country markets have been identified, companies usually then use standard techniques to segment the markets within countries using such variables as demographic/economic factors, life styles, consumer motivations, geography, buyer behaviour, psychographics, etc.

The problem, however, is that depending on the information base, it may be difficult to fully formulate secondary segmentation bases and achieve consistency across markets. The approach can run the risk of leading to a differentiated marketing approach, which may leave the company with a very fragmented international strategy.

Transnational segmentation

If a company is to try and achieve a consistent and controlled marketing strategy across all its international markets, it needs a transnational approach to its segmentation strategy. To achieve a transnational segmentation approach, the country as a unit of analysis is too large to be of operational use. An alternative approach is to examine the individual decision maker using such variables as demographic, psychographic and behavioural criteria.

Demographic variables have obvious potential as cross-national segmentation criteria. The most commonly used variables include sex, age, income level, social class and educational achievement Psychographic segmentation involves using 'lifestyle' factors in the segmentation process. Appropriate criteria are usually of an inferred nature and concern consumer interests and perceptions of 'way of living' in regard to work and leisure habits and include activities, interests and opinions. Objective criteria, normally of a demographic nature may also be helpful when defining life segments. *Research International*, researching the transnational segments of young adults, globally divided them into four broad categories. '*Enthusiastic materialists*' are optimistic and aspirational and to be found in developing countries and emerging markets like India and Latin America. '*Swimmers against the tide*' on the other hand demonstrate a degree of underlying pessimism and tend to live for the moment and are likely to be found in southern Europe. In northern Europe, the US and Australasia are the '*New realists*', looking for a balance between work and leisure with some underlying pessimism in outlook and, finally, the '*complacent materialists*' defined as passively optimistic and located in Japan.

Behavioural variables also have a lot of potential as a basis for global market segmentation. In particular, attention to patterns of consumption and loyalty in respect of product category and brand can be useful, along with a focus on the context for usage. Variables such as the benefit sought or the buying motivations may be used. Behaviourally defined segments may be identified in terms of a specific aspect of behaviour that is not broad enough to be defined as a 'lifestyle'. An example of this is the extremely wealthy travellers who tend to buy the same fashion brands, stay at the same hotels and buy the same luxury products. This group not only includes the wealthy from traditionally wealthy nations but also those newly rich entrepreneurs from previously closed economies

Despite the attractiveness of using individualistic characteristics, it is apparent that there is strong potential for significant differences in the patterns of consumer behaviour within global segments derived using this method. Also international similarities in lifestyle and behaviour do tend to be specific, and relevant primarily to specialist products and niche markets.

Parallels can be drawn for the Business to Business market, where the nature of the product or service and the overall market context might determine whether a country based

312

CROSS CULTURAL MARKETING STRATEGIES

approach or a transnational approach is most appropriate. For example, a country based segmentation approach might be most appropriate where there are many customers located in each country that frequently require high levels of local support from a service provider. A transnational approach might be the most appropriate in a situation where the exporter has a few potential customers located around the world with specialised requirements.

As more and more SMEs build up timely and robust customer information through web enabled traffic either by email, web traffic, or online purchasing, their ability to do this effectively has been greatly enhanced as a recent survey carried out by GetResponse (2010) identified.

ILLUSTRATION 4: USING WEB TRAFFIC TO DEVELOP SEGMENTATION STRATEGIES

Email traffic now gives SMEs much more potential to be creative yet practical in the way they segment their customer base. According to GetResponse's (2010) Email Marketing Trends Study, over half (59.4%) of small and medium-sized firms segment their consumer lists and email leads according to their recipients' professed interests. Well over a third of SMEs also segment their customers by their click rate activity. This of course gives SMEs the opportunity not to just segment customers by what they look like but how they behave and perhaps more important, how they seek their information. This gives small firms a unique insight into how best to talk and communicate with their customers, irrespective of what culture they sit in. Purchasing behaviour is also a useful segmentation criterion for companies who offer online purchasing. Nearly 30% of SME's segment customers by their customers purchase history.

However passive characteristics such as demographics are still seen as vital with nearly a third of SMEs using demographics as a segmentation criteria.

Simon Grabowski, founder of GetResponse, said: 'Today's marketers are mindful of the importance of delivering relevant content and one-to-one messaging based on preferences and behaviours. It's all about putting the human element back into marketing'.

Adapted from: www.marketscan.co.uk/ March 2010

Such approaches as these enable marketers to design strategies at a cross cultural segment level and so take a more consumer-orientated approach to international marketing. In prioritising markets, SMEs who may operate in a large number of geographical markets but with few customers may need to use existing customer data as their primary information base for segmenting existing and potential customers. Some writers argue that companies still need a secondary segmentation stage to identify the key countries where these transnational segments can be found and that country environments (legal, political, social, and economic) necessitate different marketing mix strategies, such as promotion and distribution.

Targeting approaches

For SMEs the key decision of targeting therefore will largely result from the methodology they have used to segment their international markets. If they have used a culturally or geographically based methodology the major targeting decision will relate to which country markets they are going to select and then how they should develop a market share within each country. Given the limited resources of SMEs and the narrow margin for failure it is vital that their method of targeting country markets is effective.

Firms that establish a domestic base first before selecting further country market involvement develop either through an incremental process of country market diversification, or by concentrating in a few countries following an initial expansion period. In this case the SME's may concentrate their activities in a small number of markets in which a significant market share can be built. SMEs often select countries because of the close psychic distance, the network of contacts they have made there or because they are able to piggyback on a larger organisation in that market.

Following a market-concentration strategy enables a firm to achieve market specialisation, economies of scale, market knowledge, and a high degree of control. For these reasons government support agencies often recommend that small firms follow a market concentration strategy in order to concentrate resources and achieve a greater market share. However, this conflicts with the views of the SME following a niche marketing strategy where with such a small potential market share in any one market greater profitability is viewed as being best achieved by spreading across a number of markets.

Many SMEs successfully operating across a number of cross cultural markets view themselves as international niche marketers, not necessarily as exporters to a particular foreign country market. Once they have exploited that particular niche, they look elsewhere in order to develop and for this reason they follow a market diversification strategy. Thus customer development in a number of cross cultural markets is more important than market share acquisition in the country they had already entered. This is particularly important for 'Born Global' firms that are building a business around new technology. They must develop relationships with key customers in the markets that will be most influential in the diffusion of the new idea. Parrish et al. (2006) explain how niche marketing can be used in a mature sector, such as the global textile sector, to increase competitiveness, despite the presence of strong rivals.

Firms can also become a strong force in a narrow specialised market of one or two segments across a number of country markets. An example of one such company is Macalloy in illustration 5.

ILLUSTRATION 5 MACALLOY

Macalloy is a medium-sized company based in the UK that has grown very rapidly. It manufactures and supplies tensioning devices used in construction projects to support the roofs of large buildings and bridges, such as Burj Al Arab Hotel, Dubai, Korean World Trade Centre Pyramid, and the Millau Viaduct, illustrated on its website at www.macalloy.co.uk. It has a significant share of a niche market which it has exploited by targeting clients that develop and build such projects. The company uses it networks to scan the environment and ensure that it hears of any proposed project at an early stage. Whilst the company builds its capability to deliver and support projects in particular regions or countries where it expects growth in major construction, its main focus is to target the major global companies that undertake these major capital projects.

Adapted from: www.macalloy.co.uk. March 2010

CROSS CULTURAL MARKETING STRATEGIES

If a firm has used transnational approaches to segment their markets they may be well placed to develop a market diversification strategy and expand into a number of cross cultural markets whilst only seeking to gain a superficial presence in each one. This market diversification approach reduces market risks, enables firms to exploit the economies of flexibility and be more adaptable to different market needs.

Often firms following a market diversification strategy are more proactive than SMEs pursuing a market concentration approach and attach greater importance to the pursuit of minimising market risk by operating in a number of different markets.

As said before, web based marketing has made it easier for SMEs to operate across country borders and made it much easier for SMEs to view their international markets in terms of customers, and not necessarily in terms of countries. This is leading many SMEs to seek the most profitable customers irrespective of the number of countries in which they are located. This is important as it gives them the means of focussing their strategies towards the needs of their customers and a much clearer view of how their products should be positioned in those markets. However, Servais et al. (2007) explain that even born global SMEs use the internet only to a limited extent to sell their products but rather use it as a tool to support existing relationships.

Generic positioning strategies

Having identified the target segments, the SME must then develop its unique and distinct positioning by building upon its source of competitive advantage. In order to create competitive advantage, Porter (1985) suggested that firms should adopt one of three generic strategies: cost leadership, which requires the firm to establish a lower cost base than its local or international competitors; a focussed strategy, where the firm concentrates on one or more narrow segments and thus builds a specialist knowledge of the target segment; or differentiation, where the firm emphasises particular benefits in the product, service, or marketing mix, that customers might perceive to be both important and a significant improvement over competitive offers.

It is very difficult in cross cultural marketing for SMEs to follow a cost leadership strategy or even entertain aspirations of being the cheapest in their markets. Those SME's that adopt a low-cost strategy to achieve cost leadership can be potentially vulnerable to price competition, either from local firms in the foreign country market or larger multinationals temporarily cutting prices to force the SME out of that market. Usually successful firms will choose to build competitive advantage by avoiding price competition and focussing on the achievement of margins through focus or differentiation. The problem for small firms pursuing a low-cost strategy is that it may lead them to put too much emphasis on internal matters in their efforts to simply contain costs rather than delivering superior value in the international market. To be successful on cross cultural markets, SMEs need to overcome the double hurdle of managing costs whilst at the same time, competing on added value.

Given the limited ability of small firms to pursue a low-cost strategy, superior performance is often viewed as being best achieved by delivering superior customer value through differentiated products/services for carefully selected market niches. Thus it is not the product/service strength alone that is a critical factor in cross cultural markets, but how the firm builds competitive advantage by creating superior value for its customers through its total product and service offer, supported by the effective use of the marketing mix.

Firms seek to differentiate their products from competitors in cross cultural markets either by product innovation or by adding value through additional services, for example, by

315

offering high levels of customer support and technical advice. SMEs competing in international markets do so with limited resources, and so any cross cultural marketing strategy they pursue must be developed within that context. Successful firms will invest resources either in developing the capability to add value to their product offering to targeted customers worldwide or invest resources in ensuring they maintain superior product performance ahead of competitors worldwide in specific targeted cross cultural niches.

Many SMEs base their cross cultural marketing strategy on the generic strategy that has given them competitive advantage in domestic markets and then attempt to apply this same successful strategy in international markets. Again, however, their limited resources often force them to make a change to their strategy. They may have largely used a pull strategy in their domestic marketing and thus directed much of their promotional activity at their ultimate customers, whereas in international markets they frequently adopt a less costly push strategy. This means the firm promotes only to the intermediaries in the distribution channel and expects them to promote (or push) the products and services to the final customer.

Of fundamental importance to the development of an effective cross cultural marketing strategy for some SMEs is having a very strong position in the home country. US firms have benefited from having a huge potential domestic market. By contrast SME's from emerging markets and from countries with smaller domestic markets often have to export merely to survive. There can, be some dangers in entering sophisticated markets without a clear plan and robust business model. even though Crick and Spence (2005) found that internationalisation strategy formation for high performing SMEs is not always systematic and capable of being described by one single theory. Some firms take an opportunistic approach towards their internationalising strategy and it is necessary to take a more holistic view of the organisation and its context to explain its decisions.

Balabanis and Katsikea (2003) explain the further dimensions and suggest that there is some evidence to suggest that an entrepreneurial approach, which involves risk-taking and being proactive and innovative in developing strategies is useful in international marketing development.

A small number of dynamic SMEs challenge the assumptions on which markets are based and create uncontested markets (Kim and Mauborgne, 2005) where they are able to grow very rapidly. Cirque du Soleil and Dyson (see illustration) are examples of companies that grew very quickly to become global players by meeting the common needs and interests of global customers. There is of course the danger that the most successful companies eventually get swallowed up by the multinationals. Two companies that adopted an ethical stance in business were taken over by global giants, Bodyshop by L'Oréal, and Ben and Jerry's by Unilever.

ILLUSTRATION 6 FAST GROWTH FIRMS

For SMEs the key to achieving fast growth and major international success is not about just being cheaper or offering slightly better value than their bigger, more powerful competitors but creating a new market that makes competitors irrelevant. Two organisations that have done this are Dyson and Cirque du Soleil.

Cirque du Soleil at www.cirquedusoleil.com started off as a small group of French street performers. The company challenged the idea that a circus should have animals, which were expensive to keep. Moreover, many potential customers believed that it was no longer really acceptable to keep animals caged in circuses. Also circuses were largely targeted at children, but this meant a limit to ticket prices. Instead they created spectacular shows, without animals, for adults that combined performance, art and music to become a worldwide phenomenon.

After many years of trying, inventor James Dyson released a revolutionary vacuum cleaner onto the UK market that dispensed with the need for a bag and achieved better cleaning performance than its rivals. The cleaners were also a change from convention. They were brightly coloured, had a highly functional, chunky design, and the dirt that had been collected was clearly visible. They were priced much higher than the competition, but because there was no direct competition the company grew rapidly to become a worldwide success. The company has continually innovated (www.dyson.co.uk). For example, it had to produce a much smaller cleaner than normal for the Japanese market because of the small size of apartments. This, however, had a side benefit. At the same the company was trying to develop a new hand drier for public lavatories but was having trouble designing a sufficiently small but powerful motor. The development of the motor for the Japanese vacuum cleaners proved to be the solution for the hand drier problem.

NETWORK DEVELOPMENT

The primary focus in this chapter has been examining the cross cultural marketing strategies of SMEs. So far we have examined the varying levels of involvement SME's have in cross cultural markets and discussed the need for an SME to select an appropriate segmentation approach to target priority customer groups across cultures. We have also looked at how SMEs establish a competitive positioning. However central to the achievement of a viable long-term, cross cultural marketing strategy is the way the SME manages it organisational activities across international markets. SME's have very limited resources to build any organisational structures and so rely heavily on developing a network of partners across markets in order to implement their cross cultural strategies. Research has shown that successful SMEs appear to exhibit particular competence in their ability to build and utilise a series of relationships as a cost effective (time and resources) way of identifying new market opportunities and reducing the risk of entering unknown markets.

The networking model can provide SMEs with the resources and the means to compete effectively in cross cultural markets. Through a global network many smaller firms without the resources themselves can access the expertise, market knowledge and routes to market which they could not achieve alone. Hardman et al. (2005) suggest that to compete effectively with the largest competitors, small organisations have to achieve virtual scale by working in alliances to achieve the necessary leverage. The internet can facilitate this and the success of the use of professional social networking sites has helped smaller firms access much wider business networks across cultures and markets. Previous to this, SMEs often only had the resources to access business networks close to where they were based.

Harris and Wheeler (2005) focus on the role of inter-personal relationships in the internationalisation process and explain that strong, deep relationships are developed in wide social/personal and business situations that do not just provide information and access to networks but, more importantly, can be influential in directing strategy and can lead to the transformation of the firm. A number of studies of born global firms have been made in different country contexts. Mort and Weerawardena (2006) have researched born global firms and highlighted the importance of relationships and networking in enabling the identification and exploitation of market opportunities and facilitating the development of knowledge-intensive products.

A relational strategy is often central to the firm's long-term objective of maintaining their competitiveness in cross cultural markets over time by giving the firm a number of strategic advantages:

- Providing access to markets;
- Building barriers to entry by competitors;
- Improving the level of support to the end user;
- Tying in customers to longer term commitments to market development;
- Improving the speed of access to and accuracy of information on market changes;
- Building repeat business;
- Providing the connections to hold the cross cultural marketing strategy together;
- Improving the effectiveness of communication links.

Firms build partnerships of varying degrees of intensity and use these relationships to enhance their capability to compete in different cultures. These relationships are valuable for a number of reasons. They help the SME to quickly gain the knowledge and information needed for cost effective market entry, to build barriers to competition by establishing a locally responsive, adaptable, and flexible distribution channel, as well as ensuring their customers in different markets around the world obtain effective service. The relationships can, therefore, be the firms' major communication link to their cross cultural markets, both in relaying communications to the market to help build the firm's competitive advantage and relaying information back from the market which provides input into the decision making processes of the firm. Relationships are the process by which the strategy is built, organised, and implemented; it is the glue, a vital piece of the jigsaw.

Asian firms are typically most committed to relationship development as a central element of their cross cultural marketing strategy. Indeed it appears that some Asian firms develop their segmentation strategy around selecting target markets where there are strong cultural ties, as illustration 7 shows.

ILLUSTRATION 7 CROSS CULTURAL MARKETING CHINESE STYLE

Chinese entrepreneurs are developing their cross cultural marketing strategies by using existing networks of contacts. They operate through a network of family and 'clan' relationships in different geographies, political and economic systems. This approach reflects the Chinese culture and the Confucian tradition of hard work, thrift, and respect for one's social network.

This provides the rationale for retaining a small business approach to cross cultural marketing that is capable of a variety of business solutions at relatively low risk. However, Chinese management recognises the need for innovation and growth, and to encourage greater openness to outsiders if they wish to compete effectively in cross cultural markets.

CROSS CULTURAL MARKETING STRATEGIES

Relationship development plays an important role in enabling firms to build the capability to achieve sustainable competitive advantage over the long-term. Central to this is that through their relationships firms develop their knowledge base of the changes occurring in cross cultural markets, thus enabling them to anticipate and deal with the challenges and changes in the marketplace. They use relationships to improve the quality of their decision making by seeking assurances that the decisions that they make are valid and appropriate for the culture of the market in which they are competing. As the managing director of a firm, operating in many different international markets remarked,

> Our information comes from customers around the world, but it's not just customers. Your contacts are in banking and in shipping, and they enable you to actually draw up a picture of what is really happening so you understand the culture of the country, not just what people want you to know.

Networks and relationships therefore can critical to the success of SMEs all over the globe competing in across different cultural markets.

SUMMARY OF KEY IDEAS

Traditionally, explanations for the success of SMEs in cross cultural markets have been sought in the marketing mix paradigm. This has meant the focus of research studies have been on explaining marketing transactions and exchanges rather than a long term strategic focus on competitiveness. Thus traditionally the literature on cross cultural marketing for smaller firms has generally viewed marketing as being treated as a tactical issue by the firms and neglected concern for such things as strategic positioning, the importance of developing a sustainable competitive advantage, quality issues, customer retention, and building relationships.

In practice successful firms develop strategies based on delivering customer satisfaction to their target segments, thus ensuring high levels of customer retention by providing a high quality total product and service offer. In this way they are able to establish clear positioning that is distinctive compared to local and other multinational competition? Central to the achievement of these objectives is the relational strategy developed by the SME and the success they have in developing an integrated network of partners across the cross cultural markets in which they operate.

REVIEW QUESTIONS

1. How can the smaller business compensate for its lack of resources and expertise in cross cultural marketing when trying to enter new markets?

2. How might a small specialist supplier of games software segment its international markets?

3. Many SMEs use their networks of relationships to research their markets. What advantages and pitfalls might there be in adopting this approach?

4. Competitive relationships are increasingly becoming more important in achieving a

---

319

global competitive advantage for SMEs. Why is this so? What are the implications for the making of strategic marketing decisions in a global market?

5. For a cross cultural industry that has been affected significantly by internet marketing, explain how the drivers of internet marketing have affected the way SMEs compete on that market and how their cross cultural marketing strategies have changed.

TEAM ACTIVITIES

1. Identify a particular SME that has successfully managed to compete in across international markets that have seen substantial change. Examine the reasons why they have succeeded to achieve a competitive marketing advantage in such cross cultural markets.
2. Identify the principle challenges that SMEs are likely to face over the next decade. What does your team think are the possible implications of these challenges for SMEs competing on cross cultural markets?
3. What type of information should be collected by an SME trying to develop a cross cultural marketing strategy?
4. Your team have changed from being in a marketing department in a large global business to being the marketing department of a small firm, selling to eight different countries. What differences in terms of strategy, resources, and operations would your team expect to see, and what might the implications be for the team when developing a marketing strategy for your new firm?
5. The biggest challenge for SMEs is growing internationally in a period of recession, in your teams discuss the problems SMEs face in such periods and identify ways in which entrepreneurial management can help to overcome such problems in developing internationally.

CASE STUDY: WILLIAMSON

Williamson is a UK medium-sized business that manufactures specialist kitchen knives. It has exported its products into a number of country markets within Europe and other countries in the world with which typically the UK has had traditional ties. The company is seeking to develop its business in emerging markets that are growing more rapidly than its existing markets. The company markets its products in retail markets for consumers and also through trade channels into the hospitality and catering industry.

As Europe moves closer towards economic integration and retailers and distributors increase their internationalisation, Williamson has found that retailers are increasingly buying on a region-wide basis. The diversity of the brand names and product lines that they have built up in order to meet the specific cultural needs of individual markets is becoming increasingly difficult to sustain as they aim to develop a more efficient and cohesive cross cultural marketing strategy. They have decided they can no longer defend their competitive position in these markets using their existing strategy and have had to refocus their thinking.

Typically, SMEs develop internationally by exporting to countries one after another, so segmenting their markets principally on geographic but perhaps too on cultural criteria and then as they develop their international markets also develop more sophisticated criteria for further segmenting their markets. Williamson has traditionally aimed to develop a strategy to satisfy the varying demands of each market and have segmented their markets on a country by country basis.

They have now started working towards reorienting their international strategy to develop a more integrated approach with a more cohesive and unified brand image. As Mark Darcy, the Managing Director, said:

> As the world becomes more and more integrated then whatever is happening in one market is vitally important to what is happening in another market. You can't consider, for example, Belgium as existing on an island and having nothing to do with what's happening, say in Sweden. You have got to make sure that you're making a similar offering in your policies, they have got to be relevant to the country involved but you do need to be aware of what is happening in other markets.

The first building block of the change in orientation was to move to a customer-based segmentation approach across their international markets. Through this process, they have identified four clusters across their markets. At the same time, they have undertaken a rationalisation exercise in the number of brands and product lines offered. The result has meant that for each market cluster identified they are competing on three price points for each product line:

> Broadly speaking we look for a good, better and best offering in whatever market in which we're operating. In the Iberian cluster, for example, there is a good, better and best offering appropriate to the needs of the market where the best offering is on par with the good offering in Northern Scandinavia.

The stimulus for the change to their strategy has come from the critical changes that they found that were taking place in international markets. It was crucial for Williamson that they built a knowledgeable understanding of those factors and assessed the implications of market changes on the way they developed their strategy rather than simply accepting them in a passive way and relying on quickly reacting to any consequences. They recognised the need to reorient their strategic thinking and develop a potential solution.

The key element in this strategy reorientation process was gaining the insights from their multiple levels of customers. Williamsons did not have the resources to carry out formal market research. Instead they have relied on their network of contacts, both informal and their supply chain partners, to help identify the changes in the environment in the various countries in which they are operating, particularly the relevant political, economic, and legal changes. They have noted that the most important changes have occurred in the competitive landscape with new cheaper alternative suppliers offering competitive products. These new competitors appear suddenly and unexpectedly and Williamson have often found it difficult to predict where the next challenge would come from as they have fought to retain and build relationships with their multinational retailer customers.

Finally, Williamson has noticed that their customers appear to be much more knowledgeable about their products and use social networking sites to discuss the merits of their product against their competitors. Williamson is rather frustrated that it is not able to use easily the positive communications and deal with the negative communications on such sites.

Questions

1. Fully evaluate the advantages and disadvantages of Williamson using their networks and relationships in the markets in which they operate for building an information base to develop a cross cultural marketing strategy.
2. What approach would you advise Williamson to take to develop a segmentation approach that could form the basis of a cross cultural global strategy.

REFERENCES

Agndal, H. and Chetty, S. (2007) The impact of relationships on changes in internationalisation strategies of SME's. *European Journal of Marketing*, 41(11/12), 1449–1474.

Andersson, S. (2004) Internationalization in different industrial contexts. *Journal of Business Venturing*, 19(6), 851–875.

Balabanis, G. I. and Katsikea, E. S. (2003) Being an entrepreneurial exporter: Does it pay? *International Business Review*, 12(2), 233–252.

Crick, D. and Chaudhry, S. (2010) An investigation into UK-based Asian entrepreneurs' perceived competitiveness in overseas markets. *Entrepreneurship and Regional Development*, 22(1), 5–23.

Crick, D. and Spence, M. (2005) The internationalisation of 'high performing' UK high tech SME's: a study of planned and unplanned strategies. *International Marketing Review*, 14(2), 167–185.

Darley, W. K. and Blankson, C. (2008) African culture & business markets: Implications for marketing practices. *Journal of Business & Industrial Marketing*, 23(6), 374–383.

Grimes, A., Doole, I. and Kitchen, P. J. (2007) Profiling the capabilities of SME's to compete internationally. *Journal of Small Business and Enterprise Development*, 14(1), 64–80.

Hardman, D., Messinger, D. and Bergson, S. (2005) Virtual scale: Alliances for leverage, resilience report. *Booz, Allen, Hamilton*. 14 July. www.strategy+business.com

Harris, S. and Wheeler, C. (2005) Entrepreneurs' relationships for internationalisation: Functions, origins and strategies. *International Business Review*, 14(2), 187–207.

Kim, W. C. and Mauborgne, R. (2005) Blue ocean strategy: How to create uncontested market space and make competition irrelevant. *Harvard Business Press*, 179–180.

Loane, S (2006) The role of the internet in the internationalisation of small and medium companies. *Journal of International Entrepreneurship*, 3, 263–277.

Mangold, W. G. and Faulds, D. J. (2009) Social media: The new hybrid element of the promotion mix. *Business Horizons*. 52, 357–365.

McNaughton, R. B. (2003) The number of export markets that a firm serves: Process models versus the born-global phenomenon. *Journal of international Entrepreneurship*, 1(3), 297–311.

Mort, G. S. and Weerawardena, J. (2006) Networking capability and international entrepreneurship. *Journal of International Marketing Research*, 23(5), 549–572.

Mulhern, F. (2009) 'Integrated marketing communications: From media channels to digital connectivity. *Journal of Marketing Communications*, 15(2), 85.

Parrish, E., Cassill, N. and Oxenham, W. (2006) Niche marketing strategy for a mature market place. *Marketing Intelligence and Planning*, 24(7), 694–707.

Porter, M. E. (1985) *Competitive Advantage: Creating and Sustaining Superior Performance*. The Free Press, New York.

CROSS CULTURAL MARKETING STRATEGIES

Servais, P., Madsen, T. K. and Rasmussen, E. S. (2007) Small manufacturing frims involvement in international e-business activities. *Advances in International Marketing*, 2007(17), 297–317.

Singh, R. K., Garg, S. K. and Desmukh, S. G. (2010) The competitiveness of SME's in a globalized economy; observations from China and India. *Management Research Review*, 33, (1), 54–65.

www.britishchambers.org.uk/zones/media/articles-and-comments/don-t-forget-to-do-your-homework. html

www.britishchambers.org.uk/policy/pdf/Language_Survey2.pdf BCC Language Survey the Impact of Foreign Languages on British Business May 2004

FURTHER READING

Doole, I. and Lowe, R. (2008) *International Marketing Strategy, Analysis, Development and Implementation International*, 5th ed. Cengage Learning.

Chapter 20

Marketing planning in small businesses

Frances Ekwulugo

LEARNING OBJECTIVES

After reading the chapter, you will be able to
- Understand the implications of planning for SMEs;
- Understand the marketing planning process;
- Identify the major steps in the marketing planning process;
- Explain what a marketing plan should include;
- Develop the skills required to carry out a marketing plan task.

INTRODUCTION

This chapter discusses the process and importance of marketing planning for SMEs. It is often contended that the formal marketing approach is inappropriate for SMEs largely on account of their relatively small size and structural fluidity. Although SMEs are more flexible than large businesses, they tend to apply a more flexible and informal approach to their management systems. It is believed that the embedded attributes of SMEs militate against conventional planning, but the reality is that a formal approach to marketing planning affords the SME a sense of direction and focus. To deal with this topic, first, we start our discussion by trawling through some of the broader issues that might affect the planning process in SMEs and then focus on the structure of a marketing plan.

CONTRIBUTIONS OF SMEs TO THE ECONOMY

Small businesses are the growth engine of the economy – this is probably true of most economies of the world (Stanworth and Purdy (2003). In the UK, for example, SMEs represent at least 90% of the employers in numerical count and employ about 50% of the workforce. Statistics across different parts of the world mirror similar trends. The success of SMEs comes, in part, from them supposedly being more efficient, flexible, and responsive than their large corporate counterparts. However, large firms have the ability to obtain economies of scale in some industries and are therefore able to exploit resource-capacity advantages. Furthermore, it is claimed that more than 50% of small businesses fail during the first four years of their inception, with the figure much higher in some sectors (Perry, 2001). In part, the underlying reason for this trend is SMEs' inability to systematise their planning processes, thus leading to crises or even failure. Such a high failure rate does not augur well for any economy.

There is a general consensus that the performance of SMEs is important for both the economic and the social development of any country (Brickkmann et al., 2010). From the economic perspective, SMEs have a number of benefits that enable them to grow to become big businesses. Hence, they are seen as the seeds of future big businesses and sources of national economic growth (Kotey, 2005). The advantages that SMEs have over the large-scale competitors are due to their ability to adapt more easily to market conditions (Basu and Goswami, 1999). In many cases, they are able to withstand adverse economic situations due to their flexibility. For example, they could quickly respond to increases in demand and other market exigencies without much delay (Jamal, 2005). Some writers, however, argue that being small makes them more vulnerable during economic downturns (Stanworth and Purdy, 2003). Nevertheless, SMEs add value to the economic system. Additionally, SMEs induce improvements in the efficiency of domestic markets by intensifying competition and making productive use of scarce resources, which facilitates long-term economic growth (LDA, 2004).

The crucial concern is how to nurture SMEs so that they can develop into maturity, sustain their operations, or transition into larger businesses. Essentially, from a marketing perspective, the ability to plan is critically important. This requires developing higher levels of sensitivity to sources of resources, constraints in obtaining resource inputs, assessment of market potentials, possible setbacks in market entry strategies, and general operational dynamics. In practice, SMEs are confronted with a range of constraints, most of which militate against marketing planning efficacy.

CONSTRAINTS

Small businesses experience various problems that constrain their activities, such as ownership and succession crises, lack of access to finance, lack of skills, regulatory issues, access to international markets, lack of support services from support agencies, and inadequate equipment and technology. Start-up capital is a major barrier. It is reported that up to 50% of new businesses cease trading within five years because of poor resources. Only very few that appear to be resilient survive, but they register very limited significant growth, if they grow at all. (Stanworth and Purdy, 2003). However, many studies have reported that not all SMEs want to grow. Some prefer to remain small or retain the 'family business' status. This is not a disadvantage, providing such decisions are arrived at strategically. A small business, playing at the niche level, can achieve success if it 'fills the market'; this is an important lesson from market segmentation. For a range of other growth-oriented firms, the lack of the specialist skills (e.g., managerial skills) that are needed for business development may stunt growth. One way to overcome this barrier is through planning; in this way, firms avoid surprises of severe shock events in their operating environments. Thus, there is an increasing need to plan, not only to provide a basic business plan but also to become adept in conducting market research, financial planning, and capability audits for startups; however, many SMEs are deficient in these areas (Kraus et al., 2006).

MANAGEMENT STYLE

A vast number of SMEs are owner-managed, and it has been identified that the culture of the owner-managers influences how the business is run (Fraser, 2004). In some cases, the owner is directly involved in every important decision on day-to-day issues (e.g., customer enquiries, financial control, production, employee recruitment and rent reviews). Obviously, there are bound to be a number of problems associated with this type of set up. As the owner-manager does everything, naturally some of the required skills to deal with the complex issues in the businesses may be missing (Smallbone et al., 2005; Cook et al., 2003). Overall, studies on the management of SMEs show that their lack of management skills impedes their performance (Smallbone et al., 2005). The question, therefore, is, do the SMEs have adequate management skills to make the right decisions for an effective performance? This is partly a planning issue.

There are now some emerging global dimensions to SMEs' management and planning issues, and these have tended to challenge some of the assumptions about small businesses. Increasingly, many SMEs import goods from abroad and also sell overseas. As a result, they may require large sums of capital and knowledge to deal with international customers (Kotey, 2005). Against this background of SME internationalisation, the importance of best, proven, managerial practices to embed entrepreneurial activities cannot be overestimated. It is unsurprising, then, that companies are urged to be market oriented in order to improve performance

Small businesses typically develop and implement marketing strategies within severely resource-constrained environments. For this reason, some people may be tempted to suggest that marketing may be an unnecessary luxury in SMEs (Blankson and Omar, 2002). However, many authors have found that SMEs do practise marketing but in rather idiosyncratic ways in many instances, especially in the context of family businesses (Blankson and Omar, 2002).

The functions and purpose of management – towards marketing planning

Traditionally, management consists of five functions: planning, organising, communicating, co-ordinating, and controlling. Planning is concerned with setting out objectives; quantifying the targets of achievement for each objective; communicating these targets to other people in the organisation; and selecting the strategies, tactics, policies, programmes, and procedures for achieving the objectives. A marketing plan, which is the outcome of planning marketing tasks, is a document produced to guide the marketing of goods and services of a given organisation: 'Marketing planning is simply a logical sequence and a series of activities leading to the setting of marketing objectives and the formulation of plans for achieving them' (McDonald, 2007, p. 27). Globally, change is occurring at an accelerating rate, with many uncertainties, challenges, and opportunities affecting business operations. Therefore, making marketing decisions requires knowledge and understanding of what the actual situation is, what decisions are likely to arise from the situation, and how the decision itself could be influenced. Therefore, planning involves what to do in the future (objectives), how to do it (strategy), when to do it, and who should do it (tactics). Marketing planning appears to be a simple step-by-step approach, but, in reality, it is very complex. Consequently, there is a need for a formalised process to enable firms to achieve their stated objectives. The approach of relying only on sales forecasts and budgeting is inadequate and outmoded. Marketing planning is more comprehensive and equally more strategic than merely budgeting and sales forecasting.

QUESTIONS EMBEDDED IN MARKETING PLANNING

A marketing plan answers the following questions:

Where are we now (current situation)?

A marketing plan is produced within a context, and this context should be taken into consideration. The SME context is unique to each sector. For example, the possible lack of finance and of managerial skills may necessitate an evaluation of marketing effectiveness, ensuring that internal activities and external factors are properly analysed in relation to the specific context of the SME. An in-depth analysis of the context enables the owner-manager to understand where the business wants to be.

Where do we want to be (objectives)?

Most businesses have mission statements, which are broad statements of the purpose of the business. Business objectives are formulated around the mission statement. Understanding the present position of a firm will logically point the business in the next development direction.

How do we get there (strategy)?

The strategy is normally developed to achieve the stated objectives. It is built around two key areas: the target market and the competitive advantage sought. The ploy is to identify customers and analyse their characteristics, needs, and wants for the purpose of providing 'value' to them. To gain a competitive advantage, the plan will examine the strategies of competitors in comparison with the company's offerings.

How do we know we have arrived (evaluation and control)?

Through planning, organising, and control, organisational tasks are coordinated to achieve marketing effectiveness. Managers control these activities, resources, and people to get the expected results. However, the chosen method of control and evaluation will depend on the values of the manager and on certain organisational contingencies, but the likely impact of managerial style on individuals and groups must be taken into account. The implementation of a successful plan will depend on these matters and on the skills and knowledge which the manager possesses.

THE IMPLICATIONS OF MARKETING PLANNING

Importance

Most SMEs are either unaware of the importance marketing planning or consider such activities to be unhelpful. The usual complaint is a lack of time to spend on what are seen as unnecessary routine tasks. SMEs may not be sure if the planning process is worth the time invested in it, even when they do not know what marketing entails. However, the need for SMEs to understand the external and internal factors which are likely to affect them should be acknowledged. It is equally important for SMEs to understand their customers, specifically, their characteristics and buying behaviours. Marketing planning will help bring all of these together and enable SMEs to exploit future opportunities (Blankson and Omar, 2002).

Planning problems

There are many planning problems in SMEs, and the need to undertake marketing planning could be influenced by the following:

- weak support from top management;
- lack of a plan for planning;

- lack of line management support;
- hostility;
- lack of skills;
- lack of information;
- lack of resources;
- inadequate organisational structure;
- confusion over planning terms;
- number in lieu of written objectives and strategies;
- too much detail, too far ahead;
- once a year ritual;
- separation of operational planning from strategic planning;
- lack of integration.

UNDERSTANDING THE ENVIRONMENT: EXTERNAL ENVIRONMENTAL INFLUENCES

Small businesses are struggling to survive nationally and internationally (Basu and Goswami, 1999). For an organisation to survive and prosper, it must understand and adjust to the external environment (Drucker, 1954). Lack of response to the environment will result in the inability of businesses to meet the needs and wants of their stakeholders (Kotler, 2003). Responding to the environment means matching the capabilities of the organisation with the changing environment. This scenario has meant that the success of SMEs depends in a large part on the formulation and implementation of a viable strategy (Perry, 2001). Here, strategy means the way things are done in the organisation, which is reflected in a firm's short- and long-term responses to the challenges and opportunities posed by the business environment. All indications show that the external environment is generally assumed to be uncontrollable, and it is outside the influence of the organisation (Kotey, 2005). However, external environmental factors are dynamic; they change all the time and therefore influence the SME in major ways.

Competition

The growing number of SMEs has intensified competition among small businesses (Barrett et al., 2002) on the one hand and large businesses on the other. For example, large supermarket chains in the UK, such as Tesco and Sainsburys, are now competing with SMEs in some areas of activity. Whilst some argue that this trend has increased supplier diversity and improved the quality of goods provided (Ram and Smallbone, 1999), many are worried about the future of the SMEs. Therefore, competitive analysis, as a part of the marketing planning process, has taken on a new and central dimension.

THE ANALYSIS STAGE

Market research: The first step in marketing planning is information gathering and analysis. This helps to identify the right market audience and how they could be targeted. It must be noted that the quality of information gathered and the level of analysis will influence decisions made.

Internal Audit: The internal environment could be analysed under the following headings: production, market share, product management, distribution, price, promotion

MARKETING PLANNING IN SMALL BUSINESSES

Table 20.1 PEST factors

Political	legislation, human rights, regulatory constraints, e.g., labelling, product quality, packaging, trade practices, advertising, pricing
Economic	inflation, unemployment, energy, price volatility, materials
Social	education, immigration, emigration, religion, environment, population distribution, and dynamics
Technology	production technology, the internet, cost saving, materials, components, equipment, machinery, methods and systems, and availability of substitutes

finance, sales, profitability, marketing mix variables, human resources, location, and company image.

Customer: For the marketing planning process to be effective, organisations need to be consumer/customer-driven. Thus, it is important to establish why buyers should buy from a local SME and not from the competition. It is equally important for the SME to differentiate its own business from the competition and be able to identify the USP (unique selling proposition). To retain customers, there is a need to develop relationships with them, and to educate, develop, and be able to alter their understanding and attitude towards the firm's product. Developing relationships is particularly important, especially in business-to-business markets.

External analysis: This includes analysing the range of forces, namely, political, economic (in their entirety), and social (demography, culture and attitudes, and consumer), and the technological environment. Table 20.1 shows some examples of the external variables.

The market: To understand the market, the following areas need to be analysed: the total market in terms of size, growth, and trends; market characteristics, development, and trends; prices; physical distribution channels; customer/consumers; and industry practices. It is equally important to analyse competitors and examine demand and supply situations as well as identify who the customers are. Additionally, the analysis should include the identification of the competitive forces in the marketplace. Two concepts that could be used to achieve this are (1) Porter's five forces (entry barriers, buyers' powers, suppliers' power, availability of substitutes, extent of rivalry, and switching costs) and (2) the industry concept of competition (number of sellers and degree of differentiation, entry barriers, exit barriers, cost structures, vertical integration, and global reach). Some other variables to be covered include major competitors, size, market shares/coverage, market standing/reputation, production policies, marketing methods, extent of diversification, personnel issues, international links, profitability, and key strengths and weaknesses.

CONTENTS OF A MARKETING PLAN

Conventionally, the constituent aspects of the marketing plan are as follows:

- SWOT analysis;
- assumptions;
- marketing objectives;
- marketing strategy;
- schedules;
- contingency plan;

329

- financial statements;
- sales forecasts;
- budgets;
- control and evaluation.

Each stage is discussed succinctly as follows:

SWOT analysis: Managers need to understand the organisation's current situation before they can create appropriate strategies; this involves environmental scanning and analysis. They also need to know where their products stand in the market and be able to set realistic objectives. SWOT analysis summarises the audit under the headings of strengths, weaknesses, opportunities, and threats and should be included in the plan. Strengths and weaknesses refer to the company's internal environment, whilst opportunities and threats refer to the external environment. Conducting a SWOT analysis enables organisations to be more focussed. Most SMEs do not tap into their core strengths and thereby miss future opportunities. A SWOT analysis could be subjective, but it does work when it is carefully conducted and can lead to the articulation of marketing objectives (see Table 20.2 for an example of the elements of SWOT).

Assumption: Assumptions are based on real facts and estimates of what can be achieved in consideration of past performance.

Marketing objectives: Objectives are clear statements of what the business intends to achieve. Objectives should be SMART, that is, specific, measurable, attainable, realistic, and timed. To produce a SMART objective, the marketing audit should be taken into consideration to make sure it is based on realistic estimations.

Think and discuss: setting objectives

Examine the objectives of any SME with which you are familiar (you can check out the internet, if more practical). How well do you think these objectives are met?

Table 20.2 Examples of SWOT factors

Strengths	Weaknesses
Abundant financial resources	Lack of strategic direction
Well-known brand name	Limited financial resources
Raking in industry	Weak spending on R and D
Economies of scale	High cost of production
Superior product quality	Poor marketing skills
Committed employees	Under-trained employees
Opportunities	**Threats**
Rapid market growth	Entry of foreign competitors
Rival firms are complacent	Introduction of new substitute products
Changing customer needs/tastes	Product life cycle in decline
Opening of foreign markets	Changing customer needs/taste
New uses of product	Rival firms adopt new strategies
Government deregulation	Increased government regulation
Demographic shifts	Economic downturn
	New technology

MARKETING PLANNING IN SMALL BUSINESSES

Marketing Strategy: To meet the objectives, there is a need to establish strategies. Strategies describe how organisations could achieve their stated marketing objectives. The marketing strategy is usually expressed in terms of the 4 'P's (marketing mix). It is the marketer's challenge to find or develop these 'Ps' in such a way that will meet customers' needs and wants relatively more efficiently than the competition. There are two models that may usefully affect the setting of strategies: the Product Life Cycle (PLC) and the Boston Consulting Matrix (BCG) (these are discussed elsewhere in the book). Also, the Ansoff matrix could provide a useful guide.

For firms to create a strong strategy, they should understand the complexity of customers, competitors, suppliers, channels, and the market. Analysing the internal environment and the external environment will help to understand all the difficulties in the market, as a good plan is based on understanding the market. To formulate a strong strategy, it is important to align the SWOT factors: strength to opportunity and weakness to threat.

Think box: product management

Assume you are the manager of a medium size cosmetic company. Sales for most of your product lines are down because the tastes of women are changing and there are more quality cosmetics in the market that are cheaper than yours.

Discuss the moves you will make to arrest the situation.

Most small businesses treat the marketing strategy as a haphazard activity and make no effort to relate it to the main aim and objectives of the marketing plan. Small businesses should formulate strategies in their own way (not necessarily copying the strategy of big companies). Strategies could be set around the 4 P headings set out in Table 20.3.

Table 20.3 Marketing mix (strategies)

Product	• variety • performance • feature • design • packaging • brand name
Price	• discount • geographical pricing • payment terms • credit terms
Promotion	• advertising • public relations • trade promotion • direct marketing • digital marketing • sales promotion
Distribution	• pre-sale services • point of sale services • post-sale services • support staff • tasks and responsibilities

331

SCHEDULE OF WHAT/WHERE/HOW

The schedule will show the programme for the implementation of action plans and indicate the element of the action plan that is to be carried out by each member of staff and their responsibilities as well as the timetable for carrying them out. This may not be in the main body of the marketing plan, but it could be included in the appendix.

Contingency Plans: A good plan will always have a back-up or contingency plan that will be put into operation if any of the assumptions of the original plan do not materialise.

Financial Statements: The final part of the planning process is to show, in numeric and financial terms, what the outcome of the strategy will be in terms of revenues, costs, and profit.

Budget: Last, there is a need to develop a budget that projects the revenues, expenditures, profits, and cash flows over the planning period. Managers should evaluate the plan and expenditure to determine whether activities and cost are on track.

Control and Evaluation: Considering the marketing audit, control is based on forecasts, budgets, schedules, and metrics. The forecast is prepared based on the optimistic data on previous and future projection of sales and costs. Budgets are prepared based on past records and predicted figures. Metrics are used to measure outcomes and activities that help to achieve the short-term objectives. Control and evaluation criteria could be performed using a range of ratios (e.g., profitability, activity, performance ratios). It is also possible to use the variables indicated in Table 20.4.

Table 20.4 Dimensions of feedback, standards and control actions

Feedback	Standards	Control/Actions
Sales figures	Against budget plus or minus	Stimulate/dampen down demand
Complaints	Number, frequency, seriousness	Corrective action
Competitors	Relative to us	Attack/defence strategies
Market size changes	Market share	Marketing mix manipulation
Costs/profitability	Ratios	Cost cutting exercises
Corporate image	Attribute measures	Internal/external communications

SUMMARY

It is commonly said that many SMEs do not embark on marketing planning. This is because they are too busy to stop and be involved in what some see as an unnecessary practice. Instead, they tend to concentrate on short-term production and financial priorities. SMEs think more in the short term than in the long term. However, planning generates motivation and increases ambition. It enables managers to forecast events and explore the opportunities available in the future. In addition, it informs managers and prepares them for future risk taking. Planning on its own does not establish success, but a well thought through and carefully implemented plan is more likely to be successful. This chapter discussed the marketing planning process for SMEs. It followed a step-by-step process which can enable managers to think through their marketing planning process. In addition, this chapter provides a basic framework for developing logical marketing plans.

MARKETING PLANNING IN SMALL BUSINESSES

CASE STUDY: DRINKUP

A family soft drink producer, Drinkup, in Oxford, UK, has been running for 20 years. The family ran a chain of restaurants for many years before closing down, and they identified a new market which they believed would be profitable. Using their catering experience, they were able to get started and accumulate a good number of customers, but the financial results of the company have been very poor during the last few years.

The drinks have exotic flavours and are sold locally to hotels and shops. The business booms in the summer months, as many shops near the parks and tourist areas stock the drinks. The retail price of the products ranges from 60p to £1 depending on the size. Drinkup buy raw materials in small quantities; for this reason, they receive a lower discount than larger companies. Drinkup has built up a good reputation, but they are two hard working generations of the family who are in control of the business. They rarely go on holiday because all of them are involved in the production process. The production is labour intensive because of a lack of investment in technology. There are 500 stores around Oxford that stock the products. The management are always in conflict in terms of the best way to run the company. The second generation believes that the old fashioned approach to managing the business should change and that the business should grow more rapidly. The company has never been engaged in any meaningful market research. Recently, the company has created questionnaires and has asked customers to fill them in, but the result of the outcome of the questionnaire has not been implemented. The company has no formal structure; as a result, the line of delegation is not very clear resulting in duplication of efforts, and there is always a problem of communication breakdown. The operating cost for production is increasing, and the low value of the pound has made the situation worse. They do no research and do not know their competitors; nor do they understand the market they are in.

The company has used a variety of methods to sell the products. However, it has been difficult to predict sales volume year by year. A detailed analysis of sales has not been made. In addition, there is a high labour turnover among the staff. The sales staff are paid a basic salary plus commission, but the sales people are not properly trained. The company advertises mainly in the local magazines and newspapers, but they have not established a systematic promotional programme. Previously, the amount of advertising done at any time depended on the existing sales volume. As sales declined, advertising was increased, with local advertising the primary advertising medium. The sales people were provided with attractive, professionally prepared brochures and samples of the product, but there were no set objectives or established quotas, and consequently, the sales people could not predit the exact annual fingures but instead had to accept whatever profit they might make. However, just as they are planning to expand, competition is increasing, and the management is concerned as to the best way forward.

QUESTIONS

1. What are the characteristics of the people who make up the soft drink market? Describe the needs and wants that are satisfied by the product.
2. What recommendations would you make to the company?

333

Tasks

Working in your teams, you are required to provide Drinkup with an outline marketing plan by applying the various tools and concepts covered in this module. Identify the marketing strategy, planning, implementation, and control.

Group Task

1. Why is a marketing plan considered to be important for SMEs?
2. What factors would you consider when scanning the external and internal environment?
3. Why is it important to understand the customer/consumer before embarking on marketing planning?
4. What measures can be used to monitor marketing outcomes?
5. What are the four phases in the development of a marketing plan?
6. Give examples of a company's marketing objectives.
7. Write a short note on the stages of a marketing plan.
8. How will a marketing plan support business goal?
9. Success for small business comes with hard work and good planning.

Let's reason together

1. 'Identifying competitors is important in development of future marketing strategy'. Discuss.
2. 'Demographic change affects business objectives and strategy'. Discuss.
3. 'The elements of goal formulation, developing distinctive competencies, determining authority relationships, deploying resources, and monitoring implementation receive more effective attention when small businesses engage in formal planning'. Discuss.

Technology

Nearly all businesses use information technology to operate efficiently. Technology is essential to any small business, and growth depends on how the company can acquire and utilise technology effectively. The use of IT to process orders, maintain financial records, communicate with customers and suppliers, and carry out forecasting is now widespread. Data from all these is a valuable source of information for the marketing plan. To remain competitive requires planning for IT in order to cope with the changing environment. Also, technology is used for tracking and control in planning. The planning team in the process should recognise the company's future IT needs and prioritise them. For a small business, consideration should be given to what can be achieved within a reasonable timeline and the company's capability. An IT plan should be part of the company's main plan. A written plan for technology should contain:

- a technology vision statement;
- a description of strategy;
- a timeline;
- a budget plan.

Task

List the various types of information useful for internal market research that could be generated by company databases.

REFERENCES

Barrett, G., Jones, T., McEvoy, D. and McGoldrick, C. (2002) The economic embeddedness of immigrant enterprises in Britain. *International Journal of Entrepreneurial Behaviour and Research*, 8 (1/2), 11–31.

Basu, A. and Goswami, A. (1999) South Asian entrepreneurship in Great Britain: Factors influencing growth. *International Journal of Entrepreneurial Behaviour and Research*, 5 (5), 251–275.

Blankson, C. and Omar, O. (2002) Marketing practices of African and Caribbean small businesses in London UK. *Qualitative Market Research: An International Journal*, 5(2), 123–134.

Brickkmann, J., Grichric, D. and Kapsa, D. (2010) Should entrepreneurs plan or just storm the castle? A meta-analysis on contextual factors impacting the business planning-performance relationship in small firms. *Journal of Business Venturing*, V25, P24–P40.

Cook, M., Ekwulugo, F. and Fallon, G. (2003) Start up motivation factors in UK African Caribbean SMEs: An exploratory study. *Proceedings of the 4th International Conference*. London. 9–12 April 2003, P21.

Drucker, P. (1954) *The Practice of Management*: New York: Harper and Row Publishers.

Eisenmann, T. R. (2002) The effect of CEOs equity ownership and firm diversification on risk taking. *Strategic Management Journal*, 23, (6), 53–534.

Fadahunsi, A., Smallbone, D. and Supri, S. (2000) Networking and ethnic minority development: Insight from a North London Study. *Journal of Small Business and Enterprise Development*, 5(3), 228–240.

Fraser, D. (2004) Center for small and medium sized enterprises Warwick Business School. A Report on the 2004 UK Survey of SME Finance. University of Warwick.

Hankinson, A. (2000) The key factors in the profiles of small firm owner-managers that influence business performance. The South Coast Small Firms Survey, 1997–2000 *Journal of Industrial and Commercial Training*, 32, (3), 94–99.

Jamal, A. (2005) Playing to win: An explorative study of marketing strategies of small ethnic retail entrepreneurs in the UK. *Journal of Retailing and Consumer Services*, 12(1), 1–13.

Jocumsen, G. (2004) How do small business managers make strategic marketing decisions? A model of process. *European |Journal of Marketing*, 38(5/6), 659–674.

Kotey, B. (2005) Goals, management practices, and performance of family SMESs. *International Journal of Entrepreneurial Behaviour and Research*, 11(1), 3–24.

Kotler, P. (2003) *Marketing Management Analysis and Planning, Implement and Control*, 11th ed. Englewood Cliffs, NJ, Prentice Hall.

Kraus, S., Harns, R. and Schwarz, E.J. (2006) Strategic planning in smaller enterprises – new empirical findings. *Management Research News*, 29(6), 334–344.

London Development Agency (LDA) (2004) London BME action plan business support advice.

McDonald, M. (2007) *Marketing Plans: How to Prepare Them, How to Use Them*, 6th ed. Elsevier, Butterworth-Heinemann, Oxford.

Miles, R. E. and Snow, C. S. (1978) *Organisational Strategy, Structure, and Process*. McGraw-Hill, New York.

Mintzberg, H. (1994) The fall and rise of strategic planning. *Harvard Business Review*, 72, 107–114.

Mitter, S. (1986) Industrial restructuring and manufacturing homework. *Capital and Class*, 27, 37, 80.

O'Regan, N. and Ghobadian, A. (2004) Re-visiting the strategy-performance question: An empirical analysis. *International Journal of Management, and Decision*, 5(2/3), 144–170.

Perry, S. C. (2001) The relationship between, written business plans and the failure of small business in the US. *Journal of Small Business Management*, 39(3), 201–208.

Porter, M. E. (1980) *Competitive Strategy*. Free Press, New York.

Ram, M. and Smallbone, D. (1999) Ethnic minority Enterprises in Birmingham, paper presented at the 2nd Ethnic Minority Enterprises Seminar, London, November.

Reeves, F. and Ward, R. (1984) West Indian Business in Britain. In R. Ward and R. Jenkins (Eds.), *Ethnic Communities in Business: Strategies for Economic Survival*. Cambridge University Press, Cambridge.

Smallbone, D., Bertotti, M. and Ekanem, I. (2005) Diversity in ethnic minority business, the case of Asians in London's creative industries. *Journal of Small Business and Enterprise Development*, 12(1), 41–56.

Stanworth, J. and Purdy, D. Mascarenhas-Keyes (2003) SMEs facts and issues. www.smallbusiness-group.org.uk.
Whitehead, E. and Purdy, D. Mascarenhas-Keyes (2006) Ethnic minority businesses in England; Report on the Annual Small Business Survey 2003 Ethnic Boost Small Business Service March URN 06/958.

Chapter 21

Contemporary issues in entrepreneurship marketing
Sustainability, ethics, and social responsibility

Sonny Nwankwo and Darlington Richards

> **LEARNING OBJECTIVES**
>
> *After reading the chapter, you should be able to:*
> - Develop an understanding of some of the potent contemporary issues (sustainability, ethics and social responsibility) confronting SMEs;
> - Develop an understanding of Entrepreneurship Marketing;
> - Understand how these might impact SMEs in their marketing operations;
> - Demonstrate an awareness of how these issues might be managed or integrated into marketing decision processes;
> - Understand that higher levels of sensitivity to sustainability, ethics and social responsibility values could contribute to marketing excellence and sustainable entrepreneurship.

INTRODUCTION

Markets and market environments are changing; so are the operating market conditions in contemporary times. Today's operating market conditions, given their ever-growing level of turbulence and complexity, are likely to be profoundly impactful and strategically more demanding on SMEs than ever before. Regardless of the taxonomical complications relating to how SMEs may be classified and defined or the tensions and contradictions arising from efforts to resolves these, there is no escaping the stark reality that many SMEs (especially high-growth SMEs) are increasingly exposed to meta-marketing pressures which large organisations have had to grapple with for a long time. Essentially, a recourse to 'smallness' is no longer a sufficient base to presume that SMEs are insulated from the demands, expectations and obligations that might arise from the wider macromarketing interfaces. Paradoxically, much of what has been previously explained away as extra-competition pressures (e.g., environmentalism and ethics) are increasingly finding their ways into the mainstream strategic processes of companies and, accordingly, proving to be sources of competitive strengths (see the illustrative example in Box 21.1).

To further illustrate (Box 21.2), Steve Jobs and Steve Wozniak grew their company Apple from a *value-base* that was unconventional at the time, that is, the computer industry was revolutionised by Apple by making the technology smaller, cheaper, intuitive, and accessible to everyday customers (see Box 21.1), (Biography.com Editors, 2019).

It may well be that navigating the contemporary marketplace, in all of its diverse pressure points, may turn out to be more challenging for many SMEs than most entrepreneurs currently care to admit. Severe competition, industry capacity gluts, fragmented markets, globalisation, rapid technological innovation and diffusion, depressed margins and rising costs, global crises that provoke the images of the *Great Depression* or the biblical *Armageddon*, are putting many companies between the proverbial rock and a hard place. To compound matters, businesses will be severely challenged to demonstrate higher levels of sensitivity to a much wider battery of renascent societal issues (e.g., the impact of business on the environment, attitude towards promoting sustainable consumption, preserving the ecosystems, upholding the integrity of the marketplace and contributions to sustainable communities). For many SMEs, these are likely to pose 'new marketing challenges' to which they must not only respond but are required, as a matter of good business practice, proactively integrate into their strategic processes. More specifically, a growing number of companies will be looking to emphasise their commitment to social responsibility, ethics and sustainability values in an attempt to help differentiate themselves from their competitors and to enhance their brand and reputation (Jones et al. 2008; Lai et al. 2010; Wang et al. 2015).

BOX 21.1: HOW TO LEVERAGE SUSTAINABILITY TO INCREASE BUSINESS PROFITABILITY

As Kermit the Frog lamented, 'it's not easy being green'. However, with scientists releasing increasingly alarming evidence pointing to rising sea levels, hotter summers, and the global community's escalating carbon footprint, 'being green' is frankly no longer good enough.

Eco-friendly standards that were hip and progressive in the 1980s and 90s now seem to barely scratch the surface of what's needed to shut down this greenhouse emissions time bomb. Instead, today's focus needs to be on sustainability, the idea of putting into place long-term, sustainable practices that will help alleviate further damage to the planet.

From a business perspective, sustainability shouldn't just be another progressive marketing strategy but a rallying cry that more and more companies, big and small, need to get behind if large-scale change is to be effective.

Not only are measures like LED lighting, ride-sharing initiatives and green data centres good for the environment as well as the health and well-being of your employees and local community, but the *World Economic Forum* sees parallels between eco-innovation and increases to a business' profit margins.

'Consumers, in general, prefer a sustainable business or product. Fortunately, there are plenty of businesses who took sustainability to a new level, and they [are] profiting from it tremendously. Almost all successful and profitable businesses have real sustainability measures in place, some have it even certified', Guido Bauer, the CEO of Green Globe, a Los Angeles-based company that provides sustainability certification for the travel and tourism industries in more than 80 countries, told me in an email. Bauer is one of the many eco-thought leaders I have long admired and have tried to emulate throughout my career as a high-tech entrepreneur.

Unfortunately, there are still many companies that have not yet taken sustainability seriously, according to Bauer, 'as they are unaware of the advantages'. Others, especially small businesses, may shy away from implementing eco-measures in an effort to pinch pennies.

The way I see it, companies, no matter how small, can't afford not to be sustainable, particularly those like my web and app development shop that rely heavily on one of the world's biggest polluters – the internet. (A recent study from the Department of Energy's Lawrence Berkeley National Laboratory found that US data centres use around 70 billion kilowatt-hours annually.)

Bottom line: Sustainable business practices are your social responsibility and, if you stay within your means, not as costly as you might imagine.

Looking to Apple's massive new headquarters (compared, by Steve Jobs, to a spaceship) or Tesla's sprawling 5.5 million-square-foot Giga factory under development in the Nevada desert, both to be powered by solar energy, for inspiration will likely be disheartening if you don't have a couple of billion dollars to play around with.

Facebook's cool data centre 70 miles south of the Arctic Circle in northern Sweden may also not be within the parameters of your budget, but emulating these international giants, shouldn't be your endgame.

I recommend starting small: recycle your waste, use tap water instead of bottles, take advantage of natural light in office spaces. How many of these things do you already do? Now imagine if you were continuously thinking of new ways to expand your sustainability goals.

My development team, based in a BREEAM-certified office complex, actively recycles, uses tap water and glass kitchenware. We were awarded for our efforts, taking home both Office of the Year and Smart Office of the Year accolades. We were also nominated for Healthy Office of the Year.

These are all admirable achievements that certainly have our local business community and clients talking. But my first thought upon winning was: what can we be doing better? This is the type of thinking I believe will help take companies to the next level of social responsibility.

'Sustainability concentrates on energy/water/waste, community, heritage and corporate social responsibility. Doing well in all four categories places a company into a whole different light with consumers', Bauer, an advocate of certified sustainability, told me. 'According to our in-house data, certified companies reduce operating cost by 6.8% per year and are able to reach on average a million more consumers with communicating sustainability in the correct way'.

A recent global consumer survey by Unilever (a British-Dutch consumer goods company behind such brands as Lipton, Ben and Jerry's, Dove, and Knorr) cites a $1 trillion market opportunity for businesses that effectively market themselves as eco-innovators. In fact, 21% of those polled by Unilever said, 'they would support brands that clearly conveyed the sustainability aspects of their products through their marketing and packaging'.

I can attest to this. Over the last decade, I've been meeting more and more clients who are keenly interested in sustainable practices. In fact, some are only willing to do business with companies that actively practice sustainability. Every year, I make it a goal to expand my agency's eco-efforts beyond the office, taking cues from my own engineers as well as former clients, like Zkipster, an event management app that helps cut back on needless invitation paper trails.

In addition to our waste recycling and energy saving initiatives we've implemented at all our offices, my company has also developed a food delivery startup that leverages bicycles instead of cars and recently co-founded a new urban bike-sharing platform, billed to be one of the most eco-friendly transport options on the European market when it launches this fall.

Sustainability is more than just a shrewd business move that companies can promote on their websites and in their marketing literature, among other avenues. It is an important issue for all of us as human being and stewards of this world – it's the only one we've got. Interplanetary colonisation, despite the hype it's been getting from the likes of Elon Musk and Stephen Hawking, is still just science fiction. If it one day becomes a reality, great – but in the meanwhile, let's fix what we have, one recycle bin and data centre at a time.

Source: Adapted for teaching purposes from David Semerad, Forbes Agency Council, Community, October 21, 2017.

Notes: This article says consumers have a likeness for sustainable practices and prefer sustainable products, which makes sustainability a good selling proposition. It also talks about how sustainability can serve as a firm's CSR. It gives examples of the companies who are following the trend and implementing various sustainability programs. However, it rightly points out that the entrepreneur (small businesses owners) don't need to do as the big firms are doing. It recommended they start with everyday sustainable practices.

CRITICAL THINKING QUESTIONS

1. What are some good business practices for companies to integrate when entering new markets? What are the new marketing challenges that SMEs are faced with from their competitors?

2. How do companies uphold their commitment to social responsibility, ethics, and sustainability values? Name some strategic processes that can be implemented. What strategic process would you implement? Why?

BOX 21.2: ENTREPRENEUR'S HALL OF FAME: STEVE JOBS

Love him or hate him, Steve Jobs was an incredibly influential entrepreneur who took an industry from a simple computer programming to revolutionizing technology through Apple. Apple's revolutionary products include the Apple iPod, iPhone, and iPad. His 'trade not aid' has invaluable consequences for nations and people around the world. But that is what entrepreneurs do. Entrepreneurs make change. When we look back in history many of the great achievers were thought of as 'nuts' until well after death. People scoff at things they don't know, can't understand, or believe will make change. Steve Jobs, the co-founder of Apple, was a true champion for corporate responsibility throughout the world. He viewed business in the greater context of a world that should respect nature, animals, people, and employees. He believed business has a profound influence upon social and community economics and to a greater extent, the balance of life. These ideals underpinned the strategic development of the company he co-founded.

Source: Adapted for teaching purposes from www.biography.com/people/steve-jobs

---

BOX 21.3: ENTREPRENEUR'S HALL OF FAME: ANITA RODDICK

Love her or hate her, Anita Roddick was an incredibly influential entrepreneur who took a company from a single store to a major retailer as well as take on large-scale causes especially when they impact so many lives. Her 'trade not aid' has invaluable consequences for nations and people around the world. But that is what entrepreneurs do. Entrepreneurs make change. When we look back in history many of the great achievers were thought of as 'nuts' until well after death. People scoff at things they don't know, can't understand, or believe will make change. Anita Roddick, the founder of the The Body Shop, was a true champion for corporate responsibility throughout the world. She viewed business in the greater context of a world that should respect nature, animals, people, and employees. She believed business has a profound influence upon social and community economics and to a greater extent, the balance of life. These ideals underpinned the strategic development of the company she founded.

Source: Adapted for teaching purposes from www.ltbn.com

CHARACTERISING THE MARKETPLACE

The premise of this chapter is that much of what occurs in the contemporary marketplace is governed by symbolic processes, that is, by a rich, ever-changing play of imagery about the relations between persons and things. In the identity construction of the postmodern consumer (Elliot, 1999; Hamouda, 2015), the postmodern consumer no longer consumes products for their material utilities but for the symbolic meaning of those products as portrayed in their images. Products have become commodity signs and the real consumer has become a consumer of illusions – buying images, not things. Marketing is the active nerve-centre of these unfurling processes – in the degree to which it promotes what has been termed the *consumer society* and *hedonistic lifestyle*. O'Shaughnessy and O'Shaughnessy (2008) uses the triple platform of marketing, the consumer society and hedonism to deal with some of the contestations around the 'dark side' of consumer marketing: accumulation and display of material possessions, satisfying transitory appetites and created wants, seeking positional goods for social status and social bonding, consumers taking their identity from their possessions, commodification of social life, the impact of fantasy and imagery in influencing buying, image saturated environment pressing consumer to buy. In the face of multiple pressure-points (and countervailing forces) which now seems to characterise the environment of marketing, some of the *'consumer society'* questions long asked by Nwankwo et al. (1993) remains valid:

- How do consumers feel about the state of the marketplace and interrelationships with socioeconomic systems in which it is embedded?
- What dominant values does business subscribe to? What drives these values?
- Do consumers trust business as an agency for sustainable development?
- What does the society expect of business (business being a societal institution)?
- Are consumers' views of the marketplace different from those of business?
- What is the nature of interaction among markets, marketing and society?
- What predictions can be made about the evolving marketplace?

In the beginning...

In the early periods of industrial development, attention was largely focussed on producing goods in an ever-increasing scale (the cliché, *Fordism*, is often applied to capture the mass production mentality of the era, e.g., the Ford Model T). An ethereal model of rational choice, and concepts of fixed tastes and preferences dominated economic thought (Leiss, 1983). The process of consumption was assumed to take care of itself. The marketplace was assumed to be the privileged locus for the *satisfaction of wants*. The situation is now changed dramatically, with emphasis shifting from consumer to conserver orientation. For example, the growing use of quality-of-life and ethical orientation measures are pointers to attempts to gauge the 'subjective' impact of socioeconomic circumstances on people's conception of well-being and the intersubjective aspects of consumption, that is, the relation between the individual's taste and choices and the larger social setting.

Models of the marketplace

Each of us faces a set of moral dilemma as individual consumers – for example, as consumers who care about the environment and are keen to conserve energy on the one hand but on the other, want to use our air conditioners, heaters and other appliances that consume energy. At the level of the individual, these everyday contradictions are not easy to resolve and much less so in complex organisational settings. However, individuals as well as businesses endeavour to cope based on their respective cognitive models of the marketplace. Thus, how an individual views the way the interactions take place and are resolved reflects the individual's *model of the marketplace*. Just as different people have different models of the marketplace and no single model applies to all situations, the same is true of businesses. However, from a marketing perspective, it has been suggested that a basic view will generally fit one of the following criteria (the schema was first presented by Greyer, 1973):

- Manipulative model: this model portrays marketing's role as basically that of persuading / seducing consumers to buy.
- Service model: Marketing role is to serve the consumer. This is encapsulated in the marketing concept (consumer sovereignty).

342

- Transactional model: This portrays marketing as a give-and-take operation which is mutually beneficial. Consumption is reflective of each individual's buying criteria (reasoned action).
- Relational model: Marketing's role is simply not about satisfying the individual but building a long-term partnership in which business and consumer are co-development agents.

These perspectives present marketplace interactions, particularly the consumer's situation in broad generality, as more significant than it was thought to be earlier. Many consumers are worried today about their deteriorating environment, by the additives in their food, the side effects of soap they use, the safety and reliability of the goods they buy, the pollution inherent in product usage, food mileage, carbon footprints, integrity of the marketplace (truthful consumer information, consumer education and consumer protection), etc. Increasingly, consumers are expressing a strong desire for a new value system in the marketplace and a higher quality of life in the community. Equally, there have been issues with the 'junk culture' that dominates modern society. Therefore, what is emerging is a growing trend towards re-evaluation of what we (as consumers) buy, how we buy, and the purpose of what we buy. Essentially, the prime underpinning is presumably geared towards determining which aspects of consumption do or do not truly weigh up in the quality of life scale, with minimal injury to the environment and the community. All of these present serious challenges to business – more particularly the SMEs that may have limited absorptive capacity to engage but nevertheless are expected to respond proactively for their own long-term survival. To help unpack these issues, we lean towards three conceptual prisms: sustainability, ethics, and social responsibility (SESR).

CRITICAL THINKING QUESTIONS

1. What type of moral dilemma do consumer's face? What type of marketplace interactions are responsible for how the consumer views the model of the marketplace?
2. How does the four models of the marketplace concerns affect the consumer's perspective? How can business establishments re-shape the consumer perspective in the marketplace by addressing the three conceptual prisms?
3. Is there a need for the three conceptual prisms in the marketplace? If so, why?

SUSTAINABILITY MARKETING

Marketing, as a discipline, has continued to exhibit a remarkable capacity to reinvigorate itself and chart new directions in a manner that helps us to make sense of both the continuous and discontinuous changes taking place in and around business (Nwankwo, 2004). Theorists (e.g., Kotler et al., 2009; Greyser, 1997) have chronicled the philosophical evolution of marketing to include the following epochal stages:

- Product orientation;
- Production orientation;
- Sales orientation;
- Market orientation;
- Societal marketing orientation;
- Social marketing orientation.

Also evident in the contemporary chronicle is the *relationship marketing* concept (Gummesson, 2008) and, more recently, **sustainability marketing**, which often times is referred to as **green marketing.** They both reflect and connote different sensibilities. The latter is when a company focuses on social and environmental investments as a **marketing** strategy. The former reflects the concept of sustainable marketing that an organisation should meet the needs of its present consumers without compromising the ability of future generation to fulfil their own needs (Kotler et al., 2008). However, in these regards, Sustainability Marketing is used as a broad canvass to accommodate a range of allied and related sustainability concepts, such as ecological marketing, environmental marketing which is sometimes used interchangeably with green marketing, ethical marketing, consumerism and elements of social responsibility (Fuller, 1999; Belz and Peattie, 2009).

MARKING THE BOUNDARIES OF SUSTAINABILITY MARKETING

Although issues around sustainability are not altogether new (see also Box 21.2), the resurgence of interests in sustainability marketing is largely driven by the ideals embedded in the Brundtland Report on Sustainable Development, that is, development that meets the needs of the present generation but without compromising the ability of future generations to meet their own needs (WCED, 1987). As would be expected, there are serious contentions about what constitutes sustainable development and how it should be defined (this angle of inquiry is outside the scope of this chapter but for a bespoke treatment, see, for example, Nwankwo et al., 2010). With this in mind, it is easy to appreciate the varying prisms from which marketing scholars have treated sustainability or sustainable marketing (Belz and Peattie, 2009; Jones et al., 2008; van Dam and Apeldoorn, 2008, Fuller, 1999).

Sustainability marketing is defined as "creating, producing and delivering sustainable solutions with higher net sustainable value whilst continuously satisfying customers and other stakeholder" (Charter et al., cited by Jones et al., 2008, p. 125). Fuller (1999, p. 4) explains the concept as: a process of planning, implementing, and controlling the development, pricing, promotion and distribution of products in a way that satisfies the following three criteria: (1) customer needs are met, (2) organisational goals are attained, and (3) the process is compatible with ecosystems. We can, thus, conceptualise sustainability marketing as the formulation and implementation of marketing strategies and activities (production, distribution and promotion decisions) in ways that are sensitive and respectful of both the natural and social environments. This is a clarion call for marketing processes to be conscious of the need to use ecologically resilient resources (e.g., biodegradable packaging), reduce energy consumption and waste generation, support fair trade initiatives, and promote healthier lifestyles and sustainable human ecology. These are by no means strange demands on entrepreneurs. Essentially, entrepreneurs are increasingly confronted with expectations to scale-up their awareness of the impact of their operations on the quality of the natural environment, promote sustainable business practice and ultimately strike a balance between profitability and responsible environmental stewardship. For SMEs, sustainability marketing is analogous to the enactment of *multiple logics*, balancing sustainability and profitability in entrepreneurial practice (De Clercq and Voronov, 2010). This requires 'thinking outside the box' (i.e., rethinking the *Dominant Social Paradigm*, DSP, Belz and Peattie, 2009, p. 279) because 'companies should begin to prepare for a more sustainable millennium by re-examining the social and environmental impacts of their marketing strategies' (Charter et al., cited by Jones et al., 2008).

■ **344**

CONTEMPORARY ISSUES IN ENTREPRENEURSHIP MARKETING

> **BOX 21.4: CHALLENGING QUESTIONS AND ISSUES FOR THE 21ST CENTURY**
>
> 15 Global Challenges facing humanity
>
>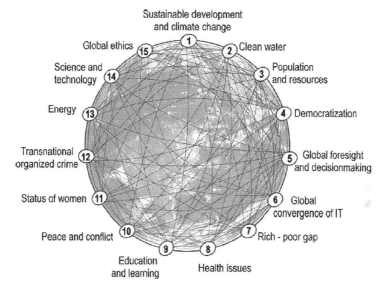
>
> Source: The millennium project
> www.millenium-project.org

Obviously, companies (both small and large) affect and are, in turn, affected by a raft of millennium challenges such as those enumerated in the Millennium Project: (see Box 21.4 and also Belz and Peattie, 2009; Fraj-Andres et al., 2008).

Some of the urgent sustainability questions confronting modern businesses include:

- How can ethical marketplaces be encouraged to help reduce poverty levels? Despite and the approbation of the Millennium Development Goals, the proportion of the world population living below the poverty threshold (less than $2 a day) has not shown much significant decline. The literature indicates that SMEs are playing significant roles in poverty alleviation. The role of Fair-Trade and Microfinance institutions in development especially in third world countries are established in development discourses (see also Viswanathan and Sridharan, 2009).
- How can growing energy demand be met safely and efficiently? How can shortages of 'life essentials' (e.g., food, oil, water, pressures on energy supplies, and other forms of life support infrastructure) be met – not now but also in the future?
- How can ethical consideration become more routinely incorporated into business decisions?
- How can sustainable development be achieved for all? The Millennium Ecosystem Assessment concluded that about 60% of the ecosystem services that support life on earth are

used unsustainably. Yet without sustainable growth, billions of people will be condemned to poverty, and much of the civilisation will collapse (State of the Future Report, 2005).

- How can population growth and resources be brought into balance? The global population has grown by 4.8 billion since 1950, now estimated to be in the region of around 7.6 billion but projected to reach 9.8 billion by 2050.
- How can incidences and spread of both curable and incurable diseases (malaria, HIV/AIDS, cancer, etc.,) and the ease of transfer from livestock to humans of unfamiliar diseases that have impacted quality of life in several regions of the world be controlled?
- How can mass movements in population groups (from rural to urban areas, from developing to developed countries) including internal displacements, as a result of wars or natural disasters, be reduced?
- How can adverse climatic conditions; resulting to severe weather conditions, growing incidences of flooding, carbon emission, and depletion of the ozone layer be reduced?

GROUP CRITICAL THINKING ACTIVITY: LET'S REASON TOGETHER EXERCISE

1. Identify two types of SMEs that play a significant role in poverty alleviation. Explain how they play a role in poverty alleviation.
2. What were their roles in social responsibility?
3. Were there any ethical concerns that needed to be addressed? If so, what were they?
4. What type of resources did these SMEs use? Did this cause a sustainable growth? If so, how? Finally, what types of resources were involved?

TOWARDS A SUSTAINABILITY MARKETING ORIENTATION

Sustainability marketing embraces a wide array of activities that spans all areas of marketing functions; encompassing how products are produced, communicated and distributed, technology in use, purpose of production, and end user/societal/sustainable concerns. The scope of activities is far-reaching; requiring full commitment and value-driven approach to entrepreneurship. It is, in fact, a requisite philosophy and culture of sustainable entrepreneurship marketing. An appropriate orientation will reflect the degree to which an SME integrates sustainability values within its entrepreneurial culture; a change in traditional marketing orientation (focussed on widening marketing scope) to sustainability marketing orientation, or SMO (with added focus on protecting social stakeholders and the natural environment). A firm's SMO may be revealed along a continuum at the opposite ends of which respectively locates a reactive, low-profile stance and a proactive, high-profile stance (see Nwankwo, 1995, for an illustrative framework for diagnosing a customer orientation). Two issues (philosophical positioning and implementation readiness) are therefore important in this respect:

- *sustainability marketing orientation* (i.e., the degree of acceptance of sustainability ideals and how the values are embedded in the philosophy of entrepreneurship);
- *sustainability marketing strategy* (the extent to which sustainability values are integrated into marketing strategy processes and implementation decisions).

These two dimensions must jell together in any firm that wishes to be taken seriously on the sustainability marketing agenda. However, the 'acid test' lies in: (1) how firms frame their understanding of sustainability marketing and (2) how they align their strategies to deliver the vision.

REDEFINING THE MUNDANE – HOW SMEs CAN MAKE PROGRESS ON SUSTAINABILITY MARKETING

In one of the most recent and comprehensive expositions of sustainability marketing Belz and Peattie (2009, pp. 271–272) argues that progress towards sustainability marketing requires the reframing and rethinking of many aspects of conventional marketing, including:

- An appreciation of social and ecological problems at macro level;
- A basic understanding of the socioecological impacts of products on a micro level;
- A change of emphasis from economic exchange to building and maintaining relationships with consumers;
- A critical reflection on the basic assumptions of marketing, its norms and values;
- Moving beyond the consideration of products and services to see the delivery of benefits to consumers in terms of providing them with solutions;
- An emphasis on the total economic and noneconomic cost of consumption instead of simply price;
- Communication as a two-way dialogue that builds relationships with consumers rather than an emphasis on the unidirectional promotion of products to them;
- The necessity of sustainability marketing transformations within and by the companies.

Figure 21.1 sets out the steps, rudimentarily, that SMEs may take to development a SMO. In doing so, they will need to address the following question:

- Purposefulness: *where* does the business want to be? Analyses at this level will lead to reconciling entrepreneurial values with sustainability ideals.
- Take a philosophical stance: *why* does the business want to be where it wants to be?
- Develop a sustainability market orientation mission. This must be futuristic and embedded within the ideals of sustainable development.

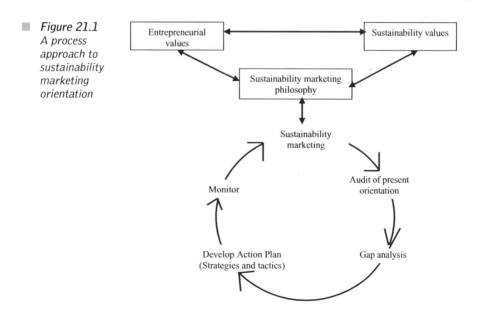

Figure 21.1 A process approach to sustainability marketing orientation

- Audit presentation orientation: **How** well balanced is the business now in terms of achieving its purpose?
- Develop action plan: **What** does the business need to do to get to where it wants to be?
- Monitor progress: **Is** the business on course towards its stated mission?

ETHICS IN ENTREPRENEURSHIP MARKETING

What is ethics?

The concept of ethics refers to the moral principles and values that generally inform the conduct of individuals. Ethics refers to accepted principles of right and wrong that govern the conduct of a person, the members of a profession, or the actions of an organisation. It is the study of what constitutes right or wrong, good or bad conduct. Ethical behaviour consists of the exhibition of those moral or ethical conducts that are considered appropriate within a society or an organisation. Interestingly enough, the concept of ethics seems to be susceptible to all kinds of interpretations, that is, it is not only interchangeably used with morality, it gets mixed up sometimes with law, etiquette, and religion. And yet there are discernible differences.

Ethics is said to be something everyone likes to talk about, especially with the current spate of questionable behaviours within organisations, yet nobody knows exactly what it is. It has even been suggested that ethics has an individual value composition, i.e., it is what the individual says it is. Because ethics, indeed moral standards, can mean different things to different people, with many varied opinions or suggestions, it makes it absolutely necessary to articulate a perspective of ethics that is both relevant and comprehendible within a context, business, profession or society.

It is generally agreed that ethics is the study of what is 'right' and 'wrong'. Of course, 'right' and 'wrong' in relation to who or what? The answers to these questions become situational, environmental, as well as circumstantial ones. This explains why reasonably ethical people may hold different and competing ethical positions on a number of issues from abortion, child labour, human rights, environmental preservation, unfair lending practices, etc. And which also explains why during the global meltdown of 2008, amidst contending widespread demands for economic and financial reliefs, many rational and even ethical people rationalised the moral hazard of bailing out some institutions.

Sources of ethical values

Where do our moral/ethical standards come from? How is it the case that within the same society there could be overlapping in ethical and moral standards? It has been suggested that many things influence us in the moral principles we hold or accept. These include early upbringing, education, the behaviour of those around us, the explicit and implicit standards of our culture, our experiences, and critical reflections of those experiences (Shaw and Barry, 2010). Ethical theorists are of the consensus that there are five sources of ethics: The Utilitarian Approach, The Rights Approach, The Fairness or Justice Approach, The Common Good Approach, and The Virtue Approach (A Framework for Thinking Ethically. ETHICS 1, (2 Winter 1988). These source differences have a way of affecting ethical thinking and rationalisation.

In these myriad of value judgments, is the normative theoretical delineation of ethical concepts based on outcomes? These are the consequentialist and non-consequentialist theories of ethics. The consequentialist theorists are of the view that the moral rightness of an action is determined solely by its outcome. That is to say, if the consequences of an act are good, then that act is ethical, if the consequences of that action are bad, then that act is unethical. Actions are desirable if they lead to the best possible balance of good consequences over bad consequences. Problems with utilitarianism include measuring the benefits, costs, and risks of an action, and the fact that the approach fails to consider justice.

The other question that arises is: consequences for whom, the individual or the group? It has been suggested that the two most important theories in this context are Utilitarianism and Egoism. Whilst Utilitarianism advocates taking into consideration everyone involved, producing the greater proportion of 'good' to the greatest number of people. Egoism contends that individual self-interest is the primary objective. 'Enlightened self-interest' could not be better explained. Utilitarianism, on the other hand, much better explains the public and organisational ethical rationale for most decisions involving distributing social benefits.

Non-consequentialist (deontology) theories of ethics contend that the diminution of ethics to outcomes or consequences trivialises the meaning and essence of ethics. Kantian (deontology) ethics, leading non-consequentialist theorists, are based on the philosophy of Immanuel Kant who argued that people should be treated as ends and never purely as means to the ends of others. 'Right' and 'wrong' should retain their intrinsic value without reference to outcome. In the context of societal complexities and a constantly evolving business environment, one cannot but wonder about the practicality of deontology. Social and business decisions cannot be devoid of cost-benefit analysis in every decision making. For example, should a business make a decision to offer free healthcare to all of its employees without considering affordability, just because it is the right and moral thing to do, without taking into consideration the cost and its impact on the businesses' bottom-line?

Ethical relativism is the other ethical concept justifiably based on the realisation that because our ethics is, among other things, a function of our peculiar culture, environment, upbringing, society, etc., it is therefore conceivable that our ethics must necessarily be open to these variabilities. In his essay, 'Is Business Bluffing Ethical?', Carr (1968) contends that business, as practiced by individual and corporations, wears the impersonal character of a game – a game that demands both special ethical standards. Essentially, business has its own norms and rules that differ from the rest of society, and a number of things that are normally thought of as wrong are really permissible in a business context.

According to Shaw and Barry (2010), examples include conscious misstatement and concealment of pertinent facts in negotiation, lying about one's age on a curriculum vitae, deceptive packaging, automobile companies' neglect of safety, and utility companies' manipulation of regulators and overcharging of electricity users.

Carr's (1968) analogy of ethical relativism with poker is both instructive and illustrative, albeit rationalising misleadingly:

> Poker's own brand of ethics is different from the ethical ideals of civilized human relationships. The game calls for distrust of the other fellow. It ignores the claim of friendship. Cunning deception and concealment of one's strength and intentions, not kindness and open-heartedness, are vital in poker. No one thinks any the worse of poker on that account. And no one should think any the worse of the game of business because its standards of right and wrong differ from the prevailing traditions of morality in our society.

The point though is that business must operate within a set of ethical rules of conduct that must take into consideration the established ideals, norms, rules and traditions of the larger society (see Box 21.5). What that means is that certain conducts for business are necessarily prohibited within a given society, as unethical.

BOX 21.5: VIEWS ON ETHICS

Ethical principles
- *Mosaic Law*: do unto others as they do to you.
- *Pareto criterion*: choose actions that are likely to benefit one or more people at the expense of none.
- *Means-end ethics*: The accumulation of wealth is essential to ensure one's survival, and growth.
- *Golden rule*: Do to other what you would wish them to do to you.
- *Professional ethics*: No one in society is above the law, so everyone must comply with legislation regardless whether or not the law appears nonsensical.
- *Non-interventionist rule*: A free-for-all business practice can create benefits for everyone.
- *Organisational ethics*: There is one rule for business and another for private life.
- *Utilitarian principle*: Taking the course of action which is likely to do the most good and the least harm.

Major theories relevant to business
- Teleology – utilitarianism: Actions are judged by their consequences.
- Deontology – the theory of rights: Acting from a sense of duty rather than concern for consequences is the basis for mortal obligation.
- Theory of justice: Decisions should be guided by equitableness, fairness, and impartiality.
- Cultural relativism: Ethical standards are culture-specific.

There is no such thing as a universal or generally acceptable ethical conduct, as ethics recognises the relativity of moral conducts within nations, organisations, and societies. What is acceptable behaviour in one nation may be considered unethical in another. Ethics becomes an issue across nations because of differing political systems, economic systems, legal systems, and cultural values. Indeed, cultural relativism also argues that ethics are culturally determined and that firms should adopt the ethics of the cultures in which they operate, in other words, '*when in Rome, do as the Romans do*'.

Perspectives: will we walk on common ground?
One day during the 19th century, a British merchant ship docked in a Chinese port. It had been a long voyage. The crew members were given shore leave and took advantage of the opportunity to refresh themselves. In the course of the night, a British sailor got into a drunken brawl and killed a Chinese coolie. The response of the local Chinese governor was immediate and exact. A posse of armed men trotted down to the quay, seized the first British sailor they met, chopped his head off, and trotted smartly back to barracks.

The captain of the merchantman was outraged. He stormed into the governor's residence to make an angry protest.

350

The governor was gently surprised. "Why are you so angry? You English; so keen on justice. I have done justice. Have a cup of tea?"

"Justice? What d'you mean justice? You executed the wrong man!"

"The wrong man? I do not understand. You kill one of mine, so I kill one of yours. That's fair isn't it? After all I could have killed 10."

Source: Adapted from the *Financial Times*, 24 December 1999, for teaching purpose only

Questions:
1. What ethical theory best describes the decision of the Chinese governor?
2. Summarise and evaluate other ethical issues raised in the case paper.

ETHICAL BEHAVIOUR IN ENTREPRENEURSHIP MARKETING

Ethical behaviour in business is one premised on the generally accepted and permitted conduct in that line of business. These may also reflect the laws and regulations that affect social and economic behaviour in that society. For SMEs, this can be very challenging largely because of their organisational and resource constraints. Given the mushrooming of SMEs and their deadly competitive drive for market share and profit, the ethical compromises can be compelling. As a result of the relative use of 'good' and 'bad' in the context of ethical behaviour in a particular business, how does one begin to rationalise the conduct of an estate agent who deliberately misrepresents the income of prospective homebuyers and thus their capacity to make mortgage payments, just because he/she must meet sales quota? Or the conduct of Banks' Sales Services' agents who go on to open accounts in customers names and send out credit cards to them without their permissions or consents (Maggie McGrath, 2017). Is it ethical to turn a blind eye to obvious falsehood? What should be the agent's ethical responsibilities? Again, is it ethical for a bank to package Credit Default Swaps (CDS) snd Collateralised Debt Obligations (CDO), trade them to unsuspecting investors, and brazenly go ahead to take out insurance protection for their eventual default, knowing full well that the underlying assets are worthless? In essence, this would mean gleefully betting on the failure of a debt instrument so created. What may be wrong with 'Insiders Trading'? Can ethical lapses be of victimless consequences? Where does the moral or ethical responsibility lie? Could the test be one of who may be 'harmed' in these outcomes? There are no easy answers (see Figure 21.2 for possibilities).

Figure 21.2
Schema for evaluating ethical/legal stances

	Legal	Illegal
Ethical	Ethical Legal	Ethical Illegal
Unethical	Unethical Legal	Unethical Illegal

TOWARDS A STRATEGIC RESPONSE

Understandably there is hardly a cut-and-dried answer to ethical questions or decision-making processes. They can be very situational. Clearly in small and medium enterprises (SMEs), the roots of unethical behaviour may be complex and generally reflect ethical dilemmas (situations where none of the available alternatives seems ethically acceptable) of small businesses; they nonetheless encompass familiar preoccupations like individual ethics, decision-making processes, leadership, performance expectations, and organisational culture. It is also the case that some of the more common areas where ethical issues arise in SMEs are employment practices, human rights, environmental pollution, corruption (both institutionalised and private), product and service quality, and durability.

In order to assist SMEs manage their ethical conundrum, and sometimes dilemmas, it is necessary to articulate some kind of ethical guidelines or code of conduct to help them and their employees navigate these myriads of situational and environmental relativities, in order to achieve a more acceptable utilitarian outcome. Because SMEs differ in their organisational focus and customer or stakeholders' expectations, it (guideline) should be rather dynamic and evolutionary. It would be different for every organisation. This indeed makes it unrealistic for a prescriptive model or form of do's and don'ts. However, a more helpful and useful ethical guideline should contain some basics. According to Lamb et al. (2011), it has a number of advantages:

- The guidelines help employees identify what their firm recognises as acceptable business practices.
- A code of ethics can be an effective internal control on behaviour, which is more desirable than external controls like government regulation.
- A written code helps employees avoid confusion when determining whether their decisions are ethical.
- The process of formulating the code of ethics facilitates discussions among employees about what is right and wrong, and ultimately leads to better decisions.

SOCIAL RESPONSIBILITY

Social responsibility (SR) refers to the idea that businesses and business people should take the social consequences of economic actions into account when making business decisions, and that there should be a presumption in favor of decisions that have both good economic and good social consequences (Hills, 2011). It is also believed to be of a business and business people having healthy concerns about the society in which they operate, the concept of *Social Community*. The newest theory in social responsibility, called *wholesome sustainability*, is best demonstrated by businesses taking into consideration both the long-range best interests of the company and the company's relationships to the larger stakeholder society in which it operates (Lamb et al., 2011; Marc, 2005).

Social responsibility proposition incorporates such varied components which demand evolving obligations that are constantly changing with the dynamism of a rapidly evolving global environment. The concept of social responsibility, in relativity terms, may mean a set of different sensibilities and expectations in the UK, the US, China, Brazil, South Africa, or even India. It should be noted therefore that SR would have particular environmental and societal need correlation to it. A recent study of businesses who said that they consider social responsibility factors when making decisions include Brazil, 62%); Canada, 54%; Australia 52%; the US 47%; India 38%; China 35%; and Mexico 26% (2007).

352

Social responsibility has four seemingly interdependent components:

- Economic (pursuit of profits);
- Legal (obey the law);
- Ethical (do what is right, fair, and just);
- Philanthropy (good corporate citizenship).

There are contentions as to the true ethical role of business, in terms of the social responsibilities of business. Do businesses have a primary and overriding purpose, as is stated in the memorandum and articles of incorporation, setting up the business? It is believed to be one of a duty of care and responsibility, to the shareholders, for whom they hold business assets in trust and cannot misapply the assets in 'giving back', and indulging general societal goodwill businesses, unless such 'extracurricular activities' are for the benefit and purposes of the business and in furtherance of generating profits/value to the shareholders. To the larger society, the business owes superior products and services, paying taxes and obeying the laws and following the regulations. Any further expectations beyond these tantamount to usurpation of the role and responsibilities of government, to whom taxes are paid.

Milton Friedman's doctrine is premised along these lines. He suggests that the only social responsibility of business is to increase profits, so long as the company stays within the rules of law. He argues that to the degree that business executives spend more money than they need to purchase delivery trucks with hybrid engines, pay higher wages in developing countries, or even donate company funds to charity, they are spending company funds outside the company's overriding primary purposes. Better to pay dividends and allow shareholders the discretionary allocation of their social goodwill.

For SMEs, SR takes on a whole new meaning and significance. Should their level of social responsibility be one of modified expectations or equal responsibility? Should they be subject to the same rules when it comes to child labour, human rights, environmental preservation, unfair lending practices, defective product liability, unfair trade practices, etc.? They should. To hold otherwise will not only be unfair but undermine the underlying premises of social ethical responsibility.

Again, SR would have varying relevance and significance to different SMEs. For example, the social responsibilities of a dry-cleaning business in relation to water and laundry chemical usage and their greenhouse impact would be different for a small retail business that has a merchandise return policy that it finds every excuse in its receipts' fine-prints to avoid. Whatever their organisational focus, it should indeed be the case that the SR of business must be one that the business recognises its obligations to the larger stakeholder society in its product and service delivery.

RESPONDING TO SR

In the absence of any consensus on what SR means, response strategies are likely to be varied; reflecting each player philosophical positioning and sensitivity to social issues. Response models generally discernible from the extant literature include:

- Regulatory model: This model is encapsulated in the cliché *'business of business is business'* – well, so long as regulations are adhered to.
- Defensive model: Perhaps, the best way to represent this model is *government of the society is not the business of business*. Therefore, business has a duty to put its interests at the foremost and protect them accordingly.

SONNY NWANKWO AND DARLINGTON RICHARDS

- Deceptive model: This response model is closely in line with the Machiavellian principle: *the end justifies the means*. Many businesses are not really 'very open and truthful' about their social responsibility credentials.
- Accommodative model: Proactively accepting to drive forward social agenda – business-driven social activism (e.g., The Body Shop).

SUMMARY

Today, more than ever before, to use a theatrical analogy, SMEs perform on a stage where other actors (e.g., conscientious stakeholders – environmentalists, consumerists) and the sets (environments of marketing) change frequently and there is no guarantee that the play will not be cancelled because of a lack of response from an unappreciative audience. Continuing with this analogy, SMEs should be certain that many of their performances will receive critical reviews from social observers, regulatory bodies, consumer-interest groups etc. Thomas Petit, in his famous book *Freedom in American Economy* reminded us that in every society there is more or less continuous interaction between social values and economic institutions. Values may be thought of as sustainability-derived normative standards which act as a filter in the articulation of ends or in pursuits of certain goals. Therefore, the concept of value will be a central tool in the analysis of how economic actors play their roles.

Indeed, sustainability, ethics, and social responsibility (SESR) values bestride modern entrepreneurial landscape like a colossus. In today's dynamic society, pressure for adaptation and responsiveness to renascent social and environmental values are proving enormous. For SMEs, it cannot be business as usual. The more the level of commitment to the emerging values, the greater the chance of success in navigating the murky waters of entrepreneurship. SESR values are not transient values. They meet the criteria of acceptance of what constitutes dominant social values in sociological interpretations because they are:

- Extensive: The proportion of the population that hold and propagate SESR values has grown exponentially.
- Durability: SESR values are not a fad.
- Intensity: SESR are not only receiving a surge of societal affirmation but also the severity of sanction connected with contra-behaviour is growing.
- Prestige of value carrier: Frontrunners in accepting and implementing SESR values are held in high esteem and, accordingly, more likely to achieve superior and sustainable market positioning.

KEY TERMS
- Sustainability values Environmentalism
- Ethical dilemma Sustainability marketing
- Social responsibility Marketplace integrity

BOX 21.6: TECHNOLOGY, SME, AND THE 21ST CENTURY

Immerging technologies have historically, been vital drivers of innovations as far back as the creation of the steam engine. The impact of technology in the 21st century is stronger than it has ever been, with new innovations changing the course of entire industries. For SMEs technology as an enabler and accelerator of change and development brings about new opportunities, as well as challenges to consider and integrate into their strategic direction.

Advances in technology present major considerations for sustainability of SMEs. While it makes it easier to reach goals and customers, technology in some respects starts to infringe on the rights of individuals, bordering on ethical considerations. SME's adopting technology must now address ethical issues as it applies to technology for sustainability and continuous adherence to corporate social responsibility. Sustainability will, therefore, be achieved by striking a balance in the adoption of technology in such a way that profits are earned while reducing the impact on environment and society (Kumar et al., 2013).

According to a recent study by the Boston Consulting Group on the relationship between SMEs' adoption of technology and their performance, SMEs that adopt technology faster tend to outperform their competitors (Michael et al., 2013). However, it is interesting to note that although digital technology provides vast opportunities for boosting efficiencies, SMEs are lagging behind in their adoption (OECD, 2018).

Questions

1. What do you perceive to be the factors contributing to the slow adoption of technology by SMEs?
2. In what ways might technology assist SMEs in responding to SR, ethics, and sustainability pressures?

REVIEW QUESTIONS

1. Explain the sustainability marketing concept? Distinguish between conventional marketing orientation and sustainability marketing orientation.

2. What role does technology play in supporting a sustainability marketing orientation?

3. In what way does technology change the competitive landscape for SMEs in terms of ethical considerations? Should ethics matter to SMEs?

4. What do you understand by 'social responsibility'? Provide examples of how an SME can adopt each of the social responsibility approaches.

5. 'Consumers and companies acting together can change the world' (Anita Roddick). Do you agree with this statement? Justify your answer.

GROUP TASK

1. Justify the logic of sustainability marketing. Using secondary sources of data, identify companies that achieved market growth as a result of adopting and implementing sustainability values.

2. Check out the following on the website: (1) One Planet Economy and (2) One Percent Club. Develop an argument, supported with real-life illustrations, to justify or debunk firms' commitments to sustainability. Should SMEs be encouraged to become members of such networks?

CASE STUDY: WHEN THERE IS NO LONGER HONOUR AMONG THIEVES

Opportunity recognition, speed, and flexibility have become the *holy grail* of successful SME operations. In the present austere economic times, small-scale money lenders, especially those operating in many inner cities, are becoming adept in their brand of 'entrepreneurial marketing'. With the recurrent company closures, loss of jobs, tight formal employment markets, lack of growth in salaried employment, and attendant family budgeting constraints, small-scale lenders are doing a brisk business and raising the bar in their entrepreneurialism. To compound matters (but good prospect for the loan sharks – as they are often referred), the banks (smarting up from near-catastrophe brought about by the recession) have not responded proactively to entreaties to lend more to business and, therefore, ease the credit crunch.

Recently, evidence of untoward practices started to surface in many parts of the UK as a result of the credit squeeze. According to an official of the Trading Standards Institute, 'we are experiencing a considerable increase in the number of people who turn to loan sharks because it is becoming harder for consumers to obtain credit. If people are looking to borrow, they need to ask the lender to see their consumer credit license as this is proof the lender is legal'. Joining the campaign against loan sharks, both the Citizen Advice and the Birmingham Illegal Money Lending Team during the National Consumer Week, in association with the Office of Fair Trading in London urged consumer to think carefully before dabbling into life-threatening situations. 'We want to get the message out there that you are likely to get ripped off if you borrow from someone without a license and could end up costing a lot more than you are expecting'. Consumer Minister, Gareth Thomas, had this to say, 'Let the unscrupulous and predatory lenders be warned – if they try to draw families into the murky world of illegal money lending, they will face investigation and prosecution by anti-loan shark teams working across the country'.

The fact is, some of the moneylenders operating in the country are not licensed. According to the Office of Fair Trading, anyone who borrows from the unlicensed moneylender is likely to get a loan on very bad terms, pay an extortionate rate of interest, be harassed if you get behind with your repayments, or be pressured into borrowing more from them to repay one debt with another.

Apart from the SME lenders, the banks have not come out unscathed. They have been accused of bringing about the conditions that are leading more and more people into debt and now discriminating against the very people they have blacklisted as poor borrowers. Recently, the UK Chancellor of the Exchequer pointed out that 'the inability to access a bank account can prevent some of Britain's poorest people from joining mainstream society by making it more difficult for them to receive pay cheques and pay bills'. While this might be at the personal or consumer level, the same applies for small businesses that depend on the banks to be able to revitalise their operations.

Consequently, it is little surprising that small time money lenders have recognised this opportunity and have been quick to respond to the growing needs for quick loans. Furthermore, they have been flexible enough to make the cost of borrowing (at face value) less tedious. While this might have brought some form of respite for small businesses and individuals who can now secure finance more easily, there seems to be a catch as the hidden cost of borrowing have given rise to questions. The ethical concerns range from: (1) exorbitant interest charges as was the case of one 'illegal loan shark charged one family an extortionate one thousand, two hundred percent interest' (ITV News, 22 March 2010); (2) use of violence rather than civil legal means to resolve credit default or repayment difficulties. Only recently, an ITV Wales investigation has found that while many families have struggled to bring home the bacon, loan sharks have grown fat from their misery. Around 100 are now thought to operate in Wales, dishing out quick cash, but threatening violence when payments are missed (ITV News, 22 March 2010).

The problem has now become so widespread that the UK government has set up a website to report loan shark activity as well as to provide advice for potential borrowers. Whilst all of these are going on, however, some questions need to be asked: is there a need to regulate entry into financial services by SMEs? Should moneylender SMEs in the sector be made to advertise their ethical/ or corporate social responsibility ethos on their websites? Is it only a few of these small-time lenders that seem to be tarnishing the image of the sector? Are there any industry standards in this sector and who are the key leaders?

Student activity:

What are the key ethical issues raised in this case?
What would be your suggestions for resolving the issues you have identified?
Assume that you have been hired by a group of 'industry players' to help development an ethical statement. Give your presentation. You should be ready to outline what principles you considered and rationalised in finalising your assignment.

Compiled from news sources

Sources: ITN (24 March 2010) Banks told to 'give bank account to everyone'. Online at: http://uk.news.yahoo.com/4/20100324/tuk-banks-told-to-give-bank-account-to-e-dba1618.html [accessed 24 March 2010]

ITV News (2010) Loan Shark Despair. ITV News, 11 March. Online at: www.itv.com/wales/loan-shark-dispair68690/ [accessed 24 March 2010]

(ITV News, 22 March 2010) Loan Shark Victim. Online at: www.itv.com/lifestyle/thismorning/reallife/loansharkvictim/

Directgov (n.d) Targeting unlicensed money lenders. Online at: http://stoploan sharks.direct.gov.uk/index.html [accessed 24 March 2010]

REFERENCES

Belz, F. and Peattie, K. (2009) *Sustainability Marketing*. Chichester, Wiley.

Carr, A. (1968) Is business bluffing ethical? *Harvard Business Review*, 46, January–February.

De Clercq, D. and Voronov, M. (2010) Balancing sustainability and profitability in entrepreneurial practice: An institutional logics perspective. Paper presented at the ICSB 2009 World Conference, Seoul, 21–24 June.

Elliot, R. (1999) Symbolic meaning and postmodern consumer culture. In Brownlie, D., Saren, M., Wensley, R. and Whittington, R. (eds.), *Rethinking marketing: towards critical marketing accounting*. London: Sage Publications.

Fraj-Andres, E., Martinez-Salinas, E. and Matute-Vallejo, J. (2008) A multidimensional approach to the influence of environmental marketing and orientation on the firm's organizational performance. *Journal of Business Ethics*, 88, 263–286.

A framework for thinking ethically. *Ethics*, 1(2) (Winter 1988). www.scu.edu/ethics/practicing/decision/framework.html

Fuller, D. (1999) *Sustainable Marketing: Managerial-Ecological Issues*. Thousand Oaks, CA: Sage.

Greyser, S. (1997) Janus and Marketing: The Past, Present, and Prospective Future of Marketing. In Lehman, D. and Jocz, K. (Eds.), *Reflections on the Futures of Marketing*. Marketing Science Institute, Cambridge, MA.

Gummesson, E. (2008) *Total Relationship Marketing*, 3rd ed. Butterworth-Heinemann, Oxford.

Hamouda, M. (2015) The Postmodern Consumer: An Identity Constructor? In Robinson, Jr. L. (Eds.), *Marketing Dynamism & Sustainability: Things Change, Things Stay the Same . . . Developments in Marketing Science: Proceedings of the Academy of Marketing Science*. Springer, Cham.

Hills, C. (2011) *International Business, Competing in the Global Market Place*, 8th ed. McGraw-Hill, New York.

Jones, P., Clarke-Hill, C., Comfort, D. and Hillier, D. (2008) Marketing and sustainability. *Marketing Intelligence & Planning*, 26(2), 123–130.

Kotler, P., Armstrong, G., Wong, V., Saunders, J. (2008) 'Principles of Marketing', 5th edn, Harlow: Pearson Education Limited.

Kotler, P., Keller, K., Brady, M., Goodman, M. and Hansen, T. (2009) *Marketing Management*. Pearson Educational Ltd., Hallow.

Kumar, V., Rahman, Z. and Kazmi, A. A. (2013) Sustainability marketing strategy: An analysis of recent literature. *Global Business Review*, 14(4), 601–625.

Lai, C. S., Chiu, C. J., Yang, C. F. and Pai, D. C. (2010) The effects of corporate social responsibility on brand performance: The mediating effect of industrial brand equity and corporate reputation. *Journal of Business Ethics.*, 95(3), 457–469.

Lamb, C., Hair, J. and McDaniel, C. (2011) *Marketing 4*. South-Western, 32–34.

Leiss, W. (1983) The icons of the marketplace. *Theory, Culture and Society*, 1(3), 10–21.

Marc, G. (2005) Will social responsibility harm business? *The Wall Street Journal*, 18 May, 2005, A2.

McGrath, M. (2017) Wells Fargo to pay $110 million to settle class action suit over phony account scandal. www.forbes.com/sites/maggiemcgrath/2017/03/28/wells-fargo-to-pay-110-million-to-settle-class-action-suit-over-phony-account-scandal/#4c73777967e6

Michael, D., Aggarwal, N., Kennedy, D., Wenstrup, J., Rubmann, M., Borno, R., Chen, J. and Bezerra, J. (2013) Ahead of the curve: Lessons from small-business leaders. http://image-src.bcg.com/Images/Ahead_of_the_Curve_Oct_2013_tcm9-94245.pdf

Nwankwo, S. (1995) Developing a customer orientation. *Journal of Consumer Marketing*, 12(5), 5–15.

Nwankwo, S. (2004) Apocalypse in marketing practices: Socio-cultural embeddedness of market orientation in African economies. *International Journal of Applied Marketing*, 3(1), 58–77.

Nwankwo, S., Chaharbaghi, K. and Boyd, D. (2010) Sustainable development in Sub-Saharan African: Issues of knowledge development and agenda setting. *International Journal of Development Issues*, 8(2), 119–133.

Nwankwo, S., Richardson, B. and Montanheiro, L. (1993) Consumer issues in the evolving environment: Characterisations of the UK marketplace *Journal of Consumer Studies*, 17, 313–323.

Organization for Economic Corporation and Development (OECD) (2018) *Strengthening SMEs and Entrepreneurship for Productivity and Inclusive Growth*.www.oecd.org/cfe/smes/ministerial/documents/2018-SME-Ministerial-Conference-Key-Issues.pdf

O'shaughnessy, J. and O'shaughnessy, N. (2008) Marketing, the Consumer Society and Hedonism. In Tadajewski, M. and Brownlie, G. (Eds.), *Critical Marketing: Issues in Contemporary Marketing*. John Willey, Chichester, 187–210.

Shaw, W. and Barry, V. (2010) *Moral Issues in Business*, 11th ed. Thomson Publishing, Wadsworth.

van Dam, Y. and Apeldoorn, P. (2008) Sustainable Marketing. In Tadajewski, M. and Brownlie, D. (Eds.), op cit. 253–269.

Viswanathan, M. and Sridharan, S. (2009) From subsistence marketplaces to sustainable marketplaces: A bottom-up perspective on the role of business in poverty alleviation. *Ivey Business Journal*, 73(2).

Wang, D. H. M., Chen, P. H., Yu, T. H. K. and Hsiao, C. Y. (2015) The effects of corporate social responsibility on brand equity and firm performance. *Journal of Business Research.*, 68(11), 2232–2236.

World Commission on Environment and Development (WCED) (1987) *Our Common Future*. Oxford, WCED.

Chapter 22

The future of SME marketing and operations
Critical change drivers

Emmanuel Adugu

LEARNING OBJECTIVES

By the end of this book chapter, the successful reader will be able to:
- Assess the level of awareness of the American public with respect to developments in robotics and computers, and their potential for changing nature of jobs;
- Determine the extent to which the American public is supportive of workplace automation in the context of risks of automation of their own jobs in particular, and the broader society in general;
- Recognise the fact that advances in artificial intelligence and computers hold varied opportunities for creative entrepreneurs to use their skills and create jobs that may benefit society.

INTRODUCTION

In recent years, there have been remarkable developments in robotics and artificial intelligence. These advances are rapidly transforming people's jobs and lives and the way they work, especially in developed countries. In the United States, these technological advances have the potential to automate human activities and reshape the way Americans live and work (PEW, 2017a). They have the ability to transform people's livelihood systems and businesses profoundly. In that context, rapid technological advances have the potential to ease people's lives and improve their business and personal dealings (Rus, 2015). Today, these technologies are mostly being used in certain settings to perform routine tasks that are repeated throughout the day. Such advances allow machines to perform cognitive and physical tasks that are currently being performed by humans. In the future, robots and computers with advanced capabilities may be able to do most jobs. This may be considered as one of the most important threats to job growth, with serious consequences in terms widening inequality and Americans having difficulty in finding jobs.

As the tasks that artificial intelligence and robots cannot perform are shrinking, machines will replace human beings for jobs that currently exist. In that context, the following are potential developments that may substantially impact society: a future where robots and computers can do many human jobs; the development of algorithms that can evaluate and hire job candidates; development of driverless vehicles; and development of robot caregivers for older adults. In effect, these developments may drastically reduce or make redundant the need for humans in both blue-collar and white-collar jobs. If this trend holds, society may be getting closer to the end of work. However, in cases where technology automation results in elimination of jobs, that could serve as an opportunity for entrepreneurs to create jobs for those retrenched to acquire new skills to make them more useful to society.

It is important to note at this point that the notion that 'machines are coming to take our jobs' has been there for hundreds of years. New technologies are now doing many things that used to be in the domain of people only and some skills have become worthless, and those who hold the wrong ones have little to offer employers (Brynjolfsson and McAfee, 2014a, 2014b). In today's economy and that of the future, people need to acquire skills that are robot-proof so that machines will not take their jobs.

An increasing number of research indicates that technological progress in robotics and automation may result in job loses or lower wages when these (technological innovations are substituted for labor (Frey and Osborne, 2013; Arntz et al., 2016; McKinsey Global Institute, 2016; Decanio, 2016). Table 22.1 depicts technological unemployment estimated by leading institutions. This suggests that the pace of technological innovation has sped up, leaving many people behind, as a consequence of not having the skills to participate in the economy.

It is apparent that a lot of people are being left behind as a consequence of technological advances. These developments may be disrupting human labor market thereby signaling the end of work, especially for those who skills have become worthless or redundant. However, it is worthy of note that even as technology makes certain jobs redundant, it also creates new jobs and complements existing ones (Autor, 2015; OECD, 2017). The main goal of this book chapter is to examine the complex linkage between job automation, entrepreneurship, and the future of work. In that context, the chapter seeks to answer the following specific research questions:

Table 22.1 Leading institutions and their estimates of technological unemployment

Organisation	Estimate of technological unemployment
PricewaterhouseCoopers	38% of jobs in America, 30% of jobs in UK, 21% in Japan and 35% in Germany at risk to automation.
University of Oxford	47% of workers in America at high risk of jobs replaced by automation.
OECD	OECD average: 9% of jobs at high risk. Low risk of complete automation but an important share (between 50%–70%) of automatable tasks at risk.
World Bank	2/3 of all jobs in developing countries are susceptible to automation.
ILO	ASEAN-5: 56% of jobs at risk to automation in next 20 years.
McKinsey	60% of all occupations have at least 30% technically automatable activities.
Roland Berger	Western Europe: 8.3m jobs lost in industry against 10m new jobs created in services by 2035.

Source: Adapted from: Frey and Osborne (2015); Roland Berger (2016); McKinsey Global Institute (2016); PwC (2017); World Bank (2016); Chang and Phu (2016) In Balliester and Elsheikhi (2018)

RESEARCH QUESTIONS

1. What is the relationship between the importance that the American public places on 'working and having a job' and advances in robotics and computers?
2. Are Americans aware of developments in robotics and computers and their potential for changing the nature of many jobs?
3. To what extent is the American public supportive of workplace automation?
4. What is the American public's view on the risks of automation of their own jobs and the professions and jobs of others?
5. What are the positive and negative impact of widespread job automation?
6. In the event that robots and computers are capable of doing many human jobs, what policies would the public support in dealing with its impact on individuals in particular, and the broader society in general?
7. How does the advances in artificial intelligence and computers facilitate entrepreneurship in the American economy?

DATA AND MEASUREMENT OF VARIABLES

This chapter is based on survey data seeking to gauge the opinions of Americans on advances in robotics and artificial intelligence. The data set used, which is nationally representative was collected from May 1–15, 2017, with a sample size of 4,135. The survey was conducted by Pew Research Center. The Pew Research Center is a nonpartisan 'fact tank' that is based in Washington, DC. It provides information on science and technology, US policy, global attitudes and trends, public opinion, and demographic trends shaping the US and the world.

Sociodemographic variables

Sociodemographics variables collected include age, gender, level of education and employment status. Age is measured in years. About 21% and 60% of the respondents were between 18–29 years and 30–69 years respectively. The rest were 65 years and over. Gender is coded as a dichotomous variable (female coded 2 and male coded 1). In the sample, about 48.2% (1991) were male and 51.8% (2144) female. With respect to level of education, 30% of the sample completed college education, 33% had some college education, whereas 37% were high school graduates or less. Most respondents (37%) earn less than US$30,000 per annum. About 35% and 28% of them earn between US$30,000–74,999 and US$75,000 respectively.

The importance of work in our lives

Why do we work? Do we work for money, leisure or what? The virtue of work is normally culturally determined. As Schwartz (2015, pp. 1 & 8) aptly noted:

> people do their work because it's an opportunity for social engagement. They do their tasks as part of teams, and even when they are working alone, there are plenty of opportunities for social interaction during work's quite moments. These people are satisfied with their work because they find what they do meaningful.

He continued that work facilitates engagement, meaning, challenge, discretion, autonomy, variety and gives people the chance to use their ingenuity to solve problems as they arise and develop more effective ways to get work done.

According to US National Academies of Sciences, Engineering & Medicine (2017, p. 102), work occupies a great deal of people's time and attention and has played a central role in shaping a sense of worth and identity. It is in that context that people's work plays an important role in their lives. In order to ascertain the level of importance Americans placed on work, PEW asked respondents the following question: 'Would you say that society generally places too much importance on working and having a job, not enough importance on working and having a job, or is just about right?' The response options were too much importance, not enough importance, and just about enough. The results are shown in Figure 22.1. Half of the respondents indicated that not enough importance is placed on working and having a job. This suggests that half of the American public has the perception that people do not have motivation to work. This might be due to the flawed character perspective prevalent in American society, where poverty is associated with those with poor work ethic. This needs further exploration in the context of developments in automation.

Awareness about automation

PEW Research Center created the following scenario to gauge whether new developments in robotics and computers are changing the nature of work in the US society:

> New developments in robotics and computing are changing the nature of many jobs. Today, these technologies are mostly being used in certain settings to perform routine tasks that are repeated throughout the day. But in the future, robots and computers with advanced capabilities may be able to do most of the jobs that are currently done by humans today. How much have you heard, read, or thought about this idea before today? Response options ranged from "a lot", to "nothing at all".

The results are shown in Table 22.2. A high proportion of respondents do not have any awareness about development of robot caregivers for older adults and the development of algorithms that can evaluate and hire job candidates.

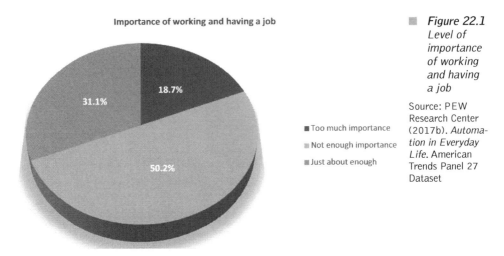

Figure 22.1 Level of importance of working and having a job

Source: PEW Research Center (2017b). *Automation in Everyday Life*. American Trends Panel 27 Dataset

THE FUTURE OF SME MARKETING AND OPERATIONS

Table 22.2 Awareness about new developments in robotics and computing

Type of technology	Level of awareness (%)		
	A lot	A little	Nothing at all
Development of robot caregivers for older adults	6.0	29.0	65.0
Development of algorithms that can evaluate and hire job candidates	8.0	33.6	57.4
*Development of driverless vehicles	34.0	60.0	6.0
Future where robots and computers can do human jobs	24.2	61.3	14.5

Source: PEW Research Center (2017b). *Automation in Everyday Life*. American Trends Panel 27 Dataset

*Question wording different for driverless vehicles. The actual question was: How much have you seen or heard about the effort to develop driverless vehicles – that is, cars and trucks that can operate on their own without a human driver?

The PEW survey asked Americans to express their views with respect to the chances of occurrence of business automation, robot deliveries, 3-D printing and doctor computer diagnosis in the next 20 years. The response options were: will definitely happen (coded 1), will probably happen (coded 2), will probably not happen (coded 3), and will definitely not happen (coded 4). They were reverse coded so that higher values were associated with greater chances of occurrence. The results are shown in Table 22.3. It appears that Americans feel that most of the technological advances have good chances of occurrences, especially the following: doctors will rely on computer programs to diagnose most diseases and determine treatments; and most stores and retail businesses will be fully automated and involve little or no human interaction between customers and employees.

Enthusiasm and worries about the development of robots

The PEW survey asked the American public about enthusiasm in relation to the development of robot caregivers; driverless vehicles; job hiring algorithms; and a future where robots and computers can do human jobs. There were four response options ranged from not at all enthusiastic (coded 4) to very enthusiastic (coded 1). They were reverse coded so that higher values were associated with greater levels of enthusiasm. Table 22.4 depicts the results. This shows that the development of robot caregivers has the highest mean enthusiasm value of 2.4, whereas the development of algorithms that can evaluate and hire job candidate has the lowest value of 2.0.

Similar to enthusiasm about the development of automation technologies, the survey asked the American public about worries with respect to the development of robot caregivers; driverless vehicles; job hiring algorithms; and future where robots and computers can do human jobs. There were four response options ranged from not at all worried (coded 4) to very worried (coded 1). They were reverse coded so that higher values were associated with greater levels of worries. Table 22.5 shows that the mean values for enthusiasm and worries on future where robots and computers can do human jobs are 2.2 and 2.9 respectively. It is obvious that Americans express more worry than enthusiasm about development of robot caregivers, driverless vehicles, job hiring algorithms, and future where robots and computers can do human jobs.

363

Table 22.3 *Chances of occurrence of business automation, robot deliveries, 3-D printing and doctor computer diagnosis*

Type of occurrence	Chances of occurrence (%)			
	Will definitely happen	Will probably happen	Will probably not happen	Will definitely not happen
Most stores and retail businesses will be fully automated and involve little or no human interaction between customers and employees (Mean = 2.8)	13.5	51.8	18.4	2.3
Most deliveries in cities will be made by robots or drones instead of humans (Mean = 2.7)	11.9	53.5	30.8	3.8
When people want to buy most common products, they will create them at home using a 3-D printer (Mean = 2.4)	6.9	36.4	49.9	6.8
Doctors will rely on computer programs to diagnose most diseases and determine treatments (Mean = 3.0)	21.0	58.3	18.4	2.3

Source: PEW Research Center (2017b). *Automation in Everyday Life.* American Trends Panel 27 Dataset

Table 22.4 *Enthusiasm about development of robot caregivers, driverless vehicles, job hiring algorithms, and future where robots and computers can do human jobs*

Type of technology	Level of enthusiasm (%)			
	Very enthusiastic	Somewhat enthusiastic	Not too enthusiastic	Not at all enthusiastic
Development of robot caregivers for older adults (Mean = 2.4)	9.1	35.0	37.9	18.0
Development of algorithms that can evaluate and hire job candidates (Mean = 2.0)	3.1	19.3	49.6	28.0
Development of driverless vehicles (Mean = 2.3)	11.5	28.5	38.5	21.7
Future where robots and computers can do human jobs (Mean = 2.2)	5.7	27.0	47.0	20.3

Source: PEW Research Center (2017b). *Automation in Everyday Life.* American Trends Panel 27 Dataset

THE FUTURE OF SME MARKETING AND OPERATIONS

Table 22.5 Worries about development of robot caregivers, driverless vehicles, job hiring algorithms, and future where robots and computers can do human jobs

Type of technology	Level of worry (%)			
	Very worried	Somewhat worried	Not too worried	Not at all worried
Development of robot caregivers for older adults (Mean = 2.5)	14.2	33.2	42.8	9.8
Development of algorithms that can evaluate and hire job candidates (Mean = 2.8)	21.3	46.2	25.5	7.0
Development of driverless vehicles (Mean = 2.6)	14.3	39.5	35.2	11.0
Future where robots and computers can do human jobs (Mean = 2.9)	24.8	47.8	23.0	4.4

Source: PEW Research Center (2017b). *Automation in Everyday Life*. American Trends Panel 27 Dataset

IMPACT OF TECHNOLOGY ON FUTURE WORK

In the context of the impact of technology on the future of work, the survey sought to find American's views on the positive and negative impact due to widespread automation of jobs. Specifically, respondents were asked the following questions: 'if robots and computers were able to perform most of the jobs currently being done by humans, do you think the following are likely or not likely to happen as a result?':

> Inequality between rich and poor would be much worse than it is today; people would have a hard time finding things to do with their lives; people would be able to focus less on work and more on the things that really matter to them in life; the economy as a whole would be much more efficient; the economy would create many new, better-paying jobs for humans; humans would find their jobs more meaningful and fulfilling since machines would mostly be doing things that humans find unappealing.

The response options were: yes, likely (coded 1) and no, not likely (coded 2). The results are shown in Table 22.6. With respect to negative outcomes (that is, inequality between rich and poor would be much worse than it is today; and people would have a hard time finding things to do with their lives), at least two-thirds of Americans have a negative outlook. On the other hand, smaller proportions of the American public expect positive outcomes from a world in which machines do most of the jobs currently done by humans.

In the event that robots and computers are able to do most of the jobs that are done by humans today, respondents were asked if they would favor or oppose a number of public policies shown in Figure 22.2. The response categories range from strongly favor (coded 1) and strongly oppose (coded 4). They were reverse coded so that higher values were associated with greater levels of support. The results show that the American public is supportive of policy solutions in terms of universal basic income and limiting robots and computers to jobs dangerous or unhealthy for humans to do.

365

Table 22.6 *Positive and negative impact from widespread automation of jobs*

	Yes, likely	No, not likely
Inequality between rich and poor would be much worse than it is today	77.1	22.9
People would have a hard time finding things to do with their lives	64.0	36.0
People would be able to focus less on work and more on the things that really matter to them in life	42.6	57.4
The economy as a whole would be much more efficient	43.4	56.6
The economy would create many new, better-paying jobs for humans	24.8	75.2
Humans would find their jobs more meaningful and fulfilling since machines would mostly be doing things that humans find unappealing	40.5	59.5

Source: PEW Research Center (2017b). *Automation in Everyday Life.* American Trends Panel 27 Dataset

Public support for policies in the event that robots and computers are capable of doing human jobs

- If the federal government created a national service program that paid people to perform tasks even if a robot or computer could do those tasks faster or cheaper
- If people had the option of paying extra to interact with a human, rather than a robot or computer, when buying a product or service
- If robots and computers were mostly limited to doing jobs that are dangerous or unhealthy for humans to do
- If the federal government provided all Americans with a guaranteed income that would allow them to meet their basic needs

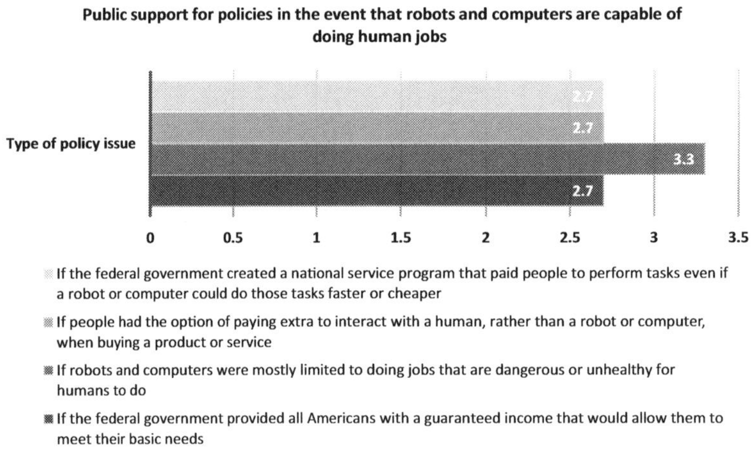

Figure 22.2 *Public support for policies in the event that robots and computers are capable of doing human jobs*

Source: PEW Research Center (2017b). *Automation in Everyday Life.* American Trends Panel 27 Dataset

Publics views was sought on government or individual responsibility in providing for displaced workers and justification of robotisation by businesses. The results are shown in Figure 22.3. The American public is evenly split on whether individuals or government are the most responsible for taking care of people whose jobs are displaced by robots or computers. Similarly, about 50% of the public feel that individuals would have an obligation to take care of their own financial well-being, even if robots and computers have already taken many of the jobs they might be qualified for. This views are consistent with Americans' controversial obsession with 'individual responsibility' while downplaying the role of government in ensuring equity.

Americans' view on the risk of automation of their 'own job or profession' and 'other jobs or professions' was surveyed. The survey asked the following question: 'How likely, if at all, do you think it is that your own job or profession will be mostly done by robots or computers in your lifetime?' The same question was asked with respect to the following professions: software engineer, legal clerk, nurse, construction worker, fast food worker, teacher, and

THE FUTURE OF SME MARKETING AND OPERATIONS

■ *Figure 22.3* American's public's views on government or individual responsibility in providing for displaced workers; and justification of robotisation by businesses

Source: PEW Research Center (2017b). *Automation in Everyday Life*. American Trends Panel 27 Dataset

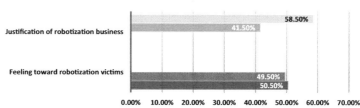

■ *Figure 22.4* American public's views on the risk of automation of jobs

Source: PEW Research Center (2017b). *Automation in Everyday Life*. American Trends Panel 27 Dataset

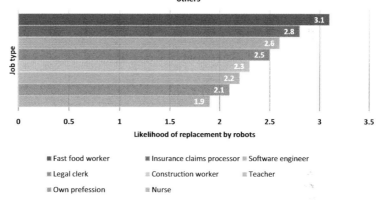

insurance claims processor. The response categories range from very likely (coded 1) to not at all likely (coded 4). They were reverse coded so that higher values were associated with greater levels of likelihood. As shown in Figure 22.4, Americans indicated a high level of confidence that their own professions will be replaced by robots or humans during their lifetimes, with just about 6% of Americans expressing the likelihood of its future occurrence. The safest job is nursing, followed by American's own jobs or professions. It is worthy of note that about two-in-five workers in banking, finance, insurance, accounting or real estate, retail, hospitality, and service indicated that their jobs are at least somewhat likely at risk of being automated in their lifetime, compared with workers in other industries such as education, healthcare, and information technology. The relatively low proportion of Americans who view their jobs at low risk suggests that some may be underestimating the possible impact of robots and computers.

BI-VARIATE ANALYSES

Bi-variate relationships between enthusiasm about robot caregiving, business automation, government guaranteed income and related variables are presented in Tables 22.7, 22.8 and 22.9 below.

EMMANUEL ADUGU

Table 22.7 *Relationship between enthusiasm and worries about robot caregiving, hiring algorithms, development of driverless vehicles, future where robots and can do many human jobs, and demographic variables*

Variable	Age	Level of education	Income
Robot caregiving enthusiasm	−0.10**	0.21**	0.13**
Robot caregiving worries	0.05**	−0.15**	−0.12**
Hiring algorithms enthusiasm	−0.09**	ns	−0.05**
Hiring algorithm worries	−0.06**	ns	Ns
Driverless vehicle enthusiasm	−0.18**	0.18**	0.11**
Driverless vehicle worries	Ns	−0.10**	−0.13**
Robots doing human job enthusiasm	−0.11**	0.11**	0.01**
Robots doing human jobs worries	0.04**	−0.12**	−0.07**

Source: PEW Research Center (2017b). *Automation in Everyday Life.* American Trends Panel 27 Dataset

**Correlation significant at 0.01 level (2-tailed); ns means correlation not significant

Table 22.8 *Relationship between business automation, robot deliveries, 3-D print products, doctor computer diagnosis, robots doing human job (enthusiasm), robots doing human jobs (worries), age, level of education, income, and effect of robotisation on own profession*

Variable	Effect of robotisation on own profession
Business automation	0.17**
Robot deliveries	0.17**
3-D print products	0.11**
Doctor computer diagnosis	0.12**
Robots doing human job (enthusiasm)	0.08**
Robots doing human jobs (worries)	0.15**
Age	−0.06**
Level of education	−0.12**
Income	−0.10**

Source: PEW Research Center (2017b). *Automation in Everyday Life.* American Trends Panel 27 Dataset

**Correlation significant at 0.01 level (2-tailed)

Examining Table 22.7, age is negatively associated with enthusiasm about robot caregiving. Americans' enthusiasms about robot caregiving is positively linked to income and level of education. On the other hand, worries about robot caregiving are negatively associated with level of education and income. The more educated an individual, the less worried he/she is about robots doing human jobs. Similarly, the higher the level of education of an individual, the more enthusiastic he/she feels about robots doing human jobs.

Table 22.8 depicts the relationship between business automation, robot deliveries, 3-D print products, doctor computer diagnosis, enthusiasm about robots doing human jobs,

THE FUTURE OF SME MARKETING AND OPERATIONS

Table 22.9 *Relationship between guaranteed income, national service program, extra payment for human interaction, limitation of robots to dangerous jobs, and sociodemographics*

Variable	Age	Level of education	Income
Government guaranteed income	−0.13**	−0.08**	−0.21**
Limit robots and computers	0.08**	ns	Ns
Extra payment for human interaction	0.07**	ns	Ns
Government program to pay people	−0.05**	−0.19**	−0.22**

Source: PEW Research Center (2017b). *Automation in Everyday Life*. American Trends Panel 27 Dataset

**Correlation significant at 0.01 level (2-tailed); ns means correlation not significant

worries about robots doing human jobs, age, level of education, income, and effect of robotisation on one's own profession. There is a positive and significant relationship between business automation, robot deliveries, 3-D print products, doctor computer diagnosis, enthusiasm about robots doing human job, worries about robots doing human jobs, age, level of education, income, and effect of robotisation on one's own profession. The feeling that one's own profession will be mostly done by robots and computers in the future has a positive correlation with expectation of business automation, robot deliveries, diagnosis and treatment of diseases, and others. On the other hand, those young, having low level of education and income, are more likely to feel that their jobs or professions will be mostly done by robots and computers in the future.

The relationship between guaranteed income, national service program, extra payment for human interaction, limitation of robots to dangerous jobs and sociodemographics is shown in Table 22.9. From Table 22.9, those who are young, with low levels of education and income are more likely to support government guaranteed income in the event that computers are able to do most jobs that are done by humans today. A similar trend holds for the scenario if the government created a national service program that paid people to perform tasks even if a robot or computer could do those tasks faster or cheaper (in the event that computers are able to do most jobs that are done by humans today).

DISCUSSION

Many Americans have the perception that society attaches importance to working and having a job. Work is an opportunity for social engagement and affords people the opportunity to use their skills and ingenuity to solve problems (Schwartz, 2015), which may ultimately facilitate life satisfaction. Unfortunately, current technological advances such as artificial intelligence and robots are resulting in acute changes, where jobs are being eliminated in some occupations and sectors of the economy.

It is unfortunate that a high proportion of the American public does not have any awareness about technological advancements such as robot care givers for adults and the development of algorithms that can evaluate and hire job candidates. This means that people are not well positioned to anticipate and respond to changing skill needs in order to thrive in a rapidly emerging digital economy. For that matter, educational institutions, government, unions, civil society, and entrepreneurs must form strategic partnerships to create awareness and empower people with relevant knowledge and skills.

369

Even though, in general, the American public is optimistic about the impact of automation on their work and lives, their attitudes consistently reflect worry and concern in relation to its consequences. Specifically, they express more worry than enthusiasm about development of robot caregivers, driverless vehicles, job hiring algorithms, and future where robots and computers can do human jobs. These worries are real and may be further linked to earning and hours worked. As OECD (2018, p. 3) aptly noted, 'Today, workers in occupations with a high risk of automation display much her rates of unemployment than those with low risks and the workers in the most automatable jobs work eight hours less per week than those in the least automatable professions'. However, looking at the jobs at risk of automation, the concern that artificial intelligence poses a threat to the social and economic well-being of American society is neither limited to so-called white-collar nor blue-collar jobs. Indeed, the risk is collar-blind.

Frey and Osborne (2017) identified three sets of tasks which currently cannot be easily automated, as their codification is challenging. These are tasks related to social intelligence, such as understanding other people's reactions in social contexts or assisting or caring for others; tasks related to creative intelligence, such as coming up with original ideas; tasks related to perception and manipulation, in particular where they are performed in unstructured, complex situations such as operating in cramped work spaces. Tasks that integrate these skills are much less vulnerable to technological change. It is in that vein that workers will have to be able to take on complex, less automatable tasks such as problem solving in novel situations while working with new technologies – further requiring literacy, numeracy, problem solving, autonomy, coordination, and collaborative skills (OECD, 2015a). Clearly, people still matter. But there is an urgent need for people to race ahead of new technology to enable them thrive in the digital economy.

Historically, technological advances hardly benefit everyone in society. As usual, some sectors of the society tend to be favored whereas others are disadvantaged. It is therefore not surprising that an overwhelming proportion of Americans are concerned that the emergence of artificial intelligence and computers will worsen the inequality between the rich and poor coupled with the feeling that people will have a hard time finding jobs. Based on the analysis from the dataset used for this chapter, it appears that those who are young, with low levels of education and income are more likely to support government guaranteed income in the event that computers are able to do most jobs that are done by humans today. These individuals may be poorly prepared with respect to creative intelligence, social intelligence, and ICT skills. This calls for relevant policy interventions, such as incentivising entrepreneurship, and skill training.

INCENTIVISING ENTREPRENEURSHIP

One major policy intervention is to incentivise entrepreneurship in the artificial intelligence domain. Dau and Cuervo-Cazurra (2014) describes entrepreneurship as the creation of fresh businesses, a collection of people who coordinate their efforts to produce fresh value-added economic activity. Entrepreneurship is generally conceptualised in the context of the ability of an individual or group to discover an opportunity or create one, and when strategically implemented, may benefit the innovator (entrepreneur, product, or service developer, etc.). There is a lot of opportunity for entrepreneurs to seize in a digital economy.

Entrepreneurs can identify new opportunities in many sectors emerging from advances in artificial intelligence in such areas as drone delivery, diagnosis and treatment of diseases,

THE FUTURE OF SME MARKETING AND OPERATIONS

and agricultural extension. Incentives may be offered in the form of tax breaks, investment capital to entrepreneurs in the afore-mentioned areas where jobs can be created and people trained with requisite skills for their benefit in particular and the economy in general. In fact, to seize on the benefits of technological change, economies need ICT specialists: workers who can code, develop applications, manage networks and manage and analyse Big Data, among other skills, which enable innovation, in a digital economy, to flourish but also support infrastructure that firms, governments, commerce, and users rely on (OECD, 2015a). As a result, entrepreneurs can develop new business models that adopt new technologies.

For job creation initiatives, entrepreneurs can organise and facilitate collaboration between artificial intelligence researchers and experts in environment, agriculture, healthcare to develop solutions to current challenges in those sectors. It is in that context Google's artificial intelligence centres are laudable. These centres are located in Tokyo, Zurich, Paris, New York, and Accra. According to Google, its artificial intelligence centres work on issues related to agriculture, health, and education. For example, in agriculture, one of Google's interest is in relation to the use of artificial intelligence in boosting agricultural productivity in developing countries, which may ultimately lead to economic growth and improved well-being. Thus in spite of public concern about roots and computers with advanced capabilities, there is still hope that individuals can be empowered to succeed in the digital economy. People need to race ahead of machines and be engaged in jobs that only humans can do.

The following scenarios and the questions that follow further deepen the reader's understanding on the complex linkage between job automation, entrepreneurship, and the future of work.

SCENARIO 1

As a result of advances in artificial intelligence and computers, today, when companies are hiring they typically have someone read applicants' resumes and conduct personal interviews to choose the right person for the job. In the future, computer programs may be able to provide a systematic review of each applicant without the need for human involvement. These programs would give each applicant a score based on the content of their resume, application, or standardised tests for skills such as problem solving or personality type. Applicants would then be ranked and hired based on those scores.

- Thinking about the possibility that job candidates might be evaluated using a computer program, how enthusiastic are you, about this possibility for society as a whole? Give reasons for your answer.
- Thinking about the possibility that job candidates might be evaluated using a computer program, how worried are you, about this possibility for society as a whole? Give reasons for your answer.
- Would you, personally, apply for a job that used this type of computer program to make hiring decisions? Why or why not?
- Do you think that these computer programs would do a better job as compared to humans when it comes to hiring candidates who fit well with the company's culture?
- Considering the fact that higher education institutions are incubators of human talent, what in your view should they (higher education institutions) play in preparing people to fit and thrive in a digital economy?

371

SCENARIO 2

A number of companies (Google, Uber, Toyota, Tesla, etc.) are developing and testing autonomous vehicles (that is cars and trucks that can operate on their own without a human driver), and many modern cars offer semi-autonomous features such as adaptive cruise control and lane-assist technology.

■ Would you, personally, want to drive in a driverless vehicle if you had the opportunity?

If driverless vehicles become widespread, which of the following do you think are likely to happen as a result?

■ Many people who drive for a living would lose their jobs.
■ Owning a car would become much less important to people.
■ Elderly and disabled people will be able to live more independently.

SCENARIO 3

In view of the fact that new developments in robotics and computing are changing the nature of many jobs currently done by humans, most deliveries in cities may be made by robots or drones instead of humans in the near future. Indicate your approval of the following statements:

■ If businesses can receive better work at lower cost by replacing humans with robots and computers, they are justified in doing so.
■ There should be limits on how many jobs businesses can replace with robots and computers, even if they can do those jobs better and more cheaply than humans can.

GROUP ACTIVITY

This book chapter reveals that advances in artificial intelligence and computers hold varied opportunities for creative entrepreneurs to use their skills. Assuming that you are an entrepreneur, create a business model to establish a robot delivery company. Your company's objective is to deliver drugs and medical equipment to remote villages in the developing world.

Chapter synopsis

The chapter demonstrates that with respect to impact of artificial intelligence and computers (specifically, whether inequality between rich and poor would be much worse than it is today; and if people would have a hard time finding things to do with their lives), at least two-thirds of Americans have a negative outlook. On the other hand, smaller proportions of the American public expect positive outcomes from a world in which machines do most of the jobs currently done by humans. The public is supportive of policy solutions in terms of universal basic income and limiting robots and computers to dangerous or unhealthy jobs.

The American public is evenly split on whether individuals or government are the most responsible for taking care of people whose jobs are displaced by robots or computers. Similarly, about 50% of the public feel that individuals would have an obligation to take care of their own financial well-being, even if robots and computers have already taken many of the jobs they might be qualified for. This views are consistent with Americans' controversial obsession with 'individual responsibility' versus government.

Americans indicated a high level of confidence that their own professions will be replaced by robots or humans during their lifetimes. The public views nursing as the safest job, followed by their own jobs or professions. The relatively low proportion of Americans who view their jobs at low risk suggests that some may be underestimating the possible impact of robots and computers. As automation eliminates some jobs and render others redundant, entrepreneurs could identify emerging new opportunities and create jobs to benefit all in society.

Question: In view of all the content in this book chapter, to what extent is technological advancement a blessing or bane to society in the 21st century?

REFERENCES

Arntz, M. et al. (2016) *The Risk of Automation for Jobs in OECD Countries.* OECD social, employment and migration working papers. OECD Publishing, Paris.

Autor, D. (2015) Why are there still so many jobs? The history and future of workplace automation. *Journal of Economic Perspectives,* 29(3), 3–30.

Balliester, T. and Elsheikhi, A. (2018) *The Future of Work: A Literature Review.* Research Department Working Paper No. 29. International Labor Organization.

Berger, R. (2016) *The Industrie 4.0 Transition Quantified.* Roland Berger GMBH, Munich.

Brynjolfsson, E. and McAfree, A. (2014a) *The Second Machine Age.* MIT, Cambridge.

Brynjolfsson, E. and McAfee, A. (2014b) *The Second Machine Age: Work, Progress, and Prosperity in a Time of Brilliant Technologies.* W. W. Norton & Co, New York.

Chang, J. and Phu, H. (2016) *The Future of Jobs at Risk of Automation in ASEAN* (ILO Working Paper No. 9). ILO, Geneva.

Dau, A. I. and Cuervo-Cazurra, A. (2014) To formalize or not to formalize: Entrepreneurship and pro-market institutions. *Journal of Business Venturing,* 29(5), 668–686.

Decanio, S. (2016) Robots and humans – complements or substitutes? *Journal of Macroeconomics,* 49, 280–291.

Frey, C. and Osborne, M. (2013) *The Future of Employment: How Susceptible Are Jobs to Computerisation?* (Working paper). University of Oxford, Oxford.

Frey, C. and Osborne, M. (2015) *Technology at Work: The Future of Innovation and Employment.* (Citi GPS reports). University of Oxford, Oxford.

Frey, C. B. and Osborne, M. A. (2017) The future of employment: How susceptible are jobs to computerization? *Technological Forecasting and Social Change,* 114(C), 254–280.

McKinsey Global Institute (2016) *Technology, Jobs and the Future of Work.* Briefing Note New York.

OECD (2015) *OECD Science, Technology and Industry Scoreboard 2015.* OECD Publishing, Paris.

OECD (2017) *OECD Digital Economy Outlook 2017.* OECD Publishing, Paris.

OECD (2018) Putting faces to the jobs at risk of automation. *Policy Brief on the Future of Work.* OECD Publishing, Paris.

PEW Research Center (2017a) *Automation in Everyday Life.*

PEW Research Center (2017b) *Automation in Everyday Life.* American Trends Panel 27 Dataset.

PwC (2017) *The Long-View: How Will the Global Economic Order Change by 2050?* PwC London. Available at: https://www.pwc.com/gx/en/world-2050/assets/pwc-the-world-in-2050-full-report-feb-2017.pdf.

Rus, D. (2015) How technological breakthroughs will transform everyday life. *Foreign Affairs,* July/ August.

Schwartz, B. (2015) *Why We Work*. TED Books, Simon & Schuster, London.

The National Academies of Sciences, Engineering and Medicine (2017). *Information Technology and the U.S. Workforce: Where Are We and Where Do We Go From Here?* The National Academies Press, Washington, DC.

World Bank Group (2016) *World Development Report 2016: Digital Dividends*. World Bank, Washington, DC. Available at: https://openknowledge.worldbank.org/handle/10986/23347 License: CC BY 3.0 IGO.

Chapter 23
Religion and the SME

Andrew Lindridge

> **LEARNING OBJECTIVES**
>
> *After reading the chapter, you will be able to:*
> - Understand what religion is, what it constitutes and why religion should not be viewed as a homogenous entity;
> - Recognise how religion affects behaviour and identity, and how this affects SMEs;
> - Appreciate how religion affects SMEs at an operational level;
> - Identify the marketing opportunities that religion offers SMEs;
> - Appreciate how religion can be used by SMEs from a strategic perspective.

Does Halal meat taste so differently from non-Halal meat? Should we be bothered or more importantly should we even care? Depending upon your ethnic background, the size of your organisation, or the country you live in, the answer may vary from indifference to strong feelings of emotion. (In case you do not know what Halal meat is, it is meat where the animal has been killed in such a way that the body is drained of its blood, as prescribed by Islamic law. At the same time prayers are said for the animal's soul as recognition for the loss of its life, which makes it in some ways more considerate than how the secular west slaughters its animals).

In fact the issue of Halal meat, in 2010, has now become a hugely political issue in secular France where a franchised burger chain recently introduced Halal meat into its burger recipes. The restaurant, situated in a Paris suburb, operating as a SME, simply responded to its predominately Muslim community needs and witnessed its sales increase rapidly over the following weeks. As far as business goes, this makes great commercial sense. After all, marketing gurus have spent years extolling the values of giving your customers what you want and reaping the profits in return.

The topical issue of religion is often inflamed by a biased media, personal ignorance, or simply naïveté, religion has become a negative force that is often perceived as the cause of all problems in a society. Religion is often seen as a negative force that is the cause of all problems in a society – a perspective, which brings us back to Halal burgers and France. The French Government has now, rightly or wrongly, decided that the issue of Halal meat is a threat to secular France. A threat so great that the French Government is now considering

ANDREW LINDRIDGE

making its sale illegal (along with Kosher–Jewish meat, and any other religion's treatment of food that can be deemed non-secular).

Is Halal a threat to our Western secular societies, should we even care, or more importantly what is religion and how does it affect SMEs? Whilst the threat, real or not, of Halal to Western society is something we do not have the space to discuss here, we will be able to answer the other questions. By the end of this chapter you should be able to articulate what religion is and the problems and opportunities it poses for SMEs.

INTRODUCTION

The term 'religion' in the 21st century is likely to provoke feelings of tension and fear for some individuals or peace and tranquility for others, but what exactly is religion? Before we explore this issue let us get one issue clear – the world may think it is getting more religious but it would appear that not all is what it seems.

Americans buy in excess of 20 million bibles every year, with each American home owning on average four bibles (*The Economist*, 2007). Yet according to a Gallup survey half of Americans are unable to name the first book of the Bible (*Genesis*), two-thirds of Americans think the Sermon on the Mount was done by the evangelical preacher Billy Graham (it was in fact Jesus), and over 25% do not realise what Easter is meant to celebrate (the resurrection of Christ and the foundation of the Christian religion). Matters are not much better when it comes to reciting the Ten Commandments (only 60% can do this), whilst 12% of Americans thought Noah was married to Joan of Arc (a French knight who helped drive the English out of France in the 15th century).

Matters are not much better for Muslims either, with the general preference being to read the Quran in its first language – old Arabic. In its original form, Arabic is difficult to understand for most Arabic speakers (who are used to a more modernised version), whilst only 20% of Muslims actually speak Arabic.

What then can SMEs conclude about religion from this? First of all religion should not be interpreted or understood from a strict perspective. Religion is often what individuals choose to interpret its meanings. Second, and perhaps most importantly, religion should be viewed from an identity perspective. It is this perspective that offers the biggest opportunity for SMEs as we shall discover.

TOWARDS AN UNDERSTANDING OF RELIGION

Religion has been described as one of the most important cultural forces and influences on human behaviour (Delener, 1990), reflecting an acceptance of another, superior being over humanity (Durkheim, 1976). Such is the influence of religion over individuals that it is often considered to be the most important aspect of a group or society's cultural values, providing a reason d'être for that culture to exist (Hefner, 1998). Religion then covers a range of topics including beliefs, narrative, practices, and symbolism that provide a sense of meaning to the individual's life. The world then has six dominant main religions: Buddhism, Christianity, Hinduism, Judaism, Islam and Sikhism. Although there are many other religions, these are the ones that most SMEs are likely to encounter.

When we consider religion and what it constitutes, it is important to recognise that religion is not a homogenous whole but rather a fragmented collection of sub-religions, all of which adhere to some shared, agreed upon similarity. This fragmentation often arises from historical or cultural re-interpretations, and whilst important in understanding religion only

376

needs to be noted here. For example, within Christianity the following religions all share a common belief in Jesus but differ in how they expect followers to live their lives: Catholics, Orthodox, and Protestants, to which we can subdivide these into further groups, including Baptists, Church of England, Quakers, and so on. Whilst SMEs need not bother themselves with how these individual differences affect them, an awareness and consideration of these differences may be beneficial.

RELIGION, IDENTITY, AND BEHAVIOUR

Having identified what religion is and the numerous sub-categories that exist within each religion, we now need to consider how religion affects an individual's identity and behaviour. This is important for SMEs to understand as this will have an effect on both their internal (such as staff) and external environments (such as marketing and strategy implications).

In understanding religion's effect on identity, and hence its relevance to SMEs, we need to consider social identity theory. Social identity theory states that an individual's self-concept, i.e., who they are, is derived from their membership of groups (Tajfel and Turner, 1986), such as religious groups. Group membership entails then roles and behaviours, which help the individual in determining their own sense of self-identity; for example, self-identifying you to your religion. This process may involve social role performance where an individual adjusts their behaviour to satisfy the group's expectations, such as adhering to religious teachings. By developing a particular social role performance, the individual is allowed to adapt their behaviours to suit the context and situation they encounter. Religion's role then in social identity is particularly important in meeting an individual's psychological needs, as religion is 'more comprehensively and potently than other repositories of cultural meaning that contribute to the construction and maintenance of individual and group identities' (Seul, 1999, p. 553).

An individual's sense of self-identity then will not only provide a means of knowing who they are but also provide a means for determining their behaviour. After all, if religion includes a set of prescribed behaviours and provides a sense of identity, then it naturally follows that religion will affect an individual's behaviour. This affect may range from the need to prayer through to observing religious rituals on prescribed dates – all important considerations for SMEs as we shall soon see.

RELIGION AND ACCULTURATION

In discussing the role of religion in identity, we also need to consider its importance from an ethnic minority perspective. Most developed economies have ethnic minority populations with differing religious orientations, and as I shall show these groups can offer SMEs important marketing opportunities. To understand then the importance of religion to these groups, we need to understand how they relate not only to their religion but also their own communities and the wider society they exist within. A complex relationship called acculturation.

Acculturation describes a 'cultural change that is initiated by the conjunction of two or more autonomous cultural systems' (The Social Science Research Council, 1954, p. 974) representing a bi-directional process, with the individual's behaviours, identification, and values related to both their ethnic and dominant culture. Therefore an individual's ethnic and dominant cultural identities represents, to varying degrees, acceptance of both cultures. One of the most relevant studies into acculturation and how to group ethnic minority individuals into differing levels of acculturation is Berry's (1990, 1992, 1997) Bi-directional

377

Acculturation Model. Berry argued that an ethnic minority individual chooses between maintenance of their ethnic cultural values and the extent that they chose to engage with the dominant host group. This approach leads to four distinct acculturation outcomes: (1) integration (equal interest in engaging with both the dominant and ethnic culture), (2) separation (rejection of the dominant culture in favour of ethnic culture), (3) assimilation (acceptance of the dominant culture and rejection of their ethnic culture), and (4) marginalisation (rejection of both cultures). The extent that an ethnic minority individual identifies with these categories will then determine not only their sense of identity but also their behaviours.

How then does religion manifest within these acculturation outcomes and why should SMEs be bothered? Research tells us that religion and its related activities are the most significant aspects of an ethnic minority's identity to be retained after language, leisure activities, and dietary habits have changed. An adherence to religion then provides a means to maintain not only the individual's cultural values and identity but also their wider group's (Burghart, 1987; Mearns, 1995; Modood et al., 1994; Vertovec, 1995; Williams, 1988).

The importance of religion to SMEs is that ethnic minorities often demonstrate higher levels of religious adherence as a means of negotiating dissonance arising from cultural interactions. Religion provides individuals then with a sense of their own ethnic self-identity in potentially difficult situations, such as dealing with experiences of racial discrimination (Dosanjh and Ghuman, 1997; Dreidger, 1975). By drawing upon religion as a tool for business may provide organisations with organisational, marketing, and strategic opportunities, as we shall now explore.

RELIGION AT AN ORGANISATIONAL LEVEL

The relevance and role of religion within SMEs is perhaps no different than that of larger organisations. Both organisational types exist in a multi-cultural world, where employees are often drawn from varying religious backgrounds; with each religious background often bringing with it different rituals, belief systems, etc., that often influence how an employee works.

Considering the role of religion within an SME presents the organisation with a broad and often diverse range of legal requirements and stipulations that may be unique to one country or a trading block of countries, such as the European Union. The purpose of this section then is not to laboriously list every legal act that may or may not affect SMEs but instead to explore the more generic implications of religion on the SME and its employees. However, as the British Chartered Management Institute argues the emphasis on religion and the organisation lies in the management understanding not only religious differences but also the wider legal implications. Religious issues may include rules and regulations regarding the wearing of the hijab (the headscarf worn by female Muslims), yarmulkes (skulls caps worn by Jewish males), crosses, turbans, etc., along with prayer and meditation breaks.

However should an SME be expected to understand and accommodate all the religious needs of its employees? One perspective may argue that the approach required is one of empowering the SMEs employees to request that their religious needs are met. This need should not be seen as being difficult to implement by the SME but instead should encourage the employee to express how allowing this religious need to be met will benefit the SME. For example, if a SME has a large number of Sikh employees, then these employees may argue that if they were given time off work to celebrate Vaisakhi (the Sikh celebration marking the founding of the Khalsa – an event marking the first five people to be initiated into the now formalised Sikh religion) would respect their religious and cultural needs. In

378

return they could argue that not only would the time lost by these employees be recuperated but also that their work-life satisfaction would increase and this would indirectly increase productivity.

How should SMEs then handle religious diversity among its employees? A general collection of guidelines was offered at the 2008 American Bar Association conference by employment lawyer Michael Homans of Falster/Greenberg PC (based in Philadelphia), Ingrid Johnson of Legal Services of Edison (in New Jersey) and Kevin Henry of the Coca-Cola Bottling Co. They suggested the following workplace practices regarding religion:

DO:

- Encourage diversity;
- Promote tolerance;
- Promote nondenominational 'values' and ethics;
- Establish a mechanism to review and consider requests for accommodation;
- Encourage employees to report any discrimination or harassment;
- Train managers and HR professionals on religious discrimination, harassment, and accommodation;
- Offer employees opportunities to promote voluntary participation in religious and non-religious activities outside work hours;
- Be wary of workplace proselytising;
- Respect employee beliefs, privacy, and dignity;
- Follow best practices to avoid religious bias, as you would with any equal employment opportunity category.

DON'T:

- Mandate attendance at religious services;
- Discriminate at work based on religion or nonreligion;
- Base accommodation decisions on the religion at issue;
- Allow employees to condemn as 'evil' or 'damned' others who believe differently;
- Rely on literature of only one religion to promote values or company ethos;
- Give overly generous or solicitous accommodations to employees of one religion unless you are willing to do so for all;
- Accommodate individual conduct, speech, or religious observances that create a harassing environment for others or otherwise impinge on other employees' rights.

Source: cited/quoted from Grossman, R. J., December 2008

RELIGION AND MARKETING IMPLICATIONS

Another aspect of religion and SME is how it affects what the individual consumes (after all SMEs as we shall soon see can benefit from selling products that adhere to religious laws). To understand this we need to return to our previous discussion on social identity. If our social identity is constructed around a religion then as individuals our need to identify and reinforce that identity will encourage us to consume products that support our beliefs. We saw this earlier in the story of the French burger bar that sold Halal burgers to Muslims; French Muslims bought the burgers because it not only complimented their food tastes (representing their Western, acculturated, perspectives) but also their religious identities (as Muslims). This consumption act, although appearing to be simple – people eat burgers so why not French Muslims – represents a much more complicated set of issues.

RELIGION AND MARKETING STRATEGY

For most SMEs, marketing strategy will largely be dictated by financial limitations, so the following discussion assumes this limitation. Also, in developing a marketing strategy, various religious problems and opportunities will arise. Whilst the following discussion cannot possibly cover all the ins and outs of developing a religious friendly marketing strategy, it should provide some indication of some of the issues that should be considered.

Price

The traditional concerns that price confronts the SME with are still relevant here, such as how to price to maximise profitability or market share whilst maintaining competitiveness. However, religious considerations also need to be considered here. For example, certain religions specifically state that acts of charity are not only desirable but should be freely offered (Islam and Sikhism for instance). It is entirely feasible that a small aspect of the profit generated by selling a product is automatically attributed to a previously declared charity as a means of showing and affirming adherence to religious principles.

Product

Issues surrounding product and adherence to religious needs are complicated by differing religions often having differing demands. Whilst Christianity may not have any particular religious needs surrounding acts of consumption, other religions do. For example, from a strictly religious perspective, SMEs selling products to the Hindu religious market should not include any aspect of animal related ingredient (especially beef), whilst the Judaism and Islam strictly prevent any consumption of any part of the pig, and the list goes on.

Promotion

Promotion can be particularly problematic for SMEs without wider complications of religion being included. A good example of this was McDonald's (admittedly not an SME but a good example all the same) and the 1996 Atlanta Olympics. To celebrate the event, McDonald's printed paper bags for its takeaway meals with the various flags of competing countries. To ensure fairness and global coverage, McDonald's included the Saudi Arabian flag. The problem, and McDonald's foolishly did not recognise this, was that the Saudi Arabian flag contains a verse from the Muslim Quran; the Quran being central to the teaching of Islam was now attached to a paper bag that was to be thrown away in a bin. Saudi Arabia protested that the paper bags were distasteful and offensive to Muslims around the world (owing to the Quran verse attached to the bag being thrown away). McDonald's apologised, withdrew the bag, and learned a costly lesson.

How then should SMEs approach religion and its influence on promotion? If an SME is particularly targeting a religious group then some consideration of the religion's values and beliefs should be considered. This need not cost a lot of money, a quick chat with a local religious leader would offer valuable insights and offer powerful public relations on getting your message right – a point that McDonald's would have been wise to heed. Generally, though a number of simple rules can be applied here:

- Don't use religious symbols as this can be misconstrued by your target audience.
- Understand what religious symbols you can use. For example, in Islam the colour green is considered to be auspicious so using green in promotional materials would be deemed to be positive.
- Do not make jokes or ironic comments about religion in your promotional materials. As religion is embedded within culture, how one individual sees humour is not how another will perceive it.
- Sponsoring local religious events can often be a good means of raising your profile and showing your support for a religious community.
- If in doubt talk to someone who would be able to offer you advice; inaction can often be more cost effective than a crassly made wrong decision.

PLACE

Where the product is sold will largely depend upon what market segment that the SME is targeting. In a country where the dominant religion is used as the segmenting variable then the normal rules of place will apply. However, if the SME is targeting a minority population then it is logical that the SME will ensure that their product is sold in the areas where that population dominates. However, this approach also introduces further complications, such as potentially smaller retail outlets unable to hold large amounts of stock, credit facilities for purchasing your products may be sought, and perhaps, most importantly, a greater personal relationship between the SME and the local community may not only be sought but also vital if the SME is to succeed in that market.

Religion and consumer behaviour

If an SME is to consider targeting a religious group then it must also consider the wider social context and personal choices that influence the decision to consume a particular product (Cosgel and Minkler, 2004). For example, the social context refers not only to the laws and rules of a particular religion regarding what can be eaten (in the case of the French restaurant Halal meat) but also the informal social norms that dictate appropriate behaviours. For example, France's Muslim population is widely considered to be one of the most, from an acculturation perspective, integrated, so eating a burger that as a concept has been inherited from America does not represent any particular religious-political issue. For other countries, where integration is not so evident or political opinions differ, this may not hold true. From a marketing perspective, any SME marketing a product that targets a religious orientated group would need to consider the wider sociopolitical context that influences their potential market consumer behaviours.

Personal choices also need to be considered, as the level of religious adherence will influence the extent that they, a religious group, will purchase a product. This refers to the extent that an individual is strictly religious in their identity and related behaviours.

Previous studies in how religion affects ethnic minority groups provides further insights into both the complications and opportunities that religion offers SMEs. In particular Lindridge (2010) studied the effect of religious difference in groups of second generation British born Indians who self-identified themselves as Hindu, Muslims or Sikhs. These differences although reflective of these religious groups offer some insight into the opportunities and problems that religion offers SMEs when considering how to market their products. In particular they found that:

- Religion directly affected their participants' consumption behaviours, with their level of brand orientation directly related to their level of religious adherence. Whilst Hindus and Sikhs lack of brand orientated was directly influenced by their mother's socialisation, it was their Muslim participants felt branded products were un-Islamic – a response that was often in contradiction to their parents.
- Hindu and Sikh participants were more likely to be influenced by their level of religion and consumption behaviours at a social level than Muslims. In particular, visits to religious institutions produced a need to demonstrate consumption of clothing, etc., that conformed to their community's social expectations, often traditional Indian clothing. Instead, their Muslim participants were only concerned with meeting Islamic dress codes and often wore Western clothing to religious institutions.
- Wider family narratives around consumption inferred gender and religious differences, with fathers' and male siblings' narratives dominated by conspicuous consumption and to varying extents rejection of or being selective regarding aspects of their religion. For the males, members of these participants families, religious adherence was not prevalent in their lives, instead conspicuous consumption was used as a means to construct a social identity but also a means to demonstrate self-worth and success to their wider community – a finding that was not replicated among the female members of their families.

Whilst this example illustrates the opportunities and complexities of religion to ethnic minorities, it does illustrate the issues that SMEs face in marketing products to religious groups. How then should SMEs apply religion within a marketing context? Yankelovich and Meer's (2006) called for markets to be segmented by non-demographic means to strengthen brand identity and create emotional connections with the organisation's consumers. As Yankelovich and Meer note (2006, p. 124), 'Good segmentations identify the groups most worth pursuing – the underserved, the dissatisfied, and those likely to make a first-time purchase, for example'. This approach then supports SMEs using religion as a means of segmenting their markets on the basis of actual consumer behaviours that comply with religion's influence on consumption.

RELIGION FROM A STRATEGIC PERSPECTIVE

The final part of this chapter reviews how religion can be used by SMEs to establish a corporate strategy. Hopefully by the time you have read this you would have begun to appreciate that religion can be used by SMEs as an asset to further develop and support the organisation. It is from this perspective that we now explore religion from a strategic perspective.

In the previous section on religion and marketing I suggested that religion could be used as a marketing tool to allow SMEs to target and develop specific market segments. By focussing SMEs' often limited resources on specific niche markets, it offers opportunities for market growth and profitability. This section then continues this premise, using Michael E. Porter's (1980) work on organisational competitive advantage as a framework to illustrate how religion can be used from a strategic perspective to gain competitive advantage.

382

Competitive advantage, Porter (1980) argues, occurs when an organisation is able to undertake one activity better than its competitors and that actively is valued and sought by potential customers. To achieve competitive advantage an organisation can undertake two differing strategies:

Cost-leadership: where all input costs are reduced to the lowest possible level and the organisation competes on being the cheapest in the market. This approach tends to be short lived as often new lower cost competitors emerge and.
Differentiation: where the organisation competes on one aspect of difference from its competitors, but a difference that the market and its customers are willing to pay for.

Porter (1980) reflecting the needs of SMEs notes that within each of these strategies, a niche strategy can be pursued, i.e., cost-leadership niche or differentiation niche. The emphasis on the niche here reflects that SMEs are unable to compete in larger markets against better resourced, larger competitors. Whilst it is unlikely that SMEs will be able to compete for long on a cost-leadership basis, the differentiation-niche strategy offers an appropriate strategy.

Religion has been identified with how individuals perceive themselves, how it affects employees and potential benefits to SMEs and how it can be used within marketing strategy to increase market share and profitability. Each of these approaches has relied upon using religion as a means of achieving a desired corporate objective. It follows then the organisations could use religion as a means of achieving a niche-differentiation strategy and through this competitive advantage. How? Quite simply by focussing the organisation's strategy onto a specific religious group and then ensuring that all aspects of the organisation meets these requirements, i.e., organisational and marketing perspectives that have already been discussed.

The extent that using religion as a means of achieving competitive advantage for SMEs is increasingly becoming apparent for a number of organisations that specifically follow this approach. Perhaps the best example, and one that forms the following case study, is the emergence and growth of Mecca Cola.

CHAPTER SUMMARY

The purpose of this chapter has been to explore the business opportunities and problems that religion offers SMEs. The aim then has been to explore how religion affects not only the organisation but also its marketing and strategic decisions.

From a problem perspective, religion may be perceived as a threat or an entity that is neither understood nor appreciated in its relevance to business. This chapter has suggested that the solution is not in avoiding the issues of religion but instead embracing it by understanding what it can offer the SME.

Religion also represents opportunities for SMEs. From an employee perspective, religion can be used as a means of engaging and motivating employees, representing a win-win situation for both the SME and the employer. Marketing should also consider how religion can be used to target specific religious groups by offering products that reflect and support their religious needs. This approach lends itself to SMEs developing a niche-differentiation strategy and through this allowing the organisation to achieve a competitive advantage.

ANDREW LINDRIDGE

KEY TERMS
- Acculturation
- Competitive advantage
- Cost-leadership
- Consumer behaviour
- Differentiation
- Place
- Price
- Product
- Promotion
- Religion

REVIEW QUESTIONS

1. How important is religion in the contemporary environment of entrepreneurship marketing? Illustrate your answer with real-life examples.

2. Evaluate the connection, if any, between entrepreneurial values and marketing values in an entrepreneurship context.

CASE STUDY – MECCA COLA

Mecca Cola is a cola drink, sold in over 56 countries around the world, and which is targeted specifically at the Muslim community. The origins of Mecca Cola lie in a combination of marketing opportunity and wider Muslim discomfort over America's policies towards the Middle East. The culmination of this discomfort manifested during the 2002 build up to the American-led invasion of Saddam Hussein's Iraq, with many Muslims feeling that American policies were deliberately targeting Muslims. Anger towards American foreign policy was not solely limited to Muslims, with many non-Muslims in Europe also growing increasingly angry and despondent towards America as well. A report by the *Financial Times* at this time noted that within America, 12% of the population were willing and were boycotting American brands such as Coco-Cola, associating these brands with American Imperialism (Gapper, 2004). Being a brand associated with American culture suddenly appeared to be a commercial threat.

Mecca Cola, named after the Muslim holy city of Mecca, was launched in 2004. Tasting and looking, at first sight, like any other cola drink with its use of red and white labelling, and packaging reaffirming its identity as a cola drink allowed it to compete against more established competitors. However, closer inspection of the packaging reveals the political-social-religious origins of the brand. Labelling, includes Arabic text reading 'Don't shake me, shake your conscience' with a picture of the Mosque in Jerusalem on the other side.

384

RELIGION AND THE SME

Owing to the relatively small size of the organisation, hence its relevance as an SME example, Mecca Cola suffered from financial restraints, which affected its ability to market its product. This was resolved through relying upon the Islamic religious principles that supported the brand and hence appealed to its niche, target market. For example, 20% of Mecca Cola's profits were allocated for charity projects, with 10% going to local charities and the remainder to support Palestinian children's charities. Cost restrictions prevented paid for advertising so a dedicated website was developed (www.mecca-cola.com). The remainder of the publicity came from widespread press coverage interested in a new product that decisively and clearly aimed to be politically, religiously, and commercially provocative.

Questions

1. To what extent do you think Mecca-Cola's success is simply down to opportunism?
2. Is the use of religion by Mecca Cola merely utilising a fad that will eventually see Muslim customers returning to more popular brands such as Coca-Cola?
3. Mecca-Cola is clearly using Porter's (1980) niche-differentiation strategy. What problems do you think would other SMEs experience using a similar approach to Mecca-Cola?
4. Would the same use of religion work for other religious groups, such as a Coca-Cola aimed at the Buddhist community?

REFERENCES

Berry, J. W. (1990) Psychology of Acculturation. In Berman, J. (Ed.), *Nebraska Symposium on Motivation, 1989: Cross-Cultural Perspectives. Current Theory and Research in Motivation*, Vol. 37. University of Nebraska Press, Lincoln, 201–234.

Berry, J. W. (1992) Acculturation and adaptation in a new society. *International Migration*, 30, 69–85.

Berry, J. W. (1997) Immigration, acculturation, and adaptation. *Applied Psychology: An International Review*, 46(1), 5–34.

Burghart, R. (1987) The Perpetuation of Hinduism in an Alien Cultural Milieu. In Burghart, R. (Ed.), *Hinduism in Great Britain: The Perpetuation of Religion in an Alien Cultural Milieu*, 1st ed. Tavistock, London, 224–251.

Cosgel, M. M. and Minkler, L. (2004) Religious identity and consumption. *Review of Social Economy*, LXII(3), 339–350.

Delener, N. (1990) The effects if religious factors on perceived risk in durable goods purchase decision. *Journal of Consumer Marketing*, 7(3), 27–38.

Dosanjh, J. S. and Ghuman, P. A. S. (1997) Punjabi child-rearing in Britain: Development of identity, religion and bilingualism. *Childhood: A Global Journal of Child Research*, 4(3), 285–303.

Dreidger, L., (1975) Search of cultural identity factors: A comparison of ethnic students. *Canadian Review of Sociology and Anthropology*, 12, 150–162.

Durkheim, E. (1976) *The Elementary Forms of the Religious Life*. Allen and Unwin, London.

The Economist (2007) The Bible v the Koran, 19 December. www.economist.com/world/international/displaystory.cfm?STORY_ID=10311317

Gapper, J. (2004) Consumers prefer US brands despite foreign policy links. *Financial Times*, 23 February, 4.

Grossman, R. J. (2008) Religion at work. *HR Magazine*, December. http://findarticles.com/p/articles/mi_m3495/is_12_53/ai_n31160711/pg_9/?tag=content;col1

Lindridge, A. M. (2010) Are we fooling ourselves when we talk about ethnic homogeneity? The case of religion and ethnic sub-divisions amongst British Indians. *Journal of Marketing Management*, in press.

Mearns, D. J. (1995) *Shiva's Other Children: Religion and Social Identity Amongst Overseas Indians*. Sage, New Delhi.

Modood, T., Beishon, S. and Virdee, S. (1994) *Changing Ethnic Identities*. Policy Studies Institute, London.

Porter, M. E. (1980) *Competitive Strategy*. New York, Free Press.

Seul, J. R. (1999) 'Ours is the way of God': Religion, identity and intergroup conflict. *Journal of Peace Research*, 36(5), 553–569.

The Social Science Research Council (1954) Acculturation: An exploratory formulation. *American Anthropologist*, 56(6), 973–1002.

Tajfel, H. and Turner, J. C. (1986) The Social Identity Theory of Inter-Group Behavior. In Worchel, S. and Austin, L. W. (Eds.), *Psychology of Intergroup Relations*. Nelson-Hall, Chicago.

Vertovec, S. (1995) Hindus in Trinidad and Britain: Ethnic Religion, Reification and the Politics of Public Space. In Van der Veer, P. (Ed.), *National and Migration: The Politics of Space in the South Asian Diaspora*. University of Philadelphia Press, Philadelphia, 132–156.

Williams, R. B. (1988) *Religions of Immigrants from Indian and Pakistan: New Threads in the American Tapestry*. Cambridge University Press, Cambridge.

Yankelovich, D. and Meer, D. (2006) Rediscovering market segmentation. *The Harvard Business Review*, 84(2), 122–131.

Chapter 24

SMEs and market growth
Contemporary reflections on why and how they grow

Rula M. Al Abdulrazak and Shadi A. Razak

LEARNING OBJECTIVES

This chapter will develop your knowledge and ability to:
- Define country-of-origin-image;
- Recognise potential effects of country-of-origin-image;
- Identify the impact of digitalisation on SMEs growth;
- Examine the influence of digitalisation in SMEs, on the effect of country-of-origin-image.

INTRODUCTION

The role of small and medium-sized enterprises (SMEs) as engines of economic growth is evident in their contribution to the global economy. The report of the Global Entrepreneurship Monitor 2019 (GEM) shows that the highest global rates of total Entrepreneurial Activity or 'total early stage entrepreneurial activity' (TEA) can be found in Angola (41%), a low-income economy. Middle-income Guatemala reports 28% TEA and high-income Chile reports a 25% TEA. The UK shows reduction in TEA value since the referendum vote to leave the European Union from 8.8 in 2016 to 8.2 in 2019.[1] This suggests that the UK is falling behind the global average, however, when it comes to perceptions, the UK achieved an overall ranking of 44 in 2018 and 43 in 2017 (Bosma and Kelley, 2019), which suggests that investors and entrepreneurs perception of the UK business environment is stable and healthy. Having positive country-image and reputation as a friendly and supportive business environment thus can help the UK overcome many of the uncertainty challenges while exiting the European Union.

Despite the huge contribution of SMEs to the global economy, which is widely acknowledged and has been a focus of academic research and policymaking for decades, the literature on SME growth remains fragmented (Wiklund et al., 2009). Moreover, in spite of microenterprises accounting for around 96% of all UK businesses (Baker et al., 2015), and between 70% and 95% of all enterprises in the OECD[2] economise, limited research addressed the growth challenges facing this significant sub-set of businesses with fewer than ten employees.

A significant change in the market is seen due to the rapid development of technology and global digitalisation. Increasingly companies are reconsidering their approaches to business and traditional marketing tools and are adapting digitalised business and marketing strategies. Online tools and platforms provide new opportunities for micro-enterprises to be involved in international trade. Businesses that trade internationally appear to be more confident in the current state of their businesses and also more likely to have positive prospects of job creation due to growth. This is also true for just-me entrepreneurs (one person's business) who participate in international trade. Almost 40% of micro-enterprises achieve over 25% of their total revenue in exports (OECD, 2017). Nevertheless, country-of-origin research does not distinguish SMEs and micro-enterprises to examine the effect of country-of-origin-image on the growth of these companies.

This chapter reviews the concept of country-of-origin-image (COI) and its effect on consumers and in turn on SMEs' growth. It also reviews the entrepreneurial approach and SME growth potential and challenges in the digital era. Digitalisation of business and marketing in SMEs and its role in these businesses growth and influence on COI effect is finally examined considering future directions.

COUNTRY-OF-ORIGIN-IMAGE AND EFFECT

The country-of-origin is where a product or service is perceived to originate from. It has an impact on consumers' attitudes and behaviours towards the brand, whether the brand represents a product or a service, a corporation, or a nation. This is due to the effect of the image of the place and its inhabitants as producers, service providers, and human capital with moral values and social and individual characteristics on consumers. Srikatanyoo and Gnoth (2002, p. 140) define country-of-origin-image (COI) as peoples' 'cognitive beliefs about the country's industrialisation, national quality standard, and other information that is associated with its products and services'.

Vast research has examined country-of-origin-image. Roth and Diamantopoulos (2009) review wide range of definitions of COI and classify them into three categories based on their focus: product related country-image; country related product image; or, overall country-image. In a re-examination of these categories, Lopez et al. (2011) distinguish between three types of conceptualisation of overall country-image (CI): mental pictures or impressions of a county in the public's mind (e.g., Verlegh and Steenkamp, 1999); as a cognitive structure (e.g., Gertner and Kotler, 2004); or, as a cognitive and affective network (e.g., Verlegh, 2001). Wang et al. (2014) explore the conceptualisation of COI further identifying three main phases in COI research: associating COI with general country-image; perceiving COI as an integration of country-image and product image; and treating COI as a multidimensional concept. These phases correspond with further classifications of the conceptualisation of COI, with focus on underpinning theories that can explain country-of-origin-effect, such as attitude theory, institutional theory, and legitimacy theory (for more information, read Wang et al. 2014).

THE EFFECT OF COUNTRY-OF-ORIGIN-IMAGE ON SMALL AND MEDIUM-SIZED ENTERPRISES

For over five decades, marketing scholars have been studying the country-of-origin-effect on consumers' purchasing decision making. These studies examine the country-of-origin-effects on attitudes towards foreign products. Export promotion authorities in many countries recognise the importance of a nation's reputation in promoting local goods and the necessity to manage country-of-origin-image as a valuable asset.

388

Han (1989) classifies the effect of COI in two categories. The first has an indirect impact on consumers' decisions; a **halo effect** that influences buyers' decisions towards countries they are unfamiliar with, for example, Western perception of production in India as exotic, eastern, handmade, and cheap. Han suggests that due to the lack of information about a nation or outdated stereotypes, the images of less developed countries are expected to have the halo effect on consumers. Experiencing a country or its products forms a file of information stored in consumers' memories increasing their familiarity with the nation's products and services. This leads to the second type: the **summary effect**. More developed countries with their wide range of industrial exports usually enjoy this effect as consumers are more exposed to specific information and have experienced them directly (Han, 1990), such as Germany's reliable engineering and production. Kleppe et al. (2002) adds the **multifaceted image effect** where consumers develop a knowledge structure about a nation with associations that help them to judge the product/offer and make a decision, such as perceiving the US as the leader in advance technology, something successful global brands such as Google, Apple, and Microsoft confirm.

The relationship between brand and country-of-origin-image has been examined in a number of studies (e.g., Hynes et al., 2014). The salience of the impact of brand image and COI has been debated in these studies. Some scholars suggest that images of global brands are more salient than COI, whereas others appreciate the COI effect on local and global brands; no consensus has been established. A good example on this chicken and egg phenomenon is the Huawei, technology Chinese brand. Huawei is disrupting the global technology market dominated by huge American brands with its affordable competitive and advance technology offers, however, the Western world's perception of its country-of-origin, China, is reducing the brand trustworthiness and reliability in terms of information security at state and individuals level. Some evidence of potential risk hazards of cyberattacks in some of their products and less established Chinese policies in cybersecurity are not helping the brand promise to overcome the country-image-effect. Individual consumers in the UK, for example, may, hence, feel that they are left with a choice between their privacy and price benefits.

The wide examination of the effect of COI suggests a correlation between COI and the level of economic development of a country. For example, in a study by Gorostidi-Martinez et al. (2017), Spanish respondents viewed Chinese products as of lower quality, and as of mass-produced worldwide distribution type of products, while they believed that Chinese individuals are very hard working. Another example is evident in the results of Saffu and Scott (2009), research showing that consumers in Papua New Guinea, in the southwestern Pacific, evaluated their homemade products less favourably than foreign made products, and that COI effects influence consumers' preferences differently in the case of high-involvement products (that is a product with high impact on a consumer's quality of life such as car or smart phone) and low-involvement products (that is a product with low impact on a consumer's quality of life such as a pencil or bar of chocolate), as more consideration is given to high-involvement products. Consumers hold stereotypical views of products made in different countries but do not necessarily agree about the nature of these stereotypical views, which can be rooted in much more than the product. Kotler et al. (1993, p. 141) argue that the comprehensive view of country-image, which is not limited to the country as a producer is

> the sum of beliefs and impressions people hold about places. Images represent a simplification of a large number of associations and pieces of information connected with a place. They are a product of the mind trying to process and pick out essential information from huge amounts of data about a place.

Nations convey ranges of meanings (O'Shaughnessy and O'Shaughnessy, 2000) that represent a nation as a destination for tourists, a location for investors, and a market opportunity for traders and migrants.[3] Dinnie (2008) and many other scholars consider the country-of-origin-effect and the identity of a nation, the conceptual roots of nation branding that influences not only tourism but also local businesses ability to attract investment and international trade opportunities which are significant for their growth. For example, Qing (2016) examined country-of-origin-effect on institutional trust and found that people's trust towards New Zealand's regulatory agencies was significantly higher than towards the Chinese counterparts in two separate incidents of contamination in milk powder, one caused by a Chinese dairy corporation and the other by a New Zealand dairy company.

This effect of country-of-origin-image is even more evident in small-medium-enterprises particularly in the early stages of their lives. This is because of the limited impact their, yet to be established, brands and credibility can have on attracting national and international clients, whether in business to business sectors or business to consumers. However, the extensive research in country-of-origin effect and image focuses on large businesses and well-established brands and neglects SMEs and startups despite their need to focus on positive country-of-origin attributes to build their brand and achieve credibility. Spence and Essoussi (2010) study into SMEs brand building finds that country-of-origin of the brand can be used as secondary association to enhance brand equity in SMEs through brand identity. Since SMEs and startups have limited resources for communication, and the development of brand identity and equity, country-of-origin-image gives the brand an added value at a low cost.

ENTREPRENEURSHIP AND GROWTH OF SMALL AND MEDIUM-SIZED ENTERPRISES

Entrepreneurial companies engage in product-market innovation and take riskier ventures than larger and well-established firms; as such they are expected to be proactive innovators that take the lead (Miller, 1983). However, not all entrepreneurial companies are true innovators although they may create niche experiences. Entrepreneurship research has developed from the narrow scope of radical innovations to the creation of new economic activities (Davidsson et al., 2006). Entrepreneurship is mainly the ability to identify and pursue new business opportunities (Shane and Venkataraman, 2000).

Entrepreneurship process includes search, identification, and exploitation of business opportunities that lead a company to develop new sources of income through value creation and exchange. The major challenge for entrepreneurial company though is not only how to start but also how to survive and sustain business profitability and growth. Jacobides and Winter (2007) suggest that companies with several years of high growth are more likely to be truly entrepreneurial firms, since they have identified opportunities for growth unnoticed by others, or they are the fastest to take advantage of these opportunities. Wide-ranging studies confirm that entrepreneurship and high growth are interconnected phenomena (Davidsson et al., 2006). Entrepreneurial activity in entrepreneurially orientated companies and SMEs are positively correlated with growth (Furlan et al., 2014). This is because growth is perceived as an essential attribute of entrepreneurship.[4]

Not every high-growth company is entrepreneurial, however; although entrepreneurial leadership studies tend to allure to such believe. **Entrepreneurial cognition** (knowledge and experience) influences the ability to spot opportunities which can be enhanced if the company is led by a team of entrepreneurs. Being able to recognise market opportunities and select the most rewarding, in turn, increase small and medium-sized enterprises' ability to grow. This is because diversity of knowledge among the leadership team enhances their ability to identify opportunities, and their specialist experience offers them access to human, social and financial capital (Hallen and Eisenhardt, 2012), all of which lead to growth. **Entrepreneurs' growth motivation** is also significant in leading SMEs to grow at higher rate than larger organisations (Koryak et al., 2015). The dynamic relationship between entrepreneurial company's approach to risk and fear of failure can, however, affect the growth motivation.

Growth rate of SMEs can be determined in several ways such as: the value or volume of sales, number of employees, number of geographical regions served by the company, number of commercial partners and other institutions, number of branches, brand equity, amount of investments the company attracts, or number of years since the company was established. It is important, though, for the growth measure to be meaningful, to specify the time period and the growth ratio that is considered high-growth (Moreno and Casillas, 2007) in a specific industry and market, in a specific economic era. For example, the growth ratio expected from British SMEs and larger corporations after the UK exits the European Union market can be lower than the growth ratio expectations before leaving the EU. Sales value and net profit margin, in addition to the amount of investment the business attracts, are common measures of company growth, as they are the main mean of liquidity and sustainability of entrepreneurial SMEs.

DIGITALISATION IN SMALL AND MEDIUM-SIZED ENTERPRISES AND GROWTH

Advances in digital technologies continue to influence enterprises and individuals alike. Information technology and management studies recognise key roles that digital technologies play in improving the business landscape. Digital-technologies:

- Create opportunities to boost growth;
- Expand jobs;
- Accelerate innovation.

Digitalisation[5] changes the marketplace by offering consumers and businesses greater interactive marketplace opportunities through a wide range of timely communication platforms such as social media, e-commerce, and chatbot that help building and strengthening business-customer relationship. Moreover, digitalisation allows businesses to develop wider-scale of offers that increase convenience, transparency, and choice.

Businesses including SMEs are eager to embrace and enrich the digital environment. A myriad of technological trends, in particular, the mobile broadband, cloud-computing, big-data-analytics, internet-of-things (IoT), artificial-intelligence, and the internet-of-everything (IoE), are presenting great opportunities and challenges to today's entrepreneurs. These technologies can elevate business growth and open up new business opportunities in various different industries but embracing these digital-technologies requires new capabilities and skill set and present businesses and in particular SMEs with new challenges such as information-security.

As the pace of digitalisation builds up around the world, it is extremely imperative for SMEs to accelerate the adoption of digital technologies to spur economic growth, as they represent the majority of the total number of businesses across the world.[6] SMEs and micro-businesses are dependent on entrepreneurship initiatives, which are expected to be visionary, dynamic, and innovative. Nonetheless, research shows that SMEs often struggle with business digitalisation. Barriers and challenges may vary from infrastructure, regulatory, and administrative burdens, to insufficient access to finance and digital skills in the workforce. In a research into the Malaysian market the majority of the participant SMEs divulged plans to develop new products or services and increase online marketing, across all industries and regions. Governments believe in the impact of business digitalisation on growth (SME Corp. Malaysia and Huawei Technologies, 2018; KfW Research, 2019; IFA and Wyman, 2019) as such they are developing and funding programmes to support SMEs transformation by building their capabilities and access to infrastructure, and encouraging innovation such as *Innovate UK*.

A study in the SME utilisation of digital technologies in the UK market shows that almost all SMEs in the UK use the internet for business purposes (Baker et al., 2015), but only 20% of turnover was derived online in 2013. It is challenging that a quarter of SMEs in the UK reported that year that they do not possess basic digital skills; while there is clear evidence of a positive link between digital skill levels and turnover growth. There is also an attitudinal barrier among a minority of SMEs towards developing an online presence. This is due to two reasons: (1) a lack of awareness about the benefits and opportunities available, and (2) a lack of understanding about online security threats.

The long-term solution was embedding digital learning throughout the education system in the UK. However, to enhance digital capabilities in the shorter term few initiatives were recommended to provide digital courses and awareness-raising initiatives including cyber-security through existing industrial networks. In 2019, there are extensive activities at both the local and national levels to develop SMEs' digital capabilities in the UK. However, these dynamic technologies are progressing at high speed, and there is no sufficient evidence yet of their individual impact on business growth and on how the strands of development activities are benefiting the SMEs. The evidence varies between packages of digital skills training. Some are more thought through than others, while others are minimal in scale or dependent on limited funding.

THE USE OF TECHNOLOGY IN SMES (EXAMPLE BOX)

Silican Canal Tech Award winner icarusparts.com is a Birmingham startup who won the coveted Best Tech Startup of the year award in 2017 (Silicon canal, 2018). The founder Joe Kibbler started the company in 2016, after a long working experience in the automotive industry.

Icarusparts.com is a business idea that is based on offering a solution to make car repair less problematic and improve customer experience. This model follows the new online intermediaries' business models that focuses on price transparency and convenience, such as comparison websites (e.g., gocompare.com) and trade websites (e.g., findatrade.com) that offers list of service providers for customers to select from and receive convenient quotes. This business model benefits both customers and traders as it can increase traders' customer base due to wider exposure while pushing them to be more competitive.

Icarusparts.com sells car parts online. Customers enter their registration number and select what they need, such as new brakes, and choose the brand or the price range they are happy with. The website also offers a list of approved local garages to fit the parts for them, with a pre-agreed labour cost so customers know exactly how much they are spending. Icarusparts.com aims to provide customers a transparent pricing and user friendly online service. The company grew substantially in just two years.

The award gained icarusparts.com significant coverage, particularly on LinkedIn. It helped the business gain more credibility in the market to widen their supplier network. The business vision is to grow through market expansion and penetration by increasing their network of garages and entering multiple cities across the UK.

QUESTIONS

1. Identify enterprises that apply similar business model and think of a new business idea that can benefit from such model.
2. The company's goal is to grow in their home market across the UK, applying market penetration and national market development strategies. Do you think that they should apply product development approach and expand the business model into a new product or service? If so, why?

FUTURE DIRECTIONS OF COUNTRY-OF-ORIGIN-EFFECT IN DIGITALISED SMALL AND MEDIUM-SIZED ENTERPRISES

Patriotism is rising in politics in a way that it is affecting elections results and trade policies. This is evident in the protectionism approach to trade in the US Trump Administration. An example will be their quotas, tariff, and non-tariff barriers that limit their imports from China, in order to support American produce. The Brexit vote in the UK in 2016 can also reflect a potential protectionism approach on trade and national resources. These approaches stand against the idea of a globalised marketplace with limited trade barriers, which is the target of the World Trade Organisation (WTO). Such changes in the global market dynamics and the increased trade barriers require more focus from businesses on creating a competitive edge other than competitive pricing, as competitive pricing will become more difficult to achieve. The trade barriers will require business offers that are unique and promise a distinctive value. Strong brand is the most effective approach to achieve a unique positioning and credibility of business offers. Having a positive country-of-origin-image proved to offer a competitive edge and add value and credibility to the brand, which in turn attracts customers and leads to brand preferences. Investing in strong brand associated with favourable COI can increase international demand and help businesses avoid the disadvantages of price competition. It will also allow national brands to benefit from patriotism, as a brand that is positively associated with its home country.

Positive COI is significant in the new market conditions and, thus, startups and SMEs with less established brands, or those in the process of building a strong brand, can benefit highly from positive COI associations. This suggests SMEs to focus on industries that their home country already has a good reputation in, which in turn will open more doors for the business in international markets. However, this may mean that the home market is saturated and highly competitive, so SMEs and startups who want to serve their home market may have to focus on less-established industry regardless of the COI in this industry. In both cases whether the company is focused on serving the national or international market, taking an innovative approach to a business idea in terms of product or business model is key to success. Digitalisation and digital innovations offer a rich platform for startups and SMEs to develop mature markets through disruptive new approaches to creating value and to spotting market gap. They may also serve a niche market or create a new market through innovative offers that would improve customers' quality of life, through convenience, problem solving, and added value. CyNation is an example of a startup tackling a well-established UK market in cybersecurity with new solutions and growth ambition into the European market (see the case study for more information), while Icarusparts is focused on the national market only for growth by adding value through a new business model in the car repair market in the UK.

Entrepreneurial SMEs are deemed dynamic enough to capture and create business opportunities and manage it in a way that expedites growth, including the application of business digitalisation. Effective digitalisation of startups marketing strategies, product, and service innovations is proving to enable their brand building, which may benefit from COI association and enhance their early growth. Thus, governments across the world such as the UK, Ireland, Germany, and Malaysia are keeping a close eye on SMEs' ability to digitalise their businesses and marketing strategies and invest money and efforts into programmes that encourage SMEs' digital innovations and build their capacity and resources, including the infrastructure to enable them to digitalise effectively. These efforts include:

- Building infrastructure readiness for innovation in information communication technology (ICT);
- Enabling digital solutions to support SME business needs digitally;
- Accelerating and enhancing SMEs adoption of digital solutions to lead to innovations in new products and new business models.

Some of government's support can also be focused on specific digitalised industry to accelerate the growth of this industry and build the country's image and reputation as a leading provider of innovation in this industry, such as the UK's efforts in cyber-security, which led to a well-established market dominated by British and American companies and capable of serving other neighbouring European countries. The European market in comparison is in an earlier stage of development, hence it is an attractive market to British and international cyber-security companies and SMEs. European markets such as the Netherlands are encouraging international startups and offering support to develop their cyber-security capabilities and market as well as digitalised business offers. Examples of governments support programmes to innovation and business digitalisation are *Plug and Play* in Germany and *weXelerate* in Austria. These programmes can also be a partnership between government bodies and investors. They range from funding startups to offering development programmes and expertise and spaces to work, share ideas, and innovate.

It is vital for a startup to develop an efficient digital marketing plan that will leverage business in a highly competitive market and will promote the brand, its products, and services. The greatest benefit of digital marketing for a newly established business is cost efficiency and the ability to instantly reach online target audiences globally. A unique set of digital marketing techniques helps a startup to increase its market share and establish a strong brand in its business niche.

CASE STUDY

CyNation – small-enterprise, high-impact

One of the latest flourishing stars in cyber security in the UK is CyNation. An entrepreneurial company which was established in 2015 continues to grow rapidly, serving the UK and the European market. CyNation has seen an increase in cross-over threat that compromises organisations and individuals' privacy, security, and safety.

394

With the rapid adoption of interconnected things: home appliances, cars, and medical devices, greater increase in data and privacy breaches is expected, including fraud and identity theft, cyber extortion, and espionage. CyNation's team believes that the threat landscape is revolving around smartphones and mobile devices, internet of things, and the Cloud and IT Infrastructure.

Cyber security is a complicated and challenging market with cyber risks developing at high speed and interfering in politics, economies, security, and individuals' lives. It is also a highly competitive industry with high market entry barriers due to the need to establish the reputation of capable, credible, and trustworthy organisations with the resources to deliver and engage with businesses at different levels of risks. Much international expertise has been developed in this area; thus, new cyber security companies in the UK are competing with international as well as internal providers. Three years down the line CyNation founders, Steve Berry, executive chairman, and Shadi A. Razak, chief technology officer, reflect on the company's competitiveness and growth.

'Here at CyNation we believe in the holistic approach to cyber security and compliance. We help organisations improve their security and compliance posture by providing innovative, automated solutions and services that encompass people, processes and technology, creating an enterprise wide culture which enables organisations to become more resilient and effective against threats'.

What challenges do we face as entrepreneurs in the market, particularly in terms of growth? And how do we overcome these challenges?

The fast-paced nature of a startup requires hiring and keeping top talent. It can be difficult to find the right talent and fit for CyNation. There is fierce competition for talent, particularly in tech/deep tech roles, such as developers and dev ops engineers. This is not helped by the strict immigration rules in the UK.

Small companies have less resources, which may slow down their product development and lead to a missed opportunity. Business to business enterprise sales are also challenging because of the long sales cycle and the value placed on established brands.

Because of the high concentration of large enterprises in our target sectors and the lack of a clear, European champion for integrated risk management (IRM), we focus not only on the UK but also the Netherlands, Germany, Switzerland, and Austria. These markets represent an important opportunity for growth and expansion in the European market, as the European information risk management market is estimated to grow to $7.3 billion by 2020. With Brexit looming, however, there are several economic concerns, including the value of the GBP and possibly new export tariffs to the EU that could negatively affect our growth in Europe.

To overcome these challenges, we plan to open overseas offices to tap into talent in other markets and serve as a base for expansion into the European market. We also strive for an efficient and agile culture, enabling collaboration and cross-functional teams to overcome our limited resource capacity. By collaborating with respected partners with established brands and reputations, we can build our own reputation as they promote and distribute our solutions.

What does it mean to CyNation to be a small British company?

Even in the midst of Brexit, London is a very dynamic market. It is one of the largest centres for startups in the world and a hub for innovation. From London, we not only have access to domestic businesses or international offices of foreign businesses, but we are also close to our other target markets in Europe.

The UK is making a name for itself in cyber security and is home to many of the companies at the forefront of technology. It is incredible to be part of this network of innovative cyber companies. The UK government also sponsors several key initiatives with which we are involved. An example is the DCMS funded London Office for Rapid Cybersecurity Advancement (LORCA), which is an accelerator programme dedicated to cybersecurity innovation.

We do face challenges abroad, largely because of the uncertainty caused by Brexit and the handling of the Brexit process, but we are committed to serving our overseas target markets as well. With the reputation the UK is building for cybersecurity and the country's government-funded initiatives, and there are strong benefits to being a British cybersecurity company.

How is CyNation utilising digital marketing to overcome the challenges in the UK and international markets?

CyNation is currently focussing on website optimisation, content, and social media marketing. However, there is a need to employ other tools to increase brand awareness and online visibility, especially in the context of growth and expansion in the UK and EU markets.

Taking into consideration intense competition in the tech market, CyNation differentiates itself through the automation of its solutions, a highly focused approach to cybersecurity and compliance and excellent expertise in industry trends. This value is communicated through the company's website, social media (LinkedIn and Twitter), webinars, and tailored monthly newsletters distributed among its clients, partners, and prospect leads. CyNation aims to make existing and new customers engaged and empowers them with important information and product updates, which will have positive effects on customer loyalty in the future. This approach fosters risk-aware culture and determines a structured approach to business and strong positioning among competitors. Moreover, it will contribute to minimising current long sales cycles.

For more information see: https://cynation.com/

Case study questions

1. Explain to what extent CyNation utilise an entrepreneurial approach in developing the business, seizing opportunities, and addressing the market challenges.
2. Knowing that CyNation market value reached few millions in three years, research the cybersecurity market growth in the UK and evaluate the growth of CyNation within the market. Are the company founders reflecting a growth motivation? And why?
3. CyNation is tapping into employing more digital marketing tools to boost its online presence globally. What tools would you recommend them to use? And why?
4. What market positioning strategy CyNation is applying to differentiate their value proposition in the market? And what role country-of-origin-image plays in this strategy, particularly in the European markets they are entering?

DISCUSSION QUESTIONS

1. Discuss the halo effect and the summary effect of COI and give examples.
2. Define entrepreneurship and list entrepreneurial leadership characters. How can these characters influence SME growth?
3. Is business and marketing digitalisation important in building SME brand and credibility, and why?
4. What role governments can play in developing country-of-origin-image to support specific industries?
5. Do you think digitalisation of business and marketing can reduce the effect of COI on SMEs' growth and sustainability, and why?

A GROUP-BASED SCENARIO/ACTIVITY

Think about one of your favoured international brands and discuss with your colleagues the impact of its country-of-origin-image on your brand preference. The country-of-origin may refer to the brand home country rather than the country where a product is actually produced.

Then consider if this product is offered to you by a small company from the same country-of-origin of your preferred brand in comparison with a small company from your home country. Which one would you select, and why?

NOTES

1. In 2018, there were 5.7 million private sector businesses in the UK, down by 27,000 compared to 2017. This is the first year on year fall in the number of businesses since the UK Parliament Business Statistics series started in 2000. The UK entrepreneurship framework in GEM 2018 suggests that the UK is below the global average in government policies to support entrepreneurship and in the infrastructure, whereas it exceeds the average in tax policies and entrepreneurial finance. This suggests that financially the UK is creating an attractive business environment for entrepreneurs, but more needs to be done to support them so they can innovate and progress effectively. In comparison, Qatar and the United Arab Emirates GEM entrepreneurship framework exceeds the global average in all aspects, creating potentially an ideal business environment for startups, while Turkey matches the global average and exceeds it in internet marketing and commercial and legal infrastructure.
2. OECD is the Organisation for Economic Cooperation and Development. The OECD economies in alphabetical order are Australia, Austria, Belgium, Canada, Denmark, Finland, France, Greece, Germany, Iceland, Ireland, Italy, Japan, Luxembourg, the Netherlands, New Zealand, Norway, Portugal, Spain, Sweden, Switzerland, Turkey, the United Kingdom, and the United States.
3. Country-image can lead people from less developed nations to degrade their domestic products in favour of those from the more technologically advanced nations, whereas Europeans, Americans, and Japanese people mostly prefer their own brands.
4. Research on SME growth is developed around four main areas (Gherhes et al., 2016):
   – business capabilities and practices
   – entrepreneurial characteristics
   – entrepreneurial growth ambition
   – business environment
5. Embracing digital can be broadly categorised into computerisation and digitalisation, where computerisation means adoption of digital devices with more focus on individual usage than on

business usage; while **digitalisation** is defined as business process transformation including customer relationship management, transaction, services, and feedback in a comprehensive digital environment.

6. For example, SMEs counts for 98.5% of Malaysian businesses (SME Corp. Malaysia and Huawei Technologies, 2018), and a staggering 5.7 million businesses in the UK are SMEs, which counts for 99% of all businesses. It is even more interesting to know that 96% of all UK businesses are micro-businesses that employ less than ten employees (Baker et al., 2015).

REFERENCES

Baker, G., Lomax, S., Braidford, P., Allinson, G., Houston, M. and BMG Research and Durham University (2015) *Digital Capabilities in SMEs: Evidence Review and Re-Survey of 2014 Small Business Survey Respondents*. Department for Business Innovation and Skills, UK.

Bosma, N. and Kelley, D. (2019) *Global Entrepreneurship Monitor – 2018/2019 Global Report*, sponsored by BABSON, Universidad Del Desarrollo, and Korea Entrepreneurship Foundation – KoFE.

Davidsson, P., Delmar, F. and Wiklund, J. (2006) Entrepreneurship as Growth: Growth as Entrepreneurship. In Davidsson, P., Delmar, F. and Wiklund, J. (Eds.), *Entrepreneurship and the Growth of Firms*. Edward Elgar, Cheltenham, 21–38.

Dinnie, K. (2008) *Nation Branding: Concepts, Issues, Practice*. Butterworth-Heinemann – Elsevier, London.

Furlan, A., Grandinetti, R. and Paggiaro, A. (2014) Unveiling the growth process: Entrepreneurial growth and the use of external resources. *International Journal of Entrepreneurial Behaviour & Research*, 20(1), 20–41.

Gertner, D. and Kotler, P. (2004) How can a place correct a negative image. *Place Branding*, 1(1), 50–57.

Gherhes, C., William, N., Vorley, T. and Vasconcelos, A. C. (2016) Distinguishing micro-businesses from SMEs: A systematic review of growth constraints. *Journal of Small Business and Enterprise Development*, 23(4), 939–963.

Gorostidi-Martinez, H., Xu, W. and Zhao, X. (2017) A review of Spanish consumers' product-country-image of China. *Asia Pacific Journal of Marketing and Logistics*, 29(3), 589–615.

Hallen, B. and Eisenhardt, K. (2012) Catalyzing strategies and efficient tie formation: How entrepreneurial firms obtain investment ties. *Academy of Management Journal*, 55(1), 35–70.

Han, C. M. (1989) Country-image: Halo or summary construct. *Journal of Marketing Research*, May (26), 222–229.

Han, C. M. (1990) Testing the role of country-image in consumer choice behaviour. *European Journal of Marketing*, 24(6), 24–40.

Hynes, N., Caemmerer, B., Martin, E. and Masters, E. (2014) Use, abuse, or contribute! A framework for classifying how companies engage with country-image. *International Marketing Review*, 31(1), 79–97.

IFA-Innovation Finance Advisory, EIB Advisory and Wyman, O. (2019) *The Digitalisation of Small-and-Medium-Enterprises in Ireland- Models for Financing Digital Projects*. Department of Business, Enterprise and Innovation and the European Investment Advisory Hub, Luxembourg, March.

Jacobides, M. G. and Winter, S. G. (2007) Entrepreneurship and firm boundaries: The theory of a firm. *Journal of Management Studies*, 44(7), 1213–1241.

KfW Research (2019) *KfW SME Digitalisation Report 2018*, Zimmermann, V. (Ed.), KfW Group, Frankfurt, April.

Kleppe, I. A. Iversen, N. M. and Stensaker, I. G. (2002) Country-images in marketing strategies: Conceptual issues and an empirical Asian illustration. *Brand Management*, 10(1), 61–74.

Koryak, O., Mole, K. F., Lockett, A. Hayton, J. C., Ucbasaran, D. and Hodgkinson, G. P. (2015) Entrepreneurial leadership, capabilities and firm growth. *International Small Business Journal*, 33(1), 89–105.

Kotler, P., Haider, D. H. and Rein, I. (1993) *Marketing Places: Attracting Investment, Industry, and Tourism to Cities, States and Nations*. The Free Press, New York.

Lopez, C., Gotsi, M. and Andriopoulos, C. (2011) Conceptualising the influence of corporate-image an country-image. *European Journal of Marketing*, 45(11/12), 1601–1641.

Miller, D. (1983) The correlates of entrepreneurship in three types of firms. *Management Science*, 29(7), 770–991.

Moreno, A. and Casillas, J. C. (2007) High-growth SMEs versus non-high growth SMEs: A discriminant analysis. *Entrepreneurship and Regional Development*, 19(1), 69–88.

OECD (2017) *Entrepreneurship at a Glance 2017*. OECD Publishing, Paris. Available at: https://doi.org/10.1787/entrepreneur_aag-2017-en (Accessed 27 April 2019).

O'Shaughnessy, J. and O'Shaughnessy, N. J. (2000) Treating the nation as a brand: Some neglected issues. *Journal of Macromarketing*, 20(1), 56–64.

Qing, H. (2016) The role of institutional trust in country-of-origin effect: A comparative study of two milk powder contamination incidents. *China Media Research*, 12(2), 52–62.

Roth, K. P. and Diamantopoulos, A. (2009) Advancing the country-image construct. *Journal of Business Research*, 62(7), 726–740.

Saffu, K. and Scott D. (2009) Developing country perceptions of high- and low-involvement products manufactured in other countries. *International Journal of Emerging Markets*, 4(2), 185–199.

Shane, S. and Venkataraman, S. (2000) The promise of entrepreneurship as a field of research. *Academy of Management Review*, 25(1), 217–226.

Silicon canal news (2018) Best tech startup winner looking to expand across the UK, by *admin*, November 23. Available at: https://siliconcanal.co.uk/best-tech-startup-winner-looking-to-expand-across-the-uk/ (Accessed 22 April 2019).

SME Corp. Malaysia and Huawei Technologies (M) Sdn. Bhd (2018) *Digitalisation Survey of SMEs in 2018*. SME Corp., Malaysia.

Spence, M. and Essoussi, L. H. (2010) SME brand building and management: An exploratory study. *European Journal of Marketing*, 44(7/8), 1037–1054.

Srikatanyoo, N. and Gnoth, J. (2002) Country-image and international tertiary education. *Journal of Brand Management*, 10(2), 139–146.

Verlegh, P. W. J. (2001) *Country-of-Origin Effects on Consumer Product Evaluations*. PhD dissertation, Wageningen: Wageningen University.

Verlegh, P. W. J. and Steenkamp, J. E. M. (1999) A review and meta-analysis of country-of-origin research. *Journal of Economic Psychology*, 20, 521–546.

Wang, T., Zhou, L., Mou, Y. and Zhao, J. (2014) Study of country-of-origin image from legitimacy theory perspective: evidence from the USA and India. *Industrial Marketing Management*, 43(5), 769–776.

Wiklund, J., Patzelt, H. and Shepherd, D. A. (2009) Building an integrative model of small business growth. *Small Business Economics*, 32(4), 351–374.

Chapter 25

Developing entrepreneurial marketing competencies

Barry Ardley, Nick Taylor, and Jialin (Penny) Hardwick

LEARNING OUTCOMES:

After the reading this chapter you will be able to:
- Understand the importance of educating tomorrow's entrepreneurial marketers today;
- Recognise that students need to undergo a clearly defined learning journey in order to become future successful entrepreneurial marketers;
- Appreciate the components of a learning journey incorporating the necessary features leading to effective entrepreneurial marketing action in individual students;
- Assess and analyse the nature of the various knowledge elements and competencies that can lead to the development of an entrepreneurial identity in students.

Lack of critical competencies are generally acknowledged as a major setback among SMEs, more so in their marketing operations. In fact, the literature is replete with tensions and contestations around such issues as to how competencies should be taught and whether, in reality, they should be taught at all (Madichie et al., 2018). This chapter joins the important discussion, conscious of the fact that enterprise marketing learning, in whatever form or shape it takes, can be hugely beneficial in SME contexts and hold out a great deal of potentials to significantly influence market growth and sustainability.

INTRODUCTION

In this chapter, the authors discuss a case study of the delivery of a double semester, final year undergraduate module in Entrepreneurial Marketing (EM). We examine mainly, the teaching approach and also, some student responses to the module. These responses, in the form of an evaluation questionnaire, are from two cohorts of marketing students, who had previously not received exposure to a module of this type. For the vast majority of students, EM is a compulsory component of the third year. Whilst the bulk of the chapters in this book deal with ongoing strategic and operational issues within entrepreneurship marketing, it is important that we also consider the education of those future business people and the way in which an entrepreneurial identity can be fostered in today's learners. In constructing this chapter, we adopt the Quality Assurance Agency (QAA) model as a framework for learner development. This learning journey model is comprised of four elements (QAA, 2012, 2018). The journey starts with *entrepreneurial awareness*, being learning processes that ensure students are cognisant of what entrepreneurship involves. The model then proposes that students undergo learning that facilitates the adoption of an entrepreneurial *mind-set*. Third, students should be encouraged to develop *entrepreneurial capabilities* and finally, that *entrepreneurial effectiveness* can be demonstrated. These key imperatives present in the QAA model assisted module tutors in forming the philosophical and practical basis of an entrepreneurial marketing module delivered through the University of Lincoln's International Business School (LIBS). The current module is available to a combined cohort of BA hons marketing management, advertising and marketing, and business and marketing students. The broad aim of this chapter is to seek to illustrate how the module attempts to build an entrepreneurial identity in students, representing a way of bringing together the four elements of the QAA precepts, outlined earlier.

BACKGROUND: THE VALUE OF ENTREPRENEURIAL MARKETING EDUCATION

In the debate about the value of marketing education, a recurrent issue is the extent to which programmes adequately prepare young marketers for the demands of a modern work environment. In the influential practitioner publication Marketing Week (Rogers, 2018), this issue is starkly put by the title 'Are marketing degrees up to scratch?' In the article, the chief executive of the Royal Bank of Scotland points out that graduates need to be robust and critical thinkers, suggesting that interdisciplinary, or meta, skills have a role to play in marketing education. In this context, a university has to demonstrate that their marketing graduates have acquired skills beyond a discipline-based knowledge, encompassing areas such as critical thinking, digital technologies, networking, creativity and innovation, problem-solving, numbers, and team working (Finch et al., 2013; Ang et al., 2014). Research has identified these meta-skills are a resource for coping with vulnerability and for ensuring managers, from all disciplines, are more supple learners, able to organise, and resilient to both risk and disaster (Miles et al., 2016). It is relevant to note that in its formulation of the competencies required by today's marketers, the Chartered Institute of Marketing (CIM, 2016), features innovation, opportunity, and entrepreneurial behaviour as essential requirements.

These types of capabilities are frequently referred to as employability skills (Trough 2012), skills which are inextricably linked to entrepreneurship capabilities, the focus of this chapter. In the context of either a start-up business, or an established firm, the ability to innovate, to be creative, and to be a problem solving team worker, are vital skills that aid not only the enterprise in question but the economy and society as well. In this context, and noted some time ago by Morris et al. (2002), it was argued that responsiveness to entrepreneurialism in marketing education is underrepresented and adjustments are urgently required to the marketing curriculum. In their two documents on the topic (QAA, 2012, 2018), the value of enterprise education is linked to key arguments about the preparedness of students for the workplace. The development of capabilities in enterprise will not only help students start and develop their own businesses but assist them in becoming effective as self-employed individuals or as employees in existing organisations, where companies seek out and recruit entrepreneurially minded graduates.

ENTREPRENEURIAL MARKETING: MODULE OVERVIEW

In terms of broad aims, the entrepreneurial marketing module is designed so that students will be able to assess the nature of business enterprise, and to learn and understand the challenges, opportunities, and skills required by organisations and individuals, to make effective and enterprising decisions in the context of a changing and challenging, business environment (EM module handbook, 2018). Besides learning about enterprise, the module also aims to develop entrepreneurial marketing skills, in order to enhance student's employability. In terms of process, in semester one there is an examination of the broad elements of entrepreneurial marketing orientation and strategy, for example, innovation and opportunity identification. (Chaston, 2016). The assessed work involves, making contact with a company in order to evaluate its degree of entrepreneurial orientation and to make suggestions for possible future innovation activity, thus providing opportunity for reflection on key concepts. In term two, the theme of innovation is developed through an assessment that involves using a business model framework (Morris et al., 2005), that provides an opportunity for students to develop an approach to creating new customer value for an existing company – where again contact is encouraged – or indeed for themselves, in new ventures.

Throughout the module, attention is also focussed on the development of individual entrepreneurial marketing skills and in order to assess this component of the module, students devise their own individual competency table, which is linked to the work they do on the business model innovation. Through these aims and in the way in which the module is delivered, enterprise awareness is generated alongside an enterprise mindset and enterprise competencies are established, all of which then link to a demonstration of entrepreneurial effectiveness. Whilst the EM module is principally informed by the QAA learning journey model, it can also be seen to be inspired by a constructivist approach to education, with experience at its centre (Rami et al., 2009). The essence of constructivism is that the individual is the active creator of their own knowledge, where learners construct their own understanding and knowledge of the world through various types of experiences which they then reflect on. In the context of the EM module, students experience features of learning like entrepreneurial marketing theory, group working and negotiation, project management, and opportunity scanning, all of which they reflect on and build into their own knowledge base. Additionally, in constructivism, when an individual encounters something new, it has to be reconciled with previous ideas and experience, and as a consequence, a change may occur in what is believed (Wenger, 1998). Students are exposed to the ideas and practices of entrepreneurial marketing and in the process, many move on to adopt an entrepreneurial identity.

MODULE REVIEW: CONTENT AND DELIVERY FEEDBACK

Whilst it is very commonplace for students to complete institutional module reviews and NSS surveys, module tutors decided that it would be appropriate to gather some of their own qualitative student feedback on the delivery and content of the programme. This represented the module tutors own module evaluation process which received approval from the university ethics committee. Tutors devised a questionnaire using open ended questions, in order to elicit student responses largely based on the four QAA learning journey features. Tutors handed out the hard copy questionnaire to students at the end of two consecutive years during the final seminars, and out of a possible 69 students in one year and 53 in the other year, 101 questionnaires were returned for analysis. In terms of the structure and type of questions on the two surveys, Matthews and Ross (2010), would characterise this as the collection of semi-structured data, comprised of feelings, opinions, and beliefs. This represented student perceptions of the entrepreneurial marketing module providing tutors with insights into content and delivery. Some selected quotes are used in the following sections for illustrations of module learning issues.

DEVELOPING ENTERPRISE AWARENESS: THE CANONS OF ENTREPRENEURIAL MARKETING

The QAA documents indicate that students will acquire enterprise awareness through learning and intellectual development and the acquisition of knowledge. QAA (2012, p. 18) point out that this can include teaching about the nature of enterprise, by looking at key theories and ideas and the way in which these link to employability skills. Tutors believed the best way to approach this was to establish what we term here as the 'canons' of entrepreneurial marketing, being the key tenets of the discipline, that student needs to learn about, in order to be able to say they are entrepreneurial aware. In the first semester, the module examines and analyses key entrepreneurial orientation and strategy processes around the topics of proactiveness, innovation and creativity, opportunity identification, resource leveraging, customer intimacy, and risk management (Morrish and Deacon, 2011). The importance of these entrepreneurial orientation features was picked up by many students in our review and the following quote is typical of the type of responses. '*The module helps you understand how to be creative; it provides a course that highlights innovative thinking, which I feel is greatly needed for the future of business*'.

As a further example, there are a wide range of ways to understand opportunity and risk assessment and its different forms, and the teaching includes learning about trend analysis, visioning, and opportunity identification and networking. Additionally, these strategic issues are linked to arguments and student exercises about the importance of enterprise skill possession as without these, entrepreneurial practices cannot be executed. For Morris et al. (2013), there is scant evidence of courses and modules in universities that focus on opportunity related skills and the module attempts to incorporate these, as acknowledged by the following student quote from the evaluation. '*I now take part in opportunity scanning and see normally negative situations as an opportunity*'. Additionally, knowledge of entrepreneurial marketing also needs to extend beyond purely market based considerations, to include the resources of the firm. Consequently module learning goes beyond a limiting marketing orientation perspective (Stokes and Wilson, 2010), to one that includes the importance of a resource based view of the firm and the entrepreneurial marketer. Whilst all the students studying the module can be described as being marketers, few had been exposed to learning about enterprise and many of the previous concepts and theories are relatively unknown, where students are much more familiar with a traditional administrative based marketing framework (Hultman and Hills, 2011).

ENTERPRISE AWARENESS: HOW ENTREPRENEURIAL MARKETERS THINK

This area of developing enterprise awareness also relates to understanding the ways in which an entrepreneur thinks about business strategy. Hultman and Hills (2011) point out that mainstream marketing neglects the entrepreneur's methods, impoverishing student learning. So a key point for module tutors here is the belief that students need to understand the different ways in which the entrepreneur is a cognisant actor. In the LIBS module, students learn that EM implementation can be based on approaches to thinking that stand outside the traditional marketing textbook. Stokes and Wilson (2010) argues that the success of entrepreneurial ventures lie in managers' capabilities to go beyond proscribed, formalised, and conventional marketing. EM module tutors therefore expose students to material that highlights an approach that includes the use of nonlinear, intuitive thinking in decision making, featuring additional topics like entrepreneurial co-creation activity (Ionita, 2012).

Students are also exposed to effectuation theory and its related approaches (Nijssen, 2014), where learners are expected to appreciate that market creation can be just as an important purpose for the firm as being market serving. Consequently, students learn about some of the alternative thought processes of entrepreneurs. For example, this includes the entrepreneurial marketing model of Swenson et al. (2012), where emphasis is placed on factors like the leveraging of limited existing resources, and the use of immediate networks to help drive innovation rather than the reliance on future projections. Networks do not feature particularly in mainstream marketing texts and the EM module places emphasis on this, where students are encouraged to understand how and why networks are valued by entrepreneurial marketers (Carson and Gilmore, 2000). A number of students picked up on the importance of this feature, exemplified by the following quote. '*Learning about building up a network was really interesting because this area is very important for the future working life*'.

THE BUSINESS MODEL: DEVELOPING ENTREPRENEURIAL MINDSETS AND CAPABILITIES

Reflecting the point from the QAA that learning is not linear (QAA, 2018) and that it can have diverse starting points, the second and third features of the model proposed by the QAA relate to developing an entrepreneurial mindset and an entrepreneurial capability in students. At this stage with awareness of what entrepreneurial marketing activity is, the focus in the module shifts in the second semester, to a learning mode where not only knowledge is developed but the student's skill base as well. In particular, the module in the second semester focuses partly on developing generic skills in enterprise. QAA (2012) argue that this can be achieved through group based simulations where team working skills are a desired outcome, and an entrepreneurial mindset is built through action and reflection. The QAA further indicates that entrepreneurial competence is demonstrated when a student designs a service or product that meets an identified need, or where they can envisage an opportunity and suggest potential actions based on it. Both the aims of achieving a suitable mindset and capabilities is given shape and direction through the central focus of the second semester's work, which is based around the development of an organisation's business model.

There is a substantial literature on the area of business models, their development, renewal, and possible reinvention (see Crick and Crick, 2018). From an EM perspective, business models are about mainly process of innovation, particularly when firms focus on developing a unique business model. A recognition that it is necessary to know about business models also reflects Tollin's (2008) argument that strategic marketing managers now

404

view it as a central task to not only be involved in developing new products but also in the construction and implementation of the firm's overall strategy. This represents a challenge for new marketers, something they need to understand (Finch et al., 2013), where novices must learn to be able to work with other functional and operational areas of the business. In the context of the EM module at LIBS, students are expected to devise an innovation for an existing company where they learn about and apply a template that is discussed and applied by Morris et al. (2005). Students have to populate the template, one based around questions concerning the type of new value, who the value is for, what resources the firm can draw on, how the innovation is to be positioned, how money will be made, and what the longer term aim is. Making business models a central feature of the EM module for the second semester is generally received favourably by students, as indicated by the following quote. *'Learning about the business model, knowing what needs to be part of the business model, is very important and useful, it gave us some confidence for when we will be out there in the real world'*.

In practical terms, students have to devise an innovation and a value proposition and to either develop a new business model, or modify an existing one, for the company of the assignment. For this group based assignment, which is very much about students managing an innovation project over several weeks, module tutors have had submitted a wide variety of ideas. These have ranged from proposals like new customer service initiatives, website offerings, and digital platforms, through to manufacturing product ideas and new types of retail outlets. Module tutors do ask students to make contact with external companies to help facilitate the innovation, and this further assists in developing students networking knowledge and skills. Preparing and presenting a business model and a related innovation means that students need to not only understand and learn about business models but to apply themselves to a project requiring self-discipline, organisation, resilience, creativity, and a degree of risk management, where their own entrepreneurial marketing qualities have the opportunity to be show cased. Ideas need translating into actions, and although this is largely a business simulation exercise, students have the opportunity to display an entrepreneurial mindset and display in a group, entrepreneurial capabilities and effectiveness.

ENTREPRENEURIAL MARKETING CAPABILITIES: THE COMPETENCY TABLE

In the process of working on the business model and the innovation, students are asked to construct a competency table that is designed to illustrate the nature of the skills they use in completing the business model task. On one side of the table are the skills they select and on the other side, the evidence for these skills. The basic table can be embellished with brief references and definitions of the skills and also, a summary statement of how they might like to develop. Taking into account where they are now and their career aspirations, students are asked to reflect on the last of the features of the QAA model, that of their own entrepreneurial effectiveness. The skills present on the competency table are the ones which students select themselves, but they are encouraged to consider including on the table, key competencies discussed and taught on the module. The list most select from include capabilities like team working, project management, opportunity identification, innovation, creativity, motivation, project management, ethics, networking, oral and written communication, digital technology, and problem solving. These all seem critical skills that entrepreneurial marketing need to possess in the workplace (Mitchelmore and Rowley, 2010; O'Leary, 2017). These are the type of entrepreneurial skills that the QAA (2012, 2018) wishes to develop in students, skills also stressed in the European Commission's influential Entrecomp framework (Bacigalupo et al., 2016). Generally, there is praise for the competency table. One student commented that, '*I think the reflective table is useful, as it assesses an individual's strength and weaknesses, so they know which area to improve*'.

THE STUDENT AND AN ENTREPRENEURIAL IDENTITY

A key feature of an enterprise mindset as indicated by the QAA relates to personal identity, and this represents a good way to bring together some of the features of the module. For the tutors a key outcome is the attempt to develop in students, an entrepreneurial identity incorporating enterprise awareness, an enterprise mindset and enterprise skills. These, on a combined basis, should help to propel the student towards a true state of entrepreneurial effectiveness on entering the job market (QAA, 2018). The idea of performing entrepreneurially is the focus of activity in the module, and there is an ever present discourse of entrepreneurialism (Down and Reveley, 2004). This is realised in terms of a programme including lectures for knowledge dissemination, individually directed assignments, seminars involving case studies, presentations, and simulations, face-to-face meetings with students individually and in groups, workshops, and the use of related module materials, like websites, blogs, and set readings. Students are encouraged to appropriate the importance of a discourse around entrepreneurship and develop in turn an enterprising identity, as employees, and as possible future owners. Whilst there are differing perspectives on what the notion of identity represents, it broadly relates to the idea of who someone is, who they imagine themselves to be, and how they might act in particular situations and contexts (Zundel and Quinn, 2007).

The EM module reflects a view that individual identities are constructed through experience, interactions, and participation in discourse (Davies and Harré, 1990), where in the student's case, an identity gets realised through participating in the full range of learning activities related to entrepreneurialism, outlined in this chapter. Whilst for the vast majority of students the module is compulsory, the adoption of an entrepreneurial identity is not forced on course participants, as highlighted in the following quote from our evaluations. In the module space is provided for reflection and different views. '*I believe I have developed an entrepreneurial identity, but I haven't been forced to*'. In bringing together the key components discussed in this chapter, one respondent captured the link between entrepreneurial awareness, entrepreneurial mindsets, skill sets, and effectiveness, by stating, '*I feel I've learnt more and further improved my entrepreneurial skills and my thinking and attitude towards this*'. This point reflects the QAA's (2018) position, where it is indicated that students should ideally be involved not only in learning activities that create enterprise awareness but also engage in activities that develop and expand their enterprise capabilities, processes that will help them ultimately to become entrepreneurially effective employees and or employers.

SUMMARY

In the process of undertaking the learning tasks outlined here, students are adopting all the elements of the QAA learning journey model, to a lesser or greater extent. Alongside this, a constructivist approach to education stresses the importance of experience and learning, meaning that the EM module goes some considerable way in forming an entrepreneurial identity in students. As a result, by using the learning journey model of the QAA as a way to formalise the delivery of the EM module, this chapter has sought to show how enterprise can be embedded in a marketing degree. In recapping, this learning journey model is comprised of four elements, starting with entrepreneurial awareness. First, in the EM module, an entrepreneurial orientation framework is introduced and discussed, involving learning

DEVELOPING ENTREPRENEURIAL MARKETING COMPETENCIES

processes that ensure students are cognisant of what entrepreneurship involves. The QAA model then proposes that students undergo learning processes that facilitate the adoption of an entrepreneurial mindset. Here, the module asks students to develop an innovation around a business model framework where they have to think entrepreneurially whilst at the same time use competencies that are enterprise based, where this capability reflects the third element of the learning journey model. Finally, the model advocates that students should be encouraged to demonstrate entrepreneurial effectiveness. This is achieved through the students completing a competency table, where they are asked to indicate what enterprise skills they used in the execution of the innovation project; they then reflect on these.

The module therefore, enables students to explore and implement their own competencies around behaviours like opportunity identification, team working, risk management, innovation, resource management and creativity. The case is, at the end of the module, that most students demonstrate at least a basic capability in these various elements of entrepreneurialism. This is done by way of the competency tables and the innovation project, where many see themselves as developing entrepreneurial effectiveness, alongside an entrepreneurial mind- and skillset. For the student, the entrepreneurial marketing learning journey on completion of the module is far from over, however. On moving into employment – either in a firm or on their own – or perhaps moving onto more specialised courses, enterprise effectiveness will be enhanced. This will probably be achieved in a nonlinear fashion. For example, on entering work, the level of enterprise awareness can potentially be enhanced alongside skill progression, attitudes, and effectiveness, depending on the nature of the role. As this point demonstrates, the entrepreneurial marketing module at LIBS represents only the start of the journey and not the end.

KEY TERMS

■ Future entrepreneurial marketers
■ The entrepreneurial marketing learning journey
■ Entrepreneurial awareness, Entrepreneurial mindsets
■ Entrepreneurial capabilities, Entrepreneurial effectiveness
■ Constructivism and Entrepreneurial Marketing learning

REVIEW QUESTIONS

1. What are the reasons for developing an entrepreneurial identity in students?

2. What type of extra-curricular activities could be added into the student experience in order to assist the development of entrepreneurial effectiveness?

3. The entrepreneurial learning journey of students will continue in the workplace. If the student is not self-employed, what initiatives could their employer put in place to help them become more enterprising?

4. Is there a case that says enterprise education needs to be more widely embedded in the UK education system generally?

5. What particular types of employment skills are valued in the SME and why?

407

CASE STUDY

Like an SME: the Virgin Group ethos and new ventures

Richard Branson decided to title his bestselling book *Like a Virgin* but he could have added '*Like an SME*'. The Virgin group might be perceived as being about big business, but in a number of ways, it acts like it was an entrepreneurial SME. In highlighting this feature of Virgin, Richard Branson has pointed out that the company prides itself in being a challenger brand, always retaining an entrepreneurial mindset, an approach redolent of the small successful business. In this context, Virgin was one of the first business incubators because it hatched itself. Over time, using capital raised by other parts of the brand, the Virgin group has turned many innovative ideas into start-ups and then into fully fledged businesses. When Virgin companies have reached a point where they are making an impact, they still seek to stay true to the roots and spirit of emergent entrepreneurialism by working with small businesses and start-ups. This suggests a strong cultural affinity with the small business sector and its ethos. This type of small business spirit thrives in the group, which includes many well-known names, such as Virgin Mobile, Money, Radio, Hyperloop, Sport, and Voyages.

Linked closely to the Virgin business approach is the nature of the entrepreneurial competencies and knowledge that staff possess. Through empowered employees, who consistently monitor customer feedback and deliver a high quality service to the customer, Virgin brands seek to continually improve the customer's experience through innovation. Typically, when any new venture is started, it is based on hard research and analysis, where the industry is rigorously reviewed. It is not a pure textbook route to success however, as employees will then put themselves in the customer's shoes, in order to see what could make the innovation better. An employee in marketing, working with the Virgin group comments on the process.

'Just thinking as individuals ourselves, what do we believe consumers would want? .... We do a lot of our marketing thinking by imagining how we would feel as a customer, and that has given us an awful lot of what we need to know and understand, to move the company on'.

In carrying out these twin processes, fundamentally important strategic questions get asked. For example, is there an opportunity for restructuring a market and creating competitive advantage? Is the customer confused or badly served? Is this an opportunity for building the Virgin brand? How can Virgin add to customer perceived value? How will it interact with other businesses? Is there an appropriate trade-off between risk and reward?

New entrepreneurial ventures are often steered by people seconded from other parts of Virgin, who bring with them a trademark management style combined with skills and experience. Partnerships with other companies – quite often small firms – are created in order to pool industry specific skills, knowledge, and operational expertise. So contrary to what some people may think, Virgin's constant expansion and eclectic empire is neither random nor reckless. Each successive venture demonstrates a devotion to picking the right market and the right opportunity, and part of this is about calculated risk taking, a key small firm entrepreneurial attribute. Once the new venture is up and running, several factors contribute to making it a success. These are the power of the Virgin name and Richard Branson's personal reputation, the unrivalled network of contacts and partners and a Virgin management style that

DEVELOPING ENTREPRENEURIAL MARKETING COMPETENCIES

ensures talent is empowered to flourish. Added to this, Virgin has minimal management layers, no bureaucracy, a small board and no massive global Headquarters. These are all features of an entrepreneurial small business and, in turn, represent the key elements that the Virgin group has embedded into its own culture and strategy.

CASE QUESTIONS AND TASKS

1. From the case, identify four key entrepreneurial marketing competencies that should be possessed by an individual, indicating why they are important.
2. Identify two other key competencies not in the case that are useful to have, saying why.
3. What are the benefits to an organisation of developing individual 'competency profiles'?
4. Do you identify with the Virgin culture? Why, or why not?

Sources:

Aaker, D. and Joachimsthaler, E., (2012). Brand leadership. Simon and Schuster, Ardley B C A phenomenological perspective on the work of the marketing manager, Lambert academic publishing, Branson, R., 2013. Like a virgin: Secrets they won't teach you at business school. Random House, LIBS Entrepreneurial marketing module teaching resources www.virgin.com/richard-branson/why-i-do-business-small-businesses

---

GROUP BASED ACTIVITY

Information

Assume you are a leadership team in a successful and growing SME tool hire company. You supply tools and expertise to small builders, individual customers, and also local firms who complete public building repairs and renovations. You have decided that initially, all staff with a marketing and business role will complete a competency profile as a basis for future discussion with managers.

Task

In your group, design the profile deciding on the skills you think should be included, providing at the same time the indicative evidence for each competence selected.

TECHNOLOGY, THE SME, AND 21ST-CENTURY ENTREPRENEURIAL MARKETING COMPETENCIES

A new phenomenon of 21st-century marketing, having an undoubted effect on entrepreneurs, is the emergence of new models of the competencies required to perform effectively that incorporate digital. These include the Modern Marketing Model (M3) from Econsultancy, the Five Cs model from Keith Weed, and the Professional

409

Competencies Model from the Chartered Institute of Marketing. This means practitioners and teachers have to think about the realignment of established entrepreneurial marketing competencies, with newer ones. In considering this, it is important that organisations, learners, and tutors realise that it is important to be able to reconcile digital and classic marketing. This means avoiding the problem of a silo approach that sees digital and established marketing as separate entities. If the two areas cannot be integrated, then growth opportunities for the individual entrepreneurial marketer and their firms will be severely restricted. In other words, the marketing discipline does not just want strategy formulators who cannot operationalise in a digital context, and likewise, it does not want just digital technicians who lack marketing knowledge and the related strategic entrepreneurial aspects.

One model which reconciles these two issues is the Professional Marketing Competencies model of the Chartered Institute of Marketing referred to earlier. This provides a guide to the skills, attitudes, and behaviours that are expected of marketers. In the context of the chapter here, the model indicates that one key behaviour is the ability to be entrepreneurial, the skill to spot or create opportunities, which is then linked to innovation, the ability to formulate new ideas. These are at the core of entrepreneurial marketing and in the 21st century need connecting, however, to digital skills, which in turn are highlighted in the CIM model. This is achieved through the competence of Digital Integration. This means displaying competences in technical digital skills, thus facilitating the delivery of opportunity and innovation. These technical skills must be seen in the context of strategic entrepreneurial aims and include such competencies as search engine optimisation, marketing automation, social media marketing, email marketing, mobile, and digital analytics. In the 21st century it is a case of both these two skill and strategy competencies being owned and updated by the entrepreneurial marketer at all stages in their career.

Questions
1. Provide some an example of where opportunity identification means using digital competencies.
2. What recent innovations have occurred on online platforms?
3. Find online and research, one of the other two marketing models indicated earlier and summarise how digital competence is a central aspect of its implementation.

REFERENCES

Ang, L., D'Alessandro, S. and Winzar, H. (2014) A visual-based approach to the mapping of generic skills: its application to a marketing degree. *Higher Education Research and Development*, 33(2), 181–197.

Bacigalupo, M., Kampylis, P., Punie, Y. and Van den Brande, G., (2016) *EntreComp: The Entrepreneurship Competence Framework*. Publication Office of the European Union, Luxembourg.

Carson, D. and Gilmore, A. (2000) SME marketing management competencies. *International Business Review*, 9(3), 363–382.

Chaston, I. (2016) *Entrepreneurial Marketing: Sustaining Growth in All Organisations*. Palgrave Macmillan, London.

CIM (2016) Professional-marketing-competencies. www.cim.co.uk/membership/professional-marketing-competencies/ (Accessed 6 April 2019).

Crick, J. M. and Crick, D. (2018) Angel investors' predictive and control funding criteria: The importance of evolving business models. *Journal of Research in Marketing and Entrepreneurship*, 20(1), 34–56.

Davies, B. and Harré, R. (1990) Positioning: The discursive production of selves. *Journal for the theory of Social Behaviour*, 20(1), 43–63.

Down, S. and Reveley, J. (2004) Generational encounters and the social formation of entrepreneurial identity 'Young Guns and Old Farts'. *Organization*, 11(2), 233–250.

EM Module handbook (2018) *Entrepreneurial marketing, 2018–19*. LIBS, University of Lincoln, unpublished.

Finch, D., Nadeau, J. and O'Reilly, N. (2013) The future of marketing education: A practitioner's perspective. *Journal of Marketing Education*, 35(1), 54–67.

Hultman, C. M. and Hills, G. E. (2011) Influence from entrepreneurship in marketing theory. *Journal of Research in Marketing and Entrepreneurship*, 13(2), 120–125.

Ionita, D. (2012) Entrepreneurial Marketing: A new approach for challenging times. *Management and Marketing for the Knowledge Society*, 17(1), 131–150.

Madichie, N. O., Gbadamosi, A. and Nwankwo, S. (2018) Entrepreneurialism in a London University: A Case Illustration. In Ferreira, J., Fayolle, A., Ratten, V. and Roposo, M. (Eds.), *Entrepreneurial Universities: Collaboration, Education, and Policies*. Edward Elgar, London, Cheltenham, 88–104.

Matthews, B. and Ross, L. (2010) *Research Methods: A Practical Guide for the Social Sciences*. Pearson, Harlow.

Miles, M. P., Lewis, G. K., Hall-Phillips, A., Morrish, S. C., Gilmore, A. and Kasouf, C. J. (2016) The influence of entrepreneurial marketing processes and entrepreneurial self-efficacy on community vulnerability, risk, and resilience. *Journal of Strategic Marketing*, 24(1), 34–46.

Mitchelmore, S. and Rowley, J. (2010) Entrepreneurial competencies: A literature review and development agenda. *International Journal of Entrepreneurial Behavior and Research*, 16(2), 92–111.

Morris, M. H., Schindehutte, M. and Allen, J. (2005) The entrepreneur's business model: Toward a unified perspective. *Journal of Business Research*, 58(6), 726–735.

Morris, M. H., Schindehutte, M. and LaForge, R. W. (2002) Entrepreneurial marketing: A construct for integrating emerging entrepreneurship and marketing perspectives. *Journal of Marketing Theory and Practice*, 10(4), 1–19.

Morris, M. H., Webb, J. W., Fu, J. and Singhal, S. (2013) A competency-based perspective on entrepreneurship education: Conceptual and empirical insights. *Journal of Small Business Management*, 51(3), 352–369.

Morrish, S. C. and Deacon, J. H. (2011) A tale of two spirits: Entrepreneurial marketing at 42 below vodka and Penderyn Whisky. *Journal of Small Business & Entrepreneurship*, 24(1), 113–124.

Nijssen, E. (2014) *Entrepreneurial Marketing: An Effectual Approach*. Routledge, London.

O'Leary, S. (2017) Developing entrepreneurial and employability attributes through marketing projects with SMEs. *Journal of Research in Marketing and Entrepreneurship*, 19(1), 77–90.

QAA (2012) Enterprise and entrepreneurship education: Guidance for UK higher education providers. www.qaa.ac.uk (Accessed 29 June 2018).

QAA (2018) Enterprise and entrepreneurship education: Guidance for UK higher education providers. www. qaa.ac.uk (Accessed 15 July 2018).

Rami, J., Lorenzi, F. and Lalor, J. (2009) The application of constructivist assessment practices in a teacher-training programme: A tool for developing professional competencies. In *British Educational Research Association Annual Conference*, University of Manchester.

Rogers C. (2018) Are marketing degrees up to scratch? www.marketingweek.com/2018/10/25/marketing-degrees-up-to-scratch/ (Accessed 4 April 2019).

Stokes, D. and Wilson, N. C. (2010) Entrepreneurship and marketing education: Time for the road less travelled? *International Journal of Entrepreneurship and Innovation Management*, 11(1), 95–108.

Swenson, M. J., Rhoads, G. K. and Whitlark, D. B. (2012) Entrepreneurial marketing: A framework for creating opportunity with competitive angles. *Journal of Applied Business and Economics*, 13(1), 47–52.

Tollin, K. (2008) Mindsets in marketing for product innovation: An explorative analysis of chief marketing executives' ideas and beliefs about how to increase their firms' innovation capability. *Journal of Strategic Marketing*, 16(5), 363–390.

Trough, F. (2012) *Brilliant Employability Skills*. Prentice Hall, Harlow.

Wenger, E. (1998) *Communities of Practice*. Cambridge University Press, Cambridge.

Zundel, M. and Quinn, L. (2007) Identity construction in marketing management practices. *Review of Sociology*, 23, 385–409.

Chapter 26

Marketing in the informal economy
An entrepreneurial perspective and research agenda

Nnamdi O. Madichie, Anayo D. Nkamnebe, and Ignatius U. Ekanem

LEARNING OBJECTIVES

After reading this chapter, you should be able to:
- Explain the contribution of the informal sector to the development of both developed and emerging market economies;
- Discuss the prevalence of the informal economy across regions and sectors;
- Evaluate respective measurement metrics, and reports on the sector undertaken by governments around the world;
- Assess and critique the myths and realities associated with marketing in the informal economy;
- Recommend alternative entrepreneurial marketing strategies for businesses in the informal sector.

INTRODUCTION

The informal economy refers to the paid production and sale of goods and services which are unregistered by, or hidden from, the state for tax and/or benefit purposes but which may still be legal in all other respects (Williams and Windebank, 1998). As such, the informal economy includes only paid work that is illegal because of its non-declaration to the state for tax and/or social security purposes. Paid work in which the good and/or service itself is illegal (e.g., drug trafficking) is thus considered unpaid work (Williams, 2007, p. 350).

It is worth highlighting that the discussion on SME marketing seems to have focused primarily on the formal economy with a concomitant neglect of marketing practices within the informal economy. Paradoxically, the bulk of small business activities in developing countries (especially micro enterprises in which a significant proportion of the population is engaged) is hugely accounted for through the informal economy (Nkamnebe and Madichie, 2010).[1] Furthermore, the numerous independent and unregistered businesses across the globe that account for as much as 60% of global economic output have been part of the informal economic system. With the globalisation of markets, the prevalence of informal economy has persisted and indeed expanded due to the ease with which it can be imported

MARKETING IN THE INFORMAL ECONOMY

through migratory pipelines – for example, ethnic minority businesses spread across different parts of London, job displacement and strict enforcement of regulations force many consumers and producers into the informal economy (see Nkamnebe and Madichie, 2010).

In developing world contexts, however, it has been recognised for several decades that the undeclared sector acts as 'an incubator for business potential and . . . transitional base for accessibility and graduation to the formal economy', and that many undeclared workers show 'real business acumen, creativity, dynamism and innovation' (ILO, 2002, p. 54). In the past few years, a similar view of undeclared work[2] has started to emerge in Europe (Renooy et al., 2004; Williams and Round, 2009; Nkamnebe and Madichie, 2010). But what exactly is undeclared work and how does it relate to the topic on the informal sector? The next section provides the multifarious definitions of the sector, which is primarily informal economy-driven.

KEY FEATURES OF THE INFORMAL ECONOMY

The phrase *informal sector* has proved difficult to be given a universalistic definition. As a result of this, different meanings and estimates have been attempted in its measurement. In most cases these definitions and measurements vary widely and tend to militate against reasonable conclusions and generalisations. Most often, the informal sector has been mistaken for deleterious activities such as smuggling, black market, illegal transactions, underground sector, and unofficial transactions (see Williams, 2007). Despite these unpopular labels of the informal sector from 'cash-in-hand work', through the 'shadow economy', or 'underground sector', it remains a construct that has been in constant flux – both theoretically and practically. This constantly evolving pattern thus makes it difficult to *observe, study, define, and measure*. Despite this fluidity, attempts have been made by economists and social scientists to define and – even more tedious – measure it. As expected, the result of such efforts has yielded as many definitions as there are authors. One of the popular definitions of the informal economy conceptualises the informal economy as the paid production and sale of goods and services which are unregistered by or hidden from the state for tax and/or benefit purposes but which are legal in all other respects (Williams and Round, 2009). Taking this as a working definition, the sector remains informal by falling outside the regulatory framework of most governments for tax purposes.

The regulatory framework

Evidently, small business marketers, who are the predominant operators in the informal economies, can be distinguished from their mainstream counterparts on the basis of business registration. An unregistered business (typical of an informal economic activity) is most unlikely to pay taxes even though it might not necessarily be engaged in unlawful activities. On this basis, SME marketers should not be confused with those other operators that engage in criminal activities such as arms dealing, child trafficking and brothel operations (especially in the UK where the practice is illegal). To illustrate this point, two theoretical perspectives have been used to explain the emergence of the informal economy. The first is the argument that the increasing informalisation is a direct consequence of government over regulation of the economy, which leaves these small players little room for survival. Under such circumstances, the informal economy tends to provide a strategic choice for survival. Harney (2006, p. 374) for instance captured this reality in his description of a typical informal Neapolitan neighbourhood of La Pignasecca in Naples, Italy, thus:

413

by the early afternoon the municipal police are gone so the street vendors set up their cardboard tables, lay their tarpaulin and sheets and arrange their goods – inexpensive children's electronic toys, kitchenware, linen, lingerie, binoculars, calculators, perfume, posters of pop stars, and football players – on the main thoroughfare without fear of fines.

The second perspective sees the informal economy as

> an unavoidable expression of the uneven development inherent in late capitalism. . . (thus) evasion of regulation is simply part and parcel of a cost-cutting imperative on the part of small entrepreneurs struggling for survival in the marginal and diminishing market space left over by the expansion of corporate capital.
>
> (Jones et al., 2006, p. 358)

Following this orthodoxy, capitalism provides a key driver of the informal economy as those displaced from the formal sector take solace in the informal economy. Furthermore, Nkamnebe (2006) argued that most Sub-Saharan African (SSA) economies may find it difficult to catch up with the dominant economies and would, therefore, resort to the informal economy for survival. This somewhat explains the increasing expansion of the informal economy in developing economies with a burgeoning entrepreneurship base as epitomised by the case of Eastern Nigeria (see, for example, Igwe et al., 2018, 2019). Arguably, the emergence and growth of the informal economy is predicated upon a myriad of economic, political, cultural, and migratory influences (see Williams, 2005a, 2005b; Jones et al., 2006; Nkamnebe and Madichie, 2010; Olomi et al., 2018). While the difficulty of defining an informal economy has been recognised due to the shifts in the nature of the construct, the framework in Table 26.1 suggested by Schneider (2002) and further developed by others,[3] may be helpful for developing a middle ground definition of the concept.

MEASURING THE INFORMAL ECONOMY

Until now, measurement methods have ranged from techniques that indirectly measure its magnitude by using proxy indicators to methods that attempt to directly measure its

Table 26.1 A taxonomy of types of underground economic activities

Type of activity	Monetary transactions		Non-Monetary Transactions	
Illegal Activities	Trade with stolen goods: drug dealing and manufacturing; prostitution, gambling, smuggling, and fraud		Barter of drugs, stolen goods, smuggling, etc. Production or growing drugs for personal use. Theft for own use.	
	Tax Evasion	*Tax Avoidance*	*Tax Evasion*	*Tax Avoidance*
Legal Activities	Unreported income from self-employment: Wages, salaries and assets from unreported work related to legal services and goods	Employee discounts, fringe benefits	Barter of legal services and goods	All do-it-yourself work and neighbour help

Source: Adapted from Schneider (2002)

414

MARKETING IN THE INFORMAL ECONOMY

prevalence (for reviews, see Bajada, 2002; Thomas, 1999; Renooy et al., 2004; Williams, 2005a; Williams and Windebank, 1998). So far as indirect methods are concerned, proxy indicators used to assess its prevalence range from non-monetary indicators such as the prevalence of very small enterprises and electricity demand, monetary proxies such as the number of large denomination notes in circulation, the cash-deposit ratio or level of cash transactions, and income/expenditure discrepancies either at the household and/or national level. Over time, however, there has been a waning interest in these indirect proxy measurement methods (Thomas, 1999; OECD, 2002; Williams, 2006).

The strong consensus that has emerged is that indirect methods are not only relatively inaccurate as measures of size but also limited in their usefulness for understanding the distribution and nature of such work. This is the conclusion of both OECD experts in their handbook on measurement methods and the most recent European Commission report on undeclared work,[4] as well as a host of academic evaluations of direct and indirect methods. Therefore, much greater emphasis has been placed on more direct survey methods to measure the magnitude of such work (OECD, 2002; Renooy et al., 2004; Williams, 2006). Reflecting this, the European Commission recently evaluated the feasibility of conducting a direct survey of undeclared work across the European Union (European Commission, 2005).

In the UK, Her Majesty's Revenue and Customs (HMRC) commissioned consultants to develop methodologies for conducting direct surveys of the informal economy (Her Majesty's Revenue and Customs, 2005). The major impetus for these direct surveys of the informal economy is the current poverty of knowledge on its size and distribution. Until recently, most direct surveys have tended to be small-scale, usually conducted on specific localities which take the household as the unit of analysis and focus on off-the-books transactions in the domestic services sector (e.g., Williams, 2007a, 2007b; Leonard, 1994; Pahl, 1984; Warde, 1990; Williams, 2005a, 2005b, 2006; Williams and Windebank, 2001).

The current shift towards direct surveys rather than relying on indirect proxy indicators has its own share of criticisms, usually from the users of indirect methods, is that direct surveys naively assume that respondents will reveal to them, or even know, the prevalence of informal work. Yet the evidence appears to be that direct surveys produce fairly reliable and valid data. For example, Pahl (1984) found that when the results from individuals as suppliers and purchasers were compared, the same level of informal work was discovered. Similar conclusions have been identified in previous studies (e.g., Leonard, 1994; Nkamnebe and Madichie, 2010; Williams, 2006, 2007a, 2007b). The implication is that respondents are not secretive about their informal work. Just because it is activity hidden from or unregistered for tax and/or social security purposes does not mean that respondents are unwilling to discuss it with researchers.

However, it is important to recognise that the direct (household) surveys so far conducted have been carefully and delicately designed with data on informal work being gathered usually within the context of a broader study of 'household work practices' (Williams, 2006). That is to say, they have tended to investigate the practices households use to get a variety of domestic tasks completed and whether household members undertake tasks for other households (either on a paid or unpaid basis) in order to identify the prevalence and nature of informal work.

Even if honesty of response (and thus reliability of the data) does not appear to be a valid critique of most well-designed direct survey methods, two salient criticisms of direct methods remain. On the one hand, direct approaches have so far largely investigated only informal work used in relation to service provision in particular (especially domestic services) and final demand (spending by consumers on goods and services) more generally, rather

415

than intermediate demand (spending by businesses). Final demand, however, accounts for just two-thirds of total spending. There exists a strong case for extending direct investigations to include business surveys rather than solely household surveys. On the other hand, most direct surveys have so far tended to be confined to small-scale, often qualitative studies, of particular localities, groups, or sectors. The result is that it has been difficult to gain any representative picture at the national level of the overall prevalence, nature, and distribution of informal work.

Overall, small-scale, mostly locality-specific studies have been conducted and there has been a heavy emphasis on using the household as the unit of analysis as well as only examining domestic service provision rather than taking business as the unit of analysis and examining the full range of goods and services provision. In late 2004 the UK's Small Business Service took the decision to include a series of questions on informal work in a nationally representative survey of small businesses so as to provide the first national business survey of the prevalence and impacts of such work. Essentially, most operators in the informal economy are largely the poor and middle income developing or emerging economies and/ or ethnic minorities and immigrants in the more advanced economies. Arguably, they are mainly occupants of the so-called *bottom* or *base of the pyramid (BoP)* that have been recognised as constituting a substantial portion of the economic activities of modern economies. For instance, Humphreys (2004) estimated the total purchasing power of all ethnic minorities in the US for 2009 amounted to about US$1.5 trillion. Anderson and Billou (2007, p. 14) captured the potential of this market thus:

> Consumers at the very bottom of the economic pyramid – those with per capita incomes of less than $1,500 – number more than 4 billion. For more than a billion people – roughly one-sixth of the world's population – per capita income is less than $1 per day.

The 20 largest emerging economies include more than 700 million such households, with a total annual income estimated at some US$1.7 trillion, and this spending power was approximately equal to Germany's annual gross domestic product about a decade ago (Prahalad and Hart, 2002). The spending power of Brazil's poorest 25 million households, for example, amounts to US$73 billion per annum, while China's poor residents account for 286 million households with a combined annual income of US$691 billion. India has 171 million low-income households with a combined US$378 billion in income (Anderson and Billou, 2007).

This chapter, therefore, examines the nature, size and dynamics of informal economy and discusses marketing strategies that are applicable in such setting at the end of the chapter.

THE ANNUAL SMALL BUSINESS REPORT 2005

The 2004/2005 Annual Small Business Survey undertaken by the Small Business Service (SBS) sought to gauge the needs of small businesses, assess their main concerns and to identify the barriers that prevent them from fulfilling their potential. The survey was based on telephone interviews with a large sample of 7,505 UK small businesses. The telephone interviews for this survey were conducted in the fourth quarter of 2004 and the first quarter of 2005 (Williams and Round, 2009; Williams, 2007a, 2007b). When constructing the sampling frame, the intention was not to reflect the distribution of firms by size in the UK or their geographical distribution. Instead, more micro (one to nine employees), small business (ten to 49 employees), and medium-sized businesses (50–249 employees) were sampled than would be required to match the proportion in the UK economy (and fewer sole traders and partnerships without employees), and more firms in Wales and Scotland were sampled so that these countries' businesses could be analysed in detail.

The decision by the SBS to include questions on the prevalence and impact of the informal economy in this 2004/05 survey arose directly out of a Small Business Council (2004) report that sought to evaluate the extent and nature of the informal economy and propose ways of tackling small businesses working on an off-the-books basis. In that national report, a lack of evidence was identified concerning not only the overall magnitude of this 'hidden enterprise culture' but also the economic sectors, businesses, and geographical areas in which such work took place. Both the Small Business Council (2004) report and the government response to its recommendations (Williams and Round, 2009) agreed that improving the evidence base was a necessary precursor to concerted and targeted public policy action.

As the Rt. Hon. Alun Michael, Minister of State for Industry and the Regions, states in the foreword to the government response to the SBC report (Small Business Council, 2004): 'We do not have as clear a picture as we would like of the scale and nature of the informal economy' (SBS, 2005, p. 1). While the full report, summing up the government's perception of its knowledge on the informal economy, stated that 'the size and composition of the informal economy is uncertain' (SBS, 2005, p. 5), the report concluded in the final paragraph that 'more research is required both into the size and character of the informal economy' (SBS, 2005, p. 19). This explicit recognition of the lack of an evidence base was further reinforced later that year by an Office of National Statistics (ONS) report on data sources on the informal economy. This concluded that there is currently little or no extensive data available of the magnitude and distribution of the informal economy (ONS, 2005).

Reflecting the wider emerging consensus that indirect methods, which measure the informal economy using proxy indicators, are both unreliable and invalid (OECD, 2002; Renooy et al., 2004), these reports were thus highlighting the lack of any direct national survey of the extent and distribution of such work. Given this background context of government recognition of the lack of extensive direct surveys of the informal economy. Until 2007, most direct surveys of the informal economy have taken the household as the unit of analysis and focused upon provision in the domestic services sector (e.g., Leonard, 1994; Pahl, 1984; Warde, 1990). The few studies that have taken businesses as the unit of analysis have been small-scale ethnographic studies based on face-to-face qualitative interviews conducted by academics and focusing on a small number of firms in particular localities working in a specific sector. This SBS survey was thus the first study in an advanced economy to conduct an extensive survey of businesses with regard to the prevalence and impacts of informal work. Indeed, given that small businesses employing less than 250 comprise 99.9% of all enterprises in the UK economy (Williams and Round, 2009), this survey comprises a relatively comprehensive portrait of UK business opinion.

Extending the discussion beyond the confines of the UK economy, another separate study by Guesalaga and Marshall (2008) used the buying power index (BPI) methodology to evaluate the size of the informal economy (BOP). The use of this latter approach was in order to estimate the business opportunities as measured by the purchasing power of these economies. According to these authors the justification for using the BPI in the context of low-income consumers is twofold. First, this approach has been successful in measuring the relative buying power of people in specific geographic areas, in many different contexts – thus making the instrument valid and generally acceptable. Second, most of the literature on BOP assesses the opportunities in the low-income sector based on a purchasing power driven by population, income, or both, without considering the 'expenditure' dimension (see Madichie, 2018 for a case illustration from the Congo). As highlighted in Box 26.1, the

South African business environment has witnessed immense change in the last few years with the influx of Chinese entrepreneurs seeking acceptance in that context (see Ndoro, Louw, and Kanyangale, 2019).

> ## BOX 26.1: CHINESE IMMIGRANT ENTREPRENEURSHIP IN SOUTH AFRICA
>
> This study explores how Chinese immigrant entrepreneurs who own small retail businesses in the Eastern Cape province of South Africa draw from their social capital to operate their small businesses. The study followed a qualitative research design in which 21 in-depth interviews were conducted. The findings show that the Chinese immigrant entrepreneurs used different forms of social capital to operate their small retail businesses in the host business environment. Drawing from their social capital, the Chinese immigrant entrepreneurs were able to respond to opportunities and challenges in the host business environment. Social capital embedded in relationships and networks between the Chinese immigrant entrepreneurs and different stakeholders was central to the operations of the small retail businesses.
>
> Source: Ndoro, T. T. R., Louw, L., & Kanyangale, M. (2019). Practices in operating a small business in a host community: a social capital perspective of Chinese immigrant entrepreneurship within the South African business context. *International Journal of Entrepreneurship and Small Business*, 36(1–2), 148–163.

MARKETING IN THE INFORMAL ECONOMY

Early thinking was that informal economy only existed in the 'underground' or 'black' markets that are prevalent in the developing economies of the world. However, recent evidence conceptualises market informality as a global phenomenon.[5] Initial predictions of the modernisation theory of the 1950s and 1960s, suggested that informality was a consequence of underdevelopment that would disappear as soon as the undeveloped economies became more advanced. Indeed, Schneider (2002) used the estimation of informal economy sizes of 110 developing, transition, and OECD countries to illustrate the global dimension of informal marketing dynamics. With the increasing size and pervasive nature of the informal economy across the globe, and the prevalence of micro, small and medium-sized enterprises in this sector, a focus on SME marketing in the informal sector has become practically interesting. Such focus affords 21st-century marketers the robust knowledge base for hybridising formal and informal markets.

As McGregor (2005) once argued – from the perspective of a Canadian study – that there was a collection of marketplace imperfections around which consumer movement issues are conventionally organised – product choice and safety; package and labelling; pricing strategies; information and advertising; selling; promotion and distribution; complaints and redress; repairs and warranties; consumer education; and protection of consumers' interests. She went on to assert that patronising SMEs exposed consumers to many challenges and potential market failures (see McGregor, 2005, p. 12), which include questionable selling practices, poor complaints handling, and unclear repairs and warranties practices.

To highlight some of the dark sides of the informal market, two special issues of the *International Journal of Social Economics*[6] were dedicated to the informal economy and organised

MARKETING IN THE INFORMAL ECONOMY

crime. In one of the papers from these issues, Walle (2008) highlighted some very instructive insights into the growing blurred boundaries between the formal and informal economy. Walle (2008, p. 657) considers the informal economy as 'those income generating activities occuring oustide the state's regulatory framework . . . the scope and character of the informal economy are defined by the very regulatory framework it evades'. In other words, informal economic activities are untaxed, unlicensed, and largely unregulated economic activities usually characterised by their small scale of operation. Tripp (2001) suggested that although these activities may be defined as illicit (such as some of the marketing practices of Lebanese in West Africa – see Box 26.2) depending on the country in question, they nevertheless account for the majority of new jobs created in African economies.[7]

BOX 26.2: THE INFORMAL ECONOMY'S DARKSIDE – LEBANESE IN WEST AFRICA

The Lebanese community across West Africa is thought to be between 80,000 and 250,000 strong. Although many Africans openly state how much they hate the Lebanese in their respective countries, but the latter's seed seems to have been sown into the fabric of West African economics, politics, and culture. The Lebanese tenacity, aptitude for business and drive to succeed mean they have been not only continued to do business but have also thrived in both the formal and informal economy. It is more likely they chose to go to West Africa because at around that time American countries tightened their entry requirements after high levels of immigration during the previous century. The French government also ran a recruiting campaign in Beirut looking for middlemen to work the boom in West African groundnut farming, at a time of agricultural crisis in Lebanon. The Lebanese in West Africa have always been merchants, using their connections abroad to source goods for import, and – like other migrant groups – they use their family networks to keep their costs down. As a result they have built a strong economic presence across the region. Lebanese businesses have become the backbone of most markets in West Africa, spanning numerous sectors from car importing, mining, oil services and defence contracts – to the more shadowy worlds of gun-running, diamond-smuggling, and crude-oil theft. Doing business in politically volatile West Africa is not easy. With a poorly functioning legal system, contracts and other business agreements can be virtually worthless. The Lebanese have discovered that the best way of surviving, where the regime you're doing business with could be overthrown tomorrow, is to court the powerful – whomever they are. And an aspiring West African 'big man' knows he has to do business with the Lebanese if he has any hope of getting rich.

Source: Walker, A. (2010) Tenacity and risk – the Lebanese in West Africa. *BBC News*, 25 January. Online at: http://news.bbc.co.uk/2/hi/8479134.stm [Accessed 9 April 2010]

However, there could be three identifiable categories of markets – legal market for goods and services, a market of illegal goods and services (i.e., organised crime) and an informal market for legal goods and services. These markets have begun to exhibit blurred boundaries in a variety of ways and often merging. Citing the case of Brussels, Walle (2008, p. 658) highlights how in most cases formal and informal markets share a mutual sort of significance. The location of numerous official European institutions in

419

Brussels has not only attracted non-governmental organisations and other lobby groups whose demands for services such as courier, catering, cleaning, and even babysitting have also arisen. Services in these sectors have been provided for by the informal sector often due to the rather lax attitude towards formal regulation as they are hard to monitor.

Despite the conflicting conclusions over the nature and size of the informal economy, the general impression is that the size of the global informal market is robust enough to warrant coordinated strategies to harness. Going by the recent global economic crisis, it has become clear that no economy in the world is immune from failure, thus making even the largest economies and *Fortune 500* corporations consider investing in sectors hitherto considered unprofitable. Indeed, at the height of the recent global financial crisis, the Organised Private Sector (OPS) in an emerging market context such as Nigeria alluded to the fact that the informal economy was the 'backbone' of that economy (see end of chapter case study for an illustration). The same holds true in most economies of the world where the informal sector is perceived to be a dominant player (see Table 26.2 for some

Table 26.2 Selected sizes of informal economies in the world

Region	% of GDP	Highest	Middle	Lower
Africa	42% for the years 1999/2000.	Zimbabwe (59.4%), Tanzania (58.3%), and Nigeria (57.9%)	Mozambique (40.3%), Cote d'Ivoire (39.9%), and Madagascar (39.6%).	Botswana (33.4%), Cameroon (32.8%), and South Africa (28.4%).
Asia	26% of official GDP for the years 1999/2000.	Thailand (52.6%), Sri Lanka (44.6%), and Philippines (43.4%).	India (23.1%), Israel (21.9%), Taiwan, and China (19.6%)	Singapore (13.1%), Japan (11.3%). On average the Asian developing.
South and Latin America	% of GNP is 41%.	Bolivia (67.1%), Panama (64.1%), and Peru (59.9%).	*N/A*	Chile (19.8%), Argentina (25.4%).
Transition Economies	38% for the year 1999/2000.	Georgia (67.3%), Azerbaijan (60.6%), Ukraine (52.2%)	Bulgaria (36.9%), Romania (34.4%).	Hungary (25.1%), the Czech Republic (19.1%), Slovak Republic (18.9%).
West European OECD	18% for the year 1999/2000.	Greece (28.6%), Italy (27.0%).	Denmark (18.2%), Germany (16.3%)	Austria (10.2%), Switzerland (8.8%).
North America and Pacific OECD Countries	13.5%.	Canada (16.3%), Australia (15.3%), the New Zealand (12.7%) and the United States (8.8%).		

Source: Nkamnebe and Madichie (2010, p. 425)

MARKETING IN THE INFORMAL ECONOMY

of the statistics in the last decade, 1999–2000). Accordingly, the informal economy in developing countries and other underserved markets deserve increasing attention – both academic and policy.

Guesalaga and Marshall (2008, p. 413) captured this emerging trend:

> with markets in the developed economies experiencing slow growth. . ., private companies should look for business opportunities in emerging markets with low-income consumers; that is, at the bottom of the pyramid (BOP). There is an untapped potential for marketing to this sector, which is composed of approximately four billion people worldwide.

The main argument for targeting the bottom-of-the pyramid market is that there is significant purchasing power in this segment.[8] As Madichie (2018) points out in the case of a sartorial subculture in the Congo, these difficult to understand group have started venturing into entrepreneurship on the fringes from a long period of being fashion connoisseurs to the emerging entrepreneurial quest.

BOX 26.3: TECHNOLOGY, SME, AND THE 21ST CENTURY

SMES and especially those in the developing world, have begun to catch or provide alternative growth trajectories, especially in a sector that has started to claim its place on the world stage in the 21st century. Two chapters from a recently published book provide some insight into this growing trend. In the first of these, entitled *The African New Media Digital Revolution: Some Selected Cases from Nigeria* by Bolat (2019), explores the historical timeline of and changes in the media landscape and presents an empirical investigation of new media SMEs, reflecting on their journeys in establishing technological enterprises, the media used, and the resources that were critical to manage and run these businesses, as well as general commentary on the enablers and barriers of this development. In the second contribution entitled *The Impact of New Media (Digital) and Globalisation on Nollywood*, Madichie et al. (2019) investigated the Nigerian movie industry (aka Nollywood) in the light of digitalisation and new media. The article examined and highlighted how two major forces – new technologies and globalisation – have impacted (and are still impacting) upon Nollywood, drawing on theories of value chain in production, distribution, and marketing of cultural products, and its internationalisation.

Sources:
- Bolat, E. (2019). The African New Media Digital Revolution: Some Selected Cases from Nigeria. In Taura, N. D., Bolat, E., and Madichie, N. O (Eds.) *Digital Entrepreneurship in Sub-Saharan Africa* (67–87). Palgrave Macmillan, Cham.
- Madichie, N. O., Ajakaiye, B. O., and Ratten, V. (2019). The Impact of New Media (Digital) and Globalisation on Nollywood. In Taura, N. D., Bolat, E., and Madichie, N. O (Eds.) *Digital Entrepreneurship in Sub-Saharan Africa* (89–121). Palgrave Macmillan, Cham.

Discussion questions:

1   To what extent do you think new technologies have impacted upon the entertainment sector?
2   What other adjacent sectors can you see a similar trend? Use examples to support your points.

BOX 26.4: LET'S REASON TOGETHER

The following study presents both the 'legal' and 'illegal' aspects of the market in antiquities, specifically cultural objects which are transported from source countries to countries where they are sold or auctioned. The article defines the concept of antiquity and then examines the origin of objects, those involved in the market in different capacities, the question of how the origin of objects are examined, and the scope of the market. The analysis shows that structural and cultural characteristics of the market renders it susceptible to organised crime.

Questions

1. Is criminality of this type of market only existent in the informal economy?
2. The study provides a number of examples as illustrations. In groups of three or four, discuss any three of these.

Massy, L. (2008) The antiquity art market: between legality and illegality, *International Journal of Social Economics*, 35(10), 729–738. https://doi.org/10.1108/03068290810898936

CASE STUDY – THE NIGERIAN INFORMAL ECONOMY

The International Labour Organization (ILO) categorises a country's informal sector to include employers and their staff in the informal sector, self-employed people and workers not covered by labour unions and protection such as domestic staff (Bromley and Wilson, 2018). Because of limited resources and inadequate capital, informal businesses have been known to exploit every opportunity, both legal and illegal, to generate profit and foster growth since these businesses are not governed by regulatory bodies (Arimah, 2001; Webb et al., 2009; Khan, 2018). In addition, the informal sector businesses are always easy to set up as they are not particularly labour or capital intensive, and utilise local/easily sourced materials. Furthermore, most informal sector entrepreneurs do not require formal training to set up businesses.

In the case of Nigeria, for example, young people and women have limited access to well-equipped public-sector institutions as only a few tertiary institutions cater to these groups. Similarly, public libraries are almost non-exiting (Yousalzai et al., 2015). The lack of information and communication technology equipment also

MARKETING IN THE INFORMAL ECONOMY

presents a barrier for the poor to access the internet. These lack of adequate facilities have led to vocational training and technical colleges being weak, limited in supply, and ill-equipped. There is also a lack of suitable career advisory services for the young and growing population. These institutional voids are further compounded by high costs of transportation, communication, storage, and other overhead costs that further stretch already limited finances of the informal economy and made it impossible for this sector to thrive.

Despite these challenges, the informal economy has significantly reduced poverty in most vulnerable communities (Igwe et al., 2018). It is therefore pertinent to argue that if the environment within which the informal economy operates is adequate and conducive, it can enable businesses improve productivity and possibly compete favourably with the formal sector. Thus, the environment does not only create limits for businesses and individuals it also facilitates opportunities for competitiveness. Indeed, the IMF (2017) has reported on how the Nigerian informal economy has grown at the rate of 8.5% between 2015 and 2017 and accounts for 65% of GDP. Therefore, the informal sector in Nigeria is a significant sector that has helped absorb unemployment in the labour market. Furthermore, research evidence has shown that the informal sector in Nigeria is marginalised. Davies and Thurlow (2010) suggest two reasons for this marginalisation.

- First, both the private and public sectors have neglected the informal economy.
- Second, the education systems train students to be employed thus, but ignore self-employment or entrepreneurship.

Fasanya and Onakoya (2012) also argue that government policies have long failed to avert unemployment and despite much policies by successive regimes, unemployment persists and if not for the informal sector, the economy of Nigeria would be in disarray. Ultimately, the informal economy has contributed significantly to the country's economy despite numerous challenges.

Questions:
1. What challenges are faced by the Nigerian informal economy? Are these challenges similar in any other countries/ regions you are familiar with?
2. Given the contribution of the informal economy to Nigeria's GDP, should the government regulate the informal economy?
3. What should the government do to assist the informal sector?

SUMMARY

1. The informal economy refers to the paid production and sale of goods and services which are unregistered by, or hidden from, the state for tax and/or benefit purposes but which may still be legal in all other respects.
2. As such, the informal economy includes only paid work that is illegal because of its non-declaration to the state for tax and/or social security purposes.
3. Two theoretical perspectives have been used to explain the emergence of the informal economy: first, the increasing informalisation is a direct consequence

of government over regulation of the economy. Second, the view of the informal economy as 'an unavoidable expression of the uneven development inherent in late capitalism', which made the evasion of regulation part and parcel of a cost-cutting imperative on the part of small entrepreneurs struggling for survival in a diminishing market space.

4. Most operators in the informal economy are largely the poor and middle income developing or emerging economies and/or ethnic minorities and immigrants in the more advanced economies.

5. The informal economy is by definition unregistered by and/or hidden from the state. As such, estimating its prevalence is a difficult task. Until now, measurement methods have ranged from techniques that indirectly measure its magnitude by using a proxy.

6. The current shift towards using direct surveys rather than relying on indirect proxy indicators also has its criticisms as it naively assumes that respondents will reveal to them, or even know, the prevalence of informal work.

REVIEW QUESTIONS

1. What are the key features of the informal economy?

2. Measuring the informal economy can be fraught with difficulties. Discuss some of the measurement difficulties.

3. According to the Small Business Service, '*We do not have as clear a picture as we would like of the scale and nature of the informal economy*'. Discuss this statement with examples and illustrations of the main characteristics of the informal economy compared to the formal economy.

NOTES

1. See also Minnis, J. R. (2006). Nonformal education and informal economies in sub-Saharan Africa: Finding the right match. *Adult Education Quarterly*, 56(2), 119–133.

2. See the following: Pfau-Effinger, B. (2009). Varieties of undeclared work in European societies. *British Journal of Industrial Relations*, 47(1), 79–99; Gumbrell-McCormick, R. (2011). European trade unions and 'atypical' workers. *Industrial Relations Journal*, 42(3), 293–310; Williams, C. C. (2014). Out of the shadows: a classification of economies by the size and character of their informal sector. Work, *Employment and Society*, 28(5), 735–753; Williams, C. C., & Lansky, M. A. (2013). Informal employment in developed and developing economies: Perspectives and policy responses. *International Labour Review*, 152(3–4), 355–380; Putniņš, T. J., & Sauka, A. (2015). Measuring the shadow economy using company managers. *Journal of Comparative Economics*, 43(2), 471–490; Williams, C. C., Shahid, M. S., & Martínez, A. (2016). Determinants of the level of informality of informal micro-enterprises: Some evidence from the city of Lahore, Pakistan. *World Development*, 84, 312–325; Williams, C., & Horodnic, I. A. (2016). Cross-country variations in the participation of small businesses in the informal economy: an institutional asymmetry explanation. *Journal of Small Business and Enterprise Development*, 23(1), 3–24; Williams, C., & Kedir, A. M. (2017).

Evaluating the impacts of starting up unregistered on firm performance in Africa. *Journal of Developmental Entrepreneurship*, 22(03), 1750017; Williams, C., & Horodnic, I. A. (2017). Explaining the informal economy in post-communist societies: A study of the asymmetry between formal and informal institutions in Romania. In *The Informal Economy in Global Perspective* (pp. 117–140). Palgrave Macmillan, Cham.

3. See for example, Williams, C. C., Martinez–Perez, A., & Kedir, A. M. (2017). Informal entrepreneurship in developing economies: The impacts of starting up unregistered on firm performance. *Entrepreneurship Theory and Practice*, 41(5), 773–799; Borozan, D., Arneric, J., & Coric, I. (2017). A comparative study of net entrepreneurial productivity in developed and post-transition economies. *International Entrepreneurship and Management Journal*, 13(3), 855–880; Mathias, B. D., Lux, S., Crook, T. R., Autry, C., & Zaretzki, R. (2015). Competing against the unknown: the impact of enabling and constraining institutions on the informal economy. *Journal of Business Ethics*, 127(2), 251–264; Ruzek, W. (2014). The informal economy as a catalyst for sustainability. *Sustainability*, 7(1), 23–34.

4. See the following link for an update. https://ec.europa.eu/social/main.jsp?catId=1298&langId=en At the EU level, undeclared work is defined as "any paid activities that are lawful as regards their nature, but not declared to public authorities, taking into account differences in the regulatory systems of the Member States". Undeclared work may come in different forms. The most common type is work carried out in a formal undertaking, partially or fully undeclared. Partially undeclared work is sometimes also called 'under-declared work', 'envelope wages' or 'cash-in-hand'. Another type is undeclared 'own account' or self-employed work, where self-employed persons provide services either to a formal enterprise or to other clients, such as households. Undeclared work occurs in all kind of economic sectors, both within countries and across borders. It is often carried out in sectors like construction, renovation or repair works, gardening, cleaning, provision of childcare or HORECA (Hotel / Restaurant / Catering – food services).

5. Examples exist across the developed world from the consumer transactions with SMEs in Canada (McGregor, 2005); to the case of rural England (Williams, 2007); and the matrix approach to informal markets adopted for the European Union (Walle, 2008).

6. See Ponsaers, P., Shapland, J. & Williams, C. (2008a) Special Issue: The informal economy and its links to organised crime – part 1, *International Journal of Social Economics*, Vol 35, Issue 9; Ponsaers, P., Shapland, J., & Williams, C. (2008b) Special Issue: The informal economy and its links to organised crime – part 2, *International Journal of Social Economics*, Vol 35, Issue 10.

7. It may be worth exploring the growing Chinese influences in most parts of sub-Saharan Africa. For example, Alon, I., Yeheskel, O., Lerner, M., Zhang, W. (2013). Internationalization of Chinese entrepreneurial firms. *Thunderbird International Business Review*, 55, 495–512; Carmody, P. (2017). The new scramble for Africa. John Wiley & Sons; Bräutigam, D., & Xiaoyang, T. (2011). African Shenzhen: China's special economic zones in Africa. *The Journal of Modern African Studies*, 49(1), 27–54; Ndoro, T. T. R., Louw, L., & Kanyangale, M. (2019). Practices in operating a small business in a host community: a social capital perspective of Chinese immigrant entrepreneurship within the South African business context. *International Journal of Entrepreneurship and Small Business*, 36(1–2), 148–163.

8. Consider the following article: Williams, C. C., & Kedir, A. M. (2017). Evaluating the impacts of starting up unregistered on firm performance in Africa. Journal of Developmental Entrepreneurship, 22(03), 1750017. This study evaluates the link between starting up unregistered and future firm performance in the entrepreneurship process in Africa. The widespread assumption has been that firms starting up unregistered in the informal economy suffer from poor performance compared to those starting up registered and in the formal economy.

REFERENCES

Al-Mataani, R., Wainwright, T. and Demirel, P. (2017) Hidden entrepreneurs: Informal practices within the formal economy. *European Management Review*, 14(4), 361–376.

Alon, I., Yeheskel, O., Lerner, M. and Zhang, W. (2013) Internationalization of Chinese entrepreneurial firms. *Thunderbird International Business Review*, 55, 495–512.

Anderson, J. and Billou, N. (2007) Serving the world's poor: Innovation at the base of the economic pyramid. *Journal of Business Strategy*, 28(2), 14–21.

Arimah, B. C. (2001) Nature and determinants of the linkages between informal and formal sector enterprises in Nigeria. *African Development Review*, 13(1), 114–144.

Awojobi, N., Ayakpat, J. and Adisa, D. (2014) Rebased Nigerian gross domestic product: The role of the informal sector in the development of the Nigerian economy. *International Journal of Education and Research*, 2(7), 301–317.

Bajada, C. (2002) How reliable are the estimates of the underground economy? *Economics Bulletin*, 3(14), 1–11.

Bromley, R. (1978) Introduction – the urban informal sector: Why is it worth discussing? *World Development*, 6(9), 1033–1039.

Bromley, R. and Wilson, T. D. (2018) Introduction: The urban informal economy revisited. *Latin American Perspectives*, 45(1), 4–23.

Bureau of African Affairs (2010) www.stat-usa.gov

Davies, R. and Thurlow, J. (2010) Formal-informal economic linkages and unemployment in South Africa. *South African Journal of Economics*, 78(4), 437–459.

European Commission (2005) Communication of the commission on undeclared work. http://europa.eu.int/comm/employment_social/ empl_esf/docs/com98–219_en.pdf

Fasanya, O. I. and Onakoya, B. A. (2012) Informal sector and employment in Nigeria: A error correction model. *Journal of Research on Humanities and Social Sciences*, 2(7), 21–27.

Guesalaga, R. and Marshall, P. (2008) Purchasing power at the bottom of the pyramid: Differences across geographic regions and income tiers. *Journal of Consumer Marketing*, 25(7), 413–427.

Harney, N. (2006) Rumour, migrants, and the informal economies of Naples, Italy. *International Journal of Sociology and Social Policy*, 26(9/10), 374–384.

Her Majesty's Revenue and Customs (HMRC). (2005) *Working Towards a New Relationship: A Consultation on Priorities for Reducing the Administrative Burden of the Tax System on Small Businesses*. HMSO, London.

Humphreys, J. (2004) The multicultural economy 2004: America's minority buying power. *Georgia Business and Economic Conditions*, 64(3), Selig Center for Economic Growth, University of Georgia, Athens, GA.

Igwe, P. A., Madichie, N. and Newbery, R. (2019) Determinants of livelihood choices and artisanal entrepreneurship in Nigeria. *International Journal of Entrepreneurial Behavior & Research*, 25(4), 674–697.

Igwe, P. A., Newbery, R., Amoncar, N., White, G. R. and Madichie, N. (2018) Keeping it in the family: exploring Igbo ethnic entrepreneurial behaviour in Nigeria. *International Journal of Entrepreneurial Behavior & Research*. ahead-of-print. Available at: https://doi.org/10.1108/IJEBR-12-2017-0492

IMF (2017) Nigeria's informal economy accounts for 65% of GDP. www.businessamlive.com/nigerias-informal-economy-accounts-65-gdp-imf/ (Accessed 6 March 2019).

International Labour Office (2002), *Decent Work and the Informal Economy*. International Labour Office, Geneva.

Prahalad, C. K. (2004) *The Fortune at the Bottom of the Pyramid: Eradicating Poverty through Profits*. Wharton School Publishing, Upper Saddle River, NJ.

Jones, T., Ram, M. and Edwards, P. (2006) Shades of grey in the informal economy. *International Journal of Sociology and Social Policy*, 26(9/10), 357–373.

Khan, E. A. (2018) The voice of informal entrepreneurs: Resources and capabilities perspective. *Journal of Developmental Entrepreneurship*, 23(03), 1850015.

Leonard, M. (1994) *Informal Economic Activity in Belfast*. Avebury, Aldershot.

Madichie, N. (2018) La Sape Couture! A constellation of consuming passion for fashion, power, and entrepreneurial emergence at the bottom of the pyramid. Refereed research paper presented at the Institute for Small Business and Entrepreneurship conference, Birmingham, 7–8 November. www.

researchgate.net/publication/327944676_La_Sape_Couture_A_Constellation_of_Consuming_Passion_for_Fashion_Power_and_Entrepreneurial_emergence_at_the_Bottom_of_the_Pyramid.

McGregor, S. (2005) Consumer transactions with SMEs: implications for consumer scholars. *International Journal of Consumer Studies*, 29(1), 2–16.

Ndoro, T. T. R., Louw, L. and Kanyangale, M. (2019) Practices in operating a small business in a host community: A social capital perspective of Chinese immigrant entrepreneurship within the South African business context. *International Journal of Entrepreneurship and Small Business*, 36(1–2), 148–163.

Nkamnebe, A. D. (2006). Globalised marketing and the question of development in the Sub-Saharan Africa (SSA). *Critical Perspectives on International Business*, 2(4), 321–338.

Nkamnebe, A. D. and Madichie, N. (2010) Entrepreneurial Marketing in Informal Economies. In Nwankwo, S. and Gbadamosi, A. (Eds.), *Entrepreneurship Marketing: Principles and Practice of SME Marketing*. Routledge, Oxford. (Chapter 26). ISBN: 978-0-415-57376-4.

Office of National Statistics (2005) *Data Sources on the Informal Economy and Entrepreneurship*. Office of National Statistics, London.

Olomi, D., Charles, G. and Juma, N. (2018) An inclusive approach to regulating the second economy: A tale of four Sub-Saharan African economies. *Journal of Entrepreneurship in Emerging Economies*, 10(3), 447–471.

Organisation for Economic Co-operation and Development (2002) *Measuring the Non-Observed Economy, Organisation for Economic Co-operation and Development*, OECD, Paris.

Pahl, R. E. (1984) *Divisions of Labour*. Blackwell, Oxford.

Prahalad, C. K. and Hammond, A. (2002) Serving the world's poor profitably. *Harvard Business Review*, 80(9), 48–57.

Prahalad, C. K. and Hart, S. L. (2002) The fortune at the bottom of the pyramid, *Strategy +. Business*, (26), 54–67. www.strategy-business.com/article/11518?pg=0

Renooy, P., Ivarsson, S., van der Wusten-Gritsai, O. and Meijer, R. (2004) *Undeclared Work in an Enlarged Union: An Analysis of Shadow Work – An In-depth Study of Specific Items*. European Commission, Brussels.

SBS (2005) *Government Response to the SBC Report on the Informal Economy*. Small Business Council, London.

Schneider, F. (2002) Size and measurement of the informal economy in 110 countries around the world, paper presented at a Workshop of Australian National Tax Centre, ANU, Canberra, Australia, July 17.

Small Business Council (2004) *Small Business in the Informal Economy: Making the Transition to the Formal Economy*. Small Business Council, London.

Thomas, J. (1999) Quantifying the black economy: Measurement without theory yet again. *Economic Journal*, 109, F381–89.

Tripp, A. (2001) *Non-Formal Institutions, Informal Economies, and the Politics of Inclusion* (Discussion Paper No. 2001/108). Washington, DC: The World Bank.

Walle, G. (2008) A matrix approach to informal markets: towards a dynamic conceptualisation. *International Journal of Social Economics*, 35(9), 651–665.

Warde, A. (1990) Household work strategies and forms of labour: Conceptual and empirical issues. *Work, Employment and Society*, 4(4), 495–515.

Webb, J. W., Bruton, G. D., Tihanyi, L. and Ireland, R. D. (2013) Research on entrepreneurship in the informal economy: Framing a research agenda. *Journal of Business Venturing*, 28(5), 598–614.

Webb, J. W., Ireland, R. D. and Ketchen, D. J. (2014) Toward a greater understanding of entrepreneurship and strategy in the informal economy. *Strategic Entrepreneurship Journal*, 8, 1–15.

Webb, J. W., Tihanyi, L., Ireland, R. D. and Sirmon, D. G. (2009) You say illegal, I say legitimate: Entrepreneurship in the informal economy. *The Academy of Management Review*, 34(3), 492–510.

Williams, C. (2005a) The undeclared sector, self-employment and public policy. *International Journal of Entrepreneurial Behaviour and Research*, 11(4), 244–257.

Williams, C. (2005b) Tackling the informal economy: Towards a co-ordinated public policy approach. *Public Policy and Administration*, 20, 38–53.

Williams, C. (2006) *The Hidden Enterprise Culture: Entrepreneurship in the Underground Economy*. Edward Elgar, Cheltenham.

Williams, C. (2007a) Tackling undeclared work in Europe: Lessons from a study of Ukraine. *European Journal of Industrial Relations*, 13(2), 219–236.

Williams, C. C. (2007b) Small business and the informal economy: Evidence from the UK. *International Journal of Entrepreneurial Behavior & Research*, 13(6), 349–366.

Williams, C. and Bezeredi, S. (2018) Evaluating the impact of informal sector competition on firm performance: Some lessons from South-East Europe. *Journal of Developmental Entrepreneurship*, 23(04), 1850025.

Williams, C. and Kedir, A. (2018) Explaining cross-country variations in the prevalence of informal sector competitors: Lessons from the World Bank Enterprise Survey. *International Entrepreneurship and Management Journal*, 1–20.

Williams, C. and Round, J. (2009) Evaluating informal entrepreneurs' motives: Evidence from Moscow. *International Entrepreneurial Behaviour & Research*, 15(1), 1355–2554.

Williams, C. and Windebank, J. (1998) *Informal Employment in the Advanced Economies: Implications for Work and Welfare*. Routledge, London.

Williams, C. and Windebank, J. (2001) Reconceptualising paid informal exchange: Some lessons from English cities. *Environment and Planning A*, 33(1), 121–140.

Yousalzai, S. Y., Saeed, S. and Muffatto, M. (2015) Institutional theory and contextual embeddedness of women's entrepreneurial leadership: Evidence from 92 countries. *Journal of Small Business Management*, 53(3), 587–604.

Contributors

Rula M. Al Abdulrazak, PhD is Branding and Global Marketing Specialist with diverse experience in oil industry, business consultancy, and higher education. She spent over a decade working with Royal Dutch Shell and the European Commission before joining academia at Royal Holloway, University of London and University of East London as Senior Lecturer. She serves as a business development consultant with great interest in supporting small and medium-sized enterprises to build strong brands and internationalise in the interconnected marketplace. The Academy of Higher Education awarded her senior fellowship status. Rula was trained as an accountant with a BSc in Economics and Management, Accounting major, and a postgraduate degree in Finance Management at Damascus University, from which she also received a postgraduate degree in Psychology and Education. At Royal Holloway, University of London, Rula completed an MBA in International Management and Marketing, and a PhD in Marketing 'The Branded Nation: a comparative review with reference to Syria and the United Arab Emirates', in addition to a postgraduate degree in Inspiring Skills in Teaching and Learning. She researches in branding, nation and place marketing, and cross cultural and Islamic marketing. She is also interested in digital marketing and digitalisation of businesses as a potential for growth and efficiency. Her studies include examination of cultural diplomacy and art with reference to the United Arab Emirates, Arab Spring and nation image, nation-brand state and public diplomacy, brand and social trust, religiosity, and branding. Rula is an editor and international and interdisciplinary conference organiser. She champions creative writing in academic contexts and chairs research income generation, research ethics, business consultancy, and professional training committees.

Emmanuel Adugu, PhD is a research methodologist and lecturer at the Department of Government, Sociology and Social Work at the University of West Indies, Cave Hill Campus. He is an Ohio State University-trained Development Sociologist and a certified Survey Research Methodologist. His research and publication profile focuses on future of work, civic engagement and sustainable development, political consumption, digital activism, and action research designs. He teaches courses such as social statistics, survey design and analysis, qualitative research methods, and industrial sociology.

Mathew Analogbei is PhD researcher in the Department of Marketing, University of Strathclyde, Glasgow, UK. He received his bachelor's and MBA degrees in Marketing from the University of Nigeria, Enugu, Nigeria, and MSc in Marketing from the University of Glamorgan, Wales, UK. Prior to commencing his doctoral studies in the UK, Mathew had

429

CONTRIBUTORS

taught for some years in a number of Nigerian Universities. His doctoral research focuses on Retail Internationalisation.

Barry Ardley, PhD, is currently Visiting Senior Fellow in the Department of Marketing and Tourism in the Lincoln International Business School, University of Lincoln, UK. Prior to this, he was Senior Lecturer in Marketing at the same institution, having taught modules on global marketing, entrepreneurial marketing, and relationship marketing. Before Lincoln, Barry spent a number of years working for City College Norwich, managing and delivering a range of business studies courses. Barry is a qualified teacher and before undertaking a first degree, gained commercial experience in a range of organisations in distributive services and the public sector. A member of the Chartered Institute of Marketing and a Member of the Academy of Marketing, Barry has two Master's degrees from the University of East Anglia. He obtained his PhD from De Montfort University in strategic marketing planning. He has a wide range of publications in journals and conference proceedings and is currently carrying out research in entrepreneurial marketing.

David Bamber, PhD is Director of PhD Studies at Bolton Business School (University of Bolton). He is currently researching in the areas of International Development, Marketing, and Business. He has worked as Research Fellow in Organizational Learning (University of Salford), Senior Lecturer in International Marketing (Liverpool Hope University), and External Examiner at Canterbury Christ Church University (UK) for undergraduate business programs in the UK and MBA programs in Sri Lanka. He is a foundation member of the Chartered College of Teaching. He has been track co-chair for Organisational Studies with the British Academy of Management for 15 years and has presented academic papers at 40 international peer reviewed conferences. He is a regular reviewer for the *International Journal of Contemporary Hospitality Management* and *Social Responsibility Journal*.

Wellington Chakuzira, PhD graduated with a PhD in Management from the Business Management Department at the University of Venda, South Africa. His research interests revolve around the areas of entrepreneurship and small businesses.

Ofer Dekel-Dachs, PhD is Senior Lecturer in the Economics and Marketing department of De Montfort University. he serves as a reviewer in the *Journal of Marketing Management* and the *Journal of Small Business & Entrepreneurship*. His main teaching contributions are within the areas of social media marketing, Omni channels, marketing decision making, culture and marketing, and research methods. His interdisciplinary research (economics, marketing, social psychology, and visual research) takes into account the fluent, juxtaposed, fragmented, and globalised reality of contemporary businesses. His work deconstructs the idea of linear management that treats business reality as the outcome of clearly bounded market structures, patterns and regularities. Alternatively, I develop anti-essentialist comprehension of market reality, which consists of consumers, brands, and markets as fuzzy concepts describing market reality as temporal construction negotiated between multiple stakeholders. Ofer promotes digital customer experience, mass customisation, co-branding, co-creation, open innovation, visual research, participatory research, venture communities, and born global SMEs.

Paul Dobson is Senior Lecturer at Staffordshire Business School (SBS) in Digital and Strategic Marketing, including Search Engine Optimisation, Conversion Rate Optimisation,

■ **430**

Growth Hacking, Inbound and Outbound Marketing, Mobile and Social Media Marketing, and Google Analytics. He has been lecturing and undertaking consultancy at SBS for eight years. Paul is actively involved supporting SMES including giving hands on demonstrations showing how to make digital marketing effective, this includes: marketing with YouTube and Facebook to substantially increase sales in a restaurant, improve hotels' and restaurants' search engine rankings with inbound marketing and SEO, and increase a manufacturer's B2B and B2C sales using integrated digital marketing. Paul has three master's degrees and is undertaking a PhD in Social Enterprise Marketing Strategies. He is a Senior Fellow of the Higher Education Academy, Fellow of the Chartered Management Institute, and member of the Academy of Marketing, member of the Institute of Place Management, and member of the Association of Internet Researchers. He has presented various Digital Marketing topics for the Chartered Institute of Marketing (CIM), Manchester Metropolitan University Postgraduate Research Conference, Chamber of Commerce, etc. He has also presented Using Innovative Technology and Learning at the Association of Business Schools and he has been the Regional Chair of the CIM. Prior to SBS, Paul has over 25 years' experience working in various internal and external consultancies, including working in the UK, France, and Germany. As a hobby he helps local Charities, Social Enterprises, and businesses with their digital and strategic marketing.

Isobel Doole, PhD, is Professor of International Marketing and Assistant Dean at Sheffield Business School, Sheffield Hallam University. She is an experienced marketing professional and senior academic in international marketing and in the international competitiveness of small firms. With her co-author Robin Lowe, she has built an international reputation through the highly successful textbooks *Strategic Marketing Decisions* and *International Marketing Strategy*. The latter is in its fifth edition (2008) and has sold over 70,000 copies across the globe. She is a senior examiner for the Chartered Institute of Marketing and has acted as an expert advisor on a number of governmental committees.

Ogenyi Ejye Omar, PhD is in the Department of Maketing & Enterprise, Business School, University of Hertfordshire, Hatfield, United Kingdom. Dr Omar is the Editor of the *Journal of Retail Marketing Management Research (Jrmmr)*. His papers have been published in *the Journal of Business Research; International Journal of Retail & Distribution Management; Journal of Strategic Marketing; International Journal of Public Sector Management; Service Industries Journal; Journal of Food Product Marketing; Thunderbird International Business Review*; and others. He is the author of one of the bestselling textbooks on retailing, *Retail Marketing* (2nd ed.), published by Financial Times/Pitman Publishing. He is also the author of *International Marketing*, published by Palgrave Macmillan. He has contributed chapters to several textbooks. Dr Omar is a retail marketing specialist and his current research interests are in retail marketing management, food branding and technology; disribution and supply chain management, multicultural marketing, and global retailing.

Ignatius Ekanem, PhD joined Middlesex University in 2000. He holds a PhD in Financial Management from Middlesex University exploring 'The Investment Decision-making Process in Small Manufacturing Enterprises: With Particular Reference to Printing and Clothing Industries'. His research interests are in the areas of economic regeneration, small business development, and business support needs of ethnic minority businesses, with a particular focus on the financial management practices of small businesses. He has worked on a series of research projects including several studies for the Small Business Service on social

CONTRIBUTORS

enterprise, ethnic minority owned businesses, and rural enterprises. He has also worked on the demand and supply of finance and business support for ethnic minority businesses commissioned by the British Bankers Association, the Bank of England, and the Small Business Service. His most recent projects include 'The impact of perceived access to finance difficulties' commissioned by the Small Business Service; 'Access to Bank Finance for Scottish SMEs' (for The Scottish Government), and an assessment of the government's equity finance initiatives for SMEs with growth potential (for the Department for Business, Innovation and Skills).

Frances Ngozi Ekwulugo, PhD, is Senior Lecturer in Marketing. She obtained her master's degree in Management from the University of Kent and a PhD in Management from the University of Hull. Before venturing into academia, Dr Ekwulugo had extensive experience in both private and public sectors in the UK and overseas. She has consulted extensively for public and private sector organisations in the UK. Her research interests and consulting activities are mainly in the area of small business management and marketing, particularly in emerging economies. She currently represents her university in Africa. She collaborated with Haringey Development Agency on a project sponsored by the United Nations. Dr Ekwulugo has served as a reviewer for publishing houses such as Pearson Publishers, *Journal of Entrepreneurial Education, Journal of African Business and International Management*, Palgrave, McMillan, *International Journal of Technology Management Sustainable Development*, *International Journal of Entrepreneurial Education*, and the Academy of Marketing Science. She is Chartered Marketer, Senior fellow of the Higher Education Academy, and Fellow of the European Entrepreneurship Educators Programme.

Entissar Elgadi, PhD is Assistant Professor in accounting at the largest girls' university in the world (Princess Noura bint Abdulrahaman University). Her research interests cover entrepreneurs and profitability determinants. Her other research interest extended to gender and management performance.

Teck-Yong Eng, PhD, is Professor of Marketing and Director of Centre for Research in Management at The Business School, Bournemouth University, UK. He is on the advisory board of ORT Israel for a large grant (in excess of six million Euros) funded by the European Commission Framework 7. He has consulted for various corporations and nonprofit organisations, including Business Monitor London, BPP Business School, William Jackson Food Group, and UNICO Industries, Inc., Hong Kong Mainland China. His work has been published in journals such as *Industrial Marketing Management, Journal of World Business, Journal of Marketing Management* and *Technovation*.

Peter Fraser, PhD is in the Department of Marketing & Enterprise, Business School, University of Hertfordshire, Hatfield, United Kingdom. Dr Fraser has several years of teaching experience in both undergraduate and at graduate levels. He has supervised many doctoral students in the topical areas of small business management. Dr Fraser's research interests are in small business development and arts marketing.

Ayantunji Gbadamosi [(Bsc (Hons), Msc, PhD, FHEA, FCIM, FCMI] is the Research Coordinator and The Chair of the Research and Knowledge Exchange Committee at Royal Docks School of Business and Law, University of East London, UK. He received his PhD from the University of Salford, UK. Dr 'Tunji Gbadamosi has several research outputs – journal

432

articles, chapters in edited books, edited books, monograph, conference papers, and case studies. His papers have been published in a variety of refereed journals including *Industrial Marketing Management, Journal of strategic Marketing, Journal of Brand Management, Thunderbird International Business Review, International Journal of Market Research, International Journal of Retail and Distribution Management, Marketing intelligence and Planning, Social Marketing Quarterly, Nutrition and Food Science, Young Consumers, Journal of Fashion Marketing and Management, Society and Business Review, International Journal of Consumer Studies, International Journal of Small Business and Enterprise Development, Entrepreneurship and Regional Development, International Journal of Entrepreneurship and Innovation, Journal of Place Branding and Public Diplomacy.* He is the author of the book entitled *Low-income Consumer Behaviour* and the editor of *Young Consumer Behaviour* (Routledge, 2018), *The Handbook of Research on Consumerism and Buying Behaviour in Developing Nations* (IGI Global, 2016), *Exploring the Dynamics of Consumerism in Developing Nations* (IGI, Global, 2019), and *Contemporary Issues in Marketing* (SAGE, 2019). His co-edited books are: *Principles of Marketing – A Value-Based Approach* (Palgrave, 2013), and *Entrepreneurship Marketing: Principles and Practice of SME Marketing* (Routledge, 2011). Dr Gbadamosi is an editorial board member of several journals. He has supervised several undergraduate and postgraduate students including PhD students to successful completion and served as an examiner for several doctorate degree examinations. He is the current Programme Chair of the Academy of African Business Development (AABD). His research interest lies in Consumer Behaviour, SME Marketing, Marketing to Children, and Marketing Communications. His paper won the EMERLAD Best paper award at the International Academy of African Business Development (IAABD) conference, 2014. He is listed in Who's Who in the World.

Jialin (Penny) Hardwick, PhD is Senior Lecturer in Marketing and researcher in the areas of Industrial Marketing, Entrepreneurship, and Relationship Marketing at the University of Lincoln, UK. Penny has worked as a consultant for biotechnology SMEs in Scotland and taught at the Robert Gordon University, where she was awarded a PhD in Business Administration. Penny also has an MSc in International Marketing from the University of Leeds and holds a MBA from Dundee University. In addition, Penny worked in organisations in the healthcare sector before pursuing her interests in business studies, gaining experience in managerial roles and inter-organisational collaboration, in the medical and pharmaceutical product development sector. Penny has publications in a number of business journals and has presented at conferences and is currently a post graduate programme leader in marketing at the University of Lincoln, where she also teaches on marketing related modules.

Kevin Ibeh, PhD, is Professor of Marketing and International Business at the Department of Marketing, University of Strathclyde, Glasgow, UK, where he also serves as Director of Research. His recent work, mainly on firm internationalisation and international entrepreneurship, has appeared, or is due to appear, in highly rated outlets such as *British Journal of Management, Journal of World Business, Management International Review, Industrial Marketing Management, European Journal of Marketing, Journal of Business Ethics, Small Business Economics*, and *International Small Business Journal*. A highly regarded scholar, Professor Ibeh has had recent consulting roles with the World Bank and the OECD. His book, *Contemporary Challenges to International Business*, was published by Macmillan in 2009.

Hina Khan, PhD is Lecturer in Marketing and Director of International Teaching Partnership and Development for the Lancaster University Management School, Lancaster University,

CONTRIBUTORS

UK. She also works as an independent marketing consultant. She is on the Editorial Board of the *Journal of Small Business and Enterprise Development* and reviews papers for the Academy of Marketing Science, *International Marketing Review*, and *Journal of Services Marketing*. Her research interests are consumer buying behaviour, small and medium-sized enterprise development, and emerging markets. She was awarded an outstanding reviewer 2013 award for her contribution to the *Journal of Small Business and Enterprise Development* and was also one of the three finalists for Lloyds TSB Jewel Award in 2007. She has published in international journals. She presents papers and chairs sessions at international conferences regularly.

Helena Klipan studied International Business Administration at the University of Applied Sciences Ludwigshafen and University of West Florida. She currently pursues her Doctor of Business Administration degree at Sheffield Hallam University in cooperation with Munich Business School. She has extensive experience in business management working with multinational corporations and small businesses in the global chemical and pharmaceutical industry. Helena's research focusses on the motivational level of leadership within the context of servant leadership.

Robin Lowe is Director of the Centre for Individual and Organisational Development at Sheffield Business School, Sheffield Hallam University. Through his research, consultancy, and policy development work in international trade, innovation, and entrepreneurship, Robin has made a major contribution to government policy and business support. He also has considerable experience of consulting and training with multinationals around the world, including IBM, Microsoft, Astra Zeneca, Renault Nissan, Huawei, and Batelco, as well as being an examiner and course director for the Chartered Institute of Marketing. He is the joint author of several bestselling texts in international marketing, innovation, and entrepreneurship

Nnamdi O. Madichie, PhD, is currently based at the Dundee Business School, Abertay University. Prior to this, he was Director of the Centre for Research and Enterprise at the Bloomsbury Institute London where he is currently Research Fellow. Dr Madichie is also Visiting Professor of Marketing & Entrepreneurship at the Unizik Business School in Nigeria, and External Examiner of the MSc Entrepreneurship programme at the Liverpool Business School, Liverpool John Moores University UK. He has also previously worked on industry projects with the London Development Agency in conjunction with the Mayor of London's Office and the University of East London. Dr Madichie is a Senior Fellow and the Higher Education Academy (SfHEA), Fellow of the Chartered Institute of Marketing (FCIM), and Fellow of the Chartered Management Institute (FCMI). He is also co-author of Digital Entrepreneurship in Sub-Saharan Africa Challenges, Opportunities and Prospects as part of the Palgrave Studies of Entrepreneurship in Africa series.

Vish Maheshwari, PhD is Associate Dean with student experience responsibility at Staffordshire Business School. Also, as Professor of Marketing, Vish leads research development in the broader area of Marketing but specifically within Brand Management, in collaboration with peers nationally and globally. His research and practice-led projects have been supported by European Regional Development Fund, British Academy's Newton Fund, and Santander Bank's International Research Excellence Scheme. Vish is a co-founding Chair for the Place Marketing and Branding track and Special Interest Research group (SIG) at the Academy of Marketing. He is a Fellow of Chartered Institute of Marketing; Senior Fellow of

434

the Higher Education Academy and serves as Visiting Professor at University of Sao Paulo. Vish is an active member of the Academy of Marketing Science and American Marketing Association. He serves as a member of editorial board of two emerald journals and acts as active reviewer for several reputed publication outlets. Vish has published number of journal articles and book chapters in branding and marketing management including digital marketing. He is also Senior Examiner at the Chartered Institute of Marketing. Vish completed his PhD from the University of Liverpool and since has held several academic leadership roles such as Director of Postgraduate Programmes, MBA Director, and Senior Lecturer in Marketing at various UK higher education institutions. He is an active doctoral research supervisor and has successfully supervised several doctoral candidates to completion.

Felicity Mendoza is Research Associate at Sheffield Business School, Sheffield Hallam University, where she also obtained a Master's degree in Communication Studies. She manages The Alchemy Exchange, a unique initiative which allows external organisations to access university expertise. The projects that she has worked on with external clients include market analyses for international expansion, feasibility studies to assess the potential for a new product or service and benchmarking performance against competitors. Prior to joining Sheffield Business School, Felicity's previous experience included working within facilities management, recruitment, and tourism both in the UK and Latin America.

Anayo Dominic Nkamnebe, PhD, FNIMN, FISM, FSSM (UK), is a Professor of Marketing, former Head of Department of Marketing, former Sub Dean, and current Dean Faculty of Management Sciences at Nnamdi Azikiwe University, Awka, Nigeria. Rev. Professor Nkamnebe started his academic career after an intermission in the private sector, and his research papers are presented and/or published in many regions of the world (Africa, America, Europe and Asia). He is also on the editorial board of *Emerald Emerging Markets Case Studies*, editor of *Journal of the Management Sciences* and *Marketing Journal* and *Journal of the Marketing Academy*, regional editor (Africa) of *International Journal of Social Entrepreneurship & Innovation-Inderscience-Switzerland, Journal of Chinese Entrepreneurship, African Journal of Accounting, Auditing and Finance*, and *African Journal of Economics and Management Studies in the UK*. His research interests cover the broad area of marketing and entrepreneurship with special bias for sustainability/developmental marketing and sustainability consumption, export marketing, e-business/commerce/marketing, and entrepreneurial marketing and micro and small business. Revd. Canon Professor Nkamnebe is an Ordained Priest in the Anglican Communion.

Sonny Nwankwo, PhD, is Emeritus Professor at the University of East London and the Provost of the Nigerian Defence Academy (NDA), Nigeria. He is Visiting Professor at universities across Africa, Australia, Europe, and North America. Prior to joining academia, he was a customer services manager in the telecommunication s industry.

Sanya Ojo, PhD, is a seasoned consultant and a Senior Lecturer/Researcher at the Faculty of Social Sciences, Nigerian Defence Academy Kaduna, Nigeria. His over 40 years' experience in entrepreneurship (national and transnational) informs his research interest in ethnic, transnational, and diaspora entrepreneurship, and he has published papers in these areas. His other research interest extends to international business strategy and management.

Mee Leing Ooi is Senior Lecturer in the Department of Marketing, the Faculty of Accountancy, Finance and Business, at Tunku Abdul Rahman University College. She has obtained

CONTRIBUTORS

The Institute Chartered Secretaries and Administrators qualification in 1986. Ooi received her Master of Science in Property Investment from City University, London, UK in 1994. She teaches marketing at diploma and undergraduate levels in Tunku Abdul Rahman University College. Ooi has 15 years of working experience in the financial sector. She is an associate member with the Malaysian Institute of Chartered Secretaries and Administrators, an associate member of the Malaysian Institute of Management and a certified member with the Financial Planning Association of Malaysia. Ooi has also obtained Chartered Marketer status (MCIM) from the Chartered Institute of Marketing, UK since 2016.

Jo Padmore, PhD, is subject group leader for Quantitative Methods & Statistics at The University of Sheffield Management School. She holds a first class degree in Mathematics, MSc in Statistics (Distinction), MEd, and PhD in Probability and Statistics (Sheffield). She has performed consultancy work for a number of organisations. Her current research focusses on a variety of management issues within small and medium-sized enterprises (SMEs). She is particularly interested in issues of performance measurement in SMEs and the role of quantitative methods within this context.

Abdullah Promise Opute, PhD, is a freelance academic and management consultant. Dr A-P Opute mentors, tutors, and supports (analysis – SPSS, SEM, and qualitative analysis including Grounded Theory analysis) students towards successful completion of their PhD research. Dr A-P Opute also supports organisations with technical advice in several management streams. Dr Opute is Examiner in several management fields at UK and African universities. "Best Paper" award winner at the AM-Conference, 2007, his research interest includes Inter-Functional Integration, Relationship Management, Conflict Management, Cross Cultural Management, Consumer Behaviour, Entrepreneurship and SMEs, Strategic Management Accounting, etc. He has published in a wide range of journals including *Journal of Business and Industrial Marketing, International Journal of Entrepreneurship and Small Business, International Journal of Management Education, Team Performance Management,* and *Australasian Marketing Journal,* among others. He also has book chapters in edited books published at IGI Global Publications, Routledge Publishers, Taylor & Francis Publishers, and NOVA Science Publishers Inc. He is co-guest editor (ongoing) for a special issue (*International Journal of Business and Globalisation*). Dr. A-P Opute can be contacted at: promise. opute@gpromsolutions.org

Shadi A. Razak is a cyber security and business digitisation expert, with a strong foundation in business and IT strategy. His experience in building successful businesses and expertise in information security, information management, and business digitisation made him a sought after advisor to many international blue chip companies, government organisations, financial services, and SMEs in the UK and the MENA region for the past 17 years. He has been a visiting lecturer at a number of international and British universities and is currently a Board Member and President of the Information Security Group (ISG) Alumni, Technology and Finance Society and a mentor for several FinTech and Cyber Security start-ups in the UK. Shadi lives and works in London (UK). He holds a BSc in Computer Engineering, an MSc in Information Security, and an MBA in business digitalisation and security from Royal Holloway, University of London, and the University of Sunderland, respectively.

Darlington Richards, PhD, is Associate Professor of International Business and Marketing, Earl Graves School of Business & Management at Morgan State University, Baltimore,

436

USA. His research interests include privatisation and market deregulation, market reforms, change management, and business ethics.

Paul Sergius Koku, PhD, J.D., is a Fulbrighter and Professor in the College of Business at Florida Atlantic University. He works on interdisciplinary issues including but not limited to poverty eradication, interface between finance and marketing, corporate governance, information asymmetry, boycotts, and social activism. He comments on boycott activities in the national and international media and has authored or co-authored two books. His papers have appeared in several peer-reviewed journals and book chapters. Professor Koku holds a BA (summa cum laude) with concentration in Finance from University of the Virgin Islands. He also holds MBA (Marketing) from Oregon State University, MBA (Finance), MA (Applied Economics), and a PhD in Finance and Marketing, all from Rutgers University. Professor Koku also holds the *Juris Doctor* degree from the University of Miami, School of Law.

Jane Shambare is a postgraduate student in the Faculty of Law at the University of the Western Cape. Jane's research interests are in the areas of the intersection of commercial enterprise and law, commercial crimes, and small businesses.

Richard Shambare, PhD, is Associate Professor in the School of Business & Finance at the University of the Western Cape in South Africa. His research interests are in the areas of entrepreneurship, marketing, adoption of innovations, and microfinance. He has published and presented papers at numerous international conferences in these disciplines.

Amon Simba, PhD, is a senior academic at Nottingham Business School (NBS). His role at NBS involves teaching and research in business management. Particularly, he is an expert in entrepreneurship, innovation, and strategy. He teaches undergraduate and postgraduate students at NBS in his area(s) of expertise. He is one of the staff members responsible for leading and developing the entrepreneurship course at the Business School. Amon also supervises PhD and DBA students whose studies focus on entrepreneurship, innovation, and strategy from an emerging economy perspective. He is an established researcher. He is interested on research that focuses on born-global firms/international new ventures (INVs), micro-entrepreneurship, social entrepreneurship, networking, strategic management, entrepreneurship, and regional economics among other business management topics. Alongside his teaching and researching responsibilities, Amon is an associate editor for the *Journal of Small Business & Entrepreneurship* (JSBE) and a Research Grants Board Member for the Economic and Social Research Council (ESRC) in the UK. He has published in highly ranked journals including: *Journal of Small Business Management, Journal of Small Business and Enterprise Development, International Journal of Small Business and Entrepreneurship*, and *Local Economy*.

Mike Simpson, PhD, is Senior Lecturer in Management at the University of Sheffield, Management School and teaches Operations Management and Marketing at the postgraduate level. Mike's early career was in the semi-conductor and electronics industry working at Plessey Research (Caswell) and Marconi Electronic Devices Limited, Lincoln. He has worked in a number of high technology companies and is a consultant for small and medium-sized businesses. Until quite recently he was the subject group leader for both Operations Management and Marketing. Mike has published widely on Marketing and Operations Management in SMEs.

CONTRIBUTORS

Graham Spickett-Jones has management experience in promotional marketing and lectures in Communication Theory and Marketing at the University of Hull. He has a first degree in Communication Studies, a Master's degree in Marketing and a PhD in Management, as well as professional marketing qualifications. He has published in areas that range from neuroscience to campaign research. His research interests cover the way media shape the social environment and integrated campaign practice within the professional marketing communications industry.

Nick Taylor is the teaching and education lead for the marketing and tourism group at the University of Lincoln. Nick is also Associate Professor at Grenoble Business School. Nick gained experience with a number of global companies before entering education, including Marconi, Honeywell Control Systems, and AEG. He worked for these commercial organisations in a variety of marketing and management roles and later obtained an MBA from Sheffield Hallam University. Nick took on a role in the latter organisation as Senior Lecturer, before moving to Lincoln. Alongside his experience of SMEs, Nick has published articles on small business in a range of business and marketing journals and has had work presented and published in conference proceedings. Nick leads the Lincoln International Business schools successful undergraduate and post graduate consultancy modules, where students work with local firms and organisations on marketing strategy issues.

Sue Vaux Halliday, PhD, is Marketing Subject Group Leader and Senior Lecturer, University of Surrey. She teaches and researches relational marketing focussing on trust, shared values, branding, and innovation/entrepreneurship. She advises on a KTP project transforming a small social enterprise into a market-facing sustainable business. Before joining academia she held management posts in several services firms, ultimately as Director of Marketing for a city law firm. She is a Chartered Marketer. She publishes widely, including the *European Journal of Marketing*, the *Journal of Marketing Management*, and the *Journal of Services Marketing*.

Hsiao-Pei (Sophie) Yang, PhD, is a Senior Lecturer in Marketing at Coventry University. Prior to joining academia, Sophie held several marketing posts in the private education sector and retailing sector. Her research interests are in the marketing of Higher Education, consumer behaviour of services, and entrepreneurial marketing. Sophie had published her work in journals such as the *Journal of General Management* and *Qualitative Market Research*. In addition, she had written various book chapters and case studies in areas of Services Marketing and Consumer Behavior.

Index

Page numbers in *italics* indicate figures and in **bold** indicate tables on the corresponding pages.

accelerated internationalisation 288
accessory products 116–117
acculturation and religion 377–378
advertising, paid for 179–180
advocate marketing 180
affiliate marketing 180
Agndal, H. 304
Ahmed, P. K. 247
American Marketing Association (AMA)
    14, 119
Anderson, J. 416
Andersson, S. 306
Annual Small Business Survey 416–418
Anttila, M. 3
Apple 337–338, 340–341
Armstrong, G. 54, 82, 83, 87, 88
Aspinwall, E. 64
Atherton, A. 3, 5
automation 362–363, **363–365**; impact of
    367–369, **368–369**
Avlonitis, G. 122–123
Azad, S. 87

backward flows 148
Baker, R. 151
Balabanis, G. I. 316
Baldwin, C. 290
Barringer, B. R. 122
Barrow Industries 34–35
Barry, V. 349
Barth, F. 15
Basu, A. 215
Beckman, T. N. 151
Belleflamme, P. 262, 265
Belz, F. 347
Bembom, M. 291
Bennett, R. 288
Berry, J. W. 378
Berry, L. L. 247
Berryman, J. 203
Bettis, R. A. 39, 40

Billou, N. 416
bi-variate analyses 367–369, **368–369**
Blankson, C. 206
Bloodgood, J. 279
Bolton Report 276
bootstrapping 263
Born Global Firms (BGFs) 287, 288
Born Global SMEs (BGSs): Born Global Firms
    (BGFs) and 287, 288; cloud technology
    and 289; co-creation and open innovation
    and 290; cross cultural marketing and 306;
    crowdsourcing and 289; digitalisation and
    288–289; introduction to 287; networks and
    strategic alliances and 290–291
brand awareness 178
branding 119
brand management in retailing 195–196
Branson, R. 408–409
Brassington, F. 115
Brexit 67–69
Brooksbank, R. 6
business-to-business marketing 86–87, 88;
    online 179; organisational products in
    116–117
business-to-consumer marketing 115–116
buyer behaviour: in business-to-business
    marketing 86–87; buyer's journey and
    177, 177–178; consumer decision-making
    process and 73, *73*; consumer involvement
    and 84–86, *85*; evaluation of alternatives
    in 74–75; information search and 74;
    introduction to 72–73; marketing stimuli
    and 83–84, *84*; need recognition and
    73–74; organisational buying decision
    process and 87–89, *87–89*; personal factors
    in 77–79, **79**; post-purchase evaluation in
    76–77; psychological factors in 79–83, *80*;
    purchase decisions in 75–76; religion and
    381–382; understanding factors influencing
    77, *77*
buying centre 88, *88*

439

INDEX

Campaign for Real Ale (CAMRA) 150, 154
capital products 116
Carr, A. 349
Carson, D. 122, 123
Casaló Ariño, L. V. 76
cash-in-hand work 413
Chalmers, A. F. 42
Chaudhry, S. 304
Chen, S. 65
Chetty, S. 304
Ciravegna, L. 291
Clark, E. 148
classic market relationships 224
cloud technology 289
CMK 282–283
co-creation and open innovation 290
cognition, entrepreneurial 390–391
collaborative competence in networks 236
commitment in relationship marketing and
    networks 226, 228
communication technology and marketing
    communications 166–167
competencies, entrepreneurial marketing (EM)
    see Quality Assurance Agency (QAA) model
competition: marketing planning and 328; in
    microenvironment of marketing 58–59;
    religion and 383; retail market 216–217
component parts 116
consumer behaviour *see* buyer behaviour
consumer products 115–116
consumer rights **50–51, 52**
content curation for internet marketing
    182–183, *182–183*
Content Marketing Institute 182
contingency approach 4
convenience products 115
Cost, Customers, and Competition 138
cost-leadership 383
country based segmentation 310–312, *311*
country-of-origin-image (COI) 388; effect on
    SMEs 388–390; future directions of 393–396
Coviello, N. V. 279
Crick, D. 304, 316
cross cultural marketing: by Born Global SMEs
    306; categories of international development
    and 308; characteristics of SMEs and
    301–302; domestic SMEs and 303–304;
    generic positioning strategies in 315–317;
    importance of SME activity in 302–303;
    internationalisation process and 306–308;
    international marketing segmentation and
    310–317, *311*; introduction to 300–301;
    modes of engagement in 308–309; network
    development in 317–319; networked SMEs
    and 304–305; by SMEs with concentrated
    expansion into foreign markets 305–306; by
    SMEs with dispersed expansion into foreign

markets 306; strategy development in 310;
    summary of key ideas in 319; supply chain
    SMEs and 305; targeting approaches in
    313–315
cross-elasticity 135–136
crowdfunding: advantages of 266–267;
    conceptual analysis of 264–266; critical
    evaluation of 266–269; disadvantages of
    267–269; explaining 264–265; introduction
    to 262–263; models of 265–266; policy and
    regulatory frameworks of 266; SME access
    to funding and 263–264; summary and
    implications of 269
crowdsourcing 289
Cuervo-Cazurra, A. 370
cultural values 15
Curata 182
customer orientation 17–19
Customer Relationship Management (CRM) 76
customers: behavior of (*see* buyer behaviour);
    defined to enable effective and efficient
    marketing 175–177, *176*; journey to
    sales and loyalty with *177*, 177–178; in
    microenvironment of marketing 57–58, *58*;
    orientation of 17–19
CyNation 394–396

Dau, A. I. 370
Day, G. S. 232
Deakins, D. 121
debt-based crowdfunding 266
De Buysere, K. 265
decision maker factors in international
    entrepreneurship (IE) 278–279
decision-making process, consumer 73, *73*
demand, price elasticity of 134–135
demographic environment 55–56, **56**
Denison, T. 6
Desphande, R. 61
Diamantopoulos, A. 388
Di Fatta, D. 191
differentiation 383
digitalisation 288–289; market growth and
    391–392; *see also* technology
Dinnie, K. 390
Direct Delivery System (DDS) 158–159
direct exporting 309
distribution: brewery location and 150–151;
    conclusions on *156*, 156–157; contractual
    complications and 153–154; difficulties
    caused by warehousing hops and rising oil
    prices and 154–155; horizontal competition
    and 152–153; introduction to 147–148;
    niche market 150; overview of 148–150,
    149; retail sector 151; SME relationships
    and 153; tasks of **149**; threats to the free
    economy and 154; wholesaler 152

440

INDEX

domestic SMEs 303–304
donation-based crowdfunding 266
Dovetail 238–241
Drinkup 333–334
durable products 114

economic environment 48
economic growth and SMEs 14–16, **16–17**, 324–325
economics of pricing 134
education, entrepreneurial marketing, value of 401–402
Ekwulugo, F. 191
Electrical Equipment Ltd. 8–9
email marketing 181
Engle, N. H. 151
entrepreneurial cognition 390–391
entrepreneurial identity 406
entrepreneurial marketing (EM): canons of 403; characterising the marketplace and 341–343; defined 14, 103–104, **104**; developing entrepreneurial mindsets and capabilities for 404–405; enterprise awareness in 404; ethics in 348–351, *351*; introduction to 337–340, 400–401; module overview for 402; networks for 234–237; Quality Assurance Agency (QAA) model and (*see* Quality Assurance Agency (QAA) model); service-dominant logic in **230–231**, 230–232; social responsibility in 352–354; strategic response in 352; SWOT analysis in 63–64, *63–64*; two foundational premises for *232*, 232–233, *234*; value of education in 401–402; *see also* relationship marketing and networks; sustainability marketing
entrepreneurs' growth motivation 391
entrepreneurship: definition of 15; and growth of SMEs 390–391; incentivising 370–372; international (*see* international entrepreneurship (IE)); qualities of 15–16; relationship marketing and networks and 222–223
entrepreneurship marketing research (EMR) 104–106, *105*; centrality of marketing in business and 98, 98–99; conclusions on 109–110; differences between SMEs and LSEs and 99–102, **100**, **102–103**; innovative value creation in 108–109; introduction to 97–98; opportunity identification in 105–106
environmental scanning and analysis 60–63, *62*
equity-based crowdfunding 265–266
Essoussi, L. H. 390
ethics in entrepreneurship marketing 348–351, *351*
ethnic minority market 91–92, **92–93**
European Commission 203, 266, 406, 415
evaluation of alternatives by consumers 74–75

exporting 309
external marketing environment 48

Facebook 103, 107, 178, 179
Farner, S. 252–253
Faulds, D. J. 304
Ferreira, M. P. 288
firm-specific advantages in international entrepreneurship (IE) 279–280
Focus on Gender 53
formal business networks 236
forward flows 148
four Ps of marketing 246
Fraser, P. 189
Freedom in American Economy 354
Freel, M. 121
Frey, C. 370
fuller 344
funding, SME access to 263–264
Future of Competition: Co-Creating Unique Value with Customers, The 238
future of SME marketing and operations: automation and robotics in 362–363, **363–365**; bi-variate analyses and 367–369, **368–369**; country-of-origin effect and 393–396; data and measurement of variables in 361–363, *362*, **363–365**; impact of technology on 365–367, **366**, 366–367; incentivising entrepreneurship and 370–372; introduction to 359–360, **360**; public opinions on 369–370

Gabrielsson, M. 281
Gbadamosi, A. 117
generic positioning strategies in cross cultural marketing 315–317
GetResponse 313
Gilligan, C. 119
Gilmore, A. 6
Gilthorpe, G. 254
Gnoth, J. 388
Golić, Z. 262
Google AdWords 179
Google Analytics 184
Google search engine optimisation 183–184
Gorostidi-Martinez, H. 389
Goswami, A. 215
Gousto 197–198
green marketing 344
Grimes, A. 302
Grimmer, L. 72
Gripple Limited 40–41
Gronroos, C. 246, 247
Gross Domestic Products (GDP) 48
Gross National Product (GNP) 48
growth motivation, entrepreneurs' 391
Guar, S. S. 85

441

INDEX

Guesalaga, R. 417, 421
Gummesson, E. 225, 235
Gumtree 107

Halal 375–376
Hall, W. K. 39, 40
halo effect 389
Hamel, G. 236
Han, C. M. 389
Hannon, P. D. 3, 5
Hansen, T. 85
Hardman, D. 317
Harney, N. 413–414
Harris, L. C. 6
Harris, S. 317
Hartley, S. 81
Hassan, M. 76
Heding, T. 195–196
Heene, A. 65
Hemmati, H. 87
Henderson, S. 6
Hierarchy of Needs 79, 80
Hill, J. 4
Hills, G. E. 233, 404
Hogarth-Scott, S. 5
horizontal competition 152–153
Horton, H. 82
Howe, J. 289
Hsieh, L. 19
Hultman, C. M. 404
Humphreys, J. 416
Hutt, M. D. 87

Ibrahim, N. A. 5
Icarusparts.com 392–393
incentivising of entrepreneurship 370–372
indirect exporting 309
inflation 219
informal economy, the: Annual Small
   Business Survey report, 2005, on 416–418;
   introduction to 412–413; key features of
   413–414; marketing in 418–422, **420**;
   measuring **414**, 414–416; regulatory
   framework and 413–414
information search by consumers 74
innovation: co-creation and open 290;
   entrepreneurship marketing research (EMR)
   and 108–109; marketing strategy 20–21; new
   product 121–123, *122*; product strategy 20;
   sustainable economic growth and 19–21;
   willingness to pursue 16
Instagram 107, 178
intermediaries in microenvironment of
   marketing 59–60
internal marketing: advantages and
   disadvantages of 248; defined 247;
   environment of 47–48; key elements of

247, 247–248; objectives of 248; service
   excellence achieved through use of 249–252,
   251; *see also* service excellence
international entrepreneurship (IE): barriers
   to 280–281; factors facilitating **278**,
   278–280; internationalisation and SMEs
   and 275–277, **276**; introduction to 275;
   organisational types and 277, *277*; summary
   and implications of 281–282
internationalisation 275–277, **276**; motivations
   and barriers in 306–308
*International Journal of Entrepreneurial
   Behaviour& Research* 32
International Journal of Social Economics 418
international marketing segmentation
   310–317, *311*
internet marketing: affiliate marketing 180;
   content curation for 182–183, *182–183*;
   customer journey to sales and loyalty and
   177, 177–178; defining your customers to
   enable effective and efficient 175–177,
   176; email 181; introduction to 174–175;
   mobile 181; monitoring and improvement
   of 184–185; paid for advertising and search
   engine 179–180; referral and advocate 180;
   search engine optimisation (SEO) 183–184;
   social media 178–179
Ireland, R. D. 122

Jacobides, M. G. 390
Jegeleviciute, S. 265
Jensen, J. M. 85
Jobs, S. 337–338, 340–341
Jones, M. V. 279
Jordaan, M. 101–102
*Journal of Small Business& Enterprise
   Development* 32

Kant, I. 349
Katsikea, E. S. 316
Kay, J. 235
Kent, T. 151, 212
Kerin, R. 81
Kibbler, J. 392
Kirby, D. A. 3, 4
Kleppe, I. A. 389
Knight, F. 15
Kohli, A. K. 107
Koksalan, M. 150
Kotler, P. 54, 82, 83, 87, 88, 125, 245, 389
Kraus, S. 14, 15

Laere, K. V. 65
Lamb, C. S. 352
large-scale enterprises (LSEs) 97; differences
   between SMEs and 99–102, **100**, **102–103**
Ledwith, A. 124

442

INDEX

Levitt, T. 6
Levy, M. 209
Li, D. 288
licensing 309
Lindridge, A. M. 381
LinkedIn 107, 178, 179, 393
litigation crowdfunding 266
Loane, S. 305, 308
logical distribution 148
long-term relationships with customers 179
Lopez, C. 388
Lovelock, C. 245
Luo, K. 17
Lusch, R. F. 234

macroenvironment of marketing 48–53
Madichie, N. 421
Malholtra, N. 109
Maloff, J. 288
management function model 4
management style approach 4, 325–326
Mangold, W. G. 304
market growth: country-of-origin-image and effect and 388–390; digitalisation and 391–392; entrepreneurship and 390–391; future directions of country-of-origin effect and 393–396; introduction to 387–388; technology use and 392–393
marketing communications: characteristics of SME 164, 164–165, 166; communication technology and 166–167; defined 162–164, 163; network perspective to 168–170; opportunities for, in SMEs 167–168; reasons for studying 162; summary of 170
marketing dominated organisations 37
marketing environment: environmental scanning and analysis in 60–63, 62; external 48; informal economy 418–422, 420; internal 47–48; introduction to 46–47; macroenvironment of 48–53; microenviroment of 57, 57–65; nature of SME 47–48; physical 54–56; planning and 328; SMEs' response to 64–65; summary of 66; SWOT analysis in 63–64, 63–64; technological 53–54
marketing independent organisations 38
marketing led organisations 37
marketing mix 331, **331**
marketing orientation 107–108
marketing stimuli 83–84, 84
marketing weak organisations 37–38
marketplace, characteristics of the 341–343
market segmentation, international 310–317, 311
Marks & Spencer 149
markup pricing 139–140
Marshall, P. 417, 421

Maslow, A. 79
Matthews, B. 403
McDonald, M. 6
McDougall, P. P. 277, 278, 279, 288, 291
McGregor, S. 418
McLarty, R. 5
McNaughton, R. B. 306
Mecca Cola 384–385
Meer, D. 382
mega relationships 224
Merrilees, B. 118, 119
Meyer, A. D. 18
Michael, A. 417
microenvironment of marketing 57, 57–65
Miesenbock, K. J. 279
Miles, R. E. 61, 216
Millennium Project 345
Mitchell, R. 195, 196
mobile marketing 181
modified rebuy 89
Moller, K. 3
Monroe, K. 133
Morgan Hunt Model of Relationship Marketing 226, 226
Morris, M. H. 103, 401, 403, 405
Mort, G. S. 318
Muhamad, R. 83
Mukhtar, S. M. 203
multifaceted image effect 389

nano relationships 224–225
Ndlovu, T. 291
need recognition 73–74
network development in cross cultural marketing 317–319
networked SMEs 304–305
networks and strategic alliances 290–291
New Product Development (NDP) 121–123, 122; pricing strategies and 136–137
new task 89
niche markets 150
Nkamnebe, A. D. 414
non-durable products 114
North American Industrial Classification System (NAICS) 203
Nwankwo, S. 117, 342

Oakland, J. S. 254
O'Dwyer, M. 124
Office of Fair Trading (OFT) 52
Ohmae, K. 291
Omar, O. 151, 189, 206, 212
one-on-one socialisation 106
open-mindedness 15
opportunities, leveraging of 15–16
opportunity identification 105–106
Ordanini, A. 264–265

443

INDEX

organisational buying decision process 87–89, 87–89
organisational products 116–117
Osborne, M. 370
O'Shaughnessy, J. 341
O'Shaughnessy, N. 341
Oviatt, B. M. 277, 278, 288, 291

packaging, product 119–120, *120*
Pahl, R. E. 415
paid for advertising, online 179–180
Pallett, R. A. 6
Parasuraman, A. 247
Parker, C. 193
Peattie, K. 347
Pelham, A. M. 6
Perry, S. C. 5–6
Personal Contact Networks (PCNs) 6, 117, 190, 235, 237
personal factors in decision-making 77–79, **79**
Petit, T. 354
Pettitt, S. 115
PEW Research Center 362, 363
Pfeffer, J. 254
physical environment 54–56
Piacentini, M. 82
placed trust 227–228
planning, marketing: analysis stage of 328–329, **329**; constraints on SMEs and 325; contributions of SMEs to the economy and 324–325; external environmental influences in 328; implications of 327–328; introduction to 324; management style and 325–326; plan contents in 329–331, **330–331**; questions embedded in 326–327; schedule of what/where/how in 332, **332**; summary of 332
political-legal environment 49–52
Porter, M. E. 216, 315, 382, 383
Porter's five forces framework 108
post-purchase evaluation 76–77
Prabhu, V. B. 249
Prahalad, C. K. 238, 290
predisposition 81
price elasticity of demand 134–135
pricing: economics of 134; introduction to 131–132; issue of cross-elasticity and 135–136; laws on 132–133; objectives of 137; with other marketing variables 137–138; price elasticity of demand and 134–135; return on investment and markup 139–140; role of three Cs in 138; strategies in 136–141; value 140
proactivity 15
products: branding of 119; classification of and opportunity recognition in SME *114*, 114–115; consumer 115–116; defined 113;

development of new 121–123, *122*, 136–137; introduction to product management and 112–113, *113*; levels of 117–118, *118*; managing diffusion of new 124–126; organisational 116–117; packaging of 119–120, *120*; product life cycle (PLC) and *123*, 123–124, 137; product line/product mix 119
psychological factors in decision-making 79–83, *80*
purchase decisions 75–76

Qing, H. 390
Quality Assurance Agency (QAA) model: canons of entrepreneurial marketing and 403; competency table in 405–406; content and delivery feedback in 402–403; developing entrepreneurial mindsets and capabilities and 404–405; EM module overview 402; entrepreneurial identity in 406; how entrepreneurial marketers think and 404; introduction to 400–401; summary of 406–407

Rafiq, M. 6, 247
Ramaswamy, V. 238
Ramphal, V. 168
Rana, N. P. 191
Ratnatunga, J. 4
raw materials 117
REBRAND model 250–252, *251*
Rees-Mogg, M. 266–267
referral and advocate marketing 180
regulatory framework for the informal economy 413–414
relationship marketing and networks: commitment in *226*, 228; current context for entrepreneurial **230–231**, 230–232; future direction of 237–238; introduction to 222–223; Morgan Hunt Model of *226*, *226*; roots of *223*, 223–224; service quality in 228–229, *229*; trust in *226*, 226–228; types of relationships and 224–225; *see also* entrepreneurial marketing (EM)
relativism, ethical 349
religion 375–376; acculturation and 377–378; at an organisational level 378–379; identity, behaviour, and 377; introduction to SMEs and 376; marketing implications and 379–380; marketing strategy and 380–381; place and 381–382; from strategic perspective 382–383; towards an understanding of 376–377
Rennie, M. 288
Research at the Marketing/Research Interface 233
resource pooling marketing 21

■ **444**

INDEX

retailing: brand management in context of 195–196; challenges to SME sector 212–216, **213**; characteristics of SME 205–207; conclusions on 217–218; defined 190; definition of SMEs in 203–205; industry restructuring in UK 208, **209**; market competition in 216–217; marketing challenges of offline SME 192–193; organisation of small retailer 209, 209–210, **210–212**; SME marketing and 190–192; structural outline for UK markets in 207–208, **207–208**; summary of marketing in 196–197; UK government policy and 212; use of omni-channel approach in 193–195

retailing and SME marketing: distribution and 151; introduction to 189

return on investment (ROI) 5, 6; markup pricing and 139–140

reward-based crowdfunding 266

Rice, G. R. 5

risk taking 15

robotics 362–363, **363–365**; impact of 367–369, **368–369**

Robson, A. 249

Rocks, S. 236

Roddick, A. 341

Rogers, E. M. 125

role and relevance model: assumptions in 40–41; background and history on 33–35; categories in 37; conclusions on 41–43; introduction to 31–32; managerial and policy implications of 43–44; in marketing dominated organisation 37; in marketing independent organisation 38; in marketing led organisation 37; in marketing weak organisation 37–38; origins of 32–33; relevance dimension in 36–41; research on 32; role dimension in 36–41; strategies in 38–39; types of organisations and 35

Romano, C. 4

Ross, L. 403

Roth, K. P. 388

Rue, L. W. 5

Sadarangani, P. H. 85

Saffu, K. 389

Salavou, H. 122–123

Sale of Good Acts 1979 **50**

Savage, M. 82

Saxby, C. L. 60, 61

Schiffman, L. G. 78, 82

Schneider, F. 414, 418

Schumpeter, J. A. 15, 121, 277

Schwartz, B. 361

Schwens, C. 291

Scott, D. 389

search engine marketing 179–180

search engine optimisation (SEO) 183–184

segmentation, market 310–317, *311*

self-identity 377

service-dominant logic to marketing **230–231**, 230–232

service excellence: barriers that SMEs need to overcome for 252–253; defined 248; introduction to 244–245; practical implications of barriers and challenges in 253, 253–254; significance of achieving 249; steps for successful 254–256; summary of 256–257; use of internal marketing as means to achieve 249–252, *251*; *see also* internal marketing

service marketing: defined 245; importance of 245–246, **246**

service quality 228–229, *229*

services 117

Seshoene, M. 106

seven Ps of services marketing 245–246, **246**

shadow economy 413

Shaw, W. 349

shopping products 115

Shrader, R. C. 288

Simba, A. 288, 291

Simpson, M. 190

Singer, I. 148–149

Singh, R. P. 233

Sinkula, J. M. 232

Siu, W. 3, 4

small and medium-sized enterprises (SMEs): appropriate marketing responses to characteristics of 102, **102–103**; Born Global (*see* Born Global SMEs (BGSs)); buyer behaviour and (*see* buyer behaviour); conclusions on 7, 21; cross cultural marketing by (*see* cross cultural marketing); crowdfunding in (*see* crowdfunding); defined 2–3, 99–100, **100**, 190; differences between LSEs and 99–102, **100, 102–103**; distribution in (*see* distribution); domestic 303–304; economic growth and 14–16, **16–17**, 324–325; entrepreneurial marketing in 14; entrepreneurship marketing research (EMR) and (*see* entrepreneurship marketing research (EMR)); future of (*see* future of SME marketing and operations); informal economy and (*see* informal economy, the); innovation and sustainable economic growth in 19–21; international entrepreneurship in (*see* international entrepreneurship (IE)); internet marketing and (*see* internet marketing); introduction to 1–2, 13–14; market growth and (*see* market growth); marketing, strategic thinking, and survival of 5; marketing communications in (*see* marketing communications); marketing environment in (*see* marketing

445

INDEX

environment); marketing in practice in 6–7; marketing models for 3; marketing orientation and performance in 6; networked 304–305; planning and performance by 5–6; previous research on marketing in 3; pricing in (*see* pricing); product management in (*see* products); religion and (*see* religion); retailing in (*see* retailing); role and relevance model of marketing in (*see* role and relevance model); service excellence in (*see* service excellence); strategic marketing and 17–19; structural features of 100–102; supply chain 305; theoretical approaches to marketing in 4; in the United Kingdom (*see* United Kingdom, retail sector in the)
Small Business Act for Europe **49**
Smith, A. 214
Snapchat 178
Snow, C. C. 61, 216
social agents for change 15
social identity theory 377
social media 107, 108; marketing using 178–179
social networks 107, 168
social responsibility (SR) 352–354
sociocultural environment 52–53
sociocultural factors in decision-making 81–83, 80
Solomon, M. 78, 86
South Africa, Chinese immigrant entrepreneurship in 418
Sparks, L. 214
special market relationships 224
specialty products 115
Speh, T. W. 87
Spence, M. 316, 390
Srikatanyoo, N. 388
stages/growth model 4
Stevens, A. 166
Stokes, D. 109, 404
Storey, D. 215
straight rebuy 89
strategic alliances 290–291
strategic distribution 148
strategic marketing 5, 17–19; customer orientation and 17–19; entrepreneurship marketing and 352; religion and 382–383
summary effect 389
suppliers in microenvironment of marketing 59
supply chain SMEs 305
Supported Employment Enterprises (SEEs) 33–34
sustainability marketing 343–344; characterising the marketplace and 341–343; dimensions of 346; how SMEs can make progress on 347, 347–348; introduction to 337–341; marking the boundaries of 344–346, 345

sustainable economic growth and innovation 19–21
Swenson, M. J. 404
SWOT analysis 63–64, 63–64, 329–330
Szmingin, I. 82

targeting approaches in cross cultural marketing 313–315
technological environment 53, 53–54; innovative value creation and 108–109
technology: cloud 289; impact of, on future work 365–367, **366**, 366–367; market growth and use of 392–393; *see also* digitalisation
technology enhanced marketing 20–21, 166–167, 185–186
Tollin, K. 404
Toyota 22–25
transnational segmentation 312–313
Tripp, A. 419
trust in relationship marketing and networks 226, 226–228
Twitter 107, 179

underground sector 413
United Kingdom: informal economy in the 415–418; retail sector in the: challenges to SME 212–216, **213**; conclusions on 217–218; government policy and 212; industry restructuring in 208, **209**; introduction to SMEs in 202–203; marketing in 191–196; organisation of small retailers in 209, 209–210, **210–212**; structural outline of retailers in 207–208, **207–208**
United Nations Economic Programmes (UNEP) 13
unsought products 115–116
Utilitarianism 349

Valanciene, L. 265
value pricing 140
Varadarajan, R. 18
Vargo, S. L. 234
Virgin Group 408–409
Virtual Farmers Market 171–172
Von Hippel, E. 290

Walle, G. 419
Wang, T. 388
Watkins, P. 6
Weber, M. 15
Webster Jr., F. E. 88
Weerawardena, J. 318
Weitz, B. A. 209
Welsh, R. 213, 215
West Africa, Lebanese informal economy in 419
Wheeler, C. 317
wholesalers and distribution 152

Williamson company 320–322
Wilson, N. C. 404
Wilson, R. M. S. 119
Wind, Y. 88
Winter, S. G. 390
Wirtz, J. 245
Wong, H. Y. 118, 119
Wong, K. Y. 64
word-of-mouth communications
   (WOM) 82
work, importance of 362, 362

World Bank 99
Wozniak, S. 337–338
Wright, P. L. 85

XenoGesis 295–296

Yankelovich, D. 382
YouTube 178, 179

Zaichkowsky, J. L. 84, 85
Zuckerberg, M. 103